More advance praise for *On the Irish Waterfront*—

"*On the Irish Waterfront* documents the true story of labor struggles in the Port of New York that led to the making of the classic film *On the Waterfront*. James T. Fisher's exploration of the high-stakes, true-life battle between Jesuit labor priest Pete Corridan and Irish mobster Bill 'Mr. Big' McCormack over the 'shapeup' system among dockworkers reveals the multiple, contradictory currents of justice and violence, exploitation and solidarity, that shaped prewar American Catholic culture. A remarkable story in the hands of a talented storyteller, *On the Irish Waterfront* takes readers on a rollicking journey to the bars, cathedrals, boxing gyms, back alleys, parish basements, and front parlors of the Port of New York. This much-anticipated book is classic Fisher—lively, insightful, crackling with verve and intellect, and just plain fun to read."

— AMY KOEHLINGER, author of *The New Nuns: Racial Justice and Religious Reform in the 1960s*

"James T. Fisher's treatment of the 'spiritual front' that brought the Irish Catholic priest Father Pete Corridan and the Jewish writer Budd Schulberg together in a common crusade for justice—and of their triumph, not on the waterfront, but on the silver screen—is scintillating. Fisher is a good writer and a very fine historian—intellectually sophisticated, indefatigable, wonderfully sensitive to human drama and foibles. *On the Irish Waterfront* covers an amazing amount of terrain. Urban, cultural, intellectual, and labor history all fall within Fisher's purview and magnify the importance of his work."

— BRUCE NELSON, author of *Workers on the Waterfront* and *Divided We Stand*

"What a story: religion, politics, ethnicity, labor, and a classic film. By giving a deep reading to this rich cultural mix, James T. Fisher reveals much about urban life and social change in twentieth-century America."

— JAMES M. O'TOOLE, author of *Passing for White* and editor of *Habits of Devotion*

On the Irish Waterfront

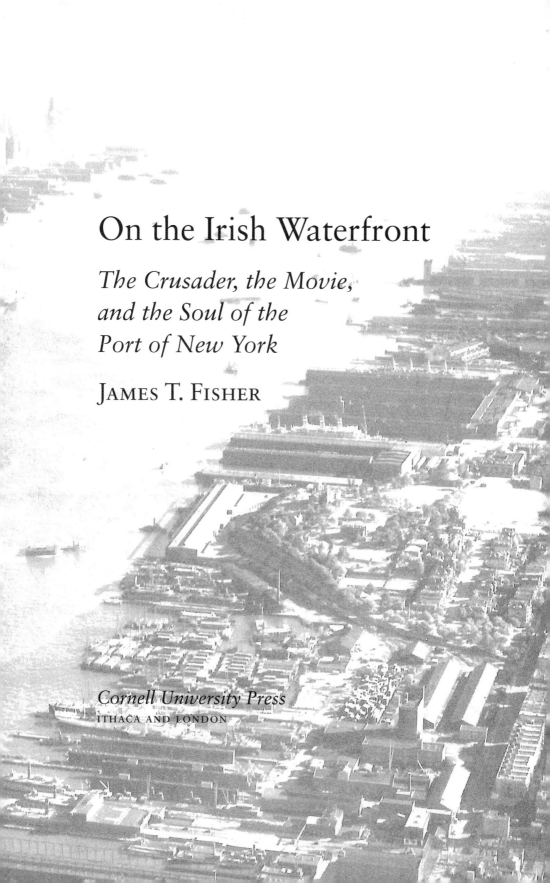

On the Irish Waterfront

*The Crusader, the Movie,
and the Soul of the
Port of New York*

JAMES T. FISHER

Cornell University Press
ITHACA AND LONDON

First published 2009 by Cornell University Press

Printed in the United States of America

Library of Congress Cataloging-in-Publication Data

Fisher, James Terence.
    On the Irish waterfront : the crusader, the movie, and the soul of the port of New York / James T. Fisher.
        p. cm. — (Cushwa Center studies of Catholicism in twentieth-century America)
    Includes bibliographical references and index.
    ISBN 978-0-8014-4804-1 (cloth : alk. paper)
    1. Stevedores—Hudson River Region (N.Y. and N.J.)   2. Irish Americans—Employment—Hudson River Region (N.Y. and N.J.)   3. Port districts—Corrupt practices—Hudson River Region (N.Y. and N.J.)   4. Church work with the working class—Hudson River Region (N.Y. and N.J.)   5. Catholic Church—Missions—Hudson River Region (N.Y. and N.J.)   6. On the waterfront (Motion picture)   I. Title. II. Series: Cushwa Center studies of Catholicism in twentieth-century America.

    HD8039.L82F57   2009
    331.7′61387164097471—dc22

2009013058

Cornell University Press strives to use environmentally responsible suppliers and materials to the fullest extent possible in the publishing of its books. Such materials include vegetable-based, low-VOC inks and acid-free papers that are recycled, totally chlorine-free, or partly composed of nonwood fibers. For further information, visit our website at www.cornellpress.cornell.edu.

Cloth printing   10 9 8 7 6 5 4 3 2 1

Cover photos—Waterfront, aerial, 1930s (courtesy of the Jersey City Free Public Library); "Striking longshoremen surge against police at Pier 90, West 50th Street, as cops block them out to let nonstriking longshoremen make their end run onto picketed pier." *New York World-Telegram and Sun,* October 29, 1951 (courtesy of the Archives of the Xavier Institute of Industrial Relations, Fordham University Library, Bronx, New York).

to James W. Reed, historian

to the dear memory of
Michael Young
(1953–2004)

All I said to kids I recruited was, "You're born and you die alone."

—Al McGuire (1928–2001)
Marquette University basketball coach
Native son of the Irish waterfront

Contents

Prologue

PETE BARRY'S PUNCH

Late in the Academy Award–winning 1954 film *On the Waterfront*, Father Pete Barry (Karl Malden) delivers a straight left to the chin of longshoreman Terry Malloy (Marlon Brando), who is sent sprawling across a barroom floor. The pretext for the punch is Terry's suggestion that the priest "go to hell" for demanding he relinquish his firearm, the first time in American film history a cleric had been addressed that way by a (nominal) parishioner. The rugged priest's real purpose is to persuade Terry to attack Johnny Friendly (Lee J. Cobb)—the mob-connected boss of a longshoremen's union local—with words, not bullets, by testifying against him at a public hearing. Just hours earlier Johnny Friendly had presided over the murder of his own consigliere, Terry's mobster brother "Charley the Gent" Malloy (Rod Steiger), killed for failing to win Terry's promise of silence.[1]

After Terry discovers and tenderly frees Charley's corpse from a long-shoreman's baling hook impaled in a redbrick alley wall, he and his girl-friend, Edie Doyle (Eva Marie Saint), narrowly escape being deliberately run down by a truck. By the time Father Barry—who along with Edie struggles throughout the film to help Terry find his conscience—arrives at Friendly's clubhouse-saloon, Terry is picking glass from his wounds and brandishing a pistol with murderous intent. The priest's resort to violence reverses the logic of the waterfront's inviolable code of silence. On the historic New York–New Jersey waterfront, truths spoken and shared with outsiders routinely prompted a violent reprisal; but Pete Barry deploys violence to *compel* just such an act of speech. The morally awakened Terry sips a beer with the priest, then hurls Charley's pistol through a glass-framed photograph of Johnny Friendly adorning the barroom wall. Hours later he shatters the waterfront code of silence by providing testimony against Friendly himself.

American movie audiences were familiar with tough, courageous Irish priests as featured in dozens of Hollywood films produced since the 1930s.

In addition to appealing to a vast urban Catholic moviegoing audience, "two-fisted" priests like Pete Barry were the favorite screen characters of Joseph I. Breen, the immensely powerful head of the film industry's self-censorship board, the Production Code Administration, which the militantly Catholic Breen wielded on behalf of "real Catholic action." Father Barry's punch readily found favor with the Code's watchdog. The vernacular expression that prompted the blow, however, brazenly violated the Code's unyielding policy that "hell" had no place in Hollywood. Breen quickly devised a solution: he personally (and successfully) intervened on behalf of the film's producer, Sam Spiegel, using his "Jesuit schooling in argumentation," in the words of historian Thomas Doherty, to persuade the Code board to make an exception for *On the Waterfront* as, in Breen's estimation, "an outstanding motion picture which deals, powerfully, with the problems of corruption among the waterfront unions in New York City, and the solution to these problems, largely through the leadership of a courageous priest."[2]

The priest in the movie was modeled explicitly after John M. "Pete" Corridan, a young New York Jesuit who crusaded for social justice in the Port of New York and New Jersey between 1946 and 1954. *On the Waterfront* originated in two events that occurred in the autumn of 1948: the delivery of a fiery speech on the Jersey City waterfront by a then unknown Corridan and the publication of a Pulitzer Prize–winning investigative series on waterfront crime by reporter Malcolm Johnson, for whom the Jesuit served as the prime source. Lengthy excerpts from Corridan's historic oration punctuated Budd Schulberg's waterfront screenplay from its earliest incarnations. Beginning with the initial version, completed in April 1951, the scripts also featured a moral conversion experienced by the priest himself after witnessing waterfront brutality. In the final cut Terry's conversion is more spectacular. But the film as a whole represented—as Joe Breen exulted—a Catholic redemption story so powerful that *On the Waterfront* would earn canonical status as an exemplary work of the "Catholic imagination."[3]

This reading of *On the Waterfront* is as limited—if not nearly so familiar—as the enduring interpretation which reduces the film to an elaborate rationalization by Schulberg and director Elia Kazan for their decisions to testify as former communists turned "friendly witnesses" before the House Committee on Un-American Activities (HUAC). This book demolishes that hoary myth. As for the Catholic reading, Pete Barry's punch looms large as an invitation to much deeper historical inquiry than is generally pursued by advocates of the "Catholic imagination" school of interpretation. The priestly blow was not a feature of the half-dozen drafts and treatments that preceded the final shooting script. Its presence in the film confirms "the mysterious way of art" (the phrase is Kazan's from a different context) to reveal the unacknowledged motivations and passions of creative artists.[4]

In the film, violence serves the priest as an "equalizer"—sometimes applied as a term of praise to Pete Corridan by ardent off-the-waterfront admirers—against rampant mob power. On the *real* New York–New Jersey waterfront, Corridan's mission was violently resisted, rebuffed, and ultimately destroyed by prominent Irish Catholics who matched Joe Breen's militant devotion and his access to the highest echelons of church authority. That truth went untreated in the Hollywood version, as in historical accounts until now. The anger and frustration Pete Corridan experienced on the Irish waterfront of history is poignantly telegraphed by Pete Barry's punch.

The Irish waterfront covered a broad expanse of political and spiritual geography on both sides of the North River, the portion of the Hudson lying between the West Side of Manhattan and Hudson County, New Jersey. It also provides the locale for the stories told in this book. A close working alliance of self-made second-generation Irish Americans presided over this most densely populated stretch of New York Harbor in the first half of the twentieth century. By that time most Irish Americans—in the New York metropolitan area as elsewhere—no longer lived in such thickly ethnic enclaves; but this Irish waterfront remnant had much incentive to endure, given the bounty that could be reaped by controlling the loading and unloading of cargoes passing through the Port of New York and New Jersey.[5] The absence of a freight rail tunnel connecting mainland Hudson County with Manhattan Island—a near-fatal flaw in the great port's infrastructure—was the guarantor of this trans-harbor cohort's power, since cargoes needed to be broken down and reprocessed on both sides of the river through a labyrinthine system involving kickbacks, shakedowns, and seemingly inscrutable negotiations conducted in the unique idiom of the Irish waterfront. For those in control of this system, as an investigator noted, "the take is beyond estimate."[6]

The lords of the waterfront evinced little or no interest in their ancestral homeland, though their story makes for a meaningful chapter in the saga of the Irish diaspora. They created instead a brand of Catholicism in the port which was as culturally and politically pervasive as that witnessed at any other time or place in North American history. Frank Hague, the long-time mayor of Jersey City, functioned more like an autocratic Old World bishop than an elected official, while the most powerful monsignor on the West Side of Manhattan doubled as ecclesiastical mob enforcer. William J. McCormack, a devoutly Catholic entrepreneur known as the waterfront's "Mr. Big," dominated the labor unions that employed his longshoremen and teamsters; the port's popular theologians blessed his operation as the purest application of papal teachings on labor-management harmony.

Although spirituality and violence are normally understood as mutually exclusive, on the Irish waterfront an intimacy with violence *confirmed* spiritual authority like no other gift. Theological reflection flourished there in a viciously competitive and almost wholly unregulated marketplace. As the church's "just war" theory afforded Catholics a way of understanding—and participating in—violence on an international scale, the Irish waterfront's popular theology yielded a kind of "just waterfront" theory to account for a world where longshoremen routinely disappeared and daylight murders went unreported. The annual April crop of bloated corpses surfacing after a winter submerged in the frosty Hudson was a harbinger of spring, signaling not the renewal of life but a new season of violence and brutality. The just waterfront required a practice of collective denial: its inhabitants learned early how not to see and what not to say about local violence. This repressive code of silence strangled the vernacular beauty of Irish American waterfront speech and instilled an overweening hostility to outsiders.[7]

The self-regulating character of that code is brilliantly conveyed in *On the Waterfront* when Pop Doyle bitterly reproaches Pete Barry, who has accompanied Pop's daughter Edie to witness the brutal pier hiring ritual known as the shapeup: "I'm surprised with you, Father, if you don't mind my sayin' so. Lettin' her see things ain't fit for the eyes of a decent girl."[8] Those things included any and all components of that very system for whose preservation Pop's son Joey had just been murdered for cooperating with outside investigators.

In 1936 the New York Jesuits opened Xavier Labor School in Chelsea—the West Side's preeminent waterfront neighborhood—designed to combat the infiltration of local unions by communists, the ultimate outsiders. But when in 1941 the school's director, Philip Carey, S.J., learned that Bill Mc-Cormack, "Mr. Big," had told employees of his stevedoring firm that they could "chew on cobblestones" if they did not care for the terms of a new contract, Father Carey resolved to help the men create their own legitimate union. Carey was promptly threatened with "utter destruction" by powerful political forces. Around that same time a West Side monsignor took Carey for a ride ending with a hint that if the Jesuit did not mind his own business, the monsignor's parishioners might burn Xavier down just as they had recently firebombed the Communist Party's Chelsea office. "We decided we were all alone," Carey lamented years after that chilling conversation. "We couldn't get anything to back us up, nothing to back us up."[9]

Carey despaired of reviving the waterfront apostolate until the much more aggressive, newly ordained Jesuit Pete Corridan was assigned to Xavier in 1946. A few New York archdiocesan priests bravely supported insurgent longshoremen in their postwar movement against waterfront oppression; but after attracting a very small cadre of "rebel disciples," Corridan was repelled as a meddler by enforcers of the Irish waterfront *sensus fidelium*. In 1948 he made the fateful decision to relocate his crusade off the waterfront, forging creative and spiritual partnerships with journalists and secular social reformers. When reporter-ally Malcolm Johnson won the 1949 Pulitzer Prize for his investigative series "Crime on the Waterfront," heavily indebted to Corridan's sources, the code of silence began to crack. No longer would longshoremen's corpses float unnoticed down the Hudson.

Budd Schulberg was then hired to write a screenplay based on Johnson's series. Corridan, promptly imploring him to create "a *Going My Way* with substance," provided invaluable waterfront guides for this self-described "Jewish humanist" who had a special gift for eliciting conversation from deeply wary Irish Catholics, including Corridan himself. These unlikely partners in the "spiritual front" (as I have dubbed the postwar, postdenominational spiritual revival the Corridan-Schulberg collaboration exemplified) could not change the waterfront's religion, so they created a version of Christian existentialism driven by the power of personal witness. Corridan instigated a series of spectacular public hearings that triggered a war for the soul of the port by making witness mandatory for denizens of the waterfront. Rarely has a ritual invocation of the Fifth Amendment privilege against self-incrimination resonated so loudly as in the hearing rooms of the New York State Crime Commission during the winter of 1952–53.[10]

This "struggle *between* Catholics for the soul of their church and the allegiance of its communicants"—as it was characterized by the historian Bruce Nelson—actually found precious few Catholics joining the reformers' side; but in many ways the conflict was no longer confined to their church. It surely was not confined to the Irish waterfront, which scarcely endured by the early 1950s apart from the desire of its most powerful remaining citizens to evade the onslaught of publicity that now depicted them as rogues, pirates, and even killers. So successful was Corridan at drawing attention to the waterfront's lurid recent history that a non-reformer like Elia Kazan was drawn there for creative and political reasons of his own. Kazan was disdainful of Corridan's church, which he likened to the Communist Party, but fascinated by the Jesuit, whom he first met late in 1952, shortly after committing himself to the waterfront film project. Corridan was raging that day against New York's Francis Cardinal Spellman, whom Kazan had earlier placed at the head of a censorship conspiracy—also involving Joe Breen—to mutilate his director's cut of *A Streetcar Named Desire*. It took Schulberg's repeated assurances to convince his friend that Corridan was in fact a priest in good standing, so taken was Kazan by the Jesuit's irreverent passion.[11]

Kazan left the theology to his screenwriter and his Jesuit collaborator, but the partnership among these three men of very different temperaments yielded a brilliantly volatile mixture of advocacy cinema and art of the highest order. The advocacy came naturally, since *On the Waterfront*'s Hoboken sets virtually doubled as local campaign headquarters for an insurgent union—ardently backed by Corridan and Schulberg—seeking to topple the entrenched International Longshoremen's Association (ILA) in an election coinciding with the final days of location shooting. On its simplest level, *On the Waterfront* works like a campaign film told from the unique advocacy perspective of the Jesuit who inspired it. Yet the film is no documentary, despite its enduring stature as the most veracious record of life in the Port of New York and New Jersey during the postwar decade.[12]

Schulberg relentlessly fought for and won from Sam Spiegel a precious gift of five minutes' screen time to honor both the spirit and letter of Pete Corridan's 1948 oration, "Christ in the Shapeup," from which the film originated. Kazan was much less interested in the waterfront of history. Though Corridan never threw a punch in anger during his apostolic work, the director sensed his rage without fully understanding its sources. Pete Barry's barroom punch conveys that rage and despair in the "mysterious way of art"; coming late in the film, it also signals an end to the battle for the soul of the port. The triumphant release of *On the Waterfront* in July 1954 followed the electoral defeat of the waterfront reformers and the effective termination of Pete Corridan's public apostolate. Schulberg felt equally thwarted; but while he immediately wrote a novel with a Corridan figure in place of Terry Malloy as protagonist, the real waterfront priest was sent packing by his Jesuit superior, largely for his refusal to abide by a clerical code of silence.

Pete Corridan nearly lost his ancestral faith while seeking a more authentic version to cover the waterfront. He was left to find his way again, working through the anger he felt over his church's willingness to protect criminal enterprises presided over by prominent communicants and his despondence at the unwillingness of the Irish waterfront's rank-and-file to fulfill his injunction to speak out in witness to truth. Corridan's apostolic work left many questions unanswered and perhaps even more unasked. In the spirit of movie producer Sam Spiegel's persistent injunction that Kazan and Schulberg "open it [the script] up again," I take a new look at the long-shrouded Irish waterfront of history.[13]

On the Irish Waterfront

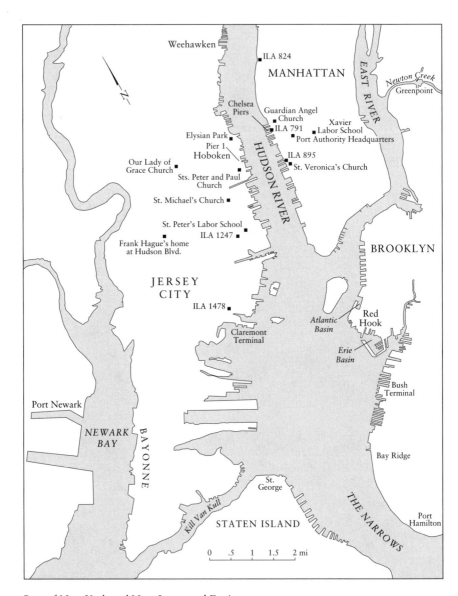

Port of New York and New Jersey and Environs

Introduction

THE PORT'S IRISH PLACES

In 1524 the Florentine explorer Giovanni da Verrazano sailed through the narrows that now bear his name into the Upper Bay of New York Harbor. He found there "a commodious and delightful" navigable shelter sufficient to accommodate safely "any laden ship." Eighty-five years later the British sea captain Henry Hudson piloted the Dutch East India Company's three-mast *Half Moon* into this "Beautiful Lake." Hudson was entranced by the "very good harbor for all windes" found in the future port's "coliseum-like interior," as it was aptly described by historian Russell Shorto. Between these journeys came other Europeans, including Esteban Gómez—a black Portuguese sailor working for the Spanish—and numerous French fur traders who encountered the Lenapes, a Native American people inhabiting the terrain that ringed the harbor.[1]

By the late nineteenth century the dazzlingly multiethnic character of the now great metropolis echoed the diverse origins of its earliest European explorers, but only one group knew the port as *their* place. For if the port made New York, the Irish made the port. Hundreds of thousands of Irish people were among the "human freight" that poured into New York Harbor after 1815, and this steady stream became a flood in the Famine years between 1845 and the early 1850s. "Despite the consistent efforts to keep the immigrants moving," wrote Robert Greenhalgh Albion in his classic *The Rise of New York Port* (1939), "a very large number remained in the city, accelerating its rapid rise in population. This was particularly true of the Irish; the Germans and English were apt to go inland at once."[2]

It was Irish immigrant workers who dug the Erie Canal beginning in 1818. The canal secured the port's future by opening a vast hinterland to trade. Many of these canal workers found their way back to newly established Irish neighborhoods in Lower Manhattan, especially the teeming Five Points, a short remove from the bustling piers near South Street on the Lower East

Side. The year 1818 also marked the inception of regularly scheduled transatlantic service between New York and Liverpool. Sailing packets with fixed routes—pioneered by the Black Ball Line—were the vehicle for New York's dizzyingly rapid ascent to world city status as the capital of global commerce. That was only the beginning. With 771 miles of wharfage, relatively little fog or ice to hamper shipping, and a growing supply of cheap labor, the Port of New York boasted natural and human resources unlike those anywhere else in North America.[3]

While the New York Irish community was occupationally stratified in the first half of the nineteenth century—featuring a substantial pre-Famine cohort of skilled artisans both Catholic and Protestant—the port was built by impoverished Irish Catholic refugees who filled the most dangerous, lowest-paying jobs found in the city. Beginning with the area around South Street, the Irish came to dominate the waterfront precincts along both shores of Lower Manhattan, working the maritime industries in every capacity, with longshoremen predominating. "Irishmen took over New York's docks" in the mid-nineteenth century, wrote Edwin G. Burrows and Mike Wallace in *Gotham:*

> On any given day five or six thousand of these "alongshoremen" moved mountains of cargo off ships and around the port, roaming from pier to pier for the "shape-ups" at which native-born stevedores amassed work crews. The work was hard, poorly paid, and erratic. While waiting for ships to arrive or weather to clear, men hung around local saloons, took alternate jobs as teamsters, boatmen, or brickmakers, and relied on the earnings of their wives and children.[4]

Stevedores hired men to load and unload ships: the work was exhausting, dangerous, and remarkably devoid of technological innovation from the mid-nineteenth to the mid-twentieth century. Longshoremen, wrote labor historian David Montgomery, were "forced to push and pull enormous weights, aided only by the most elementary inclines, pulleys, winches, hooks and screws, and above all, by their own teamwork," forged in ethnic solidarity. Since "by the 1850s the waterfront had become largely a white and Irish preserve," historian Iver Bernstein explained, Irish longshoremen developed a proprietary attitude toward it and viewed with suspicion African Americans and later immigrant workers from eastern and southern Europe, the largest cohort by far coming from southern Italy.[5]

Waterfront work was erratic, seasonal, casual, and highly localized; longshoremen lived in very close proximity to the piers in order to respond quickly to the arrival of a ship. The earliest longshoremen's unions were strictly local entities, rooted in shared ethnicity and a sense of neighborhood prerogative, a pattern that endured in the port for over a century. The carnage of the New York Draft Riots of July 1863 grew in part out of the resentment of Irish dockworkers over the recent hiring of blacks as scab labor during a strike. Though the bloodshed occurred largely north of the most populous waterfront precincts, some Irish Americans seized the opportunity to declare that "work upon the docks...shall be attended to solely by and absolutely by members of the 'Longshoremen's Association' and such white laborers as they see fit to permit upon the premises."[6]

The Irish Waterfront Emerges

A coherent Irish waterfront began to take shape in the decades after the Civil War. Prior to the war Irish dockworkers were scattered in neighborhoods along both the Lower East and Lower West sides of Manhattan, with most maritime activity originating along the southwestern shore of the East River. Waterfront life was chaotic, disorganized, and dangerous. As early as 1870 the city's antiquated wooden piers were condemned by the *New York Times* as "rotten structures, the abode of rats and the hiding places of river thieves....[I]t is at great risk that a person can walk on them in broad daylight." Irish surnames dominated the paper's account of these disorderly piers, among lessees as well as victims: the city's Common Council often made customary provision of a few thousand dollars to reimburse the likes of "Mike O'Brien or Tim McCarthy for the loss of his horse by falling through such and such a dock."[7]

Before the "spectacular thievery" of Tammany Hall boss—or "grand sachem"—William M. Tweed landed him in jail in 1872, the leader of Manhattan's Democratic organization concocted a municipal Department of Docks designed to yield a "patronage windfall" to Tammany. Reformers wished to see a master plan imposed on the chaotic waterfront; they hoped that the island's decrepit piers would be supplanted by a design to "meet needs cultural as well as commercial." But with the mayor in charge of appointments to the dock board, political needs came first as always. The department's original plan of renovation called for new bulkhead construction along both the lower Hudson and East rivers, but the focus soon shifted almost entirely to the Lower West Side, where the interests of merchants, steamship companies, and Tammany Hall—now under Irish control—converged nicely. In 1897 the department supervised construction of municipally owned piers—upwards of seven hundred feet long—on riverfront terrain between Charles and Gansevoort streets. The West Side's Irish waterfront coalesced around these imposing new structures before expanding rapidly northward up the Hudson shoreline. Between 1904 and 1909 nearly thirty-five miles of new wharves materialized.[8]

The transformation of the West Side was swift. The Irish waterfront's southern anchor, Greenwich Village, remained "a solidly middle class neighborhood that the older residents liked to call the 'American Ward'" in the years prior to the construction of new piers in the area. "The majority of the residents had English surnames as late as 1890," historian Thomas J. Shelley noted; a decade later the neighborhood was 40 percent Irish. The Village was an early beneficiary of municipally sponsored pier construction. The first masonry bulkhead was installed at the foot of Christopher Street in 1874, and piers soon covered the waterfront from there south to Canal Street. Hundreds of tenements quickly sprang up, "jammed into a warren of narrow streets." The removal of Thirteenth Avenue—built on landfill in the mid-nineteenth century at water's edge in the West Village and adjoining Chelsea—made possible the construction of enormous new piers to accommodate international shipping concerns.[9]

An Irish Catholic parish for the West Village, St. Veronica's, was established just east of the Hudson riverbank in 1887; Mass was celebrated "in a warehouse and stable" on Washington Street prior to the construction in 1890 of a basement church on Christopher Street, a very brief stroll from the tumult of Piers 45 and 46. St. Veronica's parish encompassed the compact waterfront terrain from Houston Street north to Bank Street and from Hudson Street west to the river. Most male parishioners worked as longshoremen and teamsters when work could be found; it took thirteen years for the impoverished parish to build a smallish upper church. By 1903 total attendance at Sunday Masses often exceeded six thousand souls. Poor as they were, the Irish parishioners of St. Veronica's and another longshoremen's church nearby, St. Bernard's on West Fourteenth Street, loyally supported their own parishes and aided others in even more precarious straits. According to Shelley, "Irish longshoremen who worked on the Hudson River piers became the backbone of the Italian Church of St. Anthony of Padua" on nearby West Houston Street.[10]

By the 1920s Greenwich Village was "overwhelmingly Catholic," firmly in Irish control, and a Tammany stronghold celebrated as "the cradle of New York Democracy." Moving up Manhattan Island there was Hell's Kitchen, the northern terminus of the Irish waterfront covering roughly the terrain between West Thirty-fourth and West Fifty-ninth streets from Eighth Avenue to the river. A remote rural area prior to the opening of a Hudson River Railroad station at Tenth Avenue and West Thirtieth Street in 1851, "the district grew up helter skelter," according to Luc Sante, "a malodorous environment of slaughterhouses, soap and glue factories, and waterfront effluvia, in patches that bore names like Poverty Lane and Misery Row." Hell's Kitchen drew throngs of Germans, African Americans, and especially Irish in the decades that followed, immigrants as well as those fleeing other parts of the city. As Henry J. Browne wrote of the neighborhood's flagship parish, which local tradition placed "one stop above" Hell's Kitchen, "Sacred Heart was so Irish in its beginnings, and for about half of its history, that one runs down lists of names in baptismal and marriage registers with incredulity." Browne found that of two thousand donors subscribed to help build a new church at Fifty-first Street between Ninth and Tenth avenues in 1884, only twenty-two names were not clearly Irish.[11]

Between Hell's Kitchen and Greenwich Village lay Chelsea, the heart and soul of the Irish waterfront. Chelsea originated as an Anglo-Protestant stronghold centering on "Millionaires' Row" along Twenty-third Street between Ninth and Tenth avenues and the General Theological Seminary, built two blocks to the south by the Episcopal Church in the 1820s and 1830s. Most of the surrounding neighborhood was carved out of the estate owned by the family of Dr. Clement Clarke Moore (author of "A Visit from St. Nicholas," better known as "The Night before Christmas"), whose country home once dominated the Chelsea landscape. A small cohort of Irish immigrants was attracted to Chelsea as early as the 1840s by construction sites along the Hudson River Railroad lines; others joined Scottish and German immigrants seeking work in small factories established in the neighborhood.[12]

The construction of the Chelsea Piers (1902–1910) between West Seventeenth and West Twenty-third streets provided the Irish waterfront's focal point. The monumental pier sheds designed by the firm of Warren and Wetmore—architects of the equally magnificent Grand Central Terminal—assumed iconic significance at the heart of the port for both their beauty and their advanced engineering. "Warren and Wetmore invested the fashionable Modern French façades" of the pier sheds, according to a team of New York architectural historians, "with a strikingly monumental grandeur and simplified but overscaled details. The river façades, which sheltered open observation platforms, were contrastingly festive transformations of the utilitarian steel piers which lay behind the street façades, and greeted the arriving passenger with a flutter of pennants and trophies."[13]

The Chelsea Piers drew thousands of Irish Americans to the neighborhood, including many West Side dockworkers "displaced" by the movement of shipping lines from West Village piers to their new location just blocks to the north. The *New York Times* reported in 1910 that longshoremen attached to Pier 48, at the foot of Perry Street in the West Village, "expressed regret" that they would "have to move north to be nearer their work" at the new Pier 61—barely half a mile upriver—slated for occupancy by the relocating White Star Line. West Side dockworkers lived among compatriots from the same county, if not the same village, in the west of Ireland; their residential proximity to the piers rendered the Irish waterfront's localism as intensive as at any site in the urban American experience.[14]

Ethnic Succession Irish Waterfront–Style

From this Chelsea foundation a dominant Irish Catholic waterfront ethos emerged in the years just prior to the First World War. The magnificent new pier façades suggested a waterfront cathedral: a monument to the ascendant forces of Tammany, church, and commerce that solidified Irish waterfront power. Tammany's first Irish grand sachem, "Honest John" Kelly, married the niece of New York's Archbishop John McCloskey, who became America's first cardinal in 1875. Kelly's successor once removed, Charles Francis Murphy, quietly brokered the transformation of derelict North River piers into the jewels of the Irish waterfront during his late 1890s stint as commissioner of the city's docks. Murphy became in the process the Irish waterfront's first millionaire. The Tammany-consecrated Irish American leaders of the ILA—whose headquarters was moved to Chelsea during the war—clearly shared the views of Cardinal McCloskey's successor Archbishop (later Cardinal) John Farley, who in 1907 "half-boasted, half-complained" that "New York...has only one class of people [the Irish Americans] to draw upon for the support of their own churches and schools, as well as the maintenance of so many others."[15]

It was their church, their port: from Tammany politicos—who made their fortunes from leasing, contracting, and licensing fees relating to the piers—to a small but rapidly rising entrepreneurial class who saw their waterfront opportunities from stevedoring to towboats and seized them, the waterfront belonged to the Irish. The claim staked on the world's richest piers by a vast cadre of Irish American longshoremen was akin to a hereditary birthright. As of the late 1880s, "95 per cent of the longshoremen of New York, both foreign and coastwise, were Irish and Irish-Americans," wrote Charles B. Barnes in his classic 1915 study *The Longshoremen*.[16]

The near-total Irish American dominance of the West Side's waterfront neighborhoods turned diffuse cultural forms into militantly enforced codes of conduct. An inviolable code of silence provided the foundation of cultural and religious authority on the Irish waterfront. The sources of this practice are difficult to locate precisely though its roots are evident in both rural Irish and urban American experience. If the code's origins remain suffused in a blend of myth, history, and speculation, we can trace its efficacy as wielded by the second-generation Irish Americans who ruled the West Side waterfront after 1900. These men were coolly indifferent to their ancestry: they had turf to protect, power to sustain, and fortunes yet to be won. They readily adapted cultural and religious forms designed to bolster their authority, reshaping traditionally Irish notions of deference, linguistic evasion, and tactical silence into the West Side's Irish waterfront idiom.[17]

The West Side's distinctive code of silence was prefigured in Charles Francis Murphy's post-Gilded Age waterfront deal making. The most revealing story from Tammany's well-stocked annals treats the Fourth of July celebration during which Murphy—who moved up from commissioner of docks to grand sachem in 1902 and remained there until his death in 1924—failed to join in singing "The Star Spangled Banner." When asked by a reporter why

Mr. Murphy remained silent, Tammany's secretary Thomas F. Smith replied, "Perhaps he didn't want to commit himself." On the Irish waterfront, unauthorized acts of speech and writing were viewed with the gravest suspicion. In the 1890s the reform journalist E. L. Godkin alleged that Tammany leaders feared biography more than the penitentiary. Godkin was an anti-Irish bigot but the fact remains there *are* no biographies of the leading political, labor, and entrepreneurial figures who dominated the Port of New York from 1890 to 1950, men who ranked for decades among the most powerful figures in their vast region: Frank Hague, Joseph P. Ryan, and William J. McCormack, the waterfront's "Mr. Big." These and many others who served under them in the waterfront hierarchy—along with the pastors who validated their regimes—kept personal papers strictly "in their hats," denying us knowledge of their responses to such issues as the rapid displacement of the Irish as the port's dominant constituency, an event that unfolded very early in the era of Irish waterfront supremacy.[18]

By the end of World War I Italian American dockworkers outnumbered the Irish everywhere in the port save Manhattan's West Side. Even there an Italian neighborhood initially created just east of Sixth Avenue in Greenwich Village was twice as populous by 1910 as the Irish waterfront stronghold to its west; the disparity widened further as the Italian enclave expanded following the Irish dockworker exodus to nearby Chelsea. Yet Italian Americans never achieved full access to employment on the West Village piers: for many years Italian dock workers were regularly hired by only one among the many steamship companies housed at the Chelsea Piers, where they were largely restricted to coal handling, a job beyond the pale for Irish longshoremen.[19]

An epic struggle over ethnic succession in the Port was waged most dramatically not along the West Side but directly across the North River in Hudson County, New Jersey. Hudson County was often dismissed by New Yorkers as a remote outpost, but our story locates this most distinctive of New Jersey's twenty-one counties very near to the heart of the volatile port. The Irish ruled church, state, and waterfront throughout that densely populated, immigrant-dominated community by the end of World War I. As on the West Side, Italian newcomers seeking work on the bustling piers of Hoboken and Jersey City were obliged to cross through Irish waterfront terrain. Jersey City's Italians first congregated southwest of the Irish waterfront "Horseshoe" neighborhood and later even farther inland in the city's Marion neighborhood. In Hoboken "West of Willow" (the avenue seven blocks removed from the Hudson) was an Irish euphemism for the near border of the Italian American community.[20]

Yet in Hudson County Italians not only found work on the piers but they also built a powerful civic presence between the World Wars. The distinguished journalist Richard Reeves wrote of his 1940s Jersey City childhood, "I grew up thinking America was an Italian country governed by the

Irish." The experience of a pair of cousins exemplified the difference in ethnic politics between the West Side and the Jersey side. In 1939 the talented
and ambitious Carmine De Sapio ousted Greenwich Village's Democratic
district leader Dan Finn, the third consecutive Dan Finn to hold the office in
a dynasty as old as the century. Tammany Hall responded to the shocking
electoral outcome by refusing to seat De Sapio: it took two more elections
before the dwindling machine accepted the inevitable; De Sapio finally became district leader in 1943 but enjoyed precious little patronage power on
the nearby piers still wholly dominated by the Irish.

In Hoboken Carmine's cousin Fred De Sapio became the city's first Italian
American mayor in 1947 after his "fusion" ticket of three Italian Americans
and two Irishmen ousted the long-entrenched regime of Bernard McFeely.
De Sapio soon became embroiled in Hudson County's endemic political corruption but he also did something unthinkable for a West Side politician of
any ethnicity: he reached out to the New York labor priest and reformer
John M. Corridan in early 1953, as the battle for the soul of the port reached
its peak. De Sapio's gesture was an important step in the long struggle to
produce the Corridan-inspired *On the Waterfront,* a film shot in Hoboken
based on events that took place on the West Side. The Irish waterfront was
made and unmade in encounters between the West Side's tribalism and the
fluid if volatile ethnic dynamics found along the opposing shore of Hudson
County.[21]

South Brooklyn's vast swath of New York Harbor constituted the anti-
Irish waterfront. There an ethnic "sea of every racial stock" (as onetime
Brooklyn cop and future New York City mayor Bill O'Dwyer described the
waterfront precinct he patrolled during World War I) quickly gave way in
the 1920s to Italian dominance of the borough's thriving Red Hook piers,
just as the shipping industry established its stronghold in that massive waterfront complex. Work, housing, and social and religious institutions ra-
diated from Red Hook's Columbia Street hub, forging South Brooklyn's
answer to Irish Chelsea. The Irish Americans who still ran Brooklyn's powerful Democratic machine during the 1930s and 1940s grudgingly ceded the
borough's waterfront politics and its rampant profiteering to Italian control,
alternately scorning the newcomers and dreading the political implications
of their ascent.[22]

Brooklyn also witnessed the emergence of other ethnic waterfronts. Widely
scattered enclaves of Norwegian, Polish, Hungarian, and Slavic American dockworker communities emerged there—and elsewhere around the
port—in the late nineteenth and early twentieth centuries. For decades members of these groups were generically mislabeled "Austrian" by the Irish waterfront's arbiters of ethnic identity. In fact, the communities ringing New
York Harbor grew so diverse by the 1930s—outsiders even made their way
into the residential heart of the West Side's three historic Irish strongholds—
that the "Irish waterfront" no longer designated a discreet geographic and

spiritual entity. It now symbolized retrenchment and often violent resistance against challenges to its dwindling hegemony in the port.[23]

The West Side bosses of the ILA feared one such challenge from a historically prominent population on the New York–New Jersey waterfront. African American longshoremen worked in the port from the mid-nineteenth century onward; growing patterns of housing segregation drove blacks farther from the workplace than Euro-American dockworkers. While there is evidence that Italians were regarded as non-white by some Irish longshoremen, the port's largest ethnic constituency readily controlled a large portion of waterfront turf by the late 1920s, unlike black dockworkers who were prevented by custom and force from establishing a claim to piers of their own. Largely frozen out of regular longshoremen's work gangs prior to World War II, black dockworkers were often relegated to work as "extras" handling "certain disagreeable cargoes such as bananas that had been refused by white ethnics." Shapeups for hiring blacks were often conducted far from the piers: on Lenox Avenue in Harlem, for example, "straw bosses" would "come and pick out who they wanted" from crowds of men seeking work.

By the end of World War II, between four and five thousand African American longshoremen regularly sought work in the port, including sizable contingents in Jersey City and Newark. In Brooklyn the largely African American Local 968 enrolled a membership of a thousand men, but as its president Cleophas Jacobs explained, shippers, hiring bosses, and union officials "have an agreement whereby the available work is given to the other nine [white] locals in Brooklyn, to the exclusion of our men." The waterfront Irish grew so concerned with threats to their primal claim on the port by "outsiders"—Italians, blacks, communists, or a dreaded coalition of all three—they would be caught off-guard by insurgencies from within, challenges to authority of such passionate intensity as to sometimes bewilder the Irish insurgents themselves. [24]

Cockeye Dunn Shot Me

If African American dockworkers were treated as permanent outsiders on the Irish waterfront, longshoremen of all colors were rendered virtually invisible in urban locales just beyond the piers. Public access to the New York–New Jersey waterfront ranged from daunting to near impossible, with a tangle of rail yards, streets jammed with wagons and trucks, and dangerous-looking saloons with their loitering customers forming an imposing barrier that separated the various urban publics from the piers. When outsiders did take an interest in dockworkers, their near invisibility was often cited as the waterfront's most salient feature. "You whiz by him on the West Side Highway but you don't see him," wrote Budd Schulberg in his first of many nonfiction pieces devoted to longshoremen, a December 1952 essay for the *New York Times Magazine.* "You hurry past him as you board ship for Europe or a winter cruise through the Caribbean, and you never notice his face." As late as 1955—after a string of prizewinning waterfront exposés, sensational public hearings, and an Academy Award–winning film written by Schulberg himself—he could still marvel at the willingness of the *New York Times,* a venerable West Side institution, to "live in blissful co-existence only a few blocks apart" yet light years removed from Hell's Kitchen ILA Pistol Local 824.[25]

In Greenwich Village, dock workers and civilians "studiously ignored one another," as Thomas Shelley aptly put it, even as they shared urban space. There were notable exceptions: early in the twentieth century, marauding Irish waterfront gangs like the Hudson Dusters threw "wild affairs that lasted for days and became the stuff of local legend," attracting downtown bohemians including playwright Eugene O'Neill and his friend Dorothy Day, who later founded the Catholic Worker movement. But by the 1940s tourists strolling through the neighborhood were largely oblivious to its still dominant industry and its colorful traditions. Visitors seeking a taste of Village bohemia were drawn instead to 57 Grove Street, where Charlie Parker and his bebop confreres regularly performed at the oldest jazz club in New York City, Arthur's Tavern. Next door at 59 Grove an engraved plaque on the building's exterior wall informed history buffs that in 1809 Thomas Paine, revolutionary pamphleteer and author of *Common Sense,* died in a farmhouse once located on the site.[26]

There is no plaque outside 61 Grove to commemorate a homicide committed there on the morning of January 8, 1947, which signaled the beginning of the end of the Irish waterfront. Local gangster and businessman John "Cockeye" Dunn—accompanied by a pair of confederates—gunned down Anthony Hintz in daylight as he descended the stairwell of his apartment building in the heart of bustling Sheridan Square. Andy Hintz (as in "pints") was en route to his job on Pier 51 when he took six bullets plus several kicks to the head and body. Hintz was shot because he refused to turn over Pier 51's lucrative "loading racket" to the ruthless, politically connected Dunn.

The loading racket was an unsavory West Side tradition. Truckers sent to deposit and pick up cargoes stacked pierside by longshoremen were routinely tied up for hours on jammed, narrow roadways. In the years after World War I employers grew tired of dispatching crews of workers to the piers only to have them idled by such thick congestion. It proved more efficient to employ the services of "public loaders" to move the cargoes to waiting trucks. In the 1930s waterfront entrepreneurs turned public loading from an optional service into a mandatory racket: truckers paid a steep loading fee whether they received the service or not. As Malcolm Johnson reported, "the trucker who balked at the shakedown did not get his merchandise, and his driver came home bloody."[27]

While the shapeup hiring system became the most notorious symbol of waterfront corruption, the loading racket was the port's uniquely insidious signature, a practice unknown in other harbors around the United States. The rise of the loading racket coincided with "King Joe" Ryan's tenure as ILA president. In response to the condemnation of the loaders as "organized banditti" by a shippers' group in 1930, Ryan characteristically asserted, "I think the loading situation is in very fine shape." As a wholly unregulated practice, control of the loading on a given pier was customarily acquired at gunpoint, enabling a violent racketeer like Cockeye Dunn—backed by his smooth-talking brother-in-law Eddie McGrath—to ascend to the status of legitimate businessman. Dunn eventually won control of the loading on most of the Lower West Side's piers. On Pier 51 Andy Hintz was a rare holdout. He operated as a pier foreman and boss loader, hiring both longshoremen and public loaders. But Hintz "wouldn't hire any of Dunn's hoodlums," recalled a New York detective who knew him well. "He didn't care if a guy maybe had done a little time, but he wanted no part of organized gangsters."[28]

Cockeye Dunn also harbored an older Pier 51 grudge: in 1942 a hiring boss named Edward J. Kelly had transgressed the code of silence after enduring a brutal beating by Dunn in his first bid to conquer the pier. Kelly's shocking action led to Dunn's conviction on charges of coercion, but Cockeye was soon paroled, putatively as an asset to the war effort. Dunn's well-placed backers on and off the waterfront informed parole officials that "the clergy of his locality…who are well acquainted with him" vouched for Dunn's "excellent reputation." Once back in circulation Cockeye and Eddie McGrath "moved like feudal princes through the streets of the West Side."[29]

Dunn employed public loaders on the piers he controlled and ran the fictitious union that represented his workers, a characteristic feature of the port's labor relations practices. He also ran a murder-for-hire business that seemed only to enhance his standing as a "smooth-operating waterfront cartelist" and pillar of a brutal hierarchy reinforced by culture, ethnicity, and religion. In the weeks prior to the Andy Hintz shooting, Dunn's underling Andrew "Squint" Sheridan stalked the rugged hiring boss. The vision-impaired triggerman (he had shot and killed at least one unintended victim) was, like Dunn, a product of the Catholic Protectory, a storied Northeast Bronx orphanage/reform school founded in the 1860s by an Anglo convert to Catholicism haunted by the familiar sight of "orphaned or abandoned kids, mostly Irish, who roamed the city's streets, ragged and often dangerous." Rescued from that fate Dunn and Sheridan became preeminent upholders of the West Side code, one of whose commandments dictated that recalcitrant marked men be afforded a final opportunity to capitulate.

Andy Hintz instead greeted Squint Sheridan with loud insults for Dunn and "that dressed-up consumptive brother-in-law of his," which explains why Cockeye's finger was on the trigger that morning on Grove Street. In most other respects the execution was a routine happening and went virtually unreported by the city's newspapers prior to April 1, when the Manhattan district attorney's office announced the murder indictments of Dunn, Squint Sheridan, and Daniel Gentile, alias Danny Brooks. "Longshoremen were always getting shot, or beaten over the head with baseball bats, or flung into the harbor," wrote former Manhattan assistant district attorney William Keating in 1956. "Waterfront murders were the most hopeless of cases....The murderers were usually well known, but arrests and convictions were unheard of....[T]o talk was to rat, and to rat was to stand exposed and unprotected."[30]

In 1953 the respected labor journalist Guy Richards asserted in the *New York Journal-American* that there had been "more than 100 waterfront murders since 1928." At the time of Hintz's shooting, no killer or killers had ever been convicted of their crimes. "The West Side Code," wrote journalist T. J. English, was "a tradition so sacred that even non-criminal types saw that it was adhered to....[U]nder no circumstances did anyone talk to the cops." But Hintz's wife, Maisie, did talk to the cops. When they arrived at the crime scene she impulsively reported, "I kept asking him who were the rats that shot him and he said, 'Johnny Dunn shot me.'" Andy Hintz meanwhile refused to expire in a timely manner. Perhaps seeking to deflect the heat from his wife, Hintz identified Dunn as his assailant when Cockeye was brought to the foot of his deathbed at St. Vincent's Hospital. He offered a "dying declaration" for use at Dunn's trial before succumbing on January 29, 1947.[31]

Cockeye Dunn's pitch-perfect alibi—he was dropping his children for daily Mass at their church in Queens at the time of the shooting—lost its customary efficacy when Maisie Hintz, who had fled to Miami in advance of the December 1947 trial, rematerialized to offer testimony. So too did Willie Hintz, the brother who was waiting for Andy in his car on Grove Street when Hintz was shot. Others took the stand to corroborate elements of the prosecution's case. Dunn's shell-shocked defense team could only sputter that the appearance of these witnesses proved Cockeye was being framed, since nobody from the West Side would ever testify voluntarily. His attorney alleged, "This case has an unwritten script that was designed to ensnare an innocent man," but it was in fact a time-dishonored unwritten script that was being torn up in this case. Prosecutors justifiably touted the "miracle" of testimony resulting in the conviction—and sentencing to death—of Dunn, professional assassin Squint Sheridan, and Daniel Gentile, would-be concessionaire of the numbers racket on Pier 51.[32]

Cockeye Dunn lived another eighteen months; from Death Row and beyond he remained a specter haunting the waterfront and New York City's political life. Novelists and filmmakers ruminated over the reasons for his depravity. There was nothing new in these imaginative efforts to treat an individual's criminality as the distilled essence of an inhumane social and economic order. But on the West Side Irish waterfront there was one difference: those who, like John Dunn, were most intimate with violence *did* seem to achieve not just temporal power but a kind of mythic stature for their unmediated knowledge of the world as it truly worked.

Early 1949 found Cockeye Dunn suddenly talkative in his cell at Sing Sing in the presence of New York prosecutors; but just as abruptly he turned "silent to the end," as the *New York Times* reported, when he faced his executioners on July 7. If Cockeye had talked in hopes of a reprieve—as reported at the time—the gesture was oddly resonant with a new waterfront dispensation he had inadvertently helped usher in by shooting a longshoreman whose wife spoke up, followed by the victim himself, then his brother, then a skein of witnesses with no overt link to the victim—a stream of testimony issuing from the core of this Irish waterfront oppressed by decades of fear, intimidation, and the certainty of reprisal. Dunn commenced talking at precisely the moment when Malcolm Johnson, a *New York Sun* investigative reporter, was awarded the Pulitzer Prize for a series of articles blasting open the code of silence, highlighted by his exhaustive account of Dunn, the dark prince of waterfront rackets.[33]

From Edward J. Kelly, to Maisie, Andy, and Willie Hintz, to Malcolm Johnson and the Jesuit labor priest who guided him, perhaps even to Dunn himself for making of his own violent life a story too significant to go permanently uncovered, the stories were beginning to flow by the latter 1940s. Waterfront figures lately deemed permanently untouchable were now marked for exposure. A postwar decade of struggle pitted the spiritual primacy of silence against insurgent acts of speech as witness. It was an apocryphal story, but it coursed through the "kite," the Irish waterfront's intricately encoded grapevine of rumor, innuendo, and home truth: the priest sent to hear Cockeye Dunn's final confession, it was said, couldn't understand English.[34]

PART ONE

Boys of the Irish Waterfront

Figure 1. "King Joe and the Boys." International Longshoremen's Association life president "King Joe" Ryan is seated next to John J. "Ike" Gannon, president of New York District Council ILA (from Hell's Kitchen "Pistol Local" 824). Standing are, from left to right, Paul Baker, general vice president; Gus Scannavino, international vice president representing New York; Charles P. Spencer, secretary-treasurer, Atlantic Coast District; Harry B. Hasselgren, international secretary and treasurer, New York; John V. Silke, vice president, Portland, Me. New York City, ca. 1950. Courtesy of the Archives of the Xavier Institute of Industrial Relations, Fordham University Library, Bronx, New York.

I *Chelsea's King Joe*

In 1912 a West Side boy named Joe Ryan "went down to the docks"—as he ritually testified in later years—to join his older brother Tom and throngs of Chelsea Irish working the magnificent new piers jutting into the North River. Although Joseph P. Ryan's career as a working longshoreman lasted less than a year, in 1927 he was elected president of the International Longshoremen's Association. Sixteen years later Ryan's title was amended to "life president" (see figure 1). Political cartoonist Thomas Nast died a decade before Joe Ryan went to work on the piers, but the spirit of Nast's lurid anti-Irish illustrations lived on in the ardent Ryan-bashing featured in the nation's left-leaning journals of opinion from the 1930s through the early 1950s. Unlike his higher-ups in the Irish waterfront chain of command, Joe was always pleased to supply fresh material to his legion of detractors.

Manhattan's West Side waterfront spawned smarter, tougher, greedier, and far more violent men than Joseph Patrick Ryan, but none was a truer son of the Irish waterfront than "King Joe." During his nearly three-decade reign as union kingpin, Tammany stalwart, and notorious "mob associate," Ryan was variously described in public print as a gangster, a soft touch, and a fascist; maudlin, morose, and full of blarney; a captive, a pratt-boy, and a brawler; a trencherman; an aficionado of silk underwear and bejeweled pinky rings; stubby-fingered, cauliflower-eared, and barrel-chested; a hack, a punk, and a thug; a florid plug-ugly; and a devoted family man and daily communicant at his neighborhood parish, Guardian Angel, the Shrine Church of the Sea.

Mary Shanahan Ryan died giving birth to Joe, her fourth child, in Babylon, Long Island, in 1884. James Ryan, like his wife an immigrant from County Tipperary, remarried, and when he died in 1893 his penniless widow, Bridget, arranged for her stepdaughters to board with her brother while she moved with Joe and Tom to a tiny flat on Eighth Avenue in Chelsea.[1]

Families in that West Side neighborhood were typically large, Irish, and poor; nearly everyone who could work did, including children. Married women had to adapt to the unpredictable cycles of both childbirth and their husbands' irregular work on the piers. A woman who grew up in the neighborhood recalled: "We had the Wolfs with eight kids. We had the Lynches with twelve kids.... The Applegates had about fourteen. One day, there was all of us comin' out of the house, and this man came by, and he thought it was a school."[2]

Chelsea's low-rise dwellings "meant that everybody had access to the street." The neighborhood featured a richly Irish American cultural and religious life, with ten Catholic parishes located between West Fourteenth and West Thirty-fourth streets. There was a lively Catholic Youth Organization and a Police Athletic League famed for annually providing contenders for the Golden Gloves amateur boxing championships. There was "a James Connolly Club, St. Patrick's Day organizations, Irish youth gangs, even an Irish-American community newspaper, *The Shamrock*," noted Chelsea historian Joe Doyle. Then there were the workingmen's bars: "McManus's, McIntyre's, the Bank of Ireland, Moran's, Shannon's, Wilson's, just to name a few." Life was hard, and "much of the misery was caused by the drinking," declared a longtime Chelsea resident, recalling these "liquor joints where a stiff shot of rye or gin could be had for a nickel."[3]

The ubiquity of alcoholism in Chelsea and neighboring Irish waterfront communities can scarcely be overstated: extreme forms of inwardness, silence, and familial secrecy prompted by alcoholism may even help account for the tendency of the waterfront Irish to offer less than forthright public testimony of their experience with violence and family chaos. In *You Must Remember This*, a 1989 oral history of Manhattan neighborhoods, the only Irish American Chelsea interviewee willing to treat the issue chose to be identified by a pseudonym. "Peggy Dolan" recalled: "Come Friday nights, the men would come home and get drunk.... [T]hey all got drunk. And the women would say, 'that bum, that bum, here he comes again.... But if *you* said he was a bum, well, his family would kill you." An Italian American Chelsea native was haunted for life by memories of "lovely, lovely mothers with black eyes and their kids crying."[4]

The World the "Shape" Made

If West Side men hoped to work on the piers, they needed to congregate near if not *in* the bars, an integral component of the waterfront economy. "When a ship was coming in and reached Quarantine," recalled an early longshoremen's union leader,

> a flag would be flown from its pier so a gang of longshoremen could be assembled in two or three hours before the ship docked. A hundred men looking

predicted in his 1933 memoir, "If he hasn't forgotten the tricks I taught him he ought to get along."[11]

King Joe in the Neighborhood

"From the start, affable Joe Ryan showed skill in labor politics," wrote journalist Matthew Josephson in 1946. "He possessed a facility with the English language," gangland historian T. J. English noted; "his red-meat rhetoric was frequently humorous and sentimental." Ryan's rapid ascent was also closely tied to location. The ILA's headquarters was moved to West Fourteenth Street in Chelsea early in his union career. Ryan always treated it as his local clubhouse, even after he rose to the presidency of the union in 1927, with responsibility—on paper at least—for leadership of ILA district operations along the Atlantic, Gulf, and Pacific coasts, across the Great Lakes, and in Canada and Puerto Rico. Locally, according to William J. Keating, "the union was a political auxiliary of Tammany." Ryan's ILA powerbase was an integral component of Tammany's operation in the neighborhood and the city; his chairmanship of the AFL's Central Trades and Labor Council between 1928 and 1938 strengthened his ties to such citywide political powers as Jimmy Walker, the dapper mayor whose career ended in colorful scandal in 1932.[12]

The first mayor from the Irish waterfront, James J. Walker grew up on St. Luke's Place just three blocks from the West Village piers. Like Ryan, he was a product of St. Francis Xavier School. In the late 1890s his father, William H. Walker, Tammany's commissioner of public buildings, condemned a historic cemetery belonging to Trinity Episcopal Church; it was replaced by a neighborhood park. The Kilkenny-born alderman tended his own interests while serving constituents: the new park, whose presence raised local property values, was located directly across the street from the Walker family home. The Episcopalians retained a young Anglo-American attorney, Samuel Seabury, who with his father, a prominent Episcopal theologian and pastor, helped disinter the remains of Protestant forebears so that Irish Catholic children might play on the site. As a Progressive reformer, Judge Samuel Seabury would later zealously lead the investigation into municipal corruption that brought down the mayoral regime of "Beau James" Walker, privileged son of the Irish waterfront.[13]

The Seabury family fled their Chelsea home in 1900, part of the Protestant exodus that enabled the Irish waterfront to thrive on the site. Everything Joe Ryan ever needed could be found in the neighborhood: his comfortable home at 433 West Twenty-first Street; the Mother Local at 164 Eleventh Avenue; the Joseph P. Ryan Association clubhouse on West Eighteenth Street, a "private social club" founded in 1923 that "wields much political influence," as Matthew Josephson reported two decades later.

The Tammany Tough Club at 243 West Fourteenth Street was a favored watering hole of a thriving and thirsty local political leadership during the era of Prohibition.[14]

Above all Joe Ryan had the Chelsea Piers—a cash nexus to ensure that his taste for Sulka undershorts would never strain the family budget—and his church, Guardian Angel, where he was a "bountiful trustee." Guardian Angel was located just steps from Ryan's home, replacing an earlier and much less elegant incarnation slightly nearer the Chelsea piers. The façades of the new Romanesque church, designed by John V. Van Pelt and opened in 1930, "were among the most exquisitely crafted of the period"; they "conjured up the image of a humble Lombard country church decorated piecemeal over time." Few rank-and-file longshoremen worshipped at Guardian Angel, which became known as the "stevedore's [that is, the employer's] parish." Joe and Maggie Ryan were daily communicants at Guardian Angel's 8 A.M. Mass and often returned in the afternoon to make the Stations of the Cross, a meditative devotional practice once an integral feature of Catholic life.[15]

Father (later Monsignor) John J. O'Donnell, who became Ryan's pastor in 1934, reveled in his warm alliance with the labor boss and Tammany chieftain. By the time O'Donnell assumed the pastorate of Guardian Angel, the archdiocese had long since vanquished "any major rivals within the New York Irish community; and the dominant form of politics, that associated with the Democratic Party machine, complemented, rather than contested, the influence of the church." The loyalty of their Irish parishioners, remarked historian Hugh McLeod, "gave the clergy very considerable political influence. At the same time, the connections that they had with other powerful figures in the Irish community, notably politicians, meant that the clergy were respected even by those who had no love for them," including Irish nationalists and militant labor organizers. Even John Lovejoy Elliott, an agnostic and no admirer of the Catholic Church in his role as founding director of the Hudson Guild, a venerable Chelsea settlement house, "was forced to come to terms with the neighborhood priests" in order to function openly.[16]

By the late 1920s the deepening insularity of the ILA on the Irish waterfront distanced the men not only from outside insurgencies but from their own traditions as well, ranging from Irish nationalism to collaboration with women activists to support of the rights of African American longshoremen. All of these had been in evidence as recently as August 1920, when "the first purely political strike of workingmen in the history of the United States" (in the view of the *New York Sun*) broke out on the West Side piers. Dockworkers joined forces with a women's group in support of Irish independence at a moment, wrote Joe Doyle, when "a fever for independence gripped the Irish community in New York City." The strike was touched off by the arrests of Terence MacSwiney, "lord mayor of Cork City and

a republican military commander," and the interception at sea of Austra-
lia's Irish-born Archbishop Daniel Mannix, an anti-conscription firebrand
detained by British naval forces as he sought to travel from New York to
Ireland following a triumphal speaking tour of the United States.[17]

When Mannix's ship, the *Baltic*, returned to the Chelsea Piers on August 27, the Irish Patriotic Strike commenced. The staunch support of Irish
nationalism by the charismatic Marcus Garvey—leader of the United Negro
Improvement Association—helped persuade several hundred black dockworkers to join the strike for Irish freedom. The three-and-a-half-week walkout "had little effect on Britain's decision to grant Ireland independence,"
wrote Bruce Nelson, but it did lead to the integration—if short-lived—of
African Americans into the Chelsea Piers workforce, the experience of
diaspora and oppression briefly uniting black and Irish dockworkers "who
had long regarded each other with suspicion and even hatred."[18]

ILA vice president Joe Ryan was not among the supporters of the strike;
he may even have "built a power base among second-generation Irish Americans" from Local 791 who joined him in opposing the first-generation
strikers. Ryan's inaction was characteristic of the Irish waterfront's intense ethnocentrism and its peculiar variant of Americanism, grounded
in a worldview that was militantly localized even by Tammany standards.
In 1932 Ryan was the last prominent Tammanyite to publicly defend the
embattled Jimmy Walker, whose breezy laxity in governance and personal
affairs offended, respectively, secular reformers and such prominent New
York Catholics as Patrick Cardinal Hayes and Alfred E. Smith, the Lower
East Side Democratic politician who had been trounced by Herbert Hoover
in 1928 in his bid to become the first Catholic elected president of the
United States. Smith kept his eye on the national picture, as did the Tammany sachems, who willingly parted company with "Beau James" despite
pro-Walker rallies organized by Ryan, who lamented that "political expe-
dience" had deprived working New Yorkers of the services—such as they
were—of a mayor "whose every official act has been in conformity with the
Americanistic policies of organized labor."[19]

Joe Ryan's vision was so parochial, his loyalty to the boys of the Irish
waterfront so intensely tribal, it is deeply incongruous to picture him as
leader of an international union with large memberships on three seacoasts
and the Great Lakes. In the 1930s Ryan's union arch-nemesis emerged in
the person of Harry Bridges, an Australian-born San Franciscan who went
to work on the docks in 1923 and a decade later led longshoremen out of a
company union and into the ILA. In 1934 a maritime strike designed to win
union control of hiring halls sent Ryan hustling to San Francisco, where he
promptly negotiated his own settlement with steamship owners as though
he had never left Chelsea. Ryan barely avoided a beating or worse when
he appeared at a mass meeting to order the men back to work. "From that
moment on," according to Bruce Nelson, King Joe "was a dead letter on the

West Coast." He fired Bridges as ILA organizer in 1936; the following year Ryan's enemy of choice took his men out of the ILA and into a new CIO outfit, the International Longshoremen and Warehousemen's Union.[20]

Ryan's "loss" of the West Coast dockworkers has generally been viewed as evidence of his ineptitude; but given Joe's indifference to the "outports" beyond New York Harbor, he may not have been sorry to see Harry Bridges go his own way. The fact that Bridges was pro-communist—and very likely a party member—served Ryan well in the contentious years to come as a convenient pretext to play the Red card whenever he was threatened by local insurgencies or by Bridges's expansionist designs on the rank and file in Atlantic coast ports. Bridges, acknowledged as a genuinely effective if stubborn union leader by even his harshest critics—apart from Ryan—remained a key player in the protracted ideological and political struggle that pitted the Left, and communists in particular, against the Catholic Church for influence in the national labor movement. That conflict was vividly dramatized in the Port of New York, notwithstanding a paucity of actual communists working its piers.[21]

In Chelsea, Irish waterfront credentials trumped all legal or moral claims emanating from outside. In April 1953—as Ryan's tenure as "life president" ebbed—a member of a U.S. Senate subcommittee investigating waterfront crime asked him about the recently indicted business agent of Local 791. Ryan smugly replied: "I can safely say that Jay O'Connor is a boy from the neighborhood. His grandfather worked as a longshoreman. His father worked as a longshoreman." Or as a neighborhood lifer put it, "In those days, the docks were Chelsea." For urban Irish Americans like Ryan, historian Christopher Shannon argued, "ethnicity is not *who* you are but *where* you are." Identity on the Irish waterfront was grounded less in a sense of ancestral heritage than in territorial privilege. Ethnographers and other social scientists who studied these waterfront communities (often sponsored by the settlement houses founded by secular reformers in Chelsea, Greenwich Village, and Hell's Kitchen) observed that the Irish, and especially Irish longshoremen, retained a strong proprietary sense even when—as in the Village—Italian Americans far surpassed them in numbers. "Hard-won Irish success, however limited, tended to make them disdainful of the new immigrant groups," as historian Thomas M. Henderson observed.[22]

While conducting research for a 1939 study of West Village longshoremen and their homes commissioned by Greenwich House, a prominent nonsectarian institution, Elizabeth Ogg was "struck by the strong feeling of superiority of the Irish-Americans, both in neighborhood life and in labor situations on the piers." She noted that "in times past the Irish were dominant on all New York piers and especially in nearby Chelsea" and now resented "the intrusion of the Italians." But it was not just the arrival of the Italians that cast a shadow over the Irish waterfront; the mobility of the Irish community itself generated strong if not always clearly articulated emotions. "As early as 1910," according to historian Marion R. Casey, "the Irish still living in Greenwich Village, Hell's Kitchen, and Chelsea were considered to be remnants of a much larger, nineteenth-century Irish population that had long since moved on to 'better surroundings'" such as the South Bronx, Bay Ridge and Sunset Park in Brooklyn, and Sunnyside in Queens.[23]

The Irish who remained in Chelsea fought for their waterfront terrain as though it was sacred space. Because the neighborhood was so densely packed with longshoremen and the union's "international" headquarters was housed there, it was natural that outside observers and natives alike would tend to view Chelsea as a microcosm of the port. As Budd Schulberg later remarked: "If you controlled 791, you controlled the West Side. If you controlled the West Side, you controlled the harbor." Joe Ryan, his surrogates, and his rivals fought so hard for control of West Side Locals 791, 824 (Hell's Kitchen), and 895 (Greenwich Village) that "the Harbor" was rendered an abstraction. An amorphous place made up of remote enclaves (many even located in a foreign state!), the port felt too vast for any single agency or force to cover.[24]

Strike in the Mile Square City

On October 21, 1919, Joe Ryan was arrested in Hoboken, New Jersey, and charged with inciting a riot. The previous year he had been elected president of the Atlantic Coast District of the ILA. He had traveled across the Hudson to the "Mile Square City" with a group of ILA leaders including the union's president, T. V. O'Connor, determined to persuade striking longshoremen to accept a modest settlement they had reached with shippers. The 1919 strike was the third in a series of "explosive, harborwide" confrontations that had closed the port for varying lengths of time since 1887. "In between," wrote historian Calvin Winslow, "there were periods of apathy and inactivity, and while trade unionism existed, it tended to be conservative, and its presence was minimal, restricted to local and sectional organizations." The 1919 longshoremen's strike—one of 3,630 job actions nationwide in that convulsive postwar year, involving dozens of industries and over 4 million workers—confirmed dockworkers' resentment of a union leadership that was at once authoritarian and overcautious.[25]

O'Connor and Ryan were booed lustily by strikers when they arrived at St. Mary's Hall in Hoboken accompanied by "six husky bodyguards. They may have expected "a friendly welcome," recalled Dick Butler, "but what they got was catcalls, curses, and some extra choice billingsgate." A riot broke out when "one of the visitors jumped off the stage and knocked down a longshoreman who was coming toward it." A court officer wrote at the time, "It is a serious matter if Hoboken working men, whether on strike or not, could not hold a meeting without having New York 'gunmen' and 'roughnecks' come over and try to break up the meeting." Butler "learned later that O'Connor on his way out of the hall was offered a shotgun by the parish priest to defend himself, but T. V. was too anxious to get away from there."[26]

In the short run the debacle undermined O'Connor's ILA presidency and enhanced Ryan's prospects, since Joe conveyed the impression of supporting his leader strictly in the name of union loyalty. The men won a raise, Butler noted, and eventually "instead of T. V. O'Connor as head of the international they got Joe Ryan, which was some improvement at least." At the same time, the incident foreshadowed the role that would be played by ILA insurgents in Ryan's ultimate downfall and also exposed his tendency to find trouble whenever he strayed from Chelsea.[27]

Of all locales "foreign" to denizens of the West Side, Hoboken should have been the least threatening to Ryan. As a veteran journalist who covered both sides of the waterfront once remarked, had a path been paved across the Hudson, Chelsea and Hoboken would have made one neighborhood. These maritime villages shared a virtually identical dialect and dominant religious preference; they also shared the prestige of port leadership in deep-sea shipping operations. But the path went unpaved, and the waterfronts of Hoboken and Chelsea developed subtle differences in the conduct of the shapeup and equally subtle yet significant differences in the politics of ethnicity.[28]

Hoboken was more ethnically fluid than Chelsea, the West Village, or Hell's Kitchen. Although Italian American longshoremen crammed into their inland enclave "west of Willow" surely did not discern much fluidity in the attitudes of the dominant Irish—from pier hiring bosses to politicians to clerics—the nature of the city's waterfront labor market after 1917 forced interaction between the groups; men scrambled from pier to pier as work became available. Two Italian parishes established by different branches of the Franciscan Order, St. Francis (1888) and St. Ann's (1900), were well situated to serve the large number of Italian immigrant dockworkers and their families. St. Ann's was especially identified with the preservation of Italian identity and traditions and fostered a strong sense of ethnic solidarity that sustained dockworkers in their struggles with Hoboken's Irish ILA leadership.[29]

On the West Side of Manhattan, Irish American longshoremen might offer financial support to a struggling local Italian parish, but they did not shape up alongside Italians on their piers, as was increasingly the case in Hoboken. That city's Irish and Italians both toiled in the shadow of an imposing German American legacy severed when, in the wake of the First World War, the United States government confiscated the pier sheds of the Hamburg-American and North German Lloyd steamship lines which had towered over the city's waterfront for decades. Their absence left a massive hole in the waterfront economy that was never completely filled, creating a competitive, cost-driven labor market that did not permit the kind of separate Irish labor aristocracies found along Manhattan's West Side, where men worked the piers in long-standing "regular" gangs.[30]

Ten days before his appearance in Hoboken with Joe Ryan, T. V. O'Connor blamed the 1919 strike on "an element of agitators...an Italian element" who ignited the strike in Brooklyn before it spread across the port. The response of O'Connor and Ryan confirms Calvin Winslow's contention that "the Irish believed the union belonged to them." In New York "the union was organized in a way which not only followed the patterns of racial and ethnic division in the city and in the industry, but also reinforced them." The union was in fact organized differently from neighborhood to neighborhood, if not from pier to pier. ILA locals in Hoboken would develop in ways reflecting the more routine—if often uneasy and occasionally quite violent— interactions of Irish and Italian Americans.[31]

If, as journalist and future sociologist Daniel Bell observed, Joe Ryan "left the Italians strictly alone," this policy greatly limited his effectiveness beyond the West Side. Yet Ryan faced sporadic opposition even on his home turf and among his fellow Irish, as evidenced in autumn 1919, when strikers in Chelsea battered an Irish American ILA district leader as he attempted to force them back to work. The waterfront Irish were never a strictly homogeneous unit, labor historians agree, but those same historians struggle to account for the habit of the men to rise up periodically against the union's corrupt leadership, only to retreat again into the inscrutable guise of "loyal opposition" when the prospect of real change conflicted with received notions of authority and its prerogatives. Joe Ryan's "life presidency" of the ILA was only as secure as the Irish waterfront's great chain of being.[32]

2   The Boss

The most powerful political figure in the port was Frank Hague, Jersey City's mayor from 1917 to 1947 and boss of Hudson County for even longer (see figure 2). "In no other American city did one man wield so much power," historian William Lemmey rightly noted. "Hague's career has no analogy in urban bossism."[1]

The house in which Frank Hague was born in 1876 was later dubbed "the Ark" because a stagnant pond often swelled to surround the modest dwelling after rainstorms. John and Margaret Hague, immigrants from County Cavan, raised their eight children—Frank was the fourth—in the city's "Horseshoe," named for the shape of the waterfront electoral district, gerrymandered by the Republican state legislature in 1871 to contain the city's mushrooming population of Irish Democratic voters.

Hague's power was rooted in the Horseshoe's waterfront gateway to New York Harbor, a site overlooked by historians, who customarily sever the city's railroads from the shipping industry in which they played such a vital role. Jersey City's rapid growth following the Civil War was generated by the railroads, which quickly supplanted the Morris Canal as the fledgling city's engine of economic development. Jersey City—which borders Hoboken on the south and towers over the Mile Square City from its Heights neighborhood—eventually boasted the largest freight rail terminal on the East Coast. Since no rail tunnel for freight was ever dug under the Hudson River—a fateful lapse symptomatic of the historic ill will between the two states—New York City remained largely beholden to waterborne trade with Hudson County even after the advent of motorized trucks and the opening of the George Washington Bridge in 1931. The New York Central Railroad stood alone in enjoying direct rail access to Manhattan, but its freight trains crossed the Hudson via a bridge far upriver, then proceeded south, doubling back on a long journey to the West Side.[2]

Figure 2. Frank Hague with presidential candidate Franklin D. Roosevelt and New Jersey governor A. Harry Moore prior to a campaign rally at the Jersey Shore, summer 1932. Courtesy of the Jersey City Free Public Library.

In the late nineteenth century, Walt Whitman marveled at a harbor "thick as stars in the sky" with vessels, "all sorts and sizes of sail and steam[,] ... plying ferry boats, arriving and departing coasters." For decades New York Harbor was clogged with barges, lighters, car floats onto which freight cars were slid, and other vessels transporting goods to and from the great metropolis. The Erie Railroad employed seven hundred men in its lighterage operation alone.[3]

This bi-state commerce between Jersey City (and, to a lesser extent, Weehawken) and the West Side of Manhattan was both the lifeblood of the port and its most vexing feature: one port, two states. The two waterfronts ensured decades of mutual mistrust exacerbated by the haughty attitude of Manhattan's civic elites. Hudson County was itself cut off from the continental landmass by a latticework of estuaries, creeks, and two rivers that emerged from a vast salt marsh before wending their way into Newark Bay. These features—along with its overwhelmingly immigrant Catholic populace—likewise aggravated the mutual alienation of Hudson County from the Garden State's mainland. This densely populated waterfront county and its people were generally misunderstood, feared, and isolated, a reputation many of its residents cultivated with relish. Yet New Yorkers who regarded this Jersey shore as an alien backwater neglected at their peril a fundamental truth: the key to enduring power in the region was held by those who were most adept at covering the waterfront.

By the time Frank Hague entered politics in 1897, the property of the nine major railroads serving Jersey City consumed more than one-third of the city's terrain, extending far to the west of the water's edge; the massive acreage of docks, sidings, and yards occupied more urban space than many smaller cities in their entirety. Every major railroad serving the gargantuan New York market but one—the New York Central enjoyed a bridge crossing at distant Albany—"came to an abrupt halt at the Hudson River." In Jersey City, as historian Jill Jonnes noted, "there sprawled the terminals and ferry depots for the Pennsylvania and Erie railroads, as well as those of the New York, Ontario & Western Railroad, and the New York, Susquehanna & Western. The Central of New Jersey terminal sat slightly downriver in Communipaw and also served the Baltimore & Ohio, the Philadelphia & Reading, and the Lehigh Valley railroads."[4]

Jersey City's forbidding industrial waterfront was unlike anything found in Manhattan. On that side of the river "an almost continuous yard of the New York Central Railroad" ran up the West Side from the Battery to Riverside Drive. The tracks covered long stretches of Tenth and Eleventh avenues; mayhem at grade level crossings on both thoroughfares led to their popular renaming as "Death Avenue." This ribbon of rail yard with its "territory of warehouses containing a wealth of plunder" was a ripe target for casual thieves who struck quickly and disappeared into the surrounding streets clogged with traffic and merchants.[5]

Jersey City was different: its vast, concentrated acreage of harborside rail yards and terminals made for a separate waterfront empire and an urban political culture "where life is more simple and direct," as Daniel Bell noted, and "politics more brutal and unadorned." Describing Jersey City's unique and "essential pattern" of life, urban theorist Kevin Lynch wrote in 1960, "Everything stops at the barrier of the railroad-industrial-dock area on the Hudson"; everything started there too.[6]

Jersey City's railroads were built by Irish immigrants, men from Connaught and Munster who dug a crucial tunnel through the Palisades in the late 1850s, linking waterfront rail terminals with tracks laid in the meadowlands to the west and the vast continent that lay beyond. When in September 1859 a contractor announced that payment of wages would be delayed, a relatively peaceful protest of railroad workers was spun by a local newspaper editor into the "terrible riot of the tunnel men[,]...a mongrel mass of ignorance and crime and superstition." By 1870 the Jersey City waterfront was identified as the natural habitat of the foreign rabble. Conflating ethnic geography with social decay in the same way his paper had treated the docksides of Lower Manhattan, a *New York Times* reporter lamented that "Quality Row" in downtown Jersey City had had its views of the river and harbor spoiled by "the slimiest, dirtiest shore in this part of the country. When the tide is down, on a hot day, it is absolutely sickening. Old bits of carpet and clothing, ragged baskets, old tin kettles, bottles, and various articles of household crockery, all covered by green slime, are to be seen." By 1900, nearly 10 percent of Jersey City's 206,000 inhabitants were Irish-born; the vast majority lived in the waterfront precincts.[7]

The "Mayor of Cork Row" was Nat Kenny, proprietor of one of forty saloons found in the Horseshoe. Kenny launched Frank Hague's political career in 1897 by putting him up for election as constable in a bid to undermine a political rival. Kenny had been unable to find a taker for the contest until he approached Hague, a sixth-grade expellee and erstwhile employee of the Erie Railroad who had gained some notoriety as the manager of a neighborhood pugilist. Hague agreed to run for constable but told Kenny he would need "about seventy-five dollars, if I'm to make friends." Over the next half-century Frank Hague made far more dollars than friends; but his regime enjoyed the often grudging respect of Irish Americans—and the militant support of local Catholic pastors—and this was sufficient to maintain his iron grip on the city.[8]

The "Hague People"

As the head of a second-generation Irish political machine, Hague was the first boss to craft a persona that expressed the aspirations and moral sensibilities of the ascendant Jersey City Irish. Monsignor John Sheppard of St. Michael's parish in the Horseshoe was an early supporter of the Hague regime. Working with Sheppard, wrote William Lemmey, "Hague made Catholicism the city's quasi-official religion and never separated matters of Church and State." Sheppard's "influence and his power were enormous," his successor at St. Michael's acknowledged in a 1953 memoir. In 1913 Sheppard endorsed Hague in the pages of the parish bulletin when his young parishioner successfully ran for a seat on the city commission.[9]

Monsignor Sheppard shared genuine if paternalistic Progressive sympathies with Hague, who supported women's suffrage and quickly incorporated female voters within his "family-oriented organization." Hague did not drink or smoke and was "shyly polite around women," according to historian Barbara Burns Petrick. "Perhaps these were the qualities that recommended him" to the monsignor, described by political scientist Richard J. Connors as "thoroughly puritanical in his outlook." Hague eventually rewarded the loyalty of female voters by securing the election of women to the state assembly and the Hudson County Board of Chosen Freeholders; he also appointed the city's first policewoman in 1924. "Hague's congresswoman," Mary Norton—the daughter of impoverished Irish immigrant parents who was "almost as poorly educated" as the Boss himself—loyally served his regime in the U.S. House of Representatives from 1925 to 1951.[10]

As commissioner of public safety, Hague cracked down on indolent and corrupt cops, personally supervised raids on vaudeville theaters, and crusaded against prostitution and narcotics trafficking, highly publicized feats that in 1917 propelled him to the mayoralty, where he succeeded a most unlikely figure, Mark Fagan, an Irish Catholic Republican. A secular-minded reformer, Fagan was swept out of office in part because his plan to spend $3 million building new public schools found little support in a city whose population was nearly 75 percent Catholic. Under Hague's rule, municipal employees routinely cleared snow from the steps of parochial schools on city time; public school facilities were appropriated as needed for Catholic fund-raising activities. In the words of Barbara Burns Petrick, "the city's two sets of schools were informally, if not legally, unified." There were two free school options: "parochial schools for Catholic children who could find the room and public schools for those who could not." Catholic schoolchildren referred to the public Henry Snyder High School as "St. Henry's"; the monumental Dickinson High was known as "St. Richard's-on-the-Hill."[11]

"Hagueism was more than a political machine," wrote Jersey City historian Bob Leach. "It was a vast social order, organized upward from the neighborhood level and outward to include all spheres of social activity. It incorporated the schools, the churches, the police, lawyers, doctors, labor unions, and fraternal organizations." The "Hague people" who helped the Boss run Jersey City shared his Irish Catholicism and a general consensus as to a proper moral order for the community. Though Hague was described as "puritanical," his sensibilities were clearly rooted in a particular form of urban Irish Catholic morality. Prostitution, for example, was not tolerated (though not unheard of), but gambling was acceptable as long as it was controlled by Hague people, such as Joseph "Newsboy" Moriarty, anointed "king of the numbers racket" in the mid-thirties. As a Jersey City

cop described him, Newsboy Moriarty "was never a mobster. Just a numbers man—and not mean, either."[12]

Dozens of priests along with a few clergymen from other denominations
took their place on Jersey City's payroll as chaplains (including a priest who
earned his stipend as chaplain for the county maintenance garage). Unlike
in New York City, where Tammany and the Catholic archdiocese thrived
on a symbiotic relationship and "the power and status of Catholic priests
and Democratic politicians was mutually reinforcing," in Jersey City Hague
set the tone, both moral and political, while the church—or more precisely
the churches—followed his lead. Jersey City and neighboring Newark an-
chored the Roman Catholic diocese of Newark; when it was elevated to
archdiocesan status in 1937, Archbishop Thomas J. Walsh rose with it. But
"even bishops were loath" to take on Hague, who ruled, in historian Dermot Quinn's words, "by a hundred little fears."[13]

The contrast between these archdioceses facing each other across the Hudson grew even sharper with the ascension of Francis Spellman to archbishop
of New York in 1939. Spellman "clashed repeatedly with those whose views
he opposed," recalled William O'Dwyer, New York City's mayor from 1946
to 1950. "He watched the legislative halls for any enactments which would
in any way hamper the teachings of the church or would seem to encroach
upon what is regarded as the church or tamper with its temporal welfare."
Newark's archdiocesan leadership generally respected the decentralized localism that dominated Jersey political custom. Archbishop Walsh largely refrained from involvement in the politics of Democratic-owned and operated
Hudson County. As Richard J. Connors concisely explained, "there was no
real Catholic *Church* in Jersey City, only a number of autonomous parishes,
little related to each other in their routine activities."[14]

Frank Hague skillfully manipulated the system; his organization worked
to "perpetuate the natural fragmentation of Catholic church life in Jersey
City" by providing "the integrating mechanism for the city as a whole,"
with the staunch support of individual pastors who both shared his values
and stood to benefit greatly from the unfettered exercise of his power. According to novelist and historian Thomas Fleming (whose father, Teddy,
ran Jersey City's Sixth Ward for the Boss in conjunction with Monsignor
Joseph Meehan of All Saints parish): "Organization was a sacred word.
The word 'machine' was never used.... An organization implied that there
was this hierarchy—from the top down—all these different levels of importance, different duties, different responsibilities." In this sense Frank Hague
was clearly the dominant *religious* leader in Hudson County and the de
facto ruling Catholic. Parishes were simply fused to the machine. "Hague
demanded that his ward leaders and precinct captains take an active role
in Church activities," noted William Lemmey. "Mass on Sunday, involvement in the Holy Name Society, Knights of Columbus, and Communion
breakfasts were mandatory. Ward and precinct leaders cultivated goodwill

by securing jobs, hiring parish halls for political meetings, rallies, and other parish activities."[15]

As a result, recalled veteran political reporter and St. Patrick's parish product John Farmer: "Church and state knew no separation in the Jersey City of my youth. Together they presided over a strict private morality and a thriving public pilferage." Not precisely a theocracy, Jersey City featured a model of politics and religion whereby the "church" was shaped by extra-ecclesial forces beginning with an Irish waterfront *sensus fidelium* featuring a close acquaintance with violence as spiritual foundation.[16]

"Hague's political technique was a blend of violence and benevolence," affirmed Thomas Fleming. While serving as commissioner of public safety in 1916 Hague pursued across the county line into Newark a man suspected of killing Nat Kenny's son Frank. Hague made the collar personally and later pummeled the suspect at Jersey City police headquarters. Mayor Hague's few brave local critics absorbed more than their share of beatings at the hands of the "Zeppelin Squad" (or "Zepps"), an elite, handpicked cadre of police officers who cracked heads and "deported" undesirables via the Manhattan ferry. Other enforcers were informally deputized, especially on election days: in 1920 an uninvited group of visiting Princeton University students determined to safeguard polling places were kicked and beaten "by a dozen Jersey City men" who "sent them crying, with concussions, back to their ivy-covered walls." In 1929 the driver of a city bus "deliberately backed right through" the entrance of "an anti-Hague local club headquarters," and in 1937 "a group of some 30 longshoremen wielding baseball bats drove a half-dozen state troopers from a polling place." Victims of election violence were not limited to opponents: "once, an eight-year-old girl was accidentally hit in the head by one of the sluggers and killed." It is not difficult to see why Jersey City historian J. Owen Grundy—a Protestant—urged a political scientist to "picture this era as a reign of terror."[17]

Hague's legitimacy, like that of Joe Ryan, was grounded in his upbringing in a brawler's world that was inherited, not made, and that afforded opportunities for redemption within a rigidly moral order. His regime was the model for the hierarchical structure of the Irish waterfront. All "Hague people" contributed daily to its preservation—gangster, priest, and cop alike. The organization violently forestalled threats of "disorder"—a capacious category including communists, birth control advocates, and CIO organizers among numerous other undesirables—while presiding over a waterfront reshaped in the image of its own authority. With social order ensured by his regime's intimacy with violence, Hague built an enormous medical center offering free care to all who could not pay along with some who could; its centerpiece was the Margaret Hague Maternity Hospital, opened in October 1931.

Tens of thousands of Hudson County residents began life in "the Margaret Hague," a ten-story edifice in the Art Deco style featuring "a stainless steel chandelier in the delivery room, penthouses and a movie theater on the top floor." The medical center was located halfway up the steep slope of Montgomery Street between the river and Hague's penthouse apartment on Hudson Boulevard, its multitude of buildings seemingly tilted at a jaunty angle toward the waterfront like a sly salute. Hague spent at least as much time in his mahogany-paneled office ("complete with a mysterious door to a back hallway") at the medical center as he did at City Hall. He often placed emergency calls to test response times and punched the nose of at least one intern whose cavalier attitude was deemed unacceptable.[18]

Hague's political philosophy might be termed "populist realism," a key component of this distinctly Catholic worldview that resonated across the Irish waterfront. Populist realism as practiced by Hague coupled rough sympathy for underdogs with a rougher appraisal of human nature grounded in the ever present reality of sin as revealed in human conduct. Mercy and forgiveness were deployed strategically; even these qualities bore marks of Hague's intimacy with violence.

Known as the "union mayor" early in his career, during the October 1919 longshoremen's strike Hague ordered police to deport invading (from New York) strikebreakers from the Jersey City piers. Like most Jersey citizens Hague did not care for outside agitators of any description. But he was even more fearful of homegrown disorder: when the impasse was not resolved locally and strikebreakers returned, "they were not molested." In the early 1930s Hague crushed a powerful former ally, labor leader Theodore Brandle, over disputes pitting Brandle's Ironworkers Union against contractors building the medical center and the Pulaski Skyway, an ominous-looking three-mile-long bridge over the Passaic and Hackensack rivers and the forbidding industrial landscape that lay between. "Hague proceeded to take over almost every union in Jersey City," recalled Thomas Fleming. "He then proclaimed the city free of labor troubles and invited industry to enjoy the enforced tranquility."[19]

Late in the decade efforts by the Congress of Industrial Organizations to bring industrial unionism to Jersey City was violently resisted, earning Hague widespread condemnation as an incipient fascist. (In one notorious episode socialist orator Norman Thomas was virtually kidnapped by police, who then "dumped him onto the Pavonia Avenue Ferry bound for Manhattan.") Hague's flagship International Longshoremen's Association was an affiliate of the older American Federation of Labor—which represented conservative trade unionism in opposition to the CIO's radical industrial-union approach—but the only distinction that mattered to Hague was that the ILA reinforced his Irish waterfront authority. The rapid ascent of the CIO in the late 1930s served to highlight the ideological issues that pitted the secular Left labor movement against Hague's authoritarian Catholic regime. Nevertheless, in 1944 Hague won election to an eighth term as mayor with CIO support after he successfully fought to force railroads to pay back taxes; a political enemy, Charles Edison (son of inventor Thomas A. Edison), had while governor engineered a massive reduction in assessments.[20]

The Boss and His Waterfront

Frank Hague's most notorious utterance, "I am the law," is revealed in context as the classic expression of populist realism. Two twelve-year-old boys, deemed incorrigible, were en route to a correctional facility when Hague intervened. After talking with the boys—who told him they ardently preferred jail to school—the mayor had them put to work instead, over the objections of local educators who cited the law requiring that twelve-year-olds attend school. "In this case," bellowed Hague, "I am the law." Thomas F. X. Smith, one of Hague's successors as Jersey City mayor, who was himself "saved from prison" by a similar intervention, recalled that "the Hague approach gave the youthful braggarts nothing to swagger about—and few wanted to talk about the severe beating they received (and their fathers, too, if *they* complained)."[21]

Hague first told his "I am the law" story in November 1937 at a Methodist church at the corner of Belmont and Bergen avenues, a stronghold of the city's uptown Protestant elite. Jersey City Methodists did not share the mayor's theological anthropology. Had Hague confined his storytelling to Catholic gatherings, "I am the law" surely would not have been repeated to outsiders, sparing Hague the derision his remarks inspired among non-Catholics. The mayor did, however, more than level the playing field between the Jersey City Irish and old-stock Protestants, beginning with his own head start. On an annual salary that never exceeded $8,000 Hague somehow maintained a palatial summer home at Deal on the Jersey Shore and a sumptuous winter redoubt in Florida, in addition to his Park Avenue apartment and Hudson Boulevard penthouse with its commanding vista of downtown, the waterfront, and the skyline of Manhattan. Although Hague's manner of living scarcely qualified him as a "man of the people," he was conceded his luxuries as long as he remained in touch with his origins and the aspirations of his core constituents. As Smith put it:

> Wasn't he one of them underneath the expensive, tailor-made suit he usually wore with a vest and stiff, high collar? That pearl stickpin, costly necktie, shining patent leather shoes, and tilted derby—weren't they only the signs of a local boy who had made good? And if Frank Hague, the kid from the Horseshoe, could make it, well, couldn't they make it, too?[22]

Similarly, journalist Matthew Josephson noted that rank-and-file dockworkers liked "the touch of brass" sported by Hague's friend Joe Ryan of the ILA. "He dresses with splendor, wearing painted neckties and pin-striped, elegantly tailored double-breasted suits. 'Next to myself, I like silk under-wear best,' he has said with a defiant laugh." Ryan himself claimed to enjoy "good food of all kinds," adding, "and I think my longshoremen want me to have it." Indeed, "no loader, bull-staller or dock cooper cuts across his path whom he doesn't call by his first name," wrote Meyer Berger in the *New York Times*. "They just call him 'Joe.' He wouldn't have it otherwise." Even one of Ryan's harshest critics, journalist Maurice Rosenblatt, conceded in 1945 that he "has not lost the common touch." While this waterfront populist realism exploited by Hague and Ryan might readily be discounted as a crudely self-justifying ideology of power, it was deeply rooted in a com-munal ethos, in a shared view of how the world worked.[23]

The dominant strain of modern Catholic social teaching is grounded in the notion of *subsidiarity,* a conviction that human dignity is best promoted at the most intimate levels of social organization: the family, the neighbor-hood, the parish. "Ruthless in business," wrote Matthew Josephson, "Ryan is charitable in private life, never forgets a friend.... [O]ften in the morning he walks along the West Side docks near his home in the Chelsea section and freely hands out dollar bills or fivers to old gaffers who hail him with: 'Hello, Joe!'"[24] Notoriously fearful of germs, Frank Hague eschewed Joe Ryan's personal touch, but his organization was likewise geared to dispense mercy if not justice at the neighborhood level. Ward leaders and surrogates understood that families were not to be evicted from their homes; the sick were visited in the hospital; the dead were buried in dignity. Yet this popu-list Catholic ethos featured a very dark side on the waterfront. Jersey City boss loader and Hague lieutenant James "Happy" Keane was once asked, strictly off the record, how he squared his devout Catholicism with the brutality of life on the piers, where troublemakers tended to disappear per-manently from view. A daily communicant whose temporal well-being was tended by a seven-foot bodyguard named Cosmo, Keane explained that while God meant for all to be created in his image and all were equal in his eyes, "a few bad apples always slipped into the barrel."[25]

A Christian social order needed to be vigilantly maintained in that water-front setting where a state of savagery was more likely to prevail. Conflict would erupt later when Catholic reformers challenged the acceptance of casual brutality as a divinely sanctioned way of life, but even then all par-ties to any dispute on the Irish waterfront acknowledged that it demanded resolution by a moral and spiritual authority grounded in their own tradi-tions. Long after the Irish lost their majority status among the dockworker population, Irish-Catholic union figures, politicians, and priests claimed this authority by custom. When custom failed, force was employed as likewise sanctioned by tradition.

During Hague's entire reign, only one non-Irishman, Michael "Mike Scat" Scatuorchio, served as a Jersey City ward leader. The city's waterfront was operated strictly under Irish auspices with a virtually unlimited bounty of swag at stake. Happy Keane and his trusty associate Cornelius McKeon were installed in their posts in the early 1930s with the intercession of Hague's good friend and Democratic crony Joe Ryan. These "loaders-in-charge," as Keane preferred to be called, managed a steady patronage flow and remitted a healthy cut from the loading racket to the mayor. They also ensured that in an era of CIO union organizing campaigns which threatened Hague's absolute rule—and which were met with violent resistance—Jersey City's AFL-affiliated ILA Local 1247 would continue to provide "a fruitful field for the service-and-favors politics of the machine."[26]

Hague's "Little Guy"

The mayor's broader interests on the waterfront were tended by John V. Kenny, son of Hague's original patron, Nat Kenny, and leader of the Second Ward, where the diminutive Kenny ("the Little Guy") could be found each day presiding "on Pavonia Avenue at the corner of Erie. Kenny used to stand on the walk in the mornings and in the day with his constituents," recalled a Jersey City native who once arranged to buy his ILA union book from Kenny on the street for the discounted price of $250. From his perch just to the waterfront side of St. Michael's Church, the parish's leading benefactor dispensed jobs and good counsel while collecting all due tribute. Hague named Kenny leader of the Second Ward in 1931, making him first among equals in the machine's upper echelon.[27]

The Second Ward enjoyed a special "mystique," as historian William Lemmey explained, because the Jersey City Irish who relocated uptown remained spiritually connected to their home turf. A 1911 graduate of the Jesuits' elite St. Peter's Prep, located in downtown Jersey City just two blocks to the waterfront side of Local 1247's offices, Kenny had already made a small fortune as a bookkeeper for the nearby Erie Railroad and from the inherited proceeds of his father's saloons. He now became de facto boss of Local 1247 and took quickly to his new duties as waterfront employment broker and bagman.[28]

"The waterfront was the scene of a violent and brutal life style, but Kenny adapted to it," Lemmey wryly noted. The organization took its cut from the payrolls of the bloated municipal bureaucracy ("the pad"), whose employees were required to kick back 3 percent of their salary in a gloomy monthly ritual known as "rice pudding day" ("rice pudding" was a local bartenders' term for the coins belonging to distracted customers that they swiped surreptitiously from the mahogany). Frank Hague's many critics on the outside never understood that kickbacks from Jersey City's public employees paled next to the bounty pouring forth from the docks, especially from the loading racket, a system that guaranteed income from every exchange made between rail cars, trucks, and barges. The Boss had departed the political scene by the time Daniel Bell accurately noted: "In Jersey City the piers still form one of the chief sources of job patronage for those faithful to the machine, and the loading concessions are one of the plums of political victory. In turn, the kickbacks from jobs, and the assessments from these prizes, finance the political machine."[29]

Frank Hague was, like John V. Kenny, a St. Michael's parish product, but a move uptown in the early years of his mayoralty made him a parishioner at St. Aedan's on Bergen Avenue, upon which he bestowed in 1931 a beautiful $50,000 high altar. (He also worshipped regularly at St. Patrick's Church, located to the south of his second home at the medical center.) One of Hague's neighbors in the luxury apartment building at nearby 2600 Hudson Boulevard—where the mayor, his stately wife, and their two children occupied the lavish penthouse—was Cornelius "Connie" Noonan, a leading associate of West Side gangster Cockeye Dunn and a menacing waterfront figure in his own right.

Noonan, whose impoverished family had been taken in by Nat Kenny at his home in the Second Ward when Connie was seven years old, joined the ILA in 1936 and later became business agent and president of the ILA's Inland Terminal Workers Union Local 1730. Noonan enjoyed great influence through his connections with the fearsome Cockeye, with whom he once shared the chores of business agent at Greenwich Village Local 21510 (predecessor of 1730 and the home base of Dunn's loading racket operation). These multidigit entities were not real unions. As Bell explained: "Dunn did not organize workers; he simply went to the employers, 'negotiated' a contract, and then told the freight handlers they belonged to his union." Connie Noonan was also an officer in Varick Enterprises, an outfit "which employed roving strong arm squads to cover piers throughout the port and make the collections" on loading fees from recalcitrant shippers. Under Noonan's leadership the loading racket was transplanted to Jersey City as a shakedown tactic, a practice unknown in other major ports.[30]

The Irish waterfront's business model was polished to near perfection by Varick Enterprises, which "quickly became so efficient," wrote *New York Sun* journalist Malcolm Johnson, that "those in control had information on every shipment of goods, whether by water or rail, arriving in the city." As a waterfront employer that controlled key segments of the ILA by threats and intimidation, Varick could quickly orchestrate a strike against recalcitrant shippers; the firm also "at one time helped elect a leader of Tammany Hall," Joe Ryan's good pal Michael J. Kennedy. (Cockeye Dunn served on a "Labor for Kennedy" committee in support of the sachem's successful 1938 run for Congress.) Connie Noonan's interlocking functions in management (Varick Enterprises) and labor (ILA organizer) was a distinctive feature of the New York–New Jersey waterfront rackets and indeed the port's unique political economy. Cockeye Dunn also held an interest in Varick: according to Dunn's confederate Daniel Gentile, Connie Noonan partnered with

Cockeye and his mobster brother-in-law Eddie McGrath in controlling Manhattan's West Side numbers racket. Connie's brother Edward Noonan was a Jersey City police captain in command of the waterfront precinct.[31]

Thanks to the spoils of office, as well as his closely tended connections with such cosmopolitan waterfront characters as the Noonan brothers, Jersey City's Frank Hague was able to enjoy a near daily luncheon table at Manhattan's luxurious Plaza Hotel or entertain guests at his Park Avenue apartment. The Boss reportedly intervened with New York City law enforcement officials on behalf of Jersey City constituents who found themselves on the wrong side of both the river and the law. New Yorkers customarily turned a scornful gaze on New Jersey, when they gazed at all. Given the unique features of the bi-state port's political economy, however, a presence on both sides of the Hudson was the key to power, wealth, and longevity on the waterfront. Frank Hague had it covered.[32]

Yet not even the Boss ruled the harbor with the potency of his close friend William J. McCormack, the prodigiously self-made entrepreneur who came to be known as the waterfront's "Mr. Big."

3   *Becoming Mr. Big*

William J. McCormack was a "fabulously powerful" businessman and proprietor of what the *New York Times* described as "a vast and somewhat mysterious" waterfront empire. Born into poverty in a coldwater flat at Washington and West Tenth Streets in Manhattan's West Village, McCormack always gave 1890 as the year of his birth. Waterfront insiders suspected he was older and with good reason: a baptismal record from St. Veronica's church officially marks his date of birth as November 10, 1887. Bill was the youngest of four children born to Julia Frances Moran and Andrew McCormack, a Famine migrant from County Monaghan who found work as a wagon driver in the teeming Washington Market along the Lower West Side waterfront. The devoutly Catholic family was allegedly too poor to send Bill to the parish school, though St. Veronica's did not charge tuition at the time; as late as 1908 the school's principal reported that "almost half of the fathers of the students were unemployed." Bill McCormack's formal education in public school ended after six years.[1]

Working by age ten, at thirteen Bill was a full-time wagon boy in the Washington Market, where, after thirty-nine years of grueling labor, Andrew McCormack was unceremoniously sent packing with half a week's pay of seven dollars, having taken sick in midweek. The struggling family moved across the river to Jersey City, where Bill and his older brother Harry went to work trucking fruits and vegetables from the "Peach Yard" at Second and Henderson streets to the nearby piers for shipment to Manhattan; they started out with "one white truck pulled by horses." A former friend from their early days in Jersey City distinguished Harry ("the plodding type") from Bill: "the kind of guy who always has his eyes on a higher level." Someone "able to handle men," Bill McCormack quickly rose to become foreman in a local trucking concern; at age twenty-three, along with Harry, he bought the firm and its downtown stable at Gregory and Van

Vorst streets. The brothers then moved with their parents into a home at 37 Van Reipen Avenue, just off Journal Square, the thriving uptown district far removed from the brawling waterfront.[2]

Upward mobility could not soften Bill and Harry, long remembered in Jersey City as "two of the toughest guys downtown." Harry, though smaller in stature than his younger brother, had "the strength of a lion and Willie wasn't far behind him." In the early 1950s, two lifelong Jersey Citizens (one a former police inspector) separately recounted a memorable incident they witnessed in 1913. During a strike of produce handlers a McCormack-owned horse-drawn truck driven by a one-legged man was intercepted along the Paterson Plank Road in Jersey City; its contents were dumped and its harnesses cut by a posse that included produce handlers' union delegate Sonny McDermott. After learning just whose property he had vandalized, a trembling McDermott made his appearance at the McCormacks' stable to explain the misunderstanding. An ex-prizefighter named Charles Gordon Maphet—also known as Cal McCarthy—described the ensuing scene:

> I heard angry shouts and I went running around to the side of the barn. There was Harry in front of the horse trough. In his arms, like you would hold a doll, he was holding Sonny McDermott, and he was dunking him in and out of the trough. When he finished, he took a horse towel from the side of the trough, and whipped McDermott across the face with it. McDermott started running and never came back.[3]

The brothers McCormack were rough customers fit for a violent marketplace. As Manhattan publicist Robin "Curly" Harris—hired by Bill McCormack to plant a fawning story in the *New York Daily News*—wrote in 1952, "trucking on the waterfront is hardly a weakling's trade[,]...and Bill's business brains were more than equaled by his fighting fists and his readiness to use them." Like Frank Hague, Bill McCormack sought to impose his will on a chaotic marketplace. The two became fast friends in the period just prior to Hague's ascension to the mayoralty. "Before they were thirty," wrote journalist Allen Raymond, "both McCormack brothers were stout pillars in Frank Hague's political machine."[4]

Hague's main man on the Jersey City waterfront, "Happy" Keane, told journalist Bob Greene off the record in 1951, "William McCormack and Frank Hague and Dan Casey [Hague's longtime commissioner of public safety] was like this, joining "three fingers of his hand closely together," an assessment independently corroborated by another informant. Hague reportedly once offered Bill McCormack a captaincy on the Jersey City police force, an offer McCormack declined. Another informant told Bob Greene, "I know that Hague made the Noonans [ILA operative–racketeer Connie and police captain Ed] on the waterfront and I wouldn't doubt that it was with McCormack's help."[5]

In the tradition of his good friend and Jersey City patron, McCormack believed that personal authority cut across lines of social class and economics; it followed that the customary enmity between labor and management could be harmonized only by the exercise of that authority. The McCormacks were waterfront employers who also functioned as Teamster organizers, exerting great influence over the extraordinarily fractious affairs of Jersey City Local 641, at whose headquarters a delegate named Jim Somers—who had been making noises about imminent plans "to take back his loading at the Peach Yard"—was shot dead during a 1914 meeting where Bill McCormack was said to be in attendance. McCormack's career-long practice of controlling by any means the unions that represented his employees gave rise to scandal when exposed off the waterfront; locally it confirmed his authenticity as a powerful self-made man.[6]

Underworld Star

The McCormacks entered the stevedoring business just prior to the entry of the United States into the First World War, expanding their interests to cover the waterfront from both sides of the North River. They had maintained ties to figures in Lower Manhattan's Washington Market, which they now parlayed into a contract to handle the loading of Argentine beef destined for troops on the battlefields of France. The rough-and-tumble of Jersey City's Peach Yard paled next to the violence on New York's docks at a time when the historic Irish gangs of the West Side were undergoing a bloody consolidation. The major players were a natty Liverpool-born hoodlum from an Irish family, Owen "Owney the Killer" Madden, leader of the most potent offshoot of the erstwhile Gophers gang, and "Tanner" Smith, boss of an eponymous crew that morphed into the Marginals then muscled its way to control of the West Side piers just prior to the 1914 advent of war in Europe, a most lucrative occurrence for stevedores.[7]

According to journalist T. J. English, Owney Madden was "a street punk and a killer" who graduated from raiding West Side rail yards to violent crimes so brazen he "transformed himself into an underworld star." When Madden was sent to prison for the November 1914 slaying of rival gang member Thomas "Little Patsy Doyle" Moore, Tanner Smith, who had recently served a year for gun possession, was "said to have 'strutted in the limelight'" of his newfound wealth and notoriety.[8]

In 1951 a former army captain responsible for loading refrigerated products at the New York piers during World War I recalled, "The McCormack brothers had extensive loading operations in lower New York at the time and they were very friendly with [Tanner] Smith." This informant once spent "a social evening" along with Bill McCormack at Smith's home on West Fourteenth Street. Smith was either a foreman in the McCormack brothers' meat-stevedoring operation or a rival or both; accounts vary. In July 1919 he was assassinated, most likely by Rubber Shaw of the Hudson Dusters, a brash West Side gang whose commercial ambitions were hindered by its leaders' predilection for cocaine. Shaw reportedly shot Tanner Smith at the Marginals' social club on West Sixteenth Street before fleeing across the river to Hoboken, where he was in turn tracked down and killed, allegedly by one Patrick "Linky" Mitchell. Mitchell was arrested, but "police couldn't make the murder rap stick."[9]

The killings of Tanner Smith and Rubber Shaw were late chapters in the horrifically violent history of the pre-Prohibition Irish gangs of New York. These events later assumed great significance in the legend of Bill McCormack when in 1952 journalist Lester Velie reported that McCormack himself had been Rubber Shaw's target. According to an informant, "Rubber Shaw came into the Avonia Club looking for Bill McCormack. He stood behind McCormack watching him play cards," then left to seek out and kill Smith instead at the nearby Marginals club. Shaw's presumed killer, "Linky" Mitchell, later worked as an enforcer at a trucking firm for which McCormack served as executive vice president, only to be murdered himself over a bootlegging dispute in "an alleged speakeasy" in 1928.[10]

Various accounts of Bill McCormack's ties to these and other gangland figures persisted for decades, serving to enhance his stature as a survivor of the West Side gang wars, a rare status he shared with Owney Madden. When quizzed about Bill McCormack by a reporter for *Collier's Weekly* in 1952, Madden coolly replied, "Why should I say anything about a friend of mine?" Madden's old friend not only survived the gang wars but also, in 1920, sold one of his businesses to a new firm, United States Trucking Corporation, where he became executive vice president and handled the firm's relations with teamsters from 1920 to 1927.[11]

"The key to McCormack's success," wrote T. J. English, "was his ability to cultivate powerful political connections, a classic first-generation Irish political trait." U.S. Trucking president James J. Riordan, a West Side Irishman, had "long idolized" Alfred E. Smith, whom he persuaded to become the firm's board chairman while the "Happy Warrior" was between terms as governor of New York. Smith brought his wealth of political connections, which included a close friendship with Frank Hague. A product of the Lower East Side's St. James parochial school who often described himself as a "graduate of the Fulton Fish Market," Smith now drew close to Bill McCormack.[12]

Through contacts he made as vice president of the trucking firm, wrote Velie, "Bill McCormack became a power in labor, business and politics." Hague and McCormack shared a passion for the regulated violence of the fight game; they were often seen together at ringside enjoying the bouts, sometimes accompanied by the far less enthusiastic Al Smith. Boxing rivaled baseball and horseracing as the dominant spectator sport of the 1920s and 1930s; championship fights were covered like major civic events. Just as the sport offered a violent means of upward mobility for the most talented pugilists—often Irish, Italian, and Jewish Americans in the 1920s—so too it provided a showcase at ringside for the ascension of figures like Bill McCormack, whose presence was duly noted alongside that of socialites and sportsmen.[13]

McCormack and Hague invested in fighters at a time when Owney Madden was the dominant figure on the New York boxing scene. Bill and Harry McCormack reportedly owned a piece of future heavyweight champion Gene Tunney (while Madden "pulled the strings behind the scenes"). According to one informant, Tunney, a fellow West Village Irish American and St. Veronica's product, trained for a championship bout at Harry McCormack's summer resort in Fair Haven on the Jersey Shore. When Al Smith was returned to Albany as governor in 1922, he promptly appointed Bill McCormack license committee chairman of the State Boxing Commission. The committee was a potent vehicle for McCormack's aspirations as a power broker and mediator: legalized prizefighting had been reinstated just two years earlier through a bill authored by state senator James J. Walker, future mayor of New York City. Governor Smith had insisted that Walker obtain the support of "at least a hundred Protestant clergymen" before he would sign the bill lest voters suspect the ambitious Smith ("a Catholic with an eye on the White House") of endorsing a law "that would primarily benefit Catholics."[14]

As chairman of the license committee, McCormack worked to sustain the broad interfaith coalition supporting the Walker Act by instilling probity in fighters and their handlers. His consultations with Governor Smith were reported in detail in the *New York Times,* as was his surprising resignation from the post in January 1924, an event linked—though this was not reported at the time—to the legendary Luis Angel Firpo–Jack Dempsey heavyweight championship bout of the previous September. An incident surrounding the fight severely strained McCormack's relationship with the Happy Warrior; it would generate renewed scrutiny in a vastly different political era nearly three decades later.[15]

The Mediator

Frank Hague's handpicked candidates regularly won New Jersey's gubernatorial elections, though as a Catholic he could not hope to compete himself for statewide office in what remained in the interwar years a heavily rural-Protestant "Garden State." Al Smith ardently backed Hague's successful 1924 bid for the chairmanship of the Democratic National Committee. Hague delivered a huge Hudson County plurality for Smith in the 1928 presidential election, but it proved insufficient to offset massive support for Republican Herbert Hoover statewide. The mayor doggedly stuck with Smith throughout his quixotic 1932 bid to wrest the party's nomination from the odds-on favorite, Franklin D. Roosevelt. As Jersey City native Thomas Fleming explained: "Nothing stirred Hague more deeply than the Irish clan spirit. Loyalty was one of the few words in the English language that made him choke up." Yet he was loyal above all to his own regime. When FDR secured the nomination, Hague demonstrated his clout by organizing a Jersey Shore rally for the candidate that attracted over 150,000 Democrats, most of whom were bused down to Sea Girt from Hudson County for the occasion, lunch included. President Roosevelt's New Deal patronage program would only strengthen the Boss's grip over Hudson County.[16]

Frank Hague, Al Smith, and even FDR—who, as former New York governor, kept a close eye on Tammany Hall—were linked by "the common problems of the New York City metropolitan area in the building of tubes and tunnels and in the regulation of river navigation," concerns that further deepened their ties to Bill McCormack. The budding industrialist's close friendship with Hague (the two remained extremely close long after Smith's public career went into eclipse), his vast connections in the transportation industry, and his influence at Tammany paved the way for McCormack to score the greatest entrepreneurial coup in the history of the port. In 1930 his fledgling Penn Stevedoring Corporation won the contract from the Pennsylvania Railroad to unload all the carrier's freight cars on its six West Side piers. Three years later he organized the Jersey Contracting Company to acquire the railroad's stevedoring work in the enormous freight yards of Hudson County, making him the first businessman to truly cover the waterfront from both sides, with a commercial power analogous to, but proportionally greater than, Hague's political clout.[17]

The Pennsylvania Railroad operated an enormous fleet of car floats dedicated to transporting produce across the river; in the absence of a freight tunnel, and in light of shortsighted railroad practices that "set the stage for their own obsolescence," McCormack consolidated enormous power in the port. His firms now handled all loading and unloading for the "Pennsy" on both sides of the river. As an unidentified longshoreman explained to an investigator around 1950 of the McCormack's bi-state produce-handling operations: "That's where all your fruits and vegetables come in.... [T]o get to any market in the city, it had to come through McCormack.... [W]hoever planned this whole thing out was plannin' that you and I and anybody else would stop eatin' if they said so." Later in the 1930s McCormack added the Erie Railroad stevedoring contract to his portfolio. He grew spectacularly wealthy in the Great Depression decade, moving with his wife and two children to a mansion on Fifth Avenue with all the trimmings.[18]

A warm relationship with Joe Ryan of the ILA yielded labor relations that were both enduringly peaceful and highly favorable to McCormack's interests. He was often described as an "old West Side friend" of Ryan's and sometimes as a "boyhood friend" of the ILA boss. (Though the discrepancy in their official ages made this seem unlikely, they were in fact born just three years apart.) The pair were surely intimate associates by the late 1920s, when Ryan—in his capacity as head of New York's Central Trades and Labor Council—intervened to help settle a Teamsters' strike against McCormack's U.S Trucking firm. "I knew if I could get Bill McCormack to sit down at the same table with the Teamsters," Ryan recalled, "they'd settle," though McCormack may not have required outside help to handle the union. McCormack also brought Ryan into Frank Hague's orbit; the labor boss remained a staunch and reliable ally of Hudson County's Boss until the bitter end.[19]

McCormack's prodigious gift for mediation made him more than just another tough guy turned self-made tycoon: a wide array of "mediating" roles was in fact the key to his vast economic and spiritual authority throughout the port. Employees of Penn Stevedoring were not members of the Railroad Brotherhood, as would be expected of men unloading rail cars; they shaped up instead under the auspices of Joe Ryan's ILA, though their wages fell well below that union's scale. Many were alcoholics trying to get their lives together following stints on the Bowery; many others were newly paroled veterans of the New York State prison system. An official from the state's Division of Parole later recalled receiving numerous applications which included a note indicating that Harry McCormack would "make immediate arrangements for this inmate's union membership upon his release." The official estimated that as many as two hundred parolees found themselves working at Penn Stevedoring.[20]

Bill McCormack evaded public scrutiny of his hiring practices and of himself for decades; the conspicuous presence on his piers of figures sporting lengthy rap sheets discouraged intrusive queries. His Christian charity in giving such men a second chance might be interpreted broadly: despite paying his workers substantially lower wages than their ILA brethren earned, McCormack's businesses enjoyed long years of untroubled labor relations. As McCormack would testify in January 1953, after mounting public pressure forced him to account for his unique role in the life of the port, "good management and the human approach to the problem," not relationships with union leaders, were the keys to his success.[21]

McCormack very rarely spoke in public, but when he did he articulated better than anyone else the core beliefs of the just waterfront and its populist realism. His local origins and self-made stature lent him an enormous advantage over the heads of steamship companies—who often were of northern European backgrounds—and rival stevedoring firms, generally managed by individuals lacking the scope of McCormack's vision and experience. They dealt crudely in the cash nexus of waterfront economics; McCormack negotiated from the strength of one whose primacy was acknowledged by waterfront consensus bolstered by spiritual undertones. Like Joe Ryan and

Frank Hague, McCormack "never forgot where he came from," wrote historian Bruce Nelson, making him an "icon" on the waterfront. The "just waterfront" tradition validated the power enjoyed by these men and erased the moral judgments of reformers. As a Chelsea native whose father grew up with Ryan succinctly put it: "They used their brawn to get to the top. And there was respect for rank.... The respect came from fear and just for the fact that they had a ranking position. It didn't matter how they achieved that. It was the same kind of hero worship for the underworld. They were the top dogs. The best were the worst criminals."[22]

Joe Ryan helmed the ILA at Bill McCormack's pleasure, and he never forgot it. According to a waterfront employer with a long history of negotiations with Ryan, "when the chips were down and a decision had to be made, he'd have to go to the telephone" to call his adviser and patron. McCormack enjoyed four decades of anonymity prior to his "exposure" as the waterfront's legendary "Mr. Big" amid a flurry of stories and revelations lasting from autumn 1951 to winter 1953. Much of the coverage treated his influence over Ryan, which sociologist Daniel Bell found a "strange but potent friendship," a "hidden" factor in ILA affairs. Waterfront insiders were prone to describe the relationship in a familiar local language. "Billy is Joe Ryan's father confessor," explained an unidentified labor negotiator in a 1952 magazine story. The unequal bond between McCormack and Ryan was surely grounded in shared Irish waterfront notions of right order and hierarchy, in turn deeply embedded in the social and religious history of the port.[23]

Moral Authority

The hegemony of Catholicism on the waterfront did not simply reinforce itself. The extraordinary devotion of Frank Hague, Joe Ryan, and Bill McCormack—each of whom was highly touted as a "daily communicant" during his lengthy career—was not an inevitable consequence of their inheritance but surely enhanced their claims to moral authority and bolstered the church's local dominance. There were also significant differences in the way these men publicly represented their faith, grounded in the natural and supernatural hierarchies each one served. While Ryan was content in his role as generous benefactor of Chelsea's tiny Guardian Angel church and ardent member of the parish chapter of the Holy Name Society, Bill McCormack's gifts of weekly crates of fresh fruit to West Side pastors scarcely hinted at the full extent of his largesse. He became a pillar of the New York archdiocese and the universal church, reaping the honors and accolades befitting a recipient of investiture as a Knight of Malta (1941), and later a Grand Knight of the Holy Sepulchre and a Knight of the Grand Cross, all bestowed by papal appointment.[24]

McCormack's faith was the basis of his self-understanding and "central to his life," as his only son and onetime heir apparent, William J. McCormack Jr., retired New York auxiliary bishop, recalled in a 2002 interview. Each time Bill McCormack, his wife, and their son and daughter returned from vacation at West Virginia's Greenbrier or a similarly elegant resort, the businessman would lead the family from Pennsylvania Station to the nearby church of St. Francis Assisi, where they knelt in prayer to thank God for their abundant blessings.[25]

Bill McCormack was the least conspicuous among a fairly substantial cohort of wealthy self-made (or sons of self-made) Irish Catholic New York businessmen that emerged between the world wars. Perhaps the most accomplished figure of this Irish ascendancy was New York Stock Exchange chairman John Aloysius Coleman, the multimillionaire "Pope of Wall Street." Like Coleman, his good friend and fellow Catholic benefactor, Bill McCormack never sought public approbation; private tribute found its way to him. Although he served in the background for the annual dinner-dance of the Joseph P. Ryan Association, a prominent event reaffirming the Irish waterfront's moral order, powerful New Yorkers clearly understood his central role. What was "originally just a water-front shindig," reported Lester Velie, McCormack turned into "New York City's most important political affair—a 'must' where many of the city's biggest men feel they have to be seen."[26]

This sumptuous Tammany-flavored celebration bestowed on the waterfront the soul of a church. Monsignor John J. O'Donnell was always prominently seated at the family table of the association's proud "standard-bearer." The summoned throngs—from shipping executives to mayors, lesser-known parish priests, and "a sprinkling of murderous hoodlums"—paid tribute to the vast machinery that powered the world in whose bounty they gratefully shared. By the mid-1930s Manhattan's Commodore Hotel had to dedicate its vast main ballroom and three adjoining spaces to accommodate 250 tables and upwards of 2,500 guests, a crowd that expanded considerably over the years.[27]

Bill McCormack generally chaired committees on "arrangements" or "receptions" for the annual gala. In 1937 Cockeye Dunn served under McCormack on the arrangements committee; the following year Dunn assisted McCormack's brother Harry on that same committee while Bill handled receptions. In sworn public testimony Bill McCormack later denied having known Dunn, who as of 1938 was just another waterfront businessman–ex-con shaping up in his evening attire. In 1951 a Jersey City informant told an investigator, "Yes, they [the McCormack brothers] were very friendly with Johnnie Dunn and [Dunn's brother-in-law] Eddie McGrath." Cockeye remained a fixture at the dinner for several years to come; he was also captured in a photograph celebrating with Joe Ryan at an affair honoring Thomas A. "Teddy" Gleason, a West Side ILA leader and future president of the international.[28]

The scandal-ridden history of the ILA dating to the 1930s turns on a set of issues prompted by the unique features of the Ryan Association's annual fêtes: Joe Ryan's installation as ILA president in 1927; Bill McCormack's ascension to the status of "respectable businessman" in the late 1920s and 1930s; the role of Cockeye Dunn and other career criminals in the union hierarchy; and the transformation of the ILA from a "legitimate, if weak, union—not unlike many other unions in the 1920s—into an organization which existed largely for the benefit of a few officials and their cronies."[29]

Ryan's position as chairman of the New York State Parole Board in the 1930s smoothed the way for ex-convicts like Dunn and Eddie McGrath to move "directly onto the ILA payroll as 'organizers.'" Ryan's status as a "mob associate" was confirmed in the late 1930s, yet his paradoxical mix of power and insecurity reflected the squeeze put on Irish gangsters by the "syndicate" or "combine" organized by Jewish and Italian American mobsters in the waning years of Prohibition. "Over the three-year period from 1931 to 1933," according to T. J. English, "virtually every high-ranking Irish American bootlegger in the Northeastern United States was systematically eliminated, gangland-style." (Owney Madden, who wisely departed the scene, was the rare exception.)[30]

Since the ILA link to Tammany Hall was a given, Irish control of the union—if only within Tammany's Manhattan sphere of influence—was conceded by the newly emerging criminal syndicates. The longshoremen's union was in fact, as English argued, "more powerful than any Mafia family. It was a legitimate organization with hegemony over a massive commercial and criminal marketplace[,]...making the waterfront the most lucrative underworld universe since Prohibition." The political power bought with Irish waterfront profits—in addition to its inherently intimidating character—helped insulate that underworld from outside scrutiny as the post-Prohibition era dawned. Although an agency endowed with the potential to reshape the port's political economy was already entering its second decade of operation, it awaited a visionary leader to contest local authority in the port.[31]

4 *The Longshoreman's Grandson*

Alone among the Irish waterfront's reigning triumvirate Bill McCormack evaded the glare of hostile publicity—at least in the late 1930s and early 1940s, when domestic politics was roiled by the specter of war and the threat of totalitarian upheaval at home. Nowhere was the anxiety felt more deeply than in metropolitan New York, where Joe Ryan and Frank Hague served as lightning rods for dark fantasies of homegrown fascism and authoritarian Catholic rites of violence. In 1938 Felice Swados of the *New Republic* ominously brooded over Ryan's "considerable body of private storm troopers." A broader species of journalistic nativism never went out of style in publications across the political spectrum. The "bull-necked, heavy-fisted" Joe Ryan's physical characteristics were blithely mocked in mainstream journals from *Fortune*—which reported that weighty matters "slipped through his stubby fingers"—to *Business Week*, which depicted the ILA chieftain handling contract negotiations with "a cauliflowered ear to the ground."[1]

Frank Hague was an even more irresistible target than King Joe. In the aftermath of his campaign against Jersey City CIO organizing in the late 1930s, Hague was repeatedly assailed in mainstream liberal publications as Jersey's (or alternately Hudson County's) "Little Hitler." His power was dreaded as an uncontainable source of "contagion," while Hudson County was described as "an 'occupied area,' set apart from the rest of the country as a fascist unit." Citing Hague's rhetorical campaign against "the tide of red 'naturalism,'" McAlister Coleman offered readers of the *Nation* an "explanation for those unacquainted with the vocabulary of Jersey Catholicism." Leftist critics were one thing; it was more difficult for Hague to discount attacks on his totalitarian regime in the mass media. A 1938 photo-essay in *Life* presented "a muckraking portrait so devastating" that Hague's people immediately confiscated every copy of the magazine from the city's multitude of newsstands and candy stores.[2]

The "un-American" insularity ascribed to the Irish waterfront by outsiders only heightened its tribalism from the middle of the Great Depression through the early years of the Second World War. Slights delivered from the outside bolstered the legitimacy of Hague and Ryan in the eyes of their core constituencies; local citizens were "affronted by the ethnic bigotry apparent in such journals as *The Nation,* which referred to the 'peat bog elite,' and they rallied around their leader."[3]

Authority in the Port

As a publicity-shy businessman, albeit one enjoying vast political connections, Bill McCormack quietly yet dramatically expanded his commercial reach in the 1930s and early 1940s until his waterfront empire "spanned the rivers and bays" from its foundation in bi-state stevedoring. He became a major force in the sand and gravel industry, in ready-mixed concrete (McCormack's Transit-Mix Concrete Corporation occupied a commanding location between Twenty-first and Twenty-third streets on the East River waterfront), and in oil tankers, gasoline stations, and dredging operations. The tireless entrepreneur's ready access to municipal contracts and licenses issued by compliant governments east and west of the Hudson smoothed the way to his growing commercial dominance in the port.[4]

Confirming the truism that nothing erodes—or liberates—the bonds of tribalism like the free marketplace, McCormack entered into lucrative partnerships with politically connected Italian and Jewish businessmen from off the waterfront, most notably Generoso Pope, an immigrant gravel baron and proprietor of the influential Italian American newspaper *Il Progresso,* and the "politically hefty" contracting magnate "Subway Sam" Rosoff. The trio enjoyed prodigious influence over Tammany's contract brokers. According to waterfront legend, Rosoff "had a New York contract to remove all cinders and ashes from city buildings, including schools. McCormack won a New York City contract to pave city streets. Rosoff would dump the ashes on an empty lot on the West Side, where they would be picked up by McCormack's trucks and used to pave the city's streets."[5]

Throughout the 1930s and 1940s Bill McCormack operated freely beyond the purview of reformers, pundits, and regulators. Jersey City remained wide-open territory, while his interests in New York City were sufficiently entrenched that the 1933 election of Mayor Fiorello La Guardia, a charismatic, progressive anti-Tammany Republican, put nary a dent in McCormack's expanding commercial empire. La Guardia, wrote journalist Lester Velie, viewed McCormack as "a solid citizen-businessman." A veteran Jesuit labor priest sneered in a 1988 interview that La Guardia was in McCormack's "back pocket: that's something you'll never see in the books."[6]

A lone potential threat to McCormack's waterfront hegemony loomed in the years prior to World War II: the as yet unleashed might of the Port of New York Authority, the agency established in 1921 after decades of "ruinous competition and rivalry between the two states" threatened to destroy the port's national preeminence. The daunting nature of this challenge was apparent even in the "bi-state" agency's name: it would take an additional half-century before "New Jersey" was affixed, acknowledging its rightful place as full partner in the port.[7]

Boundary disputes and intra-port mercantile squabbles had poisoned relations between the states from their origins in colonial America. In the early national period New York State arrogantly claimed possession of the Hudson "up to the low watermark on the western shore. As a corollary New York City declared its jurisdiction over the piers and wharves on both sides of the river." As transportation historian Brian J. Cudahy explained, "a person strolling along the edge of the Hudson on the New Jersey side of the river at low tide was, at least in the eyes of New York officials, taking a walk on New York territory." Efforts at trans-Hudson diplomacy routinely failed. "At one point," wrote historian Angus Gillespie, "things got so bitter that state policemen actually exchanged shots in the middle of the Hudson River."[8]

In the landmark case of *Ogden v. Gibbons* (1824) the United States Supreme Court voided the type of interstate steamship monopoly granted by New York to Robert Fulton in 1810, which barred New Jersey steamboat concerns from operating on the Hudson. Legal battles over the continuing raids of New Yorkers on Jersey oyster beds—not to mention "the service of New York writs upon persons standing on wharves in New Jersey"— resulted in an 1834 treaty that set state boundaries in mid-river; but the rapid development of the railroad industry later in the century generated even deeper hostilities. Railroads customarily charged the same rates for shipments from the nation's interior destined for Hudson County or Manhattan, voluntarily absorbing the additional costs incurred in floating New York–bound goods via lighter from Jersey freight rail terminals to the West Side piers. New Jersey's embryonic overseas shipping industry was in effect penalized for the advantageous location of its piers compared with the better-established operations across the river.[9]

The Garden State lost a 1917 legal battle over these rate "differentials," but it was clear by then—especially to Republican legislators and elite civic and financial powers in both states—that the port faced an irresoluble dilemma unless railroad service was coordinated to benefit business interests and citizens on both sides of the Hudson. The port's anomalous character was bluntly diagnosed in February 1918 by Calvin Tomkins, New York dock commissioner during the mayoralty of Irish American reformer John Purroy Mitchell: "New York is the only great seaport in the world divided into two parts by an unbridged and untunnelled waterway." The ultimate goal of any future "port organization," insisted Tomkins, must be a system of "all-rail transit by protracting the New Jersey roads over and under the Hudson River to New York." He identified as massive dual obstacles the intractable rivalries between railroads and the port's intense political localism; these combined to perpetuate "an immensely wasteful and dilatory expenditure for lighterage," the byzantine trans-Hudson system of exchange that powered the Irish waterfront's political-industrial nexus.[10]

The ardent desire of Calvin Tompkins and other leading progressives for a nonpolitical centralized port administration was finally realized in the 1921 compact establishing the Port of New York Authority as an independent public corporation empowered to "develop and coordinate any terminal or transportation facility within the bi-state region." A self-supporting agency, the Port Authority had jurisdiction over an area within roughly twenty-five miles' radius from the Statute of Liberty. The new agency, as urban policy analyst James W. Hughes explained in 1974, "was in effect a third state superimposed on the common port region," designed "to remove those artificial boundaries which had intensified the problems of port development."[11]

The Irish waterfront's political bosses stoutly if predictably resisted this threat of intervention by outsiders. The Port Authority's focus on rationalization of *regional* commerce—a process imposed from above at the discernment of unelected experts—clashed sharply with the waterfront political culture's premium on face-to-face deal making and local autonomy. As urban public policy scholar Jameson Doig wrote in his definitive study of the bi-state agency's first three decades, "power would be taken from the neighborhood and the ward, and from the city and state; it would be given to a group of six independent citizens" from each state, for a total of twelve appointed commissioners, "who could think widely, use the skills of an able technical staff to plan wisely, and then act benevolently to improve the economic conditions for 8 million people."[12]

Frank Hague's handpicked New Jersey governor, Edward I. Edwards, vetoed the compact creating the Port Authority only to be overridden by a vote of the state legislature. Edwards boycotted the authorization ceremony, as did Tammany-backed New York City mayor John Hylan, but there was a difference in motivation. Hague, who was already developing his own version of the regional approach enshrined in the Port Authority's mission statement, viewed the new agency as a threat to both the waterfront rackets and legitimate businesses—such as international steamship concerns—whose interests he promoted in his regime's self-interest; over time none were more faithfully served than the burgeoning bi-state enterprises of his great friend Bill McCormack. Hague would do business with the Port Authority when it advanced his causes. The politically and geographically myopic New Yorker John Hylan, by contrast, fulminated against any hint of regionalism that might serve the interests of "foreigners" from across the

Hudson; he wanted a freight tunnel built from Staten Island to Brooklyn that would cut Hudson County out of the loop altogether. "Several decades of distrust, if not actual enmity, would prevail" between New York City and the new bi-state agency.[13]

Tammany Hall's self-defeating parochialism was more than matched by the shortsighted tactics of fading railroad magnates unwilling to cooperate with the Port Authority or with one other. Tammany and the rails both earned the self-inflicted extinction awaiting them. And as Jameson Doig astutely noted, the root conflict sparked by the upstart bi-state agency was not strictly "between those who favored centralization and expertise (here represented by the Port Authority) and those who embraced localism." The Port Authority's promotion of a regionally integrated transit system, for example, was designed "to wrest control of rail policy from the national centralizers—the Interstate Commerce Commission in Washington, with its stable of experts and its allies in the railroad industry—so that the New York metropolis could take responsibility for its own regional transportation system, and thereby strengthen its own economy."[14]

The ensuing struggle for the port mobilized rival claimants seeking to shape its neo-regional approach to transportation and shipping networks. The remotely owned and operated railroads proved woefully incapable of grasping the new dispensation; they insisted on maintaining their own lighter fleets and warehouse facilities. The imperious Pennsylvania Railroad even barred rivals from using its Hell Gate Bridge to ship freight between Manhattan and Long Island. In the 1920s the railroads' "unparalleled example of self-interested, parochial behavior" was more responsible than Irish waterfront political resistance for the "complete failure of all the Port Authority's plans for coordinating rail freight, and for modernizing the piers and constructing rail tunnels that would join Manhattan and Brooklyn to the mainland." The railroads' dismissal of the Port Authority's proposal to construct two freight rail tunnels connecting Jersey City with Manhattan and Brooklyn enabled Bill McCormack to capture bi-state stevedoring contracts from the Pennsylvania and later the Erie Railroad. Their managements preferred to do business with a self-made local entrepreneur whose stake in the port could be calculated according to the traditional cash nexus.[15]

While the railroads thus proceeded to doom themselves (the loading and unloading of freight cars and lighters on either side of the Hudson was "extraordinarily expensive and laborious" compared to unloading once at a rail spur), McCormack presciently discerned that no rail tunnel would ever be built and invested in that wisdom. His own bi-state political and economic clout grew enormously during the 1930s, while the Port Authority drifted. By the time the freight tunnel issue was revisited in the mid- to late 1940s, the businessman was in a position to forestall any such action that would undermine his own commercial dominance across the port. In the meantime McCormack's rapidly growing, ever-diversifying portfolio of transportation and construction-related enterprises kept pace with the Port Authority's infrastructural investments—primarily in vehicular tunnels and bridges—to enhance the booming motorized freight industry. By the late 1930s the Port Authority was operating two tunnels and four bridges, including the majestic George Washington Bridge.[16]

The businessman and the bi-state agency were on a collision course; but contrary to McCormack-sponsored legend, the contest did not pit a grassroots entrepreneur against a haughty cabal of scheming bureaucrats hailing from points unknown. The prime architects of the Port of New York Authority's policies and vision were in fact individuals formed in the hothouse political culture of the Irish waterfront. Julius Henry Cohen—drafter of the bi-state compact that created the agency—was the son of a Tammany Hall operative and a political ally of Al Smith. Cohen's previous work as a labor mediator wedded political realities to progressive reform ambitions in a fashion emulated by the "Happy Warrior." Smith's early, risky support of the Port Authority "underscored his break with New York City's Democrats," according to Doig, or at least with those Democrats who, like John Hylan, were unwilling to think regionally for the good of the city. Over time, and especially with the ascension of Austin J. Tobin—by far the dominant figure in the bi-state agency's history—the Port of New York Authority was driven by remnants of a communal Irish waterfront ethos shorn of its tribally self-lacerating features.[17]

Nemesis

Bill McCormack did not know it yet, but Austin Tobin, the future head of the Port Authority, was his nemesis-in-waiting. Tobin was the grandson of an Irish immigrant dockworker killed at age thirty in an accident on a Brooklyn pier. Tobin's father parlayed his connections to the powerful if antediluvian Brooklyn Democratic organization of John McCooey into a career as a court stenographer. Clarence Tobin and his wife, Katharine Moran, sent Austin, the eldest (born 1903) of their four children, to the parish school of St. Francis Assisi and St. John's Catholic Prep, both located near the family's home just east of Brooklyn's landmark Prospect Park. Austin then enrolled at the Jesuit College of the Holy Cross in Worcester, Massachusetts, where he compiled a brilliant academic record while "losing" his Catholic faith, a development reportedly triggered by his discovery that "some of his class assignments were excerpts and that he was forbidden by the Catholic *Index* to read other parts of great works." Apostate or not, Tobin honored the Ignatian tradition with sufficient distinction to be named salutatorian of the class of 1925.[18]

While he remained "steadfast in refusing to take part in Catholic services during the next four decades," Tobin's "intellectual development showed clear marks of his Jesuit training," Doig suggests, especially in his intense rationalism, appreciation of debate, and devotion to the classics. Tobin also demonstrated a "playful contrariness" toward authority, a trait that colored his attitude toward not only the church but also the political organization that enjoyed near sacred status in many Brooklyn Irish homes. He "visited the local Democratic club with his father once or twice, but he felt uncomfortable in the society of party members who kept their hats on indoors and chewed cigars." Yet it was his father who took Austin to witness Al Smith campaigning on behalf of the Port Authority in 1921, an experience that helped inspire a vocation. The deeply idealistic young Tobin quickly looked beyond the Happy Warrior to the tradition of Woodrow Wilson and Theodore Roosevelt, imbibing their faith in "government as an appropriate instrument in meeting broad social goals."[19]

In 1927 Tobin found work in the Port Authority's real estate department while completing legal studies in the evening division of Fordham Law School; upon graduating he was quickly promoted by Julius Henry Cohen to assistant attorney. Working in the real estate department, Tobin grew deeply enamored of the fledgling agency's commitment to solving the "complex legal issues" that political machines evaded or manipulated for selfish interests. In the absence of taxation authority, the bi-state agency depended on fees (tolls) to retire bonds issued to finance its ambitious programs. Mastery—under Cohen's expert tutelage—of the bond markets' intricacies brought both Wall Street and federal economic policy within Tobin's purview. In the tradition of Al Smith yet unburdened by any partisan obligation, Tobin developed a pragmatic, progressive ideology grounded in the faith that his agency represented the only vehicle for the port to fulfill a potential stifled by tribalism and irrationality. When he was unexpectedly elevated to the executive director's position in 1942, Tobin quickly instilled at the Port Authority a disciplined, hierarchical, but deeply communitarian ethos designed to serve not power but a higher moral purpose. "For some who knew of Tobin's painful break with the Catholic church," wrote Doig, "the Port Authority seemed to be his re-creation of that community, now lost to his sight."[20]

If Tobin revered his agency as a surrogate religion, the port itself inspired in him a mystical devotion; he was deeply "touched by the romance of the harbor." There was also a distinct echo from the nascent progressive Catholic tradition to which Tobin was temperamentally attuned. Like Al Smith he eschewed ethnocentrism (his refusal to countenance anti-Semitism at the agency helped change its culture), recruiting talented individuals from an array of cultural and geographic backgrounds for leadership positions, including the gifted publicist Lee Jaffe, who astutely handled the agency's intricate bi-state public relations operations. Jaffe was lauded by a veteran reporter as "head and shoulders above everyone else" in her field. She built relationships with journalists and opinion makers throughout the region in support of Tobin's primary postwar objective: to save the port from extinction by reviving its tarnished grandeur.[21]

Existing Arrangements

Austin Tobin understood like few others in the automobile age that new bridges and tunnels did not a great port make. In the immediate postwar years the Brooklyn longshoreman's grandson yearned to acquire and modernize the rapidly decaying pier facilities on both sides of the harbor as his agency's signature project. Most were owned by either municipalities or railroads, forces that in their unwillingness to yield local prerogatives had scarcely acknowledged the legitimacy of the Port Authority itself.

The derelict jewels of the West Side Irish waterfront topped Tobin's wish list. His bid for Port Authority acquisition of Manhattan's decrepit piers illuminated the volatile and changing nature of power relations on the postwar waterfront, exemplified in the roles played by Tobin, Bill McCormack, and a highly enigmatic product of the Brooklyn docks, Bill O'Dwyer, New York City's mayor from January 1946 through late summer 1950. Fully aware of his agency's precarious reputation, Tobin did not lobby openly for control of the piers but worked through intermediaries who "invited" local political leaders to request studies and proposals from the Port Authority. Newark's floundering marine terminal was acquired by this route in 1947 along with the city's adjoining airport, a package deal that followed by several months the agency's acquisition of New York City's airports. That achievement saw O'Dwyer break with a seemingly omnipotent patron, the imperious "power broker" and master planner Robert Moses, who—in the total absence of any bi-state clout—was outmaneuvered in his bid to prevent Tobin from "regionalizing" the metropolitan area's three major airports.[22]

With precedent and momentum on its side along with an October 1947 invitation from O'Dwyer to submit a proposal (the mayor candidly acknowledged that most of the city's long-neglected piers were "antiquated"), the Port Authority made an alluring $114 million bid for "financing, rehabilitating and operating the vast city waterfront." Here Austin Tobin finally tasted the power of Bill McCormack. The Port Authority suffered a "resounding defeat" in September 1948 with the unanimous call by the city's Board of Estimate for the Department of Marine and Aviation to continue its (mis)management of the rapidly decaying pier facilities. O'Dwyer's initial enthusiasm for the Port Authority's bold proposal had turned to "lukewarm support" followed by outright opposition. Though corroborating evidence is scant (as in all matters involving McCormack), Daniel Bell's argument is compelling in context: the Port Authority's bid—designed to "'rationalize' a chaotic and crumbling industry and bring the port back to prominence and use"—was rejected in no small part because it "would have spoiled McCormack's control of some piers." Despite a wide array of economic and political factors weighing on the board's vote, labor historian Joshua Freeman isolates "waterfront businessmen, [ILA] leaders, and mobsters with ties to the Democratic Party" as those who were most fearful of "any threat to their existing arrangements."[23]

Bill McCormack knew these worlds intimately; he surely understood what Port Authority dominance would mean on the West Side. In August 1948 his client Joe Ryan wrote to Mayor O'Dwyer urging rejection of the agency's rehabilitation proposal. The ILA took no position on other proposals, according to Ryan, but believed—its faith unaccompanied by evidence—that Port Authority operation of the piers "would mean unemployment for our members." The politically influential Central Trades and Labor Council, formerly run by Ryan, followed suit a few days later, essentially arguing that any plan was preferable to "dealing with the Authority." A deep enmity now grew between the Port Authority and Bill McCormack, who, after repelling the agency's designs on Manhattan's waterfront, had himself anointed "the Little Man's Port Authority." This publicist-concocted appellation was grounded in the populist realism of the Irish waterfront: the port's "little men" presumably recognized McCormack as the legitimate "port authority," not the haughty "super-agency that moves a metropolis." To paraphrase a commonplace explanation for the durability of organized crime, McCormack offered himself as a port authority for those lacking ready access to the Port Authority.[24]

McCormack implicitly recognized Austin Tobin's formidable presence in the port even as he never publicly acknowledged his existence (the policy was mutual). Tobin was clearly intimate with toughness if not violence: his resemblance to the great North Jersey prizefighter Mickey Walker ("the toy bulldog") was noted often. "Tobin could be ferociously combative—a bulldog with brains—when shielding the Port Authority and its great projects from anyone who tried to stop them," according to James Glanz and Eric Lipton. He eschewed personal publicity as an unseemly violation of proper order, an Irish waterfront axiom Tobin honored more consistently than Bill McCormack. "Unlike the publicity-seeking Robert Moses," wrote Angus Gillespie, "Tobin preferred to work behind the scenes. He tried to stay out of the public eye; he encouraged his commissioners to give speeches, cut ribbons, and get their pictures in the papers." Yet he also possessed the interpersonal skills viewed as most genuine on the waterfront. "Though Tobin is publicly and professionally reserved," *Business Week* reported at a later time, "those close to him say he is a warm, compassionate person, a 'great raconteur' in social gatherings."[25]

Austin Tobin was the first Irish American to tangle with Bill McCormack in the port who had no reason to fear the entrepreneur. The difference in that respect between Tobin and Bill O'Dwyer is most instructive since the pair of Brooklynites shared at least one salient feature: a disdain for the suffocating political philosophy of the city's reigning Democratic organizations, especially their ossified folkways sustaining patterns of deference and mutual obligation. O'Dwyer, however, enjoyed far fewer political options than his younger, Holy Cross–educated contemporary. Born in 1890, the eldest of eleven whose parents were rural schoolteachers in County Mayo, Bill O'Dwyer migrated to New York at age twenty following a year of study at a Spanish Jesuit seminary. He worked in a variety of waterfront-related occupations before achieving his citizenship in 1917; along with it came a job as a patrolman covering the area around the vast Bush Terminal on the South Brooklyn waterfront. While walking the beat, O'Dwyer obtained his law degree from Fordham's evening division in 1924, a year before Tobin matriculated at the Jesuit institution.[26]

O'Dwyer was "remarkably astute," wrote a veteran New York City newspaperman, a "political charmer" who, like Tobin, was a lover of the classics, gifted with an "ability to discourse on the poetry of Byron and Keats." His distaste for machine politics, while in advance of its time, did not slow O'Dwyer's ascent in the judicial ranks, from a Kings County judgeship to election as Brooklyn district attorney in 1939, in which post he earned acclaim for spectacular convictions of Murder, Inc., assassins. He simultaneously forged connections with friends and associates of such politically ambitious underworld figures as Joe Adonis and Frank Costello, upstarts who shared O'Dwyer's disdain for the highhanded manner of Tammany sachems and outer borough party czars.[27]

When the July 1939 murder of Brooklyn rebel longshoreman Peter Panto attracted the notice of a special prosecutor investigating waterfront racketeering, O'Dwyer pulled jurisdictional rank in commandeering the case files; he closed the investigation in 1940 after winning a meaningless promise from Joe Ryan to revoke the charters of several corrupt Brooklyn ILA locals. The following year Abraham "Kid Twist" Reles—a prize informant in numerous Murder, Inc., cases, likely including Panto's killing—was sequestered in protective custody at Coney Island's Half Moon Hotel. In the early morning hours of November 11, 1941, Reles leaped or was tossed from the window of his sixth-floor room while five police guards dozed nearby. Reles was eulogized in tabloids as "the canary who could sing but not fly," a line that entered the waterfront vernacular and would find its way into a celebrated film script. The "wanted" poster bearing a mug shot of Albert Anastasia—the Brooklyn waterfront overlord and a figure of interest in the Panto slaying—was taken down by O'Dwyer's office not long after Reles's defenestration.[28]

Nineteen forty-one also saw a group of New York Democratic leaders boost O'Dwyer's mayoral prospects as a homegrown version of crimebuster Thomas E. Dewey, the Michigan-bred Republican prosecutor who parlayed his 1936 conviction of alleged mobster Charles "Lucky" Luciano into three terms as New York's governor and two unsuccessful runs for the presidency. O'Dwyer was elected to the mayoralty in 1945 on his second try, but he "began his administration under a cloud"—the same cloud that soon hung heavy over the Irish waterfront, never to lift. He was immediately dogged by charges of laxity in the investigation of Panto's murder and Reles's mysterious death, events prompting the impaneling of a Brooklyn grand jury to delve into "the strange factors which had been whispered for more than three years." These 1945 proceedings—though brushed off by the new mayor—marked the beginning of waterfront-related inquires that would eventually dominate the headlines of New York's dailies, consume thousands of hours of public hearings, and reshape the port's moral and political economy for a decade to come.[29]

Bill O'Dwyer was the second and final mayor from the Irish waterfront: the star-crossed tenures of Jimmy Walker (1926–1932) and O'Dwyer bracketed its precarious hegemony over New York City politics. Serving in eras that witnessed intermittently intense civic reform fervor, "Beau James" and "Bill-O the Boy from Bohola" both abruptly vacated the mayoralty and the city during their second terms in office. O'Dwyer pursued a much more rigorous ethic of public service than Walker but was finally undone in large part by an astoundingly mercurial temperament. Between the mayoralties of Walker and O'Dwyer, Bill McCormack ascended from the status of patronage-dependent if extremely aggressive upstart to wield a powerful, mysterious dominion over the waterfront seat in the city's permanent establishment.

His staunch resistance to the Port Authority's 1948 pier rehabilitation proposal invoked a still potent Irish waterfront source of authority. A ten-day tugboat strike that broke out in New York Harbor within weeks of O'Dwyer's January 1946 inauguration had threatened to cripple the city by stranding fuel-laden barges in the harbor. After President Truman ordered the tugboats seized, strikers voted to remain off the job. O'Dwyer called it "the worst threat ever made to the city" and took drastic action, virtually shutting New York down, "placing a city of 7,000,000 persons in a state of indefinite suspension." By the time the strike ended after ten days, reported the *World-Telegram,* "an air of unreality hung over the city. Incidents took on a staccato, dream quality; sharply etched, touched with hysteria, cockeyed." The tugboat workers were represented by an affiliate of the ILA: Joe Ryan stood by during negotiations in which McCormack was widely believed to exert a weighty influence from behind the scenes. In 1947 he played a more public role in helping avert another threatened strike; then the following year O'Dwyer finally named the industrialist chairman of a three-member citizens' committee to "save the city from a harbor-crippling work stoppage." McCormack's role as the only citizen capable of mediating tugboat politics in the harbor was effectively made permanent. In the words of Daniel Bell, he became "virtual umpire of the tugboat industry."[30]

When, during customarily tense contract negotiations in December 1948, McCormack summoned reporters to assure them that Tugboat Local 333— an ILA affiliate—"was not a strike-minded union," the message quickly found its audience. Local 333's treasurer, Joseph O'Hare, was a friend of the tycoon. Its president, "Tugboat Bill" Bradley—reportedly at odds with O'Hare and a faction he led—was another friend who would later succeed Joe Ryan after McCormack signaled his lack of confidence in the ILA leadership. McCormack was clearly admired, respected, and feared in shifting proportions: when negotiations were successfully completed, he would often gather representatives of all parties together to commune informally. In the meantime, his great sway over Ryan—with labor relations involving the vastly larger cohort of longshoremen suddenly grown volatile— saw McCormack's "extraordinary influence" in city politics peak during O'Dwyer's first term as mayor. Civic elites and editorial writers lauded McCormack for his mediating prowess in a world they could scarcely locate.[31]

Yet Bill McCormack was all talk and no action when it came to a real plan for reviving the port. From his prominent role on a Joint Committee on Port Industry convened by O'Dwyer, to lengthy reports submitted to the mayor demanding "drastic action or finis," to his calls for a "Supreme Court" of the port, to knowing assurances that "one or two purposeful, practical men" could alone straighten out the port, it was all so much bluster. Nothing was done to reverse a near hopeless situation, especially on the West Side. "So the piers rotted away and floated out to sea, along with the city's hopes for economic revitalization of its waterfront." By the end of the 1940s McCormack remained an immensely powerful figure whose personal stake in forestalling genuine innovation in the port was never publicly questioned. That would change quickly under a new dispensation shepherded by priests of his church.[32]

Vocation

In *Empire on the Hudson* Jameson Doig astutely contrasted the leadership quality of Austin Tobin—a "courage to decide"—with Bill O'Dwyer's "Hamlet-like introspection and indecision." Yet these differences of individual character also reflected the contexts in which the men operated. Tobin's political skills were largely uncompromised by partisan or tribal obligations, but as of 1948 he had yet to find a way to translate his idealistic and often moralistic "Wilsonian" vision of progressive reform into the practical idiom of Irish waterfront politics. O'Dwyer's introspection and indecision, by contrast, partly reflected a morally forgiving brand of populist realism that left him open to widely divergent judgments. While he was praised by one historian as "a fair-minded, humane, and ethnically sensitive Democrat" who earned his reputation as "an independent-minded politician and the voice of liberalism" in postwar New York City, another lamented that his "many talents" were often rendered useless "because of his subservience to the demands of his powerful underworld supporters." The precise nature of these demands was never established by investigators, but O'Dwyer was burdened throughout his career by suspicions that he "played ball with the underworld." Perhaps journalist George Walsh put it best: O'Dwyer was "a man who, in his own way, wanted to do well by his city of eight million."[33]

If O'Dwyer was a kind of brooding existentialist from the old neighborhood, a hybrid whose time had not yet come, Austin Tobin operated as one who continually asked: How does a leader get things done in the port without being dragged under the currents? He found a providential answer in his childhood religion. For even if he "left" the church, Tobin never abandoned his faith in the power of a Catholic vocation to serve the common good. His wife, Geraldine, remained deeply devout: in the 1940s she became a staunch admirer of a new generation of priest-activists, New York Jesuits such as Philip Carey, who became director of Chelsea's Xavier Labor School in 1940. Geraldine Tobin's name was on a short list of personal references adorning Father Carey's résumé, a document he compiled in support of his work as labor mediator, the role traditional Irish waterfront clerics and politicos reserved for Bill McCormack.[34]

The Port Authority was the only agency in the New York metropolitan area capable of dismantling the political culture of the Irish waterfront, a goal Austin Tobin ardently shared with Philip Carey. Born in the twentieth century, unlike nearly all of their adversaries, they shared little of the hostility to secular progressives nursed by older Irish Americans, who had witnessed too many anti-Catholic Anglo zealots masquerading as social reformers. As with so many other Irish New Yorkers of his era, Philip Carey's youth and early adulthood were haunted by stories and visions of waterfront violence generated by members of his own tribe. "It used to be...let's see...Cockeye Dunn did 32 murders," the Jesuit recalled late in a long life enriched by stories he had heard as a young priest. "McGrath did 34. Squint Sheridan, I don't know how many he did. They were all part of the machine. And if you didn't knuckle in, it was murder, it was fear, it was terror." For Carey and his silent ally Austin Tobin, the first step in reclaiming the soul of the Irish waterfront was to recast those fears and terrors not as echoes of the universe's natural order but as spiritually and communally debilitating.[35]

Bill McCormack not only represented the waterfront's natural order; he virtually owned it. The struggle for the soul of the port that would pit him against Father Phil Carey and a younger, much more vociferous Jesuit confrere—both priests ardently if discretely backed by Austin Tobin—was on its face a mismatch. Mr. Big had all the monsignors and bishops he could use in his corner and the businessman, not his clerical adversaries, spoke for the Irish waterfront's *sensus fidelium*. Genuine reform would require a markedly different sense of the faithful, especially rank and file dockworkers in the front lines of a battle for the soul of the port.

PART TWO

The Soul of the Port

Figure 3. Philip A. Carey, S.J., director, Xavier Labor School, New York City, ca. early 1950s. Courtesy of the Archives of the Xavier Institute of Industrial Relations, Fordham University Library, Bronx, New York.

5   A Labor Priest in the
Catholic Metropolis

The Jesuit labor priest Philip A. Carey never tired of describing to younger people the look and feel of the Great Depression in New York. "You couldn't imagine the absolute degradation," he told interviewer Debra Bernhardt in 1981:

> You couldn't imagine that freight cars were [idled] on sidings from New York up as far as Poughkeepsie. You couldn't imagine traveling on a train, and you were the only passenger on the entire train. And so the people began saying, "well, here you people are the clergy in the church. What the hell, it doesn't mean a damn thing to you. You don't understand our suffering. You don't understand the terrible sense of hopelessness and despair."[1]

Prompted in part by this compelling witness, Carey's fellow New York Jesuits gathered together a group of "lawyers and teachers and concerned people" early in 1936; they decided to start a school for Catholic working-men in the parish of St. Francis Xavier, at the eastern edge of Manhattan's Chelsea neighborhood. After several Jesuit scholastics—young men in training for the priesthood—served brief stints at the helm of the Xavier Labor School, the recently ordained thirty-two year old Philip Carey (see figure 3) was asked to direct the school in June 1940 until such time as, he playfully recalled, "they could get somebody properly prepared for the job." Carey remained in charge until the school finally closed in 1988, not long before his death at age eighty-one on May 27, 1989.[2]

Philip Carey was a vivid New York City character who played a formidable role in the development of a Catholic labor apostolate in the era of the CIO and beyond. He remained deeply wary of the West Side waterfront, the result of boyhood memories of his father's very brief stint as a longshoreman and his own intimate knowledge of organized criminality on the piers. Unsuited for work as a waterfront priest, he would seek another Jesuit to do the job. Together they would shift the focus of Catholic activism in the city from militant anticommunism to a much more perilous internal critique of the Irish waterfront and its powerful code of silence.

A Labor School for Chelsea

Long before the New York Jesuits took on their fellow Irish Americans, however, they played a more familiar role battling local communists. In the mid-1930s the Jesuits were well aware that poverty and unemployment such as Phil Carey witnessed helped to swell the ranks of the Communist Party. The party's Union Square headquarters were just a short walk from Xavier High School at 30 West Sixteenth Street. Xavier originated in a joint New York–Canadian Jesuit mission opened in 1847 in a formerly Protestant church building on the Lower East Side of Manhattan. The school was moved to its Chelsea location in 1850 and renamed the College of St. Francis Xavier—at the urging of Archbishop John Hughes—in honor of the martyred sixteenth-century missionary.[3]

A parish church was built the following year in this affluent, largely Protestant and "uptown" neighborhood: the Vanderbilt family lived across the street from the imposing new church, built in 1882. The College of St. Francis Xavier building was erected in 1886. The Jesuits also took possession of a home that once belonged to poet and journalist William Cullen Bryant; it later became the headquarters of the labor school. The "college," a day school for boys and young men ranging in age from nine to twenty-two, was closed in 1912, but the reconfigured Xavier High School, limited to boys of secondary school age, thrived in the decades after the First World War.[4]

Xavier's location placed the Jesuits and their young charges near the heart of New York City's extravagantly contentious political theater. In a 1960 homily at a St. Patrick's Cathedral Mass celebrating the twenty-fifth anniversary of Xavier Labor School, Joseph Fitzpatrick, a renowned Jesuit sociologist who served briefly as the school's adjunct director in the late 1930s, recalled of the period and the neighborhood that "a passer-by could not push his way through Union Square for the impassioned thousands who argued day and night about theories of revolution and reform." Fitzpatrick noted that Xavier was

> just down the block from the old Rand School where generations of socialists pleaded for social justice with an enthusiasm that put us to shame; across the corner from the Henry George School; on the same block that bustled with the activity of the Garment Workers, the Clothing Workers, the Printers and the Pressmen; a short walk away from the headquarters of the Communist Party.

In the midst of this "vigorous and beating heart of a troubled world," Fitzpatrick grandiloquently reminisced, "a small group of men met in a few little rooms at Xavier and asked themselves: 'Why is the voice of Christ not heard in the land?'"[5]

Xavier was distinctive among New York–area Jesuit high schools for its uniformed cadet regiment in which all students were enlisted. During the 1930s many of these cadets commuted via the subway station at nearby Union Square, dominated at the time by soapbox radicals of all left-wing persuasions but especially by communists. "Often the students walked by communist lectures, demonstrations and confrontations," wrote Xavier's historian. "They were supposed to keep their mouths shut and to keep on walking. Frequently, the police would hurry them into the subway stations for their own safety." Xavier officials created student lecture teams that specialized in anticommunist presentations at Knights of Columbus halls and other friendly venues. The Jesuits were especially troubled by communist designs on the labor movement, a threat far too ominous for students alone to handle.[6]

The anticommunist impulse at Xavier was grounded not only in local concerns but in an evolving international Jesuit mandate as well. In 1934 leaders of the American Jesuit "assistancy" received "the disturbing news from their Father General in Rome that the first big attempt by the Communists to take over a segment of American life was scheduled for that summer. The Jesuits were told to start finding effective means to combat the Communists by offering American workers a positive, non-Marxist program for bettering working conditions." Wlodimir Ledochowski, the Jesuit Superior General in Rome, called on his North American members to "lead the way in our Society's project of a worldwide systematic warfare against the common enemy of Christianity and civilization."[7]

In November 1935 Joseph A. Murphy, S.J., superior (or "provincial") of the Jesuit Province of Maryland and New York, informed the Xavier community that "the creation of a Labor College is considered one of the most important means for carrying out Father General's mandate concerning Communism." The prominent Jesuit John LaFarge determined that in New York City, Xavier was "the House best equipped and located for the purpose." Patrick Cardinal Hayes quickly granted archdiocesan approval, and the institute began offering courses in February 1936. Ethics, sociology, religion, and modern government were taught by Jesuit and lay faculty, many drawn from nearby Catholic colleges.[8]

Twenty Jesuit labor schools opened in the following decade, part of a broader movement that saw the emergence of nearly 150 Catholic labor schools nationwide, from the industrial cities of the Northeast and Midwest to New Orleans and San Francisco. Many were operated by local dioceses or parishes, while others were sponsored by the Association of Catholic Trade Unionists (ACTU), an independent labor organization founded in February

1937 at a meeting held "around the kitchen table" at the Catholic Workers' Mott Street House of Hospitality on Manhattan's Lower East Side.[9]

American Catholic labor schools featured "remarkably similar formats" regardless of sponsorship: "one or two nights per week for eight to ten weeks; classes running one hour[,]...a set of core courses consisting of ethics, public speaking, parliamentary procedure, and labor problems." The Jesuits who ran the Xavier School from 1936 to 1938 had no experience in labor education and precious little knowledge of the labor movement. "Like every pioneering venture, they made great mistakes," Philip Carey later acknowledged. Originally envisioned as an institute where adults might discuss social problems in a Catholic idiom, Xavier—like its counterparts in Brooklyn and Philadelphia—attracted, in Carey's unsparing estimation, "pious church mice who sought entertainment of an innocent kind, preferably in a warm place." The Xavier program quickly grew "quite academic" and "lost its purpose." By the end of 1937 a decision was made to "run the schools entirely for union members or men in a position to become members. This was the change that worked," in Carey's judgment.[10]

In 1938 a twenty-nine-year-old Jesuit scholastic, Philip E. Dobson, was appointed adjunct director of the newly renamed Xavier Institute for Industrial Relations (commonly known as Xavier Labor School). Dobson, still four years shy of ordination, was teaching at Xavier High School during his "regency," a three-year period of service often spent teaching in a Jesuit school. Deeply interested in politics—like nearly everyone raised in his native Jersey City—and militantly anticommunist, Dobson took on the additional duty with ardent enthusiasm. Offerings at the Xavier Labor School were expanded to cover what Dobson termed "the union field." New courses in parliamentary procedure, the history of trade unionism, and public speaking carried Xavier's curriculum squarely into the emerging mainstream of Catholic labor schools. Dobson shared his duties with a younger scholastic, Joseph P. Fitzpatrick, a twenty-five-year-old product of Bayonne, New Jersey. In 1939 Fitzpatrick took charge when Dobson left to begin the four-year course in theological study at Woodstock College in rural Maryland.[11]

Dobson publicly urged the Jesuits to assign a priest as full-time director at Xavier. When Joe Fitzpatrick recommended his friend Phil Carey, the Xavier community's rector replied, "You mean that little guy in the gray sweater that walks with his head down?" Fitzpatrick later recalled that a longshoremen's strike was under way at the time of Carey's initial visit. Carey asked if Fitzpatrick had "been down to the piers to talk to the men." He had not and was "amazed" to discover that Carey had "spent the afternoon down there, talk[ing] to many of the men on the picket line." Unlike the Jesuits who preceded him, Phil Carey had come to Xavier to cover the waterfront.[12]

Phil Carey's Calling

The Jesuit labor schools "took their character, at least in the beginning," according to historian Steve Rosswurm, "more from the priest-director than from their particular social contexts." The first and only permanent priest-director of Xavier Labor School was a character, but he also served in a highly distinctive social context. Philip A. Carey was born in the South Bronx to an Irish immigrant family on December 19, 1907, and grew up in the east Bronx neighborhood of Union Port, a largely German American farming community. Philip Carey and his younger brother Daniel—who also became a Jesuit priest—later offered conflicting recollections of which country towns their parents actually hailed from. But the details mattered less in Phil Carey's storytelling than the message: he came from a family of humble immigrant working people whose most precious commodity was their human dignity and whose experience of hardship was leavened with good humor and grace. The ethos of Xavier Labor School was grounded in Phil Carey's storytelling. Abstraction in politics or religion inevitably led in his view to violations of human dignity.[13]

Julia and John Carey's three sons were educated at Holy Family School on Blackrock Avenue. Their teachers, as Phil Carey remembered, were German Americans, "lovely sisters, Sisters of St. Agnes.... [T]hey were all farm girls, dairy girls from Wisconsin, and they beat the hell out of us and really they learned us something good." Parts of the Bronx remained rural during Carey's childhood—"a farmer going back and forth across his field" was "the Bronx as I knew it then"—but it was his father's debilitating experience of urban working-class life that was seared most indelibly in his memory. John Carey worked for the Third Avenue Transit Company as a trolley motorman for thirty-seven years. (Young Philip's desk at Xavier was adorned for decades with the motorman's timetable belonging to his father.) He was granted only two holidays each year: one was reserved for a family trip to Coney Island, the other to attend a Communion breakfast.[14]

The "brutality of the job was incredible," his son recalled. The men enjoyed no collective bargaining rights and received no compensation for injuries sustained on the job. In the autumn of 1916 John Carey participated in a bitter, protracted, and violent strike of the Amalgamated Association of Street Car Employees; the family subsisted on tea and toast. When John Carey returned to work, he wore a union button under his lapel. When an interviewer asked Philip Carey how his father came by his unionism, he sharply replied: "It wasn't unionism. It was a sense of what was right." The 1916 strike also bequeathed to Phil Carey a deep wariness of the West Side docks, where his father had gone "down to the waterfront to get some work" in order to support his family during the strike: "He worked the barbed wire and cement because no one would handle that.

The breathing was awful. The barbed wire tore all his clothes. There was a wonderful priest at that time at Guardian Angel, Father McGrath, who told my father after two days, 'You're not the man for this kind of work. Get back. Don't stay around here.'" The Irish waterfront would remain beyond the pale for John Carey's son in the decades that followed, even as he came to view it as a lawless frontier whose indigenous violence must be subdued.[15]

Phil Carey's vocation to the priesthood was first discerned at the age of thirteen. "I was playing ball near the Palisades," he recalled in 1986, "and saw the tremendous rocks and sand. Here with time, all this was going to be gone, mowed in the ground into sand. I thought, I'll be gone too, and if I'm only going to live a few years, they'd better be profitable." In 1921 the pastor at Holy Family parish recommended Carey for a scholarship to the Jesuits' Regis High School, where his vocation was reconfirmed. "In 1925," he said, "I decided to kiss my girlfriend goodbye" and entered the Jesuit novitiate at St. Andrew-on-Hudson, near Poughkeepsie, New York. Phil Carey was ordained in 1938, in the penultimate year of the arduous Jesuit training regimen, which included studies in the classics, philosophy, and theology in addition to experience teaching in Jesuit schools.[16]

Just before his son was ordained, John Carey urged him never to forget "the grizzly guys like me who need you," men who struggled to maintain their dignity amid unrelenting toil. Phil Carey's core conviction in running Xavier Labor School was that he "would never let this place go academic." The "sole motive in running this school," Carey explained to a correspondent in 1948, "has been to help workers train themselves for leadership within their own organizations." He told another correspondent that same year: "We try to get men who left school at an early age, who hate anything academic, to think hard thoughts about economics and philosophy and the deeper things of life. We try to give them a sense of their dignity as children of God and of their long-term vocation. And this we try to do in words of one syllable, for as the fellows tell me, 'We think with our hands.'" Carey had no doubt that his own vocation was fulfilled in relationships with students and teachers at Xavier. "The life of a Jesuit is to be where one is needed," he would often say. "These are my people." Among the places he was needed was underground, where Irish American "sandhogs" were engaged in the dangerous work of digging water tunnels and where Carey occasionally celebrated Mass.[17]

During Carey's first term at the helm, Xavier's 174 enrollees were all male and overwhelmingly Irish American. Tuition was free; a registration fee of one dollar was "asked of those who can afford it." Union officials or Catholic attorneys taught most of Xavier's courses, for as Philip Dobson acknowledged in 1939, "Jesuits tend to be too academic and theoretical in training these men." This division of labor suited Phil Carey; he was primarily interested in the formation of mature, responsible union men, for whom the lay faculty served as models of Christian fortitude. Other labor schools focused more on concrete strategies to enhance labor-management cooperation, such as the Industry Council Plan, inspired by *Quadragesimo Anno,* Pope Pius XI's landmark 1931 social encyclical.[18]

Carey understood that many students viewed the labor schools primarily as a vehicle for individual advancement. As one product of the Xavier School put it in 1948: "We were men with wife and kids to take care of.... [W]e just went to labor school to get ahead in the world." They "did not care about the intricacies of a social doctrine that had been elaborated with Latin and northern Europe in mind," wrote historian Peter McDonough. While the ACTU's New York chaplain, the prominent archdiocesan labor priest John Monaghan, "poured social encyclicals" into seminarians and labor students "like Irish whiskey," Phil Carey employed a much less formal, less clerical approach. He was content for Xavier students to embrace the pope's assertion of "the sacred rights of the workers that flow from their dignity as men and as Christians."[19]

"They are a grand crowd," Carey told the *New York World-Telegram* at the beginning of the autumn 1941 term, which saw 250 men enrolled, "solid, hard-working men, whose happiness and pride is in their families, yet who, despite fatigue of the day's work, spend the hours of the evening discussing their problems as working men." Xavier Labor School grew quickly in the months just prior to the nation's entry into World War II; seventeen satellite programs were opened in parishes and Catholic high schools from Peekskill, New York, to New Brunswick, New Jersey. Leading figures in the labor movement such as Harry Read of the CIO volunteered to teach courses. Carey had initially introduced Read to CIO chief Philip Murray, a devout Catholic; these connections enabled him to move the Jesuit labor apostolate close to the heart of a momentous conversation on the labor movement's ends and means.[20]

Carey promoted an integrated approach to teaching religion and ethics "in terms of problems that arose" in the workplace. Concerned that pious language urging the imitation of Christ was not "nearly as real as it might be," he "took cases—simple ones that had a clear Catholic principle at stake and gave them to the group." He told his students, "It's YOUR problem and you are a Leader—YOU are a Catholic!" Carey found that the men "learned much" through this approach, and it gave him "a chance to educate them to the realization that Christ came into the details of their lives in a way they never dreamed."[21]

Carey's teaching method reflected his core theology of labor. He would bluntly tell Xavier students: "Look, we work out our salvation in this world. We don't save our souls in Church or on our knees[;]...we save our souls by prayer and work[,]...work with others." Many labor priests of Phil Carey's generation shared his desire to inculcate a distinctively working-class, masculine spirituality which contrasted sharply with the Marian devotions so prevalent in mid-twentieth-century Catholicism. The Jesuits also promoted a theology of lay vocations. As Carey put it:

> The priest must sell the idea to the workingman that work is a vocation, sanctified. The priest has to present the need of co-operation among workers after the ideal of the Mystical Body of Christ. The workers know what co-operation is and what it means. The ideal of the Mystical Body, of which he is a member, gives the worker something to live for and something to work for. It gives new meaning to his life.[22]

Phil Carey's pastoral and mediating gifts were legendary, recalled his Xavier predecessor, Joseph Fitzpatrick. "Everybody trusted him, so he was a natural go-between." He looked like the Irish American actor Barry Sullivan "but was tough as steel," recalled a younger Jesuit who worked with Carey. "He was a master of kindly discretion," wrote Peter McDonough, "adept at knowing what not to say." Carey could also play hardball when needed. He occasionally warned recalcitrant employers that they could "communicate with us or take your chances with the commies."[23]

A Lift from Taxi Jack

With a practical theology in place by the early 1940s, Xavier had yet to treat the New York waterfront. This was a particularly glaring shortcoming because the convert Dorothy Day's Catholic radicalism had it covered from virtually the inception of her movement in 1933. Day loved Ernest Poole's 1915 novel *The Harbor*, perhaps because the account of the Brooklyn waterfront by her fellow Chicagoan and social reformer so closely paralleled her own romantic view of urban immigrant life. As a young socialist newly arrived in New York City just before World War I, Day found that her long walks along the Lower East Side and West Side were "made more alive" by her having read *The Harbor*. For Poole as for Day, the waterfront was synonymous with immigrant Catholicism. The novel's genteel narrator recalls overhearing his mother tell a nursemaid, "Never on any account are the children to go down the street toward the docks," where the narrator's father operated a business. "At once I wanted to go there," reports the narrator, "there" being the place of "strange, ragged boys" he knew as "Finian Mickies."[24]

In part because her father—with whom she had a troubled relationship—was wary of Catholics and tried to shield Dorothy from the disorders of city life, she grew up fascinated by and inexorably drawn to the world of immigrant urban Catholicism. "As I walked these streets back in 1917 I wanted to go and live among these surroundings," Day wrote in her classic 1952 memoir *The Long Loneliness*. "In some mysterious way I felt that I would never be freed from this burden of loneliness and sorrow unless

I did." During the war, "by her own admission" she "spent a great deal of time partying" with the Hudson Dusters, the notorious gang of West Side waterfront pirates and cocaine addicts. In the 1930s her Catholic radicalism was fired by tales of waterfront brutality. The Catholic Workers hoped by their staunch support of striking merchant seamen in 1936 to undermine the authority of ILA president Joe Ryan as a conspicuously Catholic labor leader.[25]

The strikers, led by boatswain Joe Curran, rejected a contract agreement negotiated by the leaders of their union, the International Seamen's Union (ISU). The seamen were not longshoremen under Ryan's aegis but merchant sailors described by *Fortune* magazine as "the true proletariat of the Western world, the homeless, rootless and eternally unmoneyed." During their first strike, in May 1936, more than forty seamen stayed at the Catholic Workers' House of Hospitality on Mott Street. "We got some money from the shipowners," Ryan boasted three years later of the ILA's role in crushing the strikers, "and we drove them back with baseball bats where they belonged. Then they called the strike off."[26]

During a second wildcat strike in October of that year the Catholic Workers "rented a storefront on Tenth Avenue just south of Twenty-First Street, close to strike headquarters and just around the corner from the home of Joe Ryan[,]...who was doing his best to break the strike in the interests of his friends the ship owners and the leaders of the old ISU." The storefront operation provided the strikers with coffee, food, and respite at a time when "the whole West Side of New York erupted in battles between seamen and...goon squads, thugs employed by the shipowners to break the strike."[27]

Joe Ryan was shocked by this unprecedented defiance from within his own church. The insurgent seamen were ardently backed by Harry Bridges, leader of the pro-Soviet West Coast longshoremen's union, and "some of the most able and interesting Communists in the labor movement." To Ryan it was unthinkable that any professedly Catholic organization could exhibit solidarity with such a crew. During the autumn 1936 strike Ryan convened a meeting of the AFL's Central Trades and Labor Council of New York, which he led at the time, "his musclemen hunching up and down the aisles and glaring at anyone who said a kind word for the strikers." When Catholic Worker John Cort approached Ryan and identified himself, Ryan retorted, "You go back and tell Dorothy Day she's no lady." In January 1937 the *Catholic Worker* ran a front page "Open Letter to Union Leaders, Especially Joseph P. Ryan," claiming that the brutal tactics of strikebreakers and their allies made them "in effect, Bolsheviks" for denying their brotherhood in Christ with workers seeking social justice. The seamen returned to work early that year. Joe Curran successfully organized the National Maritime Union and affiliated it with the fledgling CIO; the new union supplanted the ISU and won better contracts and working conditions for the merchant seamen.[28]

The Tenth Avenue storefront opened by the Catholic Workers was located just across West Twenty-first Street from Joe Ryan's Guardian Angel Church. From the moment the church opened at its new location in 1930 it was identified not with the longshoremen who lived in the neighborhood but with shippers, stevedores, and especially its most generous patron, the neighborhood boy turned labor statesman who now lived but a stone's throw from Guardian Angel's elegantly crafted portal. Ryan's pastor, Monsignor John J. O'Donnell, was known among fellow archdiocesan priests as "Taxi Jack" because he was rarely if ever spotted in a subway station. Phil Carey by contrast was a near ascetic in eschewing luxuries his working-class constituency could not afford.[29]

Monsignor O'Donnell was a highly prominent figure in the archdiocese. In addition to exercising unrivaled spiritual authority on the West Side (his role as port chaplain barely hints at his true power), in the mid-1940s he played a major role in launching and organizing the Alfred E. Smith Memorial Dinner, an "event of the first importance" on the archdiocesan social and charitable calendar, which annually featured appearances by national and international political luminaries. O'Donnell never shied away from controversy involving Joe Ryan or any other of his generous waterfront benefactors. By the time he met Philip Carey several years after the seamen's strike, O'Donnell had apparently grown accustomed to an even more luxurious mode of transportation than taxicabs.[30]

In a 1987 journal entry Carey recalled a fearful encounter with Guardian Angel's pastor early in the Jesuit's priesthood. As Father Carey sauntered along West Twentieth Street after watching a ship depart from Pier 60, Monsignor O'Donnell pulled up alongside in his chauffeur-driven Chrysler and offered him a ride home. (Carey later learned that the chauffeur was provided by an official of the McGrath stevedoring firm, one of the leading powers on the Irish waterfront.) After an unsettling boast about his influence over the local police precinct, O'Donnell "spoke of the Communists," informing Carey that party members had recently painted the hammer and sickle on St. Francis Assisi Church on West Thirty-first Street and on the Columbus monument on West Fifty-ninth, a particular outrage to O'Donnell because he was the state chaplain of the Knights of Columbus. O'Donnell then reportedly told Carey: "We have to be very careful of what we say from our pulpit. After this outrage, we told the congregation that the Communists must be more careful since everybody knows [where] their local headquarters is." The next day, Carey recorded, party headquarters "was burnt to the ground." (There was in fact a firebombing at the Communist Party's office in Chelsea during this period—very near Guardian Angel on Tenth Avenue in the West Twenties—though details are sketchy, and it is impossible to determine if the deed was instigated by O'Donnell's sermon.)[31]

According to Carey, O'Donnell continued, "Dorothy Day and the Catholic Worker crowd were also picketing the *Bremen*," a German liner whose entry into the port in July 1935 attracted protesters who stripped Nazi insignia from the ship. Just over a year later, according to the *New York Times,* a group of 150 communists "wearing evening clothes and masquerading as peaceful visitors" boarded the same ship at Pier 86 on the North River, sparking a wild melee in which protesters and crewmembers traded "blows with fists and swinging deck chairs."[32]

"We told them [the Catholic Workers] we might give their address from our pulpit," O'Donnell informed Carey. As the limo arrived at the entrance to the Xavier Jesuit community residence, the monsignor timed his parting shot. "And Father Carey," he inquired, "your address is 30 West 16th, isn't it?" Philip Carey's account of this dramatic initial encounter with the clerical muscle behind the Irish waterfront must be read with care. The most recent *Bremen* protest had transpired the year Xavier Labor School was opened and four years before Carey took charge. Though O'Donnell may well have cited these events as cautionary tales from the past, Carey's historical narrative feels overwrought for a relatively brief conversation in a limousine. Nevertheless, Monsignor O'Donnell's effort to link the Catholic Workers with communists was a characteristic response of many New York Catholics—lay and clerical alike—who failed to recognize that Dorothy Day and her movement were staunchly *anti*communist: the Workers' *Bremen* counterprotest was meant to draw attention to the church's support of religious freedom in totalitarian societies such as Nazi Germany.[33]

Of course, O'Donnell surely made no such distinction when the Catholic Workers set up shop during the autumn 1936 seamen's strike directly across the street from Guardian Angel. In any case, Phil Carey's recollection of O'Donnell's underlying message was clear: the enmity between Guardian Angel and Xavier—real and unrelenting over a period of fifteen years—was lodged in Carey's memory for a lifetime.

Phil Carey never surrendered his resentment of this intra-church campaign of intimidation, nor did he confine his antipathy to the privacy of an unpublished journal. He blasted John J. O'Donnell in *You Must Remember This,* a 1989 oral history of Manhattan neighborhoods. When informed that a previous interviewee—a former longshoreman—had denounced O'Donnell as "a vicious bastard…like a storm trooper," Carey replied: "No, O'Donnell wasn't a storm trooper. I wouldn't want to insult the storm troopers." Nor did he stop there. "That bum," Carey testified to author Jeff Kisseloff; "he was a horse's ass[,]…a nitwit, and Ryan used him to a fare thee well." Carey linked O'Donnell to a vast impersonal system, a waterfront dreadnought the Jesuit found terrifying:

This was an enormous machine in which the longshoremen lived. All these things were organized. All the hiring was organized. The loan-sharking was organized. The numbers games were organized, and they were a tremendous source of income to the politicians. Frequently, the men couldn't work if they didn't want to play. Among the politicians it was power, power, power. The shipping associations had it; so did the politicians and the political clubs. A guy like Ryan was simply told what to do.

Speaking with Kisseloff shortly before his death in 1989 Carey maintained, "We were trying to get the whole problem out into the open," a struggle deeply complicated by the role of his own church in the waterfront machine.[34]

Why Did God Make Man?

The Jesuits were continually prodded by Catholic Workers both east and west of the Hudson. In addition to its efforts on the West Side of Manhattan, the Catholic Worker movement waged a bold campaign against the Frank Hague regime on the left bank of the Hudson. In a January 1938 "Open Letter to the People of Jersey City," the *Catholic Worker* reminded that city's overwhelmingly blue-collar constituency that the church promoted the rights of workers to organize "for mutual protection and betterment." In the June 1938 issue, in an open letter to Hague, the editors acknowledged the paper's "special interest in Jersey City because the city is over 75 percent Catholic." Although Dorothy Day's mentor and Catholic Worker co-founder Peter Maurin was unalterably opposed to industrial unionism (he obsessively touted a back-to-the-land "green revolution"), Day viewed Hague's violent resistance to CIO organizing campaigns in Jersey City as a scandal, especially as he was solidly backed by virtually all of the prominent Catholic clerics in Hudson County.[35]

After Hague refused to allow the Catholic Workers to hold meetings in his city, they retorted that *he* was aiding communists, the same charge Day had leveled against the mayor's friend Joe Ryan. Communists "don't have to try to discredit the church," the paper charged in the open letter to Hague, "because there are too many of your type doing it already."[36]

Day's ardent disciple John Cort led a small incursion of Catholic radicals into Jersey City in the spring of 1938. Cort joined forces with fellow ACTU member George Donahue, who belonged to a fledgling underground ILA reform faction. They handed out ACTU leaflets and copies of the *Catholic Worker*, testing police response to a recent Supreme Court decision outlawing a municipal anti-littering law designed by Hague forces to prevent distribution of political materials. Cort and Donahue were quickly accosted by police officers, prompting this memorable exchange as reported by Cort:

Cop: You can't distribute that stuff here. You're littering the street.

Donahue: Number one, the Supreme Court has ruled that your anti-littering ordinance is unconstitutional. Number two, we can't help it if people drop things on the street. If anybody is littering the street, they're littering the street.

Cop: Yeah, but you're the first cause of their littering.

The patrolman "kept repeating that phrase 'first cause,'" Cort recalled. "The conversation began to sound like a discussion of metaphysics, at which point I jumped in":

Cort: If you're going to talk about first causes, then God is the real first cause because God made man.

Second cop (figuring to expose our Catholic pose): Why did God make man?

Cort (letting him have it straight from the *Baltimore Catechism*): God made man to know Him and love Him and serve Him and be happy with Him forever in heaven.

Third cop: That's funny. I thought God made man to break the law so we could have a job.

Cort and Donahue could not help but laugh. The cops soon disappeared and the pair resumed leafleting, given a temporary reprieve. "Others were not so lucky," Cort dryly noted. In this world the support of the Catholic Church for the waterfront political machine was a given, and the obligation of any Catholic—lay or clerical—was to observe its division of labor, spiritual and temporal.[37]

Phil Carey knew as much, but in August 1941 he finally decided that he could no longer avoid the waterfront. He was visited by a group of men who had confided in their parish priest but received no consolation. They were coopers who worked repairing damaged crates of fruits and vegetables shipped to Pier 28 on the Lower West Side via the Erie and Pennsylvania railroads. The produce was unloaded from car floats that crossed the Hudson from the Jersey City rail yards. After work on the pier was taken over by Penn Stevedoring, waterfront kingpin Bill McCormack's firm, and Aetna Cooperage & Stevedoring, an outfit run by McCormack's brother Harry, the men lost their overtime pay. Their employer told them to accept the Teamsters contract he was offering or prepare to "chew cobblestones." Half a century later Carey recalled with disgust that "one man was responsible for all this.... This guy hired killers. One of the killers was Cockeye Dunn; another was Squint Sheridan."[38]

Since Bill McCormack and his brother dominated the Teamsters local, which in turn controlled the rank and file through intimidation, the beleaguered coopers decided after their visit with Carey to launch their own union with the Jesuit's support. Harry McCormack quickly locked them out, and local representatives of the National Labor Relations Board denied their bid for a representation election, an extremely frustrating ordeal in which the men's struggle was repeatedly thwarted by assorted politicians and government agencies in New York, New Jersey, and Washington, D.C.[39]

When Carey brought the coopers' case before the New York State Mediation Board, he was threatened by a Tammany-bred confidant of Al Smith and Franklin Roosevelt. ("This bum," fumed Carey. "He was writing FDR's speeches.") The political operative reportedly threatened to have Carey blackballed as "the worst enemy of labor.... [Y]ou'll never raise your head again[,]...and I can do it." He had never known until that moment, Carey lamented nearly fifty years later, how far the waterfront boss's influence reached. The machine prevailed over the coopers in routine fashion, with a key assist from the McCormacks' good friend Frank Hague, who, Carey learned, "was personally interested in the case."[40]

Phil Carey came to believe that a historic "original sin" accounted for the brutal moral and economic order prevailing on both sides of the waterfront: the moment around 1930 when "politicians in Jersey" first arranged for contracts with the Pennsylvania Railroad for cleaning and servicing their cars. The concession was initially acquired by Jersey City's "Little Guy" John V. Kenny through the good offices of his mentor Frank Hague. This opening of Irish waterfront access to the mighty railroad paved the way in turn for unimaginably lucrative railroad stevedoring contracts, very shortly won by the Hague-connected entrepreneur Bill McCormack in Jersey City and on the West Side of Manhattan.[41]

The Pier 28 coopers' thwarted bid for union democracy was a turning point in Carey's apostolate and the history of Xavier Labor School. "We decided we were all alone," he recalled years after that crushing defeat: "we couldn't get anything to back us up, nothing to back us up." The coopers' case "stuck in the craw of Father Carey for many a long year," wrote journalist Allen Raymond; he "could never forget it." The "pattern of oppression" discerned by Carey figured in all subsequent narratives of crime and corruption underlying waterfront reform efforts launched from Xavier.[42]

Still, although his apostolate was committed to dismantling the West Side code of silence, the Jesuit could not bring himself to pronounce the name of Bill McCormack even fifty years later, when an interviewer asked him to divulge the name of the notorious, immensely powerful waterfront boss—dead now for nearly a quarter-century—who was responsible for the "horror" on the waterfront.[43]

The Catholic Metropolis

A shaken Phil Carey grudgingly retreated from involvement on the docks during the Second World War. His focus shifted to routing communists from the Irish-led Transport Workers Union while shoring up the spiritual foundations of the city's large and fractious Irish Catholic working class. In January 1941 he rebuffed an attempted infiltration of Xavier by a cadre from the rabidly anti-Semitic Christian Front, a "dastardly outfit" inspired by the demagogic radio priest Charles Coughlin, who remained immensely popular among the New York Irish long after he was jettisoned by the Roosevelt administration and widely condemned for his own anti-Semitism. The Christian Fronters found their way to Xavier in the course of brawling with communists in nearby Union Square. On at least one occasion they disrupted a Xavier-sponsored public lecture on interfaith relations. Carey was dismayed to witness at this tumultuous event a diocesan priest from Queens who held "the wildest opinions—utterly untenable," in particular his refusal "to adore the humanity of Christ because it was Jewish." Carey's view that the man was "a wonderfully good priest otherwise" may have reflected his willingness to take the good along with the bad in others, though ethnic tribalism was pervasive on the Irish waterfront, and he was not wholly immune to its implications.[44]

A reporter for the leftist *Nation* magazine claimed in 1945 that the Christian Front "increased its activities along the waterfront" during this period, and that Coughlinites "established a liaison" with Joe Ryan, who was uniquely appealing in his combined stature as "anti-British, isolationist, anti-Communist, and unmistakably associated with labor." While there is scant evidence to establish more than a circumstantial link between Ryan and the Coughlinites, Phil Carey's resistance to the Christian Front insulated Xavier at least partially from the virulent anti-Semitism that plagued segments of the New York Irish community in the 1930s and 1940s.[45]

Carey performed a complex role in the public life of New York City in these years, a milieu dominated by a volatile mix of ethnicity and ideology. He was fearful of communist control over key unions, an issue the CIO would defer until the postwar era, when it was engaged with a vengeance. "Communism was a problem at that particular time.... [I]t was a double loyalty, that was the basic horror of it," declared Carey, an ironic formulation given that some in the labor movement felt that Catholics in the ACTU—or students at Xavier—experienced their own divided loyalties between church and union.[46]

Carey worked very hard to undermine Mike Quill, the Irish-born co-founder and president of the Transport Workers Union, organized in secret by Quill and six others in 1934, just as Phil Carey's father was nearing the end of his long and grueling career with the Third Avenue Transit Company. The mercurial Quill was an ardent Irish Republican who emigrated to the United States in 1926 and went to work for the Interborough Rapid Transit System, an outfit that employed so many committed rebels it was dubbed the "Irish Republican Training School." Quill participated in coalition-building discussions between the organization and the Communist Party, talks that brought the nascent TWU into the orbit of the CIO in the mid-1930s and probably, according to TWU historian Joshua B. Freeman, brought Quill into "the Party itself." In the late 1930s the TWU established a labor school at its Transport Hall on West Sixty-fourth Street in Manhattan amid "a number of Irish social clubs" in the neighborhood. The school grew to accommodate 250 students ("subway guards, trackwalkers, bus drivers, signalmen and cabbies") and bore some curricular resemblance to Xavier, whose program did not, however, inculcate a desire to "fight the bosses."[47]

The TWU school formed part of the "labor movement culture" of the 1930s and 1940s. Some secular-Left labor schools received federal funding through the New Deal Workers' Education Project. Although many of the working people enrolled in these schools came from Catholic backgrounds and some surely remained loyal to the church, the left-wing labor school movement was clearly viewed in an adversarial light by the Jesuits and leaders of the ACTU, an animus returned in kind by leftists, who in New York were likely to be communists. These competing labor schools—even if their leaders studiously ignored one another—were major sites of ideological struggle between the church and the secular Left in the age of the CIO.[48]

Phil Carey harbored a deep, visceral antipathy to Mike Quill and other procommunist Irish Americans in the TWU; he remained unmoved by their appeals to Irish Republicanism. Carey insisted that his own transit worker father was uninterested in the Irish cause and "would not allow politics to be discussed in the house," since "all it does is roil up the mud and makes people hate one another." He worked instead to supplant ethnic nationalism with Christian citizenship grounded in the social teachings of the church, originally designed in part to negate the appeal of the secular Left. The anticlerical Mike Quill reciprocated the antipathy: he condemned Xavier Labor School for promoting fascism and union busting as early as 1938, when Philip Dobson was still in charge. Quill even accused the not yet ordained but clerically attired Dobson of "being a false priest, an anti-unionist parading in priest's clothes."[49]

In 1947 Carey fomented an insurrection against Quill led by Xavier alumni members of the TWU who were deeply hostile to the union's procommunist leadership. The insurgents were "trounced" in elections of a key TWU local in December 1947, yet Carey took much credit for Quill's decisive break with the Communist Party the following March. Quill had many good reasons to abandon the party—beginning with intense pressure from the CIO—but the unrelenting animus of Carey's protégés surely played some role.[50]

Rescuing Catholics from communism was a pastoral duty in which Carey took pride because he believed that it restored their human dignity. A steelworker named Jim Conroy was but "one of the many men I helped out of the communist party," he recalled many years later, "and who now play a magnificent role in American society." Mike Quill was less appreciative of the Jesuit's efforts on behalf of his soul. Carey later claimed to hold "the most profound esteem" for Quill's "skill as a trade unionist" and said he "never knew why he hated me so badly." Yet it was just as difficult for Carey to acknowledge the deeply emotional and ideological nature of the conflict. In asserting, "I wanted the men to be proud of their union; instead they always had to go around apologizing for it," Carey honored the memory of his father, but he also revealed a proprietary interest in the souls of its overwhelmingly Irish membership. If Carey did not represent an officially Catholic labor "party," the anticommunist movement he espoused for advocacy of human dignity in the workplace was tantamount to the same thing. At some level all were asked to indicate which side they were on.[51]

The struggle for the TWU was but one skirmish in a widespread effort to purge leftists from the CIO in the immediate postwar years, a campaign that—especially in New York City—was in turn part of a much larger cultural and ideological struggle pitting Irish Catholics against communists. By the late 1940s it was still much easier for Jesuit labor priests to help rout an effective, politically connected, *leftist* Irish labor leader—Quill served several terms on New York's City Council—than a thoroughly corrupted figure like Joe Ryan, whose Catholic credentials were impeccable. This issue was so emotionally charged that it has proved extraordinarily resistant to nuanced historical treatment. Anticommunist maneuvering in fact constituted a very large part of Phil Carey's cultural and ideological work of the 1930s and 1940s. It was a campaign that linked him to labor priests from coast to coast, including those out West doing battle not with a Catholic-led, gangster-controlled longshoremen's union but with a left-wing counterpart that achieved for its membership many of the goals outlined in Catholic social teachings. The movement was broad enough to link Carey with both the progressive social justice tradition of Monsignor John A. Ryan—dubbed the "Right Reverend New Dealer—and the harder-edged strategies of Father John Cronin, a Maryland priest and leading interpreter of Catholic social thought who served as prime liaison after 1945 between the church and right-wing anticommunist political figures in Washington, most notably a young Southern California congressman, Richard M. Nixon.[52]

Whether Ryan, Cronin, and Phil Carey reconciled "principled anticommunism and militant trade unionism" in the manner of Catholic labor activists treated by historian William Issel, or colluded in "alliance with the most reactionary sectors of American politics," as William Mello countered, the work of the labor priests was very near the heart of an ideological and political struggle that helped shape urban American life from the Great Depression through the era of the cold war. Phil Carey's apostolic work belied his protestations of Xavier Labor School's nonpolitical character. The Jesuit labor priests were partisans without a party. Although Carey was constrained from articulating tangible political goals, his understated cultural and ideological work helped set the direction of Catholic social action in the deeply fractious context of New York City life, in an era when the tribal bonds linking Catholics to Tammany and the outer borough Democratic organizations were slowly fraying. Phil Carey was truly a labor priest in and for the Catholic metropolis.[53]

Carey's "inland" strategy for undermining New York communists would help clear the way for a waterfront campaign he knew must be waged from his base at Xavier Labor School. By the mid-1940s he had built a working model for Catholic labor advocacy that emphasized dignity in the workplace without class conflict, justice without radicalism, Christianity without tribalism. He trusted his own pastoral gift for mediation, for discerning when to counsel action and when to practice caution. Carey always believed that the ACTU was overly "interventionist," that it functioned too much like a labor party. He wanted to change men through their contact with Xavier and then see them do right by their unions. But he also bequeathed to his future collaborator a large contradiction: he "hated the church's involvement in politics" yet found himself deeply—if not publicly—involved in the politics of the TWU in an emotionally driven fashion that belied the vaunted cool detachment of Jesuit legend.[54]

Phil Carey's abundantly Irish American New York–style pastoral skills served his constituencies well in the industries he knew intimately, especially communications, transportation, and construction. These same gifts did him no good at all on the waterfront, a much rougher world unto itself and in some very painful ways the most Irish and Catholic place there was. Carey knew justice demanded that a Jesuit frontier be opened there even though it would surely lead to trouble with the church, since the Catholics who dominated both industry and labor on the waterfront counted on priests' minding their own business when it came to the conduct of their livelihoods.

The labor priest remained haunted for life by his experience trying to help organize the coopers of Pier 28 in 1941. The waterfront was sure to be one bruising apostolate, and it called for a priest with a crusading spirit to complement Carey's pastoral and diplomatic gifts. During the Second World War a succession of Jesuits served as Carey's assistants at Xavier, but none wished to become full-time labor priests, nor were any suited to take on the waterfront. That was before the arrival at Xavier in 1946 of a street-smart young Jesuit named John M. Corridan.[55]

6 *The Crusader*

Father John O'Brien's most vivid memory of his cousin John Corridan ranged back nearly seventy-five years, to summers when the Shanahans and Corridans and O'Briens of the Upper West Side of Manhattan took a bungalow near other Kerry folk at Rockaway Beach, along the "Irish Riviera" on the south shore of Long Island in the borough of Queens. Older by a decade than O'Brien, John Michael Corridan taught O'Brien and his other younger cousins to play baseball and to analyze the lineups of the Giants, who played at the Polo Grounds in Harlem, where Corridan was born in 1911, and the Dodgers, who played at Ebbets Field in Brooklyn, where his father, Patrolman John Corridan Sr., walked a beat for the New York Police Department. O'Brien recalled that even as a very young man his cousin blended a deeply analytical intelligence with street smarts no school could teach. Most of all he remembered an older boy swimming alone: "He was a great swimmer. He would go 200 yards beyond the last rope," always alone.[1]

The elder John Corridan emigrated from the parish of Duagh in Listowel, County Kerry, to New York City as a young man. His wife, Johanna Shanahan, known as Hanna, hailed from Lisheenbawn, a Kerry farming community. She was from a family of eleven children, of whom five sisters and a brother joined her in migrating to New York. There she met and married John Corridan in Brooklyn; their five sons were born in the various boroughs where Patrolman Corridan was stationed in a career as precarious as it was brief. When he died of pneumonia shortly after Hanna gave birth to their son Robert, the young widow and her five children moved in with Hanna's brother Pat Shanahan above a small grocery store he owned at 964 Amsterdam Avenue on Manhattan's Upper West Side. Pat and his wife and their three children lived upstairs, as did Pat and Hanna's sister Liz O'Brien, her husband, and their two young children.[2]

In later years John Michael Corridan never discouraged journalists from reporting that he grew up several miles south, near the West Side docks. "Many of my relatives have worked longshore for many years and are still working longshore," he testified before a United States Senate subcommittee in May 1953, though there is no indication that he was in contact with any such relatives. Corridan understood that local credentials were essential if he was to enjoy any legitimacy on the Irish waterfront. In the early 1950s a sympathetic non-Irish journalist wrote that Corridan "had known early in life the tales of strong men formed into insurgent bands, fighting the Black and Tans. His mother recalled the sound of rifle shots as rebels were cut down." But Corridan himself was unsentimental about his Irish ancestry and rarely volunteered specific information about his family's experience among New York City's vast Irish American working class.[3]

John Corridan and his brothers attended the grammar school of Ascension parish, while Hanna worked part-time for the New York Police Department in Lower Manhattan's Old Slip Station House to supplement her husband's meager pension and the monthly welfare benefits provided to the boys. Their extended family revolved around Pat Shanahan's grocery: Pat's "council room" was located in the back of the store amid tubs of butter; from there he dispensed advice and consolation to the lively community of Kerry natives inhabiting the neighborhood.[4]

During eighth grade young John was recommended for admission to the Jesuits' Regis High School on East Eighty-fourth Street near Central Park on Manhattan's Upper East Side. Regis offered an education of extraordinary quality grounded in the *Ratio Studiorum,* the "plan of studies" that had guided Jesuit educators since its publication in 1599. Matriculation at Regis virtually guaranteed opportunities for careers in the professions or business. The metropolitan area's six Jesuit preparatory schools drew eager, motivated students who traveled by trolley, foot, and subway in a kind of ritual preenactment of the social and geographic mobility that beckoned. The student bodies of these schools in the first third of the twentieth century were overwhelmingly Irish American. The New York Jesuits (technically members of the Maryland–New York province until it was divided in 1943) were an Irish American franchise of long standing. Each year a cadre of recent Jesuit high school graduates—among them Philip Carey of the Regis class of 1925—proceeded directly to a Jesuit novitiate to launch their arduous training for the priesthood.[5]

For the Irish of New York and northern New Jersey, entry into the Jesuit order was a deeply communal act. Yet John Corridan's path to the Jesuits was characteristically independent of this tradition. A friendly, likeable youth, though "quiet and reserved in class"—where his presence was "almost forgotten until he rises for translation and renders a recitation that would do credit to [Alexander] Pope"—he was "active and fun loving after school." More interested in compiling baseball statistics than in cultivating the gifts of *eloquentia perfecta* that marked Jesuit humanism, Corridan was *in* but not fully *of* Regis; he always resisted the romanticism so often associated with the New York Irish experience. Phil Carey later recalled that Corridan described his early life as "'catch as catch can' in the days of poverty and repression"; he confessed to participating once in the theft of equipment from wealthier members of his altar boys' baseball team. Corridan's Irish American experience represents the flipside of the customary lyricism. Purposeful and wary might best describe his mood as he left Regis for the workplace in 1928.[6]

In support of the extended Upper West Side family with whom he continued to live, Corridan took a job in the back office of National City Company, a Wall Street securities firm. Rising from office boy to "correspondent" at National City, where he managed to hold on to his job in the months after the devastating stock market collapse in October 1929, he took evening courses at New York University. Then in early 1931 Corridan read René Fülöp-Miller's entertaining history *The Power and Secret of the Jesuits,* a detailed political and theological history of the order that lavishly treated virtually every scandal and intrigue in which the Society of Jesuits had ever been implicated. Comparing Jesuit founder Ignatius of Loyola to Lenin ("the greatest zealot of the sixteenth and the greatest atheist of the twentieth century"), Fülöp-Miller highlighted Ignatius's purported teaching "that man can achieve perfection by his own will and his own powers." Corridan found himself deeply drawn to the unmystical, action-oriented dimension of Jesuit thought. *The Power and Secret of the Jesuits* "crystallized Corridan's thinking. It also changed his life."[7]

Corridan's discernment of a priestly vocation through the solitary act of reading was highly characteristic. In August 1931 he entered the novitiate at St. Andrew-on-Hudson, just north of Poughkeepsie. Business for the Jesuits was booming: the entering class just ahead of Corridan's was the largest in the history of the Maryland–New York province. His class of seventy was divided between the novitiate at St. Andrew and the facility in Wernersville.[8]

The Ignatian formation process was austere and highly regimented. William A. Barry, a Jesuit who entered the order after Corridan (but well before the formation process was altered in the 1960s), described life in the novitiate as

> all-encompassing....We wore uniform clothes most of each day, called each other by our formal title (Brother Barry), and had our day organized down to the hour and minute. In the novitiate, incoming and outgoing mail was censored, and no newspapers or radio programs were allowed. Indeed, even Jesuit visitors were restricted to those invited by the novice master. There was almost no privacy; we slept in a large dormitory and prayed, studied, and read in large common rooms.

Despite the strict regimen, Jesuits were not trained for monastic retreat. "Jesuit spirituality," wrote Barry, "can be said to embody a set of creative tensions.... Jesuits are to be men 'crucified to the world,' yet actively engaged in the world; they are, indeed, expected to find God in all things."[9]

In the autumn of his first year at St. Andrew, Corridan embarked on the thirty-day "long retreat," in which novices were led through the *Spiritual Exercises* of Saint Ignatius Loyola. He was deeply attracted to the corporate spirituality of the Jesuits; the mostly silent retreat represented a test he knew he could pass. A loner, he enjoyed being on retreat in the company of others, since a distance between individuals was observed even as the novices shared conferences under the leadership of a spiritual director. This parallel spirituality of individuals grounded in adherence to a communal discipline marked the Jesuits as men "who knew who they were and where they were going[,] ... a group of winners, men with a robust, masculine spirituality." Corridan did not cultivate the traditional "interior" spirituality, yet as the Franciscan scholar Joseph Chinnici once observed, a Jesuit's performance of a public vocation created a space where private religiosity might remain a very real force. Corridan would develop a richly spiritual life as a labor priest, a highly public vocation which afforded the built-in spiritual authority enjoyed by Jesuits in all their ministries.[10]

Following his novitiate and two-year "juniorate" in classical studies at St. Andrew-on-Hudson, Corridan moved on to philosophical studies at Saint Louis University in 1935, where he was immediately pegged by his midwestern confreres as a street-smart New Yorker with, as one classmate recalled, "the Jimmy Walker flair." Corridan was appointed *manuductor,* a prestigious liaison position between students and their Jesuit supervisors. There were nearly three hundred Jesuit scholastics studying at the university in the mid-1930s. So many of them shared the name John, a classmate announced that Corridan would henceforth be known as "Pete," a moniker that stuck for the remainder of his life, especially within the Jesuit community, where he was known exclusively (as he will be known here) as Pete Corridan.[11]

The newly rechristened Pete Corridan reveled in the scholastic experience. The small army of philosophy students rose at 5 A.M. and proceeded as a group to chapel for Mass at 5:30. Listening to the radio was forbidden; newspapers could be read only on a stand in the library. Meals were taken in silence apart from the voice of whoever was chosen to read selections from spiritual literature. St. Louis was a vital center of North American Jesuit life. Here Corridan was introduced to theories of industrial democracy promoted by Joseph Husslein, a prolific Jesuit scholar on the faculty of the university's School of Social Service. After completing his studies in philosophy, Corridan remained at St. Louis for an additional year before obtaining an M.A. in economics in 1939. He then went on to teach at Canisius College in Buffalo prior to assignment at the Crown Heights Labor School in Brooklyn.

Crown Heights was run by William J. Smith, S.J., "a rather combative man" less interested in labor advocacy than in advancing Catholic social studies. Corridan was much more interested in helping working people. In a revealing February 1941 essay on the right to strike during "our national crisis" published in the Jesuits' *America* magazine, Corridan acknowledged the primacy of labor-management harmony urged in the papal social encyclicals; but given the historic tendency of wages to lag behind prices, he indicated his solidarity with "the workingman" against "the unjust employer" who compels him to strike "or against a negligent government that refuses to protect him."[12]

In late 1941 Corridan embarked on the four-year Jesuit course of theology at Woodstock, a seminary with "the charm and rustic vigor of an extended retreat," according to historian Peter McDonough, "a utopian isle apart from the seductions and perils of industrialism." Corridan evinced little interest in scholastic theology, however, apart from its implications for men of action. Woodstock's most renowned theologian was John Courtney Murray, known for his conviction that "man becomes a man by the encounter with three elemental forces, and by the mastery of them—the encounter with the earth, with woman, and with his own spirit.... [M]an is not man until by his own hard work he has bent stubborn earth to his own purposes."[13]

In the 1940s no one noted the extravagantly "gendered" character of Murray's ideology, with its stark dichotomies of "masculine reason" and "feminine unreason." If anything, this hypermasculine ideology particularly appealed to men preparing to engage the rugged environment of emerging Jesuit missions such as the labor schools, which rarely admitted women. Yet the manly Jesuit ethos also lent cover to a shyness and sensitivity that was a source of some discomfort for Pete Corridan. As a spiritual ideology favoring controlled aggression, the Jesuits' "inward, strong purposefulness" might prove useful on the Irish waterfront, all things being equal, which they were not.[14]

Shaping Up for Battle

John Michael "Pete" Corridan was ordained to the priesthood on June 18, 1944, his thirty-third birthday. He spent his fourth year of theology visiting parishes in rural Maryland and Pennsylvania. In 1945 he began his "tertianship" year at Auriesville in upstate New York, the site of the Shrine of Our Lady of Martyrs, commemorating the Jesuit confreres who had died working among Native Americans in New France in the seventeenth century. Tertianship was "designed as a recapitulation, more mature in tone but nonetheless a renewal, of the novitiate experience in which the Jesuit priest was supposed to do little studying and a good deal of praying." Corridan then joined Father Phil Carey at Xavier Labor School and was quickly assigned to the unfulfilled waterfront apostolate which had been haunting Carey since 1941, when his advocacy for the coopers from Pier 28 had ended in threats and intimidation.[15]

During this period of "discernment" Corridan benefited enormously from the work of Edward Swanstrom, a Brooklyn diocesan priest whose first assignment after ordination in 1928 was at St. Peter's parish near the South Brooklyn waterfront. Swanstrom's political philosophy dissertation, published in 1938 as *The Waterfront Labor Problem,* offered the most incisive analysis of conditions in the port since Charles Brinton Barnes's classic 1915 study *The Longshoremen.* Swanstrom added a moral and theological dimension to Barnes's social and economic portrait of waterfront labor.

Driven by the memory of impoverished families in St. Peter's parish and the appeals made by waterfront families to Catholic Charities, the Brooklyn cleric aimed "to show how serious are the social consequences of the outmoded system of hiring, and of the lack of organization in the port labor market...[,] with their resulting irregularity of employment." He trained his critique on the shapeup, the traditional system of waterfront hiring. Barnes had vividly described the scene at the Chelsea piers, where men hopeful of finding work would arrive early in the morning:

> Before long several hundred have gathered on the far side of the street from the piers. Just before seven the foreman blows his whistle for them to "shape"; that is, to take their places in a half circle in front of the pier. As far as the space allows, this semi-circular line is always kept, but the number of rows deep the men may stand is limited only by the number seeking work.

According to Swanstrom, the system had changed little since Barnes's day apart from a reduction in daily shapes from four to three.[16]

The shapeup constituted an unpredictable system of casual employment that by its nature, Swanstrom argued, degraded workers and led rapidly to the social and moral crises linked to industrial capitalism by the papal social encyclicals; on the waterfront these were manifest in loan-sharking, rampant gambling, alcoholism, and broken families. He stringently invoked these papal documents against the ILA, which resisted regularization of employment because a large and docile supply of dues-paying members sustained the corrupt system on which the union thrived. The ILA's ability to deliver wage increases "means little, or nothing at all," Swanstrom argued, "in the face of widespread irregularity of employment." He reiterated the claim of Pope Leo XIII that true associations of workingmen must help "each member to better his condition to the utmost in body, soul, and property."[17]

The Waterfront Labor Problem provided both the empirical and moral foundations for Pete Corridan's waterfront crusade. Swanstrom showed that economic data could be marshaled to serve the ends of social justice; he was also ready and willing to engage his adversaries on their own turf. When he boldly sought to promote his book at the 1939 ILA convention in New York's Commodore Hotel, the union's burly sergeant at arms promptly confiscated Swanstrom's leaflets and ushered him off the premises. Joe Ryan brashly embraced full responsibility for the ejection, explaining that Swanstrom was "not the type of priest who believes in minding his own business." Ryan had never before been compelled to articulate the "just waterfront" theory's division of church and piers into two separate Catholic spheres of influence. The papal encyclicals as wielded by Swanstrom threatened to undermine that division of temporal and spiritual labor observed by Ryan, his pastor Monsignor O'Donnell, and all parties with an investment in waterfront politics and economics.[18]

Shortly after this dramatic encounter with Ryan's hired muscle, Swanstrom turned his attention to important work off the waterfront—a wise career move surely arranged by Brooklyn diocesan officials. After the United States entered the Second World War, the shapeup was condemned as "inefficient and chaotic" by military officials concerned with this vital industry. They won a modification of the system; increasing numbers of workers henceforth secured employment in regular gangs with rights of first call on their regular piers. John V. Lyon of the New York Shipping Association continued to defend the shapeup as the historically proven method of hiring, a position that only enhanced suspicions of a collusive relationship between shippers and the ILA leadership. On the union front, Joe Ryan was named "life president" of the ILA at a 1943 convention. As historian Charles P. Larrowe characterized the wartime situation, the ILA and NYSA "seemed destined to prolong indefinitely their pattern—already 24 years old—of mutual cooperation and cordiality, coupled with complete disregard for the interests of the rank and file and the public."[19]

Sling Loads

After simmering for decades, waterfront discontent finally exploded shortly after war's end, when the ILA membership asserted its collective will in a most dramatic fashion. Early on the afternoon of October 1, 1945, a group of longshoremen from Local 791 walked off their jobs loading cargo onto the *Dalton Mann*, a vessel of the Grace Line docked at Pier 54 in Chelsea. The men were protesting their employers' refusal to limit the "sling load"—the weight borne by cargo nets that work gangs were expected to handle—to one "long ton" of 2,240 pounds. Some men were reportedly expected to handle up 7,000 pounds per sling load. The walkout quickly spread to nearby piers on the West Side and a few more along the East River. By 6 P.M., the *New York Herald Tribune* reported, "8,000 of the city's 50,000 to 60,000 longshoremen" had joined the impromptu work stoppage. Another 5,000 longshoremen struck Hudson County's piers the following day.[20]

Pete Corridan was immersed in his upstate tertianship when the strike broke out, yet it proved the foundational event of his subsequent waterfront apostolate. By the time he began his careful study of the waterfront the following year, the 1945 strike, and indeed the state of labor relations as a whole within the port, still lacked an "organizing narrative"; confusion reigned as it had during the strike itself. On October 3 the *New York Times* reported that the unauthorized strike had ended the previous afternoon when delegates from various locals voted to go back to work. Yet later that same day, as *Times* labor reporter George Horne wrote for the October 4 edition, "the entire Port of New York was paralyzed" by "an 'outlaw' strike of longshoremen, who left more than 100 transports and cargo vessels lying idle at their piers." The *New York Herald Tribune*—voice of the Republican establishment and no friend of labor—characterized the strikers as "rebellious and possibly misinformed"; the newspaper embraced Joe Ryan's explanation that a "misunderstanding" was at the root of the strike. (Ryan claimed that inoperable elevators had curtailed negotiations.) In the days to come, the waterfront labor situation enjoyed more coverage in the city's daily newspapers than in the previous two decades combined. "On September 30 few people in New York knew what a sling load was," wrote historian George Lipsitz. "Two days later nearly everybody did."[21]

For journalists, covering the waterfront proved an enduring challenge. No one knew, for example, just how many longshoremen actually worked or sought work in the Port of New York: estimates ranged from forty thousand to sixty thousand. The internal workings of the ILA were completely shrouded in mystery. The *Times* was especially candid in acknowledging the inscrutable qualities of labor relations in the port. Burned by premature claims that the strike had ended quickly, Horne reported on October 4 that the re-ignited, rapidly spreading "action was characterized by almost total confusion. Some of the strikers called it a strike while others said it was a lockout on the part of the operators." Gene Sampson, business agent of Local 791, urged a return to work, "but 1,500 men of the local had met at their headquarters, 164 Eleventh Avenue, and voted shortly after 10 A.M. to continue the strike." According to the *Times*, the vote made the strike "slightly official, as far as that body of men was concerned, although there are some 10,000 men involved in that local alone." All such figures were strictly the product of guesswork.[22]

The Communist Party deployed one lonely waterfront operative in Chelsea, Sam Madell, who "was always having a hard time with the party, trying to get them to understand the waterfront." The communists had never enjoyed influence in the ILA's Atlantic District, but amid the chaos of the October 1945 strike they enticed William Warren, a former organizer for the Transport Workers Union with precious little waterfront experience, to position himself as a rank-and-file spokesman from a base in Brooklyn. Nary a soul among the actual rank and file had ever heard of William Warren; given the ethnic dynamics of the waterfront workforce, his name must have struck some as a pseudonym. Warren's intervention, coupled with the intrusion of Harry Bridges, leftist leader of the West Coast longshoremen's union (ILWU) seeking to open a new anti-Ryan front back east, provided Ryan with a handy target: blaming the communists for the walkout surely beat blaming elevator operators.[23]

Though everyone knew there were no communists in Local 791, the men—including a key contingent of Association of Catholic Trade Union members—were sufficiently insulted by the involvement of Warren and Bridges that they went back to work. William Loughlin, shop steward for the Irish-dominated Local 895 on Pier 46 in the West Village, assured Ryan: "We are not here to overthrow you. We want no outsiders in our family fight and we will battle these Commies together." Or as longshoreman Johnny Dwyer of Pier 45 in the West Village put it: "I know I was a rebel, but they're Commie rebels. That's the difference."[24]

With the strike collapsing around him, Warren declared victory and urged longshoremen to return to work; he "slipped and hurt himself" (waterfront argot for a very bad beating) on a Brooklyn pier while attempting to shape up on October 18. The following day Warren staggered into a hastily called press conference to announce that he had been "wrongly steered" into the communist camp by Nathan Witt, left-wing attorney for the rank-and-file group. Most of the longshoremen in the port, however, remained adamantly opposed to Ryan's efforts to reach a settlement with NYSA without their consent, a customary practice that in the new postwar labor environment would not stand. Amid great uncertainty over just who legitimately represented the interests of dockworkers, Ryan and the shippers turned to an arbitrator, who granted the wage increase sought by the ILA but left the issue of sling load limits to the discretion of employers. The number of daily shapeups was reduced from three to two.[25]

The 1945 strike confirmed, as labor scholar Vernon Jensen noted in an understatement, that the "ILA leadership was not in touch with the men." If Ryan expected to retain the loyalty of the rank and file, "their consent to an agreement needed to be achieved by some form of communication." The triumph of the anticommunist West Side Irish over the smaller contingent of Brooklyn-based leftist agitators was wholly predictable (the men "were susceptible to mass movements, but perhaps not to class movements," as Jensen put it), but the strike's origins in Ryan's own "Mother Local" exposed rifts within the Irish waterfront that afforded Jesuit labor priests a rare opportunity to intervene.[26]

Despite the confusing and often bizarre character of the strike, its roots in Chelsea convinced some that Joe Ryan faced a major Irish Catholic insurgency. The memory of Edward Swanstrom's solitary 1939 incursion further emboldened clerics scandalized by Ryan's conduct to speak out for the first time. In November 1945 the labor editor of *America* magazine, Ben Masse, S.J., asserted, "The dock strike was over, but not the fight against Mr. Ryan." Masse did not claim that opposition to the shapeup was a major factor in the strike, and indeed it was not. In fact, little of the organized resistance to Ryan that Pete Corridan researched—or that he witnessed firsthand after 1946—focused principally on the shapeup, but the waterfront hiring system remained the centerpiece of his own emerging analysis in the tradition established by Swanstrom. Corridan essentially grafted Swanstrom's conclusions, grounded in conditions from an earlier era, onto the rapidly changing postwar waterfront. While this approach undermined Corridan's credibility as a waterfront expert and gravely weakened his prospects for winning the confidence of rank-and-file dockworkers, it offered the great advantage of simplicity in his looming public role as port reformer. All the ills of the waterfront could be conveyed through the potent and readily visualized symbol of an inhumane shapeup system.[27]

The equation of the shapeup with waterfront criminality, which eventually—with a very large assist from Pete Corridan—took hold in the public imagination, obscured a much more complex and variegated labor economy that was evolving throughout the port. "The shapeup was not the principal form of hiring," as labor historian Colin J. Davis asserted and as Corridan surely knew. There were several hiring systems in place in the port by 1945, ranging from the "open shape," in which all the men needed to load or unload a ship were chosen by a pier hiring foreman, to the use of "regular gangs" with rights to steady work on a given pier. "There were regular gangs at some piers" by the late 1920s, Vernon Jensen concluded in a 1964 study "based on the best information available" (which on the waterfront—it must be noted—was never very good). This prewar custom was expanded by wartime exigency, especially along the Hudson River piers worked by Irish American longshoremen. By Davis's estimate "approximately 60 percent to 75 percent of the longshoremen belonged to work gangs and were hired as such" throughout the port in the immediate postwar years. "The remaining workers were casuals shaping-up to fill temporary positions within the respective gangs."[28]

When the shapeup *was* employed, Davis argued, it "was for the most part a sham. As one observer testified, 'you will find that 99 out of a hundred times...names were submitted to that hiring boss before the men go to the shape-up.'" The ILA leadership resisted outside calls to dismantle the system because an affiliated network of specialists, including loan sharks, bookmakers, and saloonkeepers, supplemented their livelihoods from the cohort of surplus labor. Men who did not view themselves as full-time longshoremen were periodically drawn to the shapeup, which "offered them at least the hope of a day's work at relatively high hourly wages," though as critics noted, high hourly wages meant little if hours were few and far between. Many of these "extras" or "casuals" were easy marks for bookies and loan sharks, while others—including off-duty police officers, firemen, friends of friends, and the occasional civil servant looking to supplement his income with a quick shift on a busy pier—came and went as they pleased. Kickbacks to hiring bosses from part-time job seekers financed many a vacation. Even "regular" longshoremen were hesitant to embrace centralized hiring halls or any system that would undermine the highly localized, face-to-face political and social economy of the waterfront "in spite of widespread condemnation of the shape-up as 'vicious, degrading and irrational.'"[29]

The shapeup was an integral component in a hierarchical waterfront social order with deep racial and ethnic overtones. "As power shifted from the established Irish groups to others vying for control," wrote Davis, "Irishness or Irish identity did not diminish; indeed, it was strengthened." While black longshoremen in Brooklyn, often relegated to work as "extras," were more likely to be turned away by the Italian hiring bosses who dominated the vast waterfront in that borough, the system in place throughout the harbor reflected historic Irish rule and Irish prerogatives. The workers best situated to challenge the system—the men of the prestigious Irish West Side locals—had perhaps the least incentive, since they already enjoyed the privileges accruing to membership in regular gangs. Father Pete Corridan never grasped the one good reason why his fellow Irish Americans did not respond more warmly to his condemnation of the shapeup as constituting a systematic affront to human dignity: they were the ones who profited from the waterfront's social and occupational hierarchies.[30]

War veterans returning to the West Side, however, proved far less deferential than before to the men who ran the system. Johnny Dwyer grew up on West Twelfth Street and went to work on Pier 25 in 1937. When he received his first paycheck, he noticed that it did not reflect the overtime hours he had worked. When he complained, recalled Dwyer years later, the pier boss "called Johnny Dunn and a couple of his boys come lookin' for me. They said, 'You keep your mouth shut or you'll wind up in the river.' I said, 'Don't worry about me. I'm not windin' up in the river.' But next week I quit when I found out who he was." On returning to the neighborhood in 1945 after service in the South Pacific, Dwyer sought work on Pier 45 at the foot of Christopher Street in the West Village. The hiring there had long been controlled by the Thompson brothers: Eddie, who was pier foreman, and Sonny, proprietor of Sonny's West Shore Bar and Grill on West Street, an establishment frequented by loan sharks and others with a vested interest in the local labor market.[31]

When Sonny Thompson told Dwyer he could find him a job on the docks, Dwyer replied that he would find his own job, knowing these words would bring consequences. Dwyer was a member of West Village Local 895, which had not held an election in three decades. Shortly after the October wildcat strike Dwyer and some fellow veterans decided to seek an election and to make Pier 45—recently abandoned by the U.S. Navy—the focal point of their campaign. The ILA authorized an election, then supplied its own brawny voters in support of candidates chosen from points unknown, leading to a chaotic and intermittently violent scene outside the polling place, St. Veronica's church on Christopher Street. "Officers were elected for five years that none of us had ever seen before," recalled a local longshoreman. ACTU attorney Ed Scully, who provided free legal services, urged the men to level formal charges against the Thompson brothers. "A hundred men put their lives and their waterfront careers on the block by signing a court order requesting a new, free election." After the pastor of St. Veronica's, Father Martin Conboy, permitted the men to use the church hall for a "Longshore Conference" in January 1946, he was "abused and threatened," wrote journalist Allen Raymond, "and the Chancery Office was informed that the meeting was backed by Communists," a reflexive Ryan ploy that had worked every time.[32]

When the Alcoa Steamship Company and its stevedoring agent finally decided to occupy Pier 45 and offer jobs to the members of Local 895, the rebels—more incensed than ever at being labeled communists—picketed until Alcoa approached Dwyer about becoming hiring boss, a position he accepted with some trepidation. Dwyer blew the whistle for the first time in August 1946. The shapeup was modestly reformed but not replaced: regular gangs remained the norm, and extra men were hired as needed, but the loan sharks were banished, at least temporarily. The rebels of 895—with ACTU on board they now often publicly identified themselves as "the longshoremen of St. Veronica's parish"—were among Pete Corridan's earliest West Side contacts. He discerned "leadership material" in John Dwyer and sensed that "the old system was showing signs of breaking up."[33]

Corridan became the rebels' "counselor to some degree," as Raymond later wrote in a telling qualification. The Jesuit's limited advisory role reflected in part philosophical differences between the New York ACTU and Father Phil Carey, who continued to insist that labor priests should remain aloof from factional fights within unions. The men of 895 felt a strong loyalty to ACTU for the organization's bold support of their cause. By 1947 there was already some nascent suspicion of Corridan's emerging role among the rank and file; men who rarely couched their grievances in the language of workplace "dignity" were not necessarily prepared to demand an end to the shapeup and remained wary of clerical intervention on the waterfront, no matter how well meant.[34]

Corridan's most ardent supporters among West Side longshoremen were few in number and were rarely well placed even within reform factions. They were, however, deeply devoted to him, and none more than Arthur "Brownie" Brown, a "short, gadfly rebel" and "veritable sea lawyer, with a memory of waterfront history and personalities as accurately arranged and commodious as a well-ordered filing cabinet." According to an admirer, "after a lifetime of waterfront beatings," Brownie "looked like an old prize fighter." On one occasion he was thrown into the Hudson River off Christopher Street by ILA enforcers. Another attempt on his life, said Brownie, "left me with a cargo hook in me, but I fooled 'em and lived." Brownie's adventures resulted as much from his delinquent behavior as from his union activities. According to Phil Carey, "Arthur Brown had been just a drunk on the docks" when he first came to the Xavier Labor School. His association there with Carey and Corridan "changed his entire life, because we got him to understand who he truly was." This was the model of personal transformation at the heart of Carey's vision for Xavier: Brownie became the school's most visible convert, serving on the faculty while remaining Corridan's faithful liaison to the ILA rebel factions on the West Side.[35]

A Catholic Looks at the Waterfront

By autumn 1948, with his inside connection established, Pete Corridan was ready to offer a public witness on behalf of dockworkers (see figure 4). His influence at Xavier Labor School was greatly mitigated by the unwillingness of West Side longshoremen to risk being seen entering the facility. They "would slip in the back door so no would see them," Corridan later recalled. "They would come in after mass, disappearing past the sacristy so no one outside would see them come to my office." This covert operation was clearly no substitute for a public campaign. Sometime late in 1948 Corridan accepted an invitation to speak at a Communion breakfast sponsored by a Knights of Columbus chapter in Jersey City, most likely the Paulus Hook Council, then located at Jersey Avenue and York Street, just a few blocks west of the city's waterfront railroad piers.[36]

The extant undated typescript of the talk is titled "A Catholic Looks at the Waterfront." Since the breakfast was not open to the public or to reporters, it is impossible to verify either the title or the contents of the speech delivered that morning, legendarily known as "Christ in the Shapeup." "It's funny how everybody ducks the main problem of the waterfront," Corridan observed at the beginning of the manuscript version. "They plan to fix up the piers, and though the piers really need fixing, the men are in greater need than the piers." He then moved toward the controversial themes that would mark his crusade for the next six years:

> You want to know what's wrong with the waterfront? It's love of a lousy buck, whether it's one or a thousand or ten thousand[,]...God or no God. A man is going to get them in any way he can. In many ways you can't blame the mob...even if the mob is Catholic. They see Catholic-educated men chase a buck as if Christ didn't exist, and hide behind their professional Catholicity.[37]

Figure 4. John M. "Pete" Corridan, S.J., at St. Peter's Church, New Brunswick, New Jersey (a satellite of Xavier Labor School), ca. 1948. Courtesy of the Archives of the Xavier Institute of Industrial Relations, Fordham University Library, Bronx, New York.

Corridan then raised the stakes by urging his listeners to imagine Christ himself enduring the same indignities as dockworkers:

> I suppose some people would smirk at the thought of Christ in the shape. It is about as absurd as the fact that Christ redeemed all men irrespective of their race, color, or station in life....Christ also said, "If you do it to the least of mine, you do it to me." So Christ is in the shape...as sure as every man there in the state of grace is his brother and the others are called to be.[38]

The image of Christ placed squarely on the waterfront drove his theme with a cascade of ringing stanzas:

> Christ works on a certain pier. He knows that he is expected to be deaf, dumb, and blind, if He wants to work....Christ works on a pier and His back aches

because there are a fair number of the "boys" on the pier. They don't work but have their rackets at which so many wink. What does Christ think of the man who picks up a longshoreman's brass check and takes 20 per cent at the end of the week?

Corridan concluded by insisting that there was much more at stake than the amelioration of local working conditions:

> For those longshoremen who are straight and are good family men, God be praised. For those who slip every once in a while and lose hope, God have mercy. To those responsible, God grant the grace to see things on the waterfront as Christ sees them, for the time is growing short when God will show no mercy.[39]

"Pete was brilliant in putting his facts and conclusions together," Phil Carey admiringly recalled. "He was a forceful speaker." The powerful oratory of "A Catholic Looks at the Waterfront" launched Corridan's public career and was the first salvo in a cultural and political battle that would culminate in 1954 with the release of *On the Waterfront,* with actor Karl Malden as Father Pete Barry reciting verbatim from the hold of a ship lengthy excerpts from Corridan's speech during an impromptu eulogy for a slain rebel longshoreman. The story behind that film drama would unfold only gradually. On the waterfront of 1948, Corridan signaled a willingness to invest his spiritual authority fully in a dangerous cause. In another speech delivered before a Catholic group in Jersey City during this same period Corridan preached:

> The one supreme lesson that Christ taught workers by his life, was the meaning of the dignity of man—that man's dignity is a God-like dignity—that man was not only made to the image and likeness of God but was also given a share in God's divine life—that Christ, Himself, became man to restore man's God-like dignity lost in the fall of Adam—that man's God-like dignity is infinitely more valuable than the entire wealth of the world—that all men must respect that God-like dignity in themselves and in others or answer to God for it.[40]

He went on to invoke the authority of Popes Leo XIII, Pius XI, and Pius XII, powerfully and directly adapting the message of the social encyclicals to waterfront conditions of life and labor. He reminded his audience that as members of the Mystical Body of Christ, and indeed as human beings, they enjoyed the natural right to "a living wage, to decent working conditions[,]...to welfare plans and pensions—the right to share in the profits and sit at the same conference table with management and deliberate upon matters that concern both management and labor."[41]

The message of these talks was radical yet grounded squarely in the church's social teachings. A return engagement by Corridan at the Paulus

Figure 5. Corridan joined by John Holley, a layman who taught at Xavier, and Philip A. Carey, S.J., New Brunswick, New Jersey, ca. 1948. Courtesy of the Archives of the Xavier Institute of Industrial Relations, Fordham University Library, Bronx, New York.

Hook Knights of Columbus hall in May 1949 was accompanied by a press release from Xavier Labor School, which recorded the Jesuit's chagrin "that so many of those both in the industry and the union leadership are Catholic, yet give little evidence of their Catholicity in their posts of responsibility." In this presentation he challenged the reflexive anticommunism of Catholic industrialists in the port by contrasting the unregulated labor market there with the West Coast's hiring halls, established under the leadership of suspected communist Harry Bridges. He warned that in the event of war with the Soviet Union, sabotage would be less likely to occur on the West Coast than on the New York waterfront because of the chaotic hiring system in place there—"and the government knows it."[42]

Eight years after Philip Carey assumed the directorship of Xavier Labor School, the New York Jesuits finally began to fulfill his self-declared mandate to cover the waterfront. Pete Corridan's deep grounding in the social encyclicals and waterfront economics and his aura of controlled aggression—hinting at his own intimacy with violence—made him a formidable advocate (see figure 5). The Catholic Workers and the ACTU had sniped at Joe Ryan for a decade with scant results: members of these groups were easily Red-baited and marginalized despite the presence of a diocesan chaplain in the latter organization. The leading figure at ACTU, John Cort, was not only a convert from Protestantism but also "dedicated to the point of asceticism," traits sure to attract derision on the Irish waterfront.[43]

The reformer's dilemma was vividly treated in *Moon Gaffney*, New York writer Harry Sylvester's remarkable—if wildly satirical—1947 novel on the religion, politics, and copious alcohol intake of the well-established New York Irish. The novel treats a conflict pitting the entrenched society of Tammany hacks, fire captains, and their indolent pastors against Catholic radicals seeking to infuse a purified Christianity into young, upwardly mobile products of the old neighborhood now caught between these two forces. At the height of the action Linford Thomas, an apostolically Catholic character based explicitly on John Cort (to whom the novel is dedicated, along with Dorothy Day and two other Catholic activists), takes a vicious beating on a West Side pier from thugs employed by the leader of an Irish American longshoremen's union. A pair of former Notre Dame football players—one a local Irish American who has provided legal services to Thomas's reformist union—strolling in the waterfront neighborhood come to Thomas's rescue; enraged, they stand poised on the verge of killing his assailants until Thomas cries out: "In Christ's name, stop. You'll be murderers."[44]

In *Moon Gaffney* the Irish waterfront is represented in a state of savagery, its redemption attainable solely by Christian missionaries from outside the neighborhood. The emergence of Father Pete Corridan in 1948 signaled a new dispensation: a homegrown (or close enough) reformer sporting a turned-around collar with ample toughness to match the boys of the Irish waterfront.

7   *Covering the Waterfront*

On February 10, 1949, Pete Corridan offered a summary of three event-ful months on the waterfront to a San Francisco Jesuit labor priest, George Lucy. A November wildcat strike by dockworkers in the Port of New York, Joe Ryan's capitulation in grudgingly declaring the strike official, and Cock-eye Dunn's death row threat to obliterate the code of silence all figured prominently in his account; but an additional item brought Corridan him-self to the forefront. "Here is how the picture stands at the moment," the waterfront priest informed Lucy:

> The *New York Sun*, an evening newspaper, ran two front-page [series of] ar-ticles on the waterfront, one last November and December and one in January. The first series dealt with crime; the second took a positive approach to the longshoremen's problem. In the second series Ryan was painted as anti-labor and anti-union according to accepted trade union principles.

Corridan then made a stunning claim: the material for the second series was submitted to the reporter by Corridan himself and was published under the reporter's name "with very little change. This, of course, is a top se-cret." Three months later Malcolm "Mike" Johnson of the *Sun*, author of the "Crime on the Waterfront" series, was awarded the Pulitzer Prize for distinguished local reporting. In his letter Corridan was claiming co-authorship of the second series alone, not the one that earned Johnson his Pulitzer.[1]

While the details of Corridan's working arrangement with Johnson remain elusive, the Jesuit was surely the reporter's most "assiduous tipster" in the preparation of "Crime on the Waterfront" and subsequent articles for the *Sun*. As journalist Allen Raymond wrote of their partnership, "together they set off a great hue and cry against the waterfront racketeers." Corridan's work with Johnson initiated a series of fruitful collaborations with figures from the secular worlds of journalism and civic reform, resulting in a flood of spectacular exposés that shaped a narrative of the New York–New Jersey waterfront which resounded for decades to come.[2]

"Crime on the Waterfront" made its debut as the *New York Sun* hovered on the verge of extinction. In 1948 readers in Manhattan had their choice of nine English-language daily newspapers, from the leftist *PM* to the staunchly conservative *Sun*, which had been in continuous existence since September 1833. By the late 1940s, however, the *Sun* was reduced to "a museum piece," best known for its "devoted coverage of the financial markets, antiques, cat care, and motorboating." With its advertising base rapidly dwindling and little left to lose, the *Sun* unfurled Johnson's hard-hitting, lavishly illustrated crime series.[3]

Mike Johnson's beat at the *Sun* was the "rackets," a pursuit consonant with the paper's tradition of combating "indecency and rascality." The forty-four-year-old Johnson had been employed at the *Sun* since 1928, following a stint as a reporter at the *Macon Telegraph* in his native Georgia, where his life was threatened after he exposed the illegal activities of the Ku Klux Klan. "His drawl and easygoing manner hide a bulldog tenacity," *Time* magazine would later report. Hired "sight unseen" at age twenty-four by the *Sun*, Johnson worked as a rewrite man, nightclub reporter, and war correspondent in the Pacific theater. He became, wrote Murray Kempton, "by slow application, a great newspaper reporter in the old-fashioned sense: there does not seem to be a new-fashioned one."[4]

In 1946 Johnson turned full-time to covering the rackets. A series of articles on truck hijackings generated a network of waterfront sources. The *Sun* had been burned by its failure to cover Andy Hintz's January 1947 murder by Cockeye Dunn, so when Thomas Collentine, a hiring boss running a notoriously violent pier in Hell's Kitchen, was assassinated on April 29, 1948, as he left his home in the Inwood section of Upper Manhattan, the *Sun*'s city editor hastened to assign Johnson to the story. He got nowhere (Collentine's murder was never solved), but an FBI contact yielded an informant who claimed to have "the lowdown on shakedowns, thievery, kickbacks, shylocks, shape-ups, and murder" on the waterfront. Around that time Johnson met Bill Keating, the Manhattan assistant district attorney whose dogged legwork in the Cockeye Dunn case resulted in the first successful prosecution of a waterfront murder in decades. Keating provided Johnson with access to Dunn's case file, which generated countless leads the reporter pursued throughout the spring and summer of 1948. As Keating later wrote, Johnson "explored the waterfront jungle as no newspaperman had ever bothered to do."[5]

The *Sun* launched "Crime on the Waterfront" with an appropriately lurid promotion illustrated by a gangster firing into the murky waters of New York Harbor over the caption "New York's Waterfront: A Cesspool of Crime." The first installment hit the newsstands on Monday, November 8. The waterfront's "outlaw frontier" of virtually unchecked criminal activity had left the port on the brink of ruin, Johnson reported. Shippers disgusted with extortionist rackets were increasingly seeking ports to the south that were not nearly as crime-ridden. "Here, in the world's busiest port," he wrote,

> with its 906 piers, 100 ferry landings, ninety-six car-float landings and fifty-seven shipbuilding, dry dock and repair plants, criminal gangs operate with apparent immunity from the law. These gangs are well organized and their control of the piers is absolute. Their greatest weapon is terror, invoked by their strong-arm squads and their gunmen. Their power is such that they are able to levy tribute on every pound of cargo arriving at this port. This is accomplished through highly lucrative rackets controlled by gangsters.

Johnson left little doubt in his first installment that the targets of "Crime on the Waterfront" were Joe Ryan and his ILA. "The key to control by the waterfront criminals is through the unions," he explained, "particularly the powerful International Longshoremen's Association, A.F. of L., headed by Joseph P. Ryan, who has a lifetime job at $20,000 a year." The ILA's practice of installing ex-convicts as hiring bosses made the waterfront "a veritable haven" for hardened criminals who doubled as union officials and associates of a "vast crime syndicate which has national and international connections." The lifeblood of this syndicate, born of Prohibition and expanded in the 1930s to businesses both legitimate and illicit, was illegal gambling, a particularly thriving enterprise along the piers. "The take is beyond estimate," an investigator informed Johnson.[6]

In his second installment Johnson invited readers to "Meet the Boys," the Irish waterfront chieftains prominent among the "mobsters and labor racketeers" who reined over the West Side's piers. From Mickey Bowers, boss of Hell's Kitchen's "hot piers" north of Forty-second Street; to Tim O'Mara in the west thirties; to Eddie McGrath, who ran the piers below Fourteenth Street in the absence of his brother-in-law Cockeye Dunn, then awaiting execution at Sing Sing, Johnson sketched a who's who of the Irish waterfront. He did not slight the Italian presence in New York Harbor. "The East River piers and the tough South Brooklyn docks are controlled by the notorious Albert Anastasia," Johnson alleged, adding that Anastasia had been arrested on murder charges on five occasions and had been named "as a director in Murder, Inc., the organization of hired killers." Detailed rap sheets were provided for these and assorted other waterfront mugs all wedded to Joe Ryan through their control of ILA locals in the port.[7]

The *Sun*'s November 10 installment of "Crime on the Waterfront" detailed a system of organized pilferage on the piers costing shippers an estimated $50 million annually. This revelation vied for attention in the *Sun* and other papers with news that a wildcat strike had broken out in the Port of New York that same morning, idling nearly ten thousand dockworkers in Manhattan, Brooklyn, and New Jersey and bringing waterfront commerce to a standstill. Unlike the 1945 walkout, which blended into the vast post-war wave of strikes, the 1948 work stoppage stood out as a stark reminder that prosperity at home and dominance abroad depended on labor peace in the nation's busiest port. Startled travelers had to fetch their own trunks off the luxury liner piers of Hell's Kitchen, while goods destined for devastated European locales piled up on the piers of the Lower West Side.[8]

Longshoremen of the Atlantic Coast district had overwhelmingly rejected the shippers' "final offer" in balloting of November 5 and 6. On November 8 Joe Ryan met with John V. Lyon of the New York Shipping Association to hammer out a new agreement. Customarily Ryan "had taken what was offered by the shippers, usually settling for just enough to quiet rank-and-file opposition." As a stevedoring operator described the bargaining routine to Johnson, "We call Ryan in once a year or so and say, 'Joe, how much of a raise do you need to keep the boys in line?'" The 1945 strike and a more localized six-day walkout in 1947 had undermined the rank and file's traditional compliance, but Joe Ryan failed to discern that the winds were shifting direction. Although the new offer from NYSA represented "almost imperceptible gains," in the early morning hours of November 9 King Joe brazenly announced, in the company of John Lyon, "We've got a very fine agreement and we are going to recommend strongly to the membership that it accept it."[9]

According to the *New York Times,* "confusion and conflicting reports were the order of the day," evoking the now standard tone of waterfront labor coverage. In its early editions of November 9 the *Times* reported that a strike had been averted, but later that morning members of ILA Local 791 in Chelsea held a "sickout" that shut down the Cunard Line's Hudson River Piers 54 and 56. Resistance from within Ryan's own "Mother Local" was a new if potent factor. The actions of the men on the West Side Irish waterfront were rarely if ever coordinated with those of the enormous Italian-dominated locals in South Brooklyn or those in Staten Island and Hudson County, rendering impossible a coherent narrative of the looming portwide job action. The sickout at 791 skirted President Truman's Taft-Hartley injunction against a dock strike, which was to expire at midnight. The Taft-Hartley Act, passed the previous year, gave the president power to order an eighty-day "cooling-off" period before a strike could be legally authorized. Since the Marshall Plan for Europe's reconstruction required fully operative ports along the East Coast, the federal government now took a much greater interest in negotiations between shippers and the ILA than in the past.[10]

Within twenty-four hours it was clear, despite Ryan's claims of an agreement, that the new deal was no deal to the rank and file. Their walkout quickly spread from Chelsea to Brooklyn, reaching Hudson County on

November 10. With men abandoning the piers in droves, Ryan tried to pin the strike on the *Sun*. Speaking to reporters from the offices of Local 791, King Joe alleged:

> This sudden strike was caused by the articles by Malcolm Johnson, which began in the *Sun* on Monday, while we were negotiating. It was a written insult to our members. It is a serious factor in this strike. The articles tend to show our union is a front for these rackets. It is a direct insult to the Police Commissioner and the FBI. We are ready to be investigated at any time.[11]

Ryan blasted the *Sun* as anti-labor, an allegation not without merit: the paper was one of only two in the city—the *Wall Street Journal* being the other—that barred Newspaper Guild organizers. But Ryan was far less concerned with labor practices in the newspaper business than with reestablishing his moral authority over the Irish waterfront by inciting resistance to outsiders. With the work stoppage spreading to other East Coast ports, he finally gave in, grudgingly conceding on November 11, "As long as we're having a strike, let's have a strike." Ryan's capitulation signaled, as Daniel Bell noted, "the first regularly called strike in the history of the union."[12]

Ryan would learn the hard way that his consoling Irish waterfront redoubt was no more. The lingering effects of the 1945 strike and the precipitous decline of Tammany Hall were apparent in the sudden boldness of local challenges to King Joe's authority: the street corners and saloons of Chelsea and the West Village were suddenly contested sites, if not downright hostile to the life president. Longtime 791 business agent Gene Sampson emerged as Ryan's most formidable rival in the union hierarchy and the neighborhood with which it was synonymous. The son of an immigrant West Side Irish longshoreman, Sampson went to work on the Chelsea piers in 1902 and never strayed while slowly ascending the ILA ladder. Like Ryan he kept union records strictly "in his hat," but unlike the international president Sampson was content to hold forth each day from a bench inside a stevedore's office on Pier 61, just across Eleventh Avenue from Local 791's offices, which he rarely entered. Sampson openly supported the wildcat strike, though his "inscrutable" manner (in the eyes of outsiders) and sporadic deference to Ryan tended to relegate him to the role of "loyal opposition" in newspaper accounts.[13]

Gene Sampson's brother Frank was a Tammany stalwart with mild reform inclinations who assumed leadership of New York City's Democratic machine in 1947 in a coup engineered by his likeminded patron, the mercurial Irish-born mayor Bill O'Dwyer. Frank Sampson's reign as grand sachem, albeit brief, was not inconsequential: the episode revealed an Irish waterfront on the verge of devouring itself. Sampson was eased out of Tammany leadership in July 1948, replaced by Manhattan borough president Hugo Rogers, the choice of Frank Costello, reputed "Prime Minister" of organized crime, who enjoyed inordinate influence at Tammany Hall in the 1940s. Costello and Mayor O'Dwyer shared a past, details of which would captivate a nationwide television audience during the famous Kefauver hearings in January 1951. In the meantime O'Dwyer was forced to dump Frank Sampson in a move staunchly supported by Ryan, whose growing dependence on the goodwill of Brooklyn's immense Italian ILA locals left him more beholden to Costello than the erratically independent-minded Irish mayor.[14]

The Irish had always battled among themselves, but they now often did so at the bidding of others, and these betrayals left deep scars, especially with their share of the spoils diminishing rapidly. Gene Sampson's opposition to the deal Ryan cut with shippers in autumn 1948—and his subsequent support of the wildcat strike—was payback for Ryan's betrayal of his brother. Sampson now ventured a most rare violation of the code of silence to let outsiders know just how he felt. On the eventful afternoon of November 10 he and Ryan traded "bitter and inelegant words" in the presence of newspaper reporters gathered in front of Local 791's offices.[15]

Stunned at first, Ryan quickly rebounded into his most florid grandstanding mode, providing a throng of print journalists and "television operators" with a "historical resume" of the strike's background, "explaining that the press had the whole thing badly tangled up." Ryan insisted that investigators look into "the insurance partnership of Frank Sampson," a remark that prompted Gene Sampson to demand that Ryan "retract everything you said about my brother. You retract it or we'll make you retract it." Sampson then showed he was not above a little Italian- and Red-baiting by association, hollering over the din that Ryan was connected to left-wing East Harlem congressman Vito Marcantonio via their mutual crony Hugo Rogers of Tammany Hall. "After further exchanges," the *Times* reported, "the shouting died off and it was decided to eliminate the non-union observers. 'Get out,' Mr. Ryan called to the press delegation. 'We are going into executive session.'" Sampson's confrontation with Ryan was but one dramatic sign of impending breakdown in King Joe's vaunted machinery. After decades of neglect the waterfront now bore in the imagination of the great metropolis an indelible taint of corruption, which quickly spread beyond the piers to the Irish waterfront's political culture, its economy, and its religion.[16]

Opening the Partnership Front

In the days immediately preceding the November 1948 strike Pete Corridan composed an essay, "Longshoremen's Case," and submitted it on November 9 to *America* labor editor Ben Masse, S.J. Although Ryan and the ILA wage-scale committee had approved a new agreement with NYSA that

same morning, Corridan knew that the men of Local 791 were just beginning their sick-out. He attached a note for publication—written in the third
person—confirming that "his worst fears have been realized. As we go to
press, the Port of New York has been paralyzed by a widespread rank-and-
file walkout of longshoremen." Masse told Corridan that *America* could not
run the article because the newspaper of record had reported that a strike
had been averted. Corridan knew otherwise: when dockworkers walked off
the piers, "I'd scored a news beat on the *Times*." Corridan, Arthur Brown,
and some of the rebels proceeded to distribute nearly ten thousand reprints
of "Longshoremen's Case" around the harbor.[17]

The broadside firmly established Corridan's stellar public reputation as
the "waterfront priest," introducing themes he would pursue relentlessly
over the next six years. The "root of the present delicate situation," he insisted, was not the threat of communist infiltration or overtime pay or rank-
and-file disrespect for contracts. "The heart of the matter is the system of
hiring along the waterfront. Men are hired as if they were beasts of burden,
part of the slave market of a pagan era." To Corridan the shapeup "cries
against every standard of decency and justice." The issue was and would
remain human dignity and the responsibility of Christians to ensure a just
social order. "For these men are our brothers," he concluded, "redeemed
in the precious blood of Christ, and one cannot rest secure if His dignity in
them continues to be violated and outraged."[18]

The piece characteristically blended abundant statistics confirming Corridan's credentials as a waterfront expert with moral exhortation. He showed
how favoritism in hiring denied most longshoremen a living wage and deprived them of benefits; though they paid into the system, few worked sufficient hours to collect vacation pay. In the spirit of the papal social encyclicals,
Corridan demanded accountability from an industry whose enforcement of
irregular working conditions, he said, led to family breakdown and social
decay. He also called for government intervention in the form of a "Commission of Inquiry" designed to "goad the industry into living up to its
full responsibilities." Over time Corridan's scheme for strict registration of
longshoremen would take precedence over the hiring hall, an institution favored by the leftist West Coast ILWU and communist agitators in Brooklyn,
as a way to regularize waterfront employment.[19]

"Longshoremen's Case" was an integral component of a highly deliberate strategy devised by Corridan. In the words of a fellow Jesuit, "Father
Corridan wrote the article not for the case itself but for a tactical purpose."
The Brooklyn-based Back Pay Committee, a "Communist organization,"
according to Father Phil Carey, was "claiming the credit" for effective rank-
and-file advocacy. Although the party had in fact "done nothing," Carey
insisted, "because of ceaseless propaganda it seemed certain that the party
would make significant gains unless the play were taken from them." In
Corridan's strategy, this entailed focusing relentlessly on the shapeup and

moral issues of human dignity which the Left did not treat. The ongoing ideological conflict animating New York City culture and politics thus wound its way through the waterfront.[20]

From his careful analysis of Carey's failed struggle on behalf of the Pier 28 coopers, Corridan believed that the "fatal weakness" of that effort was that there had been "no airing of the case in the press so as to increase the bargaining strength of the clean element in unions, business and government." Carey had to go to the newspapers; there was no "big news event" to "bring them to him." The November 1948 strike brought Corridan to the press and the press to Corridan. Shortly after the first installment of "Crime on the Waterfront" appeared, he wrote a letter to the *Sun* that the city editor handed to Mike Johnson, urging him to "go around and see this man; he seems to know what he's talking about." Johnson immediately enlisted Corridan's vast knowledge and drew freely from his wealth of documentation. According to the veteran reporter, Corridan "can name the gangsters in control of every dock on the west side; and cite their criminal record; he can point to the mobs' political contacts in City Hall, and he can explain the most intricate type of waterfront graft which might very well involve stevedores, loaders, checkers, watchmen, policemen, and city officials." The veteran reporter was moved by the Jesuit's rough-hewn pastoral gifts. "Where I was cautious and merely implied," Johnson told a British Catholic newspaper in 1954, "Father Corridan blasted. Before I'd been a reporter. After I talked to Father Corridan he got me emotionally involved in the plight of the longshoremen—he got me hoping that something would happen to free these men." Johnson lauded Corridan's inspiration in the plainest terms: "He changed me." He in turn changed Corridan, teaching by example that the priest's most promising alliances might be forged with those from outside the waterfront.[21]

The two quickly developed a strong rapport; hints of their collaboration appear as early as November 19, when "The Dunn Case," the tenth installment of the series, displayed a sharpened focus on denizens of the Irish waterfront, beginning with the bloodcurdling story of Cockeye Dunn, presently residing on death row at Sing Sing. This and subsequent reports signaled a new insider's tone for the series hailed by a future journalistic partner of Corridan's as the "most complete and perfect picture of the close alliance between vicious criminals in the waterfront rackets and the powers of politics." It is unlikely that Mike Johnson or any other reporter could have dissected the loading racket so expertly without the benefit of Corridan's empirical and analytical resources. Johnson located Cockeye Dunn at the center of a criminal network that included his brother-in-law and fellow ex-convict Ed McGrath and extended upward to key contacts with various "respectable" figures in business and government. He offered a conservative estimate that "in the last decade at least twenty persons have been slain in the ceaseless battle for control of one of the city's richest racket territories."

Johnson also began to draw connections across the Irish waterfront, linking Dunn, for example, to his silent business partner, Frank Hague associate Connie Noonan of Jersey City, an alliance that enhanced Dunn's bid "to control the situation in Jersey as well as in New York."[22]

Johnson was now truly covering the waterfront. The Georgian might have discerned these interrelationships without help, but over time Pete Corridan's intercession lent his work much deeper authority. As Phil Carey later explained: "Pete's greatest talent was his understanding of the West Side mind: it was uncanny to witness how fast and accurately he could predict the future acts of the Irish mobs. Given one and two—he'd tell you exactly what the move at 100 would be." As "Crime on the Waterfront" progressed and Johnson became much more attuned to the life stories of West Side Irish gangsters, distinctive patterns emerged, beginning with the experience of boys raised without fathers: Cockeye Dunn's father was lost at sea when the boy was four years of age, and Dunn's stepfather was later killed in a railway accident; Eddie McGrath was only three when his immigrant father was killed in a trolley accident; Joe Ryan lost his father at age nine, the same age as Pete Corridan when *his* father died. In a variation on the theme, Dunn's vision-impaired triggerman Andrew "Squint" Sheridan lost his mother when he was five.[23]

These were the same themes of loss and premature death that pervaded Irish American immigrant culture and literature. In his biography of Boston Irish political legend James Michael Curley, Jack Beatty called the loss of fathers the "shared privation of the leading Irish-American politicians of his era," from John F. Fitzgerald (John F. Kennedy's grandfather) to Al Smith and John W. McCormack, longtime Speaker of the U.S. House of Representatives. "Their fathers worked themselves to death," wrote Beatty. "They died from the way they were obliged to live." The emotional force of this theme was tempered in "Crime on the Waterfront" by the matter-of-fact tone of Johnson's reporting and the criminal activities of his menace-to-society subjects.[24]

The intense emotions Corridan eschewed in his highly analytical writings emerged here, as it would in other works by his non-Irish, non-Catholic collaborators. "Crime on the Waterfront" featured a subtextual jeremiad on the failure of second-generation West Side Irish Americans to honor their deceased immigrant fathers. In sounding these bitter themes, Johnson's portraits of Dunn, McGrath, Sheridan, and other products of the old neighborhood mirrored Corridan's unsparing worldview. In late 1953 Corridan would tell actor Karl Malden, who was visiting Chelsea in preparation for his role as the Corridan-inspired priest in the film *On the Waterfront*: "I was born in this neighborhood [the West Side]. When I was growing up there were two ways to go. Become a priest or a hood." He told reporters the same story: "You either became a gangster or a priest." The vast majority of West Side natives were neither priests nor hoods—and Corridan did not even grow up near the waterfront—but he clearly viewed these career options as distillations of the West Side character. In that sense the gangsters represented an authentic counterpart to his priestly vocation. Malden believed that Corridan "had become the one, although in many ways, he had the personality of the other, and he stayed in the neighborhood to try to bring the two forces together by teaching."[25]

The extent of Pete Corridan's access to the pages of the *New York Sun* was confirmed in the twenty-third installment of "Crime on the Waterfront," in which Johnson extolled "Longshoremen's Case" as "eloquently present[ing]" the plight of longshoremen. On December 13 the *Sun* ran an open letter to the paper from Corridan, treating it as a news item. The Jesuit congratulated Johnson and the *Sun* "for their real service to the people of New York" in publishing Johnson's series. "Every American is opposed to Communism," Corridan asserted in a tone sure to attract the notice of Catholics, "but it is conditions such as prevail along the docks that promote the cause of Communism, not the American way of life." He urged readers to demand action from their elected representatives and hoped that "a vigorous and alert citizens' committee" might arise "to press for further action in the waterfront situation." Barely a month after publicly joining the battle, Pete Corridan emerged as the moral leader of the campaign for waterfront reform.[26]

"Crime on the Waterfront" was more damaging to Joe Ryan's reputation than the ILA strike that coincided with its publication. The union leadership decided not to mount picket lines after the strike was declared official, leaving the rank and file "isolated and uninformed about strike strategy," according to labor historian Colin Davis. "The men were left to meet in bars and street corners throughout the port to discuss strike events." A rare picket line did materialize on West Thirty-fourth Street in Manhattan on November 16 headed by Ryan himself, leading a phalanx of more than one hundred union cronies in protesting a meeting inside historic Manhattan Center. The meeting was sponsored by the leftist Brooklyn-based Back Pay Committee—disdained by Corridan and Ryan alike—which continued to press the case for "overtime on overtime" (an ongoing dispute over the definition of "overtime" used to settle dockworkers' legal claims for back pay). The participants who "booed lustily" at the mention of Ryan's name merely played to his ability to focus media attention on the meeting's alleged communist tint. The *Journal-American,* the New York newspaper with the largest readership among Catholics and working people, remained squarely in Ryan's corner throughout the strike.[27]

King Joe Takes the Bait

The federal government—concerned that the spread of the November 1948 strike to other ports would undermine delivery of Marshall Plan goods—"forced Ryan to act the role of union leader," according to Colin Davis. "To keep the confidence of the men, he had to appear to hold the line against employers trying to sneak cargo in through southern ports, while at the same time trying not to antagonize government authorities." The government was instrumental in ending the strike. Economic Cooperation Administrator Paul G. Hoffman publicly reminded the ILA of the urgency of Marshall Plan shipments, and Cyrus Ching of the Federal Mediation and Conciliation Service bluffed Ryan and John Lyon of NYSA into making a deal to avoid unspecified action from Washington. Dockworkers won modest wage gains, vacation benefits, and a welfare fund. After most New York area locals voted to accept the offered package on November 27, the men headed back to the waterfront.[28]

While Ryan managed to hold rank-and-file dissidents at bay, he could not evade the *Sun*. Ten days after the strike ended, "Crime on the Waterfront" reached its apogee in installment twenty-one, devoted to Ryan in its detailed entirety. Whereas Cockeye Dunn had been portrayed as an unregenerate psychopath, Johnson instead lavished ridicule on King Joe, depicting him as a "burly, red-faced" West Side Irishman whose forays outside the neighborhood were tinged with bathos, especially his golf outings ("enthusiastic, but no par-buster") with judges and politicians as a member of the plush Winged Foot Golf Club in leafy Westchester County. It was later revealed that his club dues were paid from a "secret anti-communist" ILA account Ryan dipped into at his discretion; just why Winged Foot needed protection from the Reds remained an open question. Johnson reported that Ryan's attempt to blame the recent strike on the *Sun* "caused only loud and derisive laughter from rank and file members of the I.L.A., who charged that Ryan had sold them out again."[29]

To allegations that he presided over a crime-ridden union, Ryan could only lamely respond, "It was all untrue." And "what about the charge that the waterfront is a haven for ex-convicts, that any ex-convict can get a job there, any time?" Johnson asked. "We welcome ex-convicts," Ryan blithely replied, adding: "Well, now maybe welcome is too broad a statement. But we believe every man, regardless of what he has done, has a right to a second chance." Ryan insisted that "ninety-nine per cent of the men in our organization are decent, hard-working, God-fearing men," but he was badly served by his insouciant swagger. During the November strike Joe had severely restricted the operations of the ILA press committee in order to minimize the damage from internal opposition. It never occurred to Ryan to save himself from embarrassment by avoiding the media or at least employing a competent handler.[30]

Joe remained jolly in his defiant fashion: "The *Sun* has been writing about some of the boys from the old ladies' home up the river who came down to the waterfront and made good," he wisecracked during the strike. "I'm proud to have them as members of this union. I'm proud to have my picture taken with them and proud to be in their company." In his cocky dismissal of the *Sun*'s charges, Ryan was like the bully who, after mocking someone, nervously looks around to make sure that others are in on the joke. This time no one was laughing.[31]

The life president dug a deeper hole in agreeing to prepare lengthy responses for a sequel to "Crime on the Waterfront." Mike Johnson's ten-part winter 1949 series "The Cause and the Remedy" portrayed Ryan "as anti-labor and anti-union"—in Corridan's words—and offered a blueprint for waterfront reform entirely of the Jesuit's making. In reprising the main themes from "Crime on the Waterfront," Johnson drew explicitly from Corridan's reform scheme without citing his source by name. "Some system of registration of longshoremen and rotation of work" would regularize employment and liberate the men from "fear of Joe Ryan and his stooges," Johnson wrote. Such language would not ordinarily be viewed as an invitation to dialogue, but Ryan—with the likely if wary assistance of ILA attorney Louis Waldman—gamely prepared a series of eight rebuttal articles for the *Sun,* the first of which appeared in the paper's February 28, 1949, edition.[32]

In his opening rejoinder Ryan desultorily conceded, "There is unquestionably room for improvement in the [waterfront] industry." Before he was allowed to elaborate, however, Johnson exercised his editorial prerogative by inserting, within brackets, an instant rebuttal to Ryan: "What improvement, Ryan?" Johnson then deftly introduced Corridan as the author of "Longshoremen's Case" and provided a lengthy excerpt to remind the *Sun*'s readers yet again that "the heart of the matter is the system of hiring along the waterfront."[33]

The ambush was on. Ryan was at a hopeless disadvantage, and not only because he was butting heads with a seasoned journalist; the reporter's main source was a priest in good standing, indeed, a priest who could match Ryan's lifetime of experience on the waterfront with his own prodigious command of facts and figures. Ryan tried to argue on the one hand that the shapeup was needed to manage the unique requirements of the shipping industry and on the other that the ILA had promoted the use of "steady gangs" on many piers, "the nearest thing to regular employment in the longshore industry." Yet "Crime on the Waterfront" had so thoroughly discredited the shapeup that Ryan was tarnished for endorsing anything short of a complete overhaul of the hiring system.[34]

King Joe was lured into a trap from which there was no escape. He predictably ignored the challenge posed by members of his own church but took customary refuge in Red-baiting, alleging repeatedly in several installments that Johnson's reporting drew on individuals "with long records of activity in pro-Communist organizations." In his rejoinder Johnson chipped away at Ryan's credibility before delivering—in the concluding installment of the entire "Crime on the Waterfront" saga—the knockout blow. If, as Ryan alleged, "I have been playing the Communists' game," wrote Johnson in the *Sun* on March 9, "I have good company." He then listed his clerical sources, beginning with Corridan and including Ben Masse of *America* and Monsignor Edward Swanstrom, the priest, he reminded Ryan, "whom you ordered ejected" from the Hotel Commodore at the 1939 ILA convention. Following Corridan's lead, Johnson strategically undermined the reflexive anticommunism that had served New York–area Catholic politicians, labor leaders, and clergymen so well since the 1930s. "Will Ryan be so reckless," Johnson concluded, "as to charge that these clergymen of his own faith also are the tools of the Communists?"[35]

Ryan was not so reckless; he was rendered nearly helpless in the court of public opinion. The *Sun* may indeed have been, as Ryan's ILA house organ sneered, "New York's labor-baiting and least-read evening newspaper," but "Crime on the Waterfront" was a journalistic sensation grounded in relentless digging and ingenious use of sources, a courageous achievement confirmed by the Pulitzer Prize bestowed on Johnson in 1949. Corridan ardently hoped that "Crime on the Waterfront" signaled the beginning of the end of the code of silence. "The situation is explosive," he wrote to George Lucy on February 10.

> John "Cockeyed" Dunn, sentenced to the chair for the murder of Hintz, a hiring boss, is telling the story of the waterfront at Sing Sing and has been granted a reprieve. Dunn can tell a story that involves people higher than Ryan. The politicians wouldn't want an investigation, but if the Dunn story breaks or anything like it, they'll have to clean up the mess on the waterfront.[36]

Corridan was determined to speed the process. On February 11 he sent Johnson a letter he had mailed to selected longshoremen, urging them to register their support for reform. "You yourself could strike a blow for the harbor crafts," he told them, "if you would write to Malcolm Johnson of the *New York Sun*.... [C]hances are Johnson would publish your letter and without revealing your name." He advised them to phrase it "something like this":

> I followed your articles in the *New York Sun* and think you did a great job. The way things stand now we get no information whatsoever from the ILA. The little information we get gets sandwiched in a lot of Communist propaganda that the front outfits distribute on the waterfront. It hurts me to think we have to depend on the Commies to give us the information we should be getting from our ILA leaders. The reforms will never come from the kind of leaders we have. The reforms will only come with a strong outside source.[37]

Corridan could not have reasonably expected longshoremen to speak out in the pages of a New York City newspaper, even with the promise of anonymity. In the absence of a strong response from the rank and file, he created his own insurgent longshoremen's newspaper, the *Crusader,* in early 1949 ("A newspaper by longshoremen for longshoremen. Anti-Communist and Anti-Ryan News, Facts, Issues on the Waterfront"). The *Crusader* attacked Ryan in Corridan's best approximation of the West Side idiom, exposing the union boss's dubious appropriation of union dues: "Ryan draws 2 checks. His salary is $1,666.67 a month. Cigar and cigarette money (his monthly expense account) is $600. For specific expense items like Railroad fare to the AFL Convention in Cincinnati last November, Joe drew a check for $304.19. No doubt the big clown had the engine switch from coal to bourbon."[38]

Years later, speaking to a fellow Kerryman in New York, Corridan uncharacteristically evoked the surreptitious tactics of Irish rebels in recounting the origins of the *Crusader.* "It had to be underground," he told writer Daniel Daly. "At the outset I didn't even want people generally to know where it was put out. I didn't want the longshoremen associated with me to become marked men." As Daly revealed, a "scenario of cloak-and-dagger measures was hatched to maintain secrecy. He used paper without a watermark and shopped for it in different stores. The typewriter used in stenciling was kept under lock and key." Corridan slipped over to Jersey City via the Hudson Tubes and mailed the incendiary newssheet from the Erie railroad station lest it be traced back to Xavier.[39]

The *Crusader* was never embraced as an authentic voice of the dissident rank and file. While it is not clear whether many or most longshoremen knew that it was a clerical production, there must have been doubts as to its authenticity. Corridan remained much more successful in his role as a source for journalists. Mike Johnson was pleased to inform him in August 1949 that a *Sun* editorial endorsing Corridan's proposal to eliminate the shapeup "was written without any suggestions from me, a fact which pleases me.... [T]hanks again for your swell cooperation." The cooperation, it seems clear, did not extend as far as Corridan's claim that *he* wrote the second series or any other of Johnson's stories; his fastidious notes *summarize* the reports, but there is no evidence he was actually writing them. It was his overall expertise that attracted the metropolitan dailies to routinely tout the Jesuit as the leading authority on waterfront labor and economics.[40]

Corridan now sought to shape the journalistic marketplace for waterfront stories with a reform angle. In October 1949 he provided a detailed prepublication critique of a *Survey* magazine article on waterfront crime that focused on the Cockeye Dunn case. Dunn and Andy Sheridan had finally trudged off to Sing Sing's electric chair on July 7, 1949, but not before, as Daniel Bell, at the time a prominent labor journalist, later reported, Dunn "sent word to the District Attorney that he wanted to 'talk.' Rumors of a statement implicating some 'Mr. Big,' a higher-up power on the waterfront, circulated freely." In the end Dunn refused to break the waterfront code of silence to save himself, though according to an unidentified priest quoted by *Survey,* "there were plenty of people sweating for fear of what Dunn might say. Some of them had run to Florida and some to Arkansas, and many were right here in New York and New Jersey, their bags packed and themselves on the rack."[41]

With the lurid Dunn case finally resolved, Corridan urged the editors of *Survey* to publish an article "on the longshoremen themselves," noting that the market for waterfront stories was diverse and growing rapidly:

> *Fortune* will have an article on the longshoremen.... *Collier's* may have an article on the school here...[and] several students from universities are doing their masters theses on certain aspects of the problems. A playwright has made inquiries for play material. Malcolm Johnson will probably re-edit and enlarge upon his articles in book form. All in all the iron curtain that hangs over the waterfront is gradually being pierced and made public and can't help but improve the condition of the longshoremen.[42]

Bell sought advice from Corridan in summer 1949 in his capacity as labor expert for *Fortune,* the business publication of Henry Luce's Time-Life empire. The presence of the ex-radical and incisive social critic on staff at *Fortune* was indicative of the ideological reconfiguration of the postwar era, a story much more complex than is found in customary accounts of the "de-conversion" or sellout of 1930s radicals to the emerging "affluent society." In the postwar period Bell blended elements of Marxian analysis with a growing appreciation of the role that ethnicity and religion played in shaping issues in the workplace and the broader political economy. Corridan supplied Bell with both empirical data and inside dope on the ILA as it embarked on another round of negotiations with shippers, depicting Joe Ryan as "trying to do a job this time due to certain external pressures" that Corridan himself had helped generate. "The men from the West Side feel that they have much more support this year than in previous years."[43]

Bell lauded Corridan in *Fortune* in December 1949 and reported that Ryan was responding to rank-and-file pressure for the first time "as a result" of the Jesuit's "vigorous public campaign to acquaint government officials with waterfront conditions." Bell continued to cover the waterfront for *Fortune;* his reports were later adapted for inclusion as a chapter in his extraordinarily influential 1961 work *The End of Ideology.* Corridan helped to shape Bell's view of the waterfront as a key site where traditional class-based analyses of labor relations no longer applied. Bell's attentiveness to organized crime as waterfront way of life was a prime source of the great intellectual authority he enjoyed in the 1950s and early 1960s. The distinguished labor reporter and columnist Murray Kempton was another great admirer of Corridan's from a leftist background. In 1949 Kempton became labor editor at the *New York Post,* the then liberal New York daily. In an undated letter to Corridan early in his stint at the paper Kempton informed the Jesuit: "I'm enclosing what I did on the piers for today. I hope it's all right; the bulk of it's your stuff."[44]

In autumn 1949 Mike Johnson compiled the stories from "Crime on the Waterfront" and other *Sun* pieces for a book, *Crime on the Labor Front,* published to rave notices in 1950. In his gripping chapter on waterfront priests Johnson reserved his most glowing tribute for Pete Corridan, a "brilliant Jesuit" with whom New York longshoremen "feel a kinship" because "he is a product of their own west side." Corridan, Johnson wrote, "attacks [Joe] Ryan with a cool precision and a carload of facts. He is a soft-spoken man, but he can be tough, tough enough to challenge the waterfront gangsters." He was so tough that he returned the mob's threats in kind. When he was heckled at a meeting, Johnson reported, Corridan coolly replied: "I know who sent you here, so go back to your bosses and deliver this message for me: tell them that if anything happens to the men I am trying to help here, I'll know who is responsible, and I'll personally see to it that they are broken throughout this port. They'll pay, and I'll see that they pay."[45]

Debating President Ryan

With his own access to the metropolitan dailies steadily dwindling, Joe Ryan decided to unmask Corridan personally. In January 1950 he agreed to appear with the Jesuit in a televised forum on the waterfront's hiring system hosted by Jack Turcott of the *New York Daily News* (owner of the television station, New York's WPIX). The program also featured Patrick J. "Packy" Connolly, Ryan's closest ally, and Dominic Usino, a veteran *Daily News* waterfront reporter and regular beneficiary of confidential information from Corridan.

Ryan opened the proceedings by invoking tradition: "The hiring system is as it has been for I don't know how long—it was in existence in 1912 when I went to work longshore—the man, the longshoreman...seeking work does the same as every other American workman. He goes down to his place of employment and seeks that work." Corridan immediately cut in to challenge Ryan from the perspective of their common faith: "Would you say that it's right, that it's the Christian thing, that one man, [a pier hiring boss] should control the destinies of 600 families merely by a pointing of the finger—you—you—you?" Connolly answered for his already flustered boss:

> Father, I was a hiring stevedore. One man don't control 600 families. We have a system of gangs where men are not hired individually. And men have worked

on the piers, the same gangs and the same pier, up to 25 years. So it's not one of those things where you go down every day. 99% of the port works on a regular gang system where them men hold their gangs. It's a permanent job, and they have security in that job.[46]

Corridan responded that apart from a few piers in Chelsea that utilized an "open shape," in which men were hired to work a ship from the time it arrived until the time it departed, most men in the port remained subject to the preferences and favoritism of hiring bosses. One alternative to the shapeup, an informal hiring hall located at Columbia Street on the Red Hook waterfront, was blasted by Corridan as "too prevalent for graft" and other vices he hinted at by referring obliquely to loan-sharking.[47]

Ryan dismissed Corridan's charges as "ridiculous" and insisted that longshoremen required no outside protection from an allegedly "vicious system at Columbia Street." He presented himself as the legitimately elected leader of a union whose members—in choosing representatives for a wage scale bargaining committee (an unwieldy collection of 125 largely self-appointed delegates)—had recently defeated "by an overwhelming majority" candidates with links to Xavier Labor School. Corridan then scored points on the issue of longshoremen's earnings, citing ILA membership figures to show that only a fraction of the thirty to thirty-five thousand men the union claimed worked in the port made more than $3,500 annually.[48]

Ryan had finally heard enough. "You're putting a picture here that's absolutely misleading and false," he sputtered at Corridan, "and we're not going to let a group of men, of decent God-fearing men, that are making their living on the waterfront, educating their families[,]...bringing them up, and they're going into the various professions, and then they're thrown into an attack like this." Nearing the end of his first season of humiliation, Ryan inelegantly, viscerally articulated a largely unspoken premise of the Irish waterfront's populist realism: work was hard and life often brutal, yet if one endured and kept his mouth shut, one's children might be spared the same fate. But Joe was too emotionally invested in this article of faith to develop the theme systematically: for all his gifts as a florid and sentimental after-dinner (and drinks) orator, Ryan was startlingly limited at the conceptual level.[49]

The televised debate revealed that the conflict between Joe Ryan and Pete Corridan operated on at least two levels: the empirical and the ideological. The Jesuit clearly won the battle of facts and figures. "Ryan and Connolly infuriated the majority of the longshoremen by their false statements" exaggerating average earnings, Corridan reported in a letter to Indiana congressman Andrew M. Jacobs. "A tremendous harbor audience tuned in," he crowed. He planned to "challenge Ryan publicly to a second debate, knowing full well he will not be allowed to accept." He even claimed that waterfront overlord William McCormack, whom he referred to only as "the business man who controls Ryan," was "quite upset by Joe's acceptance of the first debate." Ryan's desperation was apparent to observers of various persuasions, including Jack Karan of the communist *Daily Worker,* who asked: "Why was Joe Ryan on television last week? Joe never liked publicity before." Yet Karan also made a telling point in noting that although Corridan had always indicated his opposition to the West Coast hiring hall system, in the debate he cited economic data from ports utilizing hiring halls in order to discredit the shapeup. The Jesuit had yet to take a decisive position on a hiring system to replace the shape.[50]

The ideological struggle was more complicated than that. On the Irish waterfront there was less concern with Corridan's failure to articulate a reform plan than with the very idea of a priest crossing the line separating the Catholic waterfront from "the church." It was a line scrupulously observed by Joe Ryan and his pastor, "Taxi Jack" O'Donnell, a point not lost on a longshoreman who called Corridan's television appearance a "disgrace" in an unsigned letter:

Why don't you go on the Milton Berle show you sure was funny and did my friends laugh at your story of the condition on the waterfront.... All I can say as a Catholic why don't you confine your duties to the Church What a laugh the Reds must have got out of you. You a Priest trying to hurt a man [Ryan] who goes to Mass and pays many a bill for the Guardian Angel Church.[51]

Joe Ryan was by no means a beloved or respected labor leader, but on the Irish waterfront he was credited with playing by the rules of the game, grim as they were. Ryan's cryptic post-debate remark about Corridan—"the Jesuit College is going to take care of him"—reflected his conviction that the Irish waterfront's social order worked like a machine geared to expel foreign objects. Anyone from the outside was automatically suspect, turned-around collar or no turned-around collar. More than any mere outsider, Corridan now posed a genuine threat as a cleric with a demonstrated willingness to play rough when necessary. His formidable collaboration with Mike Johnson also confirmed his prowess at forging alliances with influential non-Catholics from off the waterfront. It was to the building up of this spiritual front that the Jesuit now turned his attention.[52]

8   *The Hollywood Prince*

Malcolm Johnson sold the film rights to his Pulitzer Prize–winning "Crime on the Waterfront" series in June 1949 to Monticello Film Corporation, an independent production company created solely for the purpose of turning the newspaper articles into a movie. Monticello planned to produce a full-length feature, reported the *New York Sun,* "in semi-documentary form.... [T]he picture is scheduled for production on actual locations in New York City." Monticello's head of advertising and publicity, Joseph Curtis, was the son of Jack Cohn, vice president of Columbia Pictures, and the nephew of Hollywood power broker Harry Cohn, Columbia's "famously tyrannical head of production." His title at the firm notwithstanding, Joe Curtis was the driving force behind the film project.[1]

After several commissioned treatments proved unsatisfactory, sometime in late 1949 Curtis—by now Monticello's president—and the prominent film noir director Robert Siodmak (*The Killers,* 1946; *Cry of the City,* 1948; *Criss Cross,* 1949) visited writer Budd Schulberg at his farm in New Hope, Pennsylvania. Schulberg was hired to write a screenplay based on Johnson's articles; Siodmak was slated to direct.[2]

Best known for his 1941 novel *What Makes Sammy Run,* the tale of a newspaper copyboy's frenzied, ruthless ascent from Lower East Side tenement to the life of a Hollywood mogul, by age twenty-six Budd Wilson Schulberg was a best-selling author and an exile from the Hollywood nobility of his youth as the son of B. P. Schulberg, visionary pioneer of the early studio system. As head of production at Paramount Pictures, the elder Schulberg memorably dubbed Mary Pickford "America's Sweetheart" and Louis B. Mayer "Czar of all the Rushes." He discovered Clara Bow, the "It" Girl; brought Marlene Dietrich to Hollywood; and produced *Wings* (1927), winner of the first Academy Award for Best Picture.[3]

Budd Schulberg grew up as a prince of "that glorified semi-tropical dream-factory town we call Hollywood." His playgrounds were movie sets: during breaks in production of *Ben-Hur* (1926) at MGM's Culver City studio, Budd and his best friend, Maurice Rapf, "galloped heroically around the enormous oval of the set, managing to portray both the horses pulling the chariots and the intrepid Ramon Novarro snapping his whip over the backs of the high-spirited steeds." Jackie Coogan and other child stars were regulars at birthday parties in honor of Budd, who learned early that Hollywood was a decidedly unglamorous company town: his celebrity playmates "were actually victims of child labor as inhuman as that of the scrawny ten-year-olds sent into the mines for ten hours a day." His lifelong wariness of the family "industry"—and his abhorrence of human exploitation—originated with these young performers, who were "nearly always bullied and abused by greedy and domineering parents."[4]

Budd's mother, the powerful talent agent Adeline Jaffe Schulberg, was an "energetic conveyor of culture" whose desire to "keep ahead" placed her at the forefront of early Hollywood's progressive milieu. Ad Schulberg "was really Hollywood's first lady," recalled her business partner, the legendary agent-producer Charlie Feldman. "In different times, she would have run a major studio." Ad "could be formidable," in her son's estimation, "but I always admired her and was fond of her." She later served as Budd's agent. "I once saw her kiss one of her clients," joked Schulberg. "She treated him like a son, me like a client."[5]

Budd Schulberg viewed his father as "the equal, perhaps the superior," of the legendary mogul Irving Thalberg as Hollywood's resident intellectual. B. P. was "a more profound reader and a more original mind," but he also possessed "all the traits that Irving piously disavowed: drinking, gambling, and wenching." An affair with film star Sylvia Sidney contributed to his dismissal from Paramount and the dissolution of his marriage. Budd sought a somewhat uneasy refuge on the East Coast, spending a year at Deerfield Academy in Massachusetts before entering Dartmouth College in 1932, where he wrote plays and musicals and edited the campus daily. In 1935 he was nearly expelled for passionately advocating the cause of striking marble workers in nearby Rutland, Vermont, where the Proctor family operated a dynasty in marble. The Proctors were also major benefactors of Dartmouth, whose very newspaper was now collecting food and clothing for strikers in response to Budd's "report of wives and children of the marble workers freezing and starving."[6]

The story attracted national attention and "infuriated the campus community and alumni." Dartmouth's longtime president Ernest Martin Hopkins summoned the student journalist and demanded to know what Budd would do were he in charge. Budd softly replied that he would uphold a student's right to free expression. Hopkins—no civil libertarian—reluctantly agreed with the young editor and rebuffed demands that he be "separated from the college." For all his privilege, Budd was an irresistibly likeable and deeply sympathetic individual. During the Proctor controversy he paid an impromptu weekend visit to the home of novelist Sinclair Lewis near Woodstock, Vermont. Lewis's "ill temper was notorious," and he was no friend of 1930s radical movements or the "sophomore socialism" he ascribed to his visitor from Dartmouth. Yet the cantankerous author was soon urging Budd to "call me Red." The brief interview turned into a very long and companionable weekend fueled only partly by a shared fondness for Lewis's Scotch whisky.[7]

In 1937, three years after a summer trip to the Soviet Union with his boyhood friend Maurice Rapf, Budd Schulberg joined the Communist Party. "I must say at the beginning I was a good little Communist," he later recalled. But by 1939 he was already "backsliding." He was "upset first by the Moscow Purge Trials and then by the Nazi-Soviet Non-Aggression Pact." Schulberg, now a junior writer at Selznick International Pictures, also harbored aesthetic reservations about party discipline. "I was something of a literary schizo," he later wrote, "a loyal *New Masses* subscriber and at the same time a literary freewheeler who could admire Faulkner even if he was 'reactionary' or Fitzgerald if he was 'decadent,' as they were both dismissed by the Party litterateurs." The party in turn did not care for Schulberg's attitude or his "too realistic[,]...too depressing" short stories which introduced themes and characters soon enshrined in *What Makes Sammy Run*. An advance copy of the novel was praised in the party's *People's World* newspaper in early April 1941, but the reviewer had failed to submit the notice first for clearance by party commissars. Two weeks later a negative reappraisal by the same reviewer was printed "on the basis of quite lengthy discussion." By then Schulberg considered himself a former communist.[8]

Although sometime screenwriter Dorothy Parker approvingly remarked of *Sammy*, "I never thought anyone could put Hollywood—the true shittiness of it—between covers," for the most part the film colony reacted even more harshly than the party, since numerous studio executives and publicists were convinced that they had unwittingly served as models for the title character. Louis B. Mayer recommended to members of the Motion Picture Producers Association that the Harlem-born Schulberg "be deported." (B. P. Schulberg retorted, "Where the hell are you going to send him, Catalina Island?" a remark that Budd believed hastened the end of his father's already diminished career.) Sam Goldwyn—who "had been very flattering" to Schulberg; "called me a genius"—fired Budd from a job at his studio after concluding that his initials had been borrowed for antihero Sammy Glick without permission.[9]

Schulberg entered the U.S. Navy in 1943, serving under the great film director John Ford in the Office of Strategic Services photographic unit. (He memorably interviewed Hitler's favorite filmmaker, Leni Riefenstahl, shortly after American soldiers arrested her in 1945.) Following his release from active duty in 1946, Schulberg, his wife, Victoria Anderson, and their two sons moved to a fifty-five-acre farm in Bucks County, Pennsylvania. In 1947 he published his boxing novel, *The Harder They Fall,* which the quasi-erudite ex–heavyweight champion Gene Tunney called the best novel on the fight game since George Bernard Shaw's *Cashel Byron's Profession.* Budd's devotion to boxing began at the age of six, when his father's tales of "The Great Benny Leonard" ("that's how he was always referred to in our household") sparked an infatuation with the sport and its characters. Budd's emerging religious identity was closely linked to the prowess demonstrated by Leonard—an all-time great lightweight champion—and other leading Jewish fighters of the 1920s and 1930s. He later became a prolific ringside journalist—he was the first boxing editor at *Sports Illustrated*—and sometime manager of pugilists; for a time in the 1950s he co-handled the moderately successful Trenton heavyweight Archie McBride.[10]

Schulberg enjoyed a critical success in 1950 with *The Disenchanted,* a novel whose protagonist, Manley Halliday, was "a composite of *all* the walking-wounded novelists and playwrights I had been observing through my years of growing up in Hollywood." Halliday bore an especially striking likeness to F. Scott Fitzgerald, with whom Budd had worked in 1939 on the script for *Winter Carnival,* a film set at Dartmouth. Dissatisfied with Schulberg's original treatment for the project, producer (and fellow Dartmouth alumnus) Walter Wanger told Budd he wanted to team him with another writer. When informed that the writer was Fitzgerald, Schulberg replied: "Scott Fitzgerald? Didn't he die?"[11]

Despite Fitzgerald's reputation as a washed-up relic of the Jazz Age, B. P. Schulberg was so thrilled by the prospective collaboration that he saw the duo off on a research trip to Dartmouth with two bottles of excellent champagne. The misguided gift set the tone for a "fatal weekend in Hanover." B. P. was a heavy drinker, but his son had never witnessed anyone in the late stages of a terminal addiction to alcohol. At the height of the fiasco Wanger arranged a meeting for the screenwriters with members of the Dartmouth English Department, at which time it became "pretty obvious not only that Scott was drunk but that we had no story."[12]

Amid the failed collaboration Fitzgerald grew quite fond of his young admirer; he especially enjoyed asking Budd about the early days of Hollywood, a subject of separate novels both were engaged in writing. When Schulberg sent him a copy of *What Makes Sammy Run,* Fitzgerald was relieved to discover, as he told his editor Maxwell Perkins, that "it doesn't cut into my material at all." During a December 1940 visit with the novelist Budd read the first few manuscript chapters of Fitzgerald's Hollywood novel, *The Last Tycoon.* The opening lines ("Though I haven't ever been on the screen I was brought up in pictures") produced "a queasy feeling," Budd recalled, for "those were practically my words." Fitzgerald acknowledged that "there'll be quite a few lines you'll recognize. I hope you don't mind." At the time Schulberg "wasn't sure whether I did or not."[13]

The success of *The Disenchanted* resulted in "countless offers" to Budd from Hollywood studios, but his progressive pro-labor sensibilities attracted him to "Crime on the Waterfront." There was an additional incentive for taking on the project: Joe Curtis of Monticello Films offered a co-producer's role to the ex-tycoon B. P. Schulberg, now unemployed and living in a guesthouse on his son's farm in Bucks County.[14]

A *Going My Way* with Substance

Few American writers at mid-century rivaled Budd Schulberg's wealth of life experience, but he was scarcely prepared to write a screenplay about the New York waterfront. During the winter of 1950 he contacted Mike Johnson, who immediately urged Budd to "go down to Xavier's to see Father John. He really knows the score." The following day Schulberg visited Corridan at Xavier; a day later they met again for lunch and beers at Billy the Oysterman's, a popular Chelsea establishment.[15]

In the decades to come, Schulberg spoke and wrote often about the origins of his unlikely collaboration with the New York Jesuit. "In pursuit of ideas for our film," he reported in *Holiday* magazine in 1954, "I went to see Father Corridan, a tall, semibald, fast-talking, chain smoking realist who had become a kind of unofficial brain trust for a group of dock workers campaigning against corruption, gangsterism, and the exploitation of honest, hard-working dock workers in the longshore locals." Corridan was unlike anyone Schulberg had met in his own richly varied life. His conversation "was the darnedest talk I had ever heard, a highly flavored verbal stew combining the gritty language of longshoremen with mob talk, the statistical trends of a trained economist, and the teachings of Christ." The Jesuit spoke "in vivid detail of the various mobs controlling different sections of the harbor, and of their multiple angles for illicit gain through control of the piers." Listening to Father Corridan with "growing amazement," the screenwriter recalled, "I felt myself entering a world I would not have believed possible in America, just as I might have cried 'fake!' if I had seen a movie about a Catholic priest who becomes a leader among rough-and-tumble dock-wallopers."[16]

Although Corridan envisioned the proposed film as a potent weapon in the campaign to transform the waterfront, he was simultaneously wary, cautioning Budd, "There's no percentage for us helping you turn this into another Hollywood movie." The screenwriter prevailed over the Jesuit's qualms in his winning fashion. It was at this very first meeting, Corridan later confirmed, that "the movie *On the Waterfront* was born." Nevertheless, cherished Hollywood conventions would have to be surmounted if the collaboration were to bear fruit. "'Budd,' I said, 'you can do a *Going My Way* with substance,'" Corridan stipulated. There would be no crooning Bing Crosby in this waterfront picture.[17]

Schulberg readily concurred; he then requested an expertly guided waterfront foray. "A few days later," Corridan wrote in 1954, "over a bowl of clam chowder at Billy the Oysterman's, I introduced Budd to 'Brownie.'...The triangle was complete, but not the movie." It would take more than three trying years of struggle before production on the film dawned. In the meantime the screenwriter's research proceeded in earnest. As Schulberg recalled the same incident, "A few days after I talked with Father Corridan, a veteran dock worker, who, after a lifetime of waterfront beatings, looked like an old prize fighter, took me on an extended tour of the harbor."[18]

Budd Schulberg's travels with "rebel disciple" Arthur Brown began with an unforgettable look at an early morning shapeup on the Lower West Side: "Five-hundred men hoping for work, beating their hands together for warmth, shaped themselves into a huge human horseshoe in front of the hiring boss—nominally an employee of the stevedoring company which hired the longshoremen but in actual fact a man designated by the ILA leaders." Budd and Brownie quickly repaired to a local tavern to initiate a lengthy pub crawl northward along the shores of the Hudson. As day turned to night, the tour included stops at such waterfront redoubts as McCarthy's on Little West Twelfth Street, Georgie Daggett's at Christopher and West Streets, and Eagleton's on West Fourteenth Street. In Workman's on West Street "Brownie pointed out Albert Ackalitis, a machine-gun man paroled from Sing Sing at the request of William J. McCormack's stevedore company, to be a hiring boss." In Chelsea the men visited a saloon where "a group of 'insoigents' had their unofficial headquarters. The atmosphere here was friendly to my guide, with dozens of longshoremen asking him about the water-front reforms Father Corridan was spurring."[19]

As they proceeded slowly northward Brownie warned Budd: "Things are gonna get tougher....Just keep your mouth shut and listen. If anybody asks ya about me just tell 'im we met up at Stillman's gym and got to drinkin' together." The pair made their way toward Hell's Kitchen, where, at one saloon frequented by enforcers from ILA "Pistol Local" 824, Schulberg "elbowed close to Danny St. John, hiring boss of Pier 84." At yet another gin mill favored by gangsters the avid boxing fan embraced his role with more gusto than prudence dictated, falling into lively banter about the fight game ("I said I was a Jersey sports writer") with an individual whose mien suddenly darkened when Budd asked what he did for a living. Brownie whisked Budd away before gravely explaining that his drinking companion was a former confederate of Cockeye Dunn. The remainder of the journey was "interesting but relatively uneventful."[20]

Budd Schulberg was an attentive and sympathetic listener whose work on the script that eventually became *On the Waterfront* effectively began "on that one day he [Brownie] spent with me," as the writer affirmed to Pete Corridan in August 1951, four months after completing the first draft of a screenplay. "I was surprised myself at the wealth of detail I was able to draw on, thanks to his articulateness and the impact of his conviction." Schulberg grew highly attuned to the West Side Irish idiom. Recounting an attempt on his life, Brownie told him: "I shoulda been dead years ago. I'm on borried time." His guide "didn't know it," Schulberg later acknowledged, "but he was writing my dialogue." Schulberg developed a deep and genuine affection for Brownie and other waterfront Irish Americans. He enjoyed taking a drink with them and shared many of their enthusiasms, especially for professional boxing and collegiate football (where his fondness for the Big Green of Dartmouth was more than matched by the longshoremen's fierce devotion to the Fighting Irish of Notre Dame).[21]

The pub crawl with Brownie represented a kind of ritual initiation that permanently changed Schulberg's outlook. "In subsequent months my longshoremen friends and I sat in any number of water-front bars where killers were pointed out with the frequency of movie stars recognized in Dave Chasen's Hollywood restaurant," he later wrote. These life-changing experience carried Schulberg far beyond the joints and lingo of the Irish waterfront. As he later avowed, Pete Corridan gave Budd "feelings about Christ that I never had before"; the Jesuit's example offered "the closest thing I ever came to feeling what true Christianity was all about." Schulberg viewed himself as a "Jewish humanist," an identity that only deepened over the course of his friendship with Corridan. He never formally converted to Catholicism, despite rumors to the contrary that emerged during production of *On the Waterfront* ("though they haven't converted me[,]...I respect them and feel surprisingly at home with them," Schulberg confessed to his wartime boss John Ford—a Catholic—in November 1953). Making a Catholic of the writer was never the goal for Corridan, though his influence was profound and extended to the screenwriter's family. As Ad Schulberg attested to Corridan in 1955: "I am happy about Budd's fortunate meeting with you through his interest in the Harbor problems....I know that he has benefited spiritually through his friendship with you. In fact, many members of my family have been inspired by your holiness."[22]

Corridan rarely elaborated in detail on his church's social teachings. His approach was grounded in part in a Catholic understanding of natural law as universally operative and not dependent for its validation on the claims of any particular theological tradition. "Only man is capable of knowing and loving," he once told Schulberg over beers at Billy the Oysterman's, reiterating the Catholic belief that God endows human beings with the gift of reason so that they might better know God and serve mankind. "In other words," said the priest, "all I teach 'em is the dignity of man." Corridan did not tailor his message to the religious background of his listeners. A Jesuit-educated journalistic ally recalled that he preached an exceptionally straightforward waterfront ethic: "You do something for the right reason and it is moral: that's the purest definition of it." Though the end result might conceivably leave conditions even worse than one found them, "you can't project it like that.... [Y]ou do what's moral now."[23]

The simple power of this message effected a conversion of the heart in Mike Johnson, in Budd Schulberg, and in many others who witnessed Corridan's waterfront apostolate. Johnson put it in the simplest terms: "He changed me, just as later he changed Budd Schulberg." Like Schulberg, Johnson "didn't join his team.... But the important thing is that through him...I got a new slant on life." Corridan's low-key evangelism notwithstanding, Schulberg became an ardent student of the papal social encyclicals and the activist traditions they inspired. He would become, in his own words, "a mouthpiece" for Corridan and his "insoigent" allies on the fringes of the ILA. Between 1950 and 1954, throughout the struggles to bring his waterfront screenplay to fruition, Schulberg also worked intermittently on a novel, stretching his exploration of waterfront life and the Catholic social teachings whose application, he believed, would someday transform the lives of longshoremen and their families.[24]

Schulberg's devotion to Father Pete Corridan and to the cause of waterfront justice was witnessed in the first draft of a screenplay that eventually grew into the script for *On the Waterfront*. Written over the winter of 1950–51 and completed in mid-April, "Crime on the Waterfront" was set amid the tenements, gin mills, and piers of Manhattan's Irish West Side. The opening shot was to feature a superimposed title quoting Malcolm Johnson's condemnation of the "archaic and degrading hoax" that was the shapeup. Terry Monahan, a "wiry, good-looking, high-strung kid with dark, unruly hair, and a lot of pent-up animal force" (clearly the prototype for Marlon Brando's Terry Malloy), is depicted in this version as a rebel longshoreman from the outset. It is Father Moran, the character based explicitly on Pete Corridan, who undergoes a dramatic conversion experience around which the action turns. After a recalcitrant longshoreman named Petey is "accidentally" crushed under the weight of fish barrels that fall from a sling, the mob-connected pier hiring boss, John O. "Zero" Doyle, expresses his regrets to Father Moran as the priest is about to perform last rites. "Suddenly," writes Schulberg in his directions, "Father Moran is transformed from a pious priest to the tough West Side partisan." He snaps, "Don't give me that bull" at Doyle, who leaves "with his mouth hanging open in surprise."[25]

The "Corridan figure" was the one constant over three years and seven, possibly eight, subsequent versions of Schulberg's waterfront screenplay. In each script or treatment the priest is personally transformed by firsthand observation of waterfront injustice; in each version after the first he helps inspire the moral transformation of a reluctant longshoreman who finally stands up to the mob. Since Terry Monahan is already a rebel by the time Father Moran is introduced in "Crime on the Waterfront," the power of his witness is mitigated in this initial script. It is only after Terry's body is found floating in the river that Moran cries out for justice, at a memorial service at St. Bernard's church (the name of a real longshoremen's parish on West Fourteenth Street in Chelsea). "It's high time we investigate an employment set-up that uses murder as a routine policy," the priest insists.[26]

Yet in "Crime on the Waterfront" it is Terry's sister Edie who truly incites the gathered throng of West Side longshoremen. When a mob emissary offers a gift of $500 for the family's loss, Edie screams out her condemnation of the racketeers and their "filthy money." The ensuing action unfolds "like a confessional fever," writes Schulberg, "spreading from one to the other." When a goon threatens to start throwing people out of the church meeting hall Father Moran retorts, "*You* sit down or I'll do the tossing around here." But it is Edie who persuades a cynical journalist, Al Chase, to launch a newspaper investigation that finally brings the waterfront gangsters to justice.[27]

"Crime on the Waterfront" has been largely ignored by students of *On the Waterfront;* as we shall see, its very existence has even been denied. Yet there can be no doubt that the great film originated in this draft screenplay. It may be true—as one scholar has argued—that this "hastily written" script "made the waterfront conditions a springboard for a rather conventional gangster movie." The murder of Terry Monahan two-thirds of the way into the story abruptly shifts the burden of the drama onto a waterfront outsider, a flaw that is unique to this initial draft. Yet the screenplay is a remarkable document that stands witness to Budd Schulberg's conversion not to Catholicism but to a way of seeing grounded in Pete Corridan's unfolding waterfront apostolate. At this early stage of the project Schulberg's understanding of Catholic social teaching was in its infancy, as was his willingness to depict Corridan in his most fully human dimension. In response to Terry Monahan's murder he has Father Moran confess, "I try to be a Christian— but a thing like this makes you so mad you feel like cussin'.'" Schulberg knew that Corridan already swore "worse than" a longshoreman—not that he could have faithfully represented his unpriestly vernacular in a 1951 film script.[28]

Naming Names

"Crime on the Waterfront," Budd Schulberg's completed screenplay, was "approved" by Corridan and director Robert Siodmak and shipped to Harry Cohn in Hollywood bearing the date April 14, 1951. This simple notation has loomed prominently in a debate that has flared intermittently for more than a half-century. The source of the controversy is easy to trace. On Wednesday, May 23, 1951, as the *New York Times* reported, "Budd Schulberg, novelist, testified voluntarily before the House Committee on Un-American Activities that he became a Communist during the late Nineteen Thirties but quit the party when it tried to dictate what he should write." The largely hostile reaction to Schulberg's testimony in Hollywood and among New York intellectuals and later from historians has skewed the reception of every word he subsequently wrote about the waterfront. The film script he had very recently completed would all but vanish from the evidentiary record, taking with it the potential to dismantle one of the enduring myths of America's Cold War cultural politics.[29]

Schulberg testified willingly in Room 226 of the Old House Office Building in Washington, six weeks after screenwriter Richard Collins named him as a former communist comrade in testimony before HUAC. Schulberg had known Collins since their days at Beverly Hills High School; Collins was later regaled by Budd and Maurice Rapf with stories of their 1934 trip to the Soviet Union, where the pair witnessed the First Congress of Soviet Writers and began their inexorable march toward party membership. "Recruited into the Party" by Schulberg in 1937, Collins became an ardent communist among a substantial cohort of film colony insiders.[30]

Hollywood leftists first came under suspicion by the notorious congressional panel in 1940, when Congressman Martin Dies of Texas—then chairing HUAC—descended on Los Angeles to announce that six leading members of the Communist Party worked in the local film industry. Budd Schulberg was publicly listed among that group at "just about the time" he was making his break with the party. The refusal of these barnstorming investigators to give Schulberg a chance to make his case that the list was "faulty" rankled Budd for years: in 1949 he signed a letter calling for the abolition of the committee. Two years prior to that, his friend the screenwriter Ring Lardner Jr. had been blacklisted—and later was jailed for nine months—after being held in contempt of Congress for refusing to answer questions posed by HUAC chairman J. Parnell Thomas. (Lardner had famously responded to Thomas's query as to whether he was a party member, "I could answer it but I'd hate myself in the morning.") Although Lardner was "moving away from the Party at the time of the hearings" in 1947, according to blacklist historian Victor Navasky, he and the other members of the "Hollywood Ten" were still either party loyalists or recent defectors.[31]

Budd Schulberg, by contrast, had left the party in anger more than a decade prior to being named by Richard Collins in April 1951 (a fact Collins confirmed in his testimony). Schulberg now viewed himself as a man of the noncommunist Left with a powerful antipathy for the party and its works. He remained an ardent supporter of progressive causes, including the third party presidential campaign of Henry Wallace in 1948, despite qualms—which he expressed to Wallace—that the former vice president had "unwittingly lent himself completely to the line of the Communist Party." Despite his break with the party, Schulberg remained a mainstay of the "cultural front," historian Michael Denning's term for the array of progressive artists and intellectuals joined in a loosely configured left-wing movement not limited to communists or party sympathizers.[32]

State-sponsored anticommunist crusades posed a grave challenge to this cultural front by turning friends against friends and threatening the livelihoods of creative artists. Schulberg would not have testified voluntarily before HUAC had he not been named by Collins. By May 1951, though, Schulberg understood that if he hoped to clear his own name, the names of others must be served up. He resolved to avoid naming those whose party affiliations had not been revealed by prior witnesses. In the course of his testimony Schulberg did, however, name Tillie Lerner, an author whose ties to the party had not been previously disclosed (and who as Tillie Olson went on to enjoy a distinguished literary career), but whose vocation as a fiction writer "who worked outside the Hollywood blacklist" one journalist calls a "mitigating factor" in Schulberg's reneging on his promise to himself.[33]

Schulberg likewise worked primarily outside Hollywood and indeed remained quite wary of his hometown industry. At the time of his testimony he was a best-selling novelist and highly sought-after magazine writer who had already been assured by Bennett Cerf, his exceedingly well connected publisher, that "his testimony would not matter to Random House, either way." Ring Lardner insisted that Budd unnecessarily feared the blacklist: "By that time he already had a couple of books and didn't need Hollywood." Schulberg's relative immunity from career destruction only further infuriated his growing legion of now former friends.[34]

Budd Schulberg's decision to testify before HUAC—along with similar judgments made by other prominent figures—has been dissected and debated for decades. There is little to add to a discussion of his motives, which were complex and surely involved, as are all such choices, a blend of conviction and self-interest. "My guilt is [over] what we [on the Left] did to the Czechs, not to Ring Lardner," he insisted to Navasky. "I testified because I felt guilty for having contributed unwittingly to intellectual and artistic as well as racial oppression." This rationale stands or falls less on its merits than on the predispositions of Schulberg's allies and critics, partners in a debate without end.[35]

We can nevertheless assert unequivocally that Budd Schulberg's HUAC testimony was *not* the opening act in the back story of *On the Waterfront*, since by the time he appeared before the committee he had already completed a waterfront screenplay with a theme of moral conversion at its heart. The mistaken assumption that has guided critical approaches to this superlative film may now be turned on its head: the issue here is not whether Schulberg's testimony shaped subsequent versions of the waterfront screenplay but whether the act of composing the original draft shaped his decision to testify or the character of that testimony.[36]

Forging the "Spiritual Front"

More than a half-century after the fact Schulberg did not recall seeking the counsel of his newfound Jesuit friend and creative collaborator prior to his HUAC appearance. In August 1951 Schulberg did inform Corridan that he wished to profile the Jesuit for a *Reader's Digest* series on "most memorable personalities." Though the venue was not notable for its pro-labor sympathies (and the story was never published, if indeed it was written), Schulberg told him, "I feel that your approach to labor relations should be more widely known." Budd Schulberg was a social democrat; his discovery through Pete Corridan of the labor-friendly papal social encyclicals transformed his outlook, as it did that of many others—including Catholics—who were unaware that the church possessed a semi-progressive social teaching. The broadly humanist idiom of Pete Corridan's central message ("all I teach 'em is the dignity of man") freed Catholic social thought for Schulberg from any taint of tribal separatism.[37]

In his HUAC testimony Schulberg compared his experience to that of Douglas Hyde, the former British communist who, while helping to lead the party, "was planning to join the Catholic Church. Every day in a sense he was doing both. This might seem the behavior of a very dishonest man, of a hypocrite, but I don't think it really was in that case. I think sometimes these things break slowly." What was breaking slowly for Schulberg was not a conversion to Catholicism but a spiritual transformation without a recognizable label. The original evidence is found in his April 1951 script "Crime on the Waterfront," which was wholly unlike anything he had written before. The "conviction" he witnessed in Arthur Brown, in addition to Corridan's apostolic fervor, helped form the screenplay and his spirituality.[38]

This theme was lost to history—along with the script itself—in part because Schulberg publicly aligned himself at the time with the Hungarian-born British writer Arthur Koestler, whose searing essay on his conversion to communism and subsequent bitter disillusionment was the cornerstone of *The God That Failed*, a 1949 collection of personal testimonies by prominent literary ex-communists and fellow travelers. "What he describes there is what I went through," Schulberg recalled of a three-stage process which culminates in a realization that "you have not been true to yourself." In addition to consulting with Koestler on his HUAC testimony, Schulberg found the writer "an island in the Delaware River where he could live and feel safer from possible Communist attempts on his life." Koestler's subsequent sojourn in the United States as an exceptionally bellicose anticommunist only further tarred Schulberg by association in the eyes of friends such as Maurice Rapf—blacklisted after being named by others—and Walter Bernstein, likewise named by others but who felt personally betrayed by a mentor he had "idolized" since the late 1930s. Yet in the mid-1990s Bernstein perceptively observed, after rereading transcripts of HUAC testimony, that among a group of prominent "friendly" witnesses he knew personally, only Schulberg "represents anything of himself."[39]

Schulberg's testimony works like a wide-arc narrative tracing his metamorphosis from communism to an independent liberalism grounded in a kind of existentialist spirituality. Late in the testimony he shared with the committee some findings from research for an essay he was writing on the Soviets' repression of literary freedom. "Collision with the Party Line" was completed in August 1951, but the *Saturday Review of Literature* held the piece until the following year, after the HUAC hearings were concluded. In that essay Schulberg expressed his solidarity with a passage from William Faulkner's already legendary 1950 Nobel Prize acceptance speech. Man "is immortal," Faulkner proclaimed, "not because he alone among creatures has an inexhaustible voice but because he has a soul, a spirit capable of compassion and sacrifice and endurance." One did not need a religious conversion or even a religion at all to embrace this conviction. What Budd Schulberg needed and found in Pete Corridan was a guide and partner in the "spiritual front," the loose coalition of seekers for meaning and social justice where many secular ex-leftists found a home in the post–World War II decade and beyond.[40]

Not a term in use at the time or a construct used so far by historians of the period, this spiritual front was a uniquely postwar phenomenon, a postdenominational spiritual revival deeply grounded in recent history, especially the chastening of once utopian radicals. The former Trotskyite Dwight MacDonald's 1946 essay "The Root Is Man" was a landmark testament of the spiritual front's nascent ethos, with its "critique of technology, bureaucracy, and Old Left collectivism" and its "emphasis on the moral responsibilities of the individual." Existentialism, a worldview much more compatible with a spiritual outlook than a faith in dialectical materialism, now gained great favor among American intellectuals of MacDonald's generation.[41]

Younger radicals seeking ideological autonomy—including the sociologists C. Wright Mills and Daniel Bell—willingly traded the cruder categories of Marxist thought for an embrace of "irony, paradox, ambiguity, and complexity"; themes central to the spiritual front. Bell, as we have seen, enjoyed his own fruitful spiritual front collaborative relationship with the Jesuit waterfront priest. Like Budd Schulberg, Bell was intrigued by the "realistic" labor advocacy of Pete Corridan at a time—in Bell's view—when the tradition of separate socialist labor parties had regressed into sectarian defeatism.[42]

"Even if most intellectuals remained nonbelievers," wrote historian George Cotkin, "they now adopted the language of religion in their own work and thinking, presenting themselves as chastened and savvy thinkers." Theologians Paul Tillich and Reinhold Niebuhr crafted variants of a post-tribal Christian existentialism that "gave intellectual substance to the religious revival of the postwar era," according to historian Patrick Allitt. "They were often featured in the press as spokesmen not only on religious issues but also on political and cultural affairs." Niebuhr in particular was highly influential among otherwise wholly secular Cold War intellectuals such as Arthur Schlesinger Jr. and Bell, who later acknowledged that Niebuhr's theology "became much more congenial to us" than the work of agnostic philosophers such as the pragmatist Sidney Hook, a dominant figure in prewar New York intellectual life. Though Niebuhr scorned the popular evangelical revivals ignited by the young Billy Graham in the late 1940s—and the nascent self-help tone of popular works such as Rabbi Joshua Loth Liebman's *Peace of Mind* (1946) and Monsignor Fulton J. Sheen's *Peace of Soul* (1949)—there was no containing a burgeoning postwar spiritual marketplace.[43]

This spiritual revival transformed the culture by erasing—even if partially or furtively—the boundaries between historically antagonistic religious and ethnic communities; between religion and psychology and the creative arts; and finally, during the civil rights movement, between the African American church and secular white liberals. Boundary crossing was the most conspicuous feature of the spiritual front, though for many ex-leftists a return to one's own original religious tradition could work like a conversion. When the former Marxist Will Herberg informed Niebuhr that he wished to convert to Christianity, Niebuhr urged him instead to explore the depths of his ancestral Judaism. Herberg's eclectic comparative studies of American religion were deeply informed by a blend of theology and sociology, Old Testament and New, a project that culminated in *Protestant, Catholic, Jew* (1955), aptly characterized by Allitt as "one of the twentieth century's best books about religion."[44]

Budd Schulberg's eclectic, evolving Jewish humanism was akin to that of Herberg. Schulberg's *What Makes Sammy Run* prefigured the spiritual front's fascination with the psychology of ethnic and religious identity. As Andrew R. Heinze, a historian of American Judaism, wrote, "a new wave in postwar American letters...began to swell" with the publication of the 1941 novel. By redefining "the American dream in both Jewish and psychological terms," Schulberg "opened the doors to a genre of psychologically focused fiction that became the trademark of such innovative postwar Jewish writers as Saul Bellow, Philip Roth, and Allen Ginsberg." Ginsberg's Beat poetics was consummated through his spiritual and creative partnership with Jack Kerouac, a product of the conservative French Canadian devotional subculture of Lowell, Massachusetts. This boundary-crossing quality was *constitutive* of the spiritual front's collaborative power, not merely a feature of its ethno-religious diversity.[45]

Budd Schulberg and Pete Corridan's initial 1950 encounters—couched in the hardboiled masculine argot of urban boxing aficionados—gradually evolved into an analogous kind of Jewish-Catholic existential dialogue in action, embodied in works, not conversation. Schulberg's nonfiction advocacy journalism and his waterfront screenplays advancing the crusade of a Jesuit labor priest represented a virtually unprecedented move for a man of the Left, a conundrum that the writer did not seek to evade. He struggled with a "creeping doubt" over the presence of a priest on the waterfront and indeed in his screenplay. While Schulberg was certain that Corridan's pursuit of social justice for longshoremen was totally genuine, he continued to ask himself: "What's a Catholic priest doing on the waterfront, butting into the union and political problems of longshoremen? Is this a rendering to God of the things that are Caesar's?" The screenwriter was also haunted by a painful memory from recent history. "I was approaching the phenomenon of waterfront priests with a certain blindness," he confessed. "You might even call it prejudice....Isn't there always the danger of religious demagoguery such as clouded the career of Father Coughlin?"[46]

These cultural and political issues were real and enduring. The immensely popular "radio priest" Charles E. Coughlin lost a portion of his audience in the late 1930s as his anti-Semitism accelerated rapidly, but his most militantly Catholic following only intensified. Although Coughlin was silenced by his bishop in 1942 under intense pressure from the Roosevelt administration, the figure of priest-demagogue remained a stock ingredient of leftist antifascist ideology in the United States. The "Irish-Coughlinite" worldview identified by historian Steven Fraser as a core element of the right-wing backlash against the CIO–New Deal coalition encouraged many on the Left—including Irish radicals like Mike Quill of the Transport Workers Union—to link the New York Jesuit labor priests with such allegedly proto-fascist figures as Frank Hague and Joe Ryan.[47]

The meteoric ascent of Wisconsin senator Joe McCarthy in early 1950, just as Corridan and Schulberg launched their partnership—and the militancy of Catholic support for McCarthy's destructive anticommunist crusade—presented yet another obstacle to the spiritual front. While never a notably militant anticommunist, the waterfront priest surely partook of the visceral suspicion toward leftists of all colorations that had been a universal article of faith for Catholics since the mid-1930s, when his Society of Jesus founded Xavier Labor School in large part to battle communist influence in New York City labor unions. Many local Catholics had still not accepted the idea that a figure as devout as Dorothy Day had fully relinquished her party connections even after twenty-five years (and Day had never even been a real communist, much publicity to the contrary). As late as December 1952, more than two years after being introduced to Schulberg by Corridan, Father Phil Carey could still inform a fellow Jesuit: "Budd Schulberg wrote up the plight of these men [dockworkers] in an excellent article in Sunday's *Times Magazine*. Schulberg, an ex-Commie, was moved by the Catholicism of these men in a way that was most startling."[48]

A Model of Formation

By 1951 it was abundantly clear to Pete Corridan that the Irish waterfront would never reform itself or respond to his solitary efforts. He needed his spiritual front collaborators and was amply blessed by them: first Mike Johnson of the *New York Sun*, then especially Budd Schulberg. Others were yet to come. They did not always find Corridan easy to work with; he rarely acknowledged his enormous indebtedness to them. Some years later, after being treated brusquely by Corridan, Johnson assured Phil Carey: "He was instrumental in bringing me abruptly back to reality, giving me perspective and restoring and renewing my faith in God. I shall always bless him for that." But then there was the work they shared. "I hope I am not being immodest," wrote Johnson, "when I say that in the journalistic phase of our relationship—exposing the waterfront story—I helped him as much as he helped me—painful though that may be to him now."[49]

Their mutual bond was tested when the Irish waterfront struck back. In April 1951 Joe Ryan wrote to William Randolph Hearst Jr.—owner of the International News Service, where Mike Johnson was employed in the wake of the *New York Sun*'s demise—in an effort to smear the journalist by association with Schulberg, "who was, or had been a member of the Communist Party." In his response to the charge, Johnson informed the INS: "I do not know...whether Budd Schulberg is or was a Communist....If he is, or was, it will certainly hurt the prospects of our movie and that I shall regret for we had planned a hard-hitting, honest, documentary type film." Ryan was not impressed with Schulberg's confession before HUAC: all he needed to know was that the writer was once a Red. Real communists and honestly repentant ex-communists meant far less to Ryan than phantom waterfront Reds, who served his interests much better.[50]

Schulberg wrote to Corridan in August 1951, expressing regret that "our waterfront film has hit a number of snags, the most recent one being the hesitancy of the backers to go ahead without Ryan's approval for fear of AFL opposition to the picture." Having now embraced a Catholic reform movement far more menacing to the baffled Ryan than communism, Budd Schulberg only grew more dangerous to King Joe. Far from taking refuge in Catholicism, Schulberg gradually helped reconfigure Catholic action away from its obsessive anticommunism toward internal renewal symbolized by the waterfront apostolate.[51]

Pete Corridan came to view Schulberg as a man who had exercised his free will, made a decision in conscience, and left the Communist Party without surrendering his commitment to social justice. The earnestness of his dedication exemplified the kind of moral citizenship Corridan hoped to instill in the port's longshoremen. In this sense the screenwriter became a model of Jesuit formation for Corridan, who was concerned not so much with Catholic formalism as with spiritual maturation, which in turn bolstered the habits of citizenship needed to reform the waterfront. By his variant of natural law teaching, the truths of the church's claims would become apparent when—and *only* when—men (and it was always strictly about men) were fully formed and capable of mature reasoning.

Yet Corridan made so little progress on the Irish waterfront he had to wonder if an inadequate spiritual formation was worse than none at all. "The interest of all of us in these men is that they are Catholics," he informed Philadelphia priest Henry Walsh in December 1948, "and no group is interested in promoting their welfare apart from the Communist party," a doubly peculiar admission indicating both his lack of confidence in waterfront "catechesis" and a grudging respect for the dedication of communists. One Catholic waterfront cohort appeared to him particularly susceptible. "In the New York area the communists have failed up to now to penetrate the longshore ranks, except among the Italians in Brooklyn," he informed Father Walsh. In the wake of the November 1948 walkout he had similarly alerted the young labor priest George G. Higgins: "Unfortunately the Commies made some headway in the strike among the Italian locals. The situation will bear watching, and we'll do our best to get some opening before these men are permanently captured."[52]

The Italians were especially vulnerable to "capture" by the communists because they had so little experience, in Corridan's view, with a tradition of "free" union locals. As he would later explain to a graduate student researching the waterfront's political culture, Brooklyn had been under the domination of the "Italian underworld" since the early 1920s. "I understand a free local," Corridan explained, "to be one in which although hoodlums may be members and effective at times, in matters of major importance when the rank and file turn out in large numbers, the will of the membership prevails. Many times a free local is only half a step ahead of the mob element. It is a relentless war." He clearly implied that formation of waterfront Italians as Christians and citizens was not yet complete, an attitude very widely shared by the overwhelmingly Irish-dominated Catholic clergy of New York City and the Irish waterfront's rank and file.[53]

African Americans were likewise considered particularly vulnerable to the Reds. Since few black longshoremen were Catholics, and fewer if any made their way to Xavier Labor School, the labor priests sought to broaden their spiritual authority through the auspices of the Catholic Interracial Council of New York, an apostolate founded by the Jesuit John LaFarge in 1934.

The interracial movement promoted universal solidarity in the Mystical Body of Christ over race consciousness. LaFarge's apostolate condemned racism but effectively discouraged black people from developing the same institutions of ethnic solidarity that had been so crucial for the Irish and other European Catholic immigrant groups.[54]

An analogous situation existed in the port, where African Americans were the only ethnic group denied a historic claim to piers of their own. During World War II the number of black longshoremen increased, and they found work on piers throughout the port, but after the war they were squeezed by members of white ethnic locals from Bayonne to Brooklyn intent on reclaiming their turf. In March 1949 black longshoremen from Local 968 in Brooklyn and their supporters launched a demonstration against racial injustice in Brooklyn Heights and on the West Side. Picketing outside ILA headquarters on West Fourteenth Street persisted until June 6, when thirty-eight protesting longshoremen occupied the union's nineteenth-floor offices. They planned to remain there for forty-eight hours but were forcibly ejected forty-three hours shy of their goal by "delegates of the ILA's Marine Trades Department" to the sounds of Joe Ryan's taunt, "Go back downstairs with your communist pals and let them get you some jobs." The following day 2,500 West Side dockworkers "charged into" the remaining pickets "with a cry of 'Let's get them,' along with a number of unprintable yells generally prefaced with the word 'Commie.'"[55]

"The real issue," wrote historian Bruce Nelson, "was not communism; it was the undeniable reality of racial discrimination in the employment of longshoremen on the New York waterfront." In a June 10 letter to George Hunton of the interracial council, Pete Corridan focused not on the violence but on tensions between black and Italian longshoremen in Brooklyn. Hunton was a layman, a protégé and close associate of John LaFarge driven by an apostolic fervor. Corridan trusted him to make the necessary distinction between racial justice and the need for class harmony inscribed in the social encyclicals. Though he was "inclined to believe that the greater part of the truth is on the negro side" in the conflict with the ILA and acknowledged that "race prejudice is being used as a means in this waterfront power fight," Corridan also insisted that "the disturbance has its roots in the overcrowded supply of men in relation to work opportunities in which both white and colored suffer." He observed that at least one officer of Local 968, Cleophas Jacobs, had been "palling around with the Commies." Corridan overlooked the West Side counterinsurgency against black sit-in strikers, which was led by Irish Americans, including, according to Nelson, "Irish Catholic members of West Side locals that had been leading the anti-Ryan insurgency," that is, the very men in whom the Jesuit had invested his hopes for reform.[56]

The dynamics of ethnic tribalism in the port could never be fully evaded or surmounted by the labor priests or their allies. Since relatively few Italians and precious few blacks sought out Corridan for the informal sessions in which he did his real teaching, members of these communities remained largely outside the pastoral orbit of the Jesuit labor priests. Phil Carey and Pete Corridan never acknowledged the vast array of ethnocentric assumptions on which their own spiritual politics was grounded: while Italians and blacks were viewed as needing special pastoral guidance, the Jesuits tended to approach the Irish as though they were sufficiently catechized to resist victimization by the communists or appeals to racism.

The Irish on the waterfront were indeed catechized—just well enough to reject the *priests'* message. For all their street credibility, Carey and Corridan, as Jesuits, were invested in the Eurocentric language of the social encyclicals, especially their corporatist focus on class harmony and a vision of post-tribal Christian citizenship modeled after the Mystical Body of Christ. This theme did not resonate with longshoremen concerned with economic competition in the multiethnic labor marketplace. The West Side Irish could be militantly hostile to *both* Joe Ryan and black longshoremen, a blend that must have discomfited Corridan. A "convert" like Budd Schulberg, by contrast, could embrace the crusade for social justice in its entirety, without the tribal baggage.[57]

Schulberg's solidarity with the Jesuits represented an extraordinary coup because his literary gifts were unmatched by anyone working in "official" Catholic circles at the time, when a rhetorical prudence obtained. The waterfront priest, for his part, made for one striking exception to this cultivated diffidence, and the screenwriter found his boldness deeply inspiring. Corridan's "words cut a way for me through the curtain of religious prejudice into the world of Catholic humanism—of Christian social ethics," Schulberg recalled. "He was the closest thing I ever came to feeling what true Christianity was about. Not just the soul but the guts of the New York waterfront in the tough 40s and 50s, he had chosen a dangerous road to Christian service—taking to heart and mind the challenge of Jesus: 'If you do it to the least of mine, you do it to me.'" While Corridan was "devoted to the New York waterfront," his work had "far broader and deeper implications," not just for the church but for the whole culture as it absorbed the postdenominational energies of the spiritual front.[58]

It was around the time he met Pete Corridan that Schulberg assumed the role of manager for Archie McBride, a promising heavyweight from New Jersey. When Schulberg's Random House editor Saxe Commins "lectured me about neglecting my work for what should be a hobby on the side, I tried to explain that what he was to me, a guide and nourisher, I had become to Archie." The relationship between the writer and his Jesuit collaborator was not without its occasional tensions, but it offered the partners ample opportunity for the same mutual guidance and nurturing. Working mostly separately but together when needed, Budd Schulberg and Pete Corridan became the most eloquent apostles on the port's spiritual front.[59]

9   Meeting across the River

By springtime 1950 Joe Ryan sorely needed some new allies of his own. Unlike Pete Corridan, King Joe found no solace beyond the Irish waterfront. Ryan was, however, paying closer attention to his rapidly expanding public relations challenges. His disastrous televised debate with Corridan taught him to avoid direct confrontation with implacable Jesuits. It was time for the ILA to unleash its own waterfront priest, for whom Ryan needed to look no further than his pastor, Monsignor John J. O'Donnell of Guardian Angel church. In the aftermath of the television debacle in which Corridan left Ryan playing the fool, O'Donnell weighed in for the *ILA Longshore News*. "The waterfront is my family, I honor the men who labor there," he proclaimed. "I despise the men who slander the waterfront.... [W]e have our proportionate share of crime and we have some foul balls on the water-front[,]...but I know these men, and I can say they will match any group of men in industry and come out on top."[1]

Access to an obscure house organ was one thing, but when O'Donnell entered the fray in the daily press, he found himself on the short end of comparisons with his rival, and now far better known, waterfront priest. In a February 3, 1950, editorial, the *New York World-Telegram and Sun* noted that O'Donnell had recently "told off those who are slanderously talkative about the waterfront as a place of 'extensive' crime and racketeering. We go along with Msgr. O'Donnell in recognizing that there are many honest men struggling hard to get a meager living out of serving ships in the world's greatest port." The editorialist immediately turned the tables on O'Donnell, however, declaring, "It's past time to do something to free them," starting with the elimination of the shapeup:

> Rev. John M. Corridan...[recently] offered corrective recommendations that
> were greeted by shipping companies and the union with an inactive silence still

unbroken today. We'd like to see Congress or the State Legislature change the hiring system if the companies or union don't act quickly to curb crime and give security and peace of mind and a better wage to that great mass of men praised by the port chaplain.[2]

In the months and years to come, Monsignor O'Donnell and Joe Ryan would find precious little support in the pages of the metropolitan dailies. In their quest to regain cultural and spiritual authority, the pastor and his parishioner resorted instead to a venerable tradition, the Communion breakfast. The ILA had never hosted Communion breakfasts before, though the practice was customary in other unions; during the 1940s O'Donnell himself had celebrated Mass at such events sponsored by Catholic members of a local teamsters, chauffeurs, and helpers union for which he also served as chaplain. The March 1950 edition of the *Longshore News* announced that O'Donnell would serve as "spiritual adviser" for a May 7 Communion breakfast planned by Chelsea longshoremen, inspired in part by the papal proclamation of 1950 as a Holy Year.[3]

The organizers wasted no time revealing a more pressing local motivation: "Our craft has been the subject of much unfavorable publicity, because a certain group of newspaper feature writers think the waterfront is a good source of sensational stories. This Communion breakfast is our answer to some of this nonsense." William Lynch of Local 791 was listed as organizer of the event, and Thomas "Happy" Donahue was credited with the original inspiration, though in subsequent promotions the organizers did not "publish any names (as a Committee) because being longshoremen, each one is known to you all." The committee's address was Guardian Angel church, where precious few working longshoremen worshipped.[4]

On April 29 Joe Ryan, who had the most to gain from an illusion of waterfront spiritual solidarity, issued a personal invitation to longshoremen to attend the first of a projected annual event:

Naturally, I bask in the reflected glory of the good things that you accomplish just as well as I share in the blame for anything that the public thinks is wrong on the waterfront....I deem it a grand privilege and an honor to ask all, irrespective of their religious beliefs, to honor Almighty God by turning out for the Parade from Guardian Angel Church to the Waldorf-Astoria Hotel. No other motive than pride in being a longshoreman prompts me to ask everyone to get behind this idea which will bring honor and glory to God and prestige to all of us.[5]

"Irrespective of their religious beliefs" was a rhetorical device borrowed from postwar encomiums to interfaith harmony. Ryan took for granted that any longshoreman shaping up in Chelsea was either a Catholic or fully capable of acting like one while on his Irish waterfront turf.

Monsignor O'Donnell obtained special permission from the New York archdiocese to hold the Mass on U.S. Lines' Pier 61, near Eleventh Avenue and West Twenty-first Street. The steamship company agreed to install a portable altar in its shed, making possible the first Mass ever celebrated on a pier in New York Harbor. Ryan told the *Times* that plans for the Communion breakfast represented a

> "spontaneous gesture by the men themselves." He gave his hearty approval to it, however, and called it a "clear statement" of the position taken by New York's waterfront workers. Mr. Ryan said the union's membership all over the port had shown intense interest in the plan, and were inviting longshore workers of all faiths to join with it in "showing the world what chance communism has on this waterfront."[6]

On Sunday, May 7, twelve hundred waterfront workers received Holy Communion at the "scene of their week-day labors—a New York pier," the *Times* reported. "The mass was celebrated before a candle-lit altar at the outer end of Pier 61.... [A]t the end of the mass, the men joined in singing the national anthem and the *Te Deum*" before marching to the Waldorf for breakfast. "Happy" Donahue joined O'Donnell and Ryan in leading the parade up Tenth Avenue, then eastward along Forty-eighth Street, "accompanied along the line of march by a color guard and a fife and drum corps composed of children from Guardian Angel Church." Local waterfront entrepreneurs and the ILA did very well by this event: there were color guard uniforms and sailor suits to be donated, testimonials to be placed in a handsome commemorative booklet, and a variety of other tributes to be paid. The Mass and the march provided a most imposing display of Irish waterfront power akin to the annual dinner honoring Ryan's eponymous association.[7]

The men were joined at the Waldorf by a host of Joe Ryan's friends and cronies, including Bill McCormack and his friend Vincent Impellitteri, the New York City Council president soon to assume the mayoralty upon the resignation of Bill O'Dwyer, who in August would beat a hasty retreat to the Mexican ambassadorship. Following breakfast at the Waldorf, the gathered throng heard from the Reverend William McManus, who called for the "return of a 'man's world.'" Joe Ryan was deeply grateful for the reestablishment of proper order both spiritual and temporal on the waterfront. As he explained in announcing a subsequent benefit and testimonial for Monsignor O'Donnell and the Shrine Church of the Sea: "Happily, the Monsignor, outspoken foe of the few 'foul balls' who bring shame on his and our beloved Waterfront, constantly refuses to interfere in the internal disputes in the Family of Labor and sticks exclusively to his business[,]...the Spiritual." Respect for this proper division of labor would become a constant refrain in the counterattack of waterfront realists against Jesuit reformers.[8]

"Taxi Jack" O'Donnell was Cardinal Spellman's "official representative on the waterfront," wrote Bruce Nelson. The monsignor "spoke regularly at ILA gatherings"; he always promised to "stick to my own business, which is the spiritual." O'Donnell's theology of the two Catholic spheres, as it might be labeled, represented the unofficial, rarely challenged waterfront ecclesiology of the New York archdiocese. Since the mid-1930s he had enjoyed a ferocious reputation in Chelsea for defending Irish waterfront interests, particularly those connected with his parishioner and patron Joe Ryan. A founder of the National Maritime Union and veteran of the violent counterattack to NMU organizing led by Ryan in 1936 described Guardian Angel as akin to "branch headquarters of Murder Incorporated."[9]

For all his intimidating presence, Taxi Jack's usefulness to Joe Ryan was not unlimited. "Guardian Angel was a very small parish," Phil Carey observed decades later (before it was nearly closed in 2007 for dwindling membership). "It should never have existed.... Spellman let [O'Donnell] get away with it because he was good on raising money" from his small group of benefactors, which prominently included Joe Ryan, and "from the insurance companies down around Wall Street."[10]

The bitter enmity between O'Donnell and the Xavier labor priests was the Catholic waterfront's equivalent of the vicious factional fights that rent the secular Left during this same period. For his part Pete Corridan ministered to a very small band of practicing "rebel disciples." Locked in an intractable political and theological struggle with O'Donnell and his patrons that went undisclosed despite Corridan's journalistic connections, he was unable openly to enlist the resources of Xavier parish in his cause. The potential spectacle of two priests from the same neighborhood committed to the destruction of each other's spiritual authority "gave scandal" from the church's perspective, to understate the case. The clerics waged war instead over Communion breakfasts.

O'Donnell mobilized the tradition as a show of force. To Corridan such self-serving exhibitions "violated all the norms of religious decency"; yet he himself had unveiled "A Catholic Looks at the Waterfront" at a Jersey City Communion breakfast in autumn 1948. Corridan later claimed a longshoreman had told him on the day of the first annual ILA West Side gala that "some of the biggest bums we have in the harbor, both in the union and in management, were honored at the breakfast this morning." The Jesuit cited Pope Pius XI's admonition against those Christians who "permit a deplorable cleavage in their conscience," adding, "Such lives are a scandal to the weak, and to the malicious a pretext to discredit the church."[11]

Communion breakfasts soon blanketed the waterfront. June 25, 1950, found Joe Ryan across the port in Newark, where the ILA's Warehousemen, Loaders and Checkers local hosted "the largest communion breakfast in the history of Our Lady of Mt. Carmel Church." Port Newark housed at the time a sleepy lumber terminal and little else of note: Phil Carey's view of the facility as home to "crocodiles and bulrushes" typified the view of waterfront New Yorkers. Few knew that the Port Authority had acquired control of the city's former municipal piers along with Newark Airport in 1948 and was in the process of spending $14 million in upgrades, presaging a dramatic westward shift in the port's epicenter.[12]

Located in the "Ironbound" neighborhood between the city's rail yards and Newark Bay, Mt. Carmel was a historic Italian parish in a city with a very large and vibrant Italian American community. Newark's Italian leadership was finally gaining local political clout to rival that of the Irish—and a smaller cohort of Jewish Democrats—who ran the city for decades. Marie Dolly Cuozzo, a correspondent for the *Italian Tribune* of Newark, reported on the June 25 event:

> At the completion of the communion mass, the band of Joe Basile filled the air with music. All the men who received communion lined up behind Mayor Villani, Father Callagaro and Father Fuino, who led the marchers down Ferry Street, over Adams up South Street and to the Essex House, a march of about 2½ miles. The parade itself had the spirit of a Roman holiday while the men were marching it made my heart jump with joy to see the mothers and wives, sons and daughters looking from their windows.[13]

Joe Ryan was not accustomed to celebrating in the spirit of Roman holidays. On the Jersey side—in Newark just as in Hoboken and Jersey City—Irishmen and Italians coexisted more readily than on the West Side of Manhattan. Italian American speakers at the Port Newark ILA Communion breakfast echoed their West Side Irish confreres' themes of Christian manliness as a bulwark against communist infiltration. Yet this "Americanizing" consensus was no match for the deep tensions with ethnic overtones that were brewing in neighboring Jersey City, where waterfront politics grew extraordinarily fractious in the immediate postwar period. Mayor Frank Hague had survived investigations, judicial setbacks, and disgruntled office seekers, but his brand of urban Irish Catholic politics could no longer hold back the bottled-up tide of ethnic succession.

The Waning Irish Waterfront

A "skinny kid from Hoboken" named Frank Sinatra helped bring an end to the Irish waterfront's golden age. From 1939 to 1943 Sinatra "showed up almost nightly" at Bickford's Cafeteria on Journal Square in Jersey City, not far from the apartments on Bergen and later on Audubon Avenue, where he lived with his young family. Bickford's was the favored nightly gathering place of local dissidents who expressed "dismay at Hague's every move."

The leader of these "cafeteria statesmen" was John Longo, a vocal Italian American periodically arrested by Boss Hague's cops for imaginary offenses that occasionally earned Longo very real terms of hard labor in the county jail. Longo was joined over the years at Bickford's by a coalition of Italian and Polish Americans along with a smaller contingent of Irish American Jersey Citizens.[14]

Frankie Sinatra's mother, Dolly, was a Hoboken neighborhood functionary in Hague's countywide juggernaut; the young crooner shared her interest in local politics but not her loyalty to the Boss. Sinatra's politics fell well to the left of Dolly's at this point in his career: like John Longo, he was drawn to the emerging Italian American progressive tradition represented by such New Yorkers as Vito Marcantonio, a left-wing East Harlem congressman who had previously served as Longo's defense attorney at the behest of three-term New York City mayor Fiorello La Guardia, a powerful foe of Tammany Hall and, by extension, Frank Hague. Sinatra grew friendly with John V. Kenny during his Bickford's period. The longstanding boss of Jersey City's Second Ward began "putting his political clout behind the youthful crooner, helping Sinatra obtain nightclub engagements." On April 2, 1945, Sinatra—by now the idol of "bobbysoxers" everywhere—returned the favor, performing at a concert to benefit the St. Vincent de Paul Society, housed at St. Michael's church, where Kenny regularly sponsored "a gigantic entertainment for the poor of his parish."[15]

The concert, held by local custom in a public school auditorium near St. Michael's and co-sponsored by the Second Ward Democratic Club and the allied societies of the parish, attracted 2,200 "screaming swooners," who drowned out opening acts—consisting mainly of Irish American vaudevillians—with their cries of "We want Frankie!" until they were finally rewarded with stirring renditions of "I Should Care," "Don't Blame Me," and "Night and Day." Mayor Hague made a "surprise" appearance at the concert. "I'm not here to talk politics," Hague declared after proclaiming Sinatra the "most popular young man in the world." The mayor was mistaken by Sinatra's youthful fans "for a number of people ranging from the thrush's manager to his father," but since they were not yet of voting age, the Boss was likely not alarmed.[16]

The burgeoning friendship between Kenny and Sinatra, however, signaled a new postwar fusion politics for which Hague was wholly unprepared. Several weeks after the concert, as the war in Europe neared its end, Hague played to his largest ethnic constituency in asserting his "profound sympathy" for the Italian people and calling for that nation's inclusion at the upcoming United Nations conference. Yet his system of "national" ward bosses—like the Catholic Church's system of "national" parishes—suddenly smacked of paternalism. An Italian American political insurgent accused Hague of "deceiving the Italians of Jersey City for too many years," leading them to "a veritable slaughter of their hopes and aspirations."[17]

Two years later Hague observed "what could happen to the boss who stayed on the scene a day too long." In Hoboken a "fusion" ticket of three Italians and two Irishmen waged a spirited campaign against the deeply entrenched regime of Bernard McFeely, a "tough, glum, nickel-pinching, semi-illiterate and vindictive" Hague vassal (though they were unequal politically, their contempt was wholly mutual) who outdid even the Boss in his ethnocentrism. McFeely placed so many family members on the public payroll they alone outnumbered non-Irish officeholders in the Mile Square City. The mayor "hated Italians and did his best to make life miserable for them," according to *Time* magazine. In the May 1947 election a sizeable proportion of the Italian Americans who made up 65 percent of the city's population finally had an opportunity to register their opinion of him. Votes were counted by machine for the first time in the city's history: the resulting clean sweep sent ten thousand Hobokenites into the streets for a raucous celebration of the end of two decades of misrule by the clan McFeely.[18]

Less than a month after McFeely's defeat Hague relinquished his three-decade Jersey City mayoralty, installing in his place a taciturn nephew, Frank Hague Eggers. Eggers carried out the Boss's wishes, providing even more opportunities than usual for the seventy-one-year-old Hague to conduct his business from the clubhouse at Hialeah racetrack in Florida. Hague's longtime waterfront ambassadors "Happy" Keane and Neil McKeon retained their all-important positions as hiring bosses on Jersey City's Piers D and F, respectively, ensuring that patronage and kickback cash would continue its prodigious flow in and out of these venues.[19]

While Hague turned his back on a growing body of critics, John V. Kenny listened attentively. The "Little Guy" defied the Boss's spies, loudly grumbling at Bickford's and elsewhere that Hague "seemed to be passing over loyal supporters." Like many of Joe Ryan's Irish American critics within the ILA leadership, Kenny always struggled to reconcile his decision to challenge Hague with loyalty to the Irish waterfront. "If he had not thrown me out, I probably would be a member of the machine," he often later protested.[20]

Kenny's high-stakes bid to topple Hague's regime caused him to forge alliances in the immediate postwar years with non-Irish denizens of the waterfront whose ambitions ranged far beyond ethnic political succession. A formidable North Jersey gangster, Charles "Charley the Jew" Yanowsky, launched a final bid for control of Jersey City's piers, an ambition long resisted by Hague's minions. During Frank Hague Eggers's brief mayoralty Yanowsky and Kenny were often seen driving together through the streets of Jersey City's Horseshoe district, where they distributed waterfront patronage to locales as remote as the Naval Ammunition Depot at Leonardo, New Jersey, along Raritan Bay.[21]

Kenny's burgeoning alliance with Charley Yanowsky ended on July 16, 1948, when the gangland figure was "taken for a ride," stabbed twenty-three times with an ice pick, and dumped in a field near a schoolhouse in Clifton, New Jersey. The unsolved killing was widely attributed on the waterfront to the rapidly intensifying struggle for control of the Hudson County piers in both Jersey City and Hoboken. Yanowsky's bid for control of Local 1247 passed to his brother-in-law Frank "Biffo" Di Lorenzo. The key to any successful coup was a triumph by John V. Kenny over the long-entrenched Irish waterfront machine. The battle for dominance at Local 1247 was a decisive factor shaping the funding and waging of Kenny's "Victory Ticket" campaign in the spring of 1949.[22]

Kenny's Cabbage

This explosive political climate, with millions of dollars in patronage and kickbacks at stake, was the backdrop for Pete Corridan's visit to Jersey City in late 1948, where he delivered "A Catholic Looks at the Waterfront" at a downtown Knights of Columbus hall. Corridan struggled to surmount his own Irish West Side localism but was no better prepared than Joe Ryan to engage the politics of ethnic succession Jersey-style. In June 1949 Corridan illusorily informed the Reverend R. A. McGowan, director of the Social Action Department of the National Catholic Welfare Conference, that "Father Dobson of St. Peter's in Jersey City is beginning to get the Jersey longshoremen."[23]

Philip Dobson ran a "free school for union men" established in September 1946 at St. Peter's Preparatory School on Grand Street in Jersey City. The St. Peter's Labor School bore Philip Carey's indelible handprints. Two years earlier he had suggested to his Jesuit provincial that "Father Dobson would do more for the glory of God were he to start such a school in Jersey City" than by returning to Xavier from the Crown Heights Labor School. By autumn 1948—when Corridan delivered "A Catholic Looks at the Waterfront" in the vicinity of the school—the St. Peter's Institute was attracting 339 students to courses taught by a faculty composed of Jesuits and laymen with ties to the labor movement.[24]

Jersey City's highly strategic location gave promise of a harbor finally covered on both sides by Jesuit-driven social action, but at the time of Corridan's initial Jersey City incursion the St. Peter's Labor School had yet to reach the waterfront despite its close proximity to the piers. Philip Dobson had lived in Jersey City for six years in his youth and knew well the first rule of local clerical conduct: do not risk the displeasure of Frank Hague. Then suddenly the Irish waterfront felt its first earthquake: Kenny's "Victory Slate" toppled Hague's once invincible machine on election day, May 10, 1949 (see figure 6). That night there was dancing in Jersey City "on the roofs of cars or on the grass at City Hall," where a policeman stood on the balcony "waving a broom." Patrons "stood ten deep at bars," while revelers in automobiles "moved in a long line, headlights beaming, through Journal Square, past a woman on a sound truck who repeated over and over again, 'You're free. You're free. The people of Jersey City are free.'" The Little Guy's fusion ticket included a Polish American, an Italian American, an Anglo-Republican, and an inveterate Irish American enemy of the Boss. Hague had ignored the pleas of advisers and trotted out his standard ticket, four Irishmen and a white Protestant. A jubilant John Kenny promised that the long, grim era of municipal corruption was over, but Hague knew better, having been beaten at his own game: Kenny's forces had tripled the customary local cost-per-vote gratuity from five to fifteen dollars.[25]

Not long after his defeat Hague made a phone call to Leland S. Andrews, vice president of the American Export Line, the steamship company that leased Jersey City Piers D and F. Hague told Andrews that if he did not prevent "these damn rackets" backed by Kenny from moving in on the city's piers, "there wouldn't be a damn pound of freight" left on trucks, car floats, and lighters as they departed the rail yards and piers. Hague informed Andrews that he had "made" Kenny and ominously concluded: "I want to tell you one more thing, Andrews. He likes his cabbage, and goddamn it, he's trying to get in four years what it took thirty-two years for me to get."[26]

Two months after the election Kenny's fusion partner "Biffo" Di Lorenzo— newly installed by the mayor as delegate and business agent of ILA Local 1247—and associates paid a visit to the city's American Export Line piers, demanding the immediate ouster of Hague stalwarts Happy Keane and Neil McKeon as boss loaders on Piers D and F. Keane was a special target of the new leadership of 1247 because of his long and intimate association with the vanquished Boss (the demand for Keane's ouster was accompanied by the hummed melody from "Now Is the Hour," Mayor Kenny's campaign theme song). When the steamship company balked (insisting that as an independent loader Keane operated beyond their jurisdiction), the 1247 brain trust called a strike that idled four hundred longshoremen for six weeks, prompting a frenzied series of meetings variously involving Joe Ryan, Kenny, shippers, and union officials until a compromise was reached whereby Keane relinquished Pier D but McKeon held on to the loading for Pier F.[27]

In summer 1949 Pete Corridan privately conceded "as things stand now I know very little about the Jersey set-up apart from the fact that it's a good deal different from the New York picture," but he was inexorably drawn into Hudson County waterfront politics by the Happy Keane case. In August 1949 the Jesuit was invited to meet with Keane and Manhattan assistant district attorney Bill Keating, who had successfully prosecuted the Cockeye Dunn–Andy Hintz murder case and remained deeply interested in waterfront crime throughout the port. Though it is not clear if the meeting was ever held, Keating soon became a leading Corridan ally. Happy Keane did visit Corridan to borrow a printed copy of the ILA constitution for use

Figure 6. Jubilant supporters (including throngs of policemen) swarm Jersey City's John V. Kenny the night his "Victory" ticket toppled the regime of Boss Frank Hague, May 10, 1949. Courtesy of the Jersey City Free Public Library.

in (unsuccessful) legal action against Local 1247 in a bid to regain his job. Since numerous mobbed-up ILA locals made a practice of "losing" copies of the union's constitution and bylaws, Corridan's assistance represented more than a routine courtesy. The overtures from Keane's camp indicated that the Jesuit was now viewed as a figure with some real moral authority on both sides of the Hudson, just the scenario he had craved.[28]

Meanwhile the compromise solution on Piers D and F did not obtain for long. On July 6, 1950, Kenny associates Biffo Di Lorenzo, Anthony Liucy ("Slim Lucey"), and Vincent "Cockeyed Barney" Brown visited Pier F and informed the terminal manager that Neil McKeon "would have to be removed from Pier F; that they were moving in. As a matter of fact, they already had some trucks in there that morning," the manager later testified. The invaders were chased off the pier and McKeon was urged to "stand pat" by management, but he endured a vicious beating later that afternoon; Kenny's friends then fomented a lengthy work stoppage on the pier. Joe Ryan, a longtime friend and ally of Frank Hague, ordered sympathy strikes in response by Irish American elements on piers in Hoboken and Jersey City.

A meeting was called at which Ryan reminded Mayor Kenny of the compromise deal struck the previous year, but the "Little Guy" was unable to bring peace to Pier F. This new dispute did not quite make allies of Joe Ryan and Pete Corridan, but the overture to Corridan from Ryan's friend and crony Happy Keane hinted at the shared—if perhaps unspoken—conviction of these three that the waterfront's legitimate moral order was equated with Irish Catholic control. Corridan was no admirer of Frank Hague, but the ethnic politics "fusionist" John V. Kenny was now viewed as thoroughly compromised, if not a traitor; he had no hope of reclaiming the mantle of Irish Catholic moral legitimacy on the Hudson County waterfront. A most revealing moment had occurred during Hague's telephone conversation with Leland Andrews of American Export in July 1949 (in which he made the famous remark about Kenny's affinity for "cabbage"): the old Boss condemned the new Boss for *disproportionate* greed, an "ethical" distinction characteristic of the Irish waterfront's waning moral theology, and characteristically disingenuous given Hague's heretofore unsurpassed record of plunder.[29]

The loss of Irish authority in Jersey City in 1949 and 1950 generated ominous narratives among supporters of both Corridan and the Hague-Ryan forces. In July 1949 Malcolm Johnson wrote, "The real issue is an effort by [the late Charley] Yanowsky's associates to dictate key jobs on the piers in a plan ultimately to control the Jersey waterfront." In mid-August the *Jersey Journal* reported the claim of Pier 9 boss loader James F. McGovern that "four men had come to the piers Monday and told an associate of his that 'we're in the saddle now.'" Among the group were Biffo Di Lorenzo, Slim Lucey, and "a Pier 9 man known as Tony Cheese," or Anthony Marchitto. The *Journal* also reported the dire warning of former Hudson County sheriff William McGovern that "the steamship companies will leave Jersey City because of gorilla tactics. None of these gorilla tactics were tolerated under Mayor Hague or Mayor Eggers."[30]

A *Jersey Journal* editorial succinctly lamented the price of the coup against boss loader Happy Keane: "The old order under which Keane for twenty years has dealt fairly with labor and capital at the piers gives way to a new regime." Keane—a colorful and even likeable figure in his disarmingly candid fashion but one surely intimate with waterfront violence—was now virtually canonized as an exemplar of harmonious relations between capital and labor in the Irish waterfront tradition. Keane's lawyer remarked of the new leadership at Local 1247: "Their strange power seems unending and penetrates into most highest places...labor and management were always afforded equal rights in the past and we have not had labor discord." A counternarrative gradually emerged from the Kenny forces. As a delegate from Local 1247 explained when asked why the men had not complained about alleged "contract violations" committed by Keane over the years, they "would have had their brains handed to them." Kenny later alleged that Hague employed a "dock squad" under the leadership of a "Lieutenant

Fletcher" who "assaulted" any longshoremen who complained about Hague regime favoritism in pier hiring. Kenny also claimed, "It wasn't until we come into office in 1949 that a free election was held in any local union, not only the ILA, any of the A.F. of L. unions, any of the CIO unions."[31]

Covering the Jersey Front

Around the time of his ouster from Pier D, Happy Keane became friendly with a very young reporter for the *Jersey Journal,* Bob Greene, a recent graduate of Xavier High School in Chelsea, where he met Father Phil Carey at the adjoining labor school and came to admire greatly this "lovely man." It was Carey who alerted Greene to Malcolm Johnson's "Crime on the Waterfront" series for the *Sun* and urged him to pursue waterfront stories on the left bank of the Hudson. When Greene went to work as a journalist in Jersey City in 1949—for a weekly sum of $24.30—he discovered that nearly all of his colleagues in town supplemented their incomes by working for politicians. "The Jersey," as his paper was known across Hudson County, was militantly pro-Hague after a brief flirtation with reform in the late 1920s (Hague had retaliated by renaming the city's landmark Journal Square "Victory Square," but the original designation proved ineradicable). Many of the newspaper's employees remained on the organization's payroll during his nephew's tenure in office; Greene wrote press releases for Mayor Eggers and for "Regular Democrats for Clean Government."[32]

Greene quickly discovered that the same racket-ridden, shapeup-kickback system of hiring that Johnson had exposed on the West Side and in Brooklyn also held sway in Jersey City. Despite its hostility to Kenny, his newspaper was in no position to unearth a legacy of well-organized piracy on the city's bustling piers; but as Kenny's ILA faction grew more brazen in its demands, Greene dug deeply. He was soon rewarded with regular space as a columnist. As reformer Bill Keating later noted admiringly, Greene "uprooted more scandal about the Jersey docks and their scabrous politics than had been found by generations of prosecutors, cops, and newspaper men before him." Greene grew so knowledgeable that in 1950 he became the key background source for investigators from the U.S. Senate Crime Investigating Committee preparing for New York City public hearings under the leadership of Senator Estes Kefauver. The highly publicized Kefauver Committee was more interested in gambling than in the shapeup and other waterfront rackets unique to the port, but when word of Greene's expertise crossed the river, he began receiving calls for Jersey tips from Pete Corridan. They soon embarked on a close collaboration in the tradition of his work with Mike Johnson and Budd Schulberg. Bob Greene became a lifelong friend and confidant of the Jesuit: he was the first "homegrown" Irish Catholic journalistic ally to emerge from the waterfront.[33]

There was plenty of Jersey City work to keep Greene busy. On December 1, 1950, he predicted in his column that Biffo Di Lorenzo's ouster from leadership at Local 1247 was imminent. (The *New York Times* later noted Di Lorenzo's "tough manner that was regarded by many as a false front. His greatest asset was the fact that he was Yanowsky's brother-in-law," an asset permanently relinquished in July 1948.) The following day a "special election" was held at Local 1247 headquarters: Di Lorenzo and Slim Lucey were out; four rivals installed themselves as new officers. The victors promptly summoned a photographer to capture the moment of triumph for George Donahue, "Cockeyed Barney" Brown (wearing his trademark dark glasses), Armand Faugno, and Anthony "Tony Cheese" Marchitto, misidentified as "Parchitto" in both the *Jersey Journal* and the *New York Times*.[34]

On December 16, under the headline "Hate, Violence Ride High on J.C. Waterfront," Greene revealed that the "election" had been conducted not with ballots but with pistols, blackjacks, and torches. Lucey and Di Lorenzo and a third individual Greene identified simply as "Joe Palooka" were accosted by a four-man "goon squad" (subsequent congressional testimony cited five invaders, including three from the new leadership cadre of Local 1247). While one squad member chased Biffo around the local's Grand Street office, another administered "a super-duper hot foot and a brutal beating" to Lucey after Slim—a former committeeman under Kenny and the mayor's friend and neighbor—refused to open a safe containing the local's union books.[35]

Bob Greene later reported that the coup was linked to a change in the fortunes of New York mobster Albert Ackalitis, who had succeeded Charley Yanowsky as "the real power behind the Di Lorenzo gang." A former member—with Yanowsky—of the notorious Arsenal Mob, "Acky" was released from New York's Auburn State Prison in April 1948. Though forbidden by his parole arrangement from entering Jersey City, while running Pier 18 on the West Side in late 1949 and early 1950 Ackalitis regularly phoned instructions to Di Lorenzo via "a tavern on Mercer Street in Jersey City known as 'Joe the Rebel's.'" In October 1950 Ackalitis was detained for an array of parole violations and returned to prison the following month, paving the way for old school Jersey City gangland figure Morris Manna to muscle Di Lorenzo out of his lucrative post at 1247 (it was Manna who reportedly dislodged Slim Lucey's teeth with the butt of a gun). The new leadership at Local 1247 represented a semi-balanced "fusion" ticket of Irish and Italian Americans with links, Greene subsequently reported, to organized crime figures in Brooklyn and Manhattan as well as Jersey City.[36]

Members of both Jersey City factions battling for control of the local had ardently supported John Kenny in his triumphant 1949 campaign. In the wake of the violent takeover and subsequent counterattacks at 1247 Biffo Di Lorenzo "managed to get the ILA to call a special election" slated for March 5, 1951; it too was "fought out on gangster lines," Greene later noted. Three days before the election a hand grenade was tossed into the offices of 1247; the ensuing blast seriously injured three members of the faction that had recently muscled its way to control of the local. Jersey City's waterfront, that rich source of passions, cash, and ethnic grievances that fueled his landmark victory over Hague's machine, now "became a political nightmare" for Kenny.[37]

The Waterfront's Law of Physics

The very large jam in which Kenny now found himself originated in grandiose schemes concocted while he was trolling the Jersey City waterfront with Charley Yanowsky. In early 1949 Kenny buoyantly promised at least two rivals—Tony Marchitto and Yanowsky's kinsman by marriage Biffo Di Lorenzo—that they would become the business agent of Local 1247 after they helped him topple the Hague regime. As a United States senator helpfully informed Marchitto at a subsequent public hearing on waterfront crime, "You represented the law of physics—two bodies can't occupy the same space at the same time." Between Kenny's May 1949 election and the onset of the Di Lorenzo–Marchitto war over physics in winter 1950–51, New Yorkers attracted to the lucrative Hudson County shipping trade saw their Jersey opportunity and took it, with various organized crime–ILA factions bidding to conquer the Jersey City beachhead Frank Hague had militantly guarded for decades. The Irish American Bowers crew from West Side "Pistol Local" 824 vied briefly for influence over Local 1247 with fellow New York invader Anthony ("Tough Tony Bender") Strollo, a reputed capo in the Genovese crime family.[38]

Strollo had a significant advantage over his rivals from the Irish waterfront: he was a friend and associate of prominent local gangster Morris Manna. They shared a mutual friendship with Albert Anastasia of Brooklyn infamy, now comfortably ensconced in his new mansion above the Palisades in Fort Lee, attracted like Strollo and so many other New Yorkers by the quality of postwar life in suburban North Jersey. Joe Adonis was another Brooklynite drawn to the Garden State. A former Democrat turned major player in Republican Party politics in affluent Bergen County, Adonis ran a nationwide gambling operation from his "inner sanctum," the back room at Duke's Bar and Grill, an establishment on Palisade Avenue in Cliffside Park known as "one of the most closely guarded headquarters of the underworld." Duke's did not welcome a "transient" trade but provided a comfortable setting for individuals and groups ("like a roll call of New York–New Jersey mobsters" in the judgment of one investigator) with a great and growing interest in the booming waterfront trade of nearby Jersey City.[39]

They were all warmly welcomed—at first. In September 1950 Mayor Kenny instructed his commissioner of public safety that special squads dedicated to the elimination of gambling and loan-sharking on the water-front were "hurting our friends and that the best thing to do would be to get rid of them." Yet Kenny's hospitality seemed only to accelerate his slide into near irrelevance on a Hudson County waterfront that soon truly merited the venerable label "outlaw frontier." By the time the offices of Local 1247 were bombed in March 1951, the mayor sensed he might lose all that was his to claim as the conqueror of Hague's machine.[40]

The full measure of Kenny's growing desperation was revealed by his announcement, on March 6, 1951—four days after the grenade exploded on Grand Street—that Father Philip Dobson, S.J., director of St. Peter's College Institute of Industrial Relations, had agreed to chair a "Citizens' Waterfront Committee" investigating the recent violence and labor conditions on the Jersey City piers. "The committee will be independent of all factions," promised Father Dobson. "It will be objective and completely impartial." Until that moment Dobson had assiduously avoided public engagement with local controversies, preferring to host periodic incursions from across the Hudson by Pete Corridan. The initial local response was highly favorable to Father Dobson, less so to the mayor: "Mr. Kenny thinks he can hide behind the clergy," charged the *Jersey Journal*. "But Father Dobson's is a free mind, and he will seek facts."[41]

The gambit quickly backfired in most spectacular fashion. Three days after accepting Mayor Kenny's invitation, Dobson resigned from the committee without explanation beyond an admission that he found it "impossible to serve." Two years later Kenny accurately if tersely informed a U.S. Senate subcommittee that the priest had bowed out "because of some ecclesiastical situation." Though no official explanation was ever proffered, it is more than reasonable to conclude that the time for a Jesuit or any local priest to tackle issues of waterfront crime in Jersey City publicly had not yet arrived. In the wake of Dobson's announcement a pro-Kenny political sheet, the *Jersey Free Press*, reported, "Ugly rumors have been bruited about[,] . . . rumors of such a nature that they can only do damage where ever they are heard." Jersey City was in fact abuzz with speculation in March 1951, much of it rooted in widespread suspicion that remnants of Frank Hague's machine, clerical department, saw to it that the time-honored Irish waterfront division of labors spiritual from temporal—and evidence of its long history in local practice—would remain undisturbed.[42]

Kenny's powerful local priestly champion, Father LeRoy McWilliams, pastor of St. Michael's parish in the Horseshoe, remained silent during the crisis over Local 1247 despite having been appointed by Kenny to the coveted post of Jersey City fire chaplain. Hague-era Irish Catholic tribalism remained a mighty spiritual and political remnant no ethnic "fusionist"—or sympathetic pastor, or Jesuit labor priest—could surmount. Kenny found no solace among the Irish waterfront's multitude of theologians, self-styled or ordained. The Citizens' Waterfront Committee never materialized: 1952 found Father Philip Dobson safely removed to Buffalo, where he served as rector of the Jesuit community at Canisius College.[43]

Two years of Jersey momentum gathering around Pete Corridan's waterfront crusade was suddenly halted. The hardened waterfront realist's argument—that outside interference in the balance of nature produced only disorder—was seemingly borne out in the Dobson affair. To help restore right order, King Joe Ryan now intervened amid warring factions of obscure New Jerseyans. Demonstrating his own newfound brand of pragmatic fusion politics, Ryan named Tony Marchitto trustee of Local 1247 then tossed "Tony Cheese" the additional charter for the dormant Local 1487, Charley Yanowsky's old Marine and Warehousemen's outfit, given new life just in time to handle the immense volume of work the U.S. Army brought to Jersey City's Claremont Terminal when it opened in July 1951.[44]

An enormous warehouse pier jutting far into the harbor near the Greenville neighborhood south of the downtown waterfront, Claremont was close to the site of the Black Tom disaster, which saw a munitions warehouse containing more than one thousand tons of TNT and other explosives blow up on July 30, 1916, possibly the handiwork of pro-German saboteurs. The Claremont Terminal was transformed by the Army Corps of Engineers into a massive depot for post–Marshall Plan shipments to European allies and American military installations overseas. After the Dade Brothers stevedoring firm won the lucrative contract to handle the pier's loading operations, Marchitto assumed the role Kenny himself had once enjoyed, doling out jobs to supplicants bearing notes they proffered to Tony Cheese like passports to his Claremont empire. So many job seekers found work there "they sometimes fell over each other in the performance of their new duties," as Bob Greene reported at the time. A chastened Mayor Kenny soon saw the light and repaired his working relationship with the union leaders. The interlocking forces of church, state, and labor on the waterfront were restored to their natural if no longer strictly Hibernian order, as revealed in a note on Mayor Kenny's letterhead, sent from Deputy Mayor William J. Flanagan to a local priest:

Father:

Have the gent from Bayonne [Kenny, like Hague before him, bossed all of Hudson County] meet Mr. Marchitto on the corner of Princeton Ave. and Linden tomorrow morning at 7:30. He need not be skilled but must carry his own hammer and saw with him. Mr. Marchitto is tall, Italian, and has a dark complexion and very little hair. He is about 40.

Yours,
Bill[45]

Soon the operation at Claremont "proved so lucrative that the New York mob, led by the Strollo brothers, took control. Anthony Strollo's brother,

Dominick, gained the upper hand and forced many Jersey City workers off the pier. Strikes, fights, and disorder ensued." John "Duke" DeNoia, front man of Duke's Bar and Grill, was installed as night hiring boss; the waterfront neophyte presided sporting shiny dress shoes and a dapper business suit before shippers demanded his ouster after three days, when he was promptly replaced by fellow newcomer Dominick Strollo. The vast freight terminal and environs blossomed into a wide-open country: a casino soon operated around the clock from a refitted boxcar; loan-sharking and horse-booking flourished nearby with all their attendant social consequences.[46]

Facing the ex–New Yorkers' brazen disregard for his patronage requirements, and with Tony Cheese Marchitto complicit in the new leadership, Kenny had yet another falling out with Marchitto over favors unperformed for a reputed organized crime figure linked to the bombing of Local 1247. Finally in the winter of 1952, as a waterfront informant later testified, "this here whole tieup...between politics and gangsters down on the waterfront" unraveled completely. Constituents bearing letters with Kenny's signature—including those sent by parish priests—were no longer welcome at the Claremont Terminal. When the mayor was briefly hospitalized for "pneumonia and phlebitis," wrote Jersey City memoirist Helene Stapinski, "word on the street was that the Mob had given Kenny a bullet in the ass."[47]

Backed against the wall, Mayor Kenny finally concluded that his last best hope was to don the mantle of anti-crime crusader. On March 6, 1952, he boldly proclaimed, "We want no branch of Murder, Incorporated, established here in Jersey City." Kenny then released a list of "undesirables" who would be barred from work on the piers of his city. When his waterfront squad sought to oust Dominic Strollo as night hiring boss because of his alleged ties to New York gangland figures, a wildcat strike was organized and Strollo was quickly reinstated. Victim of the new order he helped create, John V. Kenny knew that Joe Ryan could not cover the waterfront on his behalf, especially since nearly everyone on the mayor's list of undesirables was allied with a newly emerging Ryan-Marchitto trans-Hudson ILA entente.[48]

The mayor turned instead to a popular and very well connected local entertainer, Phil Regan, a Brooklyn-born Irish tenor known as the "singing cop," a nod to his previous career in law enforcement. Regan's performing talent was discovered when he joined the fun at a vaudeville party under his watch; he went on to perform in films and radio in the late 1930s and 1940s. With friends including Newark's leading gangster Abner "Longy" Zwillman, the singing cop managed to fix a meeting across the Hudson between Kenny and Anthony Strollo. On March 14, 1952, after first attending "a church affair" held at a public high school in Jersey City, Mayor Kenny enjoyed a night at the fights across the river followed by a conspicuous appearance at Toots Shor's saloon awaiting a prearranged signal. As midnight approached, the visiting mayor was observed by alert New York City detectives as he entered the Warwick Hotel (where Regan kept an apartment) in midtown Manhattan. Three minutes later Anthony "Tony Bender" Strollo ("holding a handkerchief to his face") arrived for his scheduled sit-down with Jersey City's mayor.[49]

Strollo's current Bergen County mailing address notwithstanding, to Kenny he was the gentleman from New York with whom the mayor now pleaded to bestow labor peace on the waterfront community where Kenny had spent his entire life and whence Frank Hague had routinely deported such "undesirables" as Strollo back to Gotham. After Manhattan district attorney Frank Hogan leaked news of the meeting in April 1952 (Hogan called it "a shocking instance of abject dependence of duly constituted civil authority upon the underworld to obtain peace on the waterfront"), Kenny retorted that the get-together with Strollo had inspired him to launch "all-out war on racketeers in Jersey City, particularly along the waterfront."[50]

No one bought the story. Most revealingly Kenny got nowhere by making the wholly plausible claim—while brandishing a photograph depicting Frank Hague, Cockeye Barney Brown, and Joe Ryan enjoying a light moment together—that "if there is anything wrong on the docks of Jersey City, it started" under his predecessor's regime. Tales of Hague only further enraged Jersey citizens: never again would a Hudson County political figure blend moral and religious authority, violence, and thievery in that primal Boss's seamless fashion. Kenny retreated from the mayoralty in 1953, settling for countywide powerbroker status and its attendant perquisites in swag. By then the army had already abandoned Claremont Terminal for the simpler waterfront lifestyle of Norfolk, Virginia. Tony Cheese Marchitto periodically backed anti-Kenny reform slates and was touted as a potential successor to Joe Ryan as president of the International. Anthony Strollo would vanish without a trace in 1962.[51]

Although John V. Kenny remained a wily and resourceful Democratic leader of Hudson County—extremely fortunate in the caliber of his enemies—his influence gradually waned in one of the most protracted denouements of any urban potentate's career. He ungraciously took Jersey City along for the downward ride. "Public services practically collapsed. Uncollected garbage lay in festering heaps," and by the 1960s the loss of Hudson County's once indomitable statewide political clout was palpable. The "Little Guy," always more personable than Frank Hague and far less militant, was finally indicted on charges of tax evasion in 1972, pled guilty on six counts, and served time in federal prison before dying in a Paramus, New Jersey, nursing home at age eighty-two in 1975. That same year, a young Irish-Italian Catholic rock 'n' roller from Kenny's beloved Monmouth County seashore released *Born to Run,* the breakthrough album for a Jersey-bred "Boss" of a different social order, Bruce Springsteen. The disc's most haunting song—especially for Jerseyans—indelibly conveyed the desperation of those driven by circumstance to risk everything in a fateful "Meeting across the River."[52]

10 *Priest and Worker*

At three o'clock on the morning of October 29, 1951, the Associated Press office in Manhattan received a call from Father Pete Corridan, informing the A.P. that he planned to make a 6 A.M. visit to the dockside meeting rooms of ILA Local 791, a stronghold in the wildcat strike that had begun fifteen days earlier on the Chelsea piers. The strike spread quickly across the port. The A.P., as Corridan expected, promptly notified all seven of the city's daily newspapers of his visit. Corridan's dramatic appearance at 164 Eleventh Avenue was reported in the evening editions of the *New York Post,* the *Journal-American,* the *Daily Mirror* and the *World-Telegram and Sun,* which described the scene as akin to "soldiers praying before entering battle." Corridan "told the men he had joined them at the meeting 'to give the lie to charges that Communists are invading the union.'" Though the visit was interpreted as a gesture in support of the strike, Corridan never explicitly endorsed the work stoppage and had in fact counseled against it. He "led the men in prayers," reported the *Journal-American,* "including this one: 'God grant that our government may order us back to work in honor. May God protect each and every one of us this day.'"[1]

While the visit with the men of Local 791 reconfirmed Corridan's public identity as the "waterfront priest," the event marked his one and only appearance in a pastoral capacity on or near the West Side piers. Corridan's bluntly phrased prayer highlighted his conviction that democratic unionism and human dignity on the waterfront could be established only through government intervention at the local, state, and federal levels. In publicly deriding the anticommunist reflex that had served Joe Ryan so well during prior challenges to his leadership, Corridan undermined a foundation of postwar urban Catholicism and signaled a new reform ethos. Even as his public stature grew, however, Corridan faced growing resistance from within the Irish waterfront and inside his own church. Two private meetings with extremely powerful figures, the first at the height of the strike, the second on Good Friday 1952, confirmed both his stature as a major waterfront player and his deep vulnerability.

The Strike and the Spin

For all the rhetorical beatings he had taken since autumn 1945, Joe Ryan appeared none the worse for wear as he presided over the ILA convention at New York's Commodore Hotel in July 1951. After accepting lavish praise from leaders of the American Federation of Labor and high-ranking political figures from New York and Washington, Ryan gaveled the festivities to a close, but not before passing his hat to raise money for a delegate who had just lost his wallet. "It is my hat," Ryan sang, "and I am proud to wear it! Any man respects that hat, he can show it. For, you know, my boys, I am Irish like the Old High Hat!" This was to be the Chelsea Irishman's final presidential appearance at an ILA convention, his downfall hastened by the rank and file at his own beloved Irish Mother Local.[2]

The October 1951 strike began, wrote Corridan in a January 1952 memorandum, "as all strikes on the waterfront do, in the Chelsea area, Local 791." At the July convention the men of 791 had "presented an elaborate set of demands" to the ILA Wage Scale Committee (including the reduction of shapeups to one per day) while sponsoring a motion affirming Ryan's tenure as "life president" of the union. The resolution, adopted unanimously at the convention, lauded Ryan's "successful campaign against the Communists who sought to invade the East Coast waterfront." On this issue there was no debate at 791, but on other fronts, as labor historian Vernon Jensen understated the case, "the Chelsea local was beset by perennial factionalism under the surface."[3]

In early October the shippers and Ryan's ludicrous 125-member wage scale committee worked out a new contract calling for a once-daily shapeup but failed to meet other demands made by Local 791 in July. The deal was approved in voting by locals in the "out ports" of the Atlantic Coast District and by a smaller margin in the Port of New York, but a majority in the Irish waterfront locals with a semblance of democratic procedure (791, 895, and 1124) voted no. The anti-Ryan faction in 791 refused to shape up on October 15 and was immediately supported by the local's business agent, Gene Sampson, whose hesitancy during previous conflicts had proved costly to his leadership aspirations. Sampson later asserted, "Our men went out because they felt that the contract negotiated by the wage scale committee did not fit into what they thought they were entitled to."[4]

The series of wildcat strikes that broke out in the port beginning in 1945 has baffled labor historians because the intensity of rank-and-file discontent with Ryan was never matched by a sustained effort to oust him. A successful coup could have originated only on the Irish waterfront, since the men there were suspicious of union insurgents from other precincts. But the hierarchical worldview that had prevailed since the late nineteenth century, and the tradition of grudging deference accorded established authority, was not easily supplanted. In the very early days of the 1951 strike Corridan's ally Johnny Dwyer, the hero of Local 895's 1946 campaign to reopen Pier 45 in the West Village, paid a visit to Ryan to register his complaint about the ratification process. King Joe reportedly told Dwyer, "You get a majority and I'll lead you." Dwyer later insisted that he went out and did just that but "came back to Ryan's office, only to have Ryan say, 'I don't listen to no minority group.'" Dwyer joined Sampson as strike leader but shared his partner's reluctance to launch an all-out challenge to Ryan's presidency; the "loyal opposition" was as militantly anticommunist as its life president. Ryan's plaint that "they have no leader I can deal with" may have been, as historian Colin Davis claimed, a "subtle snub to Gene Sampson," but it also highlighted the reluctance of West Side Irish insurgents to topple King Joe once and for all.[5]

On October 16 Ryan conceded that the West Side strikers were "honest dock workers with sincere grievances." He knew enough not to Redbait his own neighborhood. As the strike quickly spread throughout the port, however, Ryan lashed out at dockworkers from other neighborhoods. Dissidents in Brooklyn were "strictly Communist-inspired" and linked to "strong-arm squads" sent in by Harry Bridges to foment rebellion. Ryan promised to dispatch his own supporters from the West Side to "meet fire with fire. We're not looking for trouble but if that's what they want they'll get it." The phalanx never materialized, and the only organized resistance to the strike in Brooklyn came from figures such as the borough's ILA kingpin Anthony "Tough Tony" Anastasio and Paul Hall, vice president of the Seafarers International Union, neither of whose motives matched Joe Ryan's self-interest.[6]

When Anastasio attempted to keep the piers open at a Brooklyn army base on October 17, striking hatch boss Salvatore Brocco shouted, "Anyone who calls us Commies is a damn liar." The strike spread to Hudson County on October 22. Sampson, belatedly seeking port-wide support, led a convoy of fifty automobiles laden with New York dockworkers to the Jersey side to promote a united front. Apart from the Claremont Terminal, where hiring boss Tony Marchitto was beholden to Ryan for supporting his takeover of Locals 1247 and 1478, the Hudson County waterfront was soon shut down tight.[7]

There was no chance that Ryan could spin this strike to his own advantage. Four years of diligent work by Pete Corridan cultivating links to journalists were repaid handsomely in coverage of the 1951 strike. This time around the Jesuit shaped the narrative as it unfolded. Editorial writers weighed in fervidly on behalf of reform. Just one day into the job action the *New York Times* called for "official handling" of dockside corruption: "Whether it is initiated by Governor [Thomas E.] Dewey or by the proper Congressional committees may not be too important so long as the uncompleted job is tackled in a purposeful, crusading spirit by capable, fearless men who will not be turned aside by threats, political or otherwise." The *Brooklyn Eagle* joined the *Times* in calling for government intervention. The *World-Telegram and Sun* went further, imploring Dewey to appoint a special deputy attorney general to investigate the "veritable network of evil influence" on the waterfront.[8]

The persistent journalistic focus on governmental remedies neutralized the traditional anticommunist angle of strike reporting, with only the *New York Mirror* and the *Herald-Tribune* falling for Ryan's tactics in the early going. It was the visceral anticommunism of the rank and file, not the leadership, that was highlighted in much of the coverage, preempting Ryan's Red-baiting options. The *Brooklyn Eagle's* November 1 edition pictured a group of strikers from ILA Local 808 dumping "unwanted cases of canned goods in front of headquarters at 5012 3rd Ave. They claimed United Labor Action Committee, which donated food, is pro-Communist." Corridan took much of the credit for this journalistic coup, explaining that when "the party tried to louse up the men by organizing phony food drives for strikers outside some of the supermarkets," in Brooklyn "our men dumped the food into the Gowanus Canal, even though some of their families could have used it." He credited Dick Roth of the *Eagle* for helping to "discount this communist angle almost completely." Other journalistic allies placed responsibility for the strike squarely on the shoulders of the ILA's suddenly hapless-looking life president. "Ryan is finished," Murray Kempton reported in the *Post* on October 22.[9]

This working alliance of journalists and civic reformers increasingly touted Corridan as the lone "public" figure offering real solutions. On October 26, 1951, in the sixth installment of yet another waterfront exposé coinciding with an unauthorized strike, *Journal-American* labor reporter Guy Richards explicitly linked the Jesuit's work with the growing clamor for congressional intervention: "such a Federal airing of the port," remarked Richards, "has been proposed by a man who has done as much as anyone in New York to encourage the dockmen to clean up their own house—the Rev. John M. Corridan, 40-year-old 'waterfront priest.'"[10]

Richards also cited excerpts from an August 16, 1951, *CBS Reports* radio documentary, "Crime on the Waterfront." The broadcast was the most sensational installment of *Nation's Nightmare,* a six-part series on organized crime. "Crime on the Waterfront" provided listeners with a guided tour of the port, exposing alleged criminal factions that ruled the piers on the West Side and in Brooklyn as well as the Lower East Side, Staten Island, Jersey City, and Hoboken. The Peabody Award–winning documentary was reported by a team "who gathered the information at the risk of their lives," Richards noted. The broadcast also drew heavily on material gathered by the New York City Anti-Crime Committee.[11]

The NYCACC was an important new component of the Corridan alliance, blurring the boundaries between a civic reform group and a public relations vehicle. A privately funded nongovernmental body of "prominent, civic-minded citizens" headed by Spruille Braden, the patrician former U.S. ambassador to Argentina, the committee was founded in early 1951 after Senate hearings chaired by Tennessee Democrat Estes Kefauver uncovered rampant infiltration by gangsters "into more than 100 different types of legitimate businesses," including many in the New York area. In that same year a National Association of Citizens' Crime Commissions was established. As historian Lee Bernstein has explained, citizens' crime committees—often rooted in short-lived anticrime initiatives dating back to the 1920s—sought in the postwar era to "transform the state-sponsored activity of law enforcement into popular police actions." Bernstein argued that in a time of grave concern over "proper acts of citizenship," these committees were anticrime analogues to Civil Defense drills and other forms of Cold War vigilance. In the case of crime committees, "Un-Americanism" was often associated with urban ethnic criminality, and the watchdogs tended to be politically well connected and socially impeccable reformers like Braden.[12]

Although the Kefauver hearings "brushed but lightly on the subject of the New York waterfront," the Senate committee's report charged in passing that the ILA was "infested with hoodlums." Braden knew that his fledgling organization would need to move quickly on the waterfront. In April 1951 NYCACC chief of staff James D. Walsh hired as council Manhattan assistant district attorney Bill Keating, of Cockeye Dunn prosecution fame. Keating brought some badly needed street credibility to the new agency. Despite being dismissive of "societies for the suppression-of-something-or-other," he was persuaded to enlist in this reform cause by Walsh, an ex-cop, former prosecutor, and most recently special counsel to the Kefauver Committee.[13]

Keating "mobilized his network of street-level contacts: his many "longshore friends felt more secure about talking to me now that I was not the man behind the cop." The new job brought another benefit: "I was now able to deal freely with Father John M. Corridan, the vigorous Jesuit waterfront priest." In his memoir Keating noted that in 1948 Malcolm Johnson "had urged us to get together, but we couldn't. If the priests [Carey and Corridan] had been seen consorting with an assistant district attorney, underworld Paul Reveres would have assured the port that they were 'ratting to the cops.'" With Keating now working outside of official law enforcement circles, "Fathers Carey and Corridan and I were able to become fellow conspirators and close friends."[14]

Bob Greene of the *Jersey Journal* was hired by NYCACC at Corridan's strong urging in late 1951. Keating was highly impressed by Greene's "brief but brilliant career" investigating waterfront crime for the Hudson County daily. Greene had been the primary investigator on the Jersey side for the hard-hitting *CBS Reports* documentary; his connections on both sides of the river enabled Greene to assess port criminality from the broadest perspective, a viewpoint Corridan promoted even as he struggled to overcome his own residual parochialism. At NYCACC Greene worked closely with chief investigator John M. O'Mara, a former FBI agent. The Anti-Crime Committee may have looked from the outside like a plaything of upperclass do-gooders, but it was in fact driven by a team of urban Irish Catholics always pleased when the waterfront priest paid a visit to their midtown office.[15]

At the height of the October 1951 strike Keating "suggested to Braden that it would be appropriate to issue a statement explaining the origins of the strike and its basic issues." Joe Ryan and the leaders of the strike committee—Gene Sampson of Local 791 and Johnny Dwyer of Local 895 in the West Village—had recently sent dueling telegrams to President Truman: the strikers offered a return to work in exchange for an investigation of rank-and-file grievances, while Ryan promised that the purportedly Red-led walkout would soon be ended. "We'll go through them and over them," he told reporters, "but never around them."[16]

With a threat of imminent bloodshed looming over the waterfront (see figure 7), Pete Corridan joined Keating at Spruille Braden's home late on the evening of October 28, where they worked into the early hours of the morning on drafts of a telegram from Braden, in his capacity as head of NYCACC, to Governor Dewey. The erstwhile crime-busting prosecutor was urged to take action against ILA "mobsters" and "inefficiency, crime, and political corruption" on the waterfront. Braden put the shapeup at the heart of waterfront evils and quoted a familiar statement by Corridan, who "has a long and intimate knowledge of waterfront conditions": "Every American is opposed to Communism, but it is conditions such as prevail along the docks that promote the cause of Communism." Braden's telegram was prominently reported on the front pages of the *Times* and the *Herald Tribune*.[17]

It was during this session that Corridan decided to visit the meeting rooms of Local 791 early the following morning. The public had to be shown, he told Keating, "that Ryan and his backers are liars and thieves. I'm going to try something. I'm going to go down to strike headquarters at six o'clock in the morning and pray with the men, publicly." He added: "I've already told the Associated Press. If some pictures are published, it might help." Arthur Brown and others "had told their fellow rebels that they should stand by because Father John was coming." There were roughly three hundred men present in the room to greet him. They repeated after Corridan, "phrase by phrase," his prayer that the government "may order us back to work in

Figure 7. "Striking longshoremen surge against police at Pier 90, West 50th Street, as cops block them out to let nonstriking longshoremen make their end run onto picketed pier." *New York World-Telegram and Sun*, October 29, 1951. Courtesy of the Archives of the Xavier Institute of Industrial Relations, Fordham University Library, Bronx, New York.

dignity." The men's unyielding resistance to photojournalists seeking pictures could not dampen the ecstatic reaction by the New York media to Corridan's dramatic gesture. The *Daily Mirror*—after initially blaming West Coast leftist Harry Bridges for the strike—now proclaimed that Ryan's "anguished cry of communism" had been answered by "a soft-spoken, earnest Catholic priest, who leads the insurgents in prayer. Whatever happens this week, Joe Ryan is through." The *Brooklyn Eagle* declared on October 31:

> On all scores, action on the part of the Federal, the State, and the City government is called for.... The authorities—State, Federal, and local—have an obligation to tell the public the facts and to state openly what measures they propose to take in order to remedy the situation. Away with the "Shapeup!" Away with the kickback! Away with the loan sharks![18]

"The political climate changed so swiftly" after Corridan's dramatic gesture, according to Bill Keating, that "the violence was called off." Once

President Truman chose not to invoke Taft-Hartley's strike-ending provisions and a negotiated settlement proved impossible, Governor Dewey declared a state of emergency on November 2. New York State industrial commissioner Edward Corsi immediately appointed a three-member board of inquiry armed with subpoena powers and a charge to investigate the root causes of the dispute. Meanwhile steamship companies in New Jersey won an injunction against the roving New York invaders who had fomented strike support across the Hudson. With growing numbers of men anxious to get back to work before the holiday season—and a widening split in Local 791 between pro- and anti-Sampson forces—the strike committee agreed to end the walkout on November 9, day twenty-five, in hopes of focusing public attention on the ILA's unsavory electoral practices.[19]

A November 10 headline in the *World-Telegram and Sun* reflected the rank and file's new militancy: "Dockmen Back Seething with Hatred of Ryan." A "big, tough-looking" returning longshoreman helping to load a cargo of caskets onboard a freighter remarked, "If that cargo was going up to Ryan's office, I'd deliver it free." Prior to the 1951 strike Corridan and other reformers had hoped the ILA would clean its own house, end the shapeup, and come to resemble a democratic union. For the first time a critical mass of the rank and file was poised to effect real change just at the moment when Corridan's growing faith in state intervention and moral suasion generated through collaboration with outsiders had moved him further off the waterfront. The quintessential Irish American question—who do you think you are?—now assumed more than rhetorical significance for the waterfront priest.[20]

A Call from the Powerhouse

Governor Dewey's appointment of a citizen fact-finding board charged to investigate the strike was yet another personal triumph for Corridan, but there was no time to celebrate. On November 4, 1951, a Sunday afternoon, he was summoned to Cardinal Spellman's midtown Manhattan residence at the end of an extraordinary week that had begun with the prayer meeting at Local 791. Monsignor John J. O'Donnell of Guardian Angel church had leveled shocking accusations against Corridan. The Jesuit, O'Donnell alleged in a complaint made directly to Spellman, had exchanged fisticuffs with rival dockworkers while posing as a West Side longshoreman and instigated the current strike. At a hastily arranged Sunday morning meeting attended by O'Donnell and John J. McMahon, provincial of the New York Jesuits, the cardinal granted McMahon's request that Corridan be given the opportunity to defend himself in person later that afternoon. When Monsignor O'Donnell—who regularly touted his close ties to Spellman—protested that an important appointment would prevent him from returning later in the day, the visibly displeased prelate invited Father McMahon to accompany Philip Carey and Corridan to his residence despite the accuser's absence.[21]

This was church business of a most serious kind. McMahon was in Syracuse conducting his annual "visitation" of the Jesuit community at Le Moyne College when Spellman's urgent request that he come to New York was relayed to him by Carey. McMahon then called Carey's predecessor at Xavier, Joseph Fitzpatrick, S.J., and ominously predicted, "I think the Cardinal is going to tell them to get out" of the waterfront apostolate. Carey and Corridan were technically priests of the Jesuit's New York province, not the Archdiocese of New York, but the distinction meant little in the face of an explosive situation touching so many powerful figures in the archdiocese.[22]

Spellman enjoyed a warm and lengthy relationship with the New York Jesuits. A 1911 graduate of Fordham University, the cardinal was on the receiving end decades later of an exceedingly flattering authorized biography penned by the longtime president of his alma mater, the Jesuit Robert I. Gannon. John McMahon, S.J., a West Side product of St. Michael's parish—which straddled the somewhat indeterminate boundary between Chelsea and Hell's Kitchen—began his priestly training at the archdiocesan seminary at Dunwoodie in Yonkers before transferring to the Jesuits, an unusual career trajectory that afforded him exceptionally close ties with local church officials. His brother Thomas was a New York archdiocesan priest. Phil Carey referred to John McMahon as "Dunwoodie's greatest gift to us."[23]

During the meeting at Spellman's residence, Corridan explained to the cardinal (after denying that he had worked on the docks) that he initially opposed the strike but soon concluded that the men were justified in their rebellion against inhumane conditions and exploitation. He told Spellman that his prayer at Local 791 reflected a conviction that only a federal mandate could prevent the desperate men from "crawling on their bellies in front of a victory of the mob element within the port," a result that he, "as a priest," hoped to prevent. Corridan claimed that the men were so desperate two weeks into the strike, they would have welcomed Truman's invocation of the hated Taft-Hartley Act.[24]

Both extant firsthand accounts of the meeting—a 1987 letter from Carey to a New York priest and Corridan's version, presented in Allen Raymond's 1955 book *Waterfront Priest*—described Spellman as cordial and genuinely concerned with the welfare of the longshoremen. According to Carey, Spellman "asked no questions. He did say 'If you think there is something I ought to know, you know how to get into touch with me.'"[25]

"I was very proud of you and Father Carey on Sunday at our meeting with the Cardinal," Father McMahon wrote to Corridan on November 6. "It is clear that His Eminence values highly your opinions since he immediately assented to my suggestion that you and Father Carey be called in to advise him on the question—could he do anything to settle the Dock

Strike?" McMahon suggested that "you and Father Carey send a special delivery letter marked personal to His Eminence from time to time when you come across some fact or item of information that is important.... You heard his request that he be kept informed." Corridan would take that invitation to the bank, describing himself ever after as Spellman's adviser on waterfront affairs. McMahon concluded by urging "the need of great prudence in your activities and conversations. Before any major step consult the Local Superior."[26]

Carey could have told the provincial that prudence and Corridan did not readily mix. As he reminded a New York priest decades later, "in the beginning Pete told me what he was going to do but he sensed that any caution (no matter how kindly it was to be given) was interference." Over time Carey expended much of his considerable spiritual authority in quiet diplomacy on behalf of his junior partner. John McMahon, for his part, showed remarkable courage in supporting the volatile Corridan. The bottom line was that both he and Phil Carey believed that the waterfront priest's work advanced the cause of social justice to which all three men were committed by vocation and temperament. "You will never know the depth of my gratitude to Almighty God in sending us courageous superiors," Carey later wrote to a friend after McMahon had reaffirmed his solidarity with their cause. "The Provincial replied[,] 'well what are we in business for' and supports us at every possible way."[27]

The cordial meeting between the Jesuits and Spellman also reflected a significant shift in the slowly simmering rivalry between the Jesuit labor apostolate and the Association of Catholic Trade Unionists. In 1949 Spellman had suspended the $3,000 annual stipend he provided to the ACTU's New York chapter after the group supported a strike of gravediggers at the archdiocese's Calvary Cemetery in the winter of that year. Spellman initially tried to crush the strike—which started at Calvary in Queens in January, then spread a month later to another archdiocesan cemetery in Westchester County—in the Red-baiting tradition of Joe Ryan, condemning it as "an anti-American, anti-Christian evil and a strike against the church." When rhetoric failed, Spellman made scabs of future priests; on March 3 he "led seminarians in sweat shirts and dungarees through the picket line at Calvary Cemetery" to bury the dead. The ACTU did not share the enthusiasm later expressed by Spellman's Jesuit biographer for the Cardinal's actions ("a dramatic and courageous step"). The organization provided legal counsel to the strikers, infuriating Spellman and effectively ending the labor apostolate of Father John Monaghan, the ACTU's longtime New York chaplain, who now found himself castigated by "the American Pope."[28]

Philip Carey remarked at the time that although Spellman may have been right, he certainly did not *appear* to be right by antagonizing the strikers and working people throughout the city. Even this highly equivocal comment reportedly earned Carey a trip to the chancery office to explain his remarks, which were a far cry from the ACTU's advocacy position and may have reflected Carey's enduring suspicion of New York labor organizations—including those dominated by Catholics—over which he enjoyed little influence. (Carey later "blamed the fiasco on the bad advice that Spellman received from 'two thick Dutchmen,'" the Red-baiting cemetery director and the diocesan attorney, who both happened to be German American.) After 1949 Spellman wanted no part of the ACTU, even as the group intensified the militancy of its anticommunism to match his own. By contrast, Pete Corridan's cordial meeting with Spellman solidified his identity as the "waterfront priest," permanently ending claims to a comparable title by any archdiocesan clerics associated with ACTU.[29]

Priest or Worker?

"Within 48 hours a grapevine of information and conjecture about what happened in that meeting spread," wrote Allen Raymond in *Waterfront Priest*, a book virtually co-authored by Corridan. It was during this period that the Jesuit began occasionally to appear unannounced at New York's City Hall and other venues, where his presence would send reporters and assorted hangers-on scurrying for tips and gossip. Corridan was now a bona fide local waterfront celebrity, yet he was more vulnerable than ever to a most pertinent question: Just what *did* he do and on whose behalf? The job description for Jesuit labor priests remained highly fluid. By 1951 Corridan rarely taught courses at Xavier, preferring to meet informally with dockworkers at their homes or in the parish complex on West Sixteenth Street. He celebrated occasional Masses at Xavier but was not a full-time member of the parish's clerical staff. The labor school was his first and only assignment since his ordination, and as such it was the locus of his apostolic work even as it increasingly functioned as cover for his waterfront advocacy.[30]

Corridan's narrative of his own mission was clear enough. As he would explain in a 1954 interview, "from 1946 to 1951 I spent about half of my time on the waterfront problem; from 1951 on full time." He described his role as

> adviser to many groups and interests in the harbor. I became in effect a clearing house and a co-ordinator and still keep the confidence of all. As a collector of waterfront data I became a prime source for communication media. As a non-committed individual in a disinterested position I could do what none of the principals or groups or individuals could do because of constraining circumstances, namely, continually expose the nature of the problem and its consequences before every kind of forum throughout the states of New York and New Jersey and over radio and TV.

He acknowledged that priests with an interest in the waterfront had existed "before me. Unfortunately either because circumstances were not ripe, or because they could only handle the problem on a part-time basis, or because they couldn't stick with it for the duration, they could only achieve temporary results." Asked to describe his role as a representative of the church, Corridan replied: "The Church approves the work of the Institute in general. The Order to which I belong, approves my general assignment." He further asserted, "In 1951 the Cardinal asked me to be his adviser in waterfront matters where they concerned the Church." He conceded that "there is naturally some diversity of opinions which militates against unanimity of action but nothing of any importance. The vast majority of priests are definitely sympathetic to what is being attempted."[31]

Corridan's vocation was rooted in the living tradition of work performed for the greater glory of God. In 1956 the patrician Jesuit John LaFarge would produce *A Report on the American Jesuits,* a handsome volume published by Farrar, Straus and Cudahy designed to introduce the Ignatian charism to a wide array of readers beyond the Catholic subculture. Striking photographs by the renowned Margaret Bourke-White depicted American Jesuits working as astronomers, seismologists, and flight instructors in addition to their more familiar roles as college teachers and missionaries. LaFarge's chapter "Jesuit Activities" opened with a detailed treatment of the labor schools, accompanied by dramatic if carefully staged photos by Bourke-White of Philadelphia's waterfront priest, Denis Comey, S.J., gesticulating to a group of longshoremen and "descending into ship's hold to inspect controversial cargo." (Comey, like Phil Carey, served occasionally as a labor mediator, a calling not congenial to Pete Corridan's temperament.) LaFarge lauded those Jesuits who "have found themselves carried beyond the classroom into the push and pull of the labor man's struggle." Though Corridan's waterfront apostolate had effectively ended by the time LaFarge wrote his book, he was credited with developing "a behind-the-scenes power and knowledge which no one else can duplicate."[32]

LaFarge and Bourke-White captured the Jesuit mystique at the height of its power in North America. But if the labor priests embodied that certain "holy recklessness" LaFarge identified as the source of the order's unique sense of mission, there remained in the early 1950s a sharp distinction between *apostolic* work and *work* as it was commonly understood in industrialized nations. This was a highly charged issue. As Corridan and his confreres well knew, the church in France was then in the latter stages of a deeply controversial experiment with "worker-priests," in which more than one hundred members of the clergy toiled alongside industrial laborers, sharing their suffering and hope. The worker-priest movement was authorized in a bold if not quixotic effort to salvage a role for the church among the overwhelmingly disaffected French urban proletariat. Adapting the Catholic Action model of the 1920s, whereby apostolic activists served as the "leaven in the lump" of secular society, the worker-priests sought, as historian Oscar L. Arnal put it, to offer a "living paradigm of liberation praxis in the heartland of the industrial west."[33]

Many of the worker-priests toiled in factories, but the first and best known was Father Jacques Loew, the "docker-priest" of Marseilles. Loew believed that it was "no good wasting time on paper theories: the thing to do was to buy some overalls on the old-clothes market, get a job like everyone else, and then, at the end of the day's work, go off and live with the very dregs of the population—the dockers on the port." In other words, Loew explained, "dungarees, manual labor—prerequisites for the rediscovery and rescue of man." Though he viewed Marxism with suspicion, Loew readily conceded that "class struggle was an historic fact." Most worker-priests joined the Confédération générale du travail—the communist-dominated union—rather than its Christian-oriented Confédération Française des Travailleurs Chrétiens counterpart because the former enjoyed much greater support from the industrial rank and file. Some priests not only engaged in strike activity but also became union organizers and strike leaders.[34]

The worker-priest movement earned exceptionally positive notice in the American Catholic press. The "heroism of the worker-priest" was celebrated by *Commonweal* in 1949, but expressions of admiration were not limited to liberal publications: *America,* the *Catholic World,* and even the rabidly anticommunist *Brooklyn Tablet,* a diocesan organ, treated the movement with respect; the worker-priests earned favorable coverage in publications ranging from the *New Yorker* to the *Newark Italian Tribune.*[35]

In the winter of 1951 worker-priest Michel Favreau was crushed under a ton of wood on a Bordeaux pier. "Through his death," wrote Arnal, "the worker-priests had joined what they considered the ranks of the working class martyrs." Over time, however, "hostilities grew" between the Vatican and the worker-priests, with France's bishops caught in the middle; while many remained supportive of the program, others increasingly shared Rome's concern over boundary issues that had never been fully addressed. Pope Pius XII finally ordered a shutdown of the program in late 1953 and instructed the French bishops to make it look as if the orders "come from you," as the papal nuncio explained. Cardinal Achille Lienhart of Lille, once a prominent supporter of the movement, now proclaimed, "To be a priest and to be a worker are two functions, two different states of life, and it is not possible to unite them in the same person without altering the notion of the priesthood."[36]

On the New York–New Jersey waterfront this division of labor had always been most scrupulously observed; unlike in France, priests enjoyed substantial influence in the everyday affairs of communities adjoining the piers, where union members were generally quite well "catechized"— especially on the Irish waterfront—and the church had no reason to fear losing the souls of the working class. Longshoremen in New York and

New Jersey—whether Irish, Italian, or "Austrian" (as Catholic dockworkers of eastern and central European ancestry were still widely known)—did not need to be convinced that the church cared about them. In fact they tended—the Irish especially—to view the waterfront as that rare precinct where the long arm of the clergy did *not* extend.

Pete Corridan was not a "worker-priest" after the French model, but he surely was *working* on behalf of longshoremen and their families. No American priest of the postwar decade flouted so dramatically the customary boundaries between pastoral and temporal work, a trait that was especially dangerous given the spaces within which he operated. That is why "Taxi Jack" O'Donnell's explosive accusations against Corridan—whether motivated by jealousy or by a desire to rid the waterfront of his parishioner Joe Ryan's nemesis—were as revealing as they were ridiculous. Monsignor O'Donnell may not have been held in warm regard by many on the West Side, but as long as he upheld a tradition marking the piers as a clergy-free zone, he enjoyed legitimacy if not respect. While it is difficult to assess how widely O'Donnell's animus toward Corridan was shared by other priests in New York City, his vendetta against the Jesuit certainly did not compromise his conspicuous leadership role in the annual Alfred E. Smith Memorial Dinner, or his ardent leadership of gaudy sendoffs marking Cardinal Spellman's trips to and from Rome and other overseas destinations.[37]

O'Donnell *was* more aggressive than other priests of the archdiocese in sustaining the waterfront's separate spheres of Catholic influence. We might surmise that the views of his colleagues ranged from tacit assent to indifference to unspoken resentment. The archdiocesan priests associated at one time or another with advocacy for longshoremen—John P. Monaghan was the best known among a half-dozen or so—surely did not appreciate the heavy-handed antireform campaign waged by O'Donnell on the West Side, but the fact remained that Pete Corridan was the lone cleric still covering the waterfront after 1951.

Corridan was ultimately thwarted—as we shall see—by the tactical anticlericalism of the Irish waterfront; his most meaningful connections were forged instead with secular journalists, creative artists, and civic reformers, who lent him a credibility not always obtaining nearer the piers. But there was no mistaking the prophetic challenge the Jesuit posed to religious business as usual in one of the most densely Catholic places on earth. "Today it's called liberation theology," Budd Schulberg remarked in 1988. "The waterfront priests were the forerunners." Yet the wariness of the rank and file in the face of Corridan's bold apostolate suggests that they continued to ponder, in their own ways and words, liberation *from* what and *for* what?[38]

I I *An Intimacy with Violence*

The Board of Inquiry charged by Governor Dewey to investigate the causes of the autumn 1951 wildcat strike concluded that both the ILA and the strike committee were "singularly free" of communist influence, a statement of the obvious. Without isolating a single factor most responsible for the strike, the board found that dockworkers were angered over the settlement reached between the ILA and the New York Shipping Association, the union's crooked electoral practices, and the ILA leadership's conduct of its internal affairs.

The January 1952 report entered more contested terrain in claiming that the disputed contract was "validly ratified" despite the "evidence of many irregularities." Widespread acts of fraud (including ballot stuffing) were deemed insufficient to affect the result of the election. The strike committee's young legal counsel, Peter Johnson—a friend and confidant of Pete Corridan—was "appalled" that the report "ignominiously arrived at an invalid conclusion" and warned darkly of future "maritime chaos." The board's report signaled to the men that their strike had failed, since the dubious ratification process was its trigger. NYSA reserved comment on the report, while the ILA objected to its critique of labor practices—particularly the shapeup—not directly implicated in the strike.[1]

Corridan served the board as a consultant; its endorsement of the ratification process notwithstanding, the report's conclusions represented "a clear statement of his viewpoint." This was the first instance in which Corridan's desire for government intervention on the waterfront—including perhaps some advisory role for him—clashed so sharply with the interests of the dissident rank and file. The split grew wider once it became apparent that the Jesuit also enthusiastically backed Dewey's plan to enlist the New York State Crime Commission in an exhaustive investigation of the waterfront on both sides of the river, a bold initiative first urged in Spruille Braden's headline-grabbing telegram to Dewey of October 29, 1951. Dewey announced on November 20 that the NYSCC would launch "a bistate cooperative effort to combat racketeering, organized crime, and restrictive practices, which have increasingly over the past fifty years hamstrung the port of New York." The decision to mobilize the NYSCC shifted the burden of crime investigation from the Board of Inquiry to an agency given free range across the port—with the blessing of Dewey's fellow Republican, New Jersey governor Alfred E. Driscoll—in advance of exhaustive public hearings.[2]

Who Is Mr. Big?

The Board of Inquiry told the ILA to clean its own house, but Pete Corridan knew why that was impossible: during the October strike he had publicly asserted for the first time, "There is someone above Ryan who runs the waterfront." He decided to make a direct appeal to the lone individual he believed had the power to change the union's leadership. On April 11, 1952—Good Friday—Corridan enjoyed an audience with waterfront tycoon Bill McCormack at the New York Jesuit provincial's residence on East Fordham Road in the Bronx. The Jesuit and the businessman engaged in a somber three-hour conversation about the future of the port. By Corridan's account the meeting resulted from his shrewd orchestration of Catholic diplomacy: an elderly Jesuit living in the Xavier community had sought his advice in March regarding a proposed appeal to McCormack for a donation to the order; Corridan encouraged the overture; the older Jesuit met McCormack and was driven back to Xavier by the entrepreneur's chauffeur. Corridan doubted that a contribution was forthcoming but was confident "McCormack might be calling me soon thereafter." This bit of tactical "Jesuitry" left Corridan's senior confrere "a little provoked at me" once he learned more about McCormack, but it achieved the desired result.[3]

After Cardinal Spellman, William J. McCormack was arguably the most powerful Catholic in New York. He had recently been starkly contrasted with Pete Corridan in a sensational two-part exposé by journalist Lester Velie for *Collier's Weekly*. In the second of these February 1952 articles, "The Waterfront Priest Battles the Big Port's BIG BOSS," Velie described Corridan as "a man as humble in his station of life as McCormack is powerful." The Jesuit was "the guide of the longshoremen's rebellion," lending the movement "moral strength and purpose"; he was also "responsible for loosing" investigative forces that were currently "rocking" the "secret world of William J. McCormack." Not long after the *Collier's* exposé hit the newsstands, McCormack—who later told the New York State Crime Commission, "I always believe that I'm humble, too"—authorized *New York Herald Tribune* shipping news reporter Walter Hamshar to ask the

Jesuit if he wished to have a meeting. Corridan was informed that the tycoon professed "great admiration" for his work.[4]

Few if any figures of comparable magnitude in New York City's history had so successfully managed to keep their name out of the papers as had Bill McCormack. All that changed in the summer and autumn of 1951, when the quest to unmask the waterfront's "Mr. Big" grew into a near obsession. There were hints over the years, primarily from Westbrook Pegler, star columnist for the Hearst papers. "As far back as 1941," wrote Allen Raymond, Pegler (then employed by the Scripps Howard chain) "had told the story of an anonymous 'Mr. Big' dominating the teamsters' and longshoremen's unions and ruling in business enterprises requiring a great deal of political and union support for successful management." In June 1951 Daniel Bell, with a key assist from Corridan, authored a searching exposé of the ILA ("Last of the Business Rackets)," concluding that McCormack was a "man of extraordinary influence in city politics and with the longshore and teamsters unions." The pace of revelation picked up considerably with the August 16 broadcast of "Crime on the Waterfront," the *CBS Reports* documentary drawn from materials provided by Corridan's allies at the New York City Anti-Crime Committee. The narrator of the celebrated broadcast gravely intoned:

> There is a single individual so big, so influential, that he cannot be touched, and that individual is the power behind crime on the waterfront. That individual makes politicians, police, and union officials jump. That individual is "Mr. Big." We think we know his name. People who really understand the waterfront know his name, too. They all agree on who is "Mr. Big."[5]

The voice of Bill Keating of the NYCACC was heard next: "Mr. Big is an important, respectable businessman. He is a churchgoer. He contributes to charitable causes. He is a close friend of governors, mayors, and important political figures past and present." Keating supplied a concise explanation of how this "Mr. Big" came to control the port: "With money to back him, he stepped in and took over more and more unions on and off the waterfront. He found himself in a handy little position. On the one hand he controls certain key union locals. On the other he owned and operated the very businesses that those key unions serviced." This unique model of union-management relations was undeniably prevalent across the port. Just one question remained unanswered: Who is Mr. Big?[6]

The pursuit of Mr. Big now took on a life of its own in the mass media. In the September 12, 1951, issue of *People Today*, a weekly magazine, Joe Ryan was eliminated from contention in the Mr. Big sweepstakes. Far from being relieved, Ryan lashed back, assailing in the pages of the *New York Herald Tribune* the "gossip mongers" who were "peddling the slanderous invention that a 'prominent and wealthy business man influential in New

York politics' whom they melodramatically describe as 'Mr. Big' dominates the New York waterfront." In Washington, a Republican senator from Wisconsin, Alexander Wiley, inserted the *People Today* item in the *Congressional Record* with the comment, "It is the conclusion of all these various newsgathering and reporting organs that there is a single king-pin of waterfront crime, a Mr. Big." Spruille Braden of NYCACC declared: "Organized gangsters and racketeers must be driven off the waterfront.... [T]he pattern of police connivance and political corruption must be cleaned up, and the powers behind the throne, the shadowy people who hide behind a cloak of respectability—they must be exposed."[7]

On October 3, 1951, a decade after he first claimed that the New York waterfront was lorded over by a single powerful individual, Pegler revealed in the *Journal-American*:

> The Mr. Big that many gossips have been hinting about lately is Bill McCormack, who is boss of the Port of New York. He controls Joe Ryan, the president of the International Longshoremen's Association[,] ... and has authority in two big key locals of the Teamsters union. These are 282, which hauls McCormack's ready-mixed concrete and other building materials, and 202, downtown in the market district.

An acerbic and often mean-spirited curmudgeon, Pegler nevertheless had the rare courage to attach a real name to the shibboleth "Mr. Big." Catholic reformers overcame their distaste for the columnist just long enough to endorse his judgment. As labor journalist John Cort wrote in *Commonweal*: "Ordinarily I would not quote Pegler against any man. But I have checked this with those who know the waterfront inside out and they assure me without any question Pegler is right on this point." McCormack's unwanted season of notoriety had begun, wiping out decades of scrupulously tended obscurity. When he was subpoenaed by a Hudson County grand jury investigating waterfront crime two weeks after being named by Pegler, prosecutor H. K. Roberson bluntly identified McCormack as the "boss of the New York waterfront."[8]

The abiding urge to identify a Mr. Big of the waterfront was deeply rooted in the New York Irish American experience and sensibility. Since the era of "Boss" Richard Croker, grand sachem of Tammany Hall in the late nineteenth century, various figures had involuntarily held the strictly unsought title of "Mr. Big," a sobriquet that conveyed the Irish ambivalence toward authority and deference to it. On the one hand, the designation fulfilled beliefs about a necessary chain of command: *someone* must be in charge, and that someone was most likely not an elected official but "the man behind the man." At the same time, anyone who behaved as though he was entitled to the respect afforded a Mr. Big was highly susceptible to sniping from below: in Irish American parlance, "Who does he think he is?"

Public fascination with organized crime in the 1920s and 1930s led "many journalists and investigators," wrote Thomas Repetto in *American Mafia*, to pursue "hidden Mr. Bigs who pulled the strings from their mansions and boardrooms." The conspiracy obsession of the early Cold War era—nourished by the lurid work of popular New York journalists Jack Lait and Lee Mortimer, who blended salacious gossip and crime reporting with anticommunist invective—broadened the range of contenders for Mr. Big status, as the sensational televised hearings of the Kefauver Committee in New York City in March 1951 confirmed. The committee's chief counsel, Rudolph Halley, a New Yorker, was advised by a mentor prior to the hearings "always to 'go after a Mr. Big' in a congressional investigation."[9]

Gangland's "Prime Minister," Frank Costello—with his gravelly voice and the WPIX Channel 11 cameras trained on his "nervous, sometimes twitching hands" after his lawyer complained that close-ups of his face were making a spectacle of his client—seemed to fit the bill perfectly. Former New York City mayor Bill O'Dwyer, the highest-ranking public official exposed as a former associate in Costello's Kefauver Committee testimony, was likewise cast in the Mr. Big role by some pundits. Yet if O'Dwyer was truly Mr. Big, local reasoning quickly responded, he need not have sought the mayoralty or been compelled later to seek refuge in Mexico, hounded at every turn by reformers.[10]

The waterfront was the ripest territory for a putative Mr. Big to hold sway because it was unregulated, unpoliced, and operated according to arcane codes reinforced by a unique brand of violence, administered with swift efficiency. In 1949 reporter Ed Reid of the *Brooklyn Eagle* went undercover as a longshoreman to expose a gambling empire operated by an unnamed Mr. Big—later identified as one Harry Gross—with ties to "a nationwide crime syndicate." But Gross lacked the stature of intimidator needed to merit serious consideration. Amid the flurry of sensational crime exposés of the early 1950s, compromised politicians occasionally offered their own unsolicited nominations. In April 1953 a frazzled John V. Kenny, during testimony before a Senate subcommittee investigating waterfront crime, would endorse for the dishonor his Jersey City mayoral predecessor once removed. "Call Frank Hague!" Kenny impulsively cried out during the public hearings. "He's the real Mr. Big of the waterfront." By then the title had already been retired. There was only one Mr. Big on the waterfront: Frank Hague's old friend William J. McCormack.[11]

Cockeye, Bill-O, and Mr. Big

Even though Bill McCormack disdained publicity, in the face of mounting pressure he was finally compelled to respond. On January 20, 1952, ex-newspaperman and bon vivant turned publicist Robin "Curly" Harris planted a lengthy, highly flattering story on McCormack's behalf in the pages of the *New York Daily News,* "Who *Is* This Mr. Big? From Dock-Walloper to Tycoon, the New York Saga of Bill McCormack." Harris opened by accurately observing: "If you are one of the 12,000,000 people in the New York metropolitan area, or one of the countless millions who visit our city, your life has unquestionably been touched in some way by the manifold activities of a 62-year-old, 220-pound granite block of a man named William Jerome McCormack." He detailed the rags-to-riches saga of this "juvenile Hercules who was a glutton for work," the former wagon boy who had become "a millionaire many, many times over" but was "still working as hard as ever." Harris marveled at the horizontal monopoly McCormack's enterprises enjoyed, noting that his gasoline filled the city's school buses, his concrete supported many of the city's best-known buildings, and "your Christmas mail may have been processed in or out of New York by McCormack's men and not the Post Office." Yet this was nothing compared to the source of his real power: "And should you be one of the 400,000 whose livelihood comes from New York's biggest industry, its always turbulent port, you have probably been affected even more closely by McCormack, the waterfront's No. 1 tycoon and 'the little man's Port Authority.'"[12]

Harris followed this litany of McCormack's temporal powers with an affirmation of his spiritual authenticity, invoking the waterfront's populist realism: "A remarkable blend of hardness and humanity, his success has not made him forget that working people still live in places like the one where he was born." Spruille Braden had recently "hinted," said Harris, that McCormack's vast business empire was "only a front for racketeering. McCormack scoffs at all this. A deeply religious man who was made a Papal Knight of Malta several years ago and who attends Mass daily at the Church of St. Thomas More on 89th St., he answers it with the 8th Commandment: 'Thou shalt not bear false witness against thy neighbor.'" If McCormack had his religion, he also boasted an insider's authority that lent weight to his claims—echoed by Harris—that what truly plagued the port was an outmoded infrastructure and excessive pier rentals, not racketeering.[13]

Although the *Daily News* encomium was designed to silence self-appointed reformers whose knowledge of the port paled before McCormack's own, it only exposed him to additional criticism; and indeed his counterattack inadvertently helped undermine the code of silence. Insider knowledge could cut both ways. "The *Daily News* paid off some debts by practically nominating McCormack for mayor," wrote Corridan ally Dick Carter in the *Compass,* the short-lived successor to *PM,* a notable leftist daily. "The *News* has been exempt for years from paying the exorbitant shakedown fees demanded by waterfront truck loaders who handle newsprint for other papers," the kind of reference to McCormack's power over local unions that previously would never have found its way into print. Carter further observed that Colonel Ivan Annenberg, the paper's circulation manager, had served in the past alongside McCormack as a committee chairman at the annual dinner of the Joseph P. Ryan Association. "Waterfront amusement at the *News*'s extravagant portrayal of McCormack as a super *de luxe* Horatio Alger figure, and no more," Carter asserted, "was tempered with awe at the man's ability to get such stuff printed."[14]

Five days after the *Daily News* ran its tribute to Bill McCormack, Pete Corridan penned a lengthy memorandum to Father John McMahon "on the recent longshore strike and allied questions. The material contained therein will serve as a background for upcoming waterfront articles in so far as I am part of the subject matter." He listed such publications as *Collier's, Argosy, Look,* the *Saturday Evening Post,* and *Harper's,* all with New York waterfront articles in preparation or in press. "The material contained in these articles re: Father Corridan," he said, referring to himself in the third person, "is in the main a matter of public record. In so far as I was able, I sought to protect the Church." Many of these articles were amply supplemented by information from Corridan's files and those of his associates at the New York City Anti-Crime Committee, particularly Bob Greene, who had begun compiling background reports and interviews with waterfront figures during his stint as a *Jersey Journal* reporter.[15]

Lester Velie's February 9 *Collier's* installment, "Big Boss of the Big Port," exposed McCormack's influence over waterfront hiring and his control of Joe Ryan. The sequel ("A Waterfront Priest Battles the Big Port's BIG BOSS") devoted more space to McCormack than to Corridan, as though Velie had been emboldened to up the ante while writing the first piece. Here McCormack's alleged links to the murderous old-time West Side gangs were laid out in detail. He was also accused of a "plot against New York City taxpayers and home builders" stemming from his alleged collusion with other sand and gravel wholesalers to jack up prices in 1940. "McCormack's company paid $5,000 out of a total of $50,000 in fines imposed on the group," Velie solemnly reported, "and as part of the consent decree deal, the criminal charges against McCormack and the others were dismissed."[16]

This was not exactly the stuff of headlines. Velie's most "explosive questions" concerned McCormack's role in persuading Bill O'Dwyer to seek re-election as mayor in 1949. In the spring of that year District Attorney Frank Hogan dangled a possible commutation of Cockeye Dunn's death sentence in return for credible information on waterfront murders. "If Dunn told all he knew he could blow the lid off the water front and the city," Velie later wrote. Cockeye reportedly "complained that McCormack had blocked his business ambitions, but beyond that he wouldn't go." The clear implication was that the mayor and especially McCormack had much to fear should Dunn sing for his life. O'Dwyer decided in late May not to run, giving his "private blessing" to Hogan as his choice for successor. A "draft O'Dwyer" campaign was quickly launched by "a formidable group of business and labor leaders" including Bill McCormack; it disbanded just as quickly when O'Dwyer reiterated his decision not to run.[17]

Dunn was executed on July 7, 1949; *Journal-American* labor reporter Guy Richards later claimed this signaled that Cockeye "hadn't talked enough to suit Hogan. It was also a signal that Hogan had learned enough to make him entirely undesirable as a replacement at City Hall." The day following Dunn's electrocution Joe Ryan—as part of a delegation of thirty-five labor leaders—visited his old friend Bill O'Dwyer and urged him again to run; then on July 9 McCormack "was induced to make two pilgrimages to City Hall to urge O'Dwyer to change his mind." On July 11 three of New York City's five all-powerful county Democratic leaders expressed support for Hogan; the same day a "citizens' committee" that included McCormack visited O'Dwyer and finally succeeded in persuading the mayor to seek reelection.[18]

The timing of Dunn's execution may or may not have played a role in the mayor's decision: O'Dwyer surely faced significant additional political liabilities, including his alleged former ties to mobster turned Tammany kingmaker Frank Costello. His reluctance to run again may also have been linked to health concerns and the Byzantine workings of Tammany Hall and the outer borough machines. The mercurial "Bill-O" may have hoped to compel Tammany to beg him to run in return for control of the machinery, as historian George Walsh has suggested. It is also possible that President Truman—with whom he met the day before announcing his decision to run—promised to name him U.S. ambassador to Mexico after he won reelection. "One rumor circulated," historian Chris McNickle wrote of the increasingly erratic O'Dwyer's sudden change of heart, that "he was drunk at the time and perhaps 'unable to take the inevitable bump that comes from leaving power.'" Furthermore, as mob historian Virgil Peterson argued, "the offer of Dunn to talk may have been worrisome to the mayor in an election year," given O'Dwyer's history as a target of Brooklyn grand juries and Dunn's reported willingness to "provide the names of policemen and politicians involved in waterfront graft."[19]

The mayor from the Irish waterfront found himself caught in the crossfire yet again. He was clearly indebted to McCormack for his role in mediating several actual or potential tugboat strikes in New York Harbor; "Mr. Big" also intervened in a threatened subway strike and was widely believed to have served as the arbiter for virtually all labor conflicts involving teamsters and longshoremen working in the port during O'Dwyer's tenure in office. If Daniel Bell was correct to highlight McCormack's resistance to the Port Authority's attractive offer to modernize the city's rotting piers, his influence in the O'Dwyer administration was substantial indeed; yet little was made in 1949 of McCormack's role in persuading O'Dwyer to seek reelection. Socialist mayoral candidate Norman Thomas was the only opponent to raise the Cockeye Dunn issue during the general election campaign. O'Dwyer was uneventfully reelected despite behaving like someone whose mind tended elsewhere. "Officially O'Dwyer remained mayor," wrote Chris McNickle, "but in fact he ceased to govern the city." Rumors of his impending resignation circulated by March, and by September 1 he was on his way to Mexico City.[20]

The array of personal and political realities affecting O'Dwyer's decision to seek reelection in 1949 meant nothing to Jesuit Fathers Phil Carey and Pete Corridan. Bill McCormack, however, was the subject of an enormous burden of conviction borne by these men. In January 1952 Corridan reported to his superior, John J. McMahon, that two very high ranking New York City police officials "were told by Dunn at Sing Sing that he killed for McCormack." There is no doubt that both labor priests believed the condemned man told the truth on this account. Just as surely as Cockeye Dunn shot Andy Hintz in January 1947, in the spring and summer of 1949 he held a loaded weapon capable of obliterating the code of silence, finishing the job begun by his own victim Hintz. That tantalizing prospect expired along with Dunn in Sing Sing's electric chair.[21]

The conviction seemed at times to consume Phil Carey with anger and grief. Until the end of his long life he remained unable to utter McCormack's name publicly, inadvertently abetting the code of silence he so despised. Pete Corridan by contrast was driven to perform ever more aggressive acts of public witness, especially as captured in print. In the second installment of his *Collier's* exposé Lester Velie described the Jesuit as "a six-footer with the body of an athlete and the brain of a business machine." Corridan, with his "rugged" physique, matched up well against Bill McCormack in a moral struggle neatly personified by the rival Irish Catholic New Yorkers. Velie lavishly employed combat imagery in drawing the contrast between the two: he described the offices at Xavier as Corridan's "command post from which he's been warring on Bill McCormack and Joe Ryan's water-front system for six years."[22]

The presentation of this waterfront morality play in a mass-circulation national publication represented a tremendous coup for Corridan. It was no secret locally that he was playing a dual role as both subject and main source for the exposés, and the most effective way the "waterfront priest" battled the port's "Big Boss" was by facilitating stories like Velie's in which he served as protagonist. Guy Richards of the *Journal-American* thought he could detect how much help the priest had given Velie after the second *Collier's* piece hit the newsstands. "Please don't forget me," he implored Corridan, "whenever you think another good pitch or two in this newspaper would have a salutary effect—to say nothing of the time when there is a good scoop brewing around."[23]

Bill McCormack was an astonishingly powerful figure by any measure, especially for an individual so little known to the general public. His businesses were unrivaled in their coverage of the waterfront on both sides of the Hudson; his reach in politics and the Catholic Archdiocese of New York was immense. Those responsible for the *Collier's* exposé tasted Mr. Big's wrath in May 1952, when Velie and the magazine's editor Louis Ruppel were "astounded" to discover a letter of apology from publisher Clarence E. Stouch to McCormack in *Produce News*, "an obscure Manhattan vegetable and fruit trade paper." The story then found its way into the pages of *Time*, the nation's leading newsweekly. Stouch had caved in to McCormack's demand for a public retraction. The chastened publisher assured his fellow businessman, "We never intended the term 'Mr. Big,' as applied to you, to have any connotation of evil or association therewith, or to reflect on your integrity, or to imply that you are allied with racketeers, gangsters and mobsters." *Collier's* would neither republish nor permit the republication of Velie's blockbuster series. Editor Ruppel was then fired; Velie relinquished his highly lucrative post at the magazine "to freelance," noting on his way out the door that "the waterfront pieces took three months of digging."[24]

A Christian Gentleman in Action

Pete Corridan's purposes were very well served in autumn 1951–winter 1952 by the flurry of unwanted publicity surrounding Bill McCormack. It diminished by comparison the stature of Joe Ryan, now cast in the role of "office boy" to McCormack's "father confessor." The waterfront priest and his allies further demeaned King Joe as a "captive," a "pratt-boy," and a "figurehead." With waterfront power relations thus recast, Corridan seized the opportunity to fearlessly deliver an ultimatum to McCormack at their April 1952 meeting on East Fordham Road: if Ryan failed to "straighten out the I.L.A. and straighten it out soon, the whole house would come down around his ears, and a good many people would be hurt."[25]

In later noting to his provincial that "for the first time since the inception of the Joe Ryan dinner" McCormack had recently failed to serve on any of the annual event's planning committees, Corridan hinted that the entrepreneur was contemplating a change at the top, if only to preserve his own interests at a time when more efficient port operations in Philadelphia, Norfolk, and elsewhere were clamoring for New York's business. Corridan also believed that McCormack had betrayed his displeasure with Ryan by meeting with Gene Sampson on an Upper West Side street corner during the 1951 strike, where he had reportedly "guaranteed fair elections and honest balloting in the future" if the work stoppage was ended. Sampson's response has been lost to history, but at the April meeting McCormack reportedly concurred with Corridan's insistence on a closed shop and an improved ILA grievance procedure.[26]

As their meeting drew to a close, the businessman asked Corridan what else "should be changed and how." The priest asked McCormack "who could effect the changes," which would clearly begin with new leadership for the ILA. McCormack's most revealing statement came at the very end, after Corridan told him that he "would throw in the sponge" if reforms were not achieved within a year's time. McCormack, Corridan reported, "said I had an obligation to continue to do as I had been doing for the good of the city." By invoking the language of obligation, McCormack seemed to indicate that the priest was executing a duty for which he had been called, and which transcended—as part of the immutable authority structure of their church and his order—the grave conflict that separated them.[27]

Corridan in turn gave McCormack his due credit, later acknowledging that the businessman and his acolyte Joe Ryan were "children of Almighty God, as well as members of my own church." The waterfront priest's bow to McCormack's spiritual legitimacy went further than that routine concession. Mr. Big was also free of hypocrisy according to the standards of the Irish waterfront. "Certainly the big man had never posed as a reformer," wrote journalist Allen Raymond in *Waterfront Priest.* "He never invented that system of rule against which Father Corridan was crying aloud like an Old Testament prophet. McCormack had merely accepted all the hard conditions of the jungle world into which he was born, and fought his way to wealth and power within them."[28]

McCormack's bruising experience was a source of authority that could never be gainsaid by anyone hoping to reform the waterfront from within, a goal Corridan quixotically chased even as he lobbied for external investigations. The priest also believed that the Catholic rules were finally changing. The papal social encyclicals summoned a faith to penetrate and integrate all spheres of human activity, including work and commerce. The division of labor so scrupulously observed on the waterfront was now vulnerable to a critique from the highest authority. Invoking Pope Pius XI's admonition to those who "permit a deplorable cleavage in the conscience and live a life too little in conformity with the clear principles of justice and Christian charity," Corridan seized every opportunity to condemn Communion breakfasts and annual dinners honoring Catholic waterfront chieftains. This new dispensation obliged him to expose McCormack's alleged power over waterfront rackets; in light of the encyclicals and evolving Ignatian spirituality, his vocation *mandated* pursuit of social justice for longshoremen and their families.[29]

The social encyclicals were key texts weighed against the "just waterfront" tradition, which continued to generate narratives of its own; some were even written down. In January 1952, three months prior to Corridan's meeting with Mr. Big, the *St. Ann's Catholic Monitor,* published by the Italian Capuchin Fathers of St. Ann's Church in Hoboken, published a tribute to "William J. McCormack, a Christian Gentleman in Action." The unnamed author noted that during a recess in his testimony before the Hudson County grand jury, McCormack (a "tough man, fearless but fair in any fight") was approached by a female reporter from the *New York Mirror*. When she requested an interview,

> Mr. McCormack replied that, first, she should pay a visit to the Chapel of the Perpetual Rosary. Naturally, the reporter was startled by this reply. Two months had lapsed when they met again, following the second session of the Grand Jury. Again the *Mirror* representative pressed McCormack for an interview. But he had recognized her, and, very gravely, asked her if she had done as he asked. When she said she had not, McCormack told her that, since she had failed to comply with his wish, he could not grant her an interview.

It was "amazing in this materially minded world," exclaimed the author, to find a "Catholic man whose faith was a living thing, evident in every action of his private life," thus filing McCormack's business and legal affairs as well as his religious faith under the category of *private*. By inviting a reporter to share in a devotion that was meaningful to him, McCormack pointed to a world beyond the brutality and strife of the waterfront, a world where he bore his role as a privileged Catholic "very gravely." Such a dignified posture was befitting "a man whose advice is sought by politicians, labor leaders, business men, and government officials." The author of the tribute asserted, "The many times he has been called in to mediate labor difficulties (and the great respect with which labor holds him) are eloquent tribute to his success in putting the papal encyclicals to work."[30]

The man who "will not attend a conference unless he first says a rosary" once explained that his success was "very simple. Being a rich man, I understand management's troubles, and having been a working man, I can grasp labor's difficulties too." This blunt declaration spoke volumes on the Irish waterfront and was extremely disarming to his critics. It was as though he could single-handedly execute the mandate of *Quadregesimo Anno*, adapted to local conditions with regard to which Jesuit labor priests enjoyed little practical knowledge and less authority.[31]

To Pete Corridan, however, it was no longer sufficient—in light of the social encyclicals—for a man's faith merely to be evident "in every action of his private life." Yet Bill McCormack's waterfront authority was deeply grounded in local tradition, beginning with the mystique suffusing those whose close acquaintance with violence was most exalted. The industries McCormack served as mediator employed precious few students of the social encyclicals. Mr. Big had learned decades earlier to subdue the brutal instincts of others by gravely hinting at his own deep intimacy with violence, a power that increased as the businessman achieved ever greater rewards.

"He is a very tough man and an element of physical fear has deterred some persons from handling him as frankly as they deal with Frank Costello," wrote Westbrook Pegler of McCormack, inadvertently warming the hearts of Irish brawlers everywhere, grown tired of hearing that the Italians had scared them away from the prime arenas of urban combat. Who else but a man so intimate with violence could "mediate" the activities of Cock-eye Dunn, Squint Sheridan, and other volatile denizens of the waterfront, on the one hand, and on the other the civilized communities precariously bordering the docksides?[32]

Bill McCormack's intimacy with violence confirmed his spiritual authenticity on the Irish waterfront. He projected the strength to absorb stray blows from waterfront combatants; he would subdue their instincts for mayhem so that inland communities might be spared. His personal devotional life, it was intimated, supplied the strength to bear these heavy burdens for the good of the church as well. By the rules of this ethos one did not complain, rat on one's friends, or boast of accomplishments and honors, which in McCormack's case were legion. He and his worthy constituent Joe Ryan presented themselves as men who suffered and sinned like others, were absolved and consoled by the church and its sacraments, were devoted to their families, and practiced charity without ostentation. Beyond that, they owed no man an explanation for their part in a hierarchical universe not of their making. Many waterfront Catholics deeply feared these men or prayed to be delivered from them, but the largest number grudgingly acknowledged their fidelity to an unwritten code governing the world and its works.

The Equalizer

When Bill McCormack ridiculed "self-proclaimed experts whose knowledge of the waterfront must have been gained during a ferry ride to Staten Island," he drew a line that clearly separated would-be reformers from those whose allegiance to the West Side code constituted an integral part of their ethnic and religious identity. Pete Corridan credited the Dunn case with raising the "iron curtain" of silence that had shrouded the waterfront for decades. To McCormack, who denied having known Dunn and refused to say more, the rampant speculation surrounding the affair was typical of the "warped minds" that "dream up Captain Kidd lurking in the shadows of our piers."[33]

By this line of reasoning, Mr. Big's perennial duties as arrangements committee chairman for the annual dinner of the Joseph P. Ryan Association (which brought together union chieftains, political leaders, a smattering of priests, and assorted gangland types) hardly demonstrated a collusive business relationship, except to troublemakers. Critics who were "deluded into attacking the port's problems by seeking wings of purity" would "blame the port's tragedy on loan sharks, thieves, and two dollar horse players. They create," scoffed McCormack, "an overlord with God knows what hidden power."[34]

McCormack's mastery of the waterfront's spiritual idiom left Pete Corridan in a very tight spot, though it was not readily apparent amid all the accolades and journalistic tributes the Jesuit racked up in the early 1950s. His own intimacy with violence was indicated in oft-repeated stories of threats leveled against Ryan and assorted waterfront gangsters. But Corridan suffered a tremendous disadvantage: he had to talk twice as tough to overcome suspicions born of his clerical and non-waterfront pedigree, yet the tougher he talked, the clearer it became that he was a reformer, not a realist. All waterfront talkers were suspect; talkative waterfront reformers were anathema.

Bill McCormack, by not talking at all, spoke volumes to his cultural hegemony on the waterfront. He continued to let others do the talking, especially in settings guaranteed to infuriate the waterfront priest. On March 23, 1952, the United States Customs branch of the Holy Name Society held its twenty-eighth annual Communion breakfast at the Waldorf-Astoria. In the presence of Fordham University president Father Lawrence McGinley, S.J., McCormack took a bow at the behest of his good friend Harry M. Durning, collector of the Port of New York. "Bill is a very able man," intoned Durning, "a religious man, a family man, and a patriotic American who has worked on the port for 40 years." Corridan fired back. "If religion is on the decline as a moral influence in the lives of many people," he fumed, "breakfasts such as these, as much as the corrupt conditions on the waterfront, are a cause."[35]

While Corridan struggled in vain to accumulate waterfront spiritual authority, the many glowing accounts of his work featured in magazines and on radio won him a fervent national constituency. The response of an upstate New York woman was typical: "I have just read of your wonderful work among the unfortunate longshoremen and want to tell you how anxiously all decent Americans pray for a complete victory in your undertaking." A correspondent from Spokane exclaimed: "Americans, and above all, God, are with you. Keep working!" His crusade was especially attractive to co-religionists intent on broadening the church's role as a progressive social force. "As a Catholic, it is a supreme thrill to realize the progress that you have made in your determined effort to serve as an 'equalizer,'" wrote a Vermont physician after reading of Corridan's work in a March 1952 article for *Argosy* by Malcolm Johnson. "All Catholics, except probably Joe Ryan should be most proud (if one can so be), of your marvelous work." On the waterfront an "equalizer" was a concealed firearm; on the outside it designated weapons of the spirit.[36]

Folks closer to home remained deeply suspicious of both volunteer civic reformers and government interventionists. In January 1952 George Moller of Hoboken wrote to Corridan after viewing "Waterfront Boss," a CBS television docudrama on the 1947 Andy Hintz murder. The program ended with a warning that little had changed on the waterfront: "There still was a Mr. Big." Moller was reminded of "a statement that you made to the press during the recent strike about trying to see a Mr. Big to try and settle the dock strike but couldn't get anywhere near him. What I would like to know, Father," Moller asked with just a touch of sarcasm,

> is whether you really believe that one man controls the rackets on the 700 piers in the port of New York. It is extremely difficult to conceive of such a man. Why he would be a bigger man than the President of the United States and his business would transcend General Motors. And still remain unknown to the public! It seems unbelievable! Your thoughts and opinions on this matter would be greatly appreciated.[37]

From Moller's perspective Corridan's crusade violated the standards of populist realism. It was one thing to find it natural that a powerful man should reign at the top, quite another to link him obsessively with all the ills besetting the port. Yet Pete Corridan was not the only local figure preoccupied with Bill McCormack. Speculation continued to flourish over McCormack's purported intervention in the 1949 mayoral race. More than three years after the election, and less than a year after ardently requesting that Corridan provide him with a scoop, the Jesuit's journalistic ally Guy Richards disclosed "How Pier Chiefs Got Bill O'Dwyer to Stay in 1949" in a December 1952 article for the *Journal-American*. Richards's cryptic analysis was based in large part on a seven-hour interview with "multi-millionaire William J. McCormack, the waterfront's 'Mr. Big.'" Oddly, Richards quoted McCormack only once in the story, which opened with a rehash of charges that "the same small clique of waterfront leaders known as 'The Stable'" was responsible for persuading O'Dwyer to seek reelection just two days after Cockeye Dunn's customary silence was rendered permanent.[38]

In his final paragraphs Richards suddenly shifted gears to record his conviction that "tabbing McCormack as the 'Big Boss' of the port and of 'The Stable' are oversimplifications." Claiming "there is not space here" to explain this startling conclusion, Richards indicated that while Joe Ryan and other local union kingpins "have blindly followed McCormack in every move and turn"; "lacking his brains," they "haven't grown with the years." Richards offered a peculiarly insightful variant on populist realism and waterfront power relations: a portrait of a lonesome Mr. Big, his desire for the stature of "respectable businessman" finally shorn of quotation marks, thwarted by the shortcomings of his underlings. "Until they retire," Richards warned, "'The Stable's' blighting touch will hang over the port," its "alliances to thuggery" intact. Richards thus separated McCormack from his lesser associates shortly after a public waterfront inquiry designed to reconnect them began. The winter 1952–53 hearings of the New York State Crime Commission promised finally to complete the project begun by Mike Johnson in 1948 and relentlessly pursued by his Jesuit collaborator each day since: a portrait in full of the nefarious interests that covered the waterfront.[39]

PART THREE

Waterfront Apotheosis

12 *A Season for Testimony*

Anthony "Tony Mike" DeVincenzo worked as a longshoreman for twenty years on the Hudson County piers save for one day spent early in his career on Pier 90 at the foot of West Fiftieth Street in Manhattan. December 15, 1952, found DeVincenzo back in Gotham not on a West Side pier but in the New York County Court House on Centre Street, testifying at a public hearing conducted by the New York State Crime Commission. Since November 1948 a band of investigative reporters, radio and television commentators, and civic reformers—a disparate community mediated by one intensely driven waterfront priest—had attested to the scandalous conditions found along the docks. The only missing piece was a firsthand corroborating account by a working longshoreman.

The waterfront's code of silence finally cracked from the inside on December 15, day six of the hearings. Under questioning from prominent attorney Theodore Kiendl, special counsel to the NYSCC, DeVincenzo confirmed virtually everything that Pete Corridan and his allies had alleged over the past four years: the shapeup and the loading racket were the centerpieces of organized waterfront criminality, the fulcrum of loan-sharking, kickbacks, and patronage that in Hoboken dominated the waterfront and indeed the city's entire political economy. Hoboken twists exposed by DeVincenzo included the use of "short gangs"—with union officials pocketing wages of phantom employees—and "ship jumpers," undocumented workers most of whom came from a village near Bari on Italy's Adriatic coast. In Hudson County these individuals were treated as virtual indentured servants. The Mile Square City's political leadership conspired with the local ILA hierarchy, DeVincenzo alleged: they "eat and drink together and split up the money together."[1]

DeVincenzo's motivation in testifying before the NYSCC was surely as complex as that of Budd Schulberg prior to his own testimony before

HUAC in May of the previous year. Tony Mike's willingness to speak out was prompted in part by pent-up anger over decades of injustice he had witnessed on the Hoboken piers. He was also eager to settle scores with Ed Florio, the reigning boss of the Hoboken waterfront, and Michael Borelli, the city's commissioner of public safety. DeVincenzo alleged that Borelli and Florio, an ILA organizer and president of Hoboken Local 306, were responsible for his firing by Jarka Stevedoring—which controlled the loading on seven of Hoboken's nine piers—after DeVincenzo complained that Florio "was not living up to the union rules and he worked with short gangs, with aliens, and we don't want no part of it." Florio did not act alone, Tony Mike alleged, but conspired with Borelli. "You can't get a job," he said, "until you see Commissioner Borelli." DeVincenzo described Borelli and Florio as former bootleggers who had failed to entice him back in the early 1930s "to come and work in the alcohol business."[2]

Michael Borelli and Tony Mike DeVincenzo were first cousins—"born and raised" together, they "were like two brothers"—and Tony Mike had known Ed Florio "since I was a child." Florio was a driving force behind the ecumenical (two Irishmen and three Italians, including Borelli) fusion reform ticket that had ousted the graft-ridden regime of Bernard McFeely in the landmark Hoboken election of 1947. The reform moment in the Mile Square City had quickly yielded to struggles for power on the waterfront in which DeVincenzo played his part. He freely acknowledged having sought help across the river from Albert Ackalitis, racketeering boss of Pier 18 on the Lower West Side. "We got trouble with Eddie Florio and would like to straighten him out," Tony Mike implored Ackalitis at a 1949 meeting arranged by Biffo Di Lorenzo of Jersey City Local 1247. Ackalitis was a former Arsenal Mob partner of Biffo's late brother-in-law Charley Yanowsky, whose 1948 murder eliminated a key rival to Florio for countywide waterfront influence. When Florio resisted a pier work stoppage across Hudson County in 1950, Tony Mike was informed by Di Lorenzo, Ackalitis told Florio that he had thirty minutes to get his men off the piers or "we'll come in and take them out."[3]

Tony Mike DeVincenzo's explosive testimony and his candor made him an extremely compelling witness and an astonishingly brave one. As the *New York Times* reported on page one of its December 15, 1952, editions, the NYSCC's star witness "received a last-minute police guard yesterday as a result of threats against his life." Tony Mike's performance also confirmed the wisdom of the many other subpoenaed witnesses at the crime commission hearings who ardently invoked their constitutional right against self-incrimination. Waterfront labor inexorably entangled virtually everyone who worked the piers in networks woven from various shades of criminality, though most dockworkers were not criminals. Tony Mike's erstwhile patron Albert Ackalitis, for example, boasted a voluminous rap sheet. "Acky" was viewed by Pete Corridan and others as the real power behind the Hudson County piers from his perch across the river.

While reformers and journalists seized on Tony Mike's testimony to starkly contrast good and evil on the waterfront, anyone with local knowledge understood that Michael Borelli and Ed Florio scarcely differed from their predecessors. Borelli's habit of doling out waterfront jobs was exposed as a public scandal in 1952, but it was standard practice through all the years, for example, that Dan Casey (a former teamster on Manhattan's West Side and close friend of Bill McCormack) served as Frank Hague's commissioner of public safety in Jersey City.[4]

From this realist perspective there were no waterfront villains, only victims. Florio (who at the time of Tony Mike's testimony was on trial for perjury) was tough enough, but he had been on the receiving end of the first violent assault described in DeVincenzo's testimony, a June 5, 1950, revenge beating arising from a dispute over control of the loading operation on Hoboken's Pier 2. Two disgruntled longshoremen, Nunzio "Wally" Aluotto and his nephew Patty Lisa, "went to work" on the union leader with a lead pipe at the corner of Fourth and Jefferson, testified Di Lorenzo, who watched from a block away as Florio "got hit across the puss with the pipe. He got hit with the pipe and down he went. He was pleading on his knees and hollering, 'St. Anthony, help me—St. Anthony, help me.'" Finally Florio "managed to get up and walked across the street, which is about forty feet from where he got the beating[,] right into the arms of Commissioner Borelli, and they carried him inside to the Third Ward Democratic Club and sat him down."[5]

The Port of New York and New Jersey was forever changed in light of DeVincenzo's gripping testimony. Tony Mike's graphic eyewitness account viscerally confirmed the ever present reality of waterfront violence from which none were immune, not even politically connected pier overlords. It was no fluke, however, that the Italian American DeVincenzo came from Hoboken, not the West Side, for there was no code of silence like the West Side Irish waterfront's code of silence. Tony Mike DeVincenzo's bold testimony was a solitary act, yet it was also rooted in decades of Hoboken experience; ethnic communities there were just slightly less tribal and the efficacy of personal witness slightly more potent than across the river. While Joe Ryan and his cronies often touted the social mobility earned for future generations through self-sacrifice to the West Side code, the DeVincenzo family had already "made America": Tony Mike's brother Richard was a surgeon at Hoboken's St. Mary's Hospital.[6]

After five years of searching for an Irish waterfront longshoreman to stand up, Pete Corridan was handed a Hoboken gift, though it was not a complete surprise. The story of Ed Florio's beating which figured so dramatically in DeVincenzo's testimony had been broken in *Look* magazine in July 1951 by Jules Weinberg, a staunch partisan and occasional instructor at Xavier Labor School. The following April, in a high-profile waterfront exposé for *Harper's* magazine, "The Pirates' Nest of New York," renowned labor journalist Mary Heaton Vorse introduced "Tony Mike"—by first name only—as a disgruntled longshoreman who had lost his job for protesting "short-gangs."[7]

With half a century's impassioned work to her credit, Vorse now passed the torch to the waterfront priest. "The Pirate's Nest of New York" opened and closed with an evocative paean to Pete Corridan's regular-guy waterfront brilliance ("he talks of murder in a quiet, matter of fact voice"), one of the qualities that made this once unlikely successor to an earlier generation of Catholic radicals a most effective advocate. The article does not suggest that Corridan led Vorse to Tony Mike DeVincenzo as she prepared her exposé; nor is it known when the Jesuit first met the disaffected Hoboken longshoreman. What is clear is that with the NYSCC hearings, New Jersey's "Italian waterfront" came of age. DeVincenzo's gripping testimony now exerted a geographic and moral squeeze on the West Side of Manhattan, where Pete Corridan had for five years tried in vain to goad "the boys" into standing up and speaking out.[8]

After describing the June 1950 assault on Florio, DeVincenzo went on to narrate an event from just under a year later. On the evening of May 20, 1951, he was in a Hoboken social club listening to a Brooklyn Dodgers game on the radio when he received a call from Wally Aluotto, who needed a favor. Aluotto asked DeVincenzo to join him the next morning, when he was slated to take over the hiring boss position on the newly reopened Pier 3. Tony Mike initially demurred—"I don't want no part of the waterfront. I had enough"—but his friend persuaded him. The following morning DeVincenzo was taking a slow walk to the riverfront, accompanied along part of the route by two guys named Frank, who decided to stop at city hall and pay a courtesy call on a couple of newly reelected city commissioners. One of the officials greeted Tony Mike by asking, "'Did you hear the latest, a friend of yours was shot?'... [T]he whole hall was full of—full of everything about Aluotto being shot." DeVincenzo called his brother at St. Mary's Hospital, who informed him, "'Wally is dead.' And I never went down to the pier no more and went home."[9]

Wally Aluotto was gunned down by three assailants in the offices of Hoboken ILA Local 867. While eighty-three-year-old ILA organizer John Nolan "dropped to the floor behind his desk," Patty Lisa, after being grazed by a bullet, jumped out a rear window leaving behind a trail of blood. The *New York Times* later reported, "Although Aluotto had been a bitter foe of Edward Florio...and had been questioned regarding his alleged connection with the assault on Florio a few months earlier, he had been designated by Florio as the pier hiring boss, a job formerly held by Michael Murphy." Along with his brothers Francis and William, Michael Murphy had muscled his way to partial control of the Hoboken waterfront amid the disorder of the late 1940s, with the local shipping industry mired in a decades-long decline. Murphy handled the hiring on Pier 3 until shippers complained that pilferage exceeded the customary threshold and took their business else-where. The pier lay dormant for more than a year until the Murphy brothers sought control over a reopened Pier 3, a bid supported by John Nolan, with whom Aluotto was speaking at the time he was shot. Eyewitnesses identi-fied an automobile owned by Michael Murphy being driven away from the scene of the crime.[10]

The notorious Murphy brothers were subsequently indicted for murder, but the charges against Michael and Francis were dropped for lack of evi-dence; a Jersey City jury acquitted William Murphy in 1954. Wally Alu-otto's murder was never solved, joining a legion of such cases on both sides of the river.

On December 19, 1952, four days after Tony Mike DeVincenzo electri-fied a Manhattan hearing room with his testimony and fifteen minutes after a jury in Washington, D.C., had begun deliberations in his perjury trial, Ed Florio pled guilty and was sentenced to eighteen months in prison. Florio had won a change in venue due to the "hostile atmosphere" created by various highly publicized waterfront investigations, but the NYSCC hear-ings created such a sensation that there was no place left for infamous waterfront figures to evade the glare of publicity—not even those from Hoboken.[11]

The Hearings and the Picture

In late autumn 1952 Pete Corridan urged Budd Schulberg to "incorporate the waterfront commission hearings in Manhattan into his script" for a revived waterfront film project. After the project was shelved in late 1951 following threats of reprisals by Joe Ryan and his cronies, Corridan stood virtually alone in encouraging Schulberg to persist with his "Crime on the Waterfront" screenplay. In March 1952 he queried the screenwriter, "How is the movie, or shouldn't I ask?" Schulberg replied:

> As to our much delayed movie, I withdrew from it...because I had lost faith in [producer Joe] Curtis and did not care for the revisions, along the lines of "more violence and sex," he wished to make. In another month, if nothing develops, Curtis will lose his rights to the property, and at that time I am thinking of getting together with Mike Johnson with the idea of finding sounder auspices for our script.[12]

Schulberg instead acquired the film rights from Johnson. The project was revived when renowned director Elia Kazan pledged his collaboration with Budd in the summer of 1952. But it was the NYSCC hearings that truly reignited the waterfront movie.

With Kazan in Europe completing a film shoot, Schulberg returned to the West Side in late autumn 1952, turning his attention away from such "big names" as Ryan and McCormack to offer his tribute to "Joe Docks, Forgotten Man of the Waterfront." Longshoremen are "proud and open-handed and fine drinking companions when they feel they can trust you," wrote Schulberg in "Joe Docks," a high-profile feature for the *New York Times Magazine* that marked his public debut as both a waterfront writer and an advocate for Pete Corridan's cause. After reviewing the circumstances of his previous research trips Schulberg confessed, "Long after I had enough material for a dozen waterfront pictures I kept going back, drawn by these forgotten men performing a rugged, thankless job in a jungle of vice and violence where law and constitutional safeguards have never existed."[13]

Schulberg was more revealingly attentive to ethnicity in "Joe Docks" than was Pete Corridan's custom. He explained that Irish American dockworkers were rarely expected to pay off hiring bosses any longer, unlike the Italians and blacks, who "systematically kick back as much as $5 per man per day." The article was written strictly from the perspective of the West Side Irish rebels, and a small segment of them at that; the sources he quoted were thinly disguised partisans, most notably Arthur Brown. Schulberg noted that many of the "staunch Irish Catholics" who dominated Local 791 in Chelsea were "under the influence of the waterfront priest Father John Corridan[,]...who has become a kind of one-man brain trust of the rank-and-file." If he exaggerated the influence of the Jesuit within 791, he implicitly acknowledged Corridan's minimal role among the largest waterfront cohort: "Italians follow the Latin tradition of letting the wife handle the church responsibilities." As to the NYSCC hearings that were about to commence, a forty-year veteran of the piers remarked: "Well, lad, it can't make it any worse. I just hope it goes all the way."[14]

Schulberg's vivid and wholly sympathetic account of pro-Corridan West Side dockworkers represented another enormous breakthrough for the rebels. The Jesuit's direct access to outlets for his own written work remained largely confined to the pages of *America* magazine, which ran his piece "New York Port's Last Chance" a week prior to the appearance of "Joe Docks." In that brief essay Corridan cited Bill McCormack by name for the first time in print, arguing that the rank and file wanted to hear him "explain his approval of previous erroneous reports" on the state of the port (a reference to Mayor Bill O'Dwyer's Joint Committee on Port Industry, on which McCormack had served). But there was no substitute for access to the *Times;* "Joe Docks" showed why Budd Schulberg had become the best-placed "mouthpiece" (as he put it) for Corridan and his disciples. In turn it helped him convince "the rebel movement that I was not a Hollywood opportunist looking to cash in on their story, but a writer devoted to their cause." His article filled in the background that was lacking in newspaper accounts of ongoing testimony before the NYSCC, nicely complementing lengthy excerpts in a waterfront idiom that was not readily translatable into *Times*-speak.[15]

Schulberg was present in the Lower Manhattan hearing room throughout much of the public testimony elicited by the NYSCC. "I went and listened at least forty times," the screenwriter recalled, perhaps meaning forty or more individual witnesses, since the hearings lasted only twenty days.[16]

As an erstwhile "friendly" witness before HUAC, Budd Schulberg had traveled from the most familiar site of Cold War cultural politics into another that remains largely obscure more than half a century later. Yet the New York–New Jersey waterfront crime hearings—like the Kefauver hearings of winter 1951—were more spectacular and more widely covered than the various public inquiries on communist infiltration rolled out at regular intervals between 1947 and 1954. In March 1951, as historian Lee Bernstein noted, the trial of alleged communist spies Ethel and Julius Rosenberg "competed for public attention with the hearings of Senator Estes Kefauver's organized crime committee, then being televised to greater renown." The Rosenberg trial, Bernstein contended, "was no match for the Kefauver Committee's New York hearings."[17]

Although the NYSCC hearings were not televised, there was a vast disparity between the coverage of Tony Mike DeVincenzo's testimony, which blanketed front pages of the metropolitan dailies, and Budd Schulberg's May 1951 HUAC appearance, reported as a routine item on page sixteen of the *New York Times*. Crime hearings featured upwardly mobile yet very dangerous figures from a heretofore private underworld. The more familiar rituals of anticommunism performed acts of public retribution, though both sets of hearings revealed growing anxieties over the nature of authentic American citizenship.[18]

Fifty years later Schulberg was uncertain whether he had witnessed DeVincenzo's testimony firsthand. It is widely assumed that Tony Mike served as the role model for *On the Waterfront*'s Terry Malloy, the longshoreman who reluctantly, then powerfully, stands up and testifies against the waterfront mob. DeVincenzo's testimony, however, came twenty months *after* Schulberg had completed a screenplay in which two principled longshoremen—including Terry Monahan, the original incarnation of Terry Malloy—pay with their lives for their courage in resisting waterfront overlords. Versions of the screenplay written subsequent to Tony Mike's testimony explicitly cite the hearings as a source; a crime commission investigation was a fixture in every script composed after January 1953. Schulberg always insisted that Terry Malloy was a composite waterfront character not based on DeVincenzo, a claim confirmed by his 1951 "Crime on the Waterfront" screenplay.[19]

Geography, not biography, was the real gift of the NYSCC hearings to film history. Like all strangers to Hudson County, Budd Schulberg enjoyed—as of late autumn 1952—precious little knowledge of Hoboken's history, its neighborhoods, and its traditions. Tony Mike's debut on December 15 introduced a whole new cast of characters with names like "Red Stingaree" (Eugene Pensari), "The Big Kid" ("I think his first name was Tony," DeVincenzo testified), and "a fellow they used to call Frankie 'Cheese'" (not to be confused with Jersey City's "Tony Cheese" Marchitto), all from a community saturated unlike any other by waterfront life and labor, politics and passions. Tony Mike seemed to know everyone in this urban village, yet his story had a quasi-fictional, even mythic dimension because none of his characters was familiar to anyone outside the almost monastic enclosure of Hudson County. In other words, Tony Mike limned a perfect setting for a screenwriter seeking to tell a story at once "universal" yet rooted in a very distinctive place. Even if this real-life location had not yet stirred Schulberg's imagination, the seed was certainly planted.[20]

Tony Mike was but one among a cast of memorable witnesses. Perhaps decades of scorn from New York pundits prompted DeVincenzo and some fellow Jerseyans to seize their moment in the sun. Perhaps the code of silence was slightly less potent in Hudson County, where ethnic boundaries were more permeable than on the West Side. Whatever the reason, the most dramatic and colorful testimony seemed to emanate from the Jersey side. Lead counsel Theodore Kiendl's December 16, 1952, questioning of long-time Jersey City boss loader James "Happy" Keane began:

Q: You live in Jersey City?

A: Yes, sir.

Q: You're not winking at me, are you?

A: No, sir.

Q: In fact, you've never seen me before, have you?

A: I have not.[21]

With proper decorum restored, Keane went on to describe "phony elections" conducted by the ILA in the "bottom of St. Michael's Church, down in the bottom of the church," a phrase that would reverberate in subsequent versions of Budd Schulberg's screenplays even as his story remained set on the West Side. Happy Keane's testimony was laden with rhetorical flourishes: he referred to Jersey City mayor John V. Kenny as "the Squire of Silver Lake," a sarcastic allusion to Kenny's Jersey Shore vacation home along a stretch of Monmouth County seaside so popular with North Jersey Hibernians it was known as "the Irish Riviera." Other witnesses to Jersey malfeasance were similarly revealing in their unique fashion. Anthony Belfiore, an employee of a fruit importer, described his instructions to deliver cash payment of nine or ten thousand dollars to a "Mr. Lemon" to gain the release of a shipment of lemons from Sicily after a strike on Jersey City's Pier F tied up the valuable perishables. Much of Belfiore's exchange with Kiendl evoked routines by the comedians Bud Abbott and Lou Costello:

Q: You went and saw whom?

A: "Mr. Lemon."

Q: How did you know there was such a man as "Mr. Lemon"?

A: That's the word that was used.

Q: The word that was used by whom?

A: By whom?

Q: Yes.

A: You have to ask him—by whom.

Q: You are not trying to be smart now?

A: No, I'm not trying to be smart.

Q: Now, tell us: You saw a man outside of the pier, and he said to you, "If you want to move those lemons you've got to meet this man."

A: That's right.

Q: And that's all he told you?

A: That's all.

NYSCC counsel continually admonished Belfiore to "behave yourself.... [Y]ou don't have to adopt that tone of animosity and belligerency." "I adopt no tone," replied Belfiore. "That's just a way of mine, that's all."[22]

The reams of Jersey-based testimony roiled Hudson County's already overheated political culture. Proof that the waterfront could strike back came quickly: on December 10 Pete Corridan's young friend and ally Bob Greene—on loan to the NYSCC by the New York City Anti-Crime Committee—was indicted by a Hudson grand jury for suborning perjury. Greene was accused of having offered money to Biffo Di Lorenzo "to testify before the commission [NYSCC] that Mayor Kenny had had business relations with the late Charles Yanowsky," Di Lorenzo's slain mobster brother-in-law. The allegations provided Kenny with a convenient pretext for declining to appear in a scheduled public session before the NYSCC the following week. Biffo Di Lorenzo died suddenly on the eve of Tony Mike DeVincenzo's testimony—and the indictments against Greene and the others were quashed the following year—but Hudson County continued to produce the most vivid caliber of witnesses in this enduring season of waterfront testimony.[23]

Packy Connolly's Theory

The contrast between testimony offered by Hudson County waterfront citizens and West Siders was striking. Pete Corridan and Arthur Brown had taught Budd Schulberg that West Side waterfront talkers tempted a Hudson River gravesite, a view reconfirmed in December 1952 by the steady procession of Irish waterfront dockworkers eschewing the chance to play even bit parts in proceedings that moved relentlessly toward the commission's scheduled confrontation with Bill McCormack and Joe Ryan. The mere rumor that figures from Pistol Local 824 had received subpoenas to testify before the NYSCC was sufficient to prompt a one-day strike of a thousand dockworkers on the West Side in late November. When the leading citizens of Local 824 took the witness stand on December 9, delegate Harold Bowers promptly pleaded the Fifth, a privilege invoked in rapid succession later that day by his cousin Mickey Bowers and the Bowers brothers' compatriot John "Keefey" Keefe.[24]

Recourse to constitutional rights could not spare these individuals local embarrassment and even shame. They had spent their entire lives unaccountable to anyone on the outside; now they were dragged into the glare of publicity mostly due to the unrelenting crusade of a local priest, the last person one might expect to humiliate such leading citizens of the Irish waterfront. There was nowhere to hide: late in the proceedings the dapper hoodlum Eddie McGrath returned from his new home in Florida in response to a subpoena from NYSCC. McGrath's request to read a statement at the outset of his testimony was denied: only after invoking the Fifth one-hundred and fifteen times was he finally allowed to inform the commission he had refused to answer all questions because he had been "depicted as a criminal, racketeer, and gangster" in recent newspaper accounts. NYSCC counsel Theodore Kiendl had but one final question for the witness: "Are you, in fact, a racketeer, criminal, or gangster?" To which Eddie McGrath replied: "I refuse to answer on the grounds that my answer might tend to incriminate me."[25]

Joe Ryan's second in command, ILA executive vice president Packy Connolly, was more responsive than most of his West Side compatriots. Connolly's testimony painted a relentlessly bleak portrait of life in his native Hell's Kitchen. When NYSCC commissioner Joseph Proskauer invited Packy to offer his "theory" as to why so many ILA-related West Side murders went unsolved, Connolly grudgingly if accurately summarized the neighborhood's prevailing philosophy of life and death: "Well, coming from the West Side and being born there, living there all my life, anybody is liable to get killed in a fight in a saloon or some place. That's my theory of it. That is the way things happen. They have an argument and people get in trouble and they get into fights."[26]

Connolly was most unhelpful in unraveling the money trail that NYSCC officials clearly believed led directly to Joe Ryan and Bill McCormack, against whom they were building an empirical case in anticipation of the men's testimony at the conclusion of the public hearings. While they were flummoxed by recalcitrant dockworkers, damning testimony was elicited from industry figures less prone than longshoremen to take the Fifth. Though the commission dismally failed to crack the Irish waterfront's code of silence, a powerful evidentiary record was amassed from testimony of shipping executives whose sheepishness on the stand could not obscure their culpability.

One of the hearings' most revealing moments occurred on the very first day, December 3, 1952, when Ruth M. Kennedy, "a stately woman with gray hair, wearing colored glasses," as she was described in the *New York Times*, "admitted on the stand that she got up cash in envelopes and checks made out in fictitious names, for distribution to Mr. Ryan and to other I.L.A. officials." Ruth Kennedy was secretary-treasurer of Daniels and Kennedy, Inc., a stevedoring and trucking concern whose president, her nephew James C. Kennedy, admitted to having bestowed annual and semiannual payoffs (totaling $7,500 between 1947 and 1951) upon Joe Ryan in return for labor tranquility. Interrogators were determined to reconstruct the verbal exchanges between Ryan and Kennedy at the moment when the gratuity-laden envelopes hit Ryan's desk, as if to demonstrate that Joe acknowledged his culpability, at least in private. Kennedy insisted in every way possible that no words were ever traded beyond an occasional "thanks" from Ryan.[27]

A pattern of recent shakedowns by union officials and payoffs to Ryan and other ILA figures by stevedores and shippers left no doubt that the waterfront remained open for all manner of shady business long after Malcolm Johnson's "Crime on the Waterfront" had inflamed the sensibilities of civic reformers. One stevedoring firm was found to have paid for the lavish wedding of an ILA chieftain's daughter and a Miami vacation for her parents, while others admitted to lining the pockets of numerous ILA officials in return for labor comity. The commission "traced massive payments—amounting to hundreds of thousands of dollars over a five-year period—by stevedoring companies to shipping firms, evidently to buy business or good will." Stevedores also paid handsome sums to phantom employees, with paychecks finding their way into the pockets of Sing Sing alumni all along the West Side in return for the goodwill of these ILA "organizers." Witnesses testified that terminal managers for steamship companies offered "no resistance to the influx of functionless criminals" who often doubled as independent racketeer-businessmen and ILA officials.[28]

The season for hearings touched virtually every prominent waterfront figure. On January 15, 1953, NYSCC assistant chief counsel Leslie H. Arps formally requested Father John M. Corridan's appearance before the committee at a public hearing to explore "the method of employment of longshoremen in the Port of New York and the problem presented by the existence of the so-called public loaders on the piers in the Port of New York." The hearing was scheduled for January 29, the very day the commission had also designated for Bill McCormack's long-awaited testimony. On January 16 Corridan informed the Jesuit provincial, Father John McMahon, "As ever I am willing and available: a. for consultation. b. To appear before any proper governmental body not concerned with crime as such at their request."[29]

Corridan and his superior had been engaged in discernment over the most appropriate role for the waterfront priest to play in the hearings since March 1952, shortly before he was served a subpoena to appear in a private preliminary session. Corridan had never testified in a legal proceeding or crime-related public inquiry, and the Jesuits preferred that he refrain from doing so, but as he informed McMahon in March, the crime commission "feels that they would be delinquent in the eyes of the public, if they failed to call me as an expert witness on waterfront matters." He proposed that any public testimony be limited to "sociological lines," but "if they should choose to question me privately but not for the permanent record on specific criminal matters that I may have knowledge of but which will not involve any secrets I hold either under the seal [of the confessional] or as professional secrets, I would try to be helpful." He also asked to appear before the commission without legal counsel present. A failure to testify, he concluded, would be viewed as "a decision reached under the influence of present waterfront forces and therefore a scandal." As always, in broaching such delicate matters Corridan was well served by the quiet force and hidden hand of Father Phil Carey.[30]

On April 10, one day prior to his meeting with Bill McCormack at the provincial's East Fordham Road residence, Corridan provided a copy of a written statement he proposed to submit to the commission. On April 15 Father McMahon approved the statement: a Jesuit censor had simply "suggested a few verbal changes...for the purpose of improving the expression." On May 1 Corridan appeared before representatives of the NYSCC unaccompanied by an attorney. The statement he submitted in this closed session contained his most explicit recommendation to date for a rigorous system of registration for all longshoremen working in the port. Registration would "strike at the twin basic evils of the chronic oversupply of labor and the deep insecurity that men suffer as a consequence." With work regularized and an "equitable seniority system" instituted, "the men would have the same status as workers do in other industries." Corridan also proposed that "all public loaders, individuals and corporations should be licensed."[31]

Corridan's licensing and registration scheme was a classic progressive reform tactic, with the power of the state (or more precisely in this case the Port Authority or similar agency) usurping the autonomy of an inefficient and inhumane labor market. An expanded version of this reform blueprint was officially submitted to the NYSCC in January 1953—at the height of the inquiry's public phase—and released to extraordinary acclaim. Corridan's "eight-point plan" called for elimination of the shapeup and urged that public loading ("the source of a great deal of waterfront evil") be outlawed in its entirety. He also called for a new division of the port into seven centers for hiring and urged that the municipal piers in New York City be turned over to the Port Authority, as had those in Hoboken and Newark. Ever the New Yorker, he argued:

> The Port is a natural unit yet there is competition between the two states for business. New Jersey has cost advantages and now has advantage of oversight from the Port Authority.... The Port of New York Authority should be given over-all responsibility for the port even though the Port Authority and political interests are not anxious for the Port Authority to assume such responsibility.

He also urged the commission to press member firms of the New York Shipping Association "to allow rank and file longshoremen to replace the present company union with its gangster dominated leadership for a bona-fide union devoted to the interests of longshoremen."[32]

The plan was intended as a stinging rebuke to the waterfront's cherished localism and suspicion of outsiders, and so it was received. The proposals' extraordinarily widespread distribution raised Corridan's visibility in the New York area to an all-time high. The enthusiastic public response also effectively ended any remaining claim he had staked as a representative of the men, who abhorred outside interference in their affairs from any source.

On January 29, following the predictably unenlightening testimony of NYSA executive director John V. Lyon—and with Bill McCormack waiting in the wings—Kiendl announced that Father Corridan ("who has helped the longshoremen so tremendously in many ways for many years") had been invited to appear on that day, but the NYSCC had "received an answer" from "his superiors and his lawyer to the effect that by reason of his priestly offices he believes he should not appear and testify before the Commission."[33]

Mr. Big in the Dock

The stage was set in Corridan's absence for the public debut of the secretive, mysterious industry titan whose legend had flourished since his having been anointed "Mr. Big" sixteen months earlier. The tension had grown palpable in the weeks since McCormack's name was first invoked during December 16 testimony by Robert F. Burker, treasurer of the waterfront tycoon's flagship Penn Stevedoring Company. Burker "seemed rather nervous under questioning. He proved to be a very evasive witness," reported the *Times,* especially when asked about his firm's record and policy on hiring ex-convicts. Burker acknowledged that he had known McCormack for thirty years but indicated he did not know who headed the Jersey Contracting Company, though that firm and Penn Stevedoring shared offices and "are described as affiliated concerns." Burker initially contradicted testimony from earlier that day by an official of the New York State Division of Parole, who confirmed that he had paroled two hundred men from state prisons since 1944 on condition that they were employed by Penn Stevedoring. Burker finally admitted that one John "Chopsy" Plattner had approached him seeking employment for notorious gunman Albert Ackalitis, the former leader of the Arsenal Mob, who appeared on the witness stand that same day, declining to answer any questions.[34]

When his turn finally came six weeks later, Bill McCormack answered all of Kiendl's questions, after a West Side fashion. Kiendl seemed at least as intent on winning a confession of the businessman's true waterfront identity as on eliciting an admission of sharp practices. He began by probing with all due solemnity the nature of McCormack's unofficial title, the publicist-concocted appellation "the little man's Port Authority," which McCormack proudly embraced within moments of taking the witness stand. The following day, as McCormack's appearance before the commission drew to a close, Kiendl sought to bracket his testimony with an admission of his *real* title. "As a matter of fact," Kiendl boldly inquired, "on the waterfront at the present time, as a result of a half century of experience, you are 'Mr. Big,' aren't you?"

"No, sir, I am not," replied the witness.

"I don't mean it in any sinister sense," assured Kiendl. "Aren't you willing to admit that?"

"No."

Kiendl proceeded as if he hadn't heard the response. "One of the most important, most powerful influences on the New York waterfront, in the New York Harbor today?" he pressed on.

"Counselor, I don't—" McCormack began to answer before Kiendl interrupted: "Can't you just say yes or no to that and then explain? You're not willing to say that, are you?"

"I would say no," McCormack wearily replied.

"That's a full answer, isn't it?" Kiendl dejectedly conceded.

"Only two letters," the businessman assured his interrogator. "It covers everything."[35]

As Kiendl's questioning confirmed, after months of background investigation and twenty long days of public hearings, the commission continued to approach the New York waterfront from the lurid perspective of newspaper and broadcast exposés that had shaped a master narrative no one could evade: all parties were preassigned to fixed roles in the crime melodrama. As the special counsel badgered McCormack: "You have heard about crime,

crime, crime, crime, on the waterfront of the City of New York for the last twenty years [*sic*], haven't you? . . . You have read about it in the newspapers; you have seen it in the magazines; you have heard about it everywhere you['ve] gone, haven't you?" McCormack helpfully volunteered, "They've had movies about it." "There are movies about it," Kiendl concurred. "It has been drummed into your consciousness from every possible source."[36]

This was where Bill McCormack demurred. He had surely heard that a waterfront film was in the works; perhaps he had even seen one or more of the spate of "syndicate films" inspired by the Kefauver hearings, featuring characters based on Frank Costello and other leading organized crime figures who had achieved celebrity via Kefauver's probe. "Mr. Big" did not, however, accept the premise that evidence from movies and print exposés sufficiently established as incontrovertible the reality of a crime-ridden waterfront. Kiendl wanted to know why McCormack had downplayed criminality in his role as an industry figure serving on Mayor O'Dwyer's Joint Committee on Port Industry. Had he not contradicted himself by suggesting elsewhere that the port faced a precipitous decline if its facilities were not upgraded? But these were not contradictory positions: the prodigious entrepreneur fretted over commerce, not crime. It was certainly true—as George Horne of the *Times* had reported the previous August—that the report issued by McCormack's subcommittee had "whitewashed" waterfront labor conditions; but exposing the merely self-serving was never the mission of the NYSCC.[37]

Kiendl's overdependence on the waterfront's lurid narrative tradition enabled McCormack to undermine its legitimacy—and that of the hearings as a whole—precisely by treating it *as* fictionalized. The more Kiendl challenged (by citing) McCormack's prior condemnation of sensation-seeking writers (for example, "their warped minds leading them to think a fork lift is an Emily Post device for correct eating"), the more authentic he made McCormack sound by way of contrast. The entrepreneur presented himself as a world-weary realist against Kiendl's manic determination to find a crime behind every act of waterfront charity, correcting errors in virtually every detail of his biography as prompted by his interrogator's leading questions.[38]

When he relied on previously established facts, Kiendl fared much better. McCormack was unable (and unwilling) to explain, for instance, why NYSCC accountants could not locate any vouchers for nearly $1 million in "petty cash" disbursements by his firms in recent years, nor could he account for the whereabouts of two employees who the commission believed could help solve the mystery (it was suspected that the pair had recently burned documents at a McCormack-owned facility in the Bronx).[39]

The long first day of McCormack's testimony finally "developed a sensation in the last fifteen minutes," the *New York Times* reported, "over his denial that he had shaken down Tex Rickard, the late boxing promoter, for $81,500 and had been forced by Gov. Alfred E. Smith to resign from the Boxing Commission." Westbrook Pegler had described the alleged September 1923 incident (misdated in the NYSCC transcript as 1925) in his October 1951 column "exposing" McCormack as "Mr. Big." The tycoon dismissed the charge as "an alcoholic's dream"; but on January 30 the NYSCC produced an eyewitness, Francis X. McQuade, a former New York City magistrate and onetime treasurer of the corporation that owned the Polo Grounds, site of the legendary 1923 Jack Dempsey–Luis Firpo heavyweight bout.[40]

The seventy-five-year-old McQuade was the "father of Sunday baseball" in New York, a graduate of Chelsea's Xavier High School, longtime Tammany operative, and drinking and brawling partner of manager John McGraw and other legendary roughnecks with the New York Giants baseball club in the early decades of the century. McQuade's interest in sporting activities—including investments in a Havana casino—came to light in 1930 during the anti-Tammany inquiries of Judge Samuel Seabury that helped send Mayor Jimmy Walker into exile. McQuade resigned the magistrate's position, though even Seabury was compelled to acknowledge there was no evidence "showing any act of corruption."[41]

The elderly McQuade was now ailing (he interrupted his testimony "to take a couple of pills right now") but steadfast in his recollection, stating plainly that shortly after the Dempsey-Firpo bout Charles A. Stoneham of the Polo Grounds told him that McCormack had shaken down Rickard in return for a license to hold the fight and that McQuade should instruct McCormack to return the cash. The ex-magistrate testified that he quickly contacted McCormack and ordered him to return the money within two hours, which was done without any explanation. Several months later Governor Smith demanded McCormack's resignation from the Boxing Commission.[42]

Despite District Attorney Frank Hogan's pledge to explore possible perjury charges stemming from McQuade's testimony, there were no legal repercussions, but the issue was serious. As historian Jeffrey Sammons noted, "although McCormack was never formally charged, his alleged extortion was one of many questionable practices that would plague athletic commissions and the boxing profession, constantly placing the sport in jeopardy and opening it up to infiltration by organized crime." The statute of limitations on 1920s tough-guy behavior offered sufficient immunity in any case.[43]

As reporting on McCormack's testimony demonstrated, the spectacle surrounding his appearance was more significant than any legal outcome. Coverage of the NYSCC hearings by the New York dailies was lavish throughout, with no outlet more devoted to the fireworks than the *Times,* which dedicated vast swaths of its news pages to reporting and excerpted testimony. Both the hearings and the coverage reached a climax in Bill

McCormack's testimony: the *Times* portrayed him as "a silver haired, rubicund contractor," a

> caricature of the self-made man of slight education who had fought his way from poverty on the brawling waterfront to wealth and political power. He answered all Mr. Kiendl's questions directly, granting nothing, and smiling grimly as he spotted a nasty implication in the interrogation. Never once did he turn for aid to the slender, nervous lawyer [Jacob Goodstein] hovering nearby.[44]

McCormack's appearance partly satiated civic curiosity and may even have reduced slightly the menacing aura that suffused published reports prior to his debut on the witness stand. *Life* magazine quickly produced a photo essay titled "Mr. Big Becomes Less Mysterious"; though it added nothing substantive ("paternalist toward his men, powerful in politics," McCormack "wields enormous power over Joe Ryan"), Cornell Capa's photographs depicted a devoted head of a family—blessed with a large staff of servants—and hands-on tycoon. During his appearance on the witness stand McCormack announced that he had decided two years earlier to retire from all "public activity" apart from his business interests. If he left the stand January 30 with his "reputation in ruins," as *New York Times* reporters James Glanz and Eric Lipton would write a half-century later, there is no indication that his private enterprises suffered markedly.[45]

Joe Ryan was another story. King Joe followed McCormack to the witness stand on January 30 whistling "When Irish Eyes Are Smiling" and left his audience laughing to the end. During the final moments of the final day of testimony Ryan breezily acknowledged that much of the "secret anticommunist fund" with which he had been entrusted since the mid-1930s had been spent on other purposes because "I have to have a few vices." In the interim, however, his Irish sentimentality and loyalty to old friends betrayed King Joe as he ranged from sharing warm memories of Jersey Shore summers with waterfront politicos to admitting less wholesome intercessions on behalf of Eddie McGrath, Albert Ackalitis, Eddie Florio, and other characters about whom Bill McCormack feigned ignorance.[46]

Most surprising was Ryan's blithe admission of a friendship with Albert Anastasia dating back at least fifteen years. Unlike his brother Anthony, Albert had no formal affiliation with the ILA. The international union's life president testified that he only learned of Anastasia's violent takeover of three former "Camarda locals" in Brooklyn from Bill O'Dwyer back in the days when his old friend was serving as King's County district attorney. If Joe customarily "left the Italians strictly alone" to run the Brooklyn waterfront, as Daniel Bell had reported, he now boasted of many pleasurable hours spent in the company of the reputed "Lord High Executioner" of Murder, Inc., at the fights, at golf clubs, and in barbershops (including perhaps the midtown shop in whose chair Anastasia would be reclining when struck by assassins' bullets in 1957). In boasting this connection Ryan was virtually pleading to be pinned with the label "mob associate," though the same might be said of anyone who spent too much time in King Joe's company.[47]

The contrast between Joe Ryan's indefatigably good-natured bluster and Bill McCormack's steely reserve was most striking. In his own testimony McCormack had denied ever having welcomed Ryan into his home, establishing a critical distance that would grow into a yawning chasm before the year was over. As Murray Kempton wrote at the conclusion of the hearings: "They threw Joe to the mastiffs[,]...all the respectable people he calls by their first names: William J. McCormack, his best friend, and the ship owners he served so long....Friday morning, in his own darkening hour, Bill McCormack showed the door to poor Joe Ryan as to an old hound gone in the teeth."[48]

Unlike his patron and sponsor McCormack, Ryan could not help but admit that he followed all the latest reporting on waterfront crime in the papers; he seemed intent on making for good copy, consequences be damned. Joseph Patrick Ryan truly was a throwback to the days of Dick Butler and other saloon-keeping labor politicians of the West Side for whom good Irish fellowship served as an insurance policy against such jams as that in which Joe now found himself. His prospects would only darken, quickly.

13 "The Hook"

The year 1952 was high season for public testimony of many kinds. On April 10—the same day Pete Corridan submitted for his superior's approval his written testimony for the New York State Crime Commission—the renowned film and theater director Elia Kazan answered a summons to appear at a public hearing of the House Committee on Un-American Activities in Washington. Kazan presented a written statement disclosing his membership in the Communist Party "from some time in the summer of 1934 until the late winter or early spring of 1936, when I severed all connection with it permanently." Kazan had so confessed in a private "executive" session on January 14 of that year. What he failed to do in January he did now, serving up names of communists he had known in the "unit" ordered by the party to take control of the Group Theatre, "possibly the single most important theatrical enterprise in American history," in the estimation of Kazan's biographer Richard Schickel.[1]

Born in Istanbul to a family of Anatolian Greeks who immigrated to the United States in 1913, when Elia was four, Kazan worked his way through Williams College and the Yale Drama School. He joined the Group Theatre in 1932, a year after it was founded by Cheryl Crawford, Harold Clurman, and Lee Strasberg. Twenty years later, in Room 330 of the Old House Office Building in Washington, D.C., Kazan named eight onetime members of the Group's party unit, including Strasberg's wife, Paula ("We are friends today," Kazan reported), and playwright Clifford Odets, his erstwhile "best friend" and Popular Front icon as author of the Group Theatre's agitprop drama *Waiting for Lefty*. After Kazan's raised-fist cry of "Strike!" prompted a raucous, impromptu demonstration by the audience on opening night in March, 1935, the influential Marxist journal *New Masses* dubbed the unknown young actor the "Proletariat Thunderbolt."[2]

By the time of his 1952 testimony Kazan was the hottest, most "bankable" film and theater director in the nation: in 1949 alone he conquered both Hollywood—winning an Academy Award for his direction of *Gentlemen's Agreement*—and Broadway, with his staging of Arthur Miller's classic *Death of a Salesman*. Kazan then embarked on a new collaborative project with the gifted playwright, a waterfront-themed script—"The Hook"— conceived by Miller as "a play written for the screen." In early winter 1951 Kazan's prodigious energy was focused on this project, as well as on directing the film version of Tennessee Williams's *Streetcar Named Desire*, which he had staged on Broadway, and *Viva Zapata*, from a screenplay by John Steinbeck. The extraordinary young actor Marlon Brando played the lead role in both films, deepening the already close relationship he had forged with Kazan at the Actors Studio, an incubator of dramatic talent the director co-founded in New York in 1947 along with fellow Group Theatre veterans Cheryl Crawford and Robert Lewis. Kazan was certain that these diverse projects "would amplify my image as the leading progressive in the performing arts."[3]

But not even this highly successful run could defer a reckoning with Kazan's past politics. Movie moguls Darryl Zanuck and Spyros Skouras of Twentieth Century–Fox implored him to name names in the days following leaks of his inconclusive January 1952 testimony. The failure of *Streetcar*— a Warner Brothers production—to claim the Oscar for Best Picture at the March 1952 Academy Awards ceremony led to film industry conjecture that Kazan's political vulnerability hurt the film's reception, a view heightened by his loss to George Stevens (*A Place in the Sun*) for Best Director. Though Vivien Leigh, Kim Hunter, and Karl Malden all won Oscars for their performances in *Streetcar*, Zanuck and Skouras fretted over Fox's investment in the just-released *Viva Zapata*.

The once merely "controversial" director was suddenly a potential liability to his employers. Fearing the end of his Hollywood career, Kazan sought the counsel of friends. He had to testify. "There's nothing else you can do," he was reportedly advised both by the highly respected film producer Bud Lighton—with whom he had worked on *A Tree Grows in Brooklyn* (1945)—and by Lee Strasberg, the dominant figure at both the Group Theatre and the Actors Studio, who told Kazan, "I don't mind if you name me." Yet the "'horrible, immoral thing' I would do," Kazan wrote in 1988, "I did out of my true self. Everything before was seventeen years of posturing."[4]

After accepting Kazan's amended HUAC testimony on April 10, U.S. Representative Francis E. Walter windily assured him, "It is only through the assistance of people such as you that we have been able to make the progress that has been made in bringing the attention of the American people to the machinations of this communist conspiracy for world dominance." Kazan meekly offered "to do anything to help—anything you consider necessary or valuable," but his timidity turned to defiance in a post-testimony

New York Times advertisement drafted by his wife, Molly, the intensity of whose political convictions first as a staunch leftist and now as a militant anticommunist far outshone her husband's. Without question Elia Kazan was an unapologetic opportunist and a self-styled survivor, traits that if highlighted in the ad might at least have won him points for candor. He chose instead to rehash ancient quarrels with communists.[5]

"Instead of understanding, it brought me scorn and hardened the antagonism," Kazan acknowledged in his 1988 memoir. "I soon became the target of a well-organized campaign branding my act as shameful. That was to continue for many months and, in certain quarters, still persists.... When I began to move among people again, I found I was notorious, an 'informer,' a 'squealer,' a 'rat.'" Publishing his "Statement" was arguably a much poorer idea than his decision to testify, for as Schickel explained, it "made him a permanent target. By this one act he became the celebrity informer— the namer of names nearly everyone could name, the great symbolic stooge, rat fink of the era."[6]

Although Kazan later insisted that the ordeal "made a man of me," at the time he also "became aware of a hole in my professional life." At his wife's urging he contacted Budd Schulberg, whom he had never met; soon they were enjoying a weekend together at Schulberg's farmhouse in Pennsylvania. In January 1952 HUAC investigators had given Kazan a copy of Schulberg's testimony from the previous year, but Kazan already knew of the writer's battles with party cultural commissars over *What Makes Sammy Run?* He identified strongly with Schulberg's posture as a man of the Left deeply resistant to censorship or political interference with the creative process. Like Kazan, Budd "had been reviled by many of his old companions.... As we talked that first night in New Hope, there was an immediate warm sympathy between us. We became brothers." At that first meeting they discussed a potential collaboration on a film of social conflict set in the urban Northeast: Kazan suggested a project on the Trenton Six, a group of African American men who had been falsely accused of murdering a white store owner in New Jersey in 1948.[7]

Schulberg was much less interested in the Trenton Six than in the waterfront script he had completed the previous year, though an inkling of the painful history behind Kazan's recent break with Arthur Miller may have accounted for Budd's hesitance to promote his own screenplay at their first meeting. At a second meeting with Kazan in the summer of 1952 Schulberg "pushed harder for my waterfront script. That's when [Kazan] told me for the first time that he had been working on his own waterfront project with Arthur Miller," a screenplay set in Brooklyn. Without wishing to aggravate raw feelings, Schulberg, in Kazan's words, "found the screenplay" he had written, and "lying on the floor, I eagerly read it." Kazan judged the script (misidentifying "Crime on the Waterfront" as "The Bottom of the River" in his memoir, substituting the title of a subsequent treatment) "strong, true stuff but, as they say in our line, [it] needed work." Kazan then left for Bavaria to shoot *Man on a Tightrope,* but not before reconfirming his desire to work with Schulberg on the waterfront project.[8]

Arthur Miller at the Water's Edge

This burgeoning creative partnership would elicit frequent comparisons with the ill-fated Kazan-Miller collaboration on "The Hook," particularly in light of Kazan's newfound determination "to make a film about the New York Harbor and what went on there, thus to show everyone, including myself, that I hadn't backed away from my convictions and wasn't to be insulted or bullied again." The back story of "The Hook" is among the most revealing in the tortuous annals of Cold War cultural politics. Kazan and Miller had grown extraordinarily close in the years since 1946, when they collaborated on *All My Sons,* the first great triumph of Miller's career as a dramatist. Kazan "immediately felt close to" Miller, who had been inspired by the Group Theatre. "We were both out of the Depression," wrote Kazan, "both left-wingers, both had problems with our fathers, considered their business worlds antihuman."[9]

The triumph of *Death of a Salesman,* which opened on Broadway on February 10, 1949, cemented their creative and fraternal bond. In the early spring of that year Miller completed the first draft of "The Hook," a project conceived during long brooding walks from the playwright's home in Brooklyn Heights to the Red Hook waterfront, where he first noticed Italian graffiti "on walls and sidewalks" reading "*Dove* Pete Panto" (Where is Pete Panto?). When "the sentence began showing up in subway stations and chalked on Court Street office buildings," Miller "took to wandering the bars on the waterfront to pick up whatever I could about Panto," the young Brooklyn dockworker murdered in 1939 for leading a movement of Italian American insurgents against mob rule over the local piers. "Panto's revolt was getting somewhere," Brooklyn district attorney George J. Beldock asserted in 1941, shortly after the activist's remains were discovered in a "lime-lined gang graveyard the mob maintained" in Lyndhurst, New Jersey. Though "*Dove* Pete Panto" was strictly a rhetorical question by the time Miller discovered the Red Hook waterfront in 1948, "the idea of a longshoreman standing up to the arrogance of such power chilled me with awe," he wrote, even as he lamented, "I could never penetrate the permanent reign of quiet terror on the waterfront." Then suddenly a pair of Brooklynites, Vincent "Jimmy" Longhi and Mitch Berenson, materialized to guide Miller through this "dangerous and mysterious world at the water's edge that drama and literature had never touched."[10]

Unlike Budd Schulberg's intrepid waterfront navigator Arthur Brown, Longhi and Berenson were not real longshoremen but feisty communists from the American Labor Party. Jimmy Longhi was a colorful figure at the heart of Brooklyn's postwar Popular Front scene that also included folksinger Woody Guthrie, who Longhi befriended while they served together in the wartime Merchant Marine. According to Richard Schickel, Longhi was among "a small group of Stalinists inhabiting the far left of the Italian-speaking branch of the labor movement." Longhi and Berenson told Miller they had "worked with" Panto on an anti–Joe Ryan insurgency. By 1948 Longhi was a leader of the Back Pay Committee, "an amalgam of rank-and-file action and left-wing legal collaborators" who skillfully appropriated "*Dove* Pete Panto" as a rhetorical device to mobilize Italian American longshoremen against both Ryan and the Brooklyn mob.[11]

A warm rapport quickly developed between Longhi and Miller, though the playwright promptly dashed Longhi's hopes for a cash windfall in support of either the Back Pay Committee or Longhi's quixotic run for the Brooklyn congressional seat held by Joe Ryan's friend and Democratic crony John Rooney. Longhi nevertheless concocted a grandiose scheme to travel with Miller to Italy in the winter of 1948–49: he would collect letters from southern Italian kinfolk of prospective constituents while Miller conducted research. Unlikely as it may seem, Miller agreed and soon found himself sharing an impromptu lunch in Palermo with Longhi and repatriated waterfront mobster Charles "Lucky" Luciano. Apparently Longhi hoped to forge an anti-Ryan alliance between leftists and Italian American organized crime figures.[12]

The peculiar trajectory of his Italian research yielded Miller's erroneous view that "the hiring system on the Brooklyn and Manhattan waterfronts had been imported from the Sicilian countryside." (The shapeup had in fact long been a fixture on the New York docks.) After returning to Brooklyn, Jimmy Longhi was trounced in his bid for a congressional seat, but not before he persuaded Miller to write a film script championing waterfront radicalism. The playwright flatly described "The Hook" as "the screenplay about Panto's doomed attempt to overthrow the feudal gangsterism of the New York waterfront." The jarring contrast between *Salesman* and the initial draft of "The Hook," a dismal two-hundred-page exercise in Stalinist-tainted propaganda, shows just how precarious was the balance between Miller's artistic and political instincts.[13]

This version of "The Hook—rarely cited in the vast canon of Miller scholarship—features a heroic young attorney, Francis Salvo (Longhi), and his comrade, rank-and-file leader Marty Ferrera (a blend of Pete Panto and Mitch Berenson). Recent events from the Brooklyn waterfront are thinly dramatized, from the emergence of Longhi's Back Pay Committee to the clash of black longshoremen from Local 968 with union boss Dan Killian (Joe Ryan). "The Hook" rehashes party-line efforts to vilify Ryan as a fascist dating back to 1938, when King Joe was caricatured in the *New Republic* as a demagogue commanding a private army. It was as though in the absence of any real knowledge of the waterfront the playwright simply grafted ideological abstractions onto characters and situations.[14]

Miller's second, oft-cited version of "The Hook" was substantially improved, and Kazan clearly deserves much of the credit: despite qualms that Miller had done a "half-ass job finishing the script," Kazan "agreed to help prepare 'The Hook' for a movie studio." He worked hard with Miller on the final version, especially during an extended sojourn to Hollywood they shared in January 1951. The friends took up residence in producer Charlie Feldman's home and attended parties where Kazan tormented his unhappily married partner by "cheerfully, inconsequentially" enjoying a casual affair with twenty-four-year-old Marilyn Monroe (to whom Miller would later be even more unhappily married).[15]

The version of "The Hook" the duo finally presented to Darryl Zanuck of Twentieth Century–Fox reflected Kazan's far more "cinematic" instincts: Francis Salvo was excised and the ideological intimacy shared by Francis and Marty replaced by the much deeper and more complex relationship of Marty and his wife, Theresa. Marty now runs for president of his longshoremen's union local; the election is rigged by racketeers, but Marty learns he would have lost anyway since his own supporters are too fearful of losing their jobs to vote for him. In a strange twist, some of the men find sufficient courage to demand that Marty be named union delegate, a position he proudly accepts as the screenplay ends.[16]

"The Hook" garnered a quick rejection from Zanuck on the basis of "subject matter" (by Kazan's account), despite Zanuck's sterling commercial and artistic track record with the director on successful films including *A Tree Grows in Brooklyn* (1945), *Gentlemen's Agreement* (1947), and *Pinky* (1949). Zanuck's reputation as a mainstay of "Hollywood's left-wing roster" suddenly counted for little. At Columbia Pictures, Harry Cohn showed brief interest but was "seriously concerned about the 'The Hook's' characterization of organized labor as corrupt and gangster-ridden." Cohn consulted Roy Brewer, a friend of Joe Ryan's who ran the International Alliance of Theatrical and Stage Employees and was among a small group of industry figures "suspected Communists went to in order to arrange clearances from studio blacklisting." Brewer tauntingly suggested that Miller convert the film's villains from gangsters to communists to make it palatable to AFL unions sharing Brewer's fear that "the script's negative depiction of New York longshoremen would be exploited by the Communist Party." According to Richard Schickel, the subtext of these negotiations was "the implicit threat to expose Miller's Communist connections. Which worked." Miller withdrew the script, to Kazan's bafflement and dismay. When the director defended Miller to Cohn at their final meeting on the project, the producer remarked of the playwright, "I could tell just by looking at him, he's still one of them." "What about me?" asked Kazan. "You're just a good-hearted whore like me," Cohn replied.[17]

A Question of Provenance

In the context of the Red scare it is easy to see why, as Victor Navasky put it, "Kazan emerged in the folklore of the left as the quintessential informer, and Miller was hailed as the risk-taking conscience of the times." "The Hook" and its author were lionized as victims of political intimidation and Hollywood censorship, while the very different waterfront film subsequently created by Kazan and Schulberg was widely condemned as either a morally compromised work promoting reactionary politics or a pilfered version of Miller's original (or both). Miller himself surely believed the former but promoted the latter theory, informing literary scholar Christopher Bigsby in 1995 that his screenplay "was later the basis of *On the Waterfront*."[18]

Miller's biographer Martin Gottfried went so far as to ridicule the "claim that Schulberg had been working on his own waterfront screenplay at the same time as Miller: the only problem," concluded Gottfried, "is it isn't true." Yet of course it *is* true; the issue is no longer in dispute. After comparing "The Hook" with Schulberg's final 1954 screenplay, Richard Schickel dismissed Gottfried's claim for Miller's paternity of *On the Waterfront* as "absurd." But the case is closed most decisively simply by reintroducing the conclusive evidence, Schulberg's April 1951 "Crime on the Waterfront," which was completed more than a year before he met Kazan (and learned of Miller's script) and which treated themes of moral conversion on the waterfront featuring a priest and dissident longshoremen in prominent roles.[19]

The absence of a priest in "The Hook" is the most revealing element in this debate. A waterfront priest plays a pivotal role in each and every screenplay Schulberg drafted between early 1951 and late autumn 1953. Even Kazan's partisans overlook this crucial point: Schickel alludes but once to an unnamed "waterfront priest" who figures less prominently in the screenplay, he argues, than in the waterfront novel and play Schulberg subsequently wrote. (Schickel does note that "there is no priest character" in "The Hook.") Though Pete Corridan's work was in many ways *the* story to Schulberg, their "spiritual front" partnership was occluded by the great bitterness caused by the Hollywood blacklist and the animus against "friendly witnesses" such as Schulberg and Kazan. In the context of the militantly Catholic anticommunism that was so dominant at the time, a priest could be viewed—if at all—only as a reactionary element. Yet Budd Schulberg had a richer and more complex story to tell.[20]

Schulberg and Kazan did not "pillage" Arthur Miller's screenplay in creating their own waterfront film, but that does not mean Pete Corridan failed to discern the ideological value of his collaboration with an ex-communist screenwriter. The Jesuit surely had ample incentive to further immunize Budd Schulberg against a party aesthetic he had never fully embraced in the first place. Corridan cultivated great intrigue in his dealings with former and current leftists. In autumn 1948 he instructed his disciple Arthur Brown to infiltrate planning meetings of the Communist Party's "waterfront section" in order to confirm that "the Party didn't have a legitimate longshoreman sitting in on their strategy meetings other than Brownie." In June of the following year he informed an Irish American Bronx congressman that "a book, a movie and a play on the New York waterfront are to be undertaken in the near future. Unfortunately [Arthur] Miller, twice winner of the Pulitzer play Prize and at least a Party innocent, will write the play." Later that autumn the Jesuit advised an aspiring playwright that Miller "will probably write from a class warfare viewpoint."[21]

In January 1950 Corridan engaged in a secret meeting with three New York communists, including Miller's good friend Mitch Berenson, where they explored the feasibility of replacing the shapeup with a West Coast–style system of hiring halls. Corridan "refused to cooperate with them in any way," he assured his superior. He "merely said it would be ok if they wanted to drop in from time to time and talk things over."[22]

Corridan, like Joe Ryan, was haunted by the prospect of a Brooklyn alliance of blacks and Italians manipulated by communists. He continued to view members of both groups as insufficiently "catechized" in the gospel of responsible unionism to resist the lure of the Left. This great historic fear plaguing the Irish waterfront was the lone theme treated insightfully by Miller in "The Hook." "I don't want no backfire from Brooklyn," Dan Killian (Ryan) screams at a crony in the first script, which also contains a memorable scene evoking King Joe's worst fears. Amid a Brooklyn waterfront melee provoked by union goons, African American antifascist longshoreman Johnny Boles testifies to his solidarity with the battered, largely Italian American rank and file. Heroic labor lawyer Francis Salvo, standing nearby, "suddenly bursts out, translating Boles into Italian. Boles assumes the right rhythm for Francis' interruptions." The unrealized ethnic and racial alliance on the waterfront of history is here fulfilled artistically. An analogous dynamic featuring very different politics would be evident in *On the Waterfront*.[23]

For the real distinction between "The Hook" and Schulberg's "Crime on the Waterfront" screenplay—and its subsequent reworkings—was not between "resisters" and "rats" but between Popular Front Brooklyn and the "spiritual front" politics Schulberg first imbibed from Corridan on Manhattan's Irish West Side. A genuine contest of ideas was in play. These competing waterfront scripts were deeply influenced by external forces; yet in the absence of an Arthur Brown to lend authentic-sounding dialogue and local color, Miller's rendition floundered. A comparative reading of the 1950–51 Miller and Schulberg scripts offers a fascinating glimpse of the dominant cultural-ideological struggle in New York City, if not in the port itself. The secular left-wing proletarian drama of "The Hook" vied with a Catholic redemption story as imagined by an ex-communist through the mediation of an Irish American Jesuit labor priest. The Brooklyn tale enshrined in "The Hook" conforms much more neatly to the standard political-historical narrative of McCarthy-era cultural politics, and so it proved far easier for critics to embrace as authentic. Yet the West Side version was scarcely more commercially appealing to Hollywood, as the struggle to bring *On the Water-front* to the screen would demonstrate.

Revival of a Partnership

In late summer and early autumn 1952, while Elia Kazan was at work in Bavaria on *Man on a Tightrope,* Budd Schulberg renewed his collaboration with Pete Corridan and Arthur Brown. He spent hours writing in a cramped office at Xavier Labor School. Years later, "pointing to a small round table in his office," Phil Carey told a reporter, "Schulberg sat at that desk for three years talking to Arthur Browning [*sic*]...and writing the screenplay.'" The decision to cooperate so fully with the screenwriter was another legacy of Carey's traumatic experience with the coopers of Pier 28 in 1941 that left him feeling "so alone" in the face of Bill McCormack's vast political, economic, and spiritual power.[24]

Schulberg was welcomed by Father Carey in the spirit of his endless waterfront quest for "some way to reform the whole damn thing." The marathon pub crawl the writer had shared with Arthur Brown in late 1950 paled before the months of intense collaboration they now enjoyed. Schulberg made numerous lengthy forays along the West Side with Brownie and practically lived with him and his wife, Anne, in their tiny apartment. Brownie continued to feed dialogue to the screenwriter. As Schulberg later informed Anne Brown: "I will never forget our days and nights together along the waterfront and in your home: the whole spirit of our film emanated from Brownie. He was our inspiration and our guiding star to truth."[25]

The depth of Budd Schulberg's affinity for Pete Corridan and his cause was revealed to Kazan when the director met with the two men at Xavier shortly after his return from Bavaria in early November 1952. The Jesuit "was in great form that day," Schulberg recalled in 1980. According to the screenwriter, Corridan was "furious" with Cardinal Spellman for "recommending Bill McCormack as the recipient of the highest honor a layman could receive in the Church." Corridan reportedly thundered: "That goddamn powerhouse! That Spellman! Who the hell does he think he is....[T]he damn Power House could clean this mess up in five minutes if it really read the riot act to those S.O.B.s....But the whole trouble is, they see all that cabbage." After the meeting Schulberg was "as proud of Father John as if I had created him myself," but Kazan had his doubts: "Are you sure he's a priest?" he asked Schulberg. "Maybe he's working there for the waterfront rebels in disguise." The writer told Kazan he had seen too many "Hollywood movies.

We both laughed, overjoyed, excited. Father John *was* a priest, a ruddy-faced Irish version of one of those French worker-priests, and we both knew we had to write his character and his morality into our picture."[26]

Kazan had never heard of worker-priests and harbored the same suspicion of the clergy that Schulberg had brought to his own first meeting with Corridan in 1950. The difference was that Kazan never relinquished his animus, which originated when, in the absence of a Greek Orthodox church, his immigrant father had sent him to "Catholic church and catechism school." Kazan "hated it....I had a lot of dealings with Catholics, and I've always had it in for them a little bit, though I like a lot of Catholic people and have lots of Catholic friends. I thought their religion was simplistic, mechanical, and slightly hypocritical."[27]

In September 1951 Kazan endured a bruising experience after Warner Brothers surreptitiously permitted Martin Quigley of the Legion of Decency, the powerful Catholic watchdog agency, to supervise a re-edit of the director's cut of *A Streetcar Named Desire*. The twelve cuts deleting words or images Quigley found morally unacceptable spared *Streetcar* the Legion's dreaded "Condemned" rating, defiance of which was viewed by many Catholic moviegoers as tantamount to instant excommunication. Kazan endured a dismal meeting with the sanctimonious Quigley, who colluded often with Joe Breen, the militantly Catholic head of the motion picture industry's self-censorship apparatus, which had earlier demanded and won changes in the script before *Streetcar* was granted the industry's seal of approval. Kazan came away with a conviction that the church shared much in common with the Communist Party, "particularly in the underground nature of their operation." Despite the director's great admiration for Corridan's work, there would be no "spiritual front" collaboration between Kazan and the waterfront priest.[28]

Secularists like Kazan were not alone in finding the Schulberg-Corridan partnership anomalous. The Jesuit and Arthur Brown once accompanied the screenwriter on a return trip from his New York waterfront research to Schulberg's home in bucolic Bucks County. As they embarked on the rail journey after first enjoying a quantity of drinks together, the three were detained by police officers as they sauntered arm in arm across the main concourse of Manhattan's Pennsylvania Station. They were separated and questioned for over an hour in basement interrogation rooms before each finally convinced the Irish cops that a Jewish screenwriter, a wizened longshoreman, and a more than slightly inebriated Jesuit in clerical garb had legitimate business together. Schulberg told the cops that Brownie had been assigned to him for research purposes, a story easier to sell than his working relationship with a priest.[29]

Amusing as the incident grew in later retellings, it revealed an issue of growing concern for Corridan. Everyone drank on the Irish waterfront, and many learned the hard way that they had better not. Convivial drinking was viewed there as a birthright: to expect longshoremen to abstain from alcohol was akin to asking them to refrain from breathing. Waterfront saloons were the most trusted sites for exchanging news and employment information. "Without the gin mills nothin' would have been accomplished. Everythin' was done in the bar," recalled a Chelsea native. Corridan's reputation for an ability to toss back beers with the best of his rebel disciples was integral to his credibility, even if he did most of his drinking outside the gaze of West Side longshoremen. At some point in the early 1950s if not earlier Corridan crossed a line separating heavy drinkers from alcoholics. Ironically, he had always lamented the habit of men to hit the bars immediately once they were not chosen at the shapeup. Yet he could never endorse a Protestant-founded if now Irish-dominated institution like Chelsea's Longshoremen's Rest, established by the Church Temperance Society in 1910 to provide a healthy alternative to the saloon.[30]

Corridan would eventually find his way to a program of spiritual recovery from alcoholism, but in 1952 he was far from ready, though a confrere had already made a profound contribution to that fellowship. St. Louis Jesuit Edward Dowling made an unannounced visit in November 1940 to the temporary Chelsea home of Bill Wilson, co-founder of Alcoholics Anonymous. Dowling was deeply impressed with this burgeoning movement; he discerned an affinity between the "twelve-steps" of A.A. and the spiritual exercises of Ignatius Loyola. Wilson, a Vermont Protestant, came to view Dowling as "the greatest spiritual figure who has ever come into my life." Yet it was one thing for Pete Corridan to know that prominent Jesuit colleagues were supportive of A.A.—if indeed he did—but quite another to make a decision to seek help, especially in a world where attitudes about masculinity and Irish American identity were so strongly linked to the culture of convivial drinking.[31]

Budd Schulberg's capacity for copious drinking cemented his solidarity with the West Side Irish waterfront rebels. As Kazan observed, "strong drink brought his deepest sympathies to the surface, and suspicious, often short-tempered longshoremen spoke plainly to him, for they saw he had genuine concern for every sorry twist of their lives." Pete Corridan was equally compassionate; but for a member of a community so deeply invested in the spirituality of "discernment," lapses in judgment induced by alcohol were matters of grave concern. The dilemma grew especially acute as he struggled to persuade others to speak publicly and truthfully about their waterfront experience. The preliminary results of this crusade were not promising: as of early 1953 the truth had set precisely nobody free. Tony Mike DeVincenzo, for a most notable example, was out of work and facing bleak prospects. Corridan had done little public speaking to longshoremen since his appearance at Local 791 at the height of the October 1951 strike, nor had he addressed them directly in writing. With his goals now in reach, he would finally become a target fashioned of his own words.[32]

14 *Good Citizens*

On January 18, 1953, Dorothy Schiff, the influential publisher of the *New York Post,* confessed that she had recently been hoodwinked by an "invitation" to "Hear a Hot Debate" between Father John Corridan and Joe Ryan at a venue on West Twenty-fourth Street in Manhattan. Schiff "visualized the meeting as a debate between the Saint and the Devil and could hardly wait for the evening to arrive." But when Ryan failed to show, Corridan "decided not to come, either," leaving Schiff wondering what she was doing at a locale on the far West Side that "is not a convenient place for me to reach from where I live." Despite the fiasco she remained sufficiently intrigued by Pete Corridan to arrange a subsequent meeting with the waterfront priest, and she was not disappointed. "He gives the impression," she enthused in the *Post,* "of spiritual, intellectual, and physical strength." Father Corridan had "for years been moving heaven and earth to publicize the scandal of the waterfront jungle," the publisher gushed. "He has talked productively to newspapermen, magazine writers, playwrights, motion picture producers in his efforts to publicize the situation." Corridan assuaged her fears that gangland figures surely wished to see him silenced. "They have a code of their own" he assured Schiff and her readers. "They do have respect for me."[1]

The New York State Crime Commission hearings vindicated Corridan and greatly expanded his celebrity capital. He was now lionized as virtual savior of the great port. On January 13 the immensely popular NBC Radio talk show couple Tex McCrary and Jinx Falkenberg "were pleased to throw" Corridan "the Savarin bouquet" provided by their coffee-making sponsor; it was among many spiritual and rhetorical tributes tossed the Jesuit's way in the aftermath of the NYSCC hearings. "He's a father to us all," a shop steward from Greenwich Village Local 895 testified to the *Journal-American* for a January pictorial tribute, "He Covers the Waterfront."

218

Corridan's abstinence from pious verbiage did not dissuade others from lauding his heroism. "Reverend Father, God has shown you the light," wrote an admirer from Newark in a January 1953 telegram. "You have followed and done right keep up your great fight and we'll all come out all right (please God we do)." In an admiring profile of the "tall, rugged man who looks as if he could haul cargo around the docks and decks with the best of the men he knows," the *New York Times* let Corridan explain

> why I think we are making progress. There is a revolution going on along the waterfront in the thinking of the men.... [T]hey used to slip in the back door so no one would see them. They would come in after mass, disappearing past the sacristy so no one outside would see them come to my office. Now they come right in the front door, boldly, and they are starting to really talk to me.[2]

The accolades emboldened Corridan to sharpen his critique of the shipping industry's complicity in waterfront crime. Shippers and stevedores attracted more attention from the Jesuit in the months following the NYSCC hearings than in all his previous work combined. "Big business" and the "political part" of the story were neglected during the lengthy proceedings, he complained to the *Herald Tribune,* but his own record showed a much greater emphasis on the sins of the ILA and the local employers who also dominated unions, most notably William J. McCormack. Shippers finally decided to set the waterfront priest straight. Hans Isbrandtsen, managing director of his family's venerable steamship line, angrily chastised Corridan for calling the ILA a "company union," accusing the Jesuit of ignorance and oversimplification. He was not mollified when Corridan clarified his earlier remarks in a January 1953 letter to Isbrandtsen, who promptly reiterated his original charge: "I do not believe you know what a company union really means, and therefore to place these conditions on us, who individually have been fighting an uphill battle against all this racketeering, is grossly unfair—and it should not be done—least of all, it seems to me, by a priest." Isbrandtsen's defensiveness reflected the beating that shippers had taken during the recent hearings, but there was an ominous tone in his warning: "This over-simplification can very often miss the object."[3]

Union leadership and its links to organized crime, hiring issues, and human dignity on the Irish waterfront remained Corridan's passion and drove three interwoven projects he ardently pursued in 1953. The fate of these initiatives would shape his legacy as well as the soul of a new waterfront. He aimed to see Joe Ryan ousted from the ILA and a new longshoremen's union built on the ruins of the old; win political approval for a bi-state agency to regulate waterfront employment practices; and see to fruition Budd Schulberg's film project, which he felt was certain to advance the cause of waterfront reform.

The waterfront union situation was more volatile than at any other time since the ascendance of the ILA early in the century. On February 3, 1953, the AFL's executive council took "unprecedented action" in ordering the ILA to rid itself of all "racketeering, crime, corruption, and other irregular activities" if it hoped to remain affiliated with the national federation. The union was given a deadline of April 30 to respond. The damage inflicted on Joe Ryan by the NYSCC hearings motivated the AFL's bold move against his union. King Joe was in deep trouble locally as well. On January 11 Guy Richards reported in the *Journal-American* that Italian American pier bosses (who now controlled virtually the entire port beyond the West Side) had convened a closed meeting in Brooklyn to vent their anger at Ryan in the wake of his testimony. The Italian bosses "are understood to be especially roiled at the share of blame showered on them for what they regard as the backward ILA leadership coming from Ryan's office," not to mention his recent boastful claims of friendship with Albert Anastasia, an individual whose role on the Brooklyn waterfront was not a subject deemed fit for public discussion.[4]

"To All Harbor Workers"

There was rougher news out of Brooklyn for King Joe: according to Guy Richards, "a number of Ryan's West Side leaders attended [the secret January meeting] and lent silent assent to a scathing 'dressing down' based on the scandals uncovered" by the NYSCC. Joe Ryan's united Irish waterfront had finally cracked. Pete Corridan sensed the opening and struck quickly: in mid-January he launched a direct written appeal to the rank and file in his own name and partisan voice. This "mail order campaign among longshoremen," as the *New York Times* admiringly described it, offered detailed explanations of "the points in his own plan for waterfront reform." Corridan conceded to the *Times* that "if nothing comes of the Crime Commission investigation and they let things sink back into decay, then I'm through."[5]

"Who am I?" Corridan asked rhetorically in the first of his letters "To All Harbor Workers" distributed throughout the port. "I am a Jesuit priest who by reason of his vows cannot accept any honors in the Church nor receive any money for myself." With his credentials in order Corridan proceeded to remind the men of his advocacy on their behalf since the days leading up to the 1948 strike. "I have supported you in your wildcat strikes when you sought to improve your conditions in opposition to your leaders," he insisted in a less than wholly accurate claim. Determined above all to clarify features of his eight-point plan that were anathema on the waterfront, he promised that he remained "totally opposed" to "all licensing, fingerprinting, all enquiries as to whether a man has a criminal record or not."[6]

Although the specter of a remote external authority imposing rigid controls over the hiring process ensured militant resistance from the ILA rank and file, Corridan insisted that real job security could be achieved only through a system of registration administered by state and federal bureaus that, unlike the ILA or NYSA, "are sympathetic to labor and to you." Registration—a dirty word to dockworkers—was the sole means to "protect all longshoremen...against the unfair competition of others seeking your work at any time during the year." With the shapeup under siege from all directions, Corridan reiterated his opposition to West Coast–style rotation hiring halls and called instead for regular gangs working regular piers, supplemented by extra men hired from central locations around the port. In an undated second letter Corridan highlighted the port's parochialism as a major obstacle to reform:

> Two states and many cities share the Port of New York, but the port is one economic unit. Any changes for the better have to be port-wide or else new conditions for unfair competition will be created. As it is now—sections which live up to the contract, usually lose shipping to those sections where the men are not allowed to live up to the contract.[7]

The West Side Irish waterfront remained the locus of most militant resistance to his message, its bellicose parochialism only intensified by the looming void in the ILA's top leadership. A group of unnamed union staffers, "all of whom are Catholics" surely linked to Packy Connolly—Ryan's heir apparent—responded to Corridan's letters by distributing their own *Waterfront Alert*. Through the winter and spring of 1953 these West Siders traded mimeographed barbs with their longtime nemesis. The first issue of *Waterfront Alert* colorfully set the tone:

> Father John M. Corridan, S.J., the self-appointed "waterfront priest," seems to have stepped up his campaign to become the "impartial chairman" for the Port of New York waterfront. No sooner had he completed distribution of his expensively printed recommendations to the New York State Crime Commission, than he began mailing mimeographed "personal letters" to longshoremen, continuing the greatest one-man publicity campaign since Flagpole Kelly swayed with the winds. But however ambitious Father Corridan may be to make his mark in the temporal world, it ill behooves a man of God to trifle with the truth.[8]

Corridan's call for state registration of all dockworkers was condemned as "the most Un-American plan of hiring ever devised by anyone in labor circles," a dubious broadside followed by a more targeted blast linking the waterfront priest to the Port Authority, allegedly controlled by "the biggest Republican politicians and big money men [who] are not the least interested in the longshoreman except to find a better method to get more profits out of his sweat and blood." Though Corridan did not work directly with New York's Republican governor Thomas E. Dewey, he had become a de facto ally of the governor's in the immediate aftermath of the 1951 strike; they shared an ardent desire to dismantle the ILA. "Governor Dewey and the AFL are the keys now; watch their moves," Corridan urged dockworkers in his fourth circular letter. His relationship with the Democratic-controlled AFL was expressed less in collaboration than in exhortation. "The AFL is going to have to kick the ILA out of the union and reorganize the waterfront in another way," he informed the *New York Times* in February.[9]

The *Waterfront Alert* certainly was on target in linking Corridan with the exceedingly unpopular and deeply distrusted Port of New York Authority. In January 1953 he called on the bi-state agency to take control of the port's physical assets while claiming that the agency was not eager "to assume such responsibility," though its aggressive pursuit of marine terminals since 1947—successful in Newark and later in Hoboken, rebuffed on the West Side of Manhattan—indicated otherwise. Just weeks later Corridan recommended that the Port Authority "police the docks with its own force." Port Authority executive director Austin J. Tobin emerged in this period as Corridan's most powerful reform ally; he had been highly supportive of Fathers Carey and Corridan from the earliest days of their waterfront apostolate but avoided public endorsement in recognition of his delicate position at the helm of a semipublic authority.[10]

Just weeks after New York City's municipal government rejected Tobin's plan to rehabilitate Manhattan's piers, he had witnessed the power of collaboration between journalists and reformers borne out in Mike Johnson's "Crime on the Waterfront" series. Corridan himself now became the agency's prime collaborator, with public hearings, not newspapers, the chosen vehicle. On January 29, 1953, Walter B. Hedden, director of port development for the Port Authority, proposed in testimony before the NYSCC a "statutory plan" to require the registration of all dockworkers. Hedden's remarks signaled a major shift in the agency's focus from dire warnings of the port's commercial decline to a relentless condemnation of its archaic and degrading hiring systems. "Control over the moral character of the men working in the industry" was now the Port Authority's chosen route to waterfront renewal, just as it had been for Pete Corridan since 1948.[11]

Hedden testified just hours prior to the historic appearance of Bill Mc-Cormack before the NYSCC. In the months to come, each time Tobin alleged that "people were practically solicited in Sing Sing to come down on the waterfront," he pointedly signaled the difference between his agency's vision and that of McCormack, "the Little Man's Port Authority," whose practice of hiring recent inmates en masse at Penn Stevedoring had been exposed by the NYSCC. The final campaign against the Irish waterfront and its rulers was thus launched. The goal was nothing short of a coup d'état, and the animus was rooted in the events of autumn 1948, from the taunts of Joe Ryan—who told journalist Mike Johnson he was proud to have his picture taken with "some of the boys from the old ladies' home up the river who came down to the waterfront and made good"—to Mayor Bill O'Dwyer's suspicious rejection of the bi-state agency's Manhattan pier rehabilitation proposal.[12]

The former mayor and all he represented were pilloried mercilessly throughout the first half of 1953. In May, after Hedden described the failed 1948 Port Authority bid to rehabilitate Manhattan's piers in testimony before a U.S. Senate subcommittee, Senator Charles Tobey of New Hampshire queried, "Did you include in that the rehabilitation of Mayor O'Dwyer?" Bill O'Dwyer, like Joe Ryan, was depicted retrospectively not as a free citizen but as an unreformed captive of the waterfront machine—and of its overlord, "Mr. Big."[13]

Hoods, Goons, and Gangsters

Lost amid the beating administered to O'Dwyer's reputation between the winter 1951 Kefauver hearings and this 1953 onslaught was the fact that he never was charged with official misconduct during his tenure in public office, a point Estes Kefauver himself later asserted when the Tennessean voiced his belief "that William O'Dwyer is an honest man." The ex-mayor along with others far more culpable were suddenly caught up in a maelstrom whose end was foreseen by a very select few, including the waterfront priest, leaders of the Port Authority, and the Republican governors of New York and New Jersey. They all shared a conviction that a new bi-state agency must be authorized to complete the moral revolution launched in the port in 1948 by Pete Corridan and Mike Johnson. They all knew that such an agency was sure to be bitterly resisted on the waterfront, so the proposal was kept strictly under wraps; officials spoke vaguely of the need for a "Port Labor Director" to oversee licensing and registration functions.[14]

Remarkably, the Port Authority was investing its reputation in the reform politics of dockworker employment practices at a time when the agency controlled at most 10 percent of the harbor's piers. The agency had never been a significant waterfront employer; the shift in tactics was designed to confirm its new dual role as dominant entrepreneurial and moral force in the port. The envisioned offspring agency would be limited to the unpleasant but necessary tasks of supervising hiring at employment centers a safe remove from the piers; intrusively policing the lives of dockworkers; and eliminating the loan sharks, bookies, and saloonkeepers and the army of convict-enforcers who lent a certain unsavory character to the West Side, Brooklyn, and Hudson County waterfronts.[15]

Reenvisioning his agency and its jurisdiction as a kind of virtuous third state superimposed on the region, Austin Tobin no longer coveted Manhattan's rotting piers; they could stand as a symbol of the unregenerate Irish waterfront. The port's future lay in modern facilities sprouting in the ports of Newark and Elizabeth, New Jersey, with their ample "backup-space" and ready access to rail and highways. These behemoths were joined by more modest initiatives in Hoboken, Staten Island, and Brooklyn. It would not take long for the introduction of container technology to revolutionize shipping in the port, render the undersized West Side piers and Jersey City rail yards permanently useless, and make Tobin look quite prescient indeed (see figure 8). In the meantime he launched in early 1953 the first personal lobbying campaign of his long career. The day after Joe Ryan and Bill McCormack testified before the NYSCC, Tobin informed Richard W. Clarke, editor of the *New York Daily News,* that "the whole basis of our statutory plan is the conviction that practically every vestige of law enforcement has been driven from the waterfront and has left it, in every phase of its activity, a savage jungle." A system of registration or licensing was the only solution: "The power to withhold a longshoreman's license from hoods, goons and gangsters is the only way to reduce corruption, permit the decent hardworking longshoreman to earn an honest living without interference and, for a short period of probation at least, keep the released prisoner away from the aggressive temptations of the waterfront."[16]

The full text of Tobin's letter to Clarke revealed just how deeply he had imbibed the idiom of waterfront crusade. Tobin finally dropped any guise of neutrality on March 2, when he delivered an "off the record" talk to the Friendly Sons of St. Patrick in Manhattan with Phil Carey present. "After indicating the extent of the cooperation" between Xavier Labor School and the Port Authority, Tobin concluded, as Carey reported to a fellow Jesuit, that

> what confronts us along Twelfth Avenue and West Street and Third Avenue in Brooklyn is not a material problem but a moral problem. It calls for civic confession, penance and reform and not for phony explanations. That's the reason the waterfront gospel of Father John M. Corridan preached with all the courage of his soldierly progenitor, Francis Xavier, goes right to the heart of our waterfront problem.[17]

The Irish waterfront reformers now wed moral suasion to power politics in a stunning exhibition of their combined force. If Tobin had indeed "left" the Catholic Church as a student at the Jesuits' College of the Holy Cross, that was no obstacle to his friendship and alliance with Fathers Carey and Corridan. Tobin's deeply devout wife, Geraldine, later informed Pete Corridan that she often repeated a favorite prayer of his ("Lord, I shall be very busy this day. I may forget Thee, but do not Thou forget me"), a prayer

Figure 8. Jersey City freight rail terminals and piers face the piers of Manhattan's Lower West Side, early 1950s. Courtesy of the Jersey City Free Public Library.

"so brief, bold, and honest. Just as yours was, at 6 AM, October 29, 1951," the day he led striking insurgents at Local 791 in prayer that they might be sent back to work in dignity by order of President Truman. One major dilemma remained, however: Austin Tobin well knew what the men of Local 791 and ILA locals everywhere in the port now thought of his agency, but it is unlikely that he knew just how deeply rank-and-file sentiment had turned against his campaign's rugged spiritual director.[18]

To retrenching denizens of the Irish waterfront the problem was not Pete Corridan's outside connections but Pete Corridan himself. "Mine is the only plan put forth to give you job security, seniority and a monopoly on the work in the harbor without restrictive legislation," he lectured the rank and file in his third "Letter to Harbor Workers" in winter 1953. Many dockworkers in the port heartily disagreed. "Though Chelsea Local 791 had recently passed a resolution asking Corridan to 'let us run our own Union the way we want to,'" his West Side adversaries complained, "the good Father has seen fit to continue meddling into our union affairs."[19]

With a battle for control of the post-Ryan ILA looming, Corridan might have served his small coterie of dissident allies better by abstaining from the partisan fray. The deficiencies in his self-presentation as surrogate union leader were so readily exploitable by his enemies that they left his allies deeply vulnerable. The growing West Side anti-Ryan faction did not benefit from his heavy-handed rhetoric: Johnny Dwyer and other insurgents sneeringly dismissed by the *Waterfront Alert* as Corridan's "students" were more susceptible than ever to taint by association with the increasingly controversial priest.

Nor did Corridan help his cause by attacking his enemies with a rhetorical vitriol rarely witnessed in a modern cleric. "The truth is not in the punks who put out 'The Waterfront Alert,'" he wrote in his third letter. The surly tone of these missives provided his adversaries a rare opportunity to present themselves by contrast as gentle Christians: "We will do our best to keep our sheet clean and instead of calling people 'crum bums, punks, and rats,' we will still refer to such, as students[,]...pupils[,]...and such." The waterfront priest's enemies also knew how to tweak the church's scruples over behavior by clergymen that might tend to "give scandal." A postscript concluding an installment of *Waterfront Alert* read, "We are wondering what Father Carey thinks of this type of Unionism his subordinate, Father Corridan, teaches."[20]

The organized antipathy of the West Side ILA to Corridan evidenced in the *Waterfront Alert* was matched by more spontaneous expressions of the Irish waterfront rank-and-file *sensus fidelium*. In February 1953 he was subject of a West Side manifesto, an anonymous set of "Recommendations for Priests who Aspire to Be Would-Be Labor Advisers." It warned: "Confine yourself to the Church of God and what it represents. Take care of your Sunday and other collections, and let labor and the waterfront handle its own business....Immediately abolish your self appointment as the waterfront Priest, and Saviour of the waterfront."[21]

Away from the West Side there remained no discernible pattern of support for or rejection of Corridan: he was never a familiar figure along the vast South Brooklyn waterfront, while in Hudson County—where his ambition was matched by a poverty of local knowledge—the response was mixed if generally more positive than elsewhere. One Irish-born Hoboken dockworker wrote to assure him "in reply to one of your many letters...the longshoremen are with you in your fight." And an Italian American worker from the Mile Square City expressed gratitude

> for all you have done and we will pray for God to help you carry on....It is a blessing and surely an act of God that has helped you to act on our behalf....We fully approve of your recommendations....I have also distributed your extra letters to my fellow longshoremen to enlighten them and let them know we are not abandoned and have a truly great ally on our side.

Others too fearful of mob reprisals to communicate directly with Corridan were surely heartened by his advocacy, but he remained a very long way from generating the "movement culture" among dissident longshoremen necessary to counter the organized animus represented by the *Waterfront Alert*.[22]

A "Community without Walls"

The West Side ILA still counted on Monsignor John J. O'Donnell to re-mind nosy priests of the clergy's proper role in observing the waterfront's division of labor. O'Donnell baited Corridan in a letter of April 1952, not-ing that Joseph A. McCaffrey of Holy Cross parish on West Forty-second Street had asked his fellow monsignor to help an individual find work on the docks. "I explained," chided O'Donnell, "that I am of absolutely no help in this regard since I have never interfered either with Management or Labor and have never asked that one man be preferred to another." O'Donnell did, however, feel free to exercise a preferential option for his favorite neighborhood labor leader. Speaking at the Waldorf-Astoria Hotel before two thousand dockworkers gathered for the ILA's fourth annual Communion breakfast on April 25, 1953, the port chaplain praised "the decency, honesty and uprightness" of the men who worked on the scandal-plagued waterfront before proclaiming, "Joe Ryan is my friend and he will be my friend when the chips are down and when he's on top of the world again."[23]

O'Donnell cited yet again the gospel according to Taxi Jack and King Joe: "He keeps his hands off the spiritual things of my church and I keep my hands out of his business." Ryan's "business" now included an April 13 indictment by a Manhattan grand jury "on charges that he misused $11,390 of the union's funds for his personal taxes, golf club dues, expensive shirts, life insurance premiums and a relative's funeral."[24]

Pete Corridan pounded Ryan relentlessly. On the same day O'Donnell preached at the Waldorf, the waterfront priest traveled to Buffalo, where he informed members of the St. Joseph's Guild that the ILA "is rotten clear through.... [T]he only way the rank and file members can be heard is by wildcat strikes." The rhetorical clash between Corridan and O'Donnell was old news, but the conflict now widened into the public discourse of American Catholicism. As a New Yorker named John C. Carey noted in an unpublished letter to the *World-Telegram and Sun:* "We have the spec-tacle of two Roman Catholic priests, on the same day, making two directly contradictory statements about the same person and the same conditions. Can both be correct?" Carey's reform partisanship was evident in the text of his letter; his choice to frame the conflict as a fundamental division between competing Catholic worldviews was most revealing. O'Donnell and Corridan represented starkly opposing sides in a debate that would publicly erupt a decade later but was given a preview on the New York waterfront.[25]

"By the 1960s," wrote historian John T. McGreevy in *Parish Boundaries,* a study of American Catholics and race, "two moral languages—an older, highly structured communalism and a new attempt to build a 'community without walls'—challenged each other for religious and cultural recognition. Before the 1960s, these tensions rarely surfaced outside ecclesiastical circles." The New York waterfront was a telling exception. In the early 1950s the conflict between its "highly structured communalism" and Pete Corridan's reform network (an interfaith-secular coalition akin to McGreevy's "community without walls") assumed both ecclesiastical and political dimensions.[26]

The Jesuit grew more successful than ever at influencing progressive public opinion on the outside. In April 1953 Budd Schulberg authored the first tribute to Corridan published in a liberal Catholic publication. "Waterfront Priest" secured Corridan's place in the firmament of enlightened Catholics for the readers of *Commonweal,* a liberal lay-edited weekly whose influence far outweighed its modest circulation. "The most cynical agnostic could not help but feel the presence and power of Christ when Father Corridan describes the inhuman conditions he had seen on the waterfront," declared Schulberg, lauding Corridan's willingness to transgress the waterfront code of silence as a form of Christian witness. "For years," he wrote,

> while there was a general hush-hush policy regarding the fabulous "Mr. Big," William J. McCormack, who parlayed a horse and wagon into a hundred-million dollar waterfront empire, Father Corridan has been studying the connections between him and such unsavory characters as strong-arm specialist Albert Ackalitis and the notorious gunman Linky Mitchell.[27]

The stark contrast drawn between the tycoon and the priest highlighted Corridan's stature as a new era Catholic whose public witness was designed to bridge the divide between waterfront tribalism and a metropolitan citizenry still not fully convinced it should care about the plight of dockworkers and their families. Schulberg carried the message to locales where no Jesuit had access. For the next two years he devoted himself to persuading influential figures such as Lester Markel, editor of the Sunday *New York Times,* that "the Port of New York...presents a moral problem, and social problem and even security problem. You and the Bowers mob live in blissful co-existence only a few blocks apart."[28]

Pete Corridan promised to bridge that gulf just as American Catholic cultural life was acquiring a more cosmopolitan tone. Despite "spiritual front" collaborations such as that enjoyed between Corridan and Schulberg, suspicions of the church's motives lingered in some quarters, especially among the dwindling WASP cultural elite, as witnessed by the great popularity of Paul Blanshard's tracts on "American Freedom and Catholic Power" (1949) and other neo-nativist topics. John J. Ford of the Bronx lauded Corridan in February 1952, "You are certainly a positive answer to Paul Blanshard who questions whether a good Catholic can be a good U.S. citizen."[29]

Corridan's work was prominently featured in the inaugural issue of *Jubilee,* a visually striking progressive Catholic magazine launched in May 1953 by Edward Rice, a good friend and Columbia University classmate of the celebrated author and Trappist monk Thomas Merton. In "Waterfront Underground" author Dennis Howard focused even more sharply than had Schulberg on Corridan's role in the port's salvation narrative. "If the shapeup has been the father of waterfront crime, it has also been the father of waterfront revolt," he wrote, depicting Corridan's apostolate as the vehicle of liberation. "The men of the underground are already predicting that deliverance is near. If it comes, no small share of the credit will belong to Father John Corridan." Like Schulberg, Howard contrasted the Jesuit with Bill McCormack (and Joe Ryan), inaccurately reporting that all three men came up through the same rugged waterfront ranks: "World War I saw McCormack horn in on the business of loading beef destined for the AEF [American Expeditionary Force] in Europe.... Meanwhile, Johnny Corridan was growing up among the streams of bandy-legged dock wallopers." Each of the trio had subsequently made his fateful choice:

> Now, Father Corridan sees his mission as a priest among working men. Broad-backed, ham-handed, he possesses more than enough personal presence to handle the burliest denizen of the docks; yet there isn't a hint of vindictiveness in any of his dealings with riverfront saints and sinners. There is simply love, pity and a strong sense of justice. His vision of Christ in the weary, toil-smeared longshoreman is strong enough for that.[30]

Howard cited the same passage Schulberg had selected from "a memorable sermon on the docks," which now served as a virtual calling card for the celebrated Jesuit: "I suppose some people would smirk at the thought of Christ in the shape-up. It is about as absurd as the fact that He carried carpenter's tools in His hands and earned His bread by the sweat of his brow." While Schulberg cited Corridan's original 1948 oration as "one of the few times he revealed the spiritual passion" fueling his work, it was especially resonant now, at a moment when Catholic liberals were pursuing rigorous "Christocentric" theologies of social action (supplanting the immigrant church's more devotional "Mariology") and when their favored publications, like *Jubilee,* had jettisoned the thickly ornamental visual aesthetic of immigrant Catholicism in favor of the clean lines of modernism. Historian Garry Wills later captured the 1950s liberal Catholic's affinity for "steel and glass fish-shaped churches, and driftwood-swirl Madonnas, and wrought-iron abstract tracery for the stations of the cross (artily photographed in *Jubilee*)."[31]

To Howard the waterfront provided a perfect metaphor for a Catholic subculture in transition. From this perspective the morally opaque ethos of the immigrant waterfront was finally being supplanted by a transparent model of citizenship pioneered by the young Jesuit who "has pleaded with governors, senators, heads of government agencies and high union leaders." The result of Corridan's unambiguously "clean" moral citizenship "has been that the dawn has come at last for the forgotten men on the New York docks."[32]

Return of the Nativist

Citizenship was the pervasive issue in various public waterfront hearings that ground on through the spring and summer of 1953. On March 27 a subcommittee of the U.S. Senate's Committee on Interstate and Foreign Commerce opened its inquiry on waterfront racketeering and port security prompted by the recent publicity. Subcommittee chairman Charles W. Tobey—a Republican from New Hampshire—eschewed even the pretense of fact-finding objectivity that marked the previous winter's hearings of the New York State Crime Commission. "It's high time we found out who's running this country," Tobey bellowed in advance of the hearings. His avowed goal was not simply to drive the "rats" off the waterfront; he hoped to inspire a "revival of spiritual forces in our daily living and a return to the principles of Jesus Christ." Tobey's evangelical fervor conveyed a harsh message to leaders of the Irish waterfront: the bogus moral order they had sustained was to be forcibly overturned by federal intervention.[33]

The political motivation was to ensure full Senate approval of a bi-state waterfront compact even then being quietly drafted in New York and New Jersey. Tobey opened the hearings by opining, "It seems to me that in order to get a job on the docks, it is necessary to have a criminal record as the first requisite." He then proceeded to badger his witnesses—and their legal counsel—sanctimoniously, as if their criminality were a natural fact. A focus on the U.S. Army's Claremont Terminal was validated on grounds of national security, though it is likely that Tobey and his confreres simply found the Jersey City waterfront an irresistible target not fully demolished by the NYSCC. Tobey's shameless grandstanding exposed a subtext of anti-urban, anti-Irish, anti-Italian, and anti–New Jersey bigotry that went largely unnoticed against the backdrop of the waterfront "crisis."[34]

The relentlessly moralizing senator from the Granite State had discovered, while serving on the Kefauver Committee during its televised hearings, that "the majority of people heartily approved" of his histrionics, even if these included reading "into the record a letter that some interpreted as a slight on the Italian community." Now as the star of his own (albeit untelevised) show, Tobey proceeded giddily to mock the surnames of Italian American witnesses; he asked if the Jersey City street corner where Tony Marchitto met Claremont Terminal job seekers had been "fumigated." When an Irish American lawyer from Jersey City informed Tobey that he and an ailing Italian American client on the witness list lived "400 miles away" in the Garden State, the chairman snapped back, "Is that something for congratulations or commiseration?"[35]

Joe Ryan was finally dragged before Senator Tobey's circus on April 30 in an appearance that bore all the markings of a show trial, from the statement of his attorney, Lewis Waldman, explaining the circumstances of Ryan's recent indictment, to Tobey's reference to his colleague Republican senator Charles Potter of Michigan as a "member of this jury." Tobey theatrically contrasted the sacrifices of Senator Potter, "a noble American citizen" who had lost both legs in combat in France in 1945, with Ryan, who "employed the crooks and gangsters" who were soiling the waterfront. When asked by Senator Potter if he "would like to be rid of the gangster element on the waterfront," Ryan could only dimly reply, "If they are doing anything wrong, I would say yes."[36]

"If I had my way," Tobey cried out, "I would kick you out of the union today. You sanctioned these things by your silence. You didn't clean house. What is the matter with you, as an American citizen? Or aren't you an American citizen?" Tobey did not wait for a reply, but later in Ryan's testimony he revisited the theme. "Are you an American citizen?" Tobey demanded. "I think I am as good an American citizen—" began Ryan, before he was cut off by the senator. "As an American citizen...don't you feel a sense of outrage, bitterness...that you are infested with crooks and gangsters on the docks of New York; doesn't that make you mad?"[37]

After Ryan testified about giving a man with a criminal record "a chance to redeem himself" with a job on the docks, Tobey invoked one of the classic themes of nineteenth-century nativist fantasy. "Put him out on the farms across the country where he can be in the open air and not on the docks," cried the senator. Tobey even suggested that George Dade, president of the firm contracted to handle the stevedoring at Claremont, might wish to take "Joe Ryan out for a ride" on Long Island Sound on his sailboat. When informed that the water depth was only "about 40 feet" Tobey replied, "That is enough."[38]

These insults attracted little if any notice. Tobey and his subcommittee were immunized in any case against charges of anti-Catholicism by Pete Corridan's appearance before their investigative body on May 7. Tobey introduced the waterfront priest by observing, "You have made a great place for yourself in the hearts and lives of people of that district over there in New York and New Jersey." As Tobey's chief investigator, Downey Rice, noted at the outset, this was "the first time you have testified publicly," a surprising fact confirmed by the Jesuit. During his six years of tireless campaigning Corridan had made numerous trips to Washington to meet with government officials, and prepared several statements for use by investigative bodies in New York, but never actually offered public testimony during the marathon season of hearings his own work had inspired.[39]

Corridan now reiterated his long-standing contention that Joe Ryan was "a captive" of the mob, in effect disqualifying him from the right to waterfront citizenship grounded in the practice of free will. The Jesuit stood Ryan's trademark anticommunism on its head in proclaiming that an "Iron Curtain" had hung over the waterfront until 1947, prior to which date he estimated "that as many as 10 or 20 men were killed on the waterfront in a year, but you won't find that on the books" because policemen, he alleged, sometimes reported murders as heart attacks. The ILA's Packy Connolly promptly suggested that Corridan take a "vow of silence" as penance for having "slandered every longshoreman in the Port of New York and the New York Police Department"; later that summer New York district attorney Frank Hogan won an admission from Corridan that there was "no basis" for the explosive allegation.[40]

Corridan's "campaign oratory," as Hogan put it, played better in Washington than on the waterfront. "Hasn't anyone got any guts?" Tobey plaintively wailed during Corridan's appearance, "to speak with authority? There should be a red-blooded man who could clean that [waterfront] up." The assignment "would be tough," replied the Jesuit, perhaps a bit wistfully, for he was prevented by his vocation from volunteering for the job he may have felt better qualified to handle than anyone else, especially given Tobey's criteria for union leadership: "men of character and high integrity, Christian men." When Tobey asked, "Wouldn't they be a tremendous force in transforming the situation there?" Corridan replied, "They certainly could, Senator."[41]

It was publisher Dorothy Schiff's vision of the Saint and the Devil revisited: the waterfront priest was now authorized by the Congress of the United States to plant the seeds of a Christian moral order in the urban-immigrant swamp into which the port was sinking. The Jesuit had presented himself as a moral alternative to Joe Ryan since 1949, when he informed a Bronx congressman that only the bold actions taken by Phil Carey and himself had spared several longshoremen from murder. The highlighting of the enormous contrast between Ryan and Corridan by the Bible-thumping Senator Tobey was akin to receiving a public re-baptism as an authentic Christian citizen. The unregenerate—beginning with King Joe—would face the wrath of the federal government, if not God.[42]

As an honest broker and staunch advocate of union democracy, Corridan could not evade one delicate related issue in his May 7 testimony. The following day the Honest Balloting Association was set to supervise the first port-wide referendum since 1948, with longshoremen voting on the question "Are you satisfied with the present method of hiring?" This development revealed just how complicated waterfront politics had grown in the final days of King Joe's interminable ILA regime. As the *New York Times* reported on May 9, "the reason for holding the referendum was not clear." Ryan certainly did not welcome the plebiscite, since he had already acquiesced to the AFL's demands to end the shapeup, exerting his waning influence over the ILA's New York District Council to win approval of the ban on April 7. Both the union and NYSA continued to insist that regular gangs accounted for at least 80 percent of work on the piers. Yet Ryan well knew that a "yes" vote by longshoremen on May 8 would, as the *New York Times* reported, increase "the likelihood that their union...would be expelled from the American Federation of Labor" because the public outcry against the shapeup had grown so strong.[43]

Although Corridan ardently desired the union's expulsion, he knew that after his obsessively attacking the hiring system for five years, a "yes" vote would represent a stinging repudiation. He informed the Senate subcommittee that the referendum was a "loaded proposition" since "we have different methods of hiring on the waterfront," precisely the point his enemies had been making since his televised debate with Joe Ryan and Packy Connolly in January 1950. Corridan was backed into a very tight spot and could only predict, "I feel the vote will be a 'yes' vote, but I think there will be a strong 'no' vote." While he claimed that the "mob element" was behind the referendum, the anti-Ryan, anti-Corridan forces at Local 791 gleefully offered the Jesuit a civics lesson as they anticipated "a big vote for the present system of hiring." An anonymous West Side dockworker declared on the eve of the balloting, "Our union has done the democratic thing and demanded that we, the men involved, be heard by voting on the method of hiring," taunting, "We will vote as individuals[,]...something our modest waterfront priest and other so-called experts cannot do."[44]

The following day 7,020 union members voted in the affirmative while only 3,920 "opposed continuation of the system that long has been regarded as the focal point of infection for waterfront evils," as the *New York Times* reported. The West Side locals targeted by Corridan's crusade registered the greatest degree of satisfaction with the current hiring system (the vote at Local 791 was 622 "yes" to 277 "no"). Ryan nemesis Gene Sampson of 791 opined that the men there were "confused"; but they knew exactly what they were doing in voting against external intervention from any source. Most worked in regular gangs and viewed themselves as the waterfront's labor aristocracy. Ironies abounded: the *Times* reported that the strongest opposition to the shapeup came from Brooklyn locals that the NYSCC hearings had revealed as "mob"-controlled; the Brooklynites opted for a hiring hall controlled by these same locals.[45]

The results of the referendum and the public response set the tone for the post-NYSCC hearings era. Nothing the rank and file said or did mattered anymore because the growing outcry for government intervention trumped the highly tainted local sentiments of dockworkers. As the reformist landscape widened beyond Corridan's campaign, he remained the lightning rod for defenders of the West Side code. Just days after the May 8 referendum he was urged by the "son of a longshoreman" to "please now for the benefit of all of us who try to follow in the teaching of our religion back out of this gracefully." Packy Connolly linked Corridan with both Brooklyn's Tough Tony Anastasio and waterfront communists as forces that had lost the most by urging a "no" vote.[46]

Tobin Steps Up

On May 20, 1953, the New York State Crime Commission issued a report and recommendations based on thirty thousand pages of testimony collected over the previous year. The primary conclusions came as no surprise to anyone who had read a newspaper in metropolitan New York at any time since autumn 1948: the health of the great port was imperiled by inefficiency, corruption, and "deplorable conditions involving unscrupulous practices and undisciplined procedures, many of which [were] criminal or quasi-criminal in nature." The ills of the waterfront were nowhere more evident than in the shapeup, this "vicious and antiquated system" to be legislated out of existence and replaced by an industrywide system of licensing, registration, and hiring information centers drawn explicitly from Father Pete Corridan's proposals.[47]

The long season of lurid exposés was over: "the time has come for drastic action" in the form of remedial legislation that would give a newly created state agency "almost total control over waterfront workers," according to the *New York Times*. Republican dominance of statehouses and legislatures in New York and New Jersey contributed greatly to enabling the requisite bi-state aspect of the proposed scheme. With urgent prompting by governors Thomas E. Dewey of New York and Alfred E. Driscoll of New Jersey, in late June the states' legislatures established the Waterfront Commission of New York Harbor. The vote was unanimous in New York and missed unanimous passage by just one vote in New Jersey and later in the U.S. Congress.[48]

The New York Waterfront Compact authorized the creation of a bi-state agency with power to impose a uniform hiring system, eliminate the shapeup, and outlaw public loading in the port. This "classic 'Progressive' agency" would "police or discipline an industry that had failed to discipline itself." The torrent of legislation leading to the Waterfront Commission represented, Dewey gushed, "the swiftest and most complete enactment of a revolutionary approach in history." According to historian Peter B. Levy the NYSCC investigation was "the main impetus for the creation" of the commission. "Also instrumental in drawing attention to the problems on the waterfront were the highly publicized crusade of Father John Corridan—the so-called Waterfront Priest—investigative reporting by the press, and other government and private inquiries."[49]

The Jesuit's crusade in fact inspired or abetted virtually every reform initiative launched between 1948 and the inception of the Waterfront Commission. Governor Dewey would never have charged NYSCC to conduct hearings without Corridan's relentless prodding and his ability to influence public discourse through his undisputed role as preeminent waterfront authority. Austin Tobin believed that the establishment of the commission represented a triumph of his agency's behind-the-scenes collaboration with Phil Carey and especially with Pete Corridan. Yet with victory at hand, the substance and tone of Tobin's public statements suddenly grew much more subdued than his previous fiery remarks. The Port Authority's twelve commissioners were "opposed to government regulation wherever it can be avoided," he assured his audience at a June hearing convened by Dewey to consider the NYSCC recommendations for a licensing and registration scheme. "They have reached the conclusion, however, that work on the waterfront is among those occupations where unfortunately law and order depend on active and constant and vigorous state regulation."[50]

Corridan similarly retreated into a highly uncharacteristic pastoral mode, as if to evade charges of partisan collusion with Republican politicians, patrician reformers, and Port Authority bureaucrats. In his own highly muted testimony at Dewey's hearings he insisted, "My sole concern is the moral aspects of the problem under consideration insofar as they affect the spiritual well being of the longshoremen, the industry and the community at large." In the past this standard disclaimer had always been followed by bold new proposals from the Jesuit. In this case, although the NYSCC's plan very closely resembled his own (though he had wished to see public loading "outlawed in its entirety" rather than strictly regulated), he sounded oddly resigned:

> Unfortunately I cannot offer a better proposal. I don't think there is any other. I feel that it is the obligation of the government by the states to provide a climate in which the longshoremen, once they do become free and have some job security and seniority, can begin, through their own efforts or with the help of the A.F. of L., to clean up the union.[51]

After five years of persistently warning that the port was immune to reform in the absence of enduring if not permanent government intervention, Corridan now suggested that the NYSCC's recommendations be implemented on a trial basis for three years, after which time, if "the private parties are able to function normally without certain governmental aids," they "should be withdrawn." Corridan then offered an unsolicited revised assessment of the Port Authority's proper role: it did not entail handling "the labor-management problem." This last point served to run interference against Dewey's ongoing desire for the Port Authority to do just that, another indication that the Waterfront Commission's charge was composed on the fly in anticipation of overwhelming legislative support matched by massive resistance on the piers.[52]

The extremely guarded public statements by Corridan and Tobin reflected the political reality that there was nary a longshoremen in the port who would welcome a new agency wielding unprecedented power over the workplace. The allies shared an understanding that their triumph had mortally injured the Irish waterfront's spiritual foundation. Corridan's extreme vulnerability on this score was exposed at the June hearings in blistering remarks by James J. Conroy, executive secretary of the Association of Catholic Trade Unionists. "We do not believe that American workers or an American industry should be marked out for state control," Conroy asserted just hours after Corridan testified before Dewey's rubber stamp proceedings. When asked if this did not represent a "violent disagreement" with Father Corridan, Conroy acknowledged: "That's quite right. We're very good friends, and I've taught at the labor school for six years, but on this proposition we don't see eye to eye." Conroy's bitter dissent further distanced his Jesuit "friend" from the waning Irish waterfront. "It is appalling," Conroy insisted, "that anyone would recommend the licensing of the right to work as a means of attacking crime."[53]

Conroy's testimony reaffirmed the enduring hostility to the state evinced by the heirs to Catholic radicalism. This was no longer even a small part of Pete Corridan's tradition; it never was any part of Governor Dewey's, who curtly informed Conroy in mid-sentence, "You have already exceeded your time." Time was moving quickly indeed in the world of waterfront reform, so quickly that Corridan himself may not have noticed how far he had traveled not only from the likes of James J. Conroy but also from the rank-and-file longshoremen whose interests he sought to serve and whose insular mood confounded his powers of discernment.[54]

He could much more readily commune with Austin Tobin: the two men shared a language of moral reform in a Catholic idiom—perhaps more vestigial than explicit—blended with the visionary rhetoric of the modern urban planner. On July 22, 1953, with the Waterfront Commission Compact assured of passage in the U.S. House of Representatives, Tobin testified before the House Judiciary Committee, proclaiming the creation of the bi-state commission the "greatest reform that we...have ever seen in 32 years of the work of the Port Authority to promote and develop the port of New York." It had truly happened as swiftly as Governor Dewey claimed. The commission was empowered to abolish the shapeup; outlaw public loading; "register and license employers, union officials and dockworkers" (and bar those with criminal records from the piers); license port watchmen; and establish employment information centers (not centralized hiring halls) to regularize the work of both established crews and extras. The registration feature outraged organized labor even as the AFL prepared to jettison the ILA: AFL president George Meany gravely objected to "a system of regimentation which is not only unwarranted and unnecessary but smacks strongly of totalitarianism."[55]

In his own testimony at the July congressional hearings Corridan invoked national security in explaining how the federal legislation would eliminate potentially subversive illegal alien "ship jumpers." "I happen to be a priest. I am also an American citizen," he reminded members of the House subcommittee poised to approve the compact. Senator Tobey made a guest appearance to express his own support for the bill. Corridan was not a xenophobe, but Tobey was powerfully inclined that way: he viewed the ILA as akin to a foreign plague. The Granite State senator reaffirmed his great admiration for Father Corridan ("a wonderful power in the spiritual world and the material world[,] . . . an inspiration to me as I heard him testify before our committee") before launching into an apocalyptic oration blending the preacher's art with the ominous rhetorical devices familiar to listeners of radio and television broadcasts on waterfront evil enriched by Corridan's crusading spirit. "What is that huddled mass over in that pier?" Tobey intoned. "Go look at it; it is a shapeless man. It is a man made in the image of God originally. Twelve ice picks in his back—there he is, part of the crime wave on the docks of New York. . . . The Nation cries out: 'Unclean, unclean,' to the docks in New Jersey and New York." It was Senator Tobey's seventy-third birthday; he received the well-wishes of colleagues prior to making his exit. Within two days he was dead, the victim of a coronary thrombosis.[56]

Pete Corridan's peculiar collaboration with Charles H. Tobey revealed his growing dilemma. While the late senator's unhinged public deportment had borne little resemblance to the waterfront priest's rugged empiricism, many New York–New Jersey dockworkers *did* view the Jesuit as less than fully grounded in all dimensions of his subject and erratic in his advocacy. He was now linked with a political campaign to effectively disqualify the Irish waterfront from practicing self advocacy or governance by democratic majority. Though the ILA was fully responsible for its own predicament, longshoremen now suffered the harsh judgment of powerful outsiders with little sympathy for urban workers. Pete Corridan surely did not count himself among that cohort. His closest collaborators and fellow visionaries now shaped up to create the waterfront priest's final testament.

15 Saving the Picture

On the Waterfront very nearly went unrealized. In February 1953 Elia Kazan was poised for a green light from Twentieth Century–Fox, where he owed a film to producer Darryl Zanuck. Late in the previous autumn at Kazan's urging Budd Schulberg had sent the mercurial Nebraskan a thirty-seven-page outline with dialogue for a screenplay, "The Bottom of the River." A prefatory note explained, "factual background drawn from Malcolm Johnson's Pulitzer Prize winning reportage and current New York State Crime Commission investigations."[1]

The storyline had evolved significantly since Schulberg's original April 1951 version. The character Edie, who was Terry Monahan's sister in "Crime on the Waterfront," was now the sister of longshoreman Joey Doyle, killed by the mob in the opening scene before he can testify at a waterfront crime commission hearing. Here Edie and Terry Malloy (from the Monahan prototype) fall in love amid pressure on Terry to testify. The courageous waterfront priest Father Corcoran is threatened by goons working for waterfront entrepreneur George Foley. "Nobody would want to harm a priest," Corcoran is warned by the Catholic thugs, "but if he lets the trouble-makers use the Church for a meeting place, and if he insists on showing his face on the waterfront, a falling crate is just as liable to hit him as anybody else."[2]

The threat prompts a response from Father Corcoran drawn directly from an incident both Schulberg and Malcolm Johnson had cited in nonfiction articles on Pete Corridan. "I know who you are—and I think I know who your bosses are," Corcoran tells the hoods. "Give 'em this message for me. One of these days they're going to pay for those crimes. It's become my business to see that they pay." The priest's soliloquy also incorporates material drawn verbatim from "A Catholic Looks at the Waterfront," Corridan's 1948 Jersey City talk: "When good men...are made to suffer, it's a Crucifixion just the same as if it took place on Calvary. For it was our

Lord Jesus Christ who said, 'If you do it to the least of mine, you do it to me.'" Corcoran is subsequently called to the chancery office of a powerful cardinal archbishop who has heard "conflicting reports" about the priest's role on the waterfront and wants to know "exactly what is going on down there." Father Corcoran answers bluntly: "Excellency, the truth is that the situation stinks down there. I never would have believed it if I had not come to see it with my own eyes. Men are suffering under the most unchristian conditions. I'm trying to help them correct these evils.... I'm only trying to help them to help themselves to a decent, American, Christian life."[3]

The cardinal approves of Corcoran's work "so long as you're sure you know what you're doing." Since Pete Corridan's November 1951 meeting with Cardinal Spellman had never been treated in print, Schulberg surely obtained this detailed account from the Jesuit himself. In "The Bottom of the River" Terry and Edie Doyle plan to flee the waterfront, but when Father Corcoran holds a meeting for a fledgling dissident longshoremen's group, Terry cannot resist: "'Edie...I guess I gotta stick with Father Corcoran.' With a sense of inevitability, he leaves Edie there on the steps and turns back into the Church." Terry is crushed to death by the mob after he tells the police what he knows about Joey Doyle's murder. This treatment is the last to see Terry Malloy killed, despite persistent claims by many of the principals that the necessity of his death was debated until the final day of shooting *On the Waterfront*.[4]

In early January 1953 Schulberg sent Zanuck "Golden Warriors," a heavily revised, slightly shorter outline for a screenplay with dialogue. The story, still set on the Lower West Side of Manhattan, opens with a wake for Joey Doyle, but in this version Terry Malloy is a widower with a thirteen-year-old son named Jimmy, "a tough little kid allowed to run wild." Terry is a "standby" prizefighter in local clubs; during a post-bout date with his love interest, Edie, he shares his waterfront philosophy: "You gotta look out for number 1." Echoing the influence of "Father Monohan," the heroic priest in this version, Edie asks plaintively, "What about our religion?" The longshoremen in this script initially view Monohan as "a good man but awfully holy," not a flattering appraisal. But when Kid Nolan (the first incarnation of a character based on Arthur Brown) is crushed under a falling sling load for talking, "the Father delivers his sermon on the docks—Where would Christ be on the waterfront?"[5]

Later, when Terry and Edie inform Father Monohan of their plan to flee the waterfront, the priest wishes them well, but "he makes it clear that Terry's departure will dramatize the fact that it is wiser to run away from the waterfront than to talk about the mob." Terry decides to stay and talk. Jimmy then takes a beating from the leader of his father's old gang, the Golden Warriors, for being the son of a "rat." The author's didactic streak is evident in Terry's response: in Schulberg's paraphrase Terry patiently explains to Jimmy that the "code of the Golden Warriors is kid stuff...perpetrated on the waterfront because these kid gangs inevitably feed the pier gangs and that murder and every form of racket will go on as long as the curtain of silence hangs over the waterfront." In this as in each successive version of the script, Terry Malloy ultimately prevails over the mob.[6]

Worries Aplenty

On February 4, 1953, Darryl Zanuck shared his initial written response to this version with Kazan and Schulberg: "I have struggled with the problem of the waterfront story as this means a decision of great importance to the company" ("business at Fox had been bad," explained Kazan in his memoir). Zanuck liked "the basic material enormously, as I told you when I read the treatment, but I continue to be worried about the labor support" needed to permit shooting on "dock facilities." Zanuck had not cared for the Arthur Miller–Kazan collaboration on "The Hook," and now his fear of union trouble aroused by that ill-fated project was reignited. Although Zanuck's memo did not mention George Meany by name, Kazan later claimed that he and Schulberg were expected to "secure the backing" of the AFL chief if they expected a green light for their waterfront picture.[7]

The chances of winning organized labor's support for a film treating waterfront union corruption had in fact improved dramatically since January 1951, when Kazan and Arthur Miller visited Hollywood to shop "The Hook." One day prior to Zanuck's memo to the filmmakers the AFL's executive council promised to expel the ILA if the union failed to clean up its act. As president of the New York State AFL and secretary-treasurer of the national organization in the 1930s and 1940s, Meany had "kept his distance from Ryan"; he "never lifted a hand against recognized ILA corruption." But the terrible publicity generated by the ILA was more than Meany could bear: his decades-long tolerance for Joe Ryan's shenanigans was over. King Joe and the union he had ridden to wealth and power now teetered on the brink of expulsion from the labor movement.[8]

There were political worries aplenty. Zanuck revealed to the filmmakers his fear that communists abroad would exploit a waterfront film's exposé of political corruption and brutality, just as they "did to me in connection with *Grapes of Wrath.*" Kazan had continually reassured Schulberg that Zanuck's history as producer of that classic 1940 film ensured his sympathy with their point of view, but Schulberg knew the industry much better than his friend and partner. Budd's instinct was accurate: Zanuck's only concern was the box office, especially given his recent disappointment over *Zapata,* the kind of film "which nobody comes to see except the intelligentsia." But politics were never Zanuck's "main problem" with "Golden Warriors"; it was all about business. Concern over "the telling of the story" was producer-speak for dubious commercial potential. "We must not hit everything on the nose and get up on a soap box....[T]he personal story must predominate," lectured Zanuck. He drove home the point again in a February 10 memo. This time he insisted that "the only reformer in this picture should be the priest," freeing Edie Doyle to play the strictly conventional romantic interest of Terry Malloy. "Now I think that a strong, dramatic and exciting *personal* story laid against the background of the waterfront scandal can turn out to be an outstanding picture with a certain amount of dignity and with fine commercial results, providing we use the waterfront scandal as our *excuse* for telling the personal story."[9]

Zanuck also offered some casting suggestions. Karl Malden "wouldn't be bad for the priest," he wrote in a memo to Kazan and Schulberg after the first of two meetings in Hollywood with the homecoming screenwriter (the director remained in New York, immersed in preparations for the Broadway opening of Robert Anderson's highly acclaimed coming-of-age melodrama *Tea and Sympathy*). "He's tough, the right age and Irish." (In fact he was Serbian American, born Mladen Sekulovich.) Zanuck indicated a desire for "two stars such as Brando and Maggie McNamara" to play the romantic leads. In the February 10 memo and one that followed on February 12, dictated "in the presence of Budd at the conclusion of our second meeting," Zanuck insisted that the character of Jimmy, Terry Malloy's son, be excised from the script. He argued that the presence of a child diluted the erotic power of scenes between Terry and Edie: "I just cannot visualize Marlon Brando with a 13-or 14-year old son. It takes all of the bite out of it."[10]

These memos attest to Zanuck's unyielding commercial instincts and his astute story sense, inseparable traits that mitigate, if only slightly, his reputation as the man who would have killed *On the Waterfront*. Despite Zanuck's pointed critique Schulberg "did come back satisfied," according to Kazan. "Budd seemed more confident than ever that the film was going to go through; I was certain of it."[11]

On April 1, 1953, Budd Schulberg completed his first fully realized screenplay since "Crime on the Waterfront" two years earlier. "The Golden Warriors"—along with a slightly revised script that was submitted to Zanuck on May 15—attests to the profound and growing influence of Pete Corridan in shaping Budd's waterfront vision. Entire passages from Corridan's "A Catholic Looks at the Waterfront"/"Christ in the Shapeup" speech are present; the priest delivering these lines is now Father Pete Barry, in homage to Corridan's Jesuit handle; Schulberg experimented with "Father John Barry" in the May 15 version before reverting to "Father Pete" for good.[12]

The working-class Irish Catholic motifs that pervade the scripts feature a devotion to local detail rarely witnessed in writing for the American cinema. The "poor, West Side Irish neighborhood" in which the drama is set is filled not only with "Old Country Irishmen" but also with the likes of Charley Malloy, a sophisticated, ethically challenged, likely disbarred union attorney ("more politician than mobster") who fancies himself "an idealist.... Why, I nearly got kicked out of Fordham for being a Socialist." There is a lengthy, booze-sodden Irish wake for Joey Doyle, slain by the mob for talking after being lured (in the May 15 version) by Terry Malloy to a darkened pier. At the wake Joey's father, Pop Doyle, and other longshoremen speculate as to whether admission to heaven is preceded by a shapeup.[13]

In the version of "Golden Warriors" sent to Zanuck in May, Joey's sister Edie meets Father Barry as she lights a candle before a Marian shrine in St. Bernard's church (the name of a historic longshoremen's parish on West Fourteenth Street in Chelsea). "Blessed Mother of God, help me, I need you," prays Edie; "Sweet Mother—in the name of the five blessed wounds give me the strength, the strength." Edie troubles Father Barry's conscience by speaking explicitly about the duties of a Catholic, just as she later troubles Terry by insisting "it's in our religion" when he scoffs at her conviction that "we must care about each other." These thickly detailed evocations of the Irish Catholic waterfront would be excised from the shooting script, placing an even greater burden on Pete Barry's persona—and especially his "Christ in the Shapeup" speech—to convey the distinctly Catholic character of waterfront life to movie audiences everywhere.[14]

The "Dream Trip"

That speech was the heart and soul of the script Schulberg shipped to Hollywood in advance of his ecstatic May 1953 journey westward with Kazan aboard the fabled *Super Chief* for a meeting with Zanuck. The adventure enjoys a prominent place in movie industry folklore. Schulberg called it "a writer's dream trip, long lunches in the dining car, with my director exclaiming, 'I don't think you realize how great this is'... whereupon my Greek friend would go into what was becoming almost a religious litany... 'Salesman... Streetcar... Waterfront.'" It was "the nicest trip to California" Schulberg ever enjoyed, but the idyll was shattered the moment the creative partners detrained in Los Angeles. There was no limousine awaiting them; no fresh flowers adorned their suite at the Beverly Hills Hotel. Kazan told Schulberg to stop worrying, but the screenwriter had grown up in the industry. "I knew the unspoken language. No limo and no roses, no loving welcome note, and no invitation to come down to Palm Springs for the big Sunday croquet match spelled big trouble."[15]

Following a nervous weekend of "intense tennis and Polo Lounging," Kazan and Schulberg spent Monday morning, May 25, in the waiting room of the "Mussolini-sized office of the fearless producer of the *Grapes of Wrath*." According to Schulberg, Zanuck greeted the men with an effusive tribute to the latest in wide-screen movie technology: "Can you imagine *Prince Valiant* in Cinerama? All those beautiful broads in silky gowns practically on top of you! I tell you, this is an exciting business!" (Zanuck surely said or meant to say CinemaScope, the technology his studio had banked on to lure potential moviegoers away from the novelty of their television sets.) Kazan's account eschewed Zanuck's manic preliminaries, but his version of the producer's judgment of their film project was virtually identical to that of Schulberg. "'I'm not going to make this picture,' he said. 'I don't like it. In fact, I don't like anything about it.'" Both men recalled Zanuck's insistence that the material was exactly what the filmgoing public did not care to see. "Who gives a shit about longshoremen?" Kazan recalled him demanding; or in Schulberg's version, "Who's going to care about a lot of sweaty longshoremen?"[16]

Darryl Zanuck did not relish his subsequent role in *On the Waterfront* folklore. There was some truth to his protestations, notably his insistence that he did not simply deliver a "cold turn-down" at their May meeting—as Kazan and Schulberg persistently maintained—but had nurtured the project over a period of months. It is true that he worked closely with Schulberg on the story in February 1953; it is also true that he had told Fox executives and producers in March 1953 that the waterfront project would be among a very small group of films produced before the studio turned all its energies to "subjects suitable for CinemaScope" ("costumed horse operas," in Schulberg's derisive phrase). Yet Zanuck's exculpatory case was refuted by his own words. As he conceded to Kazan in July 1954, in light of Cinema-Scope's commercial potential, "I had no alternative but to back away from intimate stories even though they were good stories."[17]

Zanuck might have added that a good story with suspect popular appeal and a troubled political history surely eased the decision to back away. The major studios had equated a labor-themed waterfront film with political headaches since 1951, whether the aspiring screenwriter was Arthur Miller or Budd Schulberg. Zanuck now shared with Harry Cohn of Columbia Pictures the dubious distinction of rejecting both the underdeveloped project "The Hook" and the incandescent *On the Waterfront*. Cohn in fact rejected scripts for the latter on three occasions: Schulberg's original 1951 screenplay and the May 1953 "Golden Warriors" both before—when Kazan's agent Abe Lastfogel "sneaked one" to Cohn's office—and after Zanuck's final turndown. Zanuck's undeniable contribution to the Kazan-Schulberg property entailed some shrewd casting suggestions and a streamlined narrative structure—little consolation to the filmmakers when weighed against the producer's failure of nerve.[18]

Desperate to see the scorned film project restored to life, its creative team now turned to a flamboyant character long accustomed to courting personal and financial disaster. Sam Spiegel, as it happened, was ensconced across the hall from the room in the Beverly Hills Hotel where the dejected director and screenwriter—their expenses cut off by Fox—regrouped for a last Hollywood gasp. "A master of high risk and chutzpah" and "sometime art director," Spiegel had enjoyed (as "S. P. Eagle") but one success as a producer, *The African Queen* (1951), directed by John Huston. "A legendary high roller," as Kazan biographer Richard Schickel described him, Spiegel "had just produced a resounding flop, *Melba*, about the opera singer [Nellie Melba] who had lent her name to the toast and the peaches." At the very moment Kazan and Schulberg hit their nadir of despair—with the director muttering about making the film himself with a hand-held camera—Spiegel was holding court for guests in his suite, "smart as paint" and "smelling of expensively crushed French lilacs," in Schulberg's recollection. When the downtrodden pair declined his neighborly invitation to join in the revelry, Spiegel inquired, "Are you boys in trouble?"[19]

Early the next morning, "with the covers up to his nose," Spiegel entertained the screenwriter in his room. "The muscle of the story began to stir me," Schulberg later recalled of his pitch, "as I followed Terry Malloy through his waterfront ordeal." Wrote Kazan, "That's when the miracle happened." Spiegel suddenly looked out from under the covers and promised Schulberg: "I'll do it. We'll make the picture." The director and screenwriter largely omitted from their miracle texts details of the long personal histories both shared with Sam Spiegel. Schulberg's father, B. P., "went way back with Sam": Spiegel was sufficiently friendly with the Schulbergs that in 1936—when the fledgling but high-flying producer was jailed in England for nonpayment of bills—he was bailed out by Budd's mother, who was "living it up in London" at the time and took Spiegel's call from Brixton Prison while preparing to host her first formal British dinner party. In the late 1940s Kazan had often borrowed an upstairs bedroom in Spiegel's Hollywood home for assignations with aspiring starlets.[20]

The film colony was a small community, so it is no surprise that Kazan and Schulberg had deep connections with their new producer. Yet Kazan's agent was sufficiently concerned by Spiegel's reputation to warn his client: "Watch out for him! He has moves you've never seen before." Those moves came in handy. After first securing a financing deal from United Artists, Spiegel then took the project to Columbia Pictures' New York office, where his manic persistence—and his promise to deliver the newly "bankable" Brando for the lead role—was rewarded when Columbia made a lowball but viable offer of $800,000 in financing, hedging its bet on a high-end black and white independent film budget.[21]

Ironically, it was Darryl Zanuck who first suggested (in writing, at least) that Marlon Brando play Terry, in his February 10, 1953, memo to Kazan and Schulberg, though it is likely that Kazan already envisioned him in the role. In casting Brando for the title role in *Viva Zapata,* the director had prevailed over Zanuck's insistence that Tyrone Power be offered the part. A twenty-nine-year-old from Nebraska, Brando had appeared in a small but memorable role in Maxwell Anderson's *Truckline Café,* which opened on Broadway in late February 1946 under Kazan's direction but closed after thirteen performances. Kazan then invited Brando to refine his prodigious gift at the Actors Studio. Brando became an "overnight sensation" with his performance as Stanley Kowalski in the 1947 Broadway production of Tennessee Williams's *Streetcar Named Desire* and reprised the role for the screen version, which, like the play, was brilliantly directed by Kazan. By the time he was approached for the lead role in *Waterfront*, Brando's newly minted star status far outweighed the judgment of those who found his "mumbling" unintelligible.[22]

Elia Kazan was Brando's creative mentor: "for about three or four years, ours was a terribly close relationship," the director told French journalist Michel Ciment in 1971. "I was like his father." But in autumn 1953 Brando harbored a deep grudge over the director's HUAC testimony and rebuffed at least two offers to play Terry Malloy. Sam Spiegel was, however, a "master seducer," as Schulberg put it; he doggedly pursued the young actor even as he offered the role to Hoboken's own Frank Sinatra, fresh off the success of his performance in *From Here to Eternity*. "Frank had grown up in Hoboken, spoke perfect Hobokenese," Kazan recalled, though these credentials could not have counted for much at the time Sinatra was approached, since Hoboken had not yet been chosen as the film's location. It is highly unlikely that Kazan or Schulberg knew of the crooner turned actor's history as a former ally of John V. Kenny and other anti-Hague Hudson County insurgents; in any case, Sinatra was always a distant second choice to play Terry Malloy.[23]

According to legend, sometime in October 1953 Sam Spiegel was dining in the Stage Delicatessen on Seventh Avenue in Manhattan at three A.M. when Brando slouched in. Spiegel reportedly seized the opportunity to implore the mercurial actor: "Professional is one thing, politics is another. Separate them." Spiegel then called Kazan, who soon joined the party and succeeded in persuading Brando to take the part. "Actually the two had already talked several times," according to Brando biographer Peter Manso: "there were these secret dinners," Schulberg told Manso, "where Spiegel specifically didn't want me or Gadge [Kazan] around." Whatever the method employed, Brando's acquisition persuaded Columbia Pictures to increase its spending on the picture from a half-million dollars to $880,000, yet "even with the increased budget, Kazan knew it was going to be tight."[24]

Sinatra was livid on hearing the news from Spiegel, who then offered him the part of Father Pete Barry, only to be rebuffed by Kazan, who had already promised that role to Karl Malden. Yet another veteran of the Actors Studio, Malden had ties with Kazan that dated back to 1937, when the very young actor appeared in the Group Theatre's production of Clifford Odets's *Golden Boy*. Malden enjoyed a brief if memorable Broadway stint working with Brando and Kazan in *Truckline Café*, and the trio teamed regularly thereafter in theater and films. Their creative rapport was brilliantly affirmed in the triumphant stage and screen productions of *Streetcar*, with Malden earning an Academy Award for Best Supporting Actor for his portrayal of Harold Mitchell, the "suitor" of Blanche DuBois.[25]

Meet the New Boss

In September 1953 the artistic collaboration of Budd Wilson Schulberg and John M. Corridan, S.J., was formalized, with the Jesuit granting the screenwriter license to "use, simulate and portray [his] likeness, personality, activities and career." In November Sam Spiegel's Horizon-American Corporation acquired additional rights to Corridan's "writings, speeches, dialogue or other literary material or ideas composed or prepared by me." Corridan donated two-thirds of the $5,000 he received from the producers toward the construction of an infirmary sacristy room at the spacious new seminary for studies in philosophy the New York Jesuits were building at Shrub Oak in northern Westchester County. Facing relentless and vitriolic attack on the waterfront, he told his superior that the donation constituted "sound public policy in forestalling cheap criticism that any activity of mine on behalf of the longshoremen was in any way connected with monetary matters."[26]

On September 21, 1953, the American Federation of Labor—meeting in St. Louis for its annual convention—ignored Joe Ryan's desperate plea to take his union into receivership; the ILA was expelled from the AFL by an overwhelming vote of 79,000 to 736 (with each vote representing one hundred workers nationwide). In the wake of this unprecedented action the AFL quickly chartered a new longshoremen's union, called the ILA-AFL; Pete Corridan's rebel ally Johnny Dwyer of Greenwich Village was named general organizer for Manhattan's piers. The "stocky battler," it was reported, left his job on Pier 45, where Dwyer had helped overturn mob rule in 1946, to assume the new post. Dwyer took eight hundred members of ILA Local 895 with him. "This is the end of an eight-year struggle," the local announced, "to prove to the waterfront that a mob-dictated union could be overcome by decent, honest, hardworking representation."[27]

Less than a week later the leader of the fledgling reform union was ardently championed in "How One Pier Got Rid of the Mob," Budd Schulberg's second high-profile waterfront story for the *New York Times Magazine* in less than a year. Schulberg summarized a nearly decade-long struggle on the West Side, beginning with Dwyer's heroic resistance against the Thompson brothers on Pier 45 in 1945–46. Though he did not eliminate the shapeup after being installed as hiring boss, Schulberg reported, "what Dwyer did was to bring to it a fresh sense of fair play and judgment." When Pier 45 was idled again in 1948, Dwyer called a "mass meeting" at St. Veronica's on Christopher Street, where he accused Teddy Gleason, a rising union power on the West Side—and future longtime ILA president—"of fronting for Bill McCormack, the powerful waterfront multimillionaire, and Joe Ryan."[28]

The "dead-square and dead-game" insurgent was touted for his close ties to Pete Corridan and Xavier Labor School. Local 895 shop steward Pete Laughran described to Schulberg the moment when Corridan had prayed with the men of nearby Local 791 during the October 1951 wildcat strike. "It was like a sword cutting a path for us," Laughran marveled, "separating us from the Commies on one side and the mob on the other—a road for longshoremen to move ahead on." Yet "How One Pier Got Rid of the Mob" closed on an ominous note: "Curiously enough," Schulberg acknowledged, "the men on [Pier] 45 have not welcomed the new bi-state law as might have been expected." No genuine product of the Irish waterfront could welcome the intervention of the Waterfront Commission, a remote bi-state agency whose imprimatur from the waterfront priest now only increased the anathema.[29]

On October 15 the *New York Times* reported that Joe Ryan was no longer in control of the ILA's day-to-day operations, bringing closer the moment when Corridan might help build a new union and reshape the moral contours of the entire port. Hoping to see the number of locals in the harbor drastically reduced from seventy to fifteen, he confided in a New Orleans Jesuit labor priest his plan to install employment information centers in Manhattan, Brooklyn, and Hudson County with a common feature: men will "be going to centers located on main thoroughfares and away from the territories of the boys." In this scheme all the power would be stripped from hiring bosses who thrived from proximity to loan sharks, bookies, and assorted underworld figures. The geographic isolation would also make it easier for the AFL to "police" the halls in the men's best interest.[30]

With negotiations for a new contract between shippers and longshoremen under way, the ILA demanded that the rank and file sign loyalty cards binding them to their discredited bargaining agent. In response Corridan urged dockworkers to sign for self-protection while also submitting membership papers to the new AFL union. With applications for employment licenses due for submission to the Waterfront Commission by November 7, Corridan began fielding requests from men concerned that a criminal record might prevent them from obtaining work. The waterfront priest was clearly more confident in his own powers of discernment than those of Ryan, McCormack, or others who routinely hired ex-convicts. In recommending one such individual—a longshoreman from Pier 45 in the West Village—Corridan explained that he was aware of the gentleman's "previous criminal record but I am convinced of his complete rehabilitation. If I were not I would not have vouched for him in the New York State Crime Commission proceedings and for him again with the Bi-State Waterfront Commission."[31]

Supporters of the new AFL longshoremen's union held a mass rally at Manhattan Center on November 18, 1953, the day Joe Ryan was "retired" by the ILA at a special convention held in Philadelphia. In a final indignity, Ryan was denied the routine privilege of an opening prayer led by a Catholic clergyman. The last-minute decision of Philadelphia Jesuit labor priest Dennis J. Comey to decline the invitation resulted in a two-hour delay before ILA vice president William "Preacher" Jones of New Orleans opened the proceedings to oust Ryan by reciting the words from a Protestant hymn, "The Mercy Seat," not part of the Irish waterfront's standard repertoire. The cash-strapped ILA, whose mounting legal fees alone threatened to sink the union, "was saddled with a new cost item—an 'irrevocable' pension of $10,000 a year" to Ryan, who assumed "emeritus" status and was replaced by William "Tugboat Bill" Bradley, a taciturn McCormack-approved boat pilot with precious little experience on the piers but just as little notoriety, a quality the ILA featured in overabundance.[32]

Meanwhile the new AFL union, the *Times* reported, "apparently has almost unlimited funds," evidence of its sponsor's great desire that it succeed. The November 18 rally drew a "cheering all-male crowd" variously estimated at 4,000 or 6,500 strong (organizers contrasted the turnout with the crowd at the previous month's ILA rally at Madison Square Garden, which drew 15,000 but was allegedly packed with women and children). Peter Johnson, the young attorney who represented the strike committee during the 1951 walkout, stirred the crowd by promising the day was at hand when "you'll go in a voting booth without any racketeers, hoodlums, no Packy Connolly's, no Anastasias—just you and God."[33]

Pete Corridan was not in attendance at Manhattan Center, though he was surely there in spirit. It was slowly becoming clear that he was not a movement figure. A loner since his boyhood days at Rockaway Beach, Corridan remained a party of one with a rare gift for mobilizing the passions of others similarly accustomed to working alone, especially writers. He had emerged as the reform crusade's stellar figure but was most effective in settings where his dockworker solidarity credentials went unchecked.[34]

Labor economist Vernon Jensen wrote of Corridan's advocacy for the new union, "None was to play a more significant and colorful role than 'the waterfront priest' who had befriended many longshoremen and served as their confidant and adviser." Yet that was not precisely the nature of his apostolate. The Jesuit's real gift was as supplier of vision and courage to earnest individuals one or more steps further removed from the waterfront than he was. First among those was Budd Schulberg, who had traveled down a long road with his Jesuit mentor since their first meeting in autumn 1950, when Corridan implored the screenwriter to "make a *Going My Way* with substance." Pete Corridan had struggled even longer to reform the waterfront with a campaign for social and economic justice. Now it was time to enshrine this apostolate on film, an integral component in the campaign for a new union: "for all are friends of mine in the real waterfront struggle," wrote Corridan of the filmmakers and their local allies. On November 18, 1953—the day Joe Ryan was retired—these friends gathered in Hoboken and commenced making their movie atop the roof of a tenement at 106 Hudson Street, very near if not quite on the waterfront.[35]

16 The Mile Square City's Moment

"Yesterday was a day among days," Pete Corridan informed a reporter for the *Newark Evening News* on December 1, 1953. Corridan was interviewed in Hoboken, where a "movie, to be called 'Waterfront,' is rolling" on a city pier. The reporter linked the film directly to "a shrewd campaign on the priest's part to make the waterfront reforms complete and irrevocable." A major element of that campaign, the Waterfront Commission of the Port of New York, had just opened for business the previous day. The establishment of the bi-state commission was a personal coup for Corridan, who could be forgiven his boastful tone in the presence of the reporter. He inaccurately backdated the genesis of his waterfront work to 1945 (when he was in his final year of Jesuit training in upstate New York), claiming that longshoremen came to see him during the October wildcat strike).[1]

"I realized a long time ago," Corridan told the reporter, "that there was one hope in this situation, just one hope. That was publicity. Only by awakening the public and their officials, could anything be done about the waterfront. Since I came to that conclusion I have aimed to draw more and more publicity to the docks." As for the man known as "Father John" to "thousands of waterfront workers," the *Evening News* assured its readers, "when he walks the waterfront streets he gets greetings heartfelt and respectful. They love him as a 'regular guy.' 'It is more to the point that they be regular guys,' Father Corridan said. 'In that way the day of their delivery from the evils that beset the docks will come sooner.'" It was Corridan, the *Evening News* reported, "who kept after Budd Schulberg, the author, to whip together a script out of the [Malcolm] Johnson articles" on waterfront crime.[2] Though the *Evening News* covered Hudson as well as its home base of Essex County, the story provided no information on the choice of Hoboken as the location for the film shoot, then entering its third week in the Mile Square City. The reporter also failed to note that the entire Hoboken waterfront and most of the Port of New York and New Jersey had been shut down tight two days earlier by a wildcat strike. In protesting against the debut of the Waterfront Commission so ardently championed by Corridan, longshoremen were also defying an eighty-day no-strike injunction courtesy of the Taft-Hartley Act. The New York Shipping Association remained embroiled in contract negotiations with a union that had been unceremoniously tossed from the AFL and whose longtime and soon-to-be-convicted president had just been "retired" in disgrace. Shippers and stevedores had no idea which union—the "old" ILA or the upstart ILA-AFL—would represent the men as negotiations over a new contract loomed.[3]

The carnival-like atmosphere that suffused the opening of the Hoboken shoot was heightened by news that the National Labor Relations Board was weighing the insurgent union's bid to limit the upcoming representation election to longshoremen in the Port of New York (including New Jersey). The NLRB would rule in the AFL's favor, finding that dockworkers in the "outports" were not party to contract negotiations with NYSA. Voting was thus restricted to the cohort targeted most intensively by Corridan's campaign since 1948. It would afford him one last chance to claim rank-and-file solidarity with his crusade to cover the waterfront.[4]

"It was our advice that caused the AFL to concentrate its efforts here in New York," Corridan jubilantly informed a fellow Jesuit in early November. By New York he meant the entire port; but even with shooting under way in Hoboken, Corridan and his partisans continued to fix their gaze on Manhattan's West Side. Early in the shoot someone attached a large sticker reading "Rebel N.Y." to a dinghy tied up alongside the "Hoboken Yacht Club" at the foot of Fourth Street. It is visible in the climactic scene when Terry Malloy confronts Johnny Friendly (Lee J. Cobb as gangster boss of longshoremen's union Local 374) after testifying against him before a body much like the New York State Crime Commission. The filmmakers' floating billboard endorsement of the new AFL union was obviously not discernible from the West Side piers of Manhattan. Hoboken longshoremen voted too, but there were no stickers urging New Jersey to rebel against the ILA.[5]

The "one port" strategy of Corridan and his allies was thus hindered in its execution by the same parochialism they expected others to surmount. The battle between the ILA and the AFL was waged as intensely in Hoboken as anywhere else in the port, as the filmmakers quickly discovered. The new union's Hoboken office was opened at 332 Hudson Street, virtually on the set. Pro-ILA dockworkers could often be heard hooting barnyard epithets from nearby working piers in a pointed but vain attempt to disrupt the shoot, which went on as scheduled over thirty-five frigid, wintry days and nights. The NLRB finally scheduled the union representation election for December 22–23, just days before the film was due to wrap in Hoboken. Pete Corridan had decided to stay off the campaign trail; this movie set was more conspicuous than any lectern or pulpit. The first day he walked onto the set, "longshoremen gaped at him...and asked, 'Are you the real one or the phony one?'" They would soon learn as had so many others that he was the real one.[6]

Not a West Side Story

On the Waterfront has generated an immense volume of critical literature in the decades since its creation, but the story of Hoboken's role as the heart of the film remains obscure (see figure 9). It has been routinely described as a "New York film" by both those who knew it was actually shot in New Jersey and those who assumed it was filmed in Manhattan. Hoboken's place in the film's history is analogous in many ways to the largely unexamined role Hudson County played in the struggle for the port: a vital front in the battle but always treated as a sidelight to the main action on the West Side of Manhattan (and subordinate in importance to Brooklyn). Yet there would be no classic waterfront movie without Hoboken, just as there would have been no meaningful waterfront reform absent a Hudson County beachhead.[7]

Studies of *On the Waterfront*—with film scholar Leo Braudy's work offering a notable exception—treat Hoboken less as a real place than as a kind of primal film set, whose anonymity and unfamiliarity to viewers rendered it a perfect blank canvas on which New York filmmakers inscribed their vision. In *Celluloid Skyline: New York and the Movies*, film historian James Sanders provided an imaginative reading of the film's locations as a "self-contained universe that brimmed with meaning," making possible the reconstruction of "movie New York." The film, argued Sanders, revived New York as both a "mythic construct" and an alternative location to Hollywood for a flourishing film industry. "Produced at the dawn of postwar filmmaking in New York," wrote Sanders, "*On the Waterfront* remains perhaps the most ambitious attempt ever to orchestrate the elements of an urban locale into a unified filmic setting." In this reading cinematic Hoboken is the vehicle for the West Side waterfront's apotheosis, leaving the Mile Square City itself deeply obscured on the waterfront of history.[8]

The film's creators similarly tended alternately to overlook Hoboken and to mythologize it. In his epic 1988 memoir director Elia Kazan did not list his rich locations among "the four reasons why *On the Waterfront* was such a success." Kazan's list was compelling: from the luminous work of Marlon Brando as longshoreman Terry Malloy ("if there is a better performance by a man in the history of film in America, I don't know what it is"); to the "devotion and tenacity" of screenwriter Budd Schulberg; Kazan's own persistence ("I was tough and good on the streets"); and finally the "instinctive story sense" of producer Sam Spiegel. "*On the Waterfront* wouldn't have been made without Sam and that's a pretty positive thing to say about

Figure 9. Marlon Brando and Eva Marie Saint on the Hoboken set of *On the Waterfront,* late autumn 1953. Courtesy of the Museum of the City of New York, Theater Collection.

someone," Kazan noted with gratitude of a producer who "had raw animal courage and he had the courage in what he chose to do."[9]

Kazan did not entirely neglect Hoboken, but many of his allusions to the city are revealingly inaccurate. In treating the film's origin he explained that Schulberg had become "a partisan of a rotten union's rebels," but Kazan relocated those rebels from Manhattan's West Side in erroneously claiming that the screenwriter had already spent years of research for the film "on the streets of Hoboken and in its dockside bars" by the time they first met in spring 1952. Others naturally followed Kazan's lead. Peter Manso, for example, reported in his extremely thorough biography of Marlon Brando that Schulberg "practically lived on the Hoboken waterfront"; his description of Pete Corridan as "Hoboken's local waterfront priest" logically followed from the first premise.[10]

Kazan claimed in his memoir that he and Schulberg had "heard the legend" of Tony Mike DeVincenzo *prior* to DeVincenzo's December 15, 1952, testimony before the New York State Crime Commission. According to Kazan, "Budd knew when he had a live one; he sought the friendship of

DeVincenzo." Sometime after Tony Mike's testimony, Kazan says that he joined Schulberg for dinner at DeVincenzo's Hoboken home: "a heavy, pungent Italian meal that was served us, pasta and peppers and meat-loaded sauces and red wine." The "garlic-and-tomato-spiced dinner" made such an impression on Kazan that he later identified "this hour at Tony Mike's" as "the instant of final commitment, when I saw that, in the mysterious way of art, I was preparing a film about myself." He even claimed that it was only after this meeting that Schulberg decided "he knew enough about the people, the story, and the 'color' of the Hoboken scene to write his screenplay."[11]

Kazan's identification with Tony Mike—grounded entirely in their shared identity as defiant informers—putatively worked its way into the film script. In fact, since actress Eva Marie Saint was present at this dinner, it could not have occurred any earlier than mid-November 1953, when she was signed for the role of Edie Doyle and met Kazan for the first time. The dinner party more likely fell near the *end* of shooting; minor changes aside, it is unlikely Tony Mike's story exerted a major influence on the shooting script. Yet most commentators on the film, from proponents of the auteur theory to Marxist labor historians, have chosen to accept Kazan's word on these claims, whether they cite his Italian meal in Hoboken or not.[12]

Ironically, Kazan highlighted his identification with Tony Mike DeVincenzo to bolster his case that the film "was based on a set of real events which had nothing to do with my involvement with the Communist Party or the information I later gave [to HUAC]." His legion of adversaries saw Kazan's intense identification with Tony Mike as yet another self-justification for ratting. In their haste to confirm the wisdom that the film constituted "a thinly veiled attempt to justify informing on the former Communists and fellow travelers who had been targeted by HUAC," they looked right past the waterfront's turbulent history and saw only a story of informers. They also overlooked the existence of at least a half-dozen versions of Schulberg's script that predate the earliest possible moment Kazan could have met DeVincenzo and misinterpreted the influence of the NYSCC hearings on subsequent revisions.[13]

Those hearings were less valuable for providing a model of the "informer" than for showcasing the waterfront's code of silence and its unique modes of noncommunication, themes brilliantly conveyed in the shooting script and in the film. Each and every human relationship depicted in *On the Waterfront* bears a terrible burden of loneliness and isolation. (When Edie visits Terry's rooftop racing pigeon coop for the first time and he informs her pigeons get married just like people, Tommy, his young Golden Warrior disciple, glumly interjects, "Better.") Budd Schulberg later insisted he never met Tony Mike DeVincenzo until the cameras were rolling on the streets of Hoboken, when DeVincenzo was engaged as a "technical adviser" by Sam Spiegel, and Kazan did not know DeVincenzo until they were introduced by

Schulberg. The melodramatic notion that Kazan made a film to enshrine his identification with Tony Mike DeVincenzo was as irresistible to his critics as to the director himself, but it simply does not stand up to scrutiny as the interpretive key to the film.[14]

There is no evidence that Kazan ever discussed shooting the film in Hoboken prior to mid-autumn 1953. He treated film locations primarily as backdrops for highly personal studies in character and social psychology, a practice at which he was supremely gifted. "As he saw it," explained Kazan scholar Jeff Young, "his lifelong task was to turn psychology into behavior" in the tradition of the Method; character development always took precedence over journalistic detail or historical accuracy. During the first nine months of 1953 Kazan was busy in Manhattan preparing to stage new plays by his friends Tennessee Williams (*Camino Real*) and Robert Anderson (*Tea and Sympathy*) while contemplating future film projects, with just enough time left over to encourage Spiegel's pursuit of additional financing for the waterfront picture. On October 25 Kazan informed the *New York Times* that the still untitled movie "should be cast and set for filming in the near future"; no location was indicated.[15]

In his memoir Kazan acknowledged that Schulberg "regarded our waterfront story with greater objectivity, an objectivity I appreciated." He meant that the screenwriter was more factually oriented, since Budd was far from dispassionate; yet even Schulberg's journalistic instincts yielded to mythmaking in an August 1954 essay for *Holiday,* a popular travel magazine. Designed to promote the newly released *On the Waterfront,* "Drama in Hoboken" treated its author's growing romance with the port from a sufficiently amorphous geographical perspective as virtually to conflate the Hudson's two shores. Though Schulberg reported that his Hoboken sojourns consumed "almost a year, from the summer of 1953 through the winter months of 1954," in the script he completed on August 29, 1953, stand-in club boxer Terry Malloy still enters the ring as "the pride of the West Side."[16]

The West Side Manhattan setting had in fact remained constant since the inaugural screenplay of April 1951. Hoboken makes a cameo appearance in the April 1953 version of "Golden Warriors," but it is represented strictly as a place where troublemaking longshoremen are taken for a last ride (as in "they just found Charley in the Joisey swamps"). In the June 1953 version the Garden State is invoked simply as "that place we been usin' across the river" to dispose of problems. This imaginative rendering of New Jersey as a swampy dumping ground was haunted by the memory of dissident longshoreman Pete Panto's burial in a Lyndhurst lime pit in 1939 and colored by outside views of the state widely prevalent at the time (and since).[17]

It was not until the version dated September 30, 1953, that the drama acquired a neutral setting with neither Hoboken nor the West Side featured.

The tactically blurred sense of geography evident in "Drama in Hoboken" helped deflect attention from painful realities that *pushed* rather than *pulled* the filmmakers from the West Side to Hoboken, beginning with concerns for the safety of cast and crew. Joe Ryan was out as ILA chief, but his embittered cronies were still seething over the recent triumphs of waterfront reformers at King Joe's expense. Threats to filmmakers from the West Side Irish waterfront proved oddly fortuitous: Chelsea and environs was perpetually snarled in traffic, cramped, noisy, and visually uninspiring. Still, Schulberg had conceived and written a West Side story. A retreat to the Hudson's left bank stung at first, but in due time the Mile Square City's visual riches unfurled as revelations.[18]

Of all the figures connected with *On the Waterfront*, Budd Schulberg stood alone as deeply invested in both the artistic and the political dimensions of the project. Pete Corridan viewed the film primarily as a weapon in the ongoing struggle for the soul of the port; he alone perceived the tactical advantages of a Hudson County location. Ever since autumn 1948, when he first delivered "A Catholic Looks at the Waterfront" at a Jersey City Knights of Columbus hall, Corridan had sought to make the Jersey side of the Hudson a safe haven for militant waterfront advocacy too dangerous to pursue openly in Manhattan. His limited success was due to the volatile political culture of Jersey City in the post–Frank Hague era and the limitations of his local knowledge and understanding.

Hoboken was another challenge entirely. Unlike its much larger neighbor to the south, it offered no Jesuit schools or parishes where he could hang his hat. The reform campaign had not yet reached the Mile Square City. High-profile magazine articles by Jules Weinberg (July 1951) and Mary Heaton Vorse (April 1952) hinted at the possibility of a link between Tony Mike DeVincenzo and Pete Corridan, clearly the major source for both journalists, though not necessarily the source of their reporting on the Hoboken longshoreman. Corridan, who was never shy about accepting credit for journalistic coups, took no credit in these cases, nor did he claim any role in persuading Tony Mike to testify.[19]

Tony Mike DeVincenzo's December 1952 testimony before the NYSCC was politically fortuitous. On January 14, 1953, Hoboken mayor Fred De Sapio officially invited the Jesuit to reopen the Jersey frontier. "Your efforts to remedy conditions on both sides of New York Harbor are most commendable," wrote De Sapio; asking Corridan around "for a chat," he promised "to place at your disposal all the facilities at my official command. In my mind, your objectives are of non-political and unbiased character, and, therefore are the most effective." De Sapio was clearly motivated by an instinct for political survival, a well-justified reflex in light of what was shortly to come. He had been implicated in Hoboken's ruling waterfront clique by Tony Mike's testimony, but the aftermath was even more damaging.[20]

New York journalist Richard Carter, a Corridan ally, quickly arranged to co-write a tell-all article with DeVincenzo for the May 1953 issue of *True*, a men's magazine found in virtually every barbershop in urban America during the 1950s and 1960s. In "The Mob Said They'd Kill Me for My Story," DeVincenzo claimed that gangland waterfront kingpin Ed Florio was "as close to De Sapio and [Commissioner of Public Safety Michael] Borelli as their underwear. All the rackets suddenly blended into one streamlined shakedown. Nobody could get a job on the piers without an okay from the mayor or the police commissioner, relayed through Florio." On February 6, while preparing the article, Carter relayed a promise from Tony Mike to Pete Corridan: information on the Hoboken scene was forthcoming, including evidence that a recent "accidental" death on a pier stevedored by the Jarka Corporation was no accident.[21]

Tony Mike's notoriety inspired the waterfront priest to take his hardest look ever at the Jersey side; his avowed commitment to port-wide solutions finally began to ring true. On March 5, in an interview with the *Bayonne Times,* a newspaper serving that peninsular waterfront community at the southern tip of Hudson County, Corridan insisted that he sought a revitalized port "for the entire New York–New Jersey harbor area." He also touted the not-yet financed film project, enthusing that "the Schullberg script is powerful" and expressing hopes for "a truly realistic picture."[22]

The Pier, the Picture, the Port Authority

A realistic-looking waterfront movie to be shot on location—especially one highlighting the evils of the shapeup—demanded a pier. In September 1952 the federal government, which had controlled the decaying piers along Hoboken's southern waterfront since their confiscation from the North German Lloyd and Hamburg-America Lines in 1917, made a leasing agreement with the city contingent on the subleasing of these piers to the Port of New York Authority. The announcement was marked by a "colorful public ceremony" on September 24 presided over by Port Authority executive director Austin Tobin—making a rare public appearance—who joined two thousand Hobokenites in a parade from City Hall to the pier facility at Third and River streets.[23]

The acquisition of Hoboken's municipal piers was a tremendous coup for Tobin and Howard S. Cullman, the Port Authority's activist chairman. Hoboken had been in play since 1947, when the bi-state agency acquired the near dormant facilities at Port Newark as part of a deal that also included a lease on the coveted Newark Airport. The Port Authority assumed control of New York City's two major airports that same year but was rebuffed by the ILA and city officials in its bid to take over and completely modernize Manhattan's rotting municipal piers. Officials in Hoboken similarly resisted entreaties from the agency for nearly five years, despite the woeful condition of the city's piers, several of which had burned down or decayed beyond repair. Local prerogatives finally yielded to common sense after Tobin dangled a $21 million scheme (and a generous revenue-sharing arrangement) to restore the grandeur of the city's waterfront by renovating two piers and building from scratch the largest and most modern docking facility on the East Coast.[24]

The September 24 parade in Hoboken ended at Pier 3, which would shortly close for lack of business. On May 4, 1953, with the pier set to reopen under Port Authority auspices, hiring boss Francis "Red" Kelly was shot and killed outside the Friendly Tavern near his Park Street home just hours before he was scheduled to blow the whistle on the pier. While Wally Aluotto's May 1951 killing—likewise related to the struggle for control of hiring on Pier 3—had attracted scant attention in the New York papers, Kelly's murder received widespread coverage across the river, not only in the *Times* and other dailies but also in detailed, lavishly illustrated accounts published in *Life* (which also ran a pictorial tribute to Pete Corridan) and *Newsweek*. The slaying figured as well in ongoing waterfront crime hearings before the Tobey Committee in Washington. Everything had changed in the two years since Aluotto was killed, largely because of public pressure generated by Corridan and his allies, of whom Austin Tobin was now by far the most powerful. Tobin responded immediately to Kelly's murder by urging "prompt action by both New York and New Jersey for the adoption of laws that would end the practice of hiring longshoremen through the shape-up and the union hiring-boss."[25]

The original lessee-employer on Pier 3 and the other still functioning Hoboken piers recently acquired by the Port Authority was the Jarka Corporation, a stevedoring concern that had taken a tremendous beating in the NYSCC hearings. Jarka and its president, Frank W. Nolan, came under indictment in Manhattan in October 1953, making it much easier for the Port Authority to close one of its Jarka-operated Hoboken piers for immediate "renovation." That facility—a 940-foot double-deck finger pier at the foot of Fourth Street just to the south of the distinctive Holland America warehouse façade so visible in *On the Waterfront*—is known to longtime Hobokenites as Pier C, but prior to its mid-1950s renovation it was designated Pier 1. By any name this facility earned its true and enduring identity as the pier on which *On the Waterfront* was shot.[26]

Working piers do not simply make themselves available to filmmakers. For Austin Tobin the issue was clear and the stakes extremely high: he needed to help make the fledgling Waterfront Commission work, and he needed to drive career criminals off his Port Authority piers. The ouster of Jarka Corporation from Pier 1 was both a real and a symbolic start. The prospect of a feature film made by friends of his good friend the crusading waterfront priest was most appealing. Like his Jesuit ally, Tobin—the

Brooklyn longshoreman's grandson—equated the physical redevelopment of the port with a kind of moral rearmament which both of these driven men were loath to avow in explicitly spiritual terms. The Port Authority had a major investment to protect in Hoboken, and the collaboration of Austin Tobin and Pete Corridan was most compelling in the context of a century of struggle on the Irish waterfront.

A hundred years earlier the immigrant Irish were linked in the popular imagination with savagery. Relegated in later years to sporadic nativist fantasy—with the benighted immigrants updated to tribal waterfront chieftains and their long-suffering constituents—the theme reemerged in accounts authored by the immigrants' descendants. "The Irish, in a sense, have never strayed far from the docks, where they established a singularly dispiriting regime of political, business, and trade-union corruption," Daniel Patrick Moynihan would write in *Beyond the Melting Pot* (1963). Moynihan's elegiac account of the New York Irish was part political sociology, part jeremiad, a tradition rooted in the work of Irish American labor priests from John Monaghan to Pete Corridan. One way to end that "dispiriting regime" was by adapting secular methods to the cause of justice to break the chains of the past. It was fitting that Corridan's official role as technical (not theological) adviser on the film project positioned him in autumn 1953 to arrange quickly through his friend Austin Tobin "use of the Hoboken dock where the picture was shot." The pier made the picture: when Tobin opened Pier 1 to the filmmakers, they finally had both a picture and a Hoboken place in which to make it.[27]

With Hoboken now a viable location, figures with more ambiguous waterfront reform credentials fell in line behind the film project. Just over a week after Red Kelly's murder John J. Grogan was elected mayor of Hoboken. Grogan was a veteran of the successful campaign to oust the clan McFeely from City Hall in 1947. In 1952 voters in Hoboken approved a referendum changing the form of local government from the commission plan (as in Jersey City) to a strong mayor-and-council model. Running under the post-NYSCC slogan "End Hoboken's Disgrace," Grogan defeated his former ally and fellow city commissioner Fred De Sapio, who had remained loyal to the Hague machine's Hoboken division.[28]

On the day of Grogan's election John V. Kenny was also narrowly re-elected a Jersey City commissioner, as was his bitter rival Frank Hague Eggers, who slightly outpolled "the Little Guy" in the last hurrah for the once invincible machine of Eggers's uncle. John Grogan was president of the Marine and Shipbuilding Workers, a CIO union, and had ample incentive to enhance the reputation of organized labor in his hometown, especially at a time when pro-Kenny forces needed to find some high ground in the aftermath of the political boss's disastrous appearances at various recent public hearings. If his link to Kenny was not problematic enough, five words of Tony Mike DeVincenzo's NYSCC testimony ("Grogan, he got his take") had rendered the incoming mayor yet another Hoboken politico with a waterfront issue, though Tony Mike's much harsher condemnation of Fred De Sapio provided Grogan with temporary cover. The reformist heat was on in the Mile Square City: no politically charged waterfront movies would be made there without Mayor Grogan's approval. When the moment of "official" assent arrived, it was signaled directly to Pete Corridan.[29]

On Location with Gadge

"I'm going across the river to Hoboken like an explorer equipped with a camera," Elia Kazan informed Otis L. Guernsey Jr. of the *New York Herald Tribune* just as shooting commenced in mid-November 1953. It is likely that every member of *On the Waterfront*'s creative team shared Kazan's sense of novelty while on location. That was to be expected: Hoboken did not welcome the tourist trade in the 1950s, nor were the thousands of commuters who detrained at the magnificent 1907 beaux arts Lackawanna Terminal each workday enticed to linger as they scurried toward the Hudson Tubes or Manhattan-bound ferries. "The old joke about Hoboken being foreign territory had some truth in it," New York pundit Christopher Morley wrote in 1928. (Morley found the city refreshingly "unpolluted by sophistication.") In 1953 a *Fortune* writer opined, "Hoboken...might be geographically termed a suburb, but it boasts few more suburban amenities than the Bowery in New York."[30]

For decades after the film put Hoboken on the cinematic map, pilgrims rarely made the leap of faith required to view its locations in person. One prominent devotee, film scholar Leo Braudy, finally made his initial foray to the Mile Square City in the late 1960s, but only after a protracted buildup:

> For years before when I had visited friends [in New York City, where he did not yet live] or driven through, I would always try to use the Holland Tunnel under the Hudson, because every once in a while, craning my neck while driving along that wide street that leads up to the tunnel on the Jersey side, I thought I could see the spires of a Hoboken church I knew must be from *On the Waterfront*.

In an insightful 2005 study Braudy identified the Hoboken locations as "a central part of the film's power" but did not treat the city itself as a historic site of waterfront conflict.[31]

When "Gadge" Kazan (from "Gadget," a nickname acquired at Yale Drama School) and Budd Schulberg made their initial scouting foray across the river, they were treated to a revelation. "Hoboken sits on an escarpment," as James Sanders, described it,

> raised above a thin sliver of land at the river's edge—an area filled almost entirely (at the time) with cargo piers, warehouses, and rail lines. The city above,

the waterfront below, the cliff between them making each its own world—it was this essential topography that the filmmakers would fill with narrative and moral significance.

By the time "gritty" was flatteringly applied to cities like Hoboken in the late 1970s, the Mile Square City was just beginning its miraculous transformation to trendy destination, but in late 1953 Hoboken was indeed the quintessential gritty city: compact, densely populated, ethnically textured, deeply wary of outsiders, and boasting a seemingly infinite stock of stories like those newly told by Tony Mike DeVincenzo across the Hudson. *On the Waterfront* wondrously captured a Hoboken moment in words and pictures: the film is so powerful it overcomes all but the most determined efforts to resist perceiving it as a documentary.[32]

Kazan deeply enjoyed outdoor location shooting. Far from being the first film of its kind, as it is often described, *On the Waterfront* was only the latest in a series of his films in which locations played a central role, including *Boomerang* (Stamford, Connecticut, and While Plains, New York), *Panic in the Streets* (New Orleans), and *Viva Zapata,* with locations in the vicinity of Roma, Texas, standing in for Emiliano Zapata's village of Cuautala after plans to shoot there were scuttled by the Mexican government. Although the city (or any city) is never mentioned by name in the film itself, an establishing shot that opens *On the Waterfront* fixes its gaze squarely on the Hoboken Yacht Club (honored by its real name in the final shooting script if not the film). The "yacht club" was in fact a dilapidated "floating hutch" dangling atop the river from its perch between Pier 1 and the Fifth Street Holland America terminal. It was the discovery of this site that clinched Hoboken as the location during the initial scouting expedition of Schulberg, Kazan, and art director Richard Day. "Once we found the little yacht club," Schulberg recalled, "we knew this was the place."[33]

The yacht club location served as the offices of Johnny Friendly's Local 374. In the opening scene Terry Malloy, "a wiry, jaunty, waterfront hanger-on in his late twenties," emerges from the shack surrounded by Friendly and some very rough-looking associates. The imposing steamship *Nieuw Amsterdam* dominates the frame; barely visible through some netting is the modest Chelsea skyline across the Hudson. Terry is sent on an errand to lure to a rooftop longshoreman Joey Doyle, where he is punished—waterfront style—for the unpardonable sin of talking to crime investigators. Kazan had a prodigious gift for blending setting, story, and theme. "The point of the introduction," he told interviewer Jeff Young in 1970, "is that the whole waterfront, which is wide and enormous, is in the grip of one fist, one little clique, one little clubhouse. I could have put the entire scene inside the office. But I did it this way because it dramatized what I thought was the situation there. So it wasn't casual. It was a specific choice I made."[34]

Kazan believed that the New York artists who dominated his cast—many with Actors Studio connections—would interact well with the Hobokenites slated to play themselves in a variety of smaller roles. The film's Hoboken production office, located in the Meyers Hotel at Third and Hudson streets, functioned as a kind of "hiring hall" for locals as well as a wardrobe storage facility and gathering place for the professional cast and crew. Most of the New Yorkers "shaped up" early each morning at Ninth Avenue and Forty-first Street in Manhattan and were ferried across the river. Marlon Brando and Eva Marie Saint often traveled together—Brando in character—via the Hudson Tubes. Brando and Karl Malden were singled out by Hobokenites for their easygoing camaraderie with townspeople. "He's so regular and natural," a fifteen-year-old girl praised Brando to the *Jersey Journal*. "I think Brando is charming—not a bit stuck-up like some of the Hollywood celebrities," added Mrs. Betty March of Hoboken's Bloomfield Street.[35]

Malden's unobtrusive gift for inhabiting a character from the inside was abundantly evident in his performance as Father Pete Barry. As a lifelong Hobokenite who closely observed the actor at work on location recalled, Malden "felt the movie, he felt the part." His role as the priest represented a unique challenge to the actor because "it was the first time I had ever played a living human being."[36]

He "ended up spending eleven days with Father John" in preparation for the role. After watching Corridan "throw back a few beers" at lunchtime in a tavern, Malden "knew immediately that I could not play this man as a sanctimonious, holier-than-thou type. He himself begged me, 'Karl, don't play me like a priest. Play me like a man.'" Corridan, he thought, "was just like Hoboken—cold and tough on the edges, but filled with integrity and a helluva lot of dignity." Malden wore Corridan's hat and coat throughout the shoot and borrowed liberally—with an assist from Schulberg—from the Jesuit's baseball-inflected vernacular. He also shared Corridan's empathy and compassion for the vulnerable: a local resident was struck by the concern Malden showed one day for a "skinny, hungry kid from the neighborhood" who stood shivering in Elysian Park while Malden and Brando performed for the cameras.[37]

Another hungry kid from the neighborhood figured prominently in a film replete with nonprofessional local talent. As part of his duties as "technical adviser" Arthur Brown tended the pigeon coops on the rooftop of a tenement building at 105 Hudson Street where Terry Malloy and his Golden Warriors kept their racing pigeons. One cold morning before shooting began Tommy Hanley, a thirteen-year-old resident of the building, appeared on the rooftop and asked Brownie what he was doing; Hanley was promptly hired to feed the pigeons while Brownie visited a number of the twenty-one saloons on the block below. Tommy and his mother lived in poverty on Hoboken's "Barbary Coast," the waterfront stretch of gin mills in which he sold chances in order to pay his tuition at nearby Sts. Peter and

Paul parochial school. Brownie, who knew that Hanley's longshoreman father had been murdered on the West Side when Tommy was four months
old, promised the youngster a part in the film.[38]

"At first I thought he was bullshitting me. But before I knew it, I was on
my way to the Actors Studio in New York to audition," Hanley recalled. He
met Kazan and Schulberg at the Studio's offices on West Fifty-second Street.
They too knew the circumstances of his father's death; during Hanley's audition for a part as a Golden Warrior "they deliberately enraged me," he
recalled. Kazan, in particular, taunted the youngster, calling his father a rat
and a squealer, until Hanley "went nuts, started throwing chairs at them,
and that's what they wanted, because there's that scene where I throw a
pigeon at Brando" after Terry Malloy "rats" before the crime commission.
The filmmakers hired Hanley on the spot at the rate of $250 a week.[39]

Tommy Hanley's story was as compelling as any that emerged from
the project. The filmmakers exposed him to a waterfront reform movement he would have ignored under ordinary circumstances. His New
York relatives—some of whom were connected to Local 791 in Chelsea—
disdained Father Pete Corridan as a pariah and an unwanted invader on
their turf. Hanley developed a warm affection on the set for Karl Malden
that sparked in turn an interest in Corridan's apostolate. Two years later
Hanley began his own half-century career as a longshoreman in the port;
though initially embittered by the taunting he took from co-workers
("Mr. Hollywood"), he later dedicated himself to the cause of social justice
and union democracy championed by Corridan, a cause he discovered only
through the intervention of Brownie and the filmmakers. In transforming
Tom Hanley's worldview they practiced a vocation akin to that performed
daily by Corridan himself.[40]

Like everyone else on the set, Hanley never forgot the bitter cold. "The
temperature was zero and a cruel wind whipped off the Hudson," Schulberg
recalled. "It was so cold out there you couldn't overact," Brando recalled of
his work on the pier. "The crew had great metal barrels burning and every
kind of wood they could rip off, so that the flames were bursting out of the
barrels and the metal rims were red hot," Kazan wrote in his memoir. The
freezing wind whipping across the piers "did a great thing for the actors'
faces: it made them look like people, not actors—in fact like people who
lived in Hoboken and suffered the cold because they had no choice." The
cold imposed a kind of ascetic discipline of work and solidarity, leveling
distinctions and creating shared bonds of suffering and endurance, the very
traits enshrined in the film.[41]

Most of the extras in the shapeup scene did not have to "try" to look
like real people; they were local longshoremen hired at a daily rate of $15,
comparable to what they would have made in wages on a normal pier
workday. Mayor John Grogan had appointed municipal employee Tony
D'Amato to serve as the city's "one-man film commission" and liaison with

the filmmakers. D'Amato supervised the hiring of scores of Hobokenites who appeared in the film.

Relations between cast, crew, and townspeople were generally warm but not wholly peaceable: at one point a group of dockworkers dangled Kazan's devoted assistant director Charlie Maguire over the edge of Pier 1 in demand of immediate payment. Kazan was inspired to seek a local emissary—Joe Marotta, brother of Police Chief Arthur Marotta and the director's bodyguard—for the duration of the shoot. "Joe carried a pistol and was never more than six feet away from me throughout the picture," Kazan wrote in his memoir. "One day some hoods pushed me up against a wall and, holding me there, began to berate me, their point being that I was making the people of Hoboken look bad—yes, they were that civic-minded. But Joe walked up and they walked away." In 1971 he told a pair of interviewers that a longshoreman once walked out of a bar to "beat the shit" out of a would-be Kazan assailant. "The atmosphere was that violent. There were things I can't tell about corruption, about our paying off people—little black sacks, things like that. We were right in the midst of life on that picture, and it shows, doesn't it?"[42]

I7 The Priest in the Movie

"We shot *On the Waterfront* surrounded by people, by spectators," Elia Kazan recalled. "It was great; it was like a public trial." Budd Schulberg likewise reveled in the tumult: "Hundreds of longshoremen were in the movie...and racketeers watching from the sidelines. It was unreal. What we were putting up on the screen was happening all around us." They were also treating the most meaningful issues from the port's recent past, defining its legacy even as the struggle for its future violently raged on. The shapeup scene in *On the Waterfront* vividly recapitulates Pete Corridan's discernment process between 1946 and 1948, when he, like his fictional alter ego Father Pete Barry, "took a look for himself" and came to see the shape as the primal source of indignity and oppression on the waterfront. That witness and the subsequent conversion of this priestly figure to militant advocacy is the one story element that survived every revision of Schulberg's scripts (see figure 10). It is the soul of the film because it was the soul of Corridan's story from the time he first poured it out to the screenwriter over a quantity of beers at Billy the Oysterman's in the winter of 1950.[1]

In an earlier scene Joey Doyle's sister Edie upbraided the priest when he told her (after performing last rites over her slain brother) that he would be "in the church" if she needed him. "In the church?" she cries out. "Did you ever hear of a saint hiding in a church?" Chastened by her response, Father Barry ventures out to Pier 1 in time for the morning shapeup only to find Edie already there. "This is my parish," he now acknowledges. "I don't know how much I can do but you're right, Edie—I'll never find out if I don't come down here and take a good look for myself." Shot against the cold brick warehouses and the hard edges of Pier 1, the shapeup scene indelibly establishes the waterfront's brutality. The filmed shapeup was designed to portray men clinging desperately to their human dignity after a lifetime of abuse, now driven by hunger to descend into a free-for-all after pier foreman

Figure 10. Budd Schulberg, Father John M. Corridan, and Elia Kazan on Pier 1, Hoboken set of *On the Waterfront,* late autumn 1953. Courtesy of the Wesleyan University Cinema Archives.

"Big Mac" tosses dozens of brass tabs to the ground, the precious tickets to a four-hour payday.[2]

Arthur Miller's biographer claimed that "the tossed work checks were Miller's idea" (checks tossed skyward by a hiring boss figure in a scene found in both versions of "The Hook"), basing his assertion on Miller's reported witnessing of such a scene in Brooklyn in the late 1940s. Yet in *Crime on the Labor Front,* Malcolm Johnson repeated a story well established in New York waterfront lore since the 1930s: "The hiring boss took one look at the gaunt, desperate faces of those 500 men and lost his nerve. With a gesture of resignation he tossed the 100 checks into the air, turned, and walked away. Five hundred men fought like animals for a hundred brass checks and a half day's work."[3]

The shapeup scene in *On the Waterfront* featured performers who the director believed "were more people than they were actors." They "had to be in the same league as the scenery," Kazan later explained. "They had to be as real as the Hoboken locations. You rarely get that with actors." Film historian Brian Neve suggested that Kazan's taking "care over relatively small parts" reflected the Group Theatre tradition of linking "the individual to the broader social conflict." Kazan's good friend the former vaudevillian

Pat Henning played Kayo Dugan, the grizzled bantamweight modeled directly after Arthur Brown. Kazan cast veteran stage actor John Hamilton as Pop Doyle, Edie's bereaved, beleaguered longshoreman father. "I'd known him for a long time from around the street," Kazan recalled. "There was this sense in him of I'm a failure. I'm not going to make it. So much goodness and so much pain." Hamilton conveys better than anyone else in the film the wages of deference, the bitterness and enforced silence visited on waterfront lifers, traits that lend his brief moment of resistance at the end of the film such raw power.[4]

As the shapeup scene winds down, an agitated Father Barry exhorts the men: "What about your union? No union in the country would stand for this." Disgruntled longshoreman Jimmy Collins replies, "the waterfront's tougher—like it ain't part of America." When Jimmy's friend Moose adds, "There's not one place to even talk without getting clobbered," Father Barry replies, "The church." As the men stare at him incredulously he repeats, "The bottom of the church." This exchange signals the "liberation theology" moment in the film so cherished by Budd Schulberg, with "the bottom of the church" signifying not simply a basement sanctuary but a site of prophetic grassroots insurgency. Schulberg had quite likely heard Happy Keane testify before the New York State Crime Commission in December 1952 that fraudulent ILA elections in Jersey City were conducted "down in the bottom of the church, bottom of St. Michael's Church." In creating a waterfront of memory, Schulberg here reversed the logic of its historic authority, just as he did by inserting an African American longshoreman into the script as well as a young woman and a parish priest (not a Jesuit) who fails to mind his own business.[5]

The subsequent meeting scene—shot in the basement chapel of Sts. Peter and Paul church, a German parish founded in 1889 at Third and Hudson streets—launches an extraordinary sequence highlighting the superb Hoboken locations selected by the filmmakers. The pastor of Sts. Peter and Paul, Father John A. Weisbrod (known for his "financial acumen"), had agreed—for a consideration after the pastor of a nearby church balked—to permit filming of a scene that features goons smashing church basement windows prior to their vicious assault on Father Barry's tiny band of still reluctant insurgents. Terry Malloy—who has been sent by his brother "Charley the Gent" (Rod Steiger) to spy on the meeting—escorts Edie to safety amid the fracas. Terry and Edie are then shown scurrying from a church, which is not Sts. Peter and Paul but Our Lady of Grace, located inland down a long slope at the southwestern edge of Church Square Park.[6]

Our Lady of Grace was the oldest parish in Hoboken and spiritual home to the city's old-stock Irish Americans. The 1878 Gothic church structure was stately and imposing, but as Pete Corridan astutely pointed out to the filmmakers, the site's real value was the visual depth of field afforded by the two-square-block park that fronted the church. While the Catholic churches on the West Side of Manhattan were jammed into side streets or faced out onto busy avenues, the juxtaposition of Our Lady of Grace to Church Square Park provided all the visual elements needed to mark this urban parish clearly as the heart of a Catholic waterfront village.[7]

After the pair make their escape, Terry is accosted in the park by a drunken man who taunts him with the reminder, "You was there that night," when Joey Doyle was killed. Suddenly in mid-sentence of Terry's angrily defensive response ("Who's he calling a bum?") the location shifts to Elysian Park, along the palisade overlooking the river a half-mile to the northeast. Cinematographer Boris Kaufman used smoke pots to obscure the differences in visual background between the two locations; "this device," he explained, "enabled me to continue the sequence...and to make it flow." The flat background landscape of Church Square Park is replaced by the steep slope of Castle Point Terrace, with the effect of moving Edie and Terry nearer to the viewer just as they awkwardly engage in their first intimate conversation while crossing a playground. This sequence is consummated with such integrity that it confirms the judgment of the great French director François Truffaut: Kazan's "cinematic unit is neither the shot nor the film itself, but the scene."[8]

In a legendary semi-improvised moment during this scene Edie drops a glove while crossing Elysian Park; Terry picks it up and tries it on his own hand, prolonging their encounter and lending an intimacy Terry has never learned to convey in words. Was this bit of business "spontaneous" or rehearsed? The dropped glove is not featured in any of Budd Schulberg's scripts, despite his habit of including more directions than are typically found in screenplays. Karl Malden later indicated that Edie never dropped her glove until the take preserved on film, while Eva Marie Saint insisted that in rehearsal Brando always picked up the glove, adding: "But Marlon would never do any scene quite the same. It was exciting, like being in a play. It became the catalyst to keep me in the scene." Years later Pete Corridan told his younger Jesuit friend the film critic Neil Hurley that "he felt a spirit come over the film" during that graced moment in Elysian Park. Corridan was "a very private man, when talkative," Hurley noted in a pithy characterization of Irish waterfront sociolinguistics, "but inside quite sentimental." Shortly before Corridan's death the two engaged in a "bedside chat" in which Hurley was again reminded that "during the shooting of the entire film there was an indescribable feeling among those present that a curious force was helping to direct the picture."[9]

"The Priest" and "the Girl"

Neil Hurley provides an extraordinarily rare glimpse of Pete Corridan's interior spirituality, illuminated by a tenderly romantic scene in a film to which he was intimately linked. If Corridan's spirituality was never more private than in his public performance as the manly labor priest, his response to this moment of grace is deeply revealing. His pastoral contact with women in his work at Xavier and with waterfront insurgents was negligible. Even though Father Phil Carey, Corridan's boss, enjoyed warm pastoral relationships with women and families, especially in his later years as a beloved weekend visitor at a parish on Long Island, he was hesitant to enroll women at Xavier; precious few attended before the late 1950s. Several women who greatly admired Carey recalled his commitment to highly traditional gender roles. Jesuit social apostolates rarely if ever addressed issues from the perspective of women's experience: waterfront rackets were condemned, for example, as degrading to families because they undermined the capacity of men to function as responsible husbands and fathers.[10]

The gender politics of Jesuit labor priests was but a small element in a much wider waterfront constellation almost wholly bereft of female presence. The fictional Edie Doyle is not merely the only prominent female character in *On the Waterfront;* she is among the very few women—real or fictional—to figure in the recorded history or folklore of the New York–New Jersey waterfront (indeed a deficit reflected in this book). Women were for all practical purposes banished from the waterfront after the early 1920s—not that they ever constituted a significant presence. The few radical reformers and journalists who challenged this prohibition left the scene early; there was no repetition of the female-led Irish Patriotic Strike of 1920. Dorothy Day ceded her interest in the waterfront to the men of the Association of Catholic Trade Unionists by the late 1930s. Mary Heaton Vorse was a special case, nearing the end of a fabled career when she wrote "Pirate's Nest of New York."[11]

In her original incarnation Edie Doyle was depicted by Schulberg as a fiery crusader for waterfront justice, the sister—not the love interest—of a martyred longshoreman who would evolve into Terry Malloy in subsequent drafts. In this sense Joey Doyle is a remnant of the original Terry Monahan, now split into two characters. The evolution of the character of Edie reflected the insistence of Darryl Zanuck and others that a love story was essential to sell the picture. Kazan's rationale for casting the delicately blond (and evocatively named) Eva Marie Saint in the role coupled routinely fantasized notions of female Catholic sexuality—he sought "a truly innocent, devoted girl, a girl who had something in her that resembled the simplicity and faith that well-brought-up Catholic girls have"—common to that and later eras with his vision of a more complex feminine persona.[12]

Kazan exalted female characters whose "virtuous exterior masks powerful feelings." The gifted artist Julie Harris was Kazan's "ideal of that kind of woman," as she would reconfirm in 1955 in a sensitive yet erotically charged role as Abra, savior of the wayward Cal Trask (James Dean), under Kazan's direction in *East of Eden*. Eva Marie Saint conveyed just this quality that Kazan sought in *On the Waterfront:* she "greatly complicates" Edie's relationship with Terry Malloy, as film historian Sam Girgus argued. "It is the unity of her sexual, moral, and psychological entanglements with Brando that makes her performance so strong and convincing." Girgus noted that although Kazan was "not usually given to romance or sentimentality," he often asserted that "my favorite scenes in the film are the love scenes between Marlon and Eva Marie Saint."[13]

In *On the Waterfront* Father Pete Barry is depicted as even more "self-less" than Edie; his inner desires and the soul of his apostolate go unrevealed. Yet the similarity of his mission to that of Edie—to arouse Terry Malloy's dormant conscience—recalls Zanuck's original concern that the presence of both "the priest" and "the girl" was redundant. That Kazan also subscribed to a kind of "gendered" view of the priesthood is evident in a rhetorical question he posed to interviewer Jeff Young: "What do priests really know about life?" adding, "The waterfront priests know more, but they're still dealing with absolute right and absolute wrong," surely an inaccurate characterization of Pete Corridan's apostolic practice. Presumed innocent of the dark passions driving dockworkers and mobsters, "the priest" and "the girl" perform at times a nearly interchangeable role: they take turns ministering to Terry from atop the (moral) high ground of Elysian Park, a setting devoid of appearances by any other of the film's characters. There they challenge him at the very edge of his familiar, compromised terrain, up against the iron fence through which the shrouded skyline of Manhattan is dimly perceived like a distant silent witness.[14]

Contenders

The priest in the movie might well have proved superfluous were it not for the speech that crystallized Budd Schulberg's waterfront redemption narrative nearly three years before Elia Kazan joined the cinematic cause. Father Pete Barry's "Christ in the Shapeup" oration was shot just a few days before Christmas 1953 not in Hoboken but on the Brooklyn waterfront. This was one of two legendary scenes shot outside the Mile Square City; the other capped a final stab at communication between the brothers Charley and Terry Malloy as they share a ride in a taxicab. Kazan remembered shooting the latter scene at a "small shabby studio" in Manhattan, contrary to local legend that implausibly locates it on the streets of Hoboken. When Sam Spiegel failed to deliver on his promise of a camera-rigged car, the crew fabricated its own "cutaway" car in the studio. Since Spiegel also failed to provide rear projection for the scene, Boris Kaufman "solved the problem in the simplest way possible, by putting a small Venetian blind across the window at the back of the cab shell and shooting straight in to avoid the side windows, except for an edge that he caught with a flickering light to suggest traffic going by."[15]

"What emerged was one of the most memorable moments in twentieth-century art," Brando biographer Peter Manso asserted with all due justification. The indelible phrase plaintively uttered by Terry Malloy at the height of that scene was a product of Budd Schulberg's great affinity for prizefighters. Schulberg had hired Roger Donoghue, a former professional middleweight from Yonkers, to teach Brando to carry himself like an ex-fighter. "Unlike the other boxers Donoghue was articulate and blessed with more than the usual pug's Runyonesque gift for gab," Manso noted. One day as he swapped stories with Schulberg, Donoghue mused offhandedly that had it not been for his "Irish skin" that cut easily, "I could have been a contender."[16]

When it came time to film "Christ in the Shapeup," the Hoboken-based Holland America Line refused to allow the filmmakers to shoot inside the steamship berthed at its Fifth Street terminal. Since longshoremen extras would not be shaping up for work that day, the firm reasoned, they would have to shape for the film on their own time. The producer quickly secured the use of the Dominican freighter *Rhadames,* berthed at the Bethlehem Steel Company's South Brooklyn pier, where cast and crew spent a long day filming the "accidental" killing of Kayo Dugan under a sling load of his beloved "good Irish whiskey." Father Barry's subsequent five-minute eulogy—delivered over the body of Dugan from the ship's hold—was among the lengthier soliloquies in film history to that point and the subject of a bitter dispute between Schulberg and Sam Spiegel. The two had quarreled throughout the shoot over the producer's constant demand for changes in the script, but on "Christ in the Shapeup" the writer refused to yield: "Day after day he hammered at this until, each time he asked me for the cuts[,]...rather than repeat myself, I would simply go to the window, open it, lean my elbows on the sill and stare out in silence."[17]

Kazan ardently backed his writer. "Christ in the Shapeup" was spoken as written and written as spoken on the waterfront of history, the source of its enduring cinematic power. Kazan "reassured Spiegel that he would cut it in such a way with interspersed shots and angles that it would play much more quickly," but the reaction shots, including the throwing of debris at Father Barry (Karl Malden was badly cut by a metal can; the on-screen blood is real)—reduced the credibility of the scene, since not even the most depraved waterfront hoodlum would assault a priest. As a latecomer to the project Spiegel could not have known that this speech, like its original author, was the "soul and spirit" of the film, its message lodged at the core of every draft Schulberg had written since the winter of 1951. The screenwriter proudly acknowledged, "I simply lifted" the speech, "practically word for word," from Pete Corridan's 1948 original, adapting it strictly for narrative purposes.[18]

"Christ in the Shapeup" neatly bracketed Corridan's career in the waterfront apostolate. He first delivered "A Catholic Looks at the Waterfront" as an obscure Jesuit signaling the launch of his crusade at a Knights of Columbus hall. Five years later he was a national celebrity, his work validated in the Waterfront Commission Compact passed by an act of the United States Congress. But no public accolade or journalistic profile came so near to capturing the soul of his apostolate; there would never be another speech or broadcast to rival the cinematic "Christ in the Shapeup." The spirit of the Catholic Church's modern social teachings was never rendered so forcefully as in those five minutes of *On the Waterfront*. Pete Corridan's apostolate on the waterfront of history had stalled just as his avowed goals were being fulfilled. He never truly found his place among the community of longshoremen, settling instead for extraordinary influence with journalists, reformers, and soon the filmgoing public. Corridan's waterfront gospel was distilled onscreen more intimately and powerfully than he could ever have achieved in person. Budd Schulberg, fearing that the Jesuit's work was insufficiently highlighted in the film, would soon publish a lengthy novel with a Corridan figure as its central character.

Yet for those determined to resist the searing message presented in the film, a dozen additional novels would not have sufficed. Many reviewers panned "Christ in the Shapeup" as markedly inferior to the film's more "realistic" scenes. The renowned critic Pauline Kael, for instance, dismissed it as the "poorest scene in the film." Another critic, while praising Malden's performance, complained that the priest's "importance in the scheme of this drama seems overemphasized"; yet another actually complimented the actor for a performance "much better than the lines he is given to speak" while chastising the filmmakers for not paying "just attention to the courage and intelligence of men like Father John Corridan."[19]

The passage of time has only amplified the negative response to the character. In 1974 the French critic Michel Ciment scolded Elia Kazan in the course of an interview, "The character of the priest is too dominant." A leading reference work on American film refers to "the rather dotty Karl Malden as the local priest"; and in 2004 New York waterfront aficionado and critic Philip Lopate still found Karl Malden "unbearably hammy with his sermons."[20]

"Many reactions were provoked by the priest, I know," Kazan told yet another French interviewer for *Cahiers du cinéma* in 1966. "Why? It seems that people were indignant because I showed him as a man who had goodness." The issue for many hostile critics was not Catholicism per se but those crucial sites where religion and politics intersected. Father Pete Barry's role in persuading Terry to testify before the crime commission late in the film was facilely if understandably linked to Kazan's and Schulberg's HUAC testimonies, which in turn triggered condemnations of the film as a whole. The critic Nora Sayre drew the connection most bluntly in her

1982 study of Cold War films. Noting that Pete Barry termed Kayo Dugan's killing "a crucifixion," Sayre wrote, "One wonders if Kazan and Schulberg felt they had been crucified for their testimony and if—as very bitter ex-Communists—they had lauded the Catholic church in deference to its powers during the political investigations."[21]

The critic and film historian Peter Biskind provided a tortuous ideological reading of Pete Barry as a manipulative, "ruthless crusader" serving the interests of a "corporate liberal" social order adept at deflecting dissent. In Biskind's view—grounded like Sayre's in revisionist Cold War historiography—the cinematic priest's intentions are "coyly denied or disguised" so that Terry Malloy will believe that his decision to testify before the crime commission is rooted in his freedom rather than coercion by "a priest[,]...the government[,]...and a woman...to establish the terms that will define and circumscribe the drama: God, country, and family." Nearly all these critiques are grounded in ignorance not of Catholicism in isolation but of postwar American urban cultural history, the context in which the Jesuit labor schools played such a significant role.[22]

In the absence of that context, many critics have understandably resorted to analyses of generically "Christian" symbolism in the film: approving or disparaging alike, they cite the passion/crucifixion/resurrection of Terry Malloy, beaten nearly to death at the water's edge only to rise and free the men; or the shot of martyred longshoreman Kayo Dugan's body ascending on a pallet accompanied by Pop Doyle and Father Barry. In a tone of futile exasperation Kazan virtually pleaded with Michel Ciment to accept his denial that the shot was intended to depict Kayo's soul "rising to heaven" but to give the longshoreman's (and filmmaker's) perspective some consideration: "That's the way you get out of the hold of a boat; there's no other way. There's a narrow little iron staircase that you climb up but you can't climb up with a dead body. But [the critics] said no, it's the priest taking his soul to heaven. The fact is, I'm not in the least religious."[23]

He was not trying to be cute: it would be difficult to find a critic more hostile to Catholicism than Kazan, largely the result of his bitter experience with "a proud conspiracy" of Catholics arrayed against his masterly 1951 film version of *A Streetcar Named Desire,* a conspiracy he believed was "led by the gluttonous Pope of Fiftieth Street [Cardinal Spellman] and the men who worked under his guidance to win his approval." There was no directorial infusion of a "Catholic imagination" in this waterfront picture.[24]

Film scholar Leo Braudy offered a "more fruitful way of looking" at *On the Waterfront* beyond the framework of politics or a mechanical application of "Christian" symbolism to the movie. He distinguished between "symbols that refer to an external belief system and symbols created by the characters themselves as a way of giving their lives meaning and purpose." Joey Doyle's jacket (passed from Pop Doyle to Kayo to the African American longshoreman Luke then back to Edie), Braudy suggested, "is a much more homemade symbol" than the garment of Jesus to which it was often compared by critics. "It fits into a larger pattern in the film of clothes and coverings that is totally apparent to all the characters and reflects a waterfront reality" (as "armor" against vulnerability; as a means to "maintain a manly surface, keep the leaking wounds invisibly inside"). Braudy's astute analysis is strikingly congruent with the teaching and pastoral methods of Phil Carey and Pete Corridan: they urged Xavier students and longshoremen alike to approach problems not from the perspective of abstract church teachings but in light of the concrete situation in which they were encountered.[25]

"Mr. Upstairs"

Pete Corridan dearly loved this movie and Karl Malden's performance in it. For him, *On the Waterfront* enshrined the lonely human struggle for connection with others: all waterfront relationships are fraught with peril, sustained by mutual self-deception and a deadening resignation to "do nothing and say nothing," as Charley Malloy urges Terry in the taxicab upon offering him a coveted, lucrative position as boss loader on a new pier. "There's more to this than I thought," the younger brother ominously responds. "I'm tellin' ya there's a lot more." The film's choked-back emotional energy is powerfully released with Terry's opening to that forbidden "more." It discloses far more than his potential willingness to testify against "certain people we might know," more than his discovery of a personal conscience. Since the code of silence functioned in a communal, transpersonal context, this solitary cog in the machine suddenly holds the power to dismantle the Irish waterfront's way of not-seeing, by speaking plainly not to crime investigators but to the brother and fellow orphan with whom he has never shared an intimate moment.

That is why Charley's response in the back of the taxi is even more revealing than Terry's startling if tentative bid for freedom. Charley's initial reaction is to reassert the primacy of the organization: Johnny Friendly will not "jeopardize a set-up like that for one rubber-lipped ex-tanker." "Don't say that," gently counters Terry as he parries Charley's scripted untruths with an honest reappraisal of his own life. When Terry laments, "I could have been better," is he referring to his life or to a boxing career thwarted by Charley and the mob? "That's not the point," Charley counters. "I could have been better," Terry repeats. "There isn't much time, kid," pleads a suddenly vulnerable Charley, begging Terry to pledge his silence before they get to River Street. Terry instead forces Charley to make and take the time, even as he too understands just what awaits him there, and even as his brother pulls a gun on him, which Terry gently turns away. When Charley tries to speak again, no words are released until he finally lets it go. "How much do you weigh, son?" he asks a suddenly puzzled looking Terry. "When you weighed 168 pounds you were beautiful. You could have been another Billy Conn if not for that skunk of a manager we got you."[26]

As the emotional power of their conversation intensifies, the brothers fall more deeply into fight talk. The ring serves as stage in a drama of moral reckoning. Charley's persisting self-delusion provokes Terry into delivering the bottom line like a straight right to the jaw: "It wasn't him. It was *you*, Charley." In Schulberg's shooting script but not the film, the next line reads, "You and Johnny," an addition more faithful to the setting. It was *all* of you, charges Terry; it was the Irish waterfront, where a personal dream is destroyed by impersonal decisions in which one's brother—"You should of looked out for me a little bit"—is fully complicit. Charley finally understands: he releases Terry before being literally knocked over sideways by emotion in the back of the cab; his guard dropped long enough for the driver, naturally "one of their own," to deliver Charley as if by instinct to River Street in his final taxi ride.

Terry Malloy could have had class. Pete Corridan would have called it dignity, but it was the same thing. This is how the Irish waterfront and its code of silence would end—not in the "confessional fever" that Budd Schulberg described in his original 1951 screenplay, but in acts like Terry's that implicate the listener regardless of their response. In the 1951 version the power of spoken truth once unleashed rapidly spread "from one to another." The screenwriter now understood that things did not work that way on the waterfront of history. For if the film as a whole recapitulates Corridan's apostolic vision, its most famous scene reprises the early awkward days of Schulberg's collaboration with the waterfront priest and his rebel disciples. Corridan himself was the first to demonstrate suspicion of the outsider. "There's no percentage for us" in being party to another sappy Hollywood movie-with-priest, he warned Schulberg in the kind of language that is employed by Pete Barry throughout the film. Fight talk was indeed their only common currency. Recall that Arthur Brown told Budd to impersonate a Trenton boxing writer on their initial pub crawl.

They had no choice but to trust one another: it was not as though Corridan was winning the Irish waterfront as of autumn 1950. So these signal few waterfront Irish overturned in every way possible the tribal boundaries, embracing an ex-communist, a Jew, a writer with a fine gift for turning their own coarse words into literature. Corridan then urged Schulberg to persist with the film project through three trying years. That work of art in time proved to be the lone Irish waterfront site where a life-denying intimacy with violence (and perhaps Pete Corridan's own loneliness too) was supplanted by love and the power of personal witness.

If *On the Waterfront* is a great "Catholic" movie, it is not owing to some inherent "sacramental imagination" working in and through the artists. The creative partnerships between the waterfront priest and Budd Schulberg, between Corridan and Malden, between the cast and crew and the people of

Hoboken—all these were emblems of the innovative boundary-crossing collaborations many urban American Catholics found themselves engaged in at mid-century. Absent such collaborative generosity there is no "Catholic imagination" illuminating this film from any source.

On the Waterfront is in the end the great film and the great artwork of what I have dubbed "the spiritual front," a model of collaboration—anathema on the Irish waterfront—bestowing its light on intently discerning off-waterfront audiences everywhere. Viewers need not embrace my analysis of spiritual front cultural politics to discern Budd Schulberg's great generosity in bringing Corridan's vision to life in his script, which in places betrays the touching awkwardness of an acolyte determined to get the whole story in the picture and get it right. Critics who suggested that Father Pete Barry seemed to be performing in his own separate movie inadvertently hit on a partial truth: that was the nonexistent documentary playing in Budd's imagination ever since he first read the text of "A Catholic Looks at the Waterfront" in 1950. The fictional film was sculpted after that original model of testimony on the waterfront of history.

That same fidelity to the Jesuit's crusading spirit helps account for a seemingly gratuitous and uncontextualized brief appearance in the film of a "Mr. Upstairs": he is shown from the rear instructing his butler never to accept another call from Johnny Friendly after the union boss is exposed by Terry Malloy during televised hearings of the "crime commission." Many viewers and critics conflate "Mr. Upstairs" with the stevedoring executive who cries out, "Let's go to work!" in the film's closing scene. (That uncredited performance was given by Frank Marnell, a Hoboken school principal; the identity of "Mr. Upstairs"—body and voice—remains hidden.) Script continuity proved less vital to Schulberg in this case than his desire to honor Pete Corridan's relentless pursuit of the historical waterfront's "Mr. Big." The racketeers' overlord *needed* to be represented in this picture, no matter how fleetingly; such was Schulberg's strong conviction and his alone.[27]

In Michael Epstein's *None Without Sin,* a moving 2003 film documentary on the politically charged creative and personal relationship of Elia Kazan and Arthur Miller, a still photograph depicting Kazan and Budd Schulberg on the Hoboken set of *On the Waterfront* is displayed (see figure 10). The writer and director flank a tall, vigorous-looking, intently smiling man dressed in clerical attire, his gaze fixed directly on the camera. The individual is never identified, nor is he mentioned even once in the highly detailed documentary's lengthy treatment of the controversies surrounding the film. This omission is a traditional feature of works devoted to the waterfront movie Pete Corridan inspired. Sometimes "the surface tells the deep secret," the social critic Paul Goodman wrote in 1948. There are two deep secrets on the surface of this passionately conceived and lustrously executed movie; they are Hoboken, New Jersey, and John M. Corridan, S.J., suppliers respectively of its vista and its vision.[28]

18 *"The Corruption Goes Deep"*

Elia Kazan and his crew returned to Hoboken in late December 1953 after shooting the "Christ in the Shapeup" scene on the Brooklyn waterfront. While away on temporary location the director was asked by a *New York Times* reporter to "take inventory": "'It's good,' he mused. 'Good, I think.'...Kazan paused. 'I liked Hoboken. I'm glad we'll be going back when we finish here. All that wonderful brick background. And the feeling and sight of New York's skyline over here in the distance.' His glance included Schulberg and Brando. 'And we have this script, don't we?'" In this rare unguarded moment, feeling very good indeed about his work, Kazan came nearer than at any other time to capturing in words the film's most special attributes. Pete Corridan was likewise buoyed by the moments of grace he had witnessed on location, but his euphoria was quickly tempered by the harsh realities of waterfront politics.[1]

On December 16, 1953, the National Labor Relations Board—"acting with unusual speed in this complicated case"—mandated a longshoremen's representation election to take place within the week. The balloting coincided with the expiration of a Taft-Hartley injunction outlawing a strike while negotiations on a new contract with shippers remained at an impasse. The NLRB reasoned that no progress on a contract could be made until the men certified a bargaining unit, a judgment whose suddenness outraged New York governor Thomas E. Dewey. The AFL's George Meany condemned the NLRB's decision even to allow the ostracized ILA to appear on the ballot as a "moral disgrace." He told dockworkers: "We won't take you in the A.F.L. with the corrupt leaders that are now at the head of the old I.L.A. We don't want the gangsters; we don't want the underworld characters who are exploiting you day in and day out." Shippers cheered the hurry-up election; like rank-and-file dockworkers they always preferred the devil they knew and shunned risky changes in ways of doing business.[2]

Although the fledgling AFL-backed union had much more cash on hand heading into the election, the ILA enjoyed a clear edge in organization at the local level, especially with the election called on such short notice. The orphaned union's prospects were further bolstered when the mercurial leader of the United Mine Workers, John L. Lewis—a bitter foe of the AFL—provided a last-minute infusion of $50,000. The AFL union suffered from grossly unwarranted overconfidence: its self-designation as the "ILA-AFL" (not until July 1954 was the new union belatedly renamed the International Brotherhood of Longshoremen) blithely disregarded the waterfront's hostility to outsiders apart from those bearing cash gifts. In October 1953 Pete Corridan predicted that the ILA-AFL would win by a margin as large as three-to-one; he made no public appearances on the union's behalf during the late autumn campaign. "The priest had held himself aloof from electioneering," noted Allen Raymond. Though he was "in touch continually" with Johnny Dwyer and other insurgents, in the Jesuit's opinion "the job of tossing off the mobsters' rule was now up to the dock workers," a tactical judgment rendered in light of the beating Corridan had taken from the rank and file after his eight-point reform plan was released at the beginning of the year.[3]

Voting was conducted across the port over two days, December 22 and 23. Balloting was peaceful on the first day, with the *New York Times* reporting, "A silent—almost somber mass of men went from the piers to the polls." The longshoremen "gave no clue as to how they had voted." The AFL had decided not to counter the ILA's supply of chartered buses to take men to polling places lest they be drawn into confrontations with their adversaries. In the West Side bars "there was drinking but almost no drunkenness." Members of pro-ILA Local 791 "got out a six-piece drum and cymbal corps, led by a baton-wielding longshoreman who gave up trying to twirl the thing after dropping it several times." Gene Sampson of Local 791 had finally bolted the old ILA, but the business agent's effort to bring his brother members of the Mother Local into the AFL union failed miserably; "at a turbulent meeting in St. Bernard's Hall only twenty-one men lined up with him: the others at the session, variously estimated at four hundred to nine hundred, voted to stay with the ILA." (The local had never been accused of precision in handling numbers.) The message from 791 and the ILA as a whole was simple yet potent: "You know what to do in there. You know what you got now. You don't know what you might get."[4]

The tone of the election turned much darker the following day: "Four hundred policemen and detectives were massed around the Brooklyn polling center after street skirmishes in which three [AFL] partisans were stabbed and a fourth was beaten around the head." Harold Bowers, boss of "Pistol Local" 824, reportedly incurred a broken nose "in the hand-to-hand fighting." When the mayhem finally subsided and the votes were counted, "the margin was so narrow," reported the *Times,* "that the outcome will not be known until the board passes on 4,405 challenged ballots next week." In fact the outcome was not known for much longer than that: although the old ILA received 9,060 votes to 7,568 for the ILA-AFL, widespread reports of fraud and voter intimidation threatened to invalidate the election altogether.[5]

The apparent result was difficult to interpret. While the *Times* had embraced the view of waterfront insiders that "the [old] I.L.A. would win overwhelmingly," there were ample reasons for dockworkers to vote not so much *for* the new AFL union as *against* the ILA. In addition to the ILA's sorry record of collusion with shippers and gangsters, waterfront realists understood that the newly empowered Waterfront Commission, the nationwide labor movement, and the governors of New York and New Jersey were loath to recognize the legitimacy of the old union regardless of the election's outcome.[6]

Pete Corridan's small cadre of disciples and their fellow insurgents enjoyed little impact: the ILA-AFL was strongest in Brooklyn, where his movement was weakest. Corridan was also learning the hard way that waterfront union building implicated him in a brand of labor politics as intricate and rough as anything he had faced in the church. Paul Hall of the Seafarers International Union, a key labor movement advocate of the ILA-AFL, was known to have backed Joe Ryan's futile attempt to crush the autumn 1951 ILA wildcat strike. Dave Beck of the Teamsters, the most powerful—and reputedly most unscrupulous—trustee of the new union, totally disregarded Corridan's pleas to "keep his hands off the pier loaders" in advance of the Waterfront Commission's ban on that infamous local tradition. Beck saw his opportunity and he took it, chartering his own loaders' local, Waterfront Commission be damned. Beck surely could not be expected to emerge from this intra-industry brawl empty-handed.[7]

Corridan also found himself poised uneasily between partisan advocacy of the AFL-ILA and the unassailably honest anti-AFL convictions of his waterfront supporters and critics alike. Just prior to the December 1953 election Michael P. O'Connell, a Jersey City longshoreman with a long history of opposition to Joe Ryan, wrote him: "I know that you have always been a friend of labor, and in particular the men on the waterfront....Let me personally compliment you for your valient [*sic*] stand in behalf of all longshoremen in the port." O'Connell opined: "Meany and Beck...are only looking to take up where 'Ryan and his boys' left off....[T]hey are in effect, trying to win over the rank and file of Ryan's old union...so that they can get their pockets full of that same blood money." This surely represented the consensus view of longshoremen in the port regardless of their attitude toward Ryan and the old ILA.[8]

The rank and file shared little if any of Pete Corridan's passion for a portwide waterfront moral economy: their allegiances like their grievances remained strictly local. Even Hoboken's Tony Mike DeVincenzo withheld his decision "to devote full time to organizing work for the A.F.L.'s dock union" until after he lost a $500,000 lawsuit against three Hoboken police officials—including his cousin, former police commissioner Michael Borelli—for, of all things, "conspiring to deprive him of his personal liberty" by providing him with a round-the-clock police guard on the day prior to his December 1952 NYSCC testimony. DeVincenzo was not a typical longshoreman, but the waterfront featured thousands of such individual stories, nearly all rooted in a single pier or neighborhood. Not even a devoted expert like Corridan could begin to assess the full range of forces compelling the men to vote for one or the other of the union contenders.[9]

With Governor Dewey and George Meany now involved, Corridan anxiously eyed a much bigger picture. Each of these men wished to reconfigure the port's moral and political economy. Despite differences in focus, they shared a conviction that there was simply no place on the waterfront for the old ILA, duly chosen by the men or not. On Christmas Eve 1953 Meany declared, "We do not accept the tally as indicating the true and free choice of the longshoremen, many of whom were forced to vote under threats and actual physical assault." Once Dewey sensed that the NLRB was inclined to recertify the ILA in order to spur contract negotiations between NYSA and the union, he made "a move without parallel in the history of the NLRB," appointing a special representative "to show that coercion and intimidation surrounded the election."[10]

Dewey's "reproachful" attitude toward the NLRB, Meany's demand for an investigation of alleged voter fraud, and the *New York Times*'s denunciation of the "unregenerate" ILA and the "hasty and ill-advised" election smacked of cynicism if not desperation. Leaders of the AFL-ILA were encouraged to continue organizing the piers as though they were destined to emerge as the longshoremen's duly chosen bargaining unit. The role of the *Times* in this campaign to invalidate the ILA was most striking: it seemed as if the newspaper of record was determined to make up for decades of waterfront neglect. Between December 1952—with the launch of public hearings by the NYSCC—and spring 1954 the *Times*'s coverage of waterfront crime, punishment, and politics was extraordinary for its depth and breadth, just as the treatment of labor issues was receding nationally in the age of McCarthyism, the Korean War, and the rise of suburbia. The reporting and analyses of George Horne were brilliant throughout. If the paper's coverage was slanted toward the Corridan-Dewey-AFL cause, its dogged, detailed persistence belied subsequent claims that the New York waterfront died of civic neglect.[11]

Save Your Souls

When "the AFL union invaded what is regarded as an ILA strong point last night," the *Times* reported on February 2, 1954, Pete Corridan stood alongside Johnny Dwyer and Paul Hall at the ILA-AFL's "first Chelsea–West Side rally," held at the Cornish Arms Hotel, Eighth Avenue and Twenty-third Street. The Jesuit's entry into the highly partisan fray was marked by a bold tactical shift: for the first time in his apostolate the waterfront priest sternly instructed men on what they must do to be redeemed. "The two places where you will save or lose your souls are within the family and the job," he exhorted. "The New Deal that I have sought for you comes closer to the Christian ideal. It will give you a better opportunity to live reasonably happy and secure both within your family and your job at the docks. It will give you a better chance to save your souls." The threat of eternal damnation had never been in play in the waterfront crusade until this moment. In his fiery autumn 1948 debut in Jersey City he had proclaimed, "The time is growing short when God will show no mercy" to those most responsible for corruption and violence, but now the rank and file were personally implicated in the realm of final judgment. If the men could not see through their enslavement in terms of labor economics, Corridan signaled his willingness to invoke a much more ancient and potent tradition, a choice he must have weighed against the likelihood of an intensified anticlerical backlash from the rank and file.[12]

More than ever before he stood apart from his confreres. Although his former boss at Crown Heights Labor School, William J. Smith, S.J.—now in command at St. Peter's College Labor School—publicly urged figures at Jersey City Local 1247 to abandon the ILA for the new union, Smith also readily acknowledged the ILA-AFL's many shortcomings. "It leaves much to be desired as the ideal labor organization," he conceded in an open letter to 1247's vice president, Marty Van Heest. Smith vacillated in ways certain to discomfit wavering Jersey longshoremen who did indeed, as he acknowledged, hold a "sentimental attachment" to the old ILA. Since that attachment was grounded in part in the union's history of resisting outside interference, few could have been persuaded by Father Smith's reassurance that affiliation with the ILA-AFL brought with it the "protection of the bi-State Law and Commission which has been established to demolish the racket-ridden old ILA and to give the hard-working, honest men on the piers the opportunity of a new beginning."[13]

Father Smith's muted support was indicative of the ILA-AFL's struggle to achieve moral traction. The stirring narratives previously authored by Malcolm Johnson, Pete Corridan, and Budd Schulberg lost resonance at a moment when "rebels" like Johnny Dwyer (and Corridan himself) were so closely linked to Dave Beck, Paul Hall, and other compromised off-waterfront operatives. When Dwyer's cousin Billy McMahon—a West Side ex-prizefighter and Xavier-trained insurgent—became the focal point of a hiring conflict pitting pro-AFL Teamsters against the old ILA, the resulting "well-organized unauthorized strikes" for which the ILA was now justly infamous tied up commerce for nearly a month and heightened public animosity toward all the combatants. While New York City mayor Robert Wagner futilely pursued negotiations, violence flared periodically on contested piers throughout the port. The rebels' links to so many tainted outside forces undermined efforts to regenerate tales of heroes and villains on the Irish waterfront: power, money, and politics were now the only live story components resonant on the docks. The waterfront moral authority accrued by Corridan and his allies for nearly five years was now largely spent.[14]

At this low moment Budd Schulberg weighed in with encouraging news from the creative front, excitedly informing Corridan on March 26:

> So far I have seen only the roughest sort of cut of our picture, without sound effects, music, or the fade-outs and dissolves that give pictures a flow. But even in this primitive state, I think it is safe to say that we have something powerfully real. The cutter, composer, and special effects cameraman, practically the only people who have seen it, are terribly moved by it. I am anxious for you to see it and have asked Spiegel to have it run for you at the earliest possible date.

Schulberg was confident that the film's highly conspicuous production would help sway the upcoming vote against the old ILA. After viewing a rough cut Corridan predicted, "This means the end of the shapeup," which to him was synonymous with the Irish waterfront's ancient regime. The picture's progress must have seemed a good omen when on April 1 the NLRB invalidated the first representation election owing to ILA misconduct and ordered a new one, later set for May 26, 1954. The federal board also ruled that no parties engaged in strike activity could appear on the ballot, a move that effectively ended the latest work stoppage. Buoyant optimism reigned again in the reformers' camps: the *New York Times* forecast that "in a clean election, the great majority of longshoremen will vote to oust the present corrupt I.L.A. and install the new A.F.L union as their bargaining agent," while in the New York ILA-AFL newspaper (printed in both English and Italian) Corridan predicted a smashing victory. The Jesuit continued to insist that the shapeup was the main "source of union corruption" and its replacement by a system of permanent gangs and seniority would make the hiring boss "what he should be, the servant of the membership."[15]

In the final days of the last crusade for the soul of the waterfront the artistic and political campaigns proceeded as if in tandem. Leonard Bernstein's original score for *On the Waterfront*—the first and only such work in his long and storied career—was recorded during the final week of April at the Columbia Pictures studio in Hollywood. Sam Spiegel had been "anxious to get another prominent name on the advertising copy," according to Kazan; after viewing the rough cut, Bernstein was "swept by my enthusiasm into accepting the commission to write the score."[16]

Then on May 6 the Port Authority's Austin Tobin issued the most partisan public statement of his career to that point, endorsing the AFL union and calling for "the final overthrow of the I.L.A.'s reign of terror." Tobin opened yet another front in the war by castigating the "shabby, servile record" of the New York Shipping Association, which he accused of playing the "I.L.A. game" in the recent strike by resisting compliance with the Waterfront Commission. The shippers—a key Port Authority constituency free to take their business to ports elsewhere—were stunned by the ferocity of Tobin's attack. An "indignation meeting" was hastily called to respond, but despite the threat by one NYSA member to "knock his hat off with the blast," Tobin succeeded in drawing the battle lines more sharply than ever before.[17]

The ILA-AFL received another gift in the form of a West Coast visit to Harry Bridges by associates of Brooklyn waterfront overlord Anthony "Tough Tony" Anastasio, who managed to wring an endorsement of the old ILA from Joe Ryan's longtime adversary. The ILA was broke again: it did not have cash on hand to pay a $50,000 contempt citation and needed help wherever it could be found. Anastasio's people may have reached out to Bridges with a deal, playing into Bridges's designs on the East Coast waterfront labor force evident since nearly the inception of his ILWU. (Although his union was prominent among the Left-led outfits purged from the CIO in 1949–50, Bridges remained a formidable figure). With Joe Ryan finally out of the picture, perhaps Bridges felt it was time to move instead against George Meany and the AFL; the ILA, he claimed "is the union which the majority of longshoremen want. It led their fight against the jurisdictional raiders, the union busters, the scab herders and the politicians."[18]

Bridges's endorsement of the mob-ridden New York–based union—if not quite the labor movement equivalent of the Nazi-Soviet pact—presented an irresistible opportunity for the AFL to link a prominent suspected communist with alleged organized crime figures. Meany made the most of this rare opportunity to Red-bait the inveterately anticommunist ILA on radio broadcasts and in the newspapers. Speaking from Chicago via WABC radio on May 17, the "honest plumber" gravely warned, "The Communists, who would like nothing better than to worm their way into control of the most vital port in America, are now using their high-powered propaganda methods in behalf of the old I.L.A." Long-suffering ILA executive vice president Packy Connolly could only sputter in reply, "We cannot and will not stand idly by and be smeared with the red label by the A.F.L. or anyone else." Joe Ryan's ancient fear of a Brooklyn Italian–Communist coalition had come back to haunt his frustrated onetime heir apparent. On May 20 a small contingent of AFL dockworkers appeared at a demonstration outside Pier 45 in the West Village "dressed in imitation Russian Cossack uniforms." They carried signs declaring: "A Vote for the I.L.A. Is a Vote for Commies." The *Times* ran a photograph of these faux Cossacks under attack by automobile-borne ILA members who shot insecticide from spray guns at their adversaries.[19]

If Pete Corridan relished the spectacle of a desperate ILA, he eschewed demagoguery in the frantic period leading up to the May 26 election. He was a clear, effective, and often powerful speaker who rarely resorted to the kind of unsavory rhetoric that was the legacy of the notorious "radio priest" Charles E. Coughlin. He was more comfortable marshaling facts and figures than engaging in fiery polemics (though his winter 1953 letters "To All Harbor Workers" had revealed a growing struggle with erratic judgment). In talks "before overflow turnouts at AFL-ILA meetings throughout the harbor" (as reported in the union's newspaper) and in a May 21 letter he sent to "all longshoremen, checkers and allied craft workers" in the port, the Jesuit didactically rehashed the ILA's culpability for the "five major strikes" that had "completely paralyzed the harbor" and forty more "serious partial work stoppages" since 1945. At the same time he adopted a more prophetic tone in his last testament to the men with whom he had enjoyed a most volatile relationship for the past half-decade. "Every longshore worker in the harbor," the ILA-AFL newspaper quoted from one of his talks,

> has prayed for the day to come when he could throw off the yoke of the old ILA mob and build a genuine trade union on the waterfront. Now…that day is near, and longshoremen soon will have the opportunity to vote for the union they wish to represent them. If they wish to better their own conditions, and the conditions of their families, they have no choice but to vote for the AFL-ILA.[20]

"The Port of New York will rise or fall on the vote you cast," Corridan insisted in his written appeal. He also took a parting shot at Packy Connolly, his old debate opponent, citing Connolly's remark of the previous year that the "unholy three" of Corridan, Tony Anastasio, and the Communist Party were responsible for the ILA's woes. "Well, today Tony A. is bigger than ever in the ILA," noted the Jesuit. "Right now the communist party is supporting the ILA to the extent that Harry Bridges has supported the ILA without any reservations. I, Father Corridan, appeal to you, the dockworkers of the Port of New York, to strike a decisive blow for freedom from the Anastasias, Bridges and the mob by casting your ballots for the AFL."[21]

The response of the rank and file to Corridan's ardent appeal was swift and disheartening. While a very small number of dockworkers expressed unreserved solidarity with him (a Brooklyn checker wrote on May 20: "Father, we believe you 100%. The waterfront commission is the answer to this whole rotten mess"), the larger number not only reiterated the skepticism widely expressed prior to the first election but also provided concrete evidence that outside opportunists had succeeded in stealing their jobs. "Why should I vote AFL when it is using the same high handed tactics and employs the same type of low characters as the ILA," plaintively asked Frank Fiano of North Arlington, New Jersey, who had lost his job at Port Newark when members of Paul Hall's AFL Seafarers Union moved in. Fiano hastened to express gratitude for the work of Corridan and his fellow labor priests and disavowed any anticlerical motivation ("I am frequently in arguments with some of my ILA friends who have the stupid idea a priest should not be in the labor movement").[22]

Another sizable cohort of Catholic longshoremen reprised a much harsher view of the waterfront priest. "What I can't understand is how you a man of the church can lie so openly to the public," wrote one anonymous critic in scorning Corridan's support of Democrat George Meany, "who you know down in your heart sold the men out to [Republican] governor Dewey." The author (who identified himself simply as "a longshoreman" and added, "I would sign this but I wouldn't trust you not to give my name to the waterfront commission so they could take my pass") continued in an eight page handwritten letter:

> The papers call you the waterfront priest, I would like to know who made you the waterfront priest[.] I have been working on the waterfront for more than ten years and I mean many years more than ten years. But I never heard of you being made the priest of the waterfront. In fact I have never seen you in my life. All I know about you is what I read about you sticking your nose in someone else's affairs. I was always taught to believe that a priest or a sister was some one sacred someone that done no wrong. But seeing how you sell your services to a man that sells his own party out right in under their noses...why don't you mind your own business and but [*sic*] out of labor troubles or are you looking to feather your own nest some way?[23]

Yet another vitriolic critic tarred Corridan by association with the Alabama-born, Protestant-bred, but reportedly unchurched Paul Hall: "When a priest of the Catholic Church comes out in public and supports a union that harbors an avowed and confirmed Atheist, he should give up the cloth and cringe away from the very church of god that he represents." Other waterfront citizens pleaded with Cardinal Spellman to silence the controversial Jesuit. Monsignor John M. Fleming forwarded to Corridan letters of protest sent to the chancery office by a dockworker's wife and a "Catholic long-shoremen with five children," who reported there were over "200 Catholic boys [on his pier] and they all resent this kind of advertisement for the AF of L as we call it."[24]

The passionate intensity of Corridan's critics reflected the port's genuine *sensus fidelium*, not an orchestrated response by his longtime adversaries. There is no question that thousands of dockworkers throughout the port were disdainful of the old ILA and longed for a legitimate, democratic union; the awkward question is whether Corridan's partisan advocacy generated a backlash that worked in the ILA's favor by inciting longshoremen to defend their piers militantly against any and all threats from the outside.

The Jesuit's divisiveness went unacknowledged by the New York reformers and journalists who continued to lionize Corridan as a waterfront sage. His predictions of a crushing victory for the AFL union (echoed by Johnny Dwyer) heartened editorialists puzzled by the seeming inability of the men to discern their self-interest clearly.

On May 25, as the insolvent ILA went into receivership, the *New York Times* editorialized: "In these circumstances it should not be necessary to argue, with the longshoremen, the case for serving their own enlightened self-interest by voting A.F.L. Everything that is bad for the port is bad for them and their families." The *Times* might better have asked why indeed it was felt necessary to argue a case that had heretofore failed to compel the rank and file. The editors of the Jesuits' *America* magazine extended the same logic to its moral conclusion: "If New York dockworkers do not choose the AFL over the discredited [ILA] in the May 26 representation election, the public can justifiably conclude that the majority of them prefer intimidation, extortion and racketeering to honest unionism and decent conditions of work.... [I]f the men vote wrong this time, they have no excuse."[25]

One Door Closes...

The May 26 election "was conducted in an atmosphere of churchlike calm in contrast to the turbulence and bloodshed" that marred the previous December's balloting. Dockworkers cast their ballots at six polling places from Brooklyn to Leonardo, New Jersey, with no "reminder of the knifings, jeers and strong-arm tactics that marked the pre-Christmas vote." NLRB regional director Charles Douds extolled the "most orderly" voting he had ever witnessed. Hundreds of pro-AFL dockworkers gathered in Brooklyn to await the results at the union hall of their patron, Paul Hall of the Seafarers International; beer was on the house. According to Budd Schulberg, the "rebel" dockworkers "lifted brews together in premature celebration." While the vote seemed at first to be going their way, the final tally yielded an ILA victory by a mere 319 votes. This time the result was official; even AFL partisans later acknowledged that the election was the cleanest in waterfront memory. ILA president "Tugboat Bill" Bradley threatened an immediate strike if government officials started "kicking us around like they did before" by refusing to recertify his union.[26]

The AFL union finally threw in the towel one week after the election; its offices closed as numerous "insurgents" returned to the ILA fold. As an AFL organizer in New Jersey explained their thinking: "They say the I.L.A. has won two elections and they want no more of this bickering. The rank-and-file longshoreman is the real sufferer from all these contests. All he wants is one strong union and a chance to work." Tugboat Bill Bradley confidently proclaimed, "Regardless of what NLRB or Governor Dewey intend to do, the rank and file of longshoremen are going to stick to the I.L.A.," as he welcomed back all but a handful of high-profile former ILA officials, including most notably Gene Sampson and Johnny Dwyer.[27]

The blackballing was not enough to prevent Dwyer from dramatically bolting the failed union in September. "I want no part of the AFL or their union," he told his cheering followers at St. Veronica's Hall on Christopher Street in the West Village (site of insurgencies past that were integral to "rebel" mythology). "Forget about the AFL and go on back to the ILA." Then just two weeks later—despite a report in *Time* magazine that he had been fired before he could quit—the increasingly inscrutable Dwyer reversed course and declared his intention to remain with the AFL even as he "urged" his forces "to remain friendly to the I.L.A." Dwyer was later hired as a business agent by an affiliate of Hall's Seafarers Union. The ILA would win yet another representation election in 1956, this time by a significantly wider margin. The outlaw union was finally readmitted into the AFL in 1959. "We did some good when we kicked them out and we are now ready to take them back," was the best explanation George Meany could muster.[28]

Disenchanted ex-rebels never forgave Meany for appointing an outsider, "Ace" Keeney, to run the AFL campaign. When labor journalist Mary Heaton Vorse blasted the defeat as "totally inexcusable" and blamed Meany for failing to promote mass rallies and not making better use of television, he responded, "We wanted the opposition to look local," a revealing admission of a tactic that obviously fooled no one on the waterfront. The local rebel leadership belatedly attracted some harsh criticism from the least likely of sources. In a draft version of "The Waterfront Revisited," a lengthy 1963 article for the *Saturday Evening Post,* Budd Schulberg quoted a pseudonymous AFL dockworker's appraisal of Johnny Dwyer:

> You know how solid we all were for Johnny. He had the guts to blow the whistle on Pier 45....But Johnny wasn't big enough to run the whole harbor-wide campaign. He just didn't size up to it. And when the war was over he got himself a nice 15–20 thousand a year job with Paul Hall and left the rest of us on the beach. He did lovely while the rest of us who fought for 'im were breaking our backs for ten years.[29]

Schulberg refrained from assigning culpability to the rank and file; his magnanimous gesture was not shared by the Catholic radical and labor reporter John C. Cort. "I know that all the better labor writers have maintained that the men themselves are clean and decent, simply the victims of a pack of jackals who feed upon their unprotected vitals," he wrote in *Commonweal* three weeks after the May election. "I can't believe it any more.... [T]oo many of the men like to do a little pilfering themselves," he observed, concluding, "If it proves anything, it proves that the corruption goes deep, into the men themselves."[30]

19 *The Poetry of Success*

The New York Jesuits were badly stung by the repudiation of their controversial waterfront priest. The timing could not have been worse: while taking a beating locally from prominent waterfront Catholics for failing to reel in Corridan, the society was under fire nationally for *America* magazine's sharp editorial turn against the rapidly self-destructing anticommunist crusade of Senator Joseph McCarthy. Just three days after the defeat of the ILA-AFL, John McMahon, S.J.—the New York Jesuit leader long heroically supportive of the waterfront priest—informed the editor of the magazine that the topic of McCarthyism was now off-limits, "not out of sympathy with McCarthy supporters," explained historian Mark S. Massa, "but out of concern that the magazine's position was dividing Jesuits and that it appeared to be breaking a long-standing command not to engage in 'disputes among Catholics.'" With the end of McMahon's tenure as provincial just weeks away, the directive made it more likely that his successor would rein in if not dismantle the boldest Jesuit social apostolate of the postwar era.[1]

Although it was not immediately apparent, the failed 1954 electoral campaign had finished Pete Corridan on the waterfront of history, just as the waterfront of memory was about to burst into the public consciousness. While the Jesuit struggled in vain for the souls of dockworkers, Elia Kazan was working feverishly in his cutting room with film editor Gene Milford, who looked to resuscitate his career seventeen years after winning an Oscar for *Lost Horizon*. Neither Milford nor Kazan nor Sam Spiegel "suspected we had a film that was going to be a classic," wrote the director in his memoir. "Actually Sam was concerned that the film would be a box office failure and further lower his standing in the industry." Spiegel was not alone: Kazan recalled that Marlon Brando walked out of a screening room after viewing the rough cut without "a word, not even a goodbye," and some weeks later at another screening, according to Budd Schulberg,

Harry Cohn of Columbia Pictures "walked out of the projection room without saying good night" (Kazan caught Cohn dozing through much of the screening). After a subsequent screening for the cast, "Marlon Brando summed it up for Karl Malden: 'In and out. In and out,'" the actor's way of indicating "he felt he was in and out of character." Brando then disappeared into the night. "I thought I was a huge failure" in the role, he wrote in his memoir. "I was simply embarrassed for myself."[2]

Redemption

The tone changed decisively and for all time on the morning of July 28, 1954, when Corridan and Arthur Brown joined Schulberg, Kazan, and "half a dozen fellow 'insoigents'" outside the Astor Theater at the corner of Broadway and West Forty-fifth Street in Manhattan. There they found over three hundred moviegoers waiting in line at 9 A.M. to buy tickets for the opening matinee of *On the Waterfront*. "We were amazed to find a line around the block," Schulberg recalled:

> But we reasoned that with twenty-five thousand working longshoremen and their families, all the related workers, and the mob and their families, we'd be doing business for at least a couple of days. None of us dreamed what lay ahead. But the next morning's reviews were unqualified raves, even hailing it as a new kind of American film. It was beginning to dawn on us that we had touched a nerve.[3]

The overnight reviews *were* highly favorable ("moviemaking of a rare and high order," wrote A. H. Weiler in a tone-setting notice for the *New York Times*), but as Kazan rightly noted, "the line was the news, not the reviews. The fellows who wrote film criticism would have had to write poetry to measure our success." For Kazan the poetry was in Budd Schulberg's story: it "struck a deep human craving... [for] redemption for a sinner, rescue from damnation." The director surely counted himself and his creative partners as newly redeemed through their creative collaboration, a theme overlooked by reviewers save Philip T. Hartung in *Commonweal*, who lauded the film as "an excellent example of cooperation in picture making." As a "drama of man's victory and rise from low estate," Hartung concluded, "*On the Waterfront* is a film to stand with the best." Hartung was also among the very few reviewers to locate Pete Corridan's role accurately in the film's back story.[4]

The politics of the film and filmmakers went untreated in the initial reviews, a very brief grace period that ended in September when *New York Post* labor editor and columnist Murray Kempton—a persistently caustic critic of Joe Ryan and admirer and recipient of frequent tips from Pete

Corridan—suggested that Kazan and Schulberg "retain the innocence which brought them into the [Communist] party." The film's ending was "murky and confusing," claimed Kempton, because "the party of proletarian struggle has been written out of it and there is nothing to take its place." The British critic and filmmaker Lindsay Anderson similarly highlighted the film's final sequence in an influential condemnation of its "fascist" politics published in the leading cinema journal *Sight and Sound*. In Anderson's view the longshoremen follow the bloodied Terry Malloy back into the pier shed because they have been politically conditioned to embrace violent leaders blindly, a premise Anderson accused the filmmakers of endorsing. "Nothing expresses a sense of liberation," complained Anderson, a reading congruent with the militantly antiexistentialist perspective of Cold War Marxist orthodoxy.[5]

The specter of HUAC haunting *On the Waterfront* was first treated in late 1954 in an obscure leftist journal, the *Hollywood Review*, where blacklisted communist screenwriter (and "unfriendly" former HUAC witness) John Howard Lawson trashed the movie as "antidemocratic, antilabor, antihuman propaganda," no surprise for a film "concocted by men who wear the livery of the informer." Just over a year later the distinguished theater critic and scholar Eric Bentley bluntly asserted, "In Mr. Kazan's movie, the act of informing is virtuous"; even more "appalling," in Bentley's view, was that the film was "created in the first place to point up this virtue." Bentley was at least evenhanded in his reductionism; he was equally appalled by Kazan's erstwhile creative partner Arthur Miller's newly debuted one-act play *A View from the Bridge*, which was written, Bentley suggested, solely to expose the *evil* of informing. (Bentley did not treat the pair's tumultuous personal and political history.)[6]

Given its prestigious source, Bentley's review most clearly signaled that a season of interpretive hostility had commenced. It would endure among intellectuals and film academics for over five decades. "Along with *Citizen Kane*, it is almost impossible to instruct a course covering the history of American film without showing *On the Waterfront*," wrote film historian Tom Stempel in 2001; he listed "the House UnAmerican Activities Committee" first among historical topics prompted by a screening of the film for students. Generations of collegians enrolled in film studies and cultural history courses have been instructed in the backhanded canonization of *On the Waterfront* as the quintessential informer's film.[7]

Although the filmmakers would spend the rest of their lives warily (then wearily) negotiating this minefield, the summer and autumn of 1954 were their high season of vindication, when politics was briefly overshadowed by jubilant reports of box office triumphs, ecstatic word-of-mouth reviews, and the promise of a bonanza in the upcoming awards season. "When it comes down," Kazan later wrote of such rare artistic and popular success, "it comes down like an avalanche." If the film's box office receipts ($4.5 million in the initial domestic release) appear paltry by contemporary blockbuster standards, *On the Waterfront* was, as Richard Schickel observed, "hugely profitable in relation to its cost."[8]

More dramatic was the global reach of the filmmakers' triumph. As the buoyant, rejuvenated Sam Spiegel embarked for the Venice film festival in early August, he informed *Time,* "The festival chairman told me that *Waterfront* is the first Italian film made in America." While Spiegel was bitterly disappointed to lose the coveted "Golden Lion" (first prize) to Renato Castellani's *Romeo and Juliet,* the passage of time would reveal that the "Silver Lion" denoted that year's true benchmarks of greatness: *On the Waterfront* shared the prize with Federico Fellini's *La Strada* and Akira Kurosawa's *Seven Samurai.*[9]

Back in New York, Kazan and Schulberg affected in their comradely fashion the swagger of dockside rebels and grass-roots artists, eschewing the lure of Hollywood to remain near the waterfront for the Academy Awards ceremonies, simultaneously telecast from Hollywood and from the Century Theater in Manhattan. This time waterfront insurgents finally won an election: in a virtual clean sweep, *On the Waterfront* was named Best Picture of 1954; Budd Schulberg won for Best Original Screenplay; Elia Kazan for Best Director. Marlon Brando accepted the Oscar for Best Actor. The winning ticket was filled out by Eva Marie Saint (Supporting Actress) Boris Kaufman (Cinematography), Richard Day (Art Direction), and Gene Milford, whose triumphant comeback was confirmed with the award for Best Editing. Only the presence of three of the film's performers in the category of Best Supporting Actor (where Karl Malden, Lee J. Cobb, and Rod Steiger effectively canceled one another out) prevented the film from taking home every major award for which it was nominated.[10]

The jubilant members of *this* waterfront union (minus Brando, who remained in Hollywood), including their Jesuit collaborator, rebel "insoigents," and the "Irish Mafia" compatriots of Kazan's unsung hero, assistant director Charlie Maguire, celebrated long and ardently into the night at the House of Chan at Seventh Avenue and West Fifty-second Street. The revelry concluded at 5 A.M. in ex-prizefighter Lee Oma's Perfect Alibi tavern. In one of the film's numerous uncredited roles, Oma played the truncheon-wielding bartender in the scene in which Father Pete Barry slugs Terry Malloy before persuading him to testify before the crime commission.[11]

If these triumphant artists harbored any regret, it was that their film had not opened in time to influence the outcome of the May 26 longshoremen's election. "Corridan and the rebels thought it would definitely help their cause," recalled Budd Schulberg, but "we suspected Spiegel wanted to release it after the election, since he wasn't as involved in the cause as we were and instead wanted to separate the film from the active struggle as much as possible." For his part Pete Corridan believed that the process of making the film as an act of witness and solidarity alongside working longshoremen would sufficiently raise the consciousness of the rank and file; he was less preoccupied with the timing of its release than other partisans of the AFL union, including Catholic labor radical John Cort, who lamented that "this picture came too late to reach the New York docks before the Labor Board election. If the men had seen this movie, there is no question in my mind that more than enough would have changed sides to sink the corrupt old [union]."[12]

This viewpoint quickly became the Catholic progressive's analogue to the secular Left's reading of the film and has proved just as enduring. In his influential 1997 historical survey *American Catholic,* Charles Morris wrote, in a stirring discussion of the New York labor priests: "The second election was held just weeks before *On the Waterfront* opened in New York theaters. Longshoremen thronged to see the movie, and it almost certainly would have swung the election against the ILA." This impassioned yet flawed conviction affirms the extraordinary power of movies to shape historical understanding. The last men on earth whose opinions were likely to be swayed by a film about their own lives were dockworkers in the Port of New York and New Jersey.[13]

For nearly a decade thousands of longshoremen had expressed their disdain for Joe Ryan and his cronies in myriad ways; they scarcely needed a movie to educate them about their corrupt union, especially a film created by a coalition of outsiders with "suspect" connections of various kinds. Filmgoers from the unknown interior of America might be moved by the sight of a young blonde nearly trampled in the shapeup. Most dockworkers could only roar with laughter or jeer even as they may have grudgingly conceded the filmmakers' artistry and dedication.

On the Waterfront enshrined Pete Corridan's waterfront vision above all: it unfolded from the perspective of his hard-earned convictions on hiring and the shapeup, criminality and the debilitating code of silence. Powerful and moving as it was in so many ways, it did not fully convey (what film could?) the reality of most longshoremen's lives. The shape had not been the port's dominant hiring method for decades; the code of silence was widely viewed as a code of honor, not a burden; investigative bodies like the crime commission depicted in *On the Waterfront* were as universally scorned along the piers after the film as before. Men looking to provide for their families might have responded more warmly to an insurgency not beholden to compromised interests promoted by the AFL. For these and other good reasons the film was not an effective local advertisement for the new union. There is no good reason to believe that an earlier opening would have caused the men to vote differently.

On the very rare occasions when real longshoremen were asked about their responses to *On the Waterfront,* they tended to express anger at its depiction of their brethren as either patsies or thieves. In the late 1980s retired Chelsea dockworker Eddie Burns complained to oral historian Jeff Kisseloff: "*On the Waterfront* was a lot of bullshit. Bullshit. It was a farce as far as longshorin' was concerned. When do you see a priest and a girl go down in the ship? That Father Corridan, he was in Xavier and that's all. He never was on the dock. Just always givin' out information. He did nothin' for nobody, Corridan." Longtime pier foreman Joe Walls made the same point in a 2003 interview: Corridan had no real followers other than Brownie; the film was wholly unrealistic. Burns revealingly went even further, roundly denying that kickbacks and payoffs for jobs were at all commonplace. Here the deeply emotional component of the controversy emerged. Like many of his colleagues, Burns resented the relentlessly negative view of the West Side waterfront fostered by decades of bad publicity, much of it owing to Pete Corridan's crusade. Even the storied "rebel" leader Johnny Dwyer would live to deny "that stuff about the payoffs on the West Side. I never saw it.... [T]hat's all fantasy as far as I'm concerned." In a gentle rejoinder Father Phil Carey told Kisseloff, "John knows the bosses were paid off[,]...but a lot of them don't want to let outsiders know." Years after the last steamship had berthed at a West Side pier, the struggle for the soul of the Irish waterfront persisted.[14]

The impassioned, varied responses to *On the Waterfront* exposed both the power and the vulnerability not just of the film but of Pete Corridan's apostolate as a whole. Labor reformers, journalists, Irish Americans one generation or a few miles removed from the waterfront, and viewers in the heartland of America adored this movie. Had any of them been granted the vote, the ILA would have been routed in a smashing victory for the AFL union. Those most directly affected took a very different view, but the "outsider" status of *On the Waterfront*'s most devoted admirers does not diminish the legitimacy of their reaction or the power of the film in bearing witness. The same eclectic coalition that had helped draw attention to injustice and brutality on the waterfront now formed the core of a vastly larger audience for the film and its message of hope and redemption. For this growing spiritual front, the violent and brutal ethos of the Irish waterfront (and its equivalent neighborhoods throughout urban America) could no longer stand with or without a reformed longshoremen's union.

A large portion of the film's audience was primed for the new spiritual dispensation whose arrival *On the Waterfront* signaled. For those still in doubt, Corridan played a powerful role from behind the scenes in prompting a Catholic transition from visceral, parochial anticommunism to collaboration in the ecumenical spiritual front. William H. Mooring, a militantly Catholic Hollywood columnist syndicated in numerous diocesan newspapers, was contacted by Corridan after Mooring expressed doubt in print that Kazan and Schulberg were truly free of Marxist influence. Mooring darkly suspected that the filmmakers had highlighted no longer prevalent waterfront evils in a bid to foment anti-American sentiment among filmgoers around the world. "I must now eat some of my words," Mooring confessed after getting an earful from the waterfront priest. He was persuaded that the film depicted conditions "as they exist now." Mooring continued to suspect, however, that Kazan and Schulberg intentionally portrayed Father Pete Barry as a "lonely fighter, apparently espousing a cause in which personal convictions drove him harder than clerical authority." Corridan provided no reassurance on this score: viewers would have to decide for themselves.[15]

The enormous success of *On the Waterfront* and Corridan's effectiveness as the film's ambassador made it a fixture in seminary and Catholic secondary school curricula, a remarkable feat given its creators' backgrounds. As early as autumn 1954 a Jesuit at the novitiate at New Baden, deep in the southern Indiana countryside, sought Corridan's help in acquiring a copy of *On the Waterfront* for use in the training of novices. Phil Carey later informed Budd Schulberg that the film was screened at Chaminade, a prestigious high school on Long Island operated by priests of the Society of Mary, "to give the students some insight into what the love of God and his brothers should be." *On the Waterfront* was very widely discussed among Catholics in the middle and late 1950s in Europe, where the suppression of the worker-priests had left the church's labor apostolate in deep disarray. A Neapolitan theologian described to Corridan public sessions held to consider the "realistic element of the movie" as it corresponded to "the events of your apostolate." In Dublin, "where critics from all over the world gathered to view the film, the Roman Catholic Movie Office gave *On the Waterfront* its Grand Prix."[16]

On the Waterfront of Memory

Longshoremen and their neighborhoods still dominated New York Harbor in 1954 when the film appeared. None could have imagined that in two years' time the *Ideal-X*, "an aging tanker ship moored in Newark" owned by trucking magnate Malcolm MacLean, would launch a revolution in global shipping as the world's first container vessel. Its cargoes were loaded at the point of production in aluminum truck bodies that could be placed atop wheels and driven away from the pier without a longshoreman's traditional ministrations. By the mid-1960s, not only would containerization drastically reduce the number of working longshoremen in the port, but also the greatly increased size and weight of container ships would render the finger piers of the West Side and Hoboken obsolete. The future of the port lay in high-technology container terminals built in the outlying precincts of Port Newark and Elizabeth, supplemented by smaller specialized facilities in Bayonne and Staten Island. All of these locales were well within the historic confines of the Port of New York and New Jersey, but their seeming remoteness and the predominance of Jersey sites would inevitably generate a narrative of lamentation over the death of "the Port."[17]

The waning of the port inspired a new generation of New York–New Jersey Irish and Italian American waterfront intellectuals. *On the Waterfront* was never far from their center of consciousness. The film was re-released for the first time in 1960 as part of a double bill with *The Caine Mutiny*. In that same year a twenty-five-year-old Brooklynite named Pete Hamill went to work for the venerable *New York Post* at its Lower Manhattan headquarters, located directly across West Street from the United Fruit Company pier. "It was one of a whole string of piers that ran all the way up the North River until it began to hit the passenger liner piers in midtown," Hamill recalled. That waterfront era was nearing its end. Hamill—the eldest of seven whose parents were Belfast immigrants—had as a child often been taken to the waterfront by his mother to witness the vast luxury liners make their glorious arrivals and departures. Hamill, who left Regis High School (the alma mater of Fathers Carey and Corridan) at sixteen for work in the Brooklyn Navy Yard prior to the discovery of his journalistic vocation, always ranked *On the Waterfront* at the top of his list of favorite New York movies ("though it was made in New Jersey," as he ruefully acknowledged), lauding it as the first film in which characters sounded like the guys he grew up among. It was "the last time we saw a real working American in a movie." For the poets and intellectuals of the waterfront—and Hamill was both—the discovery of the port's riches coincided with its precipitous decline.[18]

In the 1960s and 1970s some of Hoboken's dormant piers, like many of those directly across the river on the West Side, fell into the North River; but the Mile Square City's suffering was tempered by its claim on the great film as its own. On Hoboken's Irish-Italian waterfront the film's always powerful legacy only grew, especially once the battered city began its astonishing transformation in the late 1970s and 1980s. From local playwright Louis LaRusso's *Marlon Brando Sat Right Here* (1980), to stories of generations of Hoboken schoolchildren lovingly re-creating scenes from the film, to *New York Times* reporter Anthony DePalma's deeply moving 1988 elegy for the city's bygone way of life, Hoboken was made by the waterfront movie and remained haunted by it. "I never worked a day on the piers," DePalma confessed, "but they've shadowed my whole life. I am the son of a longshoreman, the grandson of a one-time longshoreman, the nephew of three uncles who had many waterfront hours etched on their faces. Before the waterfront disappears, or is transformed into something unrecognizable, I want to know it the way my father did."[19]

That was impossible, not because of a failure of imagination on De-Palma's part but because of the film's unchallengeable status as "the definitive account of what happened" (as Carlo Rotella characterized the effect of another "gritty" post-*Waterfront* urban film, *The French Connection*). Anthony DePalma's father, Anthony ("Tony Allatime") Sr., in fact, was known as a man who worked so hard on the piers that he declined an offer to play "Terry Malloy's legs when he staggers, heavy-footed, back to the docks in defiance of the crooked bosses." Yet both Anthony DePalmas were "mesmerized by the familiar story" when the movie played on television.[20]

Hoboken's redemptive revival mined the waterfront of memory so deeply that entire chapters of the city's recent history were virtually occluded: a postwar Puerto Rican migration that coincided with a precipitous industrial decline; violent civil unrest in the summer of 1971, when "the Hoboken Riots" included a counter-riot by a cohort of the city's "few remaining longshoremen." The last of the Hoboken piers was shuttered in 1975. Then, between 1978 and 1982, "fifty-six people, most of them children, died in highly suspicious tenement fires." When the smoke cleared, the waterfront was covered by a charming walkway extending from the historic Lackawanna Station to Frank Sinatra Park, honoring that contender for the role of Terry Malloy who also helped John V. Kenny topple the Irish waterfront's most oppressive political regime.[21]

Across the entire port, as journalist William Finnegan reported in 2006, the "collective image" projected from *On the Waterfront* remains "so compelling that its scenes and characters have become part of the consciousness of the actual waterfront's protagonists today." The Waterfront Commission code-named a major investigation "Brando"; in 2007 federally appointed administrators of Bayonne ILA Local 1588, defending the commission's ongoing power over hiring, urged the public to "recall a scene in *On the Waterfront,* which is practically a documentary of how organized crime dominated the industry." The most hopeful sign that decades of mob control of Local 1588 might end was the election in 2007 of sixty-seven-year-old Tom Hanley as "recording secretary," the same position claimed in the film by Tillio (ex-heavyweight Tami Mauriello) after he is described by a clerk at the crime commission hearings as a mere "delegate." Tillio's indignant response ("Recording secretary!") provides the final light moment before Terry Malloy's dramatic testimony, which in turn precedes the killing of Terry's prize flock of pigeons by Tommy, the Golden Warrior, played by thirteen-year-old Tommy Hanley.[22]

On the Waterfront worked its way into the sinews of virtually every subsequent cinematic representation of urban ethnicity, organized crime, and the intimacy with violence. As film critic J. Hoberman noted in 2004, *On the Waterfront* "would enable *Rocky,* refract itself in *Raging Bull,* and underscore *Goodfellas.*" Hoberman might have added *The Sopranos,* among many others: the lead actor of the television series, James Gandolfini, played Charley the Gent Malloy in an ill-fated 1995 Broadway production of *On the Waterfront* adapted from the film by Budd Schulberg and Stan Silverman. An essay devoted entirely to urban rooftop scenes featuring pigeon coops and brooding would fill out quickly. (Mickey Rourke's inspired performance as Charlie Moran in the 1984 film *The Pope of Greenwich Village* merits special recognition.)[23]

At the conclusion of Martin Scorsese's *Raging Bull* (1980), a film regarded by many as the greatest cinematic achievement of the post-*Waterfront* era, Robert De Niro, as obese, morally bankrupt ex-middleweight champion Jake LaMotta, peers into a nightclub dressing room mirror while rehearsing his stilted version of Terry Malloy's "contender" remonstrance. LaMotta awkwardly mixes fragments of a punishing self-assessment with Terry's original testament, constructed in part from bits of dialogue Budd Schulberg harvested during the countless hours he had spent with fighters past and current. Unlike Terry, Jake LaMotta did "reach a peak" as a fighter before going downhill—as he reminds the battered ex-champ reflected in the mirror—but the words of the unsuccessful cinematic middleweight remain the standard against which LaMotta examines his own conscience. His artless rendition of "contender" plays like a prayer in sustaining the spiritual notes of the original, yet it is not a simple prayer, for LaMotta's enduring rage evokes the entrapment of Charley and Terry Malloy in their intimacy with violence. With this scene Scorsese has "opened it up again" just as the enigmatic Sam Spiegel continually badgered and cajoled Kazan and Schulberg to open again the script of *Waterfront* and expose its heart and soul. The indelible testimony from *Raging Bull*—like countless similar confessions recorded in art and offered in lives since summer 1954—works so powerfully *only* because Budd Schulberg's *Waterfront* script, Elia Kazan's vision, Boris Kaufman's images, and Marlon Brando's performance are so deeply embedded in the culture's consciousness, as though all urban American roads to redemption must traverse Hoboken's waterfront of memory.[24]

Epilogue

SOULS OF THE (PORT) APOSTOLATE

Father Pete Corridan remained affiliated with Xavier Labor School for thirty months following the release of *On the Waterfront,* albeit in a greatly diminished capacity. Two books published in 1955 sparked a very short-lived revival of his notoriety. Veteran journalist Allen Raymond's *Waterfront Priest* provided the first comprehensive account of the Jesuit's public apostolate. Raymond was the son of a Methodist lay preacher who traded his Ivy League, New England pedigree for a hardboiled journalistic persona cultivated over decades as a "legman," rewrite man, copyeditor, and reporter for a dozen urban newspapers, mostly in metropolitan New York. With his blend of moral rectitude and adventurousness Raymond must have reminded Corridan of an older version of Mike Johnson. (A book Raymond co-authored in 1940, *Gang Rule in New York,* was a worthy if lurid precursor to Johnson's "Crime on the Waterfront.")[1]

Years of experience rendered the Jesuit an expert literary collaborator. *Waterfront Priest* faithfully conveyed the arc of Pete Corridan's apostolate prior to concluding in a remarkably candid admission of failure. "As for the fight he has made to clean up New York's waterfront, Father Corridan says that the fight has been lost," Raymond reported. "You can't close this story with any happy ending," the priest told him. "If you're going to tell the truth, you will have to ram one fact home. The rank-and-file dockworkers have lost this fight, and they won't make another for a long time to come. I've lost," he confessed, adding, "I believe the city and the people of New York have lost." Instead,

the mobsters won. They're still on the docks. The more unscrupulous elements within the shipping industry won. They still try to maintain that surplus working force, insecure and dependent for daily bread on the daily favor of the man who blows the morning whistle. They're trying to push the old degrading shape-up into the new job information centers.[2]

As Lewis Gannett of the *New York Herald Tribune* astutely noted in his review of *Waterfront Priest,* "three figures [Corridan, Joe Ryan, and William McCormack] dominate this story, all New York City–born sons of Irish immigrants who grew up in dire poverty and became major, but very different, figures in city life." Even though Corridan was the youngest of the trio by nearly a quarter-century, the true crime tone of *Waterfront Priest* evoked the bygone days of ethnic tribalism and Tammany shenanigans, not the progressive "spiritual front" confirmed at the time by the Jesuit's recent triumph in cinematic collaboration. Raymond's "angry, impassioned" book generated little of the outraged reaction urged on the metropolitan citizenry by *New York Times* reviewer Quentin Anderson.[3]

To Pete Corridan's sorrow the one *truly* outraged reader of *Waterfront Priest* was his new Jesuit superior, Thomas E. Henneberry, S.J., who succeeded John McMahon as head of the order's New York province in June 1954. The previous December Corridan had received permission from McMahon's office to collaborate and split royalties with Raymond; the Jesuit's proceeds from *Waterfront Priest* were earmarked for support of Xavier Labor School. Father Henneberry inherited both the publishing deal and Corridan's customary expectation of freedom from undue scrutiny by his superiors. The new provincial was, like McMahon, a product of Manhattan's West Side Irish waterfront, but the similarity ended there. Whereas McMahon was a visionary risk taker, Henneberry was a company man; while gifted intellectually, he was devoted to the order's corporate ethos and enforcement of its internal authority and deeply averse to controversy of any description.[4]

Henneberry was shocked to discover that Corridan had virtually co-authored *Waterfront Priest;* he was particularly incensed by its detailed account of the now mythic November 1951 meeting at Cardinal Spellman's residence, a passage that by itself, in the provincial's view, invalidated the manuscript. "I cannot comprehend how you ever came to offer for publication to an extern [non-Jesuit] the details of a confidential meeting and the doings of a Cardinal and a Provincial," scolded Henneberry in a letter of early January 1955. "Now that I have read the 'Cardinal sections' it is clear that the notion I had a few weeks ago that his Eminence might be approached for permission to publish is strictly out. Let us rather hope that he never discovers that there was even a thought of publishing."[5]

Corridan refused to yield; his militant devotion to smashing the code of silence on the outside would not be compromised by acquiescence to its religious-life equivalent. While taking full responsibility for his own actions, he noted that Allen Raymond was "not a Catholic and although a very reasonable man, has strong views on censorship." Corridan continued:

> As he sees it—the work of a priest for social reform in a vital area was under its most serious attack from within the framework of the Church which above

all others stands for social reform. For repelling that attack Raymond—though a Protestant—believes the Church should be praised. He also maintains that if the attack had been successful, it would have been a scandal.

Since he knew there was no chance that Raymond and Henneberry would ever communicate on the matter, the waterfront priest was free to spin his writing partner's views in any way that advanced their shared cause. Nearing the end now of his public life, Corridan exposed his strategy for collaborating with "externs." Highly publicized work with non-Catholics obliged Jesuit officials to weigh the reward of keeping their mercurial celebrity in line against the risk of "giving scandal," for if they censored the waterfront priest, news would surely leak out. Father McMahon had eschewed the calculations, risking his own future by embracing the prophetic apostolate of his younger confrere. Henneberry effectively closed this chapter of American Jesuit history in a letter to Corridan written three days after Louis Gannett accurately surmised that *Waterfront Priest* "reads as if Father Corridan had conscientiously studied every page and written a good many of them," a revelation the provincial found "disturbing although not surprising."[6]

Corridan had lost the New York Jesuit leadership, but Budd Schulberg remained squarely in his corner. September 1955 saw the publication of *Waterfront*, the sprawling novel Schulberg had conceived early in the discouraging process of bringing a version of Corridan's story to fruition on the screen. Here Father Pete Barry finally takes center stage, fulfilling a pledge the author had made to himself. "I always felt," he told a reporter, "because of my involvement with Xavier, that we had short-changed the priest, that we simply didn't have room in a 90-minute movie to explore [his] ordeal." As the critic Richard Gilman—a recent (if temporary) convert from Judaism—informed the readers of the avant-garde Catholic magazine *Jubilee*, "It is Schulberg's passionate desire to bring to bear the moral principles of Catholicism under his own name on an abject and unredeemed segment of society, to see it transformed and the lesson of its transformation learned widely." Although Terry Malloy finally dies in this *Waterfront*, the shadow cast by the film remained overpowering. "Like millions of other Americans," wrote W. R. Burnett in *Saturday Review*, "I saw the movie version, and so I find it impossible to read the book freshly and judge it merely on its merits as prose fiction." *Waterfront*, the novel, was dedicated to Corridan, Brownie, Malcolm Johnson, and unnamed longshoremen slain in the Port of New York. Schulberg's inscription "1950–1955" below the dedication line memorialized a half-decade's deep engagement with the waterfront crusade.[7]

Like Schulberg, Pete Corridan turned the page of his life story in 1955. "I doubt whether I'll speak again at union meetings," he told a reporter for the *Village Voice*, then a fledgling neighborhood weekly, prior to a December speaking engagement at the venerable Greenwich House. "As a priest I was taking sides and there were members of our parish on both sides. It affected them in many ways including their religious lives." Corridan indicated an interest in pursuing the cause of affordable housing for families, an initiative that failed to materialize. Nineteen fifty-six was a lost year. On the second day of the following year Henneberry notified Corridan of his new assignment: teaching economics at LeMoyne College in Syracuse. He was expected to arrive in a week's time to make preparations for classes set to begin later that month. "Though you have been away from the classroom and from formal study for quite a while," Henneberry reminded the waterfront priest with lukewarm praise, "I am sure that you are equipped to do excellent teaching in certain areas."[8]

The Jesuits' *America* magazine reported that Corridan's transfer came "at his own request," but as Schulberg later wrote: "Believe me, it wasn't that simple. Syracuse was the last place he wanted to go. What was done to him broke his spirit, his heart and, almost, his faith." Decades later the extraordinarily distinguished labor priest George G. Higgins wasted no time in asking an interviewer, "Was it Mr. Big that drove him from the waterfront?" As Higgins was a product of the Chicago archdiocese, his suspicion shows how widespread was the standard view originating with New York Jesuits. The specter of Bill McCormack's displeasure with Corridan's apostolate hovered over conversations among the waterfront priest's contemporaries for decades. Though it provides a most dramatic storyline—and one not without merit—it is more likely that Corridan was shipped out as a result of perceived insubordination to his provincial's authority. Jesuit leaders apart from John McMahon had long since tired of the constant controversy his work aroused; there were also growing concerns about his judgment under the influence of alcohol, fears confirmed when the Jesuit "went over the hill," as he informed Budd Schulberg, shortly after arriving in Syracuse. He was reportedly sent to a secluded facility to "dry out."[9]

Pete Corridan continued to struggle with an alcohol problem in the early days of his stint at Saint Peter's College in Jersey City, where he returned to teaching in 1959. There he joined a fellowship dedicated to spiritual recovery from alcoholism and went on to enjoy extended periods of sobriety, during which he never spoke publicly of his celebrated waterfront crusade. Students at Saint Peter's admired Corridan: while one likened him to a caged tiger in the classroom, another marveled at his compassion and "magnificent presence" when lecturing on "these guys from the Bible" in his religion classes. Another former student was certain, however, that Corridan occasionally stole glances down the steep slope of Montgomery Street toward the waterfront and his haunted West Side just across the mouth of the North River.[10]

Frank Hague is buried in Holy Name Cemetery, just across West Side Avenue from the western edge of the college's compact campus; John V. Kenny's remains repose nearby. Though Corridan had little direct engagement with this pair from New Jersey's Irish waterfront, his years at Saint Peter's saw the passing of his trio of bitter adversaries. After a 1955 conviction for accepting gifts from a stevedoring firm (he was spared a jail term because of ill health), Joe Ryan took to wandering forlornly through the old neighborhood where he was once hailed as a soft touch by dockworkers down on their luck; now King Joe trudged among them. He died in June 1963 at age seventy-nine.[11]

Bill McCormack made good on his promise to retire from public life after the New York State Crime Commission hearings of 1952–53. His son and heir apparent William J. McCormack Jr. expanded the family's business profile, developing an oil-hauling operation on steel barges for Hess and Standard Oil. The younger McCormack stood poised to assume leadership of the family empire when he discerned, a few years after his father's January 1953 appearance before the NYSCC, a "late vocation" to the priesthood By 1965, when his father died at age seventy-seven, Monsignor McCormack was stationed at St. Patrick's Cathedral on Fifth Avenue in Manhattan, where he was joined in celebrating a solemn requiem Mass of Christian burial by Francis Cardinal Spellman, Bishop Fulton J. Sheen, and Bishop Terence James Cooke, who would shortly succeed Spellman as archbishop of New York. McCormack was named auxiliary bishop of New York in 1987.[12]

Monsignor John J. O'Donnell passed away in 1967, the same year as Cardinal Spellman, a year that also saw Pete Corridan leave St. Peter's College for a chaplaincy position at King's County Hospital in Brooklyn. Ministries to indigent, mentally ill, and alcoholic patients at "paupers'" hospitals on Hart Island off the Bronx coast and other remote venues were an honored component of New York Jesuit tradition. Corridan embraced that apostolate—updated in the context of a large municipal hospital—with gratitude and even joy, experiencing a spiritual renewal far from the contentious waterfront and out of the spotlight. He ministered warmly to patients and their families, including many who had suffered from violence. Associates from this period spoke often of his great and growing compassion for others.[13]

Father Pete Corridan enjoyed a rich and meaningful final decade of active ministry before a heart ailment prompted his retirement; he spent his final months at the New York Jesuit province's nursing home on Fordham University's Bronx campus, located next to the former provincial's residence where, at the height of his fame and influence, the waterfront priest had met with "Mr. Big." He died on July 1, 1984; a simple, sparsely attended funeral was held nearby at the university church.[14]

The waterfront priest's old boss and confrere Father Phil Carey bitterly lamented prior to his own death in 1989 that "only Arthur Brown came back to thank [Corridan] for all that he had done. None, not one of the others did." But Pete Corridan had never established a truly intimate rapport with his few "rebel disciples." Carey, by contrast, was surrounded by a legion of friends and admirers. Before her death in 1966 Austin Tobin's wife, Geraldine, was a member of a kind of parish without boundaries woven by Phil Carey's pastoral network. Tobin later married Rosaleen Skehan, a Port Authority attorney who, like his first wife, was listed as a reference on Father Carey's résumé, a testament to his longstanding connection with the Tobin family.[15]

Austin Tobin is best known as the man whose agency built the gargantuan World Trade Center on Manhattan's Lower West Side waterfront. The planning and execution of the Trade Center exerted a great toll on Tobin, who retired from the Port Authority in 1972. The following year he failed to attend the Trade Center's opening ceremony because, he said, "it was raining." Four years later it was Austin Tobin's "dying wish" to spend several hours alone at the site, seated in a wheelchair in the plaza that would later bear his name. The windswept and barren expanse of Austin J. Tobin Plaza symbolized for many the impersonal character of this envisioned but unrealized "vertical port," a subject of widespread derision in the Trade Center's early years. But by the time of Austin Tobin's death in 1978, New Yorkers and tourists alike were gradually developing a fondness and even a warm affection for the Twin Towers.[16]

Philip A. Carey loved being a Jesuit and a labor priest. "I've been nothing but a sociological tinker for all these years," he told interviewer Debra Bernhardt in 1981. "A sociological tinker?" she queried, as if uncertain whether Carey had pronounced "thinker" with the New York Irish touch or if he actually meant to liken himself to a wanderer, a jack-of-all-trades. He surely intended the remark to remain open to the broadest range of interpretations: "Sociological tinker, that's all."[17]

In this as in transcripts of interviews conducted with other veterans of the Irish waterfront, it is not uncommon to encounter a bit of tactical linguistic evasiveness. While some might take this for a broad rendition of "Irishness," the speech patterns of figures like Phil Carey also betray the brutal legacy of the West Side code of silence and the equally painful experiences it was designed to conceal. Carey was a charming storyteller, but he was a man who preferred to set his prayers in motion. As late as 1970 he remained a "marvel in action," as a young Jesuit wrote after spending a day with him, "for certainly he is a charismatic figure, and one would wish that somehow some of his younger brethren who are concerned about the poor could see him in action."[18]

Pete Corridan did not enjoy nearly so great an influence among younger Jesuits; his true disciples numbered precisely two. In a 1987 letter Budd Schulberg anointed Corridan and Arthur Brown "the soul of the waterfront, both with a capital and small 'w,' and I have said and written all my life that the film could never have been written without them." Schulberg always understood better than anyone else that the Irish waterfront was both a real place and more than a place. He was far too modest to add that without his own vision and persistence there would have been no waterfront movie, and perhaps no spiritual front either, so integral was his role as champion and translator of the waterfront priest's often quixotic liberationist impulse. Schulberg continued to represent this shared tradition in the decades to come. October 25, 2006, found him on Pier 40 at the foot of Houston Street, near the southern edge of Manhattan's historic Irish waterfront, helping to christen the *Rev. John M. Corridan, S.J.*, a "sleek police vessel" operated by the Waterfront Commission of New York Harbor.[19]

Pier 40 was now the site of a very heavily trafficked soccer and recreation facility and massive rooftop parking deck—and, as an occupant of desirable Manhattan real estate, the subject of heated debates over its future. All along the once forbidding "lawless jungle" of the Irish waterfront the river's edge was experiencing reclamation, on Hudson County's "Gold Coast" just as in Manhattan, where the ribbon-like Hudson River Park had transformed Pier 45—where Johnny Dwyer had risked his life challenging the menacing Thompson brothers—into a grassy expanse extremely popular with West Village sunbathers. Farther north Pier 51—whose coveted loading racket cost Andy Hintz his life in 1947—was now a maritime-themed playground. A waterfront park along the Hudson just north of the former Hell's Kitchen neighborhood preserved as relics the tangled remains of a pier shed and a float bridge, once used to transfer car floats from barge to railroad.

The West Side's Chelsea neighborhood was radically transformed in the 1990s as derelict warehouses were converted into chic art galleries; multimillion-dollar apartment units proliferated. The former headquarters of ILA Local 791 was now the home of the Sanford Meisner Theatre. Although Meisner enjoyed no connection to the waterfront of history or memory, he was a founding member of the Group Theatre and a seminal New York acting teacher whose methods deeply influenced Elia Kazan. Across the West Side Highway from the onetime home of 791 stands the Chelsea Piers recreation complex, surely one of the gaudiest and most ambitious commercial enterprises ever undertaken on a former waterfront industrial site.

Between the complex's lavish sporting facilities and the river's edge stands a wall richly adorned with blow-ups of photographs documenting the piers' working history.

The photograph on display along the wall's southern edge was taken in the shed that remains standing directly behind the viewer. This May 7, 1950, composition depicts the first Catholic Mass celebrated on a pier in the Port of New York. That Pier 61 Mass and Waldorf-Astoria Communion breakfast—following a spectacular cross-town parade—were designed to reassert the spiritual authority of Joe Ryan and the celebrant at Mass, Ryan's pastor, port chaplain John J. "Taxi Jack" O'Donnell. The photograph offers wonderful period detail: ornate patterns on the socks of worshippers are visible, as are the elaborate floral arrangements specially prepared for the occasion. A viewer will not, however, discern a single human face in the photograph. There were 1,200 longshoremen in attendance at Mass that day; their identities remain shrouded by a code of silence that covered the waterfront visually as in speech.

Across the river and visible from Pier 61 a public recreation facility has been slowly emerging in Hoboken from out of the North River. Plans for Pier C Park (boating and fishing facilities, a water play area, and a "rookery" were among prospective features subject to alteration, given the Mile Square City's historic funding vagaries) did not cite the magnificent movie filmed on the long-demolished Pier 1, as it was known at the time. The omission signaled perhaps the dawn of Hoboken's post-*Waterfront* era. For years the city's revival was yoked to the film's aura and gritty prestige. No location offered more powerful witness to the collaborative spiritual and creative prowess of Pete Corridan, Budd Schulberg, and Elia Kazan, who together so brilliantly choreographed the violent dance of the shapeup filmed on that Hoboken pier in the memorably frigid air of late November 1953.

Acknowledgments

Years of walks and talks with Carlo Rotella—on and off the waterfront—prepared me like no other experience to animate the port's vast spaces as story-enriched places. Carlo's kindred film and boxing aficionado Jim Garamone shared with me his total recall of a New York City moviegoing lifetime; Jim also accompanied me to the south shore of Long Island in May 2002 for my initial meeting with Budd Schulberg. My ongoing engagement with this supremely gifted trio—Carlo, Jim, and Budd—made of this work a most meaningful adventure. Budd is of course a major character in the book, a fact that this most unassuming of gentlemen may only now fully discern, even as he will likely demur over some of my conclusions. The numerous trips Budd and Betsy (Budd's wife) and I shared to Hoboken and back were high points in this historian's working life.

Michael Aaron Rockland and Angus Kress Gillespie gave a Rutgers graduate student his first real teaching job in 1986: their friendship—and prolific fascination with the people, bridges, tunnels, and towers that linked both shores of the North River—is a foundation on which this project was built. On August 16, 2001, Angus escorted me to One World Trade Center for a meeting with officials of the Port Authority of New York and New Jersey, who seemed both heartened and bemused that I was about to launch a course on the history of the port at Saint Peter's College, just across the harbor in Jersey City. My family and I had returned to New Jersey only weeks earlier, thanks to Saint Peter's late president, James N. Loughran, S.J., who kindly invited me to serve as Will and Ariel Durant Visiting Professor at the college.

On September 11 the class was scheduled to meet at Liberty State Park on the Jersey City waterfront to embark on field work documenting the port's history and culture. The following morning found me instead crossing the river via police boat alongside a large portion of the Saint Peter's College community, bearing supplies for rescue workers at the World Trade Center site. This book represents in part a very modest tribute to the women and men who lost their lives on September 11, 2001, and to the enduring spirit of all those who incarnated the soul of the port in the weeks and months that followed.

This long-unfolding project was blessed with wonderfully insightful and constructive readers, from Peter Quinn, historical novelist and memoirist extraordinaire of urban Irish America; to Bruce Nelson, a distinguished labor historian at Dartmouth College; to the incomparable Patrick Allitt of Emory University, who remains after two decades my role model as historian and friend. Amy Koehlinger continually reassured me that the subject of Catholic violence was legitimate, as her own groundbreaking work will soon surely confirm. Few have been so blessed with a relative as gifted at reading, writing, and theological insight as I have been across years of spirited conversation with my L.A. cousin and great friend Bob Fisher.

While serving as director of Notre Dame's Cushwa Center for the Study of American Catholicism, Scott Appleby secured the grant that helped fund the early research for this project and facilitated its publication in the series, Cushwa Center Studies of Catholicism in Twentieth-Century America. Scott not only provided a searching reading of the manuscript but also collaborated with Michael McGandy of Cornell University Press and me to dramatically improve the final product. At Cornell Amanda Heller's adept and insightful copyediting and Susan Specter's expert handling of final manuscript preparations inspired great confidence, and Dave Prout did an outstanding job of preparing the index. Scott Appleby's successor at Cushwa, Timothy Matovina, and associate director Kathleen Sprows Cummings extended much warm hospitality during the course of this project. My many friends at the University of Dayton—my other American Catholic studies home away from home—invited me back repeatedly to talk about the Irish waterfront and the movie until I felt I was finally getting the story straight. Many others kindly invited me to speak at their venues, none more memorably than Jane Sammon of the New York Catholic Worker community, where a June 2008 Friday evening session at Maryhouse truly did produce some "clarification of thought."

Patrice Kane, head of Archives and Special Collections, and preservation librarian Vivian Shen welcomed me to Fordham University's O'Hare Special Collections, Walsh Family Library, when that extraordinary resource was as new as my fledgling book project. More than a decade later I remain a most grateful and devoted patron: this book exists in no small part thanks to Patrice and Vivian's kindness, patience, and understanding. As I emerged from the Walsh library after a long day of research in spring 2000 Mark Massa, S.J., accosted me to inquire about my possible interest in a teaching position at Fordham. I was interested: Mark and the amazing Maria Terzulli of the Curran Center for American Catholic Studies have bestowed on me their good graces through all the years since. The members of Fordham's theology department likewise welcomed this cultural historian to their most collegial community, which includes a very lively cohort of graduate students pursuing American Catholic studies—Jack Downey, Kyle Haden, O.F.M., Cindy McCann, and Catherine Osborne.

I am deeply grateful for the many courtesies, leads, and images provided by archivists, librarians, and curators at numerous other locations: the late Frederick J. O'Brien, S.J., who expertly guided me through the archives of the New York Jesuit Province; Joan Miller at the Wesleyan Cinema Archives; Cynthia Harris and John Beekman of the New Jersey Room of the Jersey City Free Public Library; Mary Kinahan-Ockay at the Saint Peter's College archives; Alan Delozier at the Catholic Archdiocese of Newark archives, Seton Hall University Library; and many others at the Museum of the City of New York; Rauner Special Collections Library, Dartmouth College; Princeton University Library's Department of Rare Books and Special Collections; Harry Ransom Center, University of Texas at Austin; and the Tamiment Library and Robert F. Wagner Labor Archives at New York University. I am especially grateful for the generosity of Haynes Johnson, a Pulitzer Prize–winning journalist and author who shared with me invaluable materials relating to his father and fellow Pulitzer honoree, Malcolm "Mike" Johnson.

For tips, sources, inspiration, companionship, and combinations thereof I humbly offer thanks to Bob Armbruster, the great Hal Borden, Jeffrey M. Burns, Julie Byrne, Rodger Citron, Mindi Grieser Cromwell, Adam Davis, Julia Dillon, Roy P. Domenico, Joe Doyle, Dennis Durst, T. J. English, Michael Epstein, Tom Ferraro, the late Robert W. Greene, Paula Printon Jara, Belden Lane, Barry V. Lipinski, Joe Long, Joan Doherty Lovero, Leonard Luizzi, Ed Mahon, Jeff Marlett, Paul Myhre, Anne Pardun, Jeffrey Rosen, Luz and Michael Scotti, Bill Shea, Thomas J. Shelley, Helene Stapinski, Glenn Wallach, Matt Weiner, Steve Werner, and my dear friend through three, often turbulent decades, Denise Young.

As a young child in the mid-1960s I often heard my mother regaling friends—via late-night phone calls—with excerpts from Jimmy Breslin's *New York Herald Tribune* columns. I don't know how these friends reacted to Gracie's enthusiasm: we lived far from the city at the time; the "Trib" arrived at our home by mail each day, a day late. I avidly scoured the paper's sports and nightlife columns and surely pondered more than once the nature of "shipping news," which then featured—as I discovered decades later—a kind of rolling epitaph for the Irish waterfront. Soon the *Herald Tribune* would itself expire; of such fleeting moments are vocations made and books conceived.

Every Christmas morning since 1994 has found me standing along a very steep hillside cemetery in Oakland, California, honoring the memory of departed members of the extended Yeung, Wong, and Chew families. For the past decade Gordon and Kayris Chew have completely devoted their lives to the care and well-being of their very special grandson, Charles Vincent Fisher. To me that's heroism; to them it's the meaning of family and that's a home truth—learned late in life—I hope never to relinquish. Kay and Gordon's daughter Kristina Julie Chew, Charlie's mom, my love, has covered with me and Charlie waterfronts on both coasts and the heartland of America. We live in a country of difference, if not a different country, but Kristina's tireless devotion to Charlie, along with her teaching, mentoring, and public advocacy make all our works and days pass like a cool breeze, my chronic bouts of unbelief notwithstanding. Since the love of Charlie and Kristina endures I may finally let go of my other constant companion of the decade past, this story of the Irish waterfront.

http://irishwaterfront.wordpress.com

Notes

Prologue: Pete Barry's Punch

1. Budd Schulberg, *On the Waterfront: The Final Shooting Script* (Hollywood: Samuel French, 1980), 118.

2. Thomas Doherty, *Hollywood's Censor: Joseph I. Breen and the Production Code Administration* (New York: Columbia University Press, 2007), 174, 320–21; see also Leo Braudy, *On the Waterfront* (London: British Film Institute, 2005), 76.

3. Malcolm Johnson, *On The Waterfront* (New York: Chamberlain Bros., 2005), is a collection of the author's Pulitzer Prize–winning stories for the *New York Sun*. I treat the Johnson-Corridan partnership in detail in chapter 7, "Covering the Waterfront."

4. Elia Kazan, *Elia Kazan: A Life* (New York: Doubleday, 1988), 444. Schulberg testified in May 1951 and Kazan the following April.

5. On Irish American residential patterns, see, for example, Kerby A. Miller, *Emigrants and Exiles: Ireland and the Irish Exodus to North America* (New York: Oxford University Press, 1985), 52–23; see also chapter 1 of this book, "Chelsea's King Joe."

6. Malcolm Johnson, "Crime on the Water Front," *New York Sun*, November 8, 1948. The lack of a freight rail tunnel is a recurring motif of this book because it symbolized both the historic "irrationality" of the port's political economy and the capacity of the Irish waterfront to transform the deficit into a defining advantage. See chapter 4, "The Longshoreman's Grandson," for an extended discussion.

7. There is a scholarly literature on religion and violence. While intriguing, this material generally falls outside the scope of this study by virtue of methodology or subject matter. See, for example, the classic work of René Giraud, *Violence and the Sacred*, trans. Patrick Gregory (Baltimore: Johns Hopkins University Press, 1977); see also R. Scott Appleby, *The Ambivalence of the Sacred: Religion, Violence, and Reconciliation* (Lanham. Md.: Rowman and Littlefield, 2000), 116–17, for a discussion of violence as a choice made by and for Christians.

8. Schulberg, *On the Waterfront*, 34.

9. For Carey's travails, see chapter 5, "A Labor Priest in the Catholic Metropolis."

10. See chapter 8, "The Hollywood Prince," and chapter 12, "A Season for Testimony."

11. Bruce Nelson, *Divided We Stand: American Workers and the Struggle for Black Equality* (Princeton: Princeton University Press, 2001), 77. See chapter 13, "The Hook."

12. See chapters 15 through 19 for a fully contextualized treatment of *On the Waterfront*'s sources, production, and reception.

13. Kazan, *Elia Kazan*, 517.

Introduction: The Port's Irish Places

1. James Morris, *The Great Port: A Passage through New York* (New York: Harcourt, Brace and World, 1969), 21; Russell Shorto, *The Island at the Center of the World: The Epic Story of Dutch Manhattan and the Forgotten Colony That Shaped America* (New York: Doubleday, 2004), 32; Edwin G. Burrows and Mike Wallace, *Gotham: A History of New York City to 1898* (New York: Oxford University Press, 1999), 5–13; Tom Lewis, *The Hudson: A History* (New Haven: Yale University Press, 2005), 37–55.

2. Robert Greenhalgh Albion, *The Rise of New York Port, 1815–1860* (New York: C. Scribner's Sons, 1939), 336–52.

3. Ibid., 38–42; Donald Squires and Kevin Bone, "The Beautiful Lake: The Promise of the Natural Systems," in *The New York Waterfront: Evolution and Building Culture of the Port of New York,* ed. Kevin Bone (New York: Monacelli Press, 1997), 22, 26; Lewis, *The Hudson,* 236–37. For an excellent history of the original New York Irish neighborhood, see Tyler Anbinder, *Five Points: The Nineteenth-Century New York City Neighborhood That Invented Tap Dance, Stole Elections, and Became the World's Most Notorious Slum* (New York: Free Press, 2001).

4. Hasia R. Diner, "'The Most Irish City in the Union': The Era of the Great Migration," in *The New York Irish, ed.* Ronald H. Bayor and Timothy J. Meagher (Baltimore: Johns Hopkins University Press, 1996), 87–105; Burrows and Wallace, *Gotham,* 744.

5. David Montgomery, *The Fall of the House of Labor: The Workplace, the State, and American Labor Activism, 1865–1925* (Cambridge: Cambridge University Press, 1987), 96–99; Iver Bernstein, *The New York City Draft Riots: Their Significance for American Society and Politics in the Age of the Civil War* (New York: Oxford University Press, 1990), 27–28, 117–19.

6. Calvin Winslow, introduction to *Waterfront Workers: New Perspectives on Race and Class* (Urbana: University of Illinois Press, 1998), 10.

7. *New York Times,* April 22, June 2, and December 13, 1870.

8. David Scobey, *Empire City: The Making and Meaning of the New York City Landscape* (Philadelphia: Temple University Press, 2002), 225–26; Mary Beth Betts, "Masterplanning: Municipal Support of Maritime Transport and Commerce, 1870–1930s," in Bone, *The New York Waterfront,* 42–44, 69–70; I. N. Phelps Stokes, *The Iconography of Manhattan Island, 1498–1909, vol. 3* (1915–1928; rpt., Union, N.J.: 1998), 812.

9. Thomas J. Shelley, *Greenwich Village Catholics: St. Joseph's Church and the Evolution of an Urban Faith Community, 1829–2002* (Washington, D.C.: Catholic University of America Press, 2003), 101–2, 105–8; Stuart Waldman, *Maritime Mile: The Story of the Greenwich Village Waterfront* (New York: Mikaya Press, 2002), 42–44.

10. Regina Kellerman, ed., *The Architecture of the Greenwich Village Waterfront* (New York: New York University Press, 1989), 47; Thomas J. Shelley, "Catholic Greenwich Village: Ethnic Geography and Religious Identity in New York City, 1880–1930," *Catholic Historical Review* 89 (Winter 2003): 61; author telephone interview with Harold Blake, St. Veronica parish manager, February 5, 2007; Thomas Shelley, "'Only One Class of People to Draw upon for Support': Irish-Americans and the Archdiocese of New York," *American Catholic Studies* 112 (2001): 16.

11. Caroline Ware, *Greenwich Village, 1920–1930: A Comment on American Civilization in the Post-War Years* (Boston: Houghton Mifflin, 1935), 270; Gerald W. McFarland, *Inside Greenwich Village: A New York City Neighborhood, 1898–1918* (Amherst: University of Massachusetts Press, 2001), 43–44; Jeff Kisseloff, *You Must Remember This: An Oral History of Manhattan from the 1890s to World War II* (Baltimore: Johns Hopkins University Press, 1999), 547–52; Luc Sante, *Low Life: Lures and Snares of Old New York* (New York: Vintage Books, 1991), 18; Henry J. Browne, *One Stop above Hell's Kitchen: Sacred Heart Parish in Clinton* (South Hackensack, N.J.: CustomBook, 1977), 29, 69.

12. Burrows and Wallace, *Gotham,* 1002–8; Ackerman, *Boss Tweed,* 153–60.

13. Betts, "Masterplanning," 70–74; architectural historians Robert A. M. Stern, Gregory Gilmartin, and John Montague Massengale, authors of *New York 1900,* are quoted in Philip

Lopate, *Waterfront: A Journey around Manhattan* (New York: Crown 2004), 115–16; for Warren and Wetmore and the Chelsea Piers, see also Peter Pennoyer and Anne Walker, *The Architecture of Warren and Wetmore* (New York: W. W. Norton, 2006), 78–80.

14. *New York Times*, February 20, 1910. Even decades later the files of a Chelsea priest could include this notation: "Sixty percent of the Erie Railroad boat [lighter] crews come from the little town of Arklow, County Wicklow. They live between 18th and 21st Streets on Eighth Avenue"; see Local 996 file, box 11, folder 21, Xavier Institute of Industrial Relations Papers, O'Hare Special Collections, Walsh Family Library, Fordham University, hereafter cited as XIIR.

15. Thomas J. Shelley, *Dunwoodie: The History of St. Joseph's Seminary, Yonkers, New York* (Westminster, Md.: Christian Classics, 1993), 176; Chris McNickle, *To Be Mayor of New York: Ethnic Politics in the City* (New York: Columbia University Press, 1993), 7; for the ethnic succession at Tammany from Tweed to John Kelly, see Kenneth D. Ackerman, *Boss Tweed: The Rise and Fall of the Corrupt Pol Who Conceived the Soul of Modern New York* (New York: Carroll & Graf, 2005), 334–35.

16. Charles B. Barnes, *The Longshoremen* (New York: Survey Associates, 1915), 5.

17. There are no historical studies of the Irish American code of silence (nor of the spiritual intimacies with violence that sustained it) but the following sample of works of Irish and Irish American studies treat language, silence, culture, famine and diaspora in illuminating fashion: Robert James Scally, *The End of Hidden Ireland: Rebellion, Famine, and Emigration* (New York: Oxford University Press, 1995); Kerby A. Miller, *Emigrants and Exiles: Ireland and the Irish Exodus to North America* (New York: Oxford University Press, 1985), esp. 102–30; Peter Quinn, *Looking for Jimmy: A Search for Irish America* (New York: Overlook Press, 2007) esp. 211–69; Nathan Glazer and Daniel Patrick Moynihan, *Beyond the Melting Pot: The Negroes, Puerto Ricans, Jews, Italians and Irish of New York City* (Cambridge: MIT Press, 1963), 217–87; Kevin Kenny, *Making Sense of the Molly Maguires* (New York: Oxford University Press, 1998).

18. For Murphy, see M. R. Werner, *Tammany Hall* (Garden City, N.Y.: Doubleday, Doran, 1928), 486, 564; Herbert Mitgang, *The Man Who Rode the Tiger: The Life and Times of Judge Samuel Seabury* (New York: Fordham University Press, 1996), 68, 161; George Walsh, *Gentleman Jimmy Walker: Mayor of the Jazz Age* (New York: Praeger, 1974), 7–8, 29–30; Godkin is quoted in Mitgang, *The Man Who Rode the Tiger*, 157.

19. McFarland, *Inside Greenwich Village*, 25–36; Barnes, *The Longshoremen*, 11.

20. Author interview with Hoboken historian Leonard Luizzi, December 28, 2001.

21. http://www.themorningnews.org/archives/birnbaum_v/richard_reeves.php. For Carmine De Sapio see Warren Moscow, *The Last of the Big Time Bosses: The Life and Times of Carmine De Sapio and the Rise and Fall of Tammany Hall* (New York: Stein and Day, 1971), 31–47. For Fred De Sapio see "It Happened in Hoboken," *Newsweek* (May 26, 1947), and see chapters herein, "Meeting across the River" and "The Mile Square City's Moment."

22. Ibid., 5–12; William O'Dwyer, *Beyond the Golden Door*, ed. Paul O'Dwyer (Jamaica, N.Y.: St. John's University Press, 1987), 105; *The WPA Guide to New York City: The Federal Writers' Project Guide to 1930s New York* (1939; rpt., New York: Pantheon, 1982), 463.

23. David C. Mauk, *The Colony That Rose from the Sea: Norwegian Maritime Migration and Community in Brooklyn, 1850–1910* (Northfield, Minn.: Norwegian-American Historical Association, 1997).

24. Colin J. Davis, *Waterfront Revolts: New York and London Dockworkers, 1946–61* (Urbana: University of Illinois Press, 2003), 220–22; Bruce Nelson, *Divided We Stand: American Workers and the Struggle for Black Equality* (Princeton: Princeton University Press, 2001), 38–40, 80–82; Risa L. Faussette, "Race, Migration, and Port City Radicalism: New York's Black Longshoremen and the Politics of Maritime Protest, 1900–1920" (PhD diss., Binghamton University–State University of New York, 2002), 37–43; Colin J. Davis, "'Shape or Fight?': New York's Black Longshoremen, 1945–1961," *International Labor and Working-Class History* 62 (Fall 2002): 143–63; Kisseloff, *You Must Remember This*, 325–26.

25. Budd Schulberg, "Joe Docks, Forgotten Man of the Waterfront," *New York Times Magazine*, December 28, 1952, 3, 28–30; Budd Schulberg to Lester Markel, February 9, 1955, box 6, folder 59, XIIR.

26. Waldman, *Maritime Mile,* 42–44; for Paine's historic marker, see *The WPA Guide to New York City,* 141–42; Shelley, *Greenwich Village Catholics,* 157; Ware, *Greenwich Village,* 96, 106.

27. For the loading racket, see Craig Thompson and Allen Raymond, *Gang Rule in New York: The Story of a Lawless Era* (New York: Dial Press, 1940), 219; for the Dunn mob's role, see Malcolm Johnson, *Crime on the Labor Front* (New York: McGraw-Hill, 1950), 117–32, 165–83.

28. For Ryan's response to the "banditti" allegations, see *New York Times,* November 13, 1930; William J. Keating (with Richard Carter), *The Man Who Rocked the Boat* (New York: Harper and Brothers, 1956), 71–76, 94.

29. Keating, *The Man Who Rocked the Boat,* 62, 102–3, 119.

30. *New York Times,* April 1, 1947. The *Times* finally "tumbled to the story" with the arrests of Dunn, Sheridan, and Gentile on March 31; for the paper's coverage, see editions of April 1, 4, and 5, 1947; George Paul Jacoby, *Catholic Child Care in Nineteenth-Century New York: With a Correlated Summary of Public and Protestant Child Welfare* (Washington, D.C.: Catholic University of America Press, 1941), 123–57 (my thanks to Thomas J. Shelley for alerting me to this source); William J. Stern, "Once We Knew How to Rescue Poor Kids," *Urbanities* 8 (Autumn 1988), http://www.city-journal.org/html/8_4_urbanities_once_we_knew. html; Myron Magnet, "Old Money, Old Virtues," *Forbes* (October 8, 2001), http://www.forbes. com/forbes/2001/1008/097; Maureen Fitzgerald, *Habits of Compassion: Irish Catholic Nuns and the Origins of New York's Welfare System, 1830–1920* (Urbana: University of Illinois Press, 2006), 104–6.

31. For Richards's remark, see *New York Journal-American* January 8, 1953.The Hintz killing was the first waterfront murder to be solved. English, *The Westies,* 25.

32. For Maisie Hintz's travels, see *New York Times,* December 9, 1947; for Dunn's lawyers' allegations of a police conspiracy involving Lieutenant Joe Sullivan's brother and key witnesses, see the *Times,* December 30, 1947; for the conviction, see January 1, 1948.

33. *New York Times,* July 8, 1947.

34. The *Times*'s July 8 story on the executions of Dunn and Sheridan noted that the two were visited the morning of the executions by prison chaplain Thomas J. Donovan. Dunn himself became a prominent figure not only in journalistic accounts but also in television dramas (*Waterfront Boss,* 1952), films (*Slaughter on Tenth Avenue,* 1957), and novels (Thomas McGrath, *This Coffin Has No Handles* [1948; rpt., New York: Thunder's Mouth Press 1988]).

1. Chelsea's King Joe

1. For Ryan's early life, see Maud Russell, *Men along the Shore* (New York: Brussel and Brussel, 1966), 96–97; "Joseph Patrick Ryan," *Current Biography* 10 (1949): 539–41; Matthew Josephson, "Red Skies over the Waterfront," *Collier's,* October 5, 1946, 88.

2. Jeff Kisseloff, *You Must Remember This: An Oral History of Manhattan from the 1890s to World War II* (Baltimore: Johns Hopkins University Press, 1999), 493, 511.

3. Joe Doyle, "The Chelsea Irish and Old Westside," *Ais-Erie: The Magazine of Irish America* (Spring 1982): 8–9; Kisseloff, *You Must Remember This,* 495, 497.

4. Kisseloff, *You Must Remember This,* 495, 496.

5. Richard J. Butler and Joseph Driscoll, *Dock Walloper: The Story of "Big Dick" Butler* (New York: G. P. Putnam's Sons, 1933), 26, 29–30.

6. Marc Levinson, *The Box: How the Shipping Container Made the World Smaller and the World Economy Bigger* (Princeton: Princeton University Press, 2006), 21; Vernon H. Jensen, *Hiring of Dock Workers and Employment Practices in the Ports of New York, Liverpool, London, Rotterdam, and Marseilles* (Cambridge: Harvard University Press, 1964), 21–28; Calvin Winslow, "On the Waterfront: Black, Italian and Irish Longshoremen in the New York Harbour Strike of 1919," in *Protest and Survival: Essays for E. P. Thompson,* ed. John Rule and Robert Malcolmson (London: Merline Press, 1993), 364–66.

7. See chapter 6, "The Crusader," for discussion of various hiring methods found throughout the port.

8. Russell, *Men along the Shore,* 99–102; Malcolm Johnson, *Crime on the Labor Front* (New York: McGraw-Hill, 1950), 152.

9. For the ILA's clipped version of its own history, see http://www.ilaunion.org/history_membership.asp; Russell, *Men along the Shore,* 61–112.

10. Daniel Bell, "The Racket-Ridden Longshoremen: The Web of Economics and Politics," in *The End of Ideology: On the Exhaustion of Political Ideas in the Fifties* (Glencoe, Ill.: Free Press, 1960), 171; Butler and Driscoll, *Dock Walloper,* 47–76. For the early days of the ILA in New York, see also Howard Kimeldorf, *Reds or Rackets? The Making of Radical and Conservative Unions on the Waterfront* (Berkeley: University of California Press, 1988), 37–50; Bruce Nelson, *Divided We Stand: American Workers and the Struggle for Black Equality* (Princeton: Princeton University Press, 2001), 3–26; Calvin Winslow, "'Men of the Lumber Camps Come to Town': New York Longshoremen in the Strike of 1907," in *Waterfront Workers: New Perspectives on Race and Class,* ed. Winslow (Urbana: University of Illinois Press, 1998), 62–96.

11. Butler and Driscoll, *Dock Walloper,* 201–21; for Vaccarelli, see Salvatore J. LaGumina, "Paul Vaccarelli: The Lightning Change Artist of Organized Labor," *Italian Americana* (Winter 1996): 24–45; for samples of the ethnic caricatures of which Joseph Pulitzer's *New York World* (Vacarelli was "the Little Italian Falstaff") and other New York City newspapers were fond, see Nick Tosches's rumination on the life and times of gambler Arnold Rothstein, *King of the Jews* (New York: HarperCollins, 2005), 206. Jewish and Italian American boxers often took the ring under assumed Irish names for a variety of reasons (Frank Sinatra's father fought in Hoboken under the name Marty O'Brien), but the dynamic could work both ways. "In 1910 gang leader Paul Kelly petitioned the City Court to change his name back to Antonio Vaccarelli," reported Thomas Henderson in *Tammany Hall and the New Immigrants: The Progressive Years* (New York: Arno Press, 1976), 147. "It was a hardship to be known as Paul Kelly," he told the court, "because many people with whom he was doing business asked him if he was ashamed of an Italian name."

12. Josephson, "Red Skies over the Waterfront," 88; T. J. English, *Paddy Whacked: The Untold Story of the Irish American Gangster* (New York: HarperCollins, 2005), 233; William J. Keating (with Richard Carter), *The Man Who Rocked the Boat* (New York: Harper and Brothers, 1956), 90; for Ryan's loyal ties to Jimmy Walker, see Herbert Mitgang, *Once Upon a Time in New York: Jimmy Walker, Franklin Roosevelt, and the Last Great Battle of the Jazz Age* (New York: Free Press, 2000), 211; and George Walsh, *Gentleman Jimmy Walker: Mayor of the Jazz Age* (New York: Praeger, 1974), 302.

13. Walsh, *Gentleman Jimmy Walker,* 221–22; Herbert Mitgang, *The Man Who Rode the Tiger: The Life and Times of Judge Samuel Seabury* (New York: Fordham University Press, 1996), 5–7, 46–48.

14. Josephson, "Red Skies over the Waterfront," 88.

15. Maurice Rosenblatt, "Joe Ryan and His Kingdom," *Nation* 161 (November 24, 1945): 548; Robert A. M. Stern, Gregory Gilmartin, and Thomas Mellins, *New York 1930: Architecture and Urbanism between the Two World Wars* (New York: Rizzoli, 1987), 158.

16. Hugh McLeod, "The Culture of Popular Catholicism in New York City during the Later Nineteenth and Early Twentieth Centuries," in *Working Class and Popular Culture,* ed. Lex Heerma van Voss and Fritz van Holthoon (Amsterdam: Stichting Beeher IISG, 1988), 79; Hugh McLeod, *Piety and Poverty: Working-Class Religion in Berlin, London, and New York, 1870–1914* (New York: Holmes and Meier, 1996), 59–60; Tay Hohoff, *A Ministry to Man: The Life of John Lovejoy Elliott, a Biography* (New York: Harper, 1959), 114. In *You Must Remember This* (478), Jeff Kisseloff reported, "At times, Chelsea seemed like the stage of a morality play, where the forces of Ryan and Elliott battled for the soul of its natives." It is not clear that many Chelsea residents shared that view; Elliott was a great-nephew of the martyred abolitionist and rabid anti-Catholic Elijah Lovejoy and a disciple of Felix Adler, founder of the Ethical Culture movement, connections not likely to win him a large neighborhood following. Elliott was deeply respected, however, within the settlement house movement.

17. Joe Doyle, "Striking for Ireland on the New York Docks," in *The New York Irish*, ed. Ronald H. Bayor and Timothy J. Meagher (Baltimore: Johns Hopkins University Press, 1996), 357–73.

18. Nelson, *Divided We Stand*, 26–28; Risa L. Fausette, "Race, Migration, and Port City Radicalism: New York's Black Longshoremen and the Politics of Maritime Protest, 1900–1920" (PhD diss., Binghamton University–State University of New York, 2002), 37–45, 66–78, 211–44.

19. Doyle, "Striking for Ireland," 665, n. 70; Nelson, *Divided We Stand*, 60; Mitgang, *Once Upon a Time in New York*, 209–16; Walsh, *Gentleman Jimmy Walker*, 302.

20. Bruce Nelson, *Workers on the Waterfront: Seamen, Longshoremen, and Unionism in the 1930s* (Urbana: University of Illinois Press, 1988), 143; Johnson, *Crime on the Labor Front*, 156–57; Charles P. Larrowe, *Harry Bridges: The Rise and Fall of Radical Labor in the United States* (New York: Lawrence Hill, 1972), 47–52, 99.

21. Larrowe, *Harry Bridges*, 3.

22. Joseph P. Ryan testimony, in *Waterfront Investigation: United States Senate Subcommittee of the Committee on Interstate and Foreign Commerce*, pt. 1, *New York–New Jersey Waterfront, Washington, D.C., April 30, 1953* (Washington, D.C., 1953), 463; Christopher Shannon, "Public Enemies, Local Heroes: The Irish-American Gangster Film in Classic Hollywood Cinema," *New Hibernian Review* 9, no. 4 (2005): 48–64; Kisseloff, *You Must Remember This*, 488; Henderson, *Tammany Hall and the New Immigrants*, 83.

23. Elizabeth Ogg, *Longshoremen and Their Homes: The Story of a Housing "Case" Study Conducted under the Auspices of Greenwich House* (New York: Greenwich House, 1939), 28–29. The other settlement houses near the Irish waterfront were John Lovejoy Elliott's Hudson Guild (1895) in Chelsea and Hartley House (1897) in Hell's Kitchen, the neighborhood treated by the sociologist Elsa G. Herzfeld in *Family Monographs: The History of Twenty-four Families Living in the Middle West Side of New York City* (New York: J. Kempster Printing, 1905). Hell's Kitchen (known to social reformers as the "Middle West Side") was the most heavily studied waterfront community in works of this tradition; see the series of "West Side Studies" prepared under the direction of Pauline Goldmark for the Bureau of Social Research of the New York School of Philanthropy, published by Survey Associates in 1914; Marion R. Casey, "'From the East Side to the Seaside': Irish Americans on the Move in New York City," in Bayor and Meagher, *The New York Irish*, 399.

24. Mark Jacobson, "What Makes Budd Run?" *New York Magazine*, August 19, 2002, 30. My argument that the Irish waterfront was configured as akin to sacred space represents in part an attempt to extend the analysis presented in the definitive work by John T. McGreevy, *Parish Boundaries: The Catholic Encounter with Race in the Twentieth-Century Urban North* (Chicago: University of Chicago Press, 1996).

25. Winslow, "'Men of the Lumber Camps Come to Town,'" 63.

26. Butler and Driscoll, *Dock Walloper*, 211.

27. Ibid., 211–15; Charles P. Larrowe, *Shape-Up and Hiring Hall: A Comparison of Hiring Methods and Labor Relations on the New York and Seattle Waterfronts* (Berkeley: University of California Press, 1955), 11–14; cf. Winslow, "On the Waterfront," 355–56, 383.

28. Author interview with Robert Greene, January 15, 2004; Winslow, "'Men of the Lumber Camps Come to Town,'" 65. For an account of the shapeup in pre–World War I Hoboken, see U.S. Commission on Industrial Relations, *Final Report and Testimony Submitted to Congress by the Commission on Industrial Relations*, vol. 3 (Washington, D.C., 1916), 2116–17.

29. *St. Francis Church, Hoboken, New Jersey* (Tappan, N.Y.: Custombook, 1988).

30. McFarland, *Inside Greenwich Village: A New York City Neighborhood, 1898–1918* (Amherst: University of Massachusetts Press, 2001), 25–36; Howard B. Furer, "'Heaven, Hell, or Hoboken': The Effects of World War I on a New Jersey City," *New Jersey History* 92 (1974): 147–69. A few of the many biographies of Hoboken's native son Frank Sinatra treat the interactions of the city's Italians and Irish Americans with anecdotal flair; see Kitty Kelly, *His Way: An Unauthorized Biography of Frank Sinatra* (New York: Bantam Books, 1986), 8–12, 13–22; Anthony Summers and Robbyn Swan, *Sinatra: The Life* (New York: Alfred A. Knopf, 2005), 11–25.

31. Winslow, "On the Waterfront," 370, 373, 381.
32. Bell, "The Racket-Ridden Longshoremen," 174.

2. The Boss

1. William Lemmey, "Bossism in Jersey City: The Kenny Years, 1949–1972" (PhD diss., City University of New York, 1979), 48. There is as I write no definitive biography of Hague, nor, most likely, will one be forthcoming. The smoke wafting out of City Hall's windows from trashcan fires the night in May 1949 when Hague's regime ended consumed much of the sparse documentary evidence that was not kept strictly under the Boss's hat. Insightful sources on Hague and Jersey City include Richard J. Connors, *A Cycle of Power: The Career of Jersey City Mayor Frank Hague* (Metuchen, N.J.: Scarecrow Press, 1971); Dayton David McKean, *The Boss: The Hague Machine in Action* (Boston: Houghton Mifflin, 1940); Dermot Quinn, *The Irish in New Jersey: Four Centuries of American Life* (New Brunswick: Rutgers University Press, 2004), 151–67; Thomas F. X. Smith, *The Powerticians* (Secaucus, N.J.: Lyle Stuart, 1982); Helene Stapinski, *Five-Finger Discount: A Crooked Family History* (New York: Random House, 2001). The value of the Smith and Stapinski works is only heightened by an impressionistic quality that wonderfully captures the spirit of Hudson County's political culture. *The Powerticians* contains no index or list of sources, but the author—Jersey City's mayor in the late 1970s and early 1980s—does thank by name nearly everyone who ever supported his campaigns.

2. For the heated rivalry between Manhattan and Hudson County over port commerce, see Joan Doherty Lovero, *Hudson County: The Left Bank* (Sun Valley, Calif.: American Historical Press, 1999), 24–29, 64–77; for the freight tunnel that was never built, see James Glanz and Eric Lipton, *City in the Sky: The Rise and Fall of the World Trade Center* (New York: Times Books, 2003), 47–48; see also chapter 4, "The Longshoreman's Grandson."

3. Walt Whitman is quoted in Angus Kress Gillespie, *Twin Towers: The Life of New York City's World Trade Center* (New Brunswick: Rutgers University Press, 1999), 21.

4. Jill Jonnes, *Conquering Gotham: A Gilded Age Epic: The Construction of Penn Station and Its Tunnels* (New York: Viking, 2007), 13.

5. Craig Thompson and Allen Raymond, *Gang Rule in New York: The Story of a Lawless Era* (New York: Dial Press, 1940), 31.

6. Daniel Bell, "The Racket-Ridden Longshoremen: The Web of Economics and Politics," in *The End of Ideology: On the Exhaustion of Political Ideas in the Fifties* (Glencoe, Ill.: Free Press, 1960), 178; Kevin Lynch, *The Image of the City* (Cambridge: Technology Press and Harvard University Press, 1960), 26.

7. Douglas V. Shaw, *The Making of an Immigrant City: Ethnic and Cultural Conflict in Jersey City, New Jersey, 1850–1877* (New York: Arno Press, 1976), 10–11, 81–82.

8. McKean, *The Boss*, 28; cf. Smith, *The Powerticians*, 35.

9. Lemmey, "Bossism in Jersey City," 25; Father LeRoy McWilliams with Jim Bishop, *Parish Priest* (New York: McGraw-Hill, 1953), 57. For the advent of the commission system in Jersey City, see Steven Hart, *The Last Three Miles: Politics, Murder, and the Construction of America's First Superhighway* (New York: New Press, 2007), 44–45.

10. Barbara Burns Petrick, *Church and School in the Immigrant City: A Social History of Public Education in Jersey City, 1804–1930* (Metuchen, N.J.: Scarecrow Press, 2000), 223, 229; Connors, *A Cycle of Power*, 56, 85–86.

11. McKean, *The Boss*, 41–43; Smith, *The Powerticians*, 48–51; Petrick, *Church and School in the Immigrant City*, 209–13, 228–30.

12. Bob Leach, *The Frank Hague Picture Book* (Jersey City: Jersey City Historical Project, 1998), vii, 30; "Money Mad," *Newsweek*, July 16, 1962, 25–26.

13. Thomas J. Fleming, "I Am the Law," *American Heritage* 20 (June 1969): 40; Smith, *The Powerticians*, 98; Stapinski, *Five-Finger Discount*, 91; Hugh McLeod, "Catholicism and the New York Irish, 1880–1910," in *Disciplines of Faith: Studies in Religion, Politics and Patriarchy*, ed. Jim Obelkevich, Lyndal Roper, and Raphael Samuel (London: Routledge

and Kegan Paul, 1987), 337–50; Connors, *A Cycle of Power,* 90–91; Quinn, *The Irish in New Jersey,* 157; J. Owen Grundy, "Jersey City Politics: A Letter to Professor [Richard] Connors on Hague and His Times," February 17, 1965, copy in New York Public Library, Humanities–General Research Division, 11.

14. William O'Dwyer, *Beyond the Golden Door,* ed. Paul O'Dwyer (Jamaica, N.Y.: St. John's University, 1986), 312; Connors, *A Cycle of Power,* 89–92; for Archbishop Walsh, see Reverend Christopher Ciccarino, *Seeds of Faith, Branches of Hope: The Archdiocese of Newark, New Jersey* (Strasbourg: Éditions du Signe, 2003), 71–110.

15. Connors, *A Cycle of Power,* 89–92; author interview with Thomas Fleming, May 26, 2009; Lemmey, "Bossism in Jersey City," 26.

16. *Newark Star-Ledger,* November 11, 1999.

17. Fleming, "I Am the Law," 36–37; see also Thomas Fleming, *Mysteries of My Father: An Irish-American Memoir* (Hoboken: Wiley, 2005), a work that poignantly illustrates how the "political organization was a churning mix of ambition and resentments and inertia over which leaders presided only by constant effort" (195); Smith, *The Powerticians,* 156; Stapinski, *Five-Finger Discount,* 66–70; Grundy, "Jersey City Politics," 9.

18. *Newark Star-Ledger,* June 11, 2006.

19. Bell, "Racket-Ridden Longshoremen," 173; Charles P. Larrowe, *Shape-Up and Hiring Hall: A Comparison of Hiring Methods and Labor Relations on the New York and Seattle Waterfronts* (Berkeley: University of California Press, 1955), 14; Fleming, "I Am the Law," 38; Hart, *The Last Three Miles,* 84–95; Thomas Fleming, *New Jersey: A Bicentennial History* (New York: W. W. Norton, 1977), 185.

20. Smith, *The Powerticians,* 170–71.

21. Ibid., 121.

22. Ibid., 61.

23. Matthew Josephson, "Red Skies over the Waterfront," *Collier's,* October 5, 1946, 88; Bruce Nelson, *Divided We Stand: American Workers and the Struggle for Black Equality* (Princeton: Princeton University Press, 2001), 57; Maurice Rosenblatt, "Joe Ryan and His Kingdom," *Nation* 161 (November 24, 1945): 548; Meyer Berger, "Boss of the Dockwallopers," *New York Times Sunday Magazine,* May 14, 1944, 18.

24. For a good, brief treatment of subsidiarity, see Jean Bethke Elshtain, "Catholic Social Thought, the City, and Liberal America," in *Catholicism, Liberalism, and Communitarianism: The Catholic Intellectual Tradition and the Moral Foundations of Democracy,* ed. Kenneth L. Grasso, Gerard V. Bradley, and Robert P. Hunt (Lanham, Md.: Rowman and Littlefield, 1995), 97–114; Josephson, "Red Skies over the Waterfront," 88.

25. Author interview with Robert Greene, January 15, 2004.

26. For Hague's ethnic brokerage practices, see Joseph A. Varacalli, "Ethnic Politics in Jersey City: The Changing Nature of Irish-Italian Relations, 1917–1981," in *Italians and Irish in America: Proceedings of the Sixteenth American Conference of the American Italian Historical Association,* ed. Francis X. Feminella (Staten Island, N.Y.: American Italian Historical Association, 1985), 199–224; see also Smith, *The Powerticians,* 71, 183, and Connors, *A Cycle of Power,* 81, 95–98; testimony of James F. Keane, December 16, 1952, *Public Hearings (No. 5) Conducted by the New York State Crime Commission Pursuant to the Governor's Executive Orders of March 29, 1951, and November 13, 1952,* vol. 2 (New York, 1953), 1028–30 (hereafter cited as *NYSCC Hearings* with volume and page); Allen Raymond, *Waterfront Priest* (New York: Holt, 1955), 130–31.

27. Lemmey, "Bossism in Jersey City," 99–102.

28. Ibid.

29. Ibid., 104–5; Bell, "The Racket-Ridden Longshoremen," 178; for the sources of "rice pudding day," see Hart, *The Last Three Miles,* 75–76; for Hague's management of gambling franchises in Jersey City, see Daniel Bell, "Crime as an American Way of Life," in *The End of Ideology,* 130; Grundy, "Jersey City Politics," 11; Smith, *The Powerticians,* 15.

30. Leach, *The Frank Hague Picture Book,* 78; author interview with Robert Greene, January 15, 2004. Greene's columns and reporting for the *Jersey Journal* between 1949 and 1951 and the interviews he subsequently conducted on behalf of the New York City Anti-Crime

Commission are invaluable sources for study of the Hudson County waterfront. Extremely detailed if contradictory (and self-contradictory) material on Hague, Kenny, and the Jersey City piers is found in the five-volume *NYSCC Hearings*—for Jersey City, see especially vols. 1, 2, and 4; information on Connie and Edward Noonan is from the testimony of Daniel Gentile, January 23, 1953, 2484–85, and Cornelius J. Noonan, January 23, 1953, 2514–2607, *NYSCC Hearings*, vol. 4. Another very rich source of Hudson County testimony is *Waterfront Investigation: Hearings before a Subcommittee of the Committee on Interstate and Foreign Commerce, United States Senate, pt. 1, New York–New Jersey Waterfront* (Washington, D.C., 1953); Bell, "The Racket-Ridden Longshoremen," 168.

31. Malcolm Johnson, *Crime on the Labor Front* (New York: McGraw-Hill, 1950), 117–32, 165–83; Bell, "Racket-Ridden Longshoremen," 166–70; Thompson and Raymond, *Gang Rule in New York,* 219; Daniel Gentile testimony, *NYSCC Hearings,* 4:2484–85.

32. "Calif of Bagdad (Jersey City)," *Literary Digest,* May 22, 1937, 3.

3. Becoming Mr. Big

1. See *New York Times* obituary for William J. McCormack, July 13, 1965; Allen Raymond, *Waterfront Priest* (New York: Holt, 1955), 38–40; *New York Daily News,* January 20, 1952. McCormack's baptismal record was located by Harold Blake, St. Veronica's parish manager; telephone interview with Harold Blake, February 5, 2007. Raymond wrote in 1955, "McCormack admits today to 64 years of age and might be even five or six years older than that" (*Waterfront Priest,* 38). In testimony before the New York State Crime Commission on April 3, 1952, witness Robert Burker, after giving his own date of birth as May 30, 1885, reported of McCormack, "We were born and brought up in the same neighborhood, and we went to school together"; *NYSCC Hearings,* 2:1094–96. In box 10, folder 13, XIIR, there is a detailed typescript report on Bill McCormack of unknown origin. The typescript cites articles from *Collier's Weekly* by Lester Velie but includes additional information not found in published accounts. The factual tone of the report is consistent with materials compiled by John M. Corridan, S.J., but it is impossible to verify the authorship of the report. For St. Veronica's school, see Thomas J. Shelley, *Greenwich Village Catholics: St. Joseph's Church and the Evolution of an Urban Faith Community, 1829–2002* (Washington, D.C.: Catholic University of America Press, 2003), 108.

2. Lester Velie, "A Waterfront Priest Battles the Big Port's BIG BOSS," *Collier's Weekly,* February 16, 1952, 18; report on conversation with Inspector Michael Cusack, Jersey City Police Department, n.d., box 10, folder 26, XIIR; report on conversation with Charles Gordon Maphet (alias "Cal McCarthy"), box 10, folder 26, XIIR. The *Jersey City–Hoboken Directory* for 1915 places Andrew, William, and Harry McCormack at 37 Van Reipen Street and identifies William and Harry as truckers. The 1918 *Directory* lists Andrew and William at that address but not Harry. By 1922 there was no Jersey City listing for the trucking McCormacks, relocated by then to the West Side of Manhattan.

3. Report on conversation with Charles Gordon Maphet; cf. report on conversation with Inspector Michael Cusack. Another version of this story appears in Velie, "A Waterfront Priest Battles the Big Port's BIG BOSS," 18.

4. *New York Daily News,* January 20, 1952; Raymond, *Waterfront Priest,* 39.

5. Report on conversation with James "Happy" Keane, box 11, folder 4, XIIR; report on conversation with Charles Gordon Maphet; Report on Conversation with Inspector Michael Cusack. In his January 23, 1953, testimony Noonan acknowledged having known Bill McCormack for "at least" fifteen years, answering in such a way as to suggest that it might have been considerably longer. In a private session with investigators on August 4, 1952, Noonan volunteered the same information but denied having had any business dealings with McCormack (*NYSCC Hearings,* 4:2589–90). In his testimony of January 30, 1953, McCormack would concede only: "I think I met Connie Noonan at the fights....[H]e sat a couple of rows from us" (5:3603).

6. Unpublished typescript, n.d., box 10, folder 13, XIIR; report of conversation by Bob Greene with George Geier, former delegate Local 641 Teamsters, n.d., box 10, folder 26, XIIR.

7. Velie, "A Waterfront Priest," 19; Herbert Asbury, *The Gangs of New York: An Informal History of the Underworld* (New York: Alfred A. Knopf, 1927), 322–29; Luc Sante, *Low Life: Lures and Snares of Old New York* (New York: Vintage Books, 1991), 234.

8. For Owney Madden, see T. J. English, *Paddy Whacked: The Untold Story of the Irish American Gangster* (New York: HarperCollins, 2005), 113–25; Allan May, "Gophers, Goose Chasers, and the Early Years of Owney Madden," http://www.americanmafia.com/Allan_May_1-3-00.html.

9. Report of conversation by Bob Greene with Captain John J. Kuehns, September 14, 1951, box 10, folder 26, XIIR; Velie, "A Waterfront Priest," 19. Tanner Smith and Bill McCormack were described as "competitors" in the *New York Times,* November 19, 1953. A typescript biographical report on William J. McCormack in box 10, folder 13, XIIR, also indicated that Rubber Shaw and Linky Mitchell had previously killed Dennis "Mickish" Keating, described by Herbert Asbury in *The Gangs of New York* (324) as "an honest horseshoer" who owned the house where Tanner Smith and Owney Madden established the Winona Club, site of Smith's murder; for another version of these events, see "Transcript of an Interview with a Longshoreman," n.d., 6–9, box 11, folder 4, XIIR; for coverage of the Smith-Shaw murders, see *New York Times,* August 2 and 5, 1919, November 5, 1920. Rubber Shaw's (or "Shore's") alleged accomplice George Lewis was wounded by Shaw's assailants; he was later convicted for his role in the killing of Tanner Smith and sentenced to three years in prison.

10. Velie, "A Waterfront Priest," 19; unpublished typescript, n.d., box 10, folder 13, XIIR; *New York Times,* May 24, 1928, July 4, 1929; Asbury, *Gangs of New York,* 323; Selwyn Raab, *Five Families: The Rise, Decline, and Resurgence of America's Most Powerful Mafia Empires* (New York: St. Martin's Press, 2005), 41; English, *Paddy Whacked,* 120–21.

11. Lester Velie, "Big Boss of the Big Port," *Collier's Weekly,* February 9, 1952, 19; for Madden's Hot Springs period, see Shirley Abbot, *The Bookmaker's Daughter: A Memory Unbound* (New York: Ticknor & Fields, 1991), 14–15, 111–12. William Vincent "Big Bill" Dwyer ran the largest bootlegging operation in the United States. After Madden and his band of pirates hijacked some of his trucks, Dwyer was so impressed he brought "Owney the Killer" in as partner; see Craig Thompson and Allen Raymond, *Gang Rule in New York: The Story of a Lawless Era* (New York: Dial Press, 1940), 80–99; Virgil W. Peterson, *The Mob: Two Hundred Years of Organized Crime in New York* (Ottawa, Ill.: Green Hill, 1983), 185–86.

12. English, *Paddy Whacked,* 252; for Smith's stint at U.S. Trucking, see Matthew and Hannah Josephson, *Al Smith: Hero of the Cities; A Political Portrait Drawing on the Papers of Frances Perkins* (Boston: Houghton Mifflin, 1969), 261–63.

13. Velie, "A Waterfront Priest," 56; *New York Times,* June 30, 1933, cited the presence of McCormack and Hague among numerous political and sporting figures at the Primo Carnera–Jack Sharkey heavyweight championship bout at the Long Island City Bowl.

14. The *New York Times* reported on January 28, 1923, that "Irish" Johnny Curtin of Jersey City was training for his next fight at "Harry McCormack's estate at Fairhaven"; Raymond, *Waterfront Priest,* 39–40; for McCormack and the license committee, see *New York Times,* October 27, November 10, December 21 and 31, 1923, January 31, 1924; for Tunney and the McCormacks, see report on conversation with Cusack and with Maphet; for Tunney and Madden, see Peter Benson, *Battling Siki: A Tale of Ring Fixes, Race, and Murder in the 1920s* (Fayetteville: University of Arkansas Press, 2006), 58–59; for the Walker Act, see Roger Kahn, *A Flame of Pure Fire: Jack Dempsey and the Roaring '20s* (San Diego: Harvest Books, 1999), 202–4; and Jack Cavanaugh, *Tunney: Boxing's Brainiest Champ and His Upset of the Great Jack Dempsey* (New York: Random House, 2006), 74–77.

15. George Walsh, *Gentleman Jimmy Walker: Mayor of the Jazz Age* (New York: Praeger, 1974), 33–34. The circumstances of McCormack's resignation from the Boxing Commission are treated in Chapter 12, "A Season for Testimony."

16. Dayton David McKean, *The Boss: The Hague Machine in Action* (Boston: Houghton Mifflin, 1940), 92–93; Thomas J. Fleming, "I Am the Law," *American Heritage* 20 (June 1969): 42; Sutherland Denlinger, "Boss Hague," *Forum* (March 1938): 136. Political scientist Steven P. Erie,

in an influential study, *Rainbow's End: Irish-Americans and the Dilemmas of Urban Machine Politics, 1840–1985* (Berkeley: University of California Press, 1988), argued that Hague's regime suffered "retrenchment" in the depression years, albeit more gradually and less destructively than Tammany. At the same time, Erie acknowledges that Hague's gravest challenge would result from his having "sown the seeds of ethnic insurgency" (115), a theme I treated in detail in chapter 9, "Meeting across the River."

17. McKean, *The Boss*, 92; Raymond, *Waterfront Priest*, 40; Velie, "A Waterfront Priest," 56; author interview with Bishop William J. McCormack, May 10, 2002.

18. "Transcript of an Interview with a Longshoreman," 8.

19. Velie, "A Waterfront Priest," 56; Raymond, *Waterfront Priest*, 41.

20. Bishop William J. McCormack interview; Testimony of Richard J. Malone, December 16, 1952, *NYSCC Hearings*, 2:1072.

21. Testimony of William J. McCormack, January 30, 1953, *NYSCC Hearings*, 5:3598; *New York Times*, July 13, 1965.

22. Bruce Nelson, *Divided We Stand: American Workers and the Struggle for Black Equality* (Princeton: Princeton University Press, 2001), 55; John Corcoran, quoted in Jeff Kisseloff, *You Must Remember This: An Oral History of Manhattan from the 1890s to World War II* (Baltimore: Johns Hopkins University Press, 1999), 524–25.

23. Velie, "Big Boss of the Big Port," 39; Daniel Bell, "The Racket-Ridden Longshoremen: The Web of Economics and Politics," in *The End of Ideology: On the Exhaustion of Political Ideas in the Fifties* (Glencoe, Ill.: Free Press, 1960)," 176; John Bainbridge, *The Wonderful World of Toots Shor* (Boston: Houghton Mifflin, 1951), 24, 94.

24. *New York Times*, July 13, 1965.

25. Interview with Bishop William J. McCormack.

26. Robert A. Caro, *The Power Broker: Robert Moses and the Fall of New York* (New York: Vintage Books, 1975), 688, 722–27, 741; Velie, "Big Boss of the Big Port," 38.

27. Peterson, *The Mob*, 282–83; Raymond, *Waterfront Priest*, 43. Programs with seating charts and committee assignments for the Joseph P. Ryan Association's annual dinners, beginning with 1936, are in box 26, folder 14, XIIR.

28. William J. Keating (with Richard Carter), *The Man Who Rocked the Boat* (New York: Harper and Brothers, 1956), 94; testimony of William J. McCormack, January 29, 1953, *NYSCC Hearings*, 5:3559; report on conversation with Maphet, Keane, and Cusack.

29. Joe Ryan's second in command, Packy Connolly, replied to a waterfront investigator's query in 1951: "William McCormack?...[H]e is just a good friend of Joe Ryan's that's all. I understand he's a very respectable businessman." Report on Conversation with Patrick "Packy" Connolly, box 11, folder 4, XIIR; Charles P. Larrowe, *Shape-Up and Hiring Hall: A Comparison of Hiring Methods and Labor Relations on the New York and Seattle Waterfronts* (Berkeley: University of California Press, 1955), 17; cf. Nelson, *Divided We Stand*, 57; Keating, *The Man who Rocked the Boat*, 89.

30. Nelson, *Divided We Stand*, 58; English, *Paddy Whacked*, 192.

31. English, *Paddy Whacked*, 232.

4. The Longshoreman's Grandson

1. "The Maritime Unions," *Fortune* (September, 1937): 137; "Dock Armistice," *Business Week* (October 27, 1945): 106; Felice Swados, "Waterfront," *New Republic* 94 (February 2, 1938): 362.

2. E. T. Buehrer, "Jersey's Little Hitler," *Christian Century* 55 (June 29, 1938): 810; "Mayor Hague's Long Shadow," *New Republic* 95 (June 15, 1938): 143–44; Willard Wiener, "Hague Is the Law," *New Republic* (January 31, 1944): 143; McAlister Coleman, "Hague's Army Falls Back," *The Nation* (November 26, 1938): 559.

3. Joan Doherty Lovero, *Hudson County: The Left Bank* (Sun Valley, Calif.: American Historical Press, 1999), 99.

4. McCormack grudgingly retraced some of the outlines of his partnerships in his NYSCC testimony of January 30, 1953 (*NYSCC Hearings*, 5:3539–44). William Kornblum, *At Sea in*

the City: New York from the Water's Edge (Chapel Hill: Algonquin Books), 143–50, describes his stint as a laborer at Transit-Mix Concrete's East River facility, where elaborate preparations were daily made for the arrival of Bill McCormack in his "elegant motor yacht."

5. Allen Raymond, *Waterfront Priest* (New York: Holt, 1955), 39–40; Daniel Bell, "The Racket-Ridden Longshoremen: The Web of Economics and Politics," in *The End of Ideology: On the Exhaustion of Political Ideas in the Fifties* (Glencoe, Ill.: Free Press, 1960)," 176–77.

6. Lester Velie, "Big Boss of the Big Port," *Collier's Weekly,* February 9, 1952, 19; Leslie Braginsky interview with Philip A. Carey, S.J., November 11, 1988, courtesy of Thomas Lilly.

7. James Glanz and Eric Lipton, *City in the Sky: The Rise and Fall of the World Trade Center* (New York: Times Books, 2003), 43.

8. Lovero, *Hudson County,* 24–25, 26–29; Brian J. Cudahy, *Box Boats: How Container Ships Changed the World* (New York: Fordham University Press, 2006), 53; Angus Kress Gillespie, *Twin Towers: The Life of New York City's World Trade Center* (New Brunswick, N.J.: Rutgers University Press, 1999), 21.

9. Lovero, *Hudson County,* 28–29; Jameson W. Doig, *Empire on the Hudson: Entrepreneurial Vision and Political Power at the Port of New York Authority* (New York: Columbia University Press, 2001), 32–46.

10. Lovero, *Hudson County,* 74–76; Doig, *Empire on the Hudson,* 35–46; Thomas E. Rush, *The Port of New York* (Garden City, N.Y.: Doubleday, Page & Co., 1920), 207–11.

11. Frederick L. Bird, *A Study of the Port of New York Authority* (New York: Dun & Bradstreet, 1949), 7–14; James W. Hughes, "Realtors, Bankers, and Politicians in the New York–New Jersey Port Authority," *Society* 11 (May–June 1974): 63–64; Erwin Wilkie Bard, *The Port of New York Authority* (New York: Columbia University Press, 1942), 27–34; Doig, *Empire on the Hudson,* 3, 69, 143–57, 169–71.

12. Doig, *Empire on the Hudson,* 54.

13. Ibid., 54–73; Cudahy, *Box Boats,* 55.

14. Doig, *Empire on the Hudson,* 78.

15. Ibid., 73, 78; Glanz and Lipton, *City in the Sky,* 47–48.

16. Gillespie, *Twin Towers,* 25–30.

17. Doig, *Empire on the Hudson,* 17–18, 94–96.

18. Ibid., 17–18, 194–97; Gillespie, *Twin Towers,* 30–31.

19. Doig, *Empire on the Hudson,* 195–96; Glanz and Lipton, *City in the Sky,* 41–43.

20. Doig, *Empire on the Hudson,* 286–87.

21. Ibid., 195; Gillespie, *Twin Towers,* 31.

22. O'Dwyer astutely outflanked Moses on the airports deal while winning concessions that enabled him later to claim, implausibly, "a triumph over the arrogance and tremendous power of the Port Authority." See William O'Dwyer, *Beyond the Golden Door,* ed. Paul O'Dwyer (Jamaica, N.Y.: St. John's University Press, 1987), 242–45; for Moses and O'Dwyer, see Robert A. Caro, *The Power Broker: Robert Moses and the Fall of New York* (New York: Vintage Books, 1975), 765–71; for Tobin and Moses, see Caro, *The Power Broker,* 920–30; for Doig's very different appraisal of the contestation between the two, see *Empire on the Hudson,* 326–31.

23. For Port Newark, see Cudahy, *Box Boats,* 47–53; Michael N. Danielson and Jameson W. Doig, *New York: The Politics of Urban Regional Development* (Berkeley: University of California Press, 1982), 328–30; Doig, *Empire on the Hudson,* 353–54; for a good example of the detailed studies that bolstered Port Authority marine terminal acquisition proposals, see Port of New York Authority, *Marine Terminal Study of the New Jersey Waterfront* (New York: Port of New York Authority, 1949); for O'Dwyer's "invitation" to the Port Authority, see *New York Times,* October 21, 1947; Bell, "The Racket-Ridden Longshoremen," 177–78; Marc Levinson, *The Box: How the Shipping Container Made the World Smaller and the World Economy Bigger* (Princeton: Princeton University Press, 2006, 83–85; for O'Dwyer's turn against the Port Authority proposal and the Board of Estimate's rejection, see *New York Times,* July 20 and September 24, 1948; Joshua B. Freeman, *Working-Class New York: Life and Labor since World War II* (New York: New Press, 2000), 161.

24. *New York Times,* August 20 and 22, 1948. Publicist Robin Harris referred to McCormack as "the Little Man's Port Authority" in the *New York Daily News,* January 20, 1952; the context suggests that the term had been in circulation for some time.

25. Glanz and Lipton, *City in the Sky,* 42–43; Gillespie, *Twin Towers,* 36; "The Super-Agency That Moves a Metropolis," *Business Week,* May 11, 1968, 78.

26. For Bill's O'Dwyer's richly enigmatic story, see O'Dwyer, *Beyond the Golden Door.* The "somewhat unconventional form" of this work, "neither a biography nor an autobiography," as his brother and editor Paul O'Dwyer notes, "but rather a combination of the two," resulted from Bill O'Dwyer's great reluctance to commit his recollections to paper, in the grand tradition of the Irish waterfront. Paul, his youngest brother and a well-known human rights activist and New York City political gadfly, compiled material from Bill's papers and added his own to sections of the manuscript, which—though set apart by his initials—are likely not a full measure of his authorial role. For Bill O'Dwyer's early life and character, see also George Walsh, *Public Enemies: The Mayor, the Mob, and the Crime That Was* (New York: W. W. Norton, 1980), 35–40.

27. For O'Dwyer's political gifts and challenges, see Warren Moscow, *The Last of the Big-Time Bosses: The Life and Times of Carmine De Sapio and the Rise and Fall of Tammany Hall* (New York: Stein and Day, 1971), 62; Virgil W. Peterson, *The Mob: Two Hundred Years of Organized Crime in New York* (Ottawa, Ill.: Green Hill, 1983), 224–26; Chris McNickle, *To Be Mayor of New York: Ethnic Politics in the City* (New York: Columbia University Press, 1993), 50–51, 54–55, 68, 72. For O'Dwyer and Costello, see William Howard Moore, *The Kefauver Committee and the Politics of Crime: 1950–1952* (Columbia: University of Missouri Press, 1974), 175.

28. For "Kid Twist" Reles, see Walsh, *Public Enemies,* 92–99; Selwyn Raab, *Five Families: The Rise, Decline, and Resurgence of America's Most Powerful Mafia Empires* (New York: St. Martin's Press, 2005), 71–73; Peterson, *The Mob,* 227–32.

29. Moore, *The Kefauver Committee,* 175; Sid Feder and Burton B. Turkus, *Murder, Inc.: The Story of "the Syndicate"* (Garden City, N.Y.: Doubleday, 1952), 498–500.

30. *New York Times,* February 4 and 12, 1946; *World-Telegram* quoted in Freeman, *Working-Class New York,* 5–6; Daniel Bell, "Last of the Business Rackets," *Fortune* (June 1951): 203; see *New York Times,* December 25, 1948, for McCormack's appointment as tugboat czar.

31. *New York Times,* December 28, 1948, January 7, 12, and 15, 1949.

32. *New York Times,* May 1, 1950, March 21, 1952; Glanz and Lipton, *City in the Sky,* 49–50; Freeman, *Working-Class New York,* 161–62; Danielson and Doig, *New York,* 330–31.

33. Doig, *Empire on the Hudson,* 324, 354; McNickle, *To Be Mayor of New York,* 58, 63; Peterson, *The Mob,* 224–25; Moscow, *The Last of the Big-Time Bosses,* 58; Walsh, *Public Enemies,* 152.

34. Philip Carey's, résumé is in box 1, folder 6, XIIR.

35. *Staten Island Advance,* February 9, 1986, newspaper clipping in box 1, folder 15, XIIR.

5. A Labor Priest in the Catholic Metropolis

1. Debra Bernhardt interview with Philip Carey, S.J., February 19, 1981, New Yorkers at Work Oral History Series, Wagner Labor Archives, Tamiment Library, New York University. A similar version of Carey's depression narrative is quoted in Edward F. Boyle, S.J., "At Work in the Vineyard: The Jesuit Labor Apostolate," *In All Things* 1 (March 2000): 1.

2. Bernhardt interview; Carey's obituary is in the *New York Times,* May 29, 1989.

3. *Xavier: Reflections on 150 Years* (New York: Minert Associates, 1997); Christa Ressmeyer Klein, "The Jesuits and Catholic Boyhood in Nineteenth-Century New York City: A Study of St. John's College and the College of St. Francis Xavier, 1846–1912 (PhD diss., University of Pennsylvania, 1976), 69–72, 342–45; Pete Sheehan, "Jesuit Labor Priest Recalls Decades of Working for Workers," *Long Island Catholic,* February 23, 1989.

4. Klein, "The Jesuits and Catholic Boyhood."

5. Joseph Fitzpatrick, S.J., homily delivered at St. Patrick's Cathedral, February 7, 1960, box 12, folder 23, XIIR.

6. *Xavier,* 127.

7. John LaFarge, S.J., *A Report on the American Jesuits* (New York: Farrar, Straus, and Cudahy, 1956), 153; Ledochowski is quoted in Peter McDonough, *Men Astutely Trained: A History of the Jesuits in the American Century* (New York: Free Press, 1992), 68.

8. Joseph A. Murphy, S.J., to J. Tracy Langan, S.J., November 2, 1935, folder 2, Xavier Labor School Collection, Society of Jesus New York Province Archives (hereafter ANYP); for John LaFarge and Jesuit social ministries, see David W. Southern, *John LaFarge and the Limits of Catholic Interracialism, 1911–1963* (Baton Rouge: Louisiana State University Press, 1996), 146, 214–18, and John T. McGreevy, *Parish Boundaries: The Catholic Encounter with Race in the Twentieth-Century Urban North* (Chicago: University of Chicago Press, 1996), 38–53; Francis A. O'Malley, S.J., to Patrick Cardinal Hayes, January 20, 1936, box 12, folder 5, XIIR; for the New York archdiocese's approval of the school, see Monsignor J. Francis McIntyre to Francis A. O'Malley, January 27, 1936, boxes 12, folder 5, XIIR.

9. Boyle, "At Work in the Vineyard," 3–4; John C. Cort, *Dreadful Conversions: The Making of a Catholic Socialist* (New York: Fordham University Press, 2003), 76–82. For a frequently unreliable account of the ACTU, see Douglas P. Seaton, *Catholics and Radicals: The Association of Catholic Trade Unionists and the American Labor Movement, from Depression to Cold War* (Lewisburg, Pa.: Bucknell University Press, 1981). Seaton conflates the schools of the ACTU with Jesuit labor schools. For a highly critical review of this book by a founding veteran of the ACTU, see John C. Cort, "Through Rose-Tinted Glasses," *Commonweal* 110 (August 12, 1983): 439, 442–46. Cort's broadside launched a meaningful discourse on the relationship between Catholic radicalism, the labor movement, and the secular Left in the age of the CIO, a rich set of issues yet to be treated in full.

10. Boyle, "At Work in the Vineyard," 4; McDonough, *Men Astutely Trained,* 98; Joseph M. McShane, S.J., "'The Church Is Not for the Cells and the Caves': The Working-Class Spirituality of the Jesuit Labor Priests," *U.S. Catholic Historian* 9 (Summer 1990): 300; Philip Carey, "Catholic Labor School," undated manuscript, folder 14, Xavier Labor School Collection, ANYP.

11. Philip E. Dobson, S.J., "The Xavier Labor School, 1938–1939," *The Woodstock Letters* 68 (1939): 266.

12. Joseph P. Fitzpatrick, S.J., Homily at Funeral Mass for Philip A. Carey, S.J., May 31, 1989, Church of Saint Francis Xavier, New York City, courtesy Mike Miskell; interview with Owen Daley, S.J., April 22, 2003. Although Fitzpatrick dated the encounter to May 1940, the most recent longshoremen's strike in the port had occurred the previous November, and waterfront job actions were rare at the time. In any case, even if the date is uncertain, the point of Fitzpatrick's recollection is unmistakably clear.

13. Steve Rosswurm, "The Catholic Church and Left-Led Unions: Labor Priests, Labor Schools, and the ACTU," in *The CIO'S Left-Led Unions,* ed. Steve Rosswurm (New Brunswick, N.J.: Rutgers University Press, 1992), 122; "Dan's Notes on the Family," manuscript in box 1, folder 1, XIIR; *Irish Echo,* September 1, 1984.

14. Bernhardt interview.

15. Ibid.; for the 1916 transit strike, see Joshua B. Freeman, *In Transit: The Transport Workers Union in New York City, 1933–1966* (New York: Oxford University Press, 1989), 16–17; Jeff Kisseloff, *You Must Remember This: An Oral History of Manhattan from the 1890s to World War II* (Baltimore: Johns Hopkins University Press, 1999), 492.

16. *Staten Island Advance,* February 9, 1986; Bernhardt interview; McDonough, *Men Astutely Trained,* 137.

17. Philip A. Carey, S.J., Homily Given on the Fiftieth Anniversary of Ordination, 1988, courtesy Mike Miskell; Charles R. Morris, *American Catholic: The Saints and Sinners Who Built America's Most Powerful Church* (New York: Times Books, 1997), 215; Philip Carey to Francis A. Moore, November 18, 1948, and Philip Carey to Allen Blount, December 29, 1948, box 12, folder 21, XIIR; *New York Times,* May 29, 1989.

18. Dobson, "The Xavier Labor School," 267.

19. G. Jules Weinberg, "Priests, Workers, and Communists: What Happened in a New York Transit Workers Union," *Harper's* (December 1948): 53; McDonough, *Men Astutely Trained,* 104; for the text of *Quadragesimo Anno,* see Pius XI, "On Reconstructing the Social Order," reprinted in Terence P. McLaughlin, C.S.B., *The Church and the Reconstruction of the Modern World: The Social Encyclicals of Pius XI* (Garden City, N.Y.: Doubleday, 1957), 218–78; Thomas Lynch, "Above All Things the Truth: John P. Monaghan and the Church of New York," *Dunwoodie Review* 16 (1992–93): 137.

20. *New York World-Telegram,* September 27, 1941.

21. Joseph P. Fitzpatrick, S.J., to Philip Carey, S.J., September 14, 1940, box 13, folder 13, Joseph P. Fitzpatrick Papers, Special Collections and Archives, Fordham University; Bernhardt interview; McDonough, *Men Astutely Trained,* 112–17; Philip A. Carey, S.J., journal entry, summer 1942, 43, box 1, XIIR

22. McShane, "'The Church Is Not for the Cells and the Caves,'" 289–304; Gerald Fagan, S.J., "Profile of a Worker," *Morning Star,* September 1951 (clipping from Jesuit high school newspaper, Bombay, India, box 1, folder 15, XIIR Papers).

23. Morris, *American Catholic,* 219; McDonough, *Men Astutely Trained,* 108; author interviews with Owen Daley, S.J., February 28, 2003, April 22, 2003, November 5, 2005, March 9, 2006, and with Andy Wallace, February 26, 2003; *Newsday,* July 17, 1989.

24. Ernest Poole, *The Harbor* (New York: Macmillan, 1915), 11; Dorothy Day, *The Long Loneliness* (1952; rpt., San Francisco: HarperSanFrancisco, 1997), 51.

25. Day, *The Long Loneliness,* 51; Luc Sante, *Low Life: Lures and Snares of Old New York* (New York: Vintage Books, 1991), 225; Cort, *Dreadful Conversions,* 26–28.

26. Cort, *Dreadful Conversions,* 26–29; Murray Kempton, *Part of Our Time: Some Ruins and Monuments of the Thirties* (New York: Modern Library, 1998), 120–21.

27. Cort, *Dreadful Conversions,* 28.

28. *Catholic Worker* (January 1937), 1; Cort *Dreadful Conversions,* 29.

29. Carey's humble spirituality was treated in depth in author interview with Alice Dillon Pucknat, Jackie Dillon Hill, Thomas Lilly, and Andy Wallace, February 26, 2003, and with Mike Miskell, April 11, 2003.

30. Robert I. Gannon, S.J., *The Cardinal Spellman Story* (Garden City, N.Y.: Doubleday, 1962), 258.

31. Philip Carey, S.J., journal entry, May 29, 1987, box 1, folder 5, XIIR.

32. Ibid.; *New York Times,* July 27 and August 2, 1935, August 22, 1936. Information on the firebombing of the communists' office was provided by Joe Doyle, a leading historian of the maritime industries and labor in New York.

33. Carey, journal entry, May 29, 1987; *New York Times,* July 27, 1935.

34. Kisseloff, *You Must Remember This,* 525–27.

35. *Catholic Worker* (January 1938), 1; *Catholic Worker* (June 1938), 1.

36. *Catholic Worker* (June 1938), 1.

37. Cort, *Dreadful Conversions,* 100–101.

38. Leslie Braginsky interview with Philip A. Carey, S.J., November 8, 1988, courtesy of Thomas Lilly.

39. Allen Raymond, *Waterfront Priest* (New York: Holt, 1955), 50–58.

40. Braginsky interview; Bernhardt interview; Philip Carey, S.J., journal entry, box 1, folder 1, XIIR, 51–60; Philip A. Carey, S.J., manuscript fragment, May 18, 1987, box 12, folder 4, XIIR; Raymond, *Waterfront Priest,* 50–58.

41. For Kenny's contract with the Pennsylvania Railroad, see William Lemmey, "Bossism in Jersey City: The Kenny Years, 1949–1972" (PhD diss., City University of New York, 1979), 104–5.

42. Braginsky interview; Bernhardt interview; Raymond, *Waterfront Priest,* 54.

43. Braginsky interview.

44. Bernhardt interview; Carey journal entry, January 21, 1941, 16, box 1, unnumbered folder, XIIR.

45. Maurice Rosenblatt, "Joe Ryan and His Kingdom," *The Nation* 161 (November 1945): 549–50; for the Christian Front, see Gene Fein, "For God and Country: The Christian Front in New York City, 1938–1951" (PhD diss., City University of New York, 2006).

46. Braginsky interview.

47. Freeman, *In Transit*, 55–57; Weinberg, "Priests, Workers, and Communists," 50; for the contrast between "Red Mike" Quill's relationship with the TWU's Irish Catholic rank and file and the labor politics of the Irish waterfront, see Nelson, *Divided We Stand*, 68; for the TWU school, see L. H. Whittemore, *The Man Who Ran the Subways: The Story of Mike Quill* (New York: Holt, Rhinehart and Winston), 39, 55–56.

48. Cort, *Dreadful Conversions*, 76–81; Michael Denning, *The Cultural Front: The Laboring of American Culture in the Twentieth Century* (New York: Verso, 1996), 68–72; for a representative if late-starting communist labor school, see Marvin E. Gettleman, "'No Varsity Teams': New York's Jefferson School of Social Science, 1943–1956," *Science and Society* 66 (Fall 2002): 336–55.

49. Bernhardt interview; Freeman, *In Transit*, 140; John T. Ridge, "Irish County Societies in New York, 1880–1914," in *The New York Irish*, ed. Ronald H. Bayor and Timothy J. Meagher (Baltimore: Johns Hopkins University Press, 1996), 275–300.

50. Freeman, *In Transit*, 278–81; author interview with Owen Daley, S.J., November 25, 2005.

51. Bernhardt interview; Philip A. Carey, S.J., Comments on Xavier Labor School and History, box 12, folder 26, XIIR.

52. For a sample of contemporary Jesuit views on anticommunism and the labor school tradition, see Joseph J. Fahey, "The Making of a Catholic Labor Leader," *America* 195 (August 28–September 4, 2006): 17. John F. Cronin's *Catholic Social Principles: The Social Teaching of the Catholic Church Applied to American Economic Life* (Milwaukee: Bruce Publishing Company, 1950) served Philip Carey as both a guide to the tradition of modern Catholic social thought and an exemplar of its complex character. This volume also includes valuable extended excerpts from the authoritative teachings of the church on social and economic issues. Father Cronin's long and meaningful working relationship with Nixon began when Cronin—after helping Baltimore dockworkers resist communist infiltration of their union local in the early 1940s—uncovered information suggesting that Alger Hiss of the State Department was a communist, intelligence he later shared with Nixon—then a freshman congressman—eighteen months prior to the explosive, history-making testimony of Whittaker Chambers to the same effect. See Garry Wills, *Nixon Agonistes: The Crisis of the Self-Made Man* (Boston: Houghton Mifflin, 1970), 25–30.

53. William Issel, "A Stern Struggle: Catholic Activism and San Francisco Labor, 1934–1958," in Robert W. Cherny, William Issel, and Kieran Taylor Walsh, eds., *American Labor and the Cold War: Grassroots Politics and Postwar Political Culture* (New Brunswick: Rutgers University Press, 2004), 164; William Mello, review of Robert W. Cherny, William Issel, and Kieran Taylor Walsh, eds., *American Labor and the Cold War: Grassroots Politics and Postwar Political Culture, International Labor, and Working Class History* 67 (Spring 2005): 180.

54. Bernhardt interview; author interview with Thomas Lilly, February 26, 2003.

55. Philip Carey, manuscript fragment, May 18, 1987, which appears to be part of a letter from Philip A. Carey, S.J., to Father James Gilhooley, box 12, folder 4, XIIR.

6. The Crusader

1. Author interview with Rev. John O'Brien, December 6, 2001; Peter McDermott column, *Irish Echo*, November 1–7, 2006.

2. Allen Raymond, *Waterfront Priest* (New York: Holt, 1955), 4; Patrick Kelly Corridan to author, November 12, 1998; telephone interview with Father Peter Garry (cousin of John M. Corridan), January 30, 2007.

3. Testimony of John M. Corridan, S.J., *Waterfront Investigation: Hearings before a Subcommittee of the Committee on Interstate and Foreign Commerce, United States Senate,* pt. 1, *New York–New Jersey Waterfront,* May 7, 1953, (Washington, D.C., 1953), 560; Jules Weinberg, unpublished manuscript, box 12, folder 3, XIIR.

4. O'Brien interview; telephone interview with Patricia Garry Shanahan, May 21, 2007.

5. John W. O'Malley, S.J., "*Ratio Studiorum:* Jesuit Education, 1548–1773," http://www.bc.edu/bc_org/avpulib/digi/ratio/ratiointo.html; see also John W. O'Malley, *The First*

Jesuits (Cambridge: Harvard University Press, 1993), 200–42. For an excellent study of the origins and development of Jesuit education in New York City, see Christa Ressmeyer Klein, "The Jesuits and Catholic Boyhood in Nineteenth-Century New York City: A Study of St. John's College and the College of St. Francis Xavier, 1846–1912" (PhD diss., University of Pennsylvania, 1976).

6. Author interview with Rev. William Reilly, S.J., October 30, 2002; *The Regian* (1928): 40; Philip Carey, S.J., journal entry, July 3, 1984, box 1, folder 5, XIIR.

7. Raymond, *Waterfront Priest*, 45; René Fülöp-Miller; *The Power and Secret of the Jesuits* (New York: Viking Press, 1930); Wilfrid Parsons, S.J., review of *The Power and the Secret of the Jesuits*, *America* 43 (May 17, 1930): 131–33.

8. Reilly interview.

9. William A. Barry, S.J., "Past, Present, and Future: A Jubilarian's Reflections on Jesuit Spirituality," *Studies in the Spirituality of Jesuits* 32 (September 2000): 7.

10. Ibid., 4, 6; Jonathan Wright, *God's Soldiers: Adventure, Politics, Intrigue, and Power; A History of the Jesuits* (New York: Doubleday, 2004), 18; author conversation with Joseph P. Chinnici, OFM, March 29, 1999.

11. Author interview with William Barnaby Faherty, S.J., September 14, 2000.

12. Ibid.; for Husslein, see Stephen A. Werner, *Prophet of the Christian Social Manifesto: Joseph Husslein, S.J., His Life, Work, and Social Thought* (Milwaukee: Marquette University Press, 2001); Joseph M. McShane, S.J., "A Survey of the History of the Jesuit Labor Schools in New York: An American Social Gospel in Action," *Records of the American Catholic Historical Society of Philadelphia* 102 (Winter 1991): 43; John M. Corridan, S.J., "Outlawing of Strikes during Our National Crisis, *America* 64 (February 22, 1941): 544–45.

13. Peter McDonough, *Men Astutely Trained* (New York: Free Press, 1992), 153–54, 229–30; John Courtney Murray, S.J., "The Danger of the Vows," *Woodstock Letters* 96 (1967): 422–23.

14. Murray, "The Danger of the Vows," 425, 427. Peter McDonough treats issues of sexuality and gender in the thought of Murray and several other prominent Jesuits in "Clenched Fist or Open Palm? Five Jesuit Perspectives on Pluralism," *Studies in the Spirituality of Jesuits* 37 (Summer 2005): 4, 15–19, 32–39. See also McDonough, *Men Astutely Trained*, 429–52.

15. Philip A. Carey, S.J., to James P. Sweeney, S.J., July 30, 1945, Xavier Labor School, file folder 2, Archives New York Jesuit Province (ANYP); Philip Carey, S.J., manuscript fragment, May 18, 1987, box 12, folder 4, XIIR; Raymond, *Waterfront Priest*, 58–63.

16. Edward E. Swanstrom, *The Waterfront Labor Problem: A Study in Decasualization and Unemployment Insurance* (New York: Fordham University Press, 1938), 156; Charles B. Barnes, *The Longshoremen* (New York: Survey Associates, 1915), 60.

17. Swanstrom, *The Waterfront Labor Problem*, 36, 76.

18. Malcolm Johnson, *Crime on the Labor Front* (New York: McGraw-Hill, 1950), 221; Raymond, *Waterfront Priest*, 66.

19. Swanstrom went on to serve for many years as head of Catholic Relief Services. Daniel Bell, "The Racket-Ridden Longshoremen: The Web of Economics and Politics," in *The End of Ideology: On the Exhaustion of Political Ideas in the Fifties* (New York: Free Press, 1960), 180; Admiral E. S. Land to Joseph P. Ryan, ca. April 1942, box 2, folder 58, XIIR Papers; J. V. Lyon to Captain Granville Conway, April 17, 1942, box 2, folder 58, XIIR Papers; Charles P. Larrowe, *Shape-Up and Hiring Hall: A Comparison of Hiring Methods and Labor Relations on the New York and Seattle Waterfronts* (Berkeley: University of California Press, 1955), 26.

20. George Lipsitz, *Rainbow at Midnight: Labor and Culture in the 1940s* (Urbana: University of Illinois Press, 1994), 102–3; *New York Herald Tribune*, October 2, 1945.

21. *New York Times*, October 3 and 4, 1945; *New York Herald Tribune*, October 2, 1945; see also, for example, *New York Daily News, New York Journal-American, New York Mirror,* and *Jersey Journal,* October 1–15, 1945; Lipsitz, *Rainbow at Midnight,* 108.

22. *New York Times,* October 4, 1945.

23. Jeff Kisseloff, *You Must Remember This: An Oral History of Manhattan from the 1890s to World War II* (Baltimore: Johns Hopkins University Press, 1999), 542–43.

24. *New York Journal-American,* October 13, 1945; Lipsitz, *Rainbow at Midnight,* 104–6; Kisseloff, *You Must Remember This,* 528.

25. Bell, "Racket-Ridden Longshoremen," 198–99; Vernon H. Jensen, *Strife on the Waterfront: The Port of New York since 1945* (Ithaca, N.Y.: Cornell University Press, 1974), 40–44.

26. Jensen, *Strife on the Waterfront,* 46–53; Lipsitz, *A Rainbow at Midnight,* 106–8.

27. Benjamin L. Masse, "Story of a Strike," *America* 74 (November 10, 1941): 146–48.

28. Colin J. Davis, *Waterfront Revolts: New York and London Dockworkers, 1946–61* (Urbana: University of Illinois Press, 2003), 20–21; Vernon H. Jensen, *Hiring of Dock Workers and Employment Practices in the Ports of New York, Liverpool, London, Rotterdam, and Marseilles* (Cambridge: Harvard University Press, 1964), 25.

29. Davis, *Waterfront Revolts,* 59–60; for brief overviews of the waterfront's traditional division of labor, see Calvin Winslow, "'Men of the Lumber Camps Come to Town': New York Longshoremen in the Strike of 1907," in *Waterfront Workers: New Perspectives on Race and Class,* ed. Winslow (Urbana: University of Illinois Press, 1998), 69–72; Bruce Nelson, "Longshoremen in the Port of New York, 1850–1940," in *Dock Workers: International Explorations in Comparative Labour History, 1790–1970,* ed. Sam Davies et al. (Aldershot: Ashgate, 2000), 389; Calvin Winslow, introduction to *Waterfront Workers,* 9.

30. Davis, *Waterfront Revolts,* 24, 151–52.

31. Budd Schulberg, "How One Pier Got Rid of the Mob," *New York Times Magazine,* September 27, 1953, 17; Debra Bernhardt interview with John Dwyer, November 21, 1980, New Yorkers at Work Oral History Series, Robert F. Wagner Labor Archives, Tamiment Library, New York University; Kisseloff, *You Must Remember This,* 517, 525; William J. Keating (with Richard Carter), *The Man Who Rocked the Boat* (New York: Harper and Brothers, 1956), 102–3.

32. Schulberg, "How One Pier Got Rid of the Mob," 17; Raymond, *Waterfront Priest,* 76–78.

33. John M. Corridan, S.J., to Edward Rosenbaum, March 31, 1954, box 11, folder 28, XIIR.

34. Raymond, *Waterfront Priest,* 79; author interview with Joe Walls, March 26, 2003. When I was researching this book, Walls was among a very small cohort of surviving longshoremen with a firsthand recollection of waterfront work during the entire period of Corridan's apostolate. Walls's viewpoint differed greatly from that of the Jesuit in many respects.

35. Raymond, *Waterfront Priest,* 79; Budd Schulberg, "Drama in Hoboken," *Holiday* (August 1954): 83–84; Debra Bernhardt interview with Philip Carey, S.J., February 19, 1981, New Yorkers at Work Oral History Series, Wagner Labor Archives, Tamiment Library, New York University.

36. Raymond, *Waterfront Priest,* 72; *New York Times,* January 25, 1953. In the weeks prior to the autumn 1948 strike Corridan gave a total of four talks "to Holy Name and Knights of Columbus groups in waterfront sections in Brooklyn and Jersey City"; see Raymond, *Waterfront Priest,* 100.

37. John M. Corridan, S.J., "A Catholic Looks at the Waterfront," box 10, folder 25, XIIR Papers, 1. In September 1949 Corridan gave a similarly themed talk at a Labor Day Mass at St. Peter's Church in Jersey City; he was introduced as "Friend of the Longshoreman" rather than "waterfront priest." The talk was titled "Catholic Principles and Waterfront Christianity" (*Jersey Observer,* September 6, 1949). The first specific reference I have located to "A Catholic Looks at the Waterfront" is in a November 1949 letter from an aspiring playwright to Corridan seeking material for a waterfront drama. Corridan sent in reply "a brief of a talk on 'A Catholic Looks at the Waterfront,'" which leaves open the question of the full text's origins. See Byron V. Crane to John M. Corridan, S.J., November 8, 1949, and John M. Corridan, S.J., to Byron V. Crane, November 14, 1949, box 11, folder 34, XIIR. The first published version of "A Catholic Looks at the Waterfront" appeared as an excerpt in Johnson, *Crime on the Labor Front,* 222–23.

38. Corridan, "A Catholic Looks at the Waterfront," 2–3.

39. Ibid., 3–4.

40. Philip Carey, S.J., journal entry, July 3, 1984, box 1, folder 5, XIIR; John M. Corridan, "Labor Day Speech," box 10, folder 25, XIIR.

41. Corridan, "Labor Day Speech."

42. Press release, Xavier Labor School, May 11, 1949, box 11, folder 30, XIIR.

43. Douglas P. Seaton, *Catholics and Radicals: The Association of Catholic Trade Unionists and the American Labor Movement, from Depression to Cold War (Lewisburg: Bucknell University Press, 1981)*, 23.

44. Harry Sylvester, *Moon Gaffney* (New York: H. Holt and Company, 1947), 160–65; for a brief treatment of the novel in the context of postwar Catholic radicalism, see James Terence Fisher, *The Catholic Counterculture in America, 1933–1962* (Chapel Hill: University of North Carolina Press, 1989), 97–99.

7. Covering the Waterfront

1. John M. Corridan, S.J., to George Lucy, S.J., February 10, 1949, box 10, folder 2, XIIR.

2. Allen Raymond, *Waterfront Priest* (New York: Holt, 1955), 114.

3. Richard Kluger, *The Paper: The Life and Death of the New York Herald Tribune* (New York: Alfred A. Knopf, 1986), 432–33; William B. Scott and Peter M. Rutkoff, *New York Modern: The Arts and the City* (Baltimore: Johns Hopkins University Press, 1999), 34.

4. Author interview with Haynes Johnson, July 17, 2003; *New York Sun,* May 3, 1949; for Malcolm's Johnson obituary, see *New York Times,* June 19, 1976; Haynes Johnson, foreword to Malcolm Johnson, *On the Waterfront* (New York: Chamberlain Bros., 2005), xv–xvii.

5. William J. Keating (with Richard Carter), *The Man Who Rocked the Boat* (New York: Harper and Brothers, 1956), 176; Bob Considine, syndicated newspaper column, ca. 1955, box 11, folder 39, XIIR.

6. Malcolm Johnson, "Crime on the Water Front," *New York Sun,* November 8, 1948. The series of articles is available in Johnson, *On the Waterfront* (the 2005 reprint edition); the volume contains illuminating essays by Haynes Johnson (Malcolm's son and fellow Pulitzer Prize winner) and Budd Schulberg. In my research I used the original newspaper sources, including materials from the *New York Sun* not found in the reprint edition. When materials cited are available in both the original sources and the reprint edition, I give both, citing the *Sun* series by date. The first installment of "Crime on the Water Front," for example, is in Johnson, *On the Waterfront,* 3–7.

7. Johnson, "Crime on the Water Front," November 9, 1948; *On the Waterfront,* 8–14.

8. Johnson, "Crime on the Water Front," November 10, 1948; Johnson, *On the Waterfront,* 15–20; *New York Times,* November 9, 10, 11, and 12, 1948.

9. Colin J. Davis, "'All I Got's a Hook': New York Longshoremen and the 1948 Dock Strike," in *Waterfront Workers: New Perspectives on Race and Class,* ed. Calvin Winslow (Urbana: University of Illinois Press, 1998), 142; *New York Times,* November 9, 1948; for background on the November 1948 strike, see also Colin J. Davis, *Waterfront Revolts: New York and London Dockworkers, 1946–61* (Urbana: University of Illinois Press, 2003), 84–108.

10. *New York Times,* November 9, 1948.

11. *New York Times,* November 10 and 11, 1948; *Jersey Journal,* November 10 and 11, 1948; Vernon H. Jensen, *Strife on the Waterfront: The Port of New York since 1945* (Ithaca, N.Y.: Cornell University Press, 1974), 59–61; Davis, *Waterfront Revolts,* 88–90.

12. *New York Sun,* November 10, 1948; Daniel Bell, "The Racket-Ridden Longshoremen: The Web of Economics and Politics," in *The End of Ideology: On the Exhaustion of Political Ideas in the Fifties* (New York: Free Press, 1960), 182.

13. Charles P. Larrowe, *Shape-Up and Hiring Hall: A Comparison of Hiring Methods and Labor Relations on the New York and Seattle Waterfronts* (Berkeley: University of California Press, 1955), 34–35.

14. William O'Dwyer, *Beyond the Golden Door,* ed. Paul O'Dwyer (Jamaica, N.Y.: St. John's University Press, 1987), 105–10, 35–40; Virgil Peterson, *The Mob: Two Hundred Years of Organized Crime in New York* (Ottawa, Ill.: Green Hill, 1983), 224–26; for the Sampson-Costello-Rogers machinations, see George Walsh, *Public Enemies: The Mayor, the*

Mob, and the Crime That Was (New York: W. W. Norton, 1980), 156–60; Chris McNickle, *To Be Mayor of New York: Ethnic Politics in the City* (New York: Columbia University Press, 1993), 50–51, 54–55, 68, 72; for O'Dwyer and Costello, see William Howard Moore, *The Kefauver Committee and the Politics of Crime: 1950–1952* (Columbia: University of Missouri Press, 1974), 175.

15. *New York Times,* November 11, 1948; *New York Sun,* November 13, 1948.

16. *New York Times,* November 11, 1948; *New York Sun,* November 13, 1948.

17. John M. Corridan, "Longshoremen's Case," *America* 80 (November 20, 1948): 176–78; Raymond, *Waterfront Priest,* 106–8.

18. Corridan, "Longshoremen's Case," 177–78.

19. Corridan, "Longshoremen's Case," 178.

20. Philip A. Carey, S.J., to Thomas J. Murray, S.J., February 4, 1952, Xavier Labor School File Folder 1, ANYP.

21. John M. Corridan, S.J., "Chart of the Corridan Plan of Attack on the Waterfront Problem," box 10, folder 25, XIIR Papers; Raymond, *Waterfront Priest,* 114; *Catholic Herald,* August 6, 1954; Bob Considine, syndicated column, box 11, folder 39, XIIR. Another account of the first meeting between Corridan and Johnson is in Malcolm Johnson, "Father Gangbuster on the Docks," *Catholic Digest* (March 1952): 26–33.

22. Johnson, "Crime on the Water Front," November 19, 1948, 22, 23, 24, 26, 29, 30, December 1, 1948; *On the Waterfront,* 56–98. For another account of the Corridan-Johnson collaboration, see Philip Carey, S.J., journal entry, July 3, 1984, box 1, folder 5, XIIR; see Corridan's notes on the loading racket and waterfront crime in box 10, folder 26, XIIR; for links between the Cockeye Dunn deathwatch at Sing Sing, the 1948 strike, and "Crime on the Waterfront," see Keating and Carter, *The Man Who Rocked the Boat,* 159–79.

23. Philip Carey, S.J., journal entry, July 3, 1984, box 1, folder 5, XIIR; Johnson, "Crime on the Water Front," November 19 and 26, December 1, 1948.

24. Jack Beatty, *The Rascal King: The Life and Times of James Michael Curley (1874–1958)* (Reading, Mass.: Addison-Wesley, 1992), 19.

25. Karl Malden (with Carla Malden), *When Do I Start? A Memoir* (New York: Simon & Schuster, 1997), 241; *Catholic Herald,* August 6, 1954, box 11, folder 39, XIIR.

26. *New York Sun,* December 9 and 13, 1948.

27. Davis, *Waterfront Revolts,* 92–93; for "overtime on overtime," see Bell, "The Racket-Ridden Longshoremen," 181–82; Davis, *Waterfront Revolts,* 85–87; Jensen, *Strife on the Waterfront,* 55–59.

28. Ibid., 95–96; Corridan, "Longshoremen's Case," 178. Corridan made a trip to Washington on November 4 to consult with federal mediators and officials of the Truman administration. It is unclear if his effort at intervention played any role in the government's approach to the strike, though it is highly unlikely that he enjoyed much impact at this early stage of a public career; see Raymond, *Waterfront Priest,* 104–8.

29. Johnson, "Crime on the Water Front," December 7, 1948; *On the Waterfront,* 117–25.

30. Johnson, "Crime on the Water Front," December 7, 1948.

31. Ibid.

32. Malcolm Johnson, "Crime on the Water Front: The Cause and the Remedy," *New York Sun,* January 4, 1949; Johnson, *On the Waterfront,* 145–50.

33. Johnson, "Crime on the Water Front," January 26, 1949; *On the Waterfront,* 160.

34. Johnson, "Crime on the Water Front," February 28, 1949; Ryan's responses to the series are not included in the reprint edition.

35. *New York Sun,* March 2, 3, and 9, 1949.

36. *I.L.A. Longshore News,* November 29, 1949; for Malcolm Johnson's Pulitzer, see *New York Times,* May 3, 1949; Corridan to Lucy, February 10, 1949.

37. John M. Corridan, S.J., to Frank Frano, February 11, 1949, box 11, folder 36, XIIR.

38. *Crusader,* Special Issue, 1949, box 11, folder 7, XIIR.

39. Dennis Daly, "Corridan, S.J.," in *Kerrymen: 1881–1981* (New York: Kerrymen's Patriotic and Benevolent Association, 1981), 128–29.

40. Malcolm Johnson to John M. Corridan, S.J., August 11, 1949, box 11, folder 36, XIIR; *New York World-Telegram,* August 15, 1949; Corridan's running notes on the series are in box 10, folder 26, XIIR.

41. Bell, "The Racket-Ridden Longshoremen," 201; Beulah Amidon, "Are the Gangsters Getting Back? No, They've Never Been Away," *Survey* (November 1949): 574–78; Beulah Amidon to Philip J. Carey, October 5, 1949, box 11, folder 32, XIIR.

42. John M. Corridan, S.J., to Beulah Amidon, October 11, November 23, and December 7, 1949, and Beulah Amidon to John M. Corridan, S.J., December 2, 1949, box 11, folder 32, XIIR.

43. John M. Corridan, S.J., to Daniel Bell, September 26, 1949, box 11, folder 32, XIIR.

44. Daniel Bell, "New York's Waterfront," *Fortune* (December 1949): 210; Bell, "The Racket-Ridden Longshoremen," 175–209; Howard Brick, *Daniel Bell and the Decline of Intellectual Radicalism: Social Theory and Political Reconciliation in the 1940s* (Madison: University of Wisconsin Press, 1986), 164–71; Murray Kempton to John M. Corridan, S.J., n.d., box 11, folder 32, XIIR.

45. Mike Johnson to John M. Corridan, S.J., August 22, 1949, and Corridan to Johnson, September 16, 1949, box 11, folder 36, XIIR; Malcolm Johnson, *Crime on the Labor Front* (New York: McGraw-Hill, 1950), 221–22.

46. Transcript of televised debate on waterfront hiring practices, WPIX-TV, Channel 11, January 5, 1950, box 11, folder 37, XIIR.

47. Ibid.

48. Ibid.

49. Ibid.

50. John M. Corridan, S.J., to U.S. Rep. Andrew M. Jacobs, January 18, 1950, box 11, folder 37, XIIR; *Daily Worker,* January 19, 1950, clipping in box 11, folder 37, XIIR.

51. The Son of a Longshoreman to John M. Corridan, S.J., n.d., box 11, folder 1, XIIR.

52. Lester Velie, "A Waterfront Priest Battles the Port's Big Boss," *Collier's* (February 16, 1952): 58; *I.L.A. Longshore News* (November 29, 1949).

8. The Hollywood Prince

1. Haynes Johnson, foreword to Malcolm Johnson, *On the Waterfront* (New York: Chamberlain Bros., 2005), xxiv; Haynes Johnson, *The Age of Anxiety: McCarthyism to Terrorism* (New York: Harcourt, 2005), 233; Malcolm Johnson to Seymour Berkson, April 23, 1951, courtesy of Haynes Johnson; *New York Sun,* June 15, 1949; Martin Gottfried, *Arthur Miller: His Life and Work* (New York: Da Capo Press, 2003), 175.

2. Author interviews with Budd Schulberg, October 4, 2002, May 10, 2003; James Garamone interview with Budd Schulberg, August 2, 2003, courtesy of James Garamone.

3. Budd Schulberg, *What Makes Sammy Run* (New York: Random House, 1941); Nicholas Beck, *Budd Schulberg: A Bio-Bibliography* (Lanham, Md.: Scarecrow Press, 2001), 2, 15–19; Budd Schulberg, *Moving Pictures: Memories of a Hollywood Prince* (New York: Stein and Day, 1981), 76, 158–68; Budd Schulberg, "It Was Great to Be a Boy in Hollywood," *Holiday* (January 1955): 70–72, 74, 76, 107.

4. Schulberg, *Moving Pictures,* 125–30, 207; Beck, *Budd Schulberg,* 2.

5. Schulberg, *Moving Pictures,* 281, 464; Schulberg, "It Was Great to Be a Boy in Hollywood," 107; Beck, *Budd Schulberg,* 2–3.

6. Budd Schulberg, *The Four Seasons of Success* (Garden City, N.Y.: Doubleday, 1972), 35–37; author interview with Budd Schulberg, May 8, 2004; Garamone interview with Schulberg.

7. Beck, *Budd Schulberg,* 2; Schulberg, *Four Seasons of Success,* 35–38, 31–41.

8. Beck, *Budd Schulberg,* 7–11, 17; Matthew J. Bruccoli interview with Bud Schulberg, "The Hollywood Years," second of two interviews in "Two Conversations," *Paris Review* 160 (Winter 2001): 126; Schulberg, *Four Seasons of Success,* 95.

9. Dorothy Parker is quoted in Otto Friedrich, *City of Nets: A Portrait of Hollywood in the 1940's* (New York: Harper and Row, 1986), 70; Beck, *Budd Schulberg,* 17–18; Gare Joyce,

"Why Budd Schulberg Is Unrepentant," *The Walrus* (June 2004), www.walrusmagazine.com/article.pl?sid=04/04/27/191234&tid=1; Andrew R. Heinze, *Jews and the American Soul: Human Nature in the Twentieth Century* (Princeton: Princeton University Press, 2004), 263–64.

10. Budd Schulberg, *The Harder They Fall* (New York: Random House, 1947); Beck, *Budd Schulberg*, 3, 33–40; Budd Schulberg, "The Great Benny Leonard," in *Sparring with Hemingway and Other Legends of the Fight Game* (Chicago: Ivan R. Dee, 1995), 53–63; Schulberg, *Moving Pictures*, 103–10.

11. Budd Schulberg, "Remembering Scott," in *F. Scott Fitzgerald: New Perspectives*, ed. Jackson R. Bryer, Alan Margolies, and Ruth Progozy (Athens: University of Georgia Press, 2000), 3–17.

12. Schulberg, *Four Seasons of Success*, 91–124; *New York Times*, February 7, 2003; cf. Andrew Turnbull, *Scott Fitzgerald* (New York: Scribner, 1962), 295–97; for the Dartmouth trip, see also *New York Times*, May 1, 2005.

13. Turnbull, *Scott Fitzgerald*, 320; Schulberg, *Four Seasons of Success*, 131–35; Schulberg, "Remembering Scott," 14.

14. *New York Times*, October 26, 1949; Jerry Tallmer, "When Labor Ruled the Docks," *Downtown Express* (November 5–12, 2004), http://www.downtownexpress.com/de78/whenlaborruledthedocks.html.

15. Budd Schulberg, introduction to Allen Raymond, *Waterfront Priest* (New York: Holt, 1955), x–xi; Schulberg interview, October 4, 2002. For the most complete account Schulberg has offered of his relationship with Pete Corridan, see "An Evening with Budd Schulberg," Russo Lecture, April 29, 2003, www.fordham.edu/cs/media/index.htm.

16. Budd Schulberg, "Drama in Hoboken," *Holiday* (August 1954): 83; Budd Schulberg, "Father John Knows the Score," unpublished manuscript, 2, Budd Schulberg Deposit, Rauner Special Collections Library, Dartmouth College; Budd Schulberg, "Waterfront Priest," *Commonweal* 62 (April 3, 1953): 643. Schulberg wrote and spoke often about the startling impact of Corridan's manner of speaking; see also *New York Times*, July 11, 1954, and especially "An Evening with Budd Schulberg."

17. John M. Corridan, S.J., typescript, box 11, folder 41, XIIR. Corridan's manuscript was published in revised form as "On the Waterfront, by the 'Waterfront Priest,'" *Queen's Work* (December 1954): 8.

18. Corridan, "On the Waterfront, by the 'Waterfront Priest'"; Schulberg, "Drama in Hoboken," 83. In the published version of Corridan's story for *Queen's Work*, Corridan's account of Brownie's first meeting with Schulberg is changed from "days later" to "a few years later." This would be a most significant revision—providing ammunition to those who claim that Schulberg did not begin his research on the film script immediately after his first meeting with Corridan—were it not for the existence of a letter from Schulberg to Corridan dated August 9, 1951 (box 11, folder 38, XIIR), in which Schulberg thanks Corridan, sends his best regards to Brownie, and writes warmly of the time they had spent together on the waterfront *before* Schulberg wrote the screenplay, completed in April 1951. It is clear that Corridan's original unpublished account and Schulberg's account in *Holiday* provide the accurate chronology: the *Queen's Work* version contains an editorial error.

19. Budd Schulberg, "The Waterfront Revisited," *Saturday Evening Post*, September 7, 1963, 29; see also the reprint version in Johnson, *On the Waterfront*, 267; Schulberg, "Drama in Hoboken," 83–84; author interview with Budd Schulberg, April 29, 2003.

20. Schulberg, "Drama in Hoboken," 83–84.

21. Budd Schulberg to John M. Corridan, S.J., August 9, 1951, box 11, folder 38, XIIR; Schulberg, "Drama in Hoboken," 84; cf. Budd Schulberg, "See You at Dave's," *Holiday* (April 1951): 64–65, 67–70, 135, 137–38.

22. *New York Times*, April 26, 1987, September 14, 1994; *Newsday*, October 25, 1988; Budd Schulberg to John Ford, November 20, 1953, John Ford Papers, Lilly Library, Indiana University–Bloomington (my thanks to historian Donald Critchlow for locating this document); Adeline Schulberg to John M. Corridan, S.J., March 8, 1955, box 11, folder 38, XIIR. Gossip columnist Walter Winchell later reported inaccurately that Schulberg was taking instruction to become a Catholic (Tallmer, "When Labor Ruled the Docks").

23. Author interview with Robert Greene, January 15, 2004; Schulberg, introduction to *Waterfront Priest,* xii; Schulberg interview, October 4, 2002.

24. Bob Considine, syndicated column, box 11, folder 39, XIIR; *Catholic Herald,* August 6, 1954; Budd Schulberg, *Waterfront* (New York: Random House, 1955).

25. Budd Schulberg, "Crime on the Water Front: An Original Screenplay," 25–26, typescript, box 23, folder 1, Budd Schulberg Papers, Department of Rare Books and Special Collections, Princeton University Library. Robert Siodmak told the *New York Times* on January 7, 1951, that the film would "concentrate on New York players" and "the wonderful waterfront backgrounds." The director also indicated that "the title needed changing." His biographer reported that "the project was entitled *A Stone on the River Hudson.*" There is no evidence that a screenplay under that title ever existed; Siodmak may simply have shopped Schulberg's "Crime on the Water Front" script under a new title. See Deborah Lazaroff Alpi, *Robert Siodmak: A Biography, with Critical Analyses of His Films Noirs and a Filmography of All His Works* (Jefferson, N.C.: McFarland, 1998), 179. After *On the Waterfront* was released in 1954, according to Alpi, Siodmak "successfully sued [producer Sam] Spiegel for not crediting his participation in the screenplay, and was awarded $100,000 in damages" (179).

26. Schulberg, "Crime on the Water Front," 88 90.

27. Ibid., 90–93.

28. Schulberg, "Crime on the Water Front," 79–80; Thomas H. Pauly, *An American Odyssey: Elia Kazan and American Culture* (Philadelphia: Temple University Press, 1983), 185; for brief references to this first version of the screenplay, see Leo Braudy, *On the Waterfront* (London: British Film Institute, 2005), 16–17; Richard Schickel, *Elia Kazan: A Biography* (New York, 2005), 225; Kenneth Hey, "Ambivalence as a Theme in *On the Waterfront* (1954): An Interdisciplinary Approach to Film Study," *American Quarterly* 31 (Winter 1979): 674–75; Dan Georgakas, "Schulberg on the Waterfront," in *On the Waterfront,* ed. Joanna E. Rapf (New York: Cambridge University Press, 2003), 41–42.

29. *New York Times,* May 24, 1951.

30. Budd Schulberg testimony, May 23, 1951, in *Communist Infiltration of Hollywood Motion-Picture Industry,* pt. 3, *Hearings before the Committee on Un-American Activities, House of Representatives* (Washington, D.C., 1951), 584–608; Ronald Radosh and Allis Radosh, *Red Star over Hollywood: The Film Colony's Long Romance with the Left* (San Francisco: Encounter Books, 2005), 42–43, 178.

31. Schulberg HUAC testimony, 611–12; *New York Times,* October 31, 1947; Victor S. Navasky, *Naming Names* (New York: Viking, 1980), 80–82, 301–11.

32. Navasky, *Naming Names,* 226; Schulberg HUAC testimony, 585–89; Michael Denning, *The Cultural Front: The Laboring of American Culture in the Twentieth Century* (New York: Verso, 1996).

33. Schulberg HUAC testimony, 607–8; Joyce, "Why Budd Schulberg Is Unrepentant."

34. Beck, *Budd Schulberg,* 42–45.

35. Navasky, *Naming Names,* 242.

36. See chapter 13, "The Hook," and chapter 17, "The Priest in the Movie," for detailed treatment of perennial claims linking the genesis of *On the Waterfront* to Schulberg's HUAC testimony and that of director Elia Kazan before the same body in April 1952.

37. Budd Schulberg to John M. Corridan, S.J., August 9, 1951, box 11, folder 38, XIIR.

38. Ibid.; Schulberg HUAC testimony, 615–16. Douglas Hyde recounted his conversion in *I Believed* (New York: Putnam, 1950).

39. Author interview with Budd Schulberg, May 10, 2003; Bruccoli, "Budd Schulberg, *The Art of Fiction: The Hollywood Years,*" 129–30; for a personal narrative of a writer's disillusionment with communism that did not involve a religious conversion, see Arthur Koestler's essay in *The God That Failed,* ed. Richard Crossman (New York: Harper and Brothers, 1949), 15–75; for Koestler as disagreeable Cold Warrior, see Peter Coleman, *The Liberal Conspiracy: The Congress for Cultural Freedom and the Struggle for the Mind of Postwar Europe* (New York: Free Press, 1989) 33–34, 52; in *The Cultural Cold War: The CIA and the World of Arts and Letters* (New York: The New Press, 1999), 65, historian Francis Stonor Saunders revealed *The God That Failed* was so closely linked to CIA-backed editorial and funding sources it

"was as much a product of intelligence as the intelligentsia"; for Bernstein's unusually well balanced response to Schulberg and his testimony, see Walter Bernstein, *Inside Out: A Memoir of the Blacklist* (New York: Alfred A. Knopf, 1996), 44, 49–50, 250–51; see also Berstein's oral history in Patrick McGilligan and Paul Buhle, *Tender Comrades: A History of the Hollywood Blacklist* (New York: St. Martin's Press, 1997), 43–54.

40. Budd Schulberg, "Collision with the Party Line," *Saturday Review of Literature* (August 30, 1952): 6–8, 31–37, offers a detailed account of his attraction to and subsequent disillusionment with Soviet literature and cultural politics.

41. Gregory D. Sumner, *Dwight MacDonald and the Politics Circle: The Challenge of Cosmopolitan Democracy* (Ithaca, N.Y.: Cornell University Press, 1996), 151; Alan M. Wald, *The New York Intellectuals: The Rise and Decline of the Anti-Stalinist Left from the 1930s to the 1980s* (Chapel Hill: University of North Carolina Press, 1987); for a brief overview of themes and texts related to this spiritual front, see James T. Fisher, "American Religion since 1945," in *A Companion to Post-1945 America,* ed. Jean-Christophe Agnew and Roy Rosenzweig (Malden, Mass.: Blackwell, 2002), 44–63; Patrick Allitt, *Religion in America since 1945: A History* (New York: Columbia University Press, 2003), 1–20; Mark Silk, *Spiritual Politics: Religion and America since World War II* (New York: Simon and Schuster, 1988), 23–107.

42. Eugene McCarraher, *Christian Critics: Religion and the Impasse in Modern Social Thought* (Ithaca, N.Y.: Cornell University Press, 2000), 90–91. Bell was harshly criticized for his embrace of "realism" in labor politics by Irving Howe, a paradigmatic figure from the "Old Left"; see Wald, *The New York Intellectuals,* 315.

43. George Cotkin, *Existential America* (Baltimore: Johns Hopkins University Press, 2003), 56, 118–19; Allitt, *Religion in America since 1945,* 16–19, 26–31; Silk, *Spiritual Politics,* 33–37, 49–50, 101–7; Silk, *Spiritual Politics,* 28–29; Alexander Bloom, *Prodigal Sons: The New York Intellectuals and Their World* (New York: Oxford University Press, 1986), 188–89.

44. Allitt, *Religion in America,* 29–31.

45. Heinze, *Jews and the American Soul,* 263–64. Silk, *Spiritual Politics,* 40, makes note of Budd Schulberg's invocation of "Judeo-Christian tradition" in the introduction to the Modern Library edition of *What Makes Sammy Run;* see 40–53 for Silk's treatment of the "Judeo-Christian tradition" and postwar U.S. religion.

46. Schulberg, introduction to *Waterfront Priest,* xii.

47. Fraser is quoted in Bruce Nelson, *Divided We Stand: American Workers and the Struggle for Black Equality* (Princeton: Princeton University Press, 2001), 70.

48. Philip A. Carey, S.J., to James C. Mooney, December 30, 1952, box 3, folder 1, XIIR. For the best account of McCarthy's career and "McCarthyism," see David M. Oshinsky, *A Conspiracy So Immense: The World of Joe McCarthy* (New York: Free Press, 1983); for a well-balanced treatment of American anticommunism, see Richard Gid Powers, *Not without Honor: The History of American Anticommunism* (New York: Free Press, 1995); for an excellent historical account that neatly contextualizes Cold War conversions to Catholicism, see Patrick Allitt, *Catholic Converts: British and American Intellectuals Turn to Rome* (Ithaca, N.Y.: Cornell University Press, 1997), esp. chaps. 10 and 13.

49. Malcolm Johnson to Philip A. Carey, S.J., July 15, 1963, box 6, folder 51, XIIR.

50. Joseph P. Ryan to William Randolph Hearst Jr., April 17, 1951, and Malcolm Johnson to Seymour Berkson, April 23, 1951, both courtesy Haynes Johnson.

51. Schulberg to Corridan, August 9, 1951.

52. John M. Corridan, S.J., to Rev. Henry V. Walsh, December 2, 1948, box 11, folder 34, XIIR; John M. Corridan to Father George Higgins, December 2, 1948, box 10, folder 4.

53. John M. Corridan, S.J., to Edward Rosenbaum, April 7, 1954, box 11, folder 28, XIIR.

54. For LaFarge and the Catholic Interracial Council, see David W. Southern, *John LaFarge and the Limits of Catholic Interracialism, 1911–1963* (Baton Rouge: Louisiana State University Press, 1996).

55. *New York Times,* June 7 and 8, 1949; Martha Biondi, *To Stand and Fight: The Struggle for Civil Rights in Postwar New York City* (Cambridge: Harvard University Press, 2003), 251–56.

56. Nelson, *Divided We Stand,* 79–82; John M. Corridan, S.J., to George K. Hunton, June 10, 1949, box 11, folder 20, XIIR; Southern, *John LaFarge and the Limits of Catholic Interracialism,* 160–61.

57. Nelson, *Divided We Stand,* 81.

58. Budd Schulberg to Norman Weissman, October 4, 1984, box 12, folder 4, XIIR; Schulberg, introduction to Raymond, *Waterfront Priest,* xii.

59. Budd Schulberg, *Ringside: A Treasury of Boxing Reportage* (Chicago: Ivan R. Dee, 2006), 42.

9. Meeting across the River

1. *I.L.A. Longshore News* (February 1950): 1.

2. *New York World-Telegram and Sun,* February 3, 1950. The fading *Sun* had been absorbed by the *World-Telegram* just weeks earlier; Malcolm Johnson wrote his paper's obituary.

3. *I.L.A. Longshore News* (March 1950): 1, 4.

4. Ibid.

5. Joseph P. Ryan to Dear Sir and Brother, April 29, 1950, box 11, folder 8, XIIR.

6. *New York Times,* May 6, 1950.

7. *I.L.A. Longshore News* (May 1950); *New York Times,* May 8, 1950.

8. *New York Times,* May 8, 1950; Announcement of Annual Benefit and Testimonial for Guardian Angel Church, n.d., box 6, folder 47, XIIR.

9. Bruce Nelson, *Divided We Stand: American Workers and the Struggle for Black Equality* (Princeton: Princeton University Press, 2001), 77–78. Robert McElroy's description of Guardian Angel is in Joe Doyle's foreword to Thomas McGrath, *This Coffin Has No Handles* (New York: Thunder's Mouth Press, 1988), xi.

10. Jeff Kisseloff, *You Must Remember This: An Oral History of Manhattan from the 1890s to World War II* (Baltimore: Johns Hopkins University Press, 1999), 525.

11. Allen Raymond, *Waterfront Priest* (New York: Holt, 1955), 46–47.

12. *Italian Tribune* (Newark), June 30, 1950; *I.L.A. Longshore News* (July 1950); Philip Carey, S.J., interview with Leslie Braginsky, courtesy of Thomas Lilly; for postwar developments at Port Newark, see Marc Levinson, *The Box: How the Shipping Container Made the World Smaller and the World Economy Bigger* (Princeton: Princeton University Press, 2006), 84–85; Port of New York Authority, *Marine Terminal Survey of the New Jersey Waterfront* (New York: Port of New York Authority, 1949), 14–16; Frederick L. Bird, *A Study of the Port of New York Authority* (New York: Dun and Bradstreet, 1949), 107–11, 119–21; for Mt. Carmel, see Carmine Anthony Loffredo, "A History of the Roman Catholic School System in the Archdiocese of Newark, New Jersey, 1900–1965" (Ed.D. thesis, Rutgers University, 1967), 100–101; Charles W. Churchill, *The Italians of Newark: A Community Study* (New York: Arno Press, 1975), 96–98.

13. *Italian Tribune,* June 30, 1950; there were two ILA locals in Port Newark, "one predominantly black and one 'white'"; Nelson, *Divided We Stand,* 86.

14. Thomas F. X. Smith, *The Powerticians* (Secaucus, N.J.: Lyle Stuart, 1982), 151–53. Sinatra's Jersey City period was treated in *New York Times,* October 21, 2006.

15. Gerald Meyer, "Frank Sinatra: The Popular Front and an American Icon," *Science and Society* 66 (Fall 2002): 320–22. In the vast literature on Sinatra there is precious little on his Bickford's Cafeteria insurgent years beyond the brief account in Smith's *Powerticians;* for Sinatra's progressive politics generally, see Joseph Dorinson, "Frank Sinatra's House: Pride, Passion, and Politics," in *Frank Sinatra: History, Identity, and Italian American Culture,* ed. Stanislao G. Pugliese (New York: Palgrave Macmillan, 2004), 23–31.

16. Smith, *The Powerticians,* 152; Father LeRoy E. McWilliams (with Jim Bishop), *Parish Priest* (New York: McGraw-Hill, 1953), 190–91; *Jersey Journal,* April 3, 1945.

17. *Jersey Journal,* April 27 and 30, 1945.

18. Smith, *The Powerticians,* 179; "The McFeely," *Time,* May 26, 1947, 27–28; Martin A. Bierbaum, "Hoboken—A Comeback City: A Study of Urban Revitalization in the 1970's"

(PhD diss., Rutgers University, 1980), 87–88; "It Happened in Hoboken," *Newsweek,* May 26, 1947, 23–24; "End of a Boss," *Life,* May 26, 1947, 40–41.

19. Smith, *The Powerticians,* 178; testimony of James F. Keane, December 16, 1952, *NYSCC Hearings,* 2:1028–36.

20. Smith, *The Powerticians,* 152, 183; William Lemmey, "Bossism in Jersey City: The Kenny Years, 1949–1972" (PhD diss., City University of New York, 1979), 99.

21. Author interview with Robert Greene, January 15, 2004.

22. Raymond, *Waterfront Priest,* 131–33; *New York Times,* July 16, 1948.

23. John M. Corridan, S.J., to Rev. R. A. McGowan, June 29, 1949, box 10, folder 4, XIIR.

24. *Newark Sunday News,* September 4, 1946; *Jersey Observer,* January 23, 1947; *Jersey Journal,* February 3, 1949; Philip Carey, S.J., to James P. Sweeney, S.J., June 2, 1944, file folder 2, Xavier Labor School, ANYP; Joseph M. McShane, S.J., "A Survey of the History of the Jesuit Labor Schools in New York: An American Social Gospel in Action," *Records of the American Catholic Historical Society of Philadelphia* 102 (Winter 1991): 55; *Jersey Observer,* January 23, 1947.

25. Smith, *The Powerticians,* 179–91; Helene Stapinski, *Five-Finger Discount: A Crooked Family History* (New York: Random House, 2001), 83–92.

26. Testimony of Leland S. Andrews, December 8, 1952, *NYSCC Hearings,* 1:475.

27. Testimony of James F. Keane, December 16, 1952, *NYSCC Hearings,* 2:1028–47; Raymond, *Waterfront Priest,* 131–32; *New York Times,* July 20 and 26, 1949; *New York Sun,* July 26, 1949.

28. Frank Williams to John M. Corridan, S.J., ca. August 1943, box 11, folder 22, XIIR; testimony of Frank Williams, December 15, 1952, *NYSCC Hearings,* 2:1004–12; John M. Corridan, S.J., to Frank Williams, September 19, 1949, box 11, folder 22, XIIR; Thomas J. Armstrong to John M. Corridan, S.J., August 12 and 16, 1949, box 11, folder 22, XIIR. Corridan constructed a chronological account of the labor-political strife surrounding Local 1247 in Jersey City; see box 11, folder 22, XIIR.

29. Andrews testimony, 475, 484–85; testimony of Robert McKeon, December 16, 1952, *NYSCC Hearings,* 2:1048–56. Corridan's chronological notes for July 6 indicate "D–F struck by Ryan to prevent ouster of McKeon"; box 11, folder 22, XIIR; see *ILA Longshore News* (July 1950), clipping in box 28, folder 22, XIIR; Greene interview.

30. *New York Sun,* July 26, 1949; *Jersey Journal,* August 12 and 19, 1949.

31. *Jersey Journal,* August 12 and 19, 1949; comments by Keane's attorney and the 1247 delegate are from unidentified New Jersey newspaper clipping in box 11, folder 22, XIIR; John V. Kenny testimony, April 1, 1953, in *Waterfront Investigation: Hearings before a Subcommittee of the Committee on Interstate and Foreign Commerce, United States Senate,* pt. 1, *New York–New Jersey Waterfront* (Washington, D.C., 1953), 231.

32. Smith, *The Powerticians,* 152, 183; Lemmey, "Bossism in Jersey City," 99; Greene interview.

33. Greene interview; William J. Keating (with Richard Carter), *The Man Who Rocked the Boat* (New York: Harper and Brothers, 1956), 201.

34. *Jersey Journal,* December 1, 1950; Anthony Marchitto testimony, March 30, 1953, in *Waterfront Investigation,* 168; for Biffo Di Lorenzo, see *New York Times,* January 9, 1953; John V. Kenny testimony, April 1, 1953, in *Waterfront Investigation,* 218–19, 229.

35. *Jersey Journal,* December 16, 1950; Kenny testimony, 218–19, 229 (the identity of "Joe Palooka" is revealed on 219).

36. Raymond, *Waterfront Priest,* 133–34; for Ackalitis's arrest and parole record, see Exhibit No. 31, in *Waterfront Investigation,* 218–19, 660–62.

37. Greene interview; Raymond, *Waterfront Priest,* 133; Lemmey, "Bossism in Jersey City," 144.

38. Greene interview; Anthony Marchitto testimony, in *Waterfront Investigation,* 136; Exhibit No. 11, in *Waterfront Investigation,* 642–43; Virgil W. Peterson, *The Mob: Two Hundred Years of Organized Crime in New York* (Ottawa, Ill.: Green Hill, 1983), 284–87.

39. George Walsh, *Public Enemies: The Mayor, the Mob, and the Crime That Was* (New York: W. W. Norton, 1980), 15–18; *New York Times,* March 20, 1951; Exhibit No. 11, in *Waterfront Investigation,* 642–43; Exhibit No. 35, in *Waterfront Investigation,* 665–67.

40. Testimony of Charles S. Witkowski, December 16, 1952, *NYSCC Hearings*, 2:1146; *New York Times*, March 6, 1951; Smith, *The Powerticians*, 195–96.

41. *Jersey Journal*, March 6 and 8, 1951.

42. *Jersey Journal*, March 11, 1951; Kenny testimony, April 1, 1953, 232; *New York Times*, March 11, 1951; *Newark Sunday News*, March 11, 1951; *Jersey Free Press*, March 13, 1951.

43. McWilliams, *Parish Priest*, 241–42.

44. Marchitto testimony, 138–39; author interview with Bishop William J. McCormack, May 10, 2002.

45. For the Black Tom disaster, see Chad Millman, *The Detonators: The Secret Plot to Destroy America and an Epic Hunt for Justice* (New York: Little, Brown, 2006). The situation at Claremont Terminal was the main focus of the U.S. Senate's Waterfront Investigation in spring 1953; for Claremont Terminal, see *New York Times*, December 21, 1952; for Flanagan's letters of introduction, see Marchitto testimony, 145; *Jersey Journal*, November 5, 1951.

46. Greene interview; Lemmey, "Bossism in Jersey City," 176; Kenny testimony, 236.

47. Testimony of Joseph Napolitano, March 28, 1953, in *Waterfront Investigation*, 89; Kenny testimony, 233–43; *New York Times*, April 19, 1952; Stapinski, *Five-Finger Discount*, 92.

48. Greene interview; Kenny testimony, 233.

49. *New York Times*, April 19, 1952; Kenny testimony, 235–41; testimony of Detective James M. Cashman, April 1, 1953, in *Waterfront Investigation*, 201–3; for Anthony Strollo, see Exhibits 35, 37, in *Waterfront Investigation*, 665–69; Peterson, *The Mob*, 287–88.

50. Kenny testimony, 244; *New York Times*, April 19, 1952.

51. Kenny testimony, 244; William Lemmey, "Boss Kenney of Jersey City," *New Jersey History* 98 (Spring–Summer 1980): 9–28.

52. Thomas Fleming, *New Jersey: A Bicentennial History* (W. W. Norton, 1977), 195–98; Bruce Springsteen, "Meeting across the River," *Born to Run* (1975), Columbia Records 33795; see also Jessica Kaye, ed., *Meeting across the River: Stories Inspired by the Haunting Bruce Springsteen Song* (New York: Bloomsbury, 2005); none of the stories were inspired by John V. Kenny's meeting with Strollo; none are set anywhere along the New York–New Jersey waterfront.

10. Priest and Worker

1. Allen Raymond, *Waterfront Priest* (New York: Holt, 1955), 148–49; *New York Journal-American*, October 29, 1951; *New York World-Telegram and Sun*, October 29, 1951. The *World-Telegram* absorbed the *Sun* in 1950; see Richard Kluger, *The Paper: The Life and Death of the New York Herald Tribune* (New York: Alfred A. Knopf, 1986), 432–33.

2. Maud Russell, *Men along the Shore* (New York: Brussel and Brussel, 1966), 144–46.

3. John M. Corridan, S.J., "Confidential Report of the New York–New Jersey Waterfront," January 1952, Xavier Labor School: file folder 1, ANYP (this report is also found in box 10, folder 25, XIIR, but there is a missing page); *New York Times*, July 21, 1951; Vernon H. Jensen, *Strife on the Waterfront: The Port of New York since 1945* (Ithaca, N.Y.: Cornell University Press, 1974), 65.

4. *New York Times*, October 16 and 24, 1951; Jensen, *Strife on the Waterfront*, 69, 71.

5. Jensen, *Strife on the Waterfront*, 69; Colin J. Davis, *Waterfront Revolts: New York and London Dockworkers, 1946–61* (Urbana: University of Illinois Press, 2003), 152–53; *New York Times*, October 16 and 24, 1951.

6. Charles P. Larrowe, *Shape-Up and Hiring Hall: A Comparison of Hiring Methods and Labor Relations on the New York and Seattle Waterfronts (1955; rpt., Westport, Conn.: Greenwood Press, 1976)*, 37; *New York Times*, October 16, 17, and 18, 1951.

7. *New York Times*, October 16, 17, and 18, 1951; *Jersey Journal*, October 22, 1951.

8. Corridan's assessment of newspaper coverage is from "Chart of the Corridan Plan of Attack on the Waterfront Problem," box 10, folder 25, XIIR; *New York Times*, October 17, 1951; *Brooklyn Eagle*, October 17, 1951; *New York World-Telegram and Sun*, October 26, 1951.

9. *Brooklyn Eagle,* November 1, 1951; Raymond, *Waterfront Priest,* 142–43; *New York Post,* October 22, 1951.

10. *New York Journal-American,* October 25 and 26, 1951.

11. "Nation's Nightmare: Crime on the Water Front," CBS Radio Division documentary, transcript in box 10, folder 29, XIIR.

12. Spruille Braden, *Diplomats and Demagogues: The Memoirs of Spruille Braden* (New Rochelle, N.Y.: Arlington House, 1971), 384–85; Lee Bernstein, *The Greatest Menace: Organized Crime in Cold War America* (Amherst: University of Massachusetts Press, 2002), 84–85; for the Kefauver Committee, see William Howard Moore, *The Kefauver Committee and the Politics of Crime, 1950–1952* (Columbia: University of Missouri Press, 1974); Charles L. Fontenay, *Estes Kefauver: A Biography* (Knoxville: University of Tennessee Press, 1980), 164–86; Joseph Bruce Gorman, *Kefauver: A Political Biography* (New York: Oxford University Press, 1971), 86–102.

13. Raymond, *Waterfront Priest,* 134; William J. Keating (with Richard Carter), *The Man Who Rocked the Boat* (New York: Harper and Brothers, 1956), 183–88.

14. Keating, *The Man Who Rocked the Boat,* 183–88; see *New York City Anti-Crime Committee: Annual Report for the Year 1952,* box 10, folder 30, XIIR.

15. Keating, *The Man Who Rocked the Boat,* 201; author interview with Robert Greene, January 15, 2004; "Nation's Nightmare," 10–11.

16. Keating, *The Man Who Rocked the Boat,* 193–96; Jensen, *Strife on the Waterfront,* 73–74; *New York Times,* October 29 and 30, 1951; Raymond, *Waterfront Priest,* 147–48; *New York Post,* October 29 and 30, 1951.

17. *New York Times,* October 30, 1951; for the full text of Braden's telegram to Dewey, see box 10, folder 30, XIIR.

18. Keating, *The Man Who Rocked the Boat,* 196; Raymond *Waterfront Priest,* 149; *Brooklyn Eagle,* October 31, 1951.

19. Jensen, *Strife on the Waterfront,* 75–77; Raymond, *Waterfront Priest,* 150; Davis, *Waterfront Revolts,* 157–60; *New York Times,* November 1–10, 1951.

20. *New York World-Telegram and Sun,* November 10, 1951.

21. Father James Gilhooley to Philip Carey, S.J., May 15, 1987, and Philip Carey, S.J., to Father James Gilhooley, May 18, 1987, box 12, folder 4, XIIR; author interview with Father James Gilhooley, July 22, 1998.

22. Joseph P. Fitzpatrick, S.J., Homily at Mass of Christian Burial for Father Philip A. Carey, S.J., May 31, 1989, typescript copy courtesy of Mike Miskell.

23. Carey to Gilhooley, May 18, 1987; Gilhooley interview; Robert I. Gannon, S.J., *The Cardinal Spellman Story* (Garden City, N.Y.: Doubleday, 1962). My thanks to Monsignor Thomas J. Shelley for information on Father Thomas V. McMahon.

24. Raymond, *Waterfront Priest,* 154–57.

25. Carey to Gilhooley, May 18, 1987.

26. John J. McMahon, S.J., to John M. Corridan, S.J., November 6, 1951, box 10, folder 1, XIIR. In 1992 Corridan's friend and fellow Jesuit Neil Hurley wrote that Cardinal Spellman "gave Father Corridan a fair hearing and was convinced of his innocence from charges that he did not wear clerical garb and engaged in fisticuffs"; see Neil P. Hurley, S.J., *"On the Waterfront: Rebirth of a 'Contenduh,'"* in *Image and Likeness: Religious Visions in American Film Classics,* ed. John R. May (New York: Paulist Press, 1992), 189, n. 4.

27. Carey to Gilhooley, May 18, 1987; Philip Carey, S.J., to James Kearney, January 8, 1953, box 3, folder 1, XIIR.

28. John C. Cort, *Dreadful Conversions: The Making of a Catholic Socialist (New York:* Fordham University Press, 2003), 168–70; Thomas J. Shelley, *Dunwoodie: The History of St. Joseph's Seminary, Yonkers, New York* (Westminster, Md.: Christian Classics, 1993), 217–21; Thomas Lynch, "Above All Things the Truth: John P. Monaghan and the Church of New York," *Dunwoodie Review* 16 (1992–93): 148–53; Robert I. Gannon, S.J., *The Cardinal Spellman Story* (London: Robert Hale Ltd., 1963), 276–82.

29. Author telephone interviews with Owen Daley, S.J., February 28, 2003, November 25, 2005. In January 1952 *Catholic Digest* published "Water-Front Priest," a two-page

(59–60) pictorial feature on Father Edward Head of St. Veronica's on Christopher Street in the West Village. Assistant chaplain of the New York chapter of ACTU, Head was a former longshoreman whose mediating efforts during the autumn 1951 strike attracted little public notice. This *Catholic Digest* piece may represent the final time anyone other than Corridan was labeled a "waterfront priest" in the Port of New York.

30. Raymond, *Waterfront Priest,* 155.

31. Corridan was interviewed by a graduate student, Edward Rosenbaum, on December 28, 1953; for these quotations, see their subsequent exchange of correspondence, Edward Rosenbaum to John M. Corridan, S.J., March 31, 1954, and Corridan to Rosenbaum, April 7, 1954, box 11, folder 28, XIIR.

32. John LaFarge, S.J., *A Report on the American Jesuits* (New York: Farrar, Straus & Cudahy, 1956), 153–58.

33. Ibid., 201; Oscar L. Arnal, *Priests in Working-Class Blue: The History of the Worker Priests (1943–1954)* (New York: Paulist Press, 1986), 55, 101.

34. Arnal, *Priests in Working-Class Blue,* 72, 76, 84–86, 93.

35. Ibid., 131, 168–69; Peter McDonough, *Men Astutely Trained* (New York: Free Press, 1992), 287–88; *Italian Tribune,* July 8, 1949.

36. Arnal, *Priests in Working-Class Blue,* 82, 145, 150.

37. Gannon, *The Cardinal Spellman Story,* 258, 411.

38. Budd Schulberg quoted in *Los Angeles Times,* December 30, 1988.

11. An Intimacy with Violence

1. *Final Report to the Industrial Commissioner, State of New York, from Board of Inquiry on Longshore Industry Work Stoppage October–November 1951, Port of New York* (January 22, 1952), ii, 8, 27; *New York Times,* January 23, 1952.

2. Allen Raymond, *Waterfront Priest* (New York: Holt, 1955), 150–54; *New York Times,* October 30, November 20 and 21, December 3, 1951.

3. Raymond, *Waterfront Priest,* 178–79.

4. John M. Corridan, S.J., to John J. McMahon, S.J., April 29, 1952, box 10, folder 1, XIIR; Lester Velie, "A Waterfront Priest Battles the Big Port's BIG BOSS," *Collier's Weekly,* February 16, 1952, 57.

5. Raymond, *Waterfront Priest,* 134–35; Daniel Bell, "Last of the Business Rackets," *Fortune* (June 1951): 203; "Nation's Nightmare: Crime on the Water Front," 16, CBS Radio Division documentary, transcript in box 10, folder 29, XIIR. The transcript was published under a new title in 1952 in *Crime Detective* magazine; see "Mr. Big and the Waterfront," box 10, folder 13, XIIR.

6. "Nation's Nightmare," 16–17.

7. "Ryan Hollers as 'Big' Fire Gets Hotter," *People Today,* October 24, 1951, box 10, folder 13, XIIR; *New York Herald Tribune,* September 22, 1951.

8. "As Pegler Sees It" *New York Journal-American,* October 3, 1951; *New York World-Telegram,* February 17, 1942; for a sampling of Pegler's contentious labor journalism, see box 6, folder 58, XIIR; Oliver Pilat, *Pegler: Angry Man of the Press* (Boston: Beacon Press 1963), 51; John C. Cort, "Dirt on the Waterfront," *Commonweal,* November 23, 1951, 173; "Man on the Spot," *People Today,* November 21, 1951, box 10, folder 13, XIIR.

9. Thomas Repetto, *American Mafia: A History of Its Rise to Power* (New York: Henry Holt, 2004), 156–57; for Lait and Mortimer, see Lee Bernstein, *The Greatest Menace: Organized Crime in Cold War America* (Amherst: University of Massachusetts Press, 2002), 48–60; William Howard Moore, *The Kefauver Committee and the Politics of Crime, 1950–1952* (Columbia: University of Missouri Press, 1974), 172.

10. Moore, *The Kefauver Committee and the Politics of Crime,* 189.

11. For Harry Gross, see Ed Reid, "How We Tracked Down Brooklyn's Mr. Big," *Reader's Digest* (April 1951): 133–40; Norton Mockridge and Robert H. Prall, *The Big Fix* (New York: Holt, 1954); for Kenny, see *New York Times,* April 2, 1953. Kenny's attorney also tried to

pin the "Mr. Big" label on Frank Hague; see testimony of T. James Tumulty, April 1, 1953, in *Waterfront Investigation: Hearings before a Subcommittee of the Committee on Interstate and Foreign Commerce, United States Senate*, pt. 1, *New York–New Jersey Waterfront* (Washington, D.C., 1953), 244.

12. *New York Daily News*, January 20, 1952. In his biography of nightclub owner Bernard "Toots" Shor (*Toots* [New York: Meredith Press, 1969], 192) journalist Bob Considine wrote that Harris "had worked on special assignments for McCormack since his days as a hip Broadway and crime reporter" (without indicating the nature of these assignments).

13. *Daily News*, January 20, 1952.

14. *Compass*, February 3, 1952.

15. John M. Corridan, S.J., to John J. McMahon, S.J., January 25, 1952, box 10, folder 1, XIIR.

16. Lester Velie, "BIG BOSS of the BIG PORT," *Collier's Weekly*, February 9, 1952, 18–19, 38–40; Velie, "A Waterfront Priest Battles the Port's BIG BOSS," *Collier's Weekly*, February 16, 1952, 18–19, 56–60.

17. "A Waterfront Priest Battles the Port's BIG BOSS," 57; Raymond, *Waterfront Priest*, 121–24; Moore, *The Kefauver Committee and the Politics of Crime*, 175–76; Malcolm Johnson, *Crime on the Labor Front* (New York: McGraw-Hill, 1950), 178–81; William J. Keating (with Richard Carter), *The Man Who Rocked the Boat* (New York: Harper and Brothers, 1956), 162–64; *New York Times*, June 1, 1949; *New York Journal-American*, December 28, 1952.

18. *New York Times*, July 8, 1949; *New York Journal-American*, December 28, 1952; Raymond, *Waterfront Priest*, 123–24.

19. William O'Dwyer, *Beyond the Golden Door*, ed. Paul O'Dwyer (Jamaica, N.Y.: St. John's University Press, 1987), 328–33; Chris McNickle, *To Be Mayor of New York: Ethnic Politics in the City* (New York: Columbia University Press, 1993), 72; Virgil W. Peterson, *The Mob: Two Hundred Years of Organized Crime in New York* (Ottawa, Ill.: Green Hill, 1983), 252–53; Warren Moscow, *The Last of the Big-Time Bosses: The Life and Times of Carmine De Sapio and the Rise and Fall of Tammany Hall* (New York: Stein and Day, 1971), 86–88. George E. Walsh, *Public Enemies: The Mayor, the Mob, and the Crime That Was* (New York: W. W. Norton, 1980), focuses on battles for control of Tammany Hall; though O'Dwyer's alleged links to mobster Frank Costello figure in the story, Walsh makes no mention of the not entirely unrelated Dunn case. See testimony of William J. McCormack, January 29, 1953, *NYSCC Hearings*, 5:3546–47, for McCormack's denials of his role in persuading O'Dwyer to run again.

20. Johnson, *Crime on the Labor Front*, 181–83; Bell, "Last of the Business Rackets," 201; McNickle, *To Be Mayor of New York*, 82–83.

21. John M. Corridan, S.J., "Confidential Report of New York–New Jersey Waterfront, January 1952: Xavier Labor School," file folder 1, ANYP; cf. John M. Corridan to Rev. Father Provincial (John J. McMahon, S.J.), January 25, 1952.

22. "A Waterfront Priest Battles the Port's BIG BOSS," 57–58.

23. Guy Richards to John M. Corridan, S.J., February 29, 1952, box 11, folder 32, XIIR.

24. "Trouble at Collier's," *Time*, June 2, 1952, http://www.time.com/time/magazine/article/0,9171,857228,00.html. Stouch's apology was reprinted on the back page of the ILA's house organ, *Longshore News* (June, 1952): 4.

25. For various references to Ryan's status as a "captive" and the like, see testimony of John M. Corridan, S.J., May 7, 1953, in *Waterfront Investigation*, 566–67; transcript of John M. Corridan, S.J., speech to Chelsea longshoremen at Cornish Arms Hotel, February 1, 1954, box 11, folder 30, XIIR; "pratt-boy" is from "Ryan Hollers," *People Today*, October 24, 1951; Velie, "BIG BOSS of the BIG PORT," 39; Malcolm Johnson, "Father Gangbuster of the Docks," *Catholic Digest* (March 1952): 29; Raymond, *Waterfront Priest*, 179.

26. Corridan to McMahon, April 29, 1952.

27. Ibid.

28. Raymond, *Waterfront Priest*, 188.

29. Ibid., 47, 87.

30. *St. Ann's Catholic Monitor* (January 1952), copy in box 10, folder 13, XIIR.

31. Ibid. McCormack's musings on "being a rich man" were quoted in his *New York Times* obituary, July 13, 1965.

32. *New York Journal-American*, October 3, 1951.

33. Testimony of William J. McCormack, January 29, 1953, *NYSCC Hearings*, 5:3567–68; *New York Times*, March 21, 1952; Velie, "A Waterfront Priest Battles the Port's Big Boss," 60.

34. *New York Daily News*, January 20, 1952.

35. Raymond, *Waterfront Priest*, 47–49; *New York Times*, March 24, 1952.

36. Mrs. Len Amlaw to John M. Corridan, S.J., May 12, 1952; W. E. Campbell to Corridan, February 8, 1952; R. G. Lynch, M.D., to Corridan, February 21, 1952, box 11, folder 3, XIIR.

37. George Moller to John M. Corridan, S.J., January 17, 1952, box 11, folder 3, XIIR; *New York Times*, January 18, 1952,

38. *New York Journal-American*, December 28, 1952.

39. *Journal-American*, December 28, 1952; Raymond, *Waterfront Priest*, 122–24.

12. A Season for Testimony

1. Testimony of Anthony DeVincenzo, December 15, 1952, *NYSCC Hearings*, 2:751–83; *New York Times*, December 16, 1952. Because of the prevalence of Italian Americans and Italian nationals, the Hoboken piers resembled the Brooklyn waterfront more than the West Side of Manhattan, with one crucial difference: local Irish American ILA figures continued to exert influence over hiring in Hoboken; a pattern of intermittent cooperation and competition between the Irish and Italians existed in Hoboken as in Jersey City.

2. DeVincenzo testimony, 2:752, 764; for background on events described in DeVincenzo's testimony, see transcript of "An Interview with Longshoreman," pt. 2, 1–26, box 11, folder 4, XIIR.

3. DeVincenzo testimony, 2:753–54, 769–72; Anthony (Tony Mike) DeVincenzo (as told to Richard Carter), "The Mob Said They'd Kill Me for My Story," *True* (May 1953): 18–20, 22, 24, 26–27, 101–7.

4. *New York Times*, December 15, 1952; Allen Raymond, *Waterfront Priest* (New York: Holt, 1955), 39, 131.

5. DeVincenzo testimony, 2:777; *New York Times*, November 7, 1952. In his testimony DeVincenzo did not cite the revenge factor in the beating of Florio; this angle was treated in "Interview with a Longshoreman," 15.

6. DeVincenzo testimony, 2:780.

7. Jules Weinberg, "A Racketeer Takes Over an American City," *Look*, July 17, 1951, 42–44; Mary Heaton Vorse, "The Pirates' Nest of New York," *Harper's* (April 1952): 27–37; Ross Wetzsteon, *Republic of Dreams: Greenwich Village, the American Bohemia, 1910–1960* (New York: Simon and Schuster, 2002), 168; Gerald W. McFarland, *Inside Greenwich Village: A New York City Neighborhood, 1898–1918 (Amherst: University of Massachusetts Press, 2001)*, 120–25.

8. Vorse, "The Pirates' Nest of New York," 28.

9. DeVincenzo testimony, 2:779–80.

10. Raymond, *Waterfront Priest*, 1–2; *New York Times*, May 23 and 27, June 12 and 15, September 28, 1951, March 29, 1953.

11. *New York Times*, December 19 and 20, 1952.

12. Jerry Tallmer, "When Labor Ruled the Docks," *Downtown Express*, November 5–12, 2004, www.downtownexpress.com/de 78/whenlaborruledthedocks.html; author interview with Budd Schulberg, May 10, 2003; John M. Corridan, S.J., to Budd Schulberg, March 12, 1952; Budd Schulberg to John M. Corridan, S.J., March 31, 1952, box 11, folder 38, XIIR. For an account which claims that it was Schulberg's HUAC testimony, not storyline issues or ILA intimidation, that stopped the project, see Deborah Lazaroff Alpi, *Robert Siodmak: A Biography, with Critical Analyses of His Films Noirs and a Filmography of All His Works* (Jefferson, N.C.: McFarland, 1998), 179.

13. Budd Schulberg, "Joe Docks, Forgotten Man of the Waterfront," *New York Times Magazine,* December 28, 1952, 3, 28–30.

14. Ibid., 28, 30.

15. John M. Corridan, S.J., "New York Port's Last Chance," *America* 88 (December 20, 1952): 319; *New York Times,* December 21, 1952, April 26, 1987.

16. Tallmer, "When Labor Ruled the Docks"; Schulberg interview.

17. Lee Bernstein, *The Greatest Menace: Organized Crime in Cold War America* (Amherst: University of Massachusetts Press, 2002), 26–27, 61, 78–81.

18. Compare the *New York Times* coverage of Schulberg's testimony (May 24, 1951) with that devoted to DeVincenzo's (December 16, 1952).

19. Schulberg interview.

20. DeVincenzo testimony, 763; Sada Fretz, "Hoboken's Waterfront," in *On the Waterfront: Starring Hoboken, New Jersey* (Hoboken: Hoboken Historical Society, 2004), 6.

21. Testimony of James F. Keane, December 16, 1952, *NYSCC Hearings,* 2:1028.

22. Ibid., 1028–47; testimony of Anthony Belfiore, December 8, 1952, *NYSCC Hearings,* 1:526–30.

23. Author interview with Robert Greene, January 15, 2004; *New York Times,* December 12, 1952, September 24, 1953; for Di Lorenzo's death, see *New York Times,* January 9, 1953.

24. *New York Times,* November 27, 1952; testimony of Harold Bowers, Michael Bowers, and John Keefe, December 9, 1952, *NYSCC Hearings,* 1:699–706.

25. Testimony of Edward McGrath, January 26, 1953, *NYSCC Hearings,* 4:2850–70.

26. Testimony of Patrick Connolly, January 22, 1953, *NYSCC Hearings,* 4:2337; *New York Times,* January 23, 1953.

27. Testimony of Ruth M. Kennedy, December 3, 1952, *NYSCC Hearings,* 1:85–90; testimony of James C. Kennedy, December 3, 1952, ibid., 91–107; *New York Times,* December 4, 1952.

28. For payoffs by stevedoring firms to ILA figures, see, for example, testimony of Michael Castellana, December 4, 1952, *NYSCC Hearings,* 1:206–20; John Hutchinson, *The Imperfect Union: A History of Corruption in American Trade Unions* (New York: Dutton, 1970), 102–9; Virgil W. Peterson, *The Mob: Two Hundred Years of Organized Crime in New York* (Ottawa, Ill.: Green Hill Publishers, 1983), 288–91; see also *New York Times* coverage from throughout the hearings, featuring voluminous excerpts from testimony on payoffs, kickbacks, and bribes.

29. Leslie J. Arps to John M. Corridan, S.J., January 15, 1953; John M. Corridan S.J. to John McMahon, S.J., January 16, 1953, box 10, folder 31, XIIR.

30. John M. Corridan, S.J., to John J. McMahon, S.J., November 14, 1951; John J. McMahon, S.J., to John M. Corridan, S.J., November 16, 1951; John M. Corridan, S.J., to John J. McMahon, March 30, 1952, box 10, folder 1, XIIR.

31. John M. Corridan, S.J., to John J. McMahon, S.J., April 10 and 29, 1952; John J. McMahon, S.J., to John M. Corridan, S.J., April 15, 1952, box 10, folder 1, XIIR; "Statement of Rev. John M. Corridan, S.J., 'On Labor Conditions Affecting Waterfront Commerce in the Port of New York, Made to the New York State Crime Commission,'" May 1, 1952, box 10, folder 31, XIIR.

32. "Recommendations of Rev. John M. Corridan, S.J., 'On Labor Conditions Affecting Waterfront Commerce in the Port of New York, Submitted to the New York State Crime Commission,'" January 12, 1953, box 10, folder 31, XIIR; for the highly favorable response to his eight-point plan after it was made public, see *New York Herald Tribune,* January 12, 1953; *New York Times,* January 12, 1953.

33. *NYSCC Hearings,* 5:3513.

34. Testimony of Robert Burker, December 16, 1952, *NYSCC Hearings,* 2:1077–92; *New York Times,* December 17, 1952.

35. Testimony of William J. McCormack, January 29 and 30, 1953, *NYSCC Hearings,* 5:3515–3605; *New York Times,* January 30 and 31, 1953.

36. William J. McCormack testimony, January 29, 1953, *NYSCC Hearings,* 5:3566–67.

37. For "syndicate films" inspired by the Kefauver Committee, see Ronald W. Wilson, "Gang Busters: The Kefauver Crime Committee and the Syndicate Films of the 1950s," in *Mob*

Culture: Hidden Histories of the American Gangster Film, ed. Lee Grieveson, Esther Sonnet, and Peter Stanfield (New Brunswick, N.J.: Rutgers University Press, 2005), 67–89; *New York Times,* August 7, 1952; William J. McCormack testimony, January 29, 1953, 5:3568; *New York Times,* August 7, 1952.

38. McCormack testimony, 5:3568.

39. Ibid., 5:3569–71.

40. Ibid., 5:3569–73, 3575–78; *New York Times,* January 30, 1953; "As Pegler Sees It," *New York Journal-American,* October 3, 1951.

41. Testimony of Francis X. McQuade, *NYSCC Hearings,* January 30, 1953, 5:3667–3670; for McQuade's obituary, see *New York Times,* April 7, 1955; for McQuade and Seabury, see Herbert Mitgang, *The Man Who Rode the Tiger: The Life and Times of Judge Samuel Seabury* (New York: Fordham University Press, 1996), 189–90; George Walsh, *Gentleman Jimmy Walker: Mayor of the Jazz Age* (New York: Praeger, 1974), 240–41.

42. McQuade testimony, 5:3667–70.

43. Jeffrey T. Sammons, *Beyond the Ring: The Role of Boxing in American Society* (Urbana: University of Illinois Press, 1988), 69–70.

44. *New York Times,* January 30 and 31, 1953.

45. "Mr. Big Becomes Less Mysterious," *Life,* February 9, 1953, 16–20; James Glanz and Eric Lipton, *City in the Sky: The Rise and Fall of the World Trade Center (New York: Times Books, 2003),* 51, 66.

46. Testimony of Joseph P. Ryan, January 30, 1953, *NYSCC Hearings,* 5:3606–66, 3701–36.

47. Ibid., 5:3655–57.

48. Murray Kempton, "In His Fashion," in *America Comes of Middle Age: Columns, 1950–1962* (Boston: Little Brown, 1963), 38.

13. "The Hook"

1. Testimony of Elia Kazan, April 10, 1952, in *Communist Infiltration of Hollywood Motion-Picture Industry,* pt. 7, *Hearings before the Committee on Un-American Activities, United States House of Representatives* (Washington, D.C., 1952), 2407–14; *New York Times,* April 12, 1952; Richard Schickel, *Elia Kazan: A Biography* (New York: HarperCollins, 2005), 6.

2. Elia Kazan, *Elia Kazan: A Life* (New York: Doubleday, 1988), 78, 112–17; Schickel, *Elia Kazan,* 28–32. Michael Denning argues in *The Cultural Front: The Laboring of American Culture in the Twentieth Century* (New York: Verso, 1996), that Kazan's HUAC testimony was partly responsible for the subsequent focus on the Group Theatre as communist-dominated: "Actually, the Communists were never more than a quarter of the company, which, before the success of *Waiting for Lefty,* was seen primarily as an 'art' theater" (368–69).

3. Schickel, *Elia Kazan,* 211–21; Kazan, *Elia Kazan,* 290–303, 331–73.

4. Kazan, *Elia Kazan,* 444–65; Schickel, *Elia Kazan,* 248–69; Jeff Young, *Kazan: The Master Director Discusses His Films; Interviews with Elia Kazan* (New York: Newmarket Press, 1999), 118–21.

5. Kazan testimony, 2414; *New York Times,* April 12, 1952.

6. Kazan, *Elia Kazan,* 464–65; Schickel, *Elia Kazan,* 271–72.

7. Kazan, *Elia Kazan,* 486–89; author interview with Budd Schulberg, May 10, 2003; for accounts of the "Trenton Six" case, see http://salwen.com/trenton6.html and http://www.capitalcentury.com/1948.html.

8. Schulberg interview, May 10, 2003; Budd Schulberg, introduction to Malcolm Johnson, *On the Waterfront: The Pulitzer Prize–Winning Articles That Inspired the Classic Movie and Transformed the New York Harbor* (New York: Chamberlain Bros., 2005), xxxvii; Kazan, *Elia Kazan,* 488.

9. Kazan, *Elia Kazan,* 319–23, 358–60, 488.

10. Martin Gottfried, *Arthur Miller: His Life and Work* (New York: Da Capo Press, 2003), 116, 167–68; Arthur Miller, *Timebends: A Life* (New York: Grove Press, 1987),

146–49; George Walsh, *Public Enemies: The Mayor, the Mob, and the Crime That Was* (New York: W. W. Norton, 1980), 118–19; Sid Feder and Burton B. Turkus, *Murder, Inc.: The Story of "the Syndicate"* (Garden City, N.Y.: Doubleday, 1952), 473. Miller's account of his Brooklyn waterfront excursions is highly problematic, since Panto had been dead for nearly a decade by the time Miller claimed that graffiti were sprouting up all over Brooklyn, and his murder was common knowledge; see Arthur Miller, "Suspended in Time," in *Echoes Down the Corridor: Collected Essays, 1944–2000*, ed. Stephen R. Centola (New York: Viking, 2000), 189.

11. Schickel, *Elia Kazan*, 223–25; for a highly provocative if polemical critique of Miller's infatuation with Longhi and his causes, see Stephen Schwartz, "True Life Tales 'On the Waterfront,'" *Film History*, February 11, 2005, http://www.frontpagemag.com/articles/ReadArticle.asp?ID=16967. Longhi befriended folksinger Woody Guthrie when they served together in the Merchant Marine; see Jim Longhi, *Woody, Cisco, and Me: Seamen Three in the Merchant Marine* (Urbana: University of Illinois Press, 1997); Joe Klein, *Woody Guthrie: A Life* (New York: Ballantine Books, 1980), 275–90; for Longhi and the Back Pay Committee, see Colin J. Davis, *Waterfront Revolts: New York and London Dockworkers, 1946–61* (Urbana: University of Illinois Press, 2003), 84–86.

12. Miller, *Timebends*, 150–74; for Miller's return "from his 'soaking-up-local-color' expedition to Italy," see *New York Times*, April 25, 1948.

13. Miller, *Timebends*, 147, 154–55, 195; remarks of Vincent James Longhi, "Italians on the Waterfront," symposium presented by the John D. Calandra Italian American Institute, Queens College, CUNY, October 13, 2001.

14. Arthur Miller, "The Hook," 205-page manuscript screenplay, n.d. (ca. 1949), Arthur Miller Papers, Harry Ransom Humanities Research Center, University of Texas–Austin; Brian Neve, *Elia Kazan: The Cinema of an American Outsider* (London: I.B. Tauris, 2009), 76–78; cf. Felice Swados, "Waterfront," *New Republic* 94 (February 2, 1938): 362; Brenda Murphy, *Congressional Theatre: Dramatizing McCarthyism on Stage, Film and Television* (Cambridge: Cambridge University Press, 1999), 207–10, cites yet another version of the script that became "The Hook." I located this earlier "screen treatment," titled "Shape-Up," in a folder marked *A View from the Bridge*. "Shape-Up" is essentially a dramatization of the Pete Panto story and bears very little similarity to the first and second versions of "The Hook," which do share numerous similarities; for sources of proletarian literature and drama that influenced "The Hook," see Denning, *The Cultural Front*, 200–229.

15. Kazan, *Elia Kazan*, 401–9; Schickel, *Elia Kazan*, 227.

16. Arthur Miller, "The Hook," 156-page manuscript screenplay (1951), Arthur Miller Papers; Albert Wertheim, "A View from the Bridge," in *The Cambridge Companion to Arthur Miller*, ed. Christopher Bigsby (Cambridge: Cambridge University Press, 1997), 104–5, describes an alternative ending to a slightly longer edition of the 156-page Miller-Kazan manuscript screenplay I refer to as version two: here "the film concludes with Marty turning his back on the offer [of the delegate position] and walking toward the audience flanked by the other men." Wertheim indicates that he examined this edition of the screenplay at Lilly Library, Indiana University, which apparently holds the only version of "The Hook" not found in the Miller Papers at Ransom Humanities Research Center.

17. Judith E. Smith, *Visions of Belonging: Family Stories, Popular Culture, and Postwar Democracy, 1940–1960* (New York: Columbia University Press, 2004), 200; Gottfried, *Arthur Miller*, 175–76; Schickel, *Elia Kazan*, 229–33; Kazan, *Elia Kazan*, 403, 410–15; Wertheim, "A View from the Bridge," 103–5.

18. Victor Navasky, *Naming Names* (New York: Viking, 1980), 199; Christopher Bigsby, ed., *Remembering Arthur Miller* (London: Methuen, 2005), 262. The traditional view of American cultural historians was reaffirmed by Lary May, who, in a study treating Hollywood's retrenchment from the socially conscious films of the depression era, asserted that "The Hook" "evolve[d] into *On the Waterfront*." See Lary May, *The Big Tomorrow: Hollywood and the Politics of the American Way* (Chicago: University of Chicago Press, 2000), 216; see also my discussion of Schulberg's "Crime on the Water Front" screenplay in chapter 8, "The Hollywood Prince."

19. Gottfried, *Arthur Miller*, 230–35; Schickel, *Elia Kazan*, 227.

20. Schickel, *Elia Kazan,* 225–27; Gottfried, *Arthur Miller,* 232, does acknowledge that *On the Waterfront*'s Father Pete Barry is "based on the real-life Father John Corridan" but does not say anything about his relationship with Schulberg.

21. For "pillage," see Wertheim, "A View from the Bridge," 105; John M. Corridan, S.J., to U.S. Rep. Christopher C. McGrath, June 6, 1949, box 10, folder 15, XIIR; John M. Corridan, S.J., to Byron V. Crane, November 14, 1949, box 11, folder 34, XIIR.

22. John M. Corridan, S.J., report on meeting Mitch Berenson, January 24, 1950, box 10, folder 7, XIIR. In a brief conversation with the author following the October 13, 2001, symposium "Italians on the Waterfront," Jimmy Longhi asserted that he had never met Pete Corridan.

23. Miller, "The Hook" (205-page version), 111–13.

24. *Chief-Leader* [New York City Civil Service weekly], August 28, 1987, box 1, folder 15, XIIR; Leslie Braginsky interview with Philip Carey, S.J., courtesy of Thomas Lilly.

25. Braginsky interview with Carey; author interview with Budd Schulberg, March 19, 2003; Budd Schulberg to Anne Brown, January 8, 1973, box 6, folder 59, XIIR.

26. Budd Schulberg, "*Vale Atque Ave:* Father John M. Corridan, S.J.," Schulberg Deposit, Rauner Special Collections, Webster Hall, Dartmouth College. In the excerpted version of this tribute published in 2005, Schulberg reports that at his first meeting with Elia Kazan, Corridan described Bill McCormack as "a murderer! Maybe not with his own hands. But he gets the Ackalitises and the Cockeye Dunns…to do his dirty work." (Dunn was executed more than three years before the director first met the Jesuit.) See also Johnson, *On the Waterfront,* 305–6; cf. Budd Schulberg, afterword to Johnson, *On the Waterfront,* 143–44; James Garamone interview with Budd Schulberg, August 2, 2003, courtesy of James Garamone. Kazan's return from Bavaria is noted in the *New York Times,* November 13, 1952. For the most complete account Schulberg has offered of his relationship with Pete Corridan, see "An Evening with Budd Schulberg," Russo Lecture, April 29, 2003, www.fordham.edu/cs/media/index.htm; author interview with Budd Schulberg, October 4, 2002.

27. Young, *Kazan,* 158.

28. Gregory D. Black, *The Catholic Crusade against the Movies, 1940–1975* (New York: Cambridge University Press, 1998), 112–15; Kazan, *Elia Kazan,* 401, 417, 432–38. Kazan published a statement treating this interference by a "prominent Catholic layman" in the *New York Times,* October 21, 1951; the draft was rewritten by his wife, Molly, a collaboration that worked well in this case but would backfire in the *Times* advertisement defending his HUAC testimony.

29. Schulberg interview, March 19, 2003.

30. Jeff Kisseloff, *You Must Remember This: An Oral History of Manhattan from the 1890s to World War II* (Baltimore: Johns Hopkins University Press, 1999), 530. Information on Corridan's drinking was obtained in interviews with several of his contemporaries in the New York Province of the Society of Jesus.

31. John Samuel Tieman, "The Origins of Twelve-Step Spirituality: Bill W. and Edward Dowling, S.J.," *U.S. Catholic Historian* 13 (Summer 1995): 121–35; Ernest Kurtz, *Not-God: A History of Alcoholics Anonymous* (Center City, Minn.: Hazelden, 1991), 97–99. Dowling later adapted features of the twelve steps to the Cana Conferences, a highly influential program of marital spirituality that encouraged social activism.

32. Kazan, *Elia Kazan,* 493.

14. Good Citizens

1. *New York Post,* January 18, 1953.

2. For the "Savarin Bouquet," see J. E. Mazzei to Reverend John Corridan, January 20, 1953, box 10, folder 22, XIIR; "He Covers the Waterfront," *New York Journal-American Pictorial Review,* January 11, 1953; W. J. Cahill to John M. Corridan, S.J., January 12, 1953, box 11, folder 3, XIIR; *New York Times,* January 25, 1953.

3. Allen Raymond, *Waterfront Priest* (New York: Holt, 1955), 252; *New York Herald Tribune,* February 7, 1953; Hans Isbrandtsen to John M. Corridan, S.J., January 12, 1953; Corridan to Isbrandtsen, January 14, 1953; and Isbrandtsen to Corridan, January 16, 1953, box 11, folder 2, XIIR.

4. Vernon H. Jensen, *Strife on the Waterfront: The Port of New York since 1945* (Ithaca, N.Y.: Cornell University Press, 1974), 105; *New York Journal-American,* January 11, 1953.

5. *New York Journal-American,* January 11, 1953; *New York Times,* January 25, 1953.

6. John M. Corridan, S.J., "To All Harbor Workers," ca. January 1953, box 10, folder 35, XIIR.

7. Ibid.; John M. Corridan, S.J., "To All Harbor Workers," no. 2, ca. February 1953, box 10, folder 35, XIIR.

8. *Waterfront Alert: Special Edition,* ca. February 1953, box 11, folder 7, XIIR.

9. Ibid.; John M. Corridan, S.J., "To All Harbor Workers," no. 4, ca. February 1953, box 10, folder 35, XIIR.

10. *New York Times,* January 12 and February 18, 1953; author telephone interview with Austin Tobin Jr., May 6, 2005.

11. Testimony of Walter B. Hedden, January 29, 1953, *NYSCC Hearings,* 5:3484; *New York Times,* January 30, 1953.

12. Statement of Austin J. Tobin, Executive Director, the Port of New York Authority, July 22, 1953, in *New Jersey–New York Waterfront Commission Compact, Hearing before Subcommittee No. 3 of the Committee on the Judiciary, House of Representatives* (Washington, D.C., 1953), 90; "Crime on the Water Front," *New York Sun,* December 7, 1948; Malcolm Johnson, *On the Waterfront: The Pulitzer Prize–Winning Articles That Inspired the Classic Movie and Transformed the New York Harbor* (New York: Chamberlain Bros., 2005), 117–25.

13. Hedden testimony, *NYSCC Hearings,* 5:3492–94; testimony of Walter P. Hedden, May 7, 1953, in *Waterfront Investigation: Hearings before a Subcommittee of the Committee on Interstate and Foreign Commerce, United States Senate,* pt. 1, *New York–New Jersey Waterfront* (Washington, D.C., 1953), 558; testimony of John M. Corridan, S.J., May 7, 1953, in *Waterfront Investigation,* 565.

14. William O'Dwyer, *Beyond the Golden Door,* ed. Paul O'Dwyer (Jamaica, N.Y.: St. John's University Press, 1987), 382–83. Walter B. Hedden called for the appointment of a port labor director in his NYSCC testimony (5:3486).

15. For the Port Authority's estimate that it controlled 10 percent of the port's piers in 1953, see testimony of Austin J. Tobin, June 8, 1953, in *Record of the Public Hearings Held by Governor Thomas E. Dewey on the Recommendations of the New York State Crime Commission for Remedying Conditions on the Waterfront of the Port of New York* (New York, 1953), 15.

16. Austin J. Tobin to Richard W. Clarke, January 31, 1953, box 10, folder 22, XIIR Papers.

17. Philip A. Carey, S.J., to Dennis J. Comey, S.J., March 11, 1953, Xavier Labor School, file folder 1, ANYP.

18. Geraldine Tobin to John M. Corridan, S.J., March 3, 1955, box 12, folder 1, XIIR.

19. John M. Corridan, S.J., "To All Harbor Workers," no. 3, box 10, folder 35, XIIR; *Waterfront Alert,* ca. February 1953.

20. Corridan, "To All Harbor Workers," no. 3; *Waterfront Alert,* ca. February 1953.

21. "Recommendations for Priests Who Aspire to Be Would-Be Labor Advisers," n.d., box 11, folder 3, XIIR.

22. Patrick Cleary to John M. Corridan, S.J., ca. February–March 1953; Anthony Silvio to John M. Corridan, S.J., ca. February–March 1953, box 11, folder 1, XIIR.

23. Msgr. John J. O'Donnell to John M. Corridan, S.J., April 22, 1952, box 10, folder 22, XIIR; *New York Times,* April 14 and 27, 1953; *New York World-Telegram and Sun,* April 27, 1953.

24. *New York Times,* April 14, 1953.

25. *New York World-Telegram and Sun,* April 27, 1953; John C. Carey, letter to the editor, *World-Telegram and Sun,* May 2, 1953, box 11, folder 3, XIIR.

26. John T. McGreevy, *Parish Boundaries: The Catholic Encounter with Race in the Twentieth-Century Urban North* (Chicago: University of Chicago Press, 1996), 173; "Recommendations for Priests Who Aspire to Be Would-Be Labor Advisers."

27. Budd Schulberg, "Waterfront Priest," *Commonweal*, April 3, 1953, 643–46.

28. Ibid., 644; Budd Schulberg to Lester Markel, February 9, 1955, box 6, folder 59, XIIR.

29. John J. Ford to John M. Corridan, S.J., February 24, 1952, box 11, folder 3, XIIR; for the cultural and religious wars pitting Blanshard against Catholic intellectuals, see John McGreevy, *Catholicism and American Freedom* (New York: W. W. Norton, 2003), 166–88.

30. Dennis Howard, "Waterfront Underground," *Jubilee* 1 (May 1953): 17–23.

31. Cf. Schulberg, "Waterfront Priest," 644; Howard, "Waterfront Underground," 18; Garry Wills, *Bare Ruined Choirs: Doubt, Prophecy, and Radical Religion* (Garden City, N.Y.: Doubleday, 1972), 43.

32. Howard, "Waterfront Underground," 17–23.

33. *New York Times*, January 31, February 15 and 20, 1953.

34. *Waterfront Investigation*, March 27, 1953, 2.

35. William Howard Moore, *The Kefauver Committee and the Politics of Crime, 1950–1952* (Columbia: University of Missouri Press, 1974), 203; *Waterfront Investigation*, March 28, 1953, 131; March 30, 1953, 157; April 1, 1953, 206; April 17, 1953, 271; testimony of Joseph Napolitano, March 28, 1953, in *Waterfront Investigation*, 75–102.

36. Testimony of Joseph P. Ryan, April 30, 1953, in *Waterfront Investigation*, 433–34, 461, 484, 485; *New York World-Telegram and Sun*, April 30, 1953.

37. Ryan testimony, *Waterfront Investigation*, 461, 485.

38. Ibid., 444; testimony of George C. Dade, April 24, 1953, in *Waterfront Investigation*, 359.

39. Testimony of John M. Corridan, S.J., May 7, 1953, in *Waterfront Investigation*, 559–61, 567; Raymond, *Waterfront Priest*, 199; *New York Times*, May 8 and August 22, 1953; *New York Herald-Tribune*, May 13, 1953.

40. Corridan testimony, *Waterfront Investigation*, 566–67; *New York Times*, August 22, 1953.

41. Corridan testimony, *Waterfront Investigation*, 565–67.

42. John M. Corridan, S.J., to U.S. Rep. Christopher C. McGrath, June 6, 1949, box 10, folder 15, XIIR; for evidence of coordination in the testimonies of Corridan and an official of the Port Authority, see Hedden testimony, *Waterfront Investigation*, 545–59; Corridan testimony, *Waterfront Investigation*, 559–70.

43. *New York Times*, April 1, 7, and 8 and May 9, 1953; Jensen, *Strife on the Waterfront*, 106; Colin J. Davis, *Waterfront Revolts: New York and London Dockworkers, 1946–61* (Urbana: University of Illinois Press, 2003), 164–65.

44. *Waterfront Investigation*, May 7, 1953, 569; *Waterfront Alert*, box 11, folder 7, XIIR; *New York World-Telegram and Sun*, April 23 and May 9, 1953.

45. *New York Times*, May 9 and 10, 1953.

46. "The Son of a Longshoreman" to John M. Corridan, S.J., May 13, 1953, box 11, folder 1, XIIR; *Waterfront Investigation*, May 7, 1953, 567; *New York Herald-Tribune*, May 13, 1953; *New York Times*, August 22, 1953.

47. *Fourth Report of the New York State Crime Commission (Port of New York Waterfront)* (Albany, N.Y.), May 20, 1953, 37, 67; *New York Times*, June 14, 1953.

48. *Fourth Report*, 67; Jensen, *Strife on the Waterfront*, 99–102; *New York Times*, May 22, 1953; Peter B. Levy, "The Waterfront Commission of the Port of New York: A History and Appraisal," *Industrial and Labor Relations Review* (July 1989): 511.

49. *New York Times*, August 1, 1953; Levy, "The Waterfront Commission of the Port of New York," 509.

50. Tobin testimony, *Record of the Public Hearings*, 13.

51. Testimony of Rev. John M. Corridan, S.J., June 9, 1953, ibid., 118–19.

52. Ibid., 122.

53. Testimony of James J. Conroy, June 9, 1953, ibid., 204–8.

54. 206.

55. Tobin statement, *New Jersey–New York Waterfront Commission Compact,* 77; Vernon H. Jensen, *Hiring of Dock Workers and Employment Practices in the Ports of New York, Liverpool, London, Rotterdam, and Marseilles* (Cambridge: Harvard University Press, 1964), 42; testimony of George Meany, June 9, 1953, in *Record of the Public Hearings,* 105.

56. Statement of John M. Corridan, S.J., July 22, 1953, in *New Jersey–New York Waterfront Commission Compact,* 96–100; statement of Senator Charles H. Tobey, July 22, 1953, ibid., 15–17.

15. Saving the Picture

1. Elia Kazan, *Elia Kazan: A Life* (New York: Doubleday, 1988), 492–94; Budd Schulberg, "The Bottom of the River," typescript outline for screenplay, box 31, folder 5, Elia Kazan Papers, Wesleyan Cinema Archives, Wesleyan University.

2. Schulberg, "The Bottom of the River," 26–27. In his memoir Kazan wrote: "In midwinter...Budd gave me the first draft of the waterfront screenplay, titled *The Golden Warriors*" (*Elia Kazan,* 506). There is no evidence that Schulberg had completed a new version by this time. Kazan also inaccurately referred to Schulberg's original 1951 script as "The Bottom of the River." Schulberg did not recall writing a script other than "Crime on the Water Front" prior to the partnership with Kazan, which began in late spring 1952. It is quite likely that the thirty-seven-page "Bottom of the River" found in the Wesleyan Cinema Archives is the "thirty-five page story summary" Kazan indicated was sent to Zanuck prior to "The Golden Warriors," whose first incarnation (midwinter 1953) was not as a screenplay but as a twenty-eight-page treatment. It is clear from Zanuck's February 1953 response that this was the version under consideration at the time. See Dan Georgakas, "Schulberg on the Waterfront," in *On the Waterfront,* ed. Joanna E. Rapf (New York: Cambridge University Press, 2003), 41–42, 58, n.4.

3. Schulberg, "The Bottom of the River," 29–30; cf. John M. Corridan, S.J., "A Catholic Looks at the Waterfront," box 10, folder 25, XIIR; Malcolm Johnson, "Father Gangbuster of the Docks," *Catholic Digest* (March 1952): 29; cf. Budd Schulberg, "Waterfront Priest," *Commonweal,* April 3, 1953, 644.

4. Schulberg, "The Bottom of the River," 34.

5. Budd Schulberg, "The Golden Warriors," ca. January 1953, typescript outline for screenplay, box 31, folder 5, Kazan Papers, 1, 8, 17,

6. Ibid., 24, 26–27.

7. Darryl Zanuck to Elia Kazan, February 4, 1953, in *Memo from Darryl F. Zanuck: The Golden Years at Twentieth Century-Fox,* ed. Rudy Behlmer (New York: Grove Press, 1993), 224; Kazan, *Elia Kazan,* 506.

8. Joseph C. Goulden, *Meany* (New York: Atheneum, 1972), 187–88.

9. Darryl Zanuck to Elia Kazan, February 4, 1953, in *Memo from Darryl F. Zanuck,* 223; Kazan, *Elia Kazan,* 506.

10. Kazan, *Elia Kazan,* 395, 506; author interview with Budd Schulberg, May 10, 2003; Darryl Zanuck to Elia Kazan, February 4, 1953, 224; Darryl Zanuck to Elia Kazan and Budd Schulberg, February 10, 1953, box 31, folder 8, Kazan Papers; Darryl Zanuck to Elia Kazan and Budd Schulberg, February 12, 1953, in *Memo from Darryl F. Zanuck,* 225–28.

11. Kazan, *Elia Kazan,* 507.

12. Budd Schulberg, "Golden Warriors" (April 1, 1953), box 31, folder 2, Kazan Papers, 3, 81, 111–15; Schulberg, "The Golden Warriors" (May 15, 1953), 10–11, 83, 108–9, Schulberg Deposit, Rauner Special Collections Library, Webster Hall, Dartmouth College.

13. Schulberg, "Golden Warriors" (May 15, 1953), 11, 23, 83.

14. Ibid., 19, 78. Leo Braudy, in *On the Waterfront* (London: British Film Institute, 2005), 38–39, similarly notes, "As the script developed, many of the explicitly Christian trappings were eliminated." I place greater stress on the distinctly "Catholic" references because the final version could be said to convey a generically "Christian" sensibility throughout.

15. Budd Schulberg, afterword to *On the Waterfront: The Final Shooting Script* (Hollywood: Samuel French, 1980), 145–46; cf. Kazan, *Elia Kazan*, 506–8.

16. Kazan, *Elia Kazan*, 508; Schulberg, afterword, 146–47; cf. Braudy, *On the Waterfront*, 23–24; Richard Schickel, *Elia Kazan: A Biography* (New York: HarperCollins, 2005), 286–87.

17. Darryl Zanuck to Elia Kazan, July 15, 1954, in *Memo from Darryl F. Zanuck*, 229–30; Darryl Zanuck to All Producers and Executives, March 12, 1953, ibid., 233–34; *New York Times*, July 11, 1954; for Zanuck's infatuation with CinemaScope, see also George F. Custen, *Twentieth Century's Fox: Darryl F. Zanuck and the Culture of Hollywood* (New York: Basic Books, 1997), 320–25.

18. Kazan, *Elia Kazan*, 509–10.

19. Peter Manso, *Brando: The Biography* (New York: Hyperion, 1994), 357; Schickel, *Elia Kazan*, 288; Natasha Fraser-Cavassoni, *Sam Spiegel: The Incredible Life and Times of Hollywood's Most Iconoclastic Producer, the Miracle Worker Who Went from Penniless Refugee to Show Biz Legend, and Made Possible "The African Queen," "On the Waterfront," "The Bridge on the River Kwai," and "Lawrence of Arabia"* (New York: Little Brown, 2003), 148; Schulberg, afterword, 149.

20. Kazan, *Elia Kazan*, 511; Schulberg, afterword, 150; Fraser-Cavassoni, *Sam Spiegel*, 52, 86, 148.

21. Kazan, *Elia Kazan*, 511; for the short-lived deal with United Artists, see *New York Times*, June 13, 1953; Fraser-Cavassoni, *Sam Spiegel*, 148–50.

22. Manso, *Brando*, 306; Darryl F. Zanuck, memorandum to Elia Kazan and Budd Schulberg, February 10, 1953, box 31, folder 8, Kazan Papers; Richard Schickel, *Brando: A Life in Our Times* (New York: Atheneum, 1991), 33–37; Kazan, *Elia Kazan*, 300–301.

23. Michel Ciment, *Kazan on Kazan* (New York: Viking, 1974), 107; Kazan, *Elia Kazan*, 517; Budd Schulberg remarks, *On the Waterfront* walking tour, Hoboken, N.J., May 10, 2003.

24. Manso, *Brando*, 358–60; Andrew Sinclair, *Spiegel: The Man behind the Pictures* (London: Weidenfeld and Nicolson, 1987), 69–70; cf. Kazan, *Elia Kazan*, 515–17, which does not mention an early morning meeting at the Stage Deli; biographer Natasha Fraser-Cavassoni (*Sam Spiegel*, 155) registers her skepticism that such a meeting ever took place.

25. Manso, *Brando*, 360; Jeff Young, *Kazan: The Master Director Discusses His Films: Interviews with Elia Kazan* (New York: Newmarket Press, 1999), 127–29; Michael Denning, *The Cultural Front: The Laboring of American Culture in the Twentieth Century* (New York: Verso, 1996), 20.

26. Copies of Corridan's contracts with Budd Schulberg and Horizon-American Corporation are in box 11, folder 38, XIIR; John J. McEvoy, S.J., to John M. Corridan, S.J., December 31, 1953, box 10, folder 1, XIIR; John M. Corridan, S.J., to John McMahon, S.J., December 30, 1953, box 10, folder 1, XIIR.

27. *New York Times*, September 21, 23, and 29, October 3, 1953; *New York Journal-American*, September 29, 1953.

28. Budd Schulberg, "How One Pier Got Rid of the Mob," *New York Times Magazine*, September 27, 1953, 58; reprinted in Malcolm Johnson, *On the Waterfront: The Pulitzer Prize–Winning Articles That Inspired the Classic Movie and Transformed the New York Harbor* (New York: Chamberlain Bros., 2005), appendix, 213–20.

29. Schulberg, "How One Pier Got Rid of the Mob," 60.

30. *New York Times*, October 15, 1953; John M. Corridan, S.J., to L. J. Twomey, S.J., November 4, 1953, box 10, folder 2, XIIR; Corridan, S.J., To Whom It May Concern, December 10, 1953, box 10, folder 22, XIIR.

31. Corridan, "To Whom It May Concern."

32. *New York Times*, November 19 and 22, 1953; Allen Raymond, *Waterfront Priest* (New York: Holt, 1955), 230–31.

33. *New York Times*, November 19, 1953.

34. Author interview with Father John O'Brien, December 6, 2001.

35. Vernon H. Jensen, *Strife on the Waterfront: The Port of New York since 1945* (Ithaca, N.Y.: Cornell University Press, 1974), 121; *New York Times*, November 22, 1953.

16. The Mile Square City's Moment

1. *Newark Evening News,* December 2, 1953.

2. Ibid.

3. As if to confirm the Jesuit's view that all waterfront publicity was good publicity, the *Newark Evening News* reporter noted that Corridan "has also tried to coax a waterfront script on which Arthur Miller, the playwright[,] has been working, hoping that more attention will be focused on dock problems"; ibid.; *New York Times,* December 1, 1953.

4. *New York Times,* November 22, 1953; Vernon H. Jensen, *Strife on the Waterfront: The Port of New York since 1945* (Ithaca, N.Y.: Cornell University Press, 1974), 125.

5. John M. Corridan, S.J., to L. J. Twomey, S.J., November 4, 1953, box 10, folder 2, XIIR; Jensen, *Strife on the Waterfront,* 125–27.

6. *New York Times,* November 23, 1953; Budd Schulberg remarks, *On the Waterfront* walking tour, Hoboken, May 10, 2003; Adolph Schalk, "The Real One," *Today* (June 1955): 7.

7. *On the Waterfront* "was to be filmed in New York, partly because the location demanded it," explains a standard film history reference volume. See David Shipman, *The Story of Cinema: A Complete Narrative History from the Beginnings to the Present* (New York: St. Martin, 1982), 875. Another reference work, Tom Stempel, *American Audiences on Movies and Moviegoing* (Lexington: University Press of Kentucky, 2001), 41, noted, "Audiences...respond to the reality of the New York locations." David Caute, a prominent historian of the Left and of anticommunism, wrote in *The Dancer Defects: The Struggle for Cultural Supremacy during the Cold War* (New York: Oxford University Press, 2003), 231, "The film took as its locale the New York docks." Works that begin with this premise are often marred by numerous additional factual errors related to the film and its contexts.

8. James Sanders, *Celluloid Skyline: New York and the Movies* (New York: Alfred A. Knopf, 2001), 346, 349. Leo Braudy, *On the Waterfront* (London: British Film Institute, 2005), 26–37, skillfully recovers some original locations of key scenes in the film but does not treat Hoboken as a historical site of waterfront conflict.

9. Elia Kazan, *Elia Kazan: A Life* (New York: Doubleday, 1988), 517; Natasha Fraser-Cavasoni, *Sam Spiegel* (New York: Simon and Schuster, 2003), 148.

10. Peter Manso, *Brando: The Biography* (New York: Hyperion, 1994), 354–55; for treatments that backdate the Hoboken setting, see, for example, Kenneth Hey's generally insightful essay "Ambivalence as a Theme in *On the Waterfront* (1954): An Interdisciplinary Approach to Film Study," *American Quarterly* 31 (Winter 1979): 676.

11. Kazan, *Elia Kazan,* 499–500.

12. For favorable treatments of Kazan that accept his account of Tony Mike's role, see Richard Schickel, *Elia Kazan: A Biography* (New York: HarperCollins, 2005), 284. In an interview Budd Schulberg told Schickel he introduced Kazan to DeVincenzo; no date is given, but Schulberg did not establish contacts in Hoboken until shortly before filming commenced there; cf. Richard Schickel, *Brando: A Life in Our Times* (New York: Atheneum, 1991), 87. Tony Mike's son Salvatore DeVincenzo confirmed the presence of Eva Marie Saint at the dinner; see Sada Fretz, "Hoboken's Waterfront," in *On the Waterfront: Starring Hoboken, New Jersey* (Hoboken: Hoboken Historical Museum, 2004), 8.

13. Jeff Young, *Kazan: The Master Director Discusses His Films; Interviews with Elia Kazan* (New York: Newmarket Press, 1999), 117–18. "Thinly veiled attempt" is from Robert J. Corber, *Homosexuality in Cold War America: Resistance and the Crisis of Masculinity* (Durham: Duke University Press, 1997), 131; this work was chosen nearly at random as representative of hundreds of similar assertions found in works of film studies, cultural history, and journalism. For the standard interpretations of the film's politics, see Martin Gottfried, *Arthur Miller: His Life and Work* (New York: Da Capo Press, 2003), 232–35; Victor S. Navasky, *Naming Names* (New York: Viking, 1980), 209–10 (Navasky briefly reiterated his view in *A Matter of Opinion* [New York: Farrar, Straus and Giroux, 2005], 125); Caute, *The Dancer Defects,* 212–15; Peter Biskind, "The Politics of Power in *On the Waterfront,*" in *Gods and Monsters: Thirty Years of Writing on Film and Culture from One of America's Most Incisive Writers* (New York: Nation Books, 2004), 2–25; Biskind, *Seeing Is Believing: How*

Hollywood Taught Us to Stop Worrying and Love the Fifties (New York: Pantheon, 1983), 169–82; Nora Sayre, *Running Time: Films of the Cold War* (New York: Dial Press, 1982), 161. Alternative and generally positive (or at least ambivalent) readings are found in Braudy, *On the Waterfront;* Schickel, *Elia Kazan;* James T. Fisher, "The Priest in the Movie: *On the Waterfront* as Historical Theology," in *Theology and the New Histories* 44 (annual publication of the College Theology Society), ed. Gary Macy (1998): 167–85; Brian Neve, "The 1950s: the Case of Elia Kazan and *On the Waterfront,* in *Cinema, Politics and Society in America,* ed. Philip Davies and Brian Neve (Manchester: Manchester University Press, 1981), 97–118; Dan Georgakas, "Schulberg on the Waterfront," in *On the Waterfront,* ed. Joanna E. Rapf (New York: Cambridge University Press, 2003), 40–60.

14. Author interview with Budd Schulberg, October 4, 2002; Budd Schulberg, *On the Waterfront: The Final Shooting Script, 1st ed.* (Hollywood: Samuel French, 1980), 64. On May 10, 2003, Budd Schulberg and Hoboken historian Leonard Luizzi conducted a tour of *On the Waterfront* locations for a documentary film directed by James Garamone. During a stop at Frank Sinatra Park, former site of the Fourth and Fifth Street piers, Schulberg repeated his assertion that he first met Tony Mike DeVincenzo during the late autumn 1953 location shoot in Tony Mike's hometown.

15. Young, *Kazan,* 15; *New York World-Telegram and Sun,* April 24, 1953; *New York Times,* October 25, 1953.

16. Kazan, *Elia Kazan,* 500; Budd Schulberg, "Drama in Hoboken," *Holiday* (August 1954): 82–85; Schulberg, "Waterfront Screenplay First Draft (So Far Untitled)," August 29, 1953, 14, Schulberg Deposit, Rauner Special Collections Library, Webster Hall, Dartmouth College.

17. "Waterfront: An Original Screenplay," September 30, 1953, box 31, folder 6, Elia Kazan Papers, Wesleyan Cinema Archives, Wesleyan University; "Golden Warriors," April 1, 1953, box 31, folder 2, 127, 141, Kazan Papers, ibid.; "Golden Warriors," June 1, 1953, Schulberg Deposit.

18. "Waterfront: An Original Screenplay," September 30, 1953; Schulberg, "Drama in Hoboken," 82–85; author interview with Budd Schulberg, October 4, 2002; Budd Schulberg, "'Why Write It When You Can't Sell It to the Pictures?'" *Saturday Review,* September 3, 1955, 5. Several conversations with Mike Miskell, a lifelong Chelsea resident and former ILA employee, were very helpful toward understanding the West Side's unsuitability as a film location.

19. Jules Weinberg, "A Racketeer Takes Over an American City," *Look,* July 17, 1951, 42–44; Mary Heaton Vorse, "The Pirates' Nest of New York," *Harper's Magazine* (April 1952): 27–37.

20. Fred M. De Sapio to John M. Corridan, S.J., January 14, 1953, box 10, folder 22, XIIR; Anthony (Tony Mike) DeVincenzo (as told to Richard Carter), "The Mob Said They'd Kill Me for My Story," *True* (May 1953): 18–20, 22, 24, 26–27, 101–7.

21. Dick Carter to Corridan, February 6, 1953, box 10, folder 22, XIIR Papers.

22. *Bayonne Times,* March 5, 1953.

23. *New York Times,* September 25, 1952. My approach to the relationships between place and theme is deeply indebted to the work of Carlo Rotella; see especially his stirring chapter on *The French Connection,* "Grittiness," in *Good with Their Hands: Boxers, Bluesmen, and Other Characters from the Rust Belt* (Berkeley: University of California Press, 2002), 105–66.

24. Marc Levinson, *The Box: How the Shipping Container Made the World Smaller and the World Economy Bigger* (Princeton: Princeton University Press, 2006), 83–85; Jameson W. Doig, *Empire on the Hudson: Entrepreneurial Vision and Political Power at the Port of New York Authority* (New York: Columbia University Press, 2001), 353–54, 374–75; *New York Times,* September 20, 1952; *Jersey Journal,* October 1, 1952; Daniel Bell, "The Racket-Ridden Longshoremen: The Web of Economics and Politics," in *The End of Ideology: On the Exhaustion of Political Ideas in the Fifties* (Glencoe, Ill.: Free Press, 1960), 177–78.

25. *New York Times,* May 6, 1953; "'Clean-Up Week' on Docks," *Life,* May 18, 1953, 40–43; "Death on the Docks," *Newsweek,* May 18, 1953, 34–35; testimony of Walter P. Hedden, May 7, 1953, *Waterfront Investigation: Hearings before a Subcommittee of the Committee on Interstate and Foreign Commerce, United States Senate,* pt. 1, *New York–New Jersey Waterfront* (Washington, D.C., 1953), 550.

26. *New York Times,* October 21, 1953; Allen Raymond, *Waterfront Priest* (New York: Holt, 1955), 248. Work on the new Pier C between First and Second streets, the widest in the

port, began in September 1953; see *New York Times,* September 29, 1953. Later renamed Pier A, this facility is now the site of a large park; the renamed Pier C at Fourth Street no longer exists. In 2007 construction began on a long-delayed recreation pier on the site. For an extraordinarily well documented historical and architectural account of Hoboken's piers, see the website Historic American Buildings Survey.

27. Daniel Patrick Moynihan, "The Irish," in *Beyond the Melting Pot: The Negroes, Puerto Ricans, Jews, Italians, and Irish of New York City,* ed. Nathan Glazer and Daniel Patrick Moynihan (Cambridge: MIT Press, 1963); Raymond, *Waterfront Priest,* 136; cf. John M. Corridan, S.J., "A Criticism of *On the Waterfront,* by the 'Waterfront Priest,'" *Queen's Work* (December 1954): 8–9.

28. *New York Herald Tribune,* May 13, 1953; *New York Times,* May 13, 1953; Joseph A. Varacalli, "Ethnic Politics in Jersey City: The Changing Nature of Irish-Italian Relations, 1917–1981," in *Italians and Irish in America: Proceedings of the Sixteenth American Conference of the American Italian Historical Association,* ed. Francis X. Feminella (Staten Island, N.Y.: American Italian Historical Association, 1985), 212.

29. Testimony of Anthony DeVincenzo, December 15, 1952, *NYSCC Hearings,* 2:768; Corridan, "A Criticism of *On the Waterfront,* 8–9; author interview with Leonard Luizzi, November 2, 2002.

30. *New York Herald Tribune,* November 22, 1953; Christopher Morley, "Adventure in Hoboken," *Saturday Review of Literature,* September 8, 1928, 101; *Fortune* quoted in Melissa Holbrook Pierson, *The Place You Love Is Gone: Progress Hits Home* (New York: W. W. Norton 2006), 74; Braudy, *On the Waterfront,* 29.

31. Braudy, *On the Waterfront,* 27.

32. Sanders, *Celluloid Skyline,* 347; see the chapter on Hoboken in Mary Procter and Bill Matuszeski, *Gritty Cities* (Philadelphia: Temple University Press, 1978), 91–96.

33. Nicholas Acocella, "The Filming of *On the Waterfront,*" *Hoboken History* 18 (1997): 3; Schulberg interview, October 4, 2002; Kazan, *Elia Kazan,* 316–18, 378–83, 427–28.

34. Schulberg, *On the Waterfront,* 3–7; Young, *Kazan,* 146.

35. Acocella, "The Filming of *On the Waterfront,*" 2–15; *Jersey Journal,* December 10, 1953.

36. Author interview with Joe Sivo, July 31, 2002; Karl Malden (with Carla Malden), *"When Do I Start?" A Memoir* (New York: Simon and Schuster, 1997), 240.

37. Malden, *"When Do I Start?"* 240–43; Paul Drexel, "Waterfront Property," *New Jersey Monthly* (October 2004): 119; *New York Post,* August 3, 1954; "Reflections on the Silver Screen:" videotaped interview by Richard Brown of Karl Malden, 1992, Billy Rose Theatre Collection, New York Public Library.

38. Author interviews with Thomas Hanley, November 7, 2002, April 13, 2003; *New York Times,* July 18, 2004.

39. Drexel, "Waterfront Property," 121; Hanley interviews; William Finnegan, "Watching the Waterfront," *New Yorker,* June 19, 2006, 57.

40. Hanley interviews.

41. Jeanine Basinger, John Frazer, and Joseph W. Reed Jr., eds., *Working with Kazan* (Middletown, Conn.: Wesleyan University Press, 1973), unpaginated; Kazan, *Elia Kazan,* 521; Luizzi interview; Acocella, "The Filming of *On the Waterfront,*" 14.

42. Kazan, *Elia Kazan,* 521; Acocella, "The Filming of *On the Waterfront,*" 14; Stuart Byron and Martin L. Rubin, "Elia Kazan Interview," in *Elia Kazan: Interviews,* ed. William Baer (Jackson: University Press of Mississippi, 2000), 140.

17. The Priest in the Movie

1. Stuart Byron and Martin L. Rubin, "Elia Kazan Interview," in *Elia Kazan: Interviews,* ed. William Baer (Jackson: University Press of Mississippi, 2000), 140; *Bergen Record,* July 30, 2000; author interview with Budd Schulberg, October 4, 2002.

2. Cf. Budd Schulberg, *On the Waterfront: The Final Shooting Script* (Hollywood: Samuel French, 1980), 12, 29. Naming the hiring boss "Big Mac" may well have represented an inside allusion to "Mr. Big," William McCormack, who also directly inspired the character "Mr. Upstairs," the powerful waterfront businessman who is seen only from behind in his brief appearance in the film. Among numerous other inside jokes in the script, Edie's stray cat is disparagingly called "cock-eyed" (as in Dunn) by Pop Doyle.

3. Arthur Miller, *Timebends: A Life* (New York: Grove Press, 1987), 147; Martin Gottfried, *Arthur Miller: His Life and Work* (New York: Da Capo Press, 2003), 233; Malcolm Johnson, *Crime on the Labor Front* (New York: McGraw-Hill, 1950), 138–39.

4. Jeff Young, *Kazan: The Master Director Discusses His Films; Interviews with Elia Kazan* (New York: Newmarket Press, 1999), 113, 127, 129; Brian Neve, "The Personal and the Political: Elia Kazan and *On the Waterfront*," in *On the Waterfront*, ed. Joanna E. Rapf (New York: Cambridge University Press, 2003), 34–35.

5. Schulberg, *On the Waterfront*, 35–36; testimony of James F. Keane, December 16, 1952, *NYSCC Hearings*, 2:1028.

6. Nicholas Acocella, "The Filming of *On the Waterfront*," *Hoboken History* 18 (1997): 4–5; remarks of Hoboken historian Lenny Luizzi, *On the Waterfront* walking tour, Hoboken, May 10, 2003; *Church of Saints Peter and Paul: Hoboken, New Jersey* (South Hackensack, N.J.: Custombook, 1964), and *Church of Our Lady of Grace* (Hackensack, N.J.: Custombook, 1976), both located in Parish Histories, box 11, Archdiocese of Newark Archives, Walsh Library, Seton Hall University; see also Hoboken Board of Trade, *History of Hoboken* (Hoboken, N.J., 1907), 56–58.

7. Author interview with Rev. John O'Brien, December 6, 2001.

8. Schulberg, *On the Waterfront*, 46; Edward L. de Laurot and Jonas Mekas, "An Interview with Boris Kaufman," in Rapf, *On the Waterfront*, 162; François Truffaut, *The Films in My Life*, trans. Leonard Mayhew (New York: Simon and Shuster, 1975), 111.

9. For the differing recollections of Malden and Saint, see Leo Braudy, *On the Waterfront* (London: British Film Institute, 2005), 45; Neil Hurley, S.J., "Blending Fact and Fiction Not Always Successful—But Worked in This Instance," *Variety*, October 28, 1988, 116; Neil P. Hurley, S.J., "*On the Waterfront*: Rebirth of a 'Contenduh,'" in *Image and Likeness: Religious Visions in American Film Classics*, ed. John R. May (New York: Paulist Press, 1992), 98–99, 189, n.5.

10. Interview with Alice Dillon Pucknat and Jackie Dillon Hill, February 26, 2003. Their father, John Dillon, was president of Local 770 United Automobile Workers Union, taught for many years at Xavier Labor School, and with his family enjoyed a warm decades-long relationship with Father Carey.

11. Joe Doyle, "Striking for Ireland on the New York Docks," in *The New York Irish*, ed. Ronald H. Bayor and Timothy J. Meagher (Baltimore: Johns Hopkins University Press, 1996), 357–73; Dee Garrison, *Mary Heaton Vorse: The Life of an American Insurgent*, (Philadelphia: Temple University Press, 1989), 312–13.

12. Young, *Kazan*, 126–27, 129; Thomas H. Pauly, *An American Odyssey: Elia Kazan and American Culture* (Philadelphia: Temple University Press, 1983), 201; Elia Kazan, *Elia Kazan: A Life* (New York: Doubleday, 1988), 525, 538–39.

13. Sam B. Girgus, *Hollywood Renaissance: The Cinema of Democracy in the Era of Ford, Capra, and Kazan* (New York: Cambridge University Press, 1998), 158–61.

14. Young, *Kazan*, 129.

15. Kazan, *Elia Kazan*, 524–25. Some native Hobokenites believe that the scene was shot on River Street, with venetian blinds borrowed from the nearby Meyer's Hotel; Acocella, "On the Waterfront," 12. Brando's friend and sometime stand-in Carlo Fiore, a heroin addict, recalled, "As it happened, this scene was filmed indoors at an uptown studio, five minutes away from my junk connection," likely a reliable recollection—given the circumstances—from an otherwise unreliable source; Carlo Fiore, *Bud: The Brando I Knew* (New York: Delacorte Press, 1974), 125. For Hoboken's claim, see Sada Fretz, "Hoboken's Waterfront," in *On the Waterfront: Starring Hoboken, New Jersey* (Hoboken: Hoboken Historical Society, 2004), 11.

16. Peter Manso, *Brando: The Biography* (New York: Hyperion, 1994), 361. Budd Schulberg retold the Roger Donoghue story on the Hoboken walking tour; his most detailed account is in a videotaped interview with James Garamone, August 2, 2003, courtesy of James Garamone. For more on Schulberg and boxers, see "Budd Schulberg: The Art of Fiction CLXIX," *Paris Review* 160 (Winter 2001): 93–94. The first incarnation of "I coulda been a contender" appears in the June 1, 1953, "Golden Warriors" screenplay (115), folder 3, box 31, Kazan Papers, Wesleyan.

17. *New York Times,* December 20, 1953; Schulberg, *On the Waterfront,* 79–83 and 151–52. In *On the Waterfront* Leo Braudy reported that "in a script in Kazan's files dated 'circa 4/1/1953' all the cutaways and reaction shots are already there" (80, n. 32). This script is the first complete draft of "Golden Warriors": see 111–15 for this version's "Christ in the Shapeup" and Schulberg's directions (box 31, folder 2, Kazan Papers, Wesleyan). Though the cutaway shots were already incorporated in the script it is still likely that Spiegel insisted on cutting significant time from the scene.

18. Braudy, *On the Waterfront,* 26; Budd Schulberg, *"Vale atque Ave*—Father John M. Corridan, S.J.," Schulberg Deposit, Rauner Special Collections Library, Webster Hall, Dartmouth College; Karl Malden (with Carla Malden), *"When Do I Start?" A Memoir* (New York: Easton Press, 1997), 241.

19. Budd Schulberg, *Waterfront* (New York: Random House, 1955); for Pauline Kael's review, see http://www.geocities.com/paulinekaelreviews/o2.htnl; Pauline Kael, *I Lost It at the Movies* (Boston: Little, Brown, 1965), 47–55; "The Screen: Astor Offers *On the Waterfront,*" *New York Times,* July 29, 1954, and "The Big Sell: A Review," *Harper's* (August 1954), both reprinted in Rapf, *On the Waterfront,* 151–56.

20. Michel Ciment, *Kazan on Kazan* (New York: Viking, 1974), 110–12; David Shipman, *The Story of Cinema: A Complete Narrative History from the Beginnings to the Present* (New York: St. Martin, 1982), 876; Philip Lopate, *Waterfront: A Journey around Manhattan* (New York: Crown, 2004), 59.

21. Michel Delahaye, "Interview with Kazan," in Baer, *Elia Kazan Interviews,* 93; Nora Sayre, *Running Time: Films of the Cold War* (New York: Dial Press, 1982), 161.

22. Peter Biskind, *Seeing Is Believing: How Hollywood Taught Us to Stop Worrying and Love the Fifties* (New York: Pantheon Books, 1983), 174–76; Biskind, "The Politics of Power in *On the Waterfront,*" in *Gods and Monsters: Thirty Years of Writing on Film and Culture from One of America's Most Incisive Writers* (New York: Nation Books, 2004), 2–26 (originally published in *Film Quarterly* [Fall 1975]).

23. Ciment, *Kazan on Kazan,* 112.

24. Kazan, *Elia Kazan,* 438.

25. Braudy, *On the Waterfront,* 38–45.

26. All quotations are from Schulberg, *On the Waterfront,* 99–105.

27. Ibid., 121–40; Father John O'Brien interview.

28. Michael Epstein, *None Without Sin,* Public Broadcasting System, September 3, 2003. Paul Goodman is quoted in Daniel Belgrad, *The Culture of Spontaneity: Improvisation and the Arts in Postwar America* (Chicago: University of Chicago Press, 1998), 156.

18. "The Corruption Goes Deep"

1. *New York Times,* December 20, 1953; Neil Hurley, S.J., "Blending Fact and Fiction Not Always Successful—But Worked in This Instance," *Variety,* October 28, 1988.

2. *New York Times,* December 17–20, 1953; Vernon H. Jensen, *Strife on the Waterfront: The Port of New York since 1945* (Ithaca, N.Y.: Cornell University Press, 1974), 125–28.

3. *New York Times,* October 3, 1953, July 29, 1954; Allen Raymond, *Waterfront Priest* (New York: Holt, 1955), 237–38.

4. *New York Times,* December 23, 1953; Jensen, *Strife on the Waterfront,* 123–24.

5. *New York Times,* December 22 and 24, 1953.

6. Ibid.

7. The results of the referendum were not broken down by ILA local or polling place (unlike in the hiring system election of May 1953); *New York Times,* November 25, December 10 and 24, 1953; Raymond, *Waterfront Priest,* 235, 237, 240.

8. Michael P. O'Connell to John M. Corridan, S.J., n.d. (ca. December 1953), box 11, folder 19, XIIR.

9. For DeVincenzo's lawsuit (the first of several he would file during and after his season of notoriety), see *New York Times,* December 22, 1953.

10. *New York Times* December 25, 26, 28, and 29, 1953; Jensen, *Strife on the Waterfront,* 129.

11. *New York Times,* December 25 and 28, 1953.

12. *New York Times,* February 2, 1954; Raymond, *Waterfront Priest,* 237; John M. Corridan, S.J., text of speech to longshoremen, Chelsea Arms Hotel, February 1, 1954, box 11, folder 30, XIIR.

13. William J. Smith, S.J., to Martin Van Heest, January 28, 1954, box 11, folder 22, XIIR; for accompanying press release from St. Peter's College Institute of Industrial Relations, see box 29, folder 30, XIIR.

14. Sanford Gottlieb, "The Man Who Shut Down the Port of New York," *The Reporter,* April 27, 1954, 28–31; *New York Times,* March 5, 6, 9, and 19, 1954; Jensen, *Strife on the Waterfront,* 130–31; Raymond, *Waterfront Priest,* 242–43.

15. Budd Schulberg to John M. Corridan, S.J., March 26, 1954, box 6, folder 59, XIIR; *New York AFL Longshoreman,* April 13, 1954; *New York Times,* April 2 and 13, 1954.

16. Jon Burlingame, "Leonard Bernstein and *On the Waterfront:* Tragic Nobility, A Lyrical Song, and Music of Violence," in *On the Waterfront,* ed. Joanna E. Rapf (New York: Cambridge University Press, 2003), 124–47.

17. *New York Times,* May 7, 9, and 13, 1954.

18. Jensen, *Strife on the Labor Front,* 133; *New York Times,* May 6, 1954; Charles P. Larrowe, *Shape-Up and Hiring Hall: A Comparison of Hiring Methods and Labor Relations on the New York and Seattle Waterfronts* (1955; rpt., Westport, Conn.: Greenwood Press, 1976), 215–16.

19. *New York Times* May 18 and 20, 1954.

20. *New York AFL Longshoreman,* May 18, 1954; John M. Corridan, S.J., "Letter to All Longshoremen, Checkers and Allied Craft Workers" (in English and Italian), box 11, folder 12, XIIR.

21. Corridan, *"Letter to All Longshoremen."*

22. Tom Hendrick to John M. Corridan, S.J., May 20, 1954, box 11, folder 12, XIIR; Frank Fiano to John M. Corridan, S.J., May 23, 1954, box 11, folder 1, XIIR.

23. Letter to John M. Corridan, S.J., ca. May 1954 (letter is missing last page; it is unclear if it was signed), box 11, folder 12, XIIR.

24. Unsigned letter to John M. Corridan, S.J., May 21, 1954, box 11, folder 12, XIIR; Grace Caruso to Francis Cardinal Spellman, May 22, 1954; "A Catholic Longshoreman with Five Children" to Spellman, May 22, 1954; Msgr. John M. Fleming to John M. Corridan, S.J., May 25, 1954, box 10, folder 1, XIIR.

25. *New York Times,* May 25, 1954; *America* 91 (May 22, 1954): 207.

26. *New York Times,* May 27, 28, and 31, 1954; Budd Schulberg, "The Waterfront Revisited," *Saturday Evening Post,* September 7, 1963, 30.

27. *New York Times,* June 4, September 18 and 30, 1954; Debra Bernhardt interview with John Dwyer, November 21, 1980, New Yorkers at Work Oral History Series, Robert F. Wagner Labor Archives, Tamiment Library, New York University.

28. Joseph C. Goulden, *Meany* (New York: Atheneum, 1972), 194.

29. Ibid., 192–93; Budd Schulberg, "The Waterfront Revisited," unpublished draft version, Budd Schulberg Deposit, Rauner Special Collections Library, Dartmouth College.

30. John C. Cort, "The Hidden Seeds of Corruption," *Commonweal* 60 (June 18, 1954): 267–68.

19. The Poetry of Success

1. Mark S. Massa, *Catholics and American Culture: Fulton Sheen, Dorothy Day, and the Notre Dame Football Team* (New York: Crossroad, 1999), 75–76.

2. Elia Kazan, *Elia Kazan: A Life* (New York: Doubleday, 1988), 526–27; Budd Schulberg, introduction to Malcolm Johnson, *On the Waterfront: The Pulitzer Prize–Winning Articles That Inspired the Classic Movie and Transformed the New York Harbor* (New York: Chamberlain Bros., 2005), xl; Patricia Bosworth, *Marlon Brando* (New York: Penguin, 2001), 114; Marlon Brando (with Robert Lindsey), *Songs My Mother Taught Me* (New York: Random House, 1994), 199.

3. Kazan, *Elia Kazan*, 528–29; Schulberg, introduction, xl.

4. *New York Times*, July 29, 1954; Philip T. Hartung, "Man's Hope: A Review," in *On the Waterfront*, ed. Joanna E. Rapf (New York: Cambridge University Press, 2003), 157–58. For a sampling of reviews, see "Selected Reviews and Commentary," in Rapf, *On the Waterfront*, 151–61; see also "The Beat of a Pulse," *Newsweek*, August 2, 1954, 78; "Films," *America* 91 (August 7, 1954): 466; Kazan, *Elia Kazan*, 528.

5. Murray Kempton's review is in *New York Post*, September 17, 1954; Lindsay Anderson, "The Last Sequence of *On the Waterfront*," *Sight and Sound* 24, no. 3 (1955): 127–30.

6. Lawson's *Hollywood Review* critique of the film is quoted in Joanna E. Rapf, "Introduction: 'The Mysterious Way of Art': Making a Difference in *On the Waterfront*," in Rapf, *On the Waterfront*, 16, and in Kenneth Lloyd Billingsley, *Hollywood Party: How Communism Seduced the American Film Industry in the 1930s and 1940s* (Rocklin, Calif.: Prima Publishing, 1998), 244; Eric Bentley, "*On the Waterfront*," in *What Is Theatre? A Query in Chronicle Form* (Boston: Beacon Press, 1956), 98–102. *A View from the Bridge* opened in New York in September 1955. Bentley argued that Kazan's and Miller's outlooks were equally simplistic and inimical to true artistry (136).

7. Tom Stempel, *American Audiences on Movies and Moviegoing* (Lexington: University of Kentucky Press, 2001), 136; for a sampling of subsequent work on the politics of *On the Waterfront*, see chapter 17, "The Mile Square City's Moment."

8. Kazan, *Elia Kazan*, 528; Richard Schickel, *Elia Kazan: A Biography* (New York: HarperCollins, 2005), 306.

9. "The New Pictures," *Time*, August 9, 1954, 82–83; http://www.imdb.com/Sections/Awards/Venice_Film_Festival/1954.

10. *New York Times*, March 31, 1955.

11. For Corridan's invitation to join the Academy Awards after-party, see Elia Kazan to John M. Corridan, S.J., March 25, 1955, box 11, folder 38, XIIR.

12. Schulberg, introduction, xl; the Cort quotation is from the ACTU newspaper *Labor Leader* (November 1954), clipping in box 11, folder 39 XIIR; Cort reiterated his point in "Who Thirst after Justice," review of Allen Raymond, *Waterfront Priest, Commonweal* 62 (May 20, 1955): 189.

13. Charles Morris, *American Catholic: The Saints and Sinners Who Built America's Most Powerful Church* (New York: Times Books, 1997), 217.

14. Burns, Dwyer, and Carey are quoted in Jeff Kisseloff, *You Must Remember This: An Oral History of Manhattan from the 1890s to World War II* (Baltimore: Johns Hopkins University Press, 1999), 517–18; author interview with Joe Walls, March 26, 2003. Debra Bernhardt's taped interview with John Dwyer (November 21, 1980, New Yorkers at Work Oral History Series, Robert F. Wagner Labor Archives, Tamiment Library, New York University) is fascinating for much the same reason as Philip Carey's February 19 and March 6, 1981, session with the same interviewer. Whenever the sympathetic Bernhardt prompted Dwyer to probe deeper into issues of waterfront crime and corruption, he often cut off inquiry by remarking, "That's about it."

15. William Mooring's recantation was published in diocesan newspapers including *The Advocate* (Newark), August 28, 1954; Mooring remained a militantly Catholic culture warrior (Hollywood division), but Corridan managed to plant a seed through Mooring's reconsideration of *On the Waterfront*'s political orientation.

16. John H. Williams, S.J., to John M. Corridan, S.J., September 14, 1954, box, folder 2, XIIR; Philip Carey, S.J., to Budd Schulberg, n.d., box 6, folder 59, XIIR; unidentified theologian to John M. Corridan, S.J., February 16, 1955, box 11, folder 38, XIIR; for the Dublin accolades, see Ron Offen, *Brando* (Chicago: Henry Regnery, 1973), 88. In 1995 the Vatican

Film Office listed *On the Waterfront* among forty-five "Great Films" chosen to commemorate the hundredth anniversary of cinema; http://www.nccbuscc.org/fb/vaticanfilms.htm.

17. For the containerization revolution and its impact on the port, see Marc Levinson, *The Box: How the Shipping Container Made the World Smaller and the World Economy Bigger* (Princeton: Princeton University Press, 2006), 44–52; Brian J. Cudahy, *Box Boats: How Container Ships Changed the World* (New York: Fordham University Press, 2006).

18. Pete Hamill, *Downtown: My Manhattan* (New York: Little, Brown, 2004); see also Hamill, *A Drinking Life: A Memoir* (Boston: Little, Brown, 1994); for the re-release of *On the Waterfront*, see *New York Times* advertisement, February 21, 1960. Hamill continued to evoke the memory of the port in his fiction; See Pete Hamill, *North River* (New York: Little, Brown, 2007).

19. Louis LaRusso, *Marlon Brando Sat Right Here: A Drama in Two Acts* (Hollywood: Samuel French, 1980); Anthony DePalma, "From Fathers to Sons on the Waterfront," *New York Times Magazine*, February 21, 1988, 36–39, 50, 54–56. LaRusso's best-known play, *Lamppost Reunion* (1976), was inspired by Hoboken's favorite if fugitive son Frank Sinatra, whose near miss in casting for the part of Terry Malloy always added an extra dash of local intrigue to the film. For LaRusso's obituary, see *New York Times*, February 25, 2003.

20. Carlo Rotella, *Good with Their Hands: Boxers, Bluesmen, and Other Characters from the Rust Belt* (Berkeley: University of California Press, 2002), 146; DePalma, "From Fathers to Sons on the Waterfront," 50.

21. Melissa Holbrook Pierson, *The Place You Love Is Gone: Progress Hits Home* (New York: W. W. Norton, 2006), 106; Joseph Barry and John Derevlany, eds., *Yuppies Invade My House at Dinnertime: A Tale of Brunch, Bombs, and Gentrification in an American City* (Hoboken: Big River Publishing, 1987), xvii–xxiii.

22. William Finnegan, "Watching the Waterfront," *New Yorker*, June 19, 2006, 55; Robert J. McGuire and Robert C. Stewart, "Don't Weaken the Waterfront Commission," *Newark Star-Ledger*, January 26, 2007; Paul Drexel, "Waterfront Property," *New Jersey Monthly* (October 2004): 119. This vignette featuring Tillio does not appear in the shooting script.

23. J. Hoberman, "Still a Contender," *Village Voice*, November 1, 2004. In late spring 2008 Budd Schulberg, still working daily at age ninety-four, traveled to London to witness a new theatrical production of *On the Waterfront*.

24. Paul Giles, *American Catholic Arts and Fictions: Culture, Ideology, Aesthetics* (Cambridge: Cambridge University Press, 1992), 343.

Epilogue

1. Allen Raymond, *Waterfront Priest* (New York: Holt, 1955); Craig Thompson and Allen Raymond, *Gang Rule in New York: The Story of a Lawless Era* (New York: Dial, 1940). Raymond died just two years after *Waterfront Priest* came out; see *New York Times*, June 9, 1957.

2. Raymond, *Waterfront Priest*, 260.

3. Lewis Gannett, review of Raymond, *Waterfront Priest, New York Herald-Tribune*, March 21, 1955; Quentin Anderson review of *Waterfront Priest, New York Times Book Review*, May 15, 1955, 6.

4. John M. Corridan to John McMahon, S.J., December 30, 1953; John J. McEvoy, S.J., to John M. Corridan, S.J., December 31, 1953, box 10, folder 1, XIIR.

5. Author telephone interviews with Owen Dailey, S.J., February 28 and April 2, 2003, November 25, 2005; Thomas E. Henneberry, S.J., to John M. Corridan S.J., ca. early January 1955, box 10, folder 1, XIIR; for Henneberry's habit of mind, see Peter McDonough, *Men Astutely Trained: A History of the Jesuits in the American Century* (New York: Free Press, 1992), 155.

6. John M. Corridan, S.J., to Thomas E. Henneberry, S.J., January 18, 1955; Henneberry to Corridan, March 24, 1955, box 10, folder 1, XIIR; John M. Corridan, S.J., to Henneberry, S.J., December 26, 1954, January 18 and 24, March 25 and 29, 1955, box 10, folder 1, XIIR;

Gannett, review of Raymond, *Waterfront Priest*. For the full range of correspondence between Henneberry and Corridan, see December 16 and 31, 1954, January 26, March 4, 24, 25, and 26, 1955, box 10, folder 1, XIIR.

7. Budd Schulberg, *Waterfront* (New York: Random House, 1955); Schulberg quoted in *Newsday*, October 25, 1988; Richard Gilman, review of Budd Schulberg, *Waterfront, Jubilee* (October 1955): 50–51; W. R. Burnett, review of *Waterfront, Saturday Review*, September 24, 1955, 17.

8. *Village Voice*, December 7, 1955, 1; Thomas E. Henneberry, S.J., to John M. Corridan, S.J., January 2, 1957, box 10, folder 1, XIIR.

9. "Waterfront Priest," *America* 96 (January 26, 1957): 468; Budd Schulberg, "*Vale atque Ave*," manuscript in Schulberg Deposit, Rauner Special Collections Library, Webster Hall, Dartmouth College; author interviews with Budd Schulberg, April 29 and May 10, 2003; author interview with Msgr. George V. Higgins, May 20, 1999.

10. Author interview with Florence Dzamba, September 17, 2001; author telephone interview with Hap Moran, December 4, 2001; author interview with Robert Hinckle, April 6, 2006.

11. Hague's obituary is in *New York Times*, January 2, 1956; Joe Ryan's obituary is in *New York Times*, June 27, 1963.

12. William McCormack Sr.'s obituary is in *New York Times*, July 13, 1965; for Msgr. William J. McCormack, see http://www.catholic-hierarchy.org/bishop/bmccow.html.

13. Msgr. John J. O'Donnell's obituary is in *New York Times*, October 10, 1967; author telephone interviews with George Hunt, S.J., December 4, 2001, and Jim Joyce, S.J., February 7, 2002.

14. The obituary of John M. Corridan, S.J., is in *New York Times*, July 3, 1984.

15. Philip A. Carey, S.J., to Msgr. George G. Higgins, July 27, 1984, box 12, folder 4, XIIR. Philip A. Carey's obituary is in the *New York Times*, May 29, 1989.

16. Angus Kress Gillespie, *Twin Towers: The Life of New York City's World Trade Center* (New Brunswick, N.J.: Rutgers University Press, 1999), 122–23; Austin J. Tobin's obituary is in *The New York Times*, February 9, 1978.

17. Debra Bernhardt interview with Philip Carey, S.J., February 19, 1981, New Yorkers at Work Oral History Series, Wagner Labor Archives, Tamiment Library, New York University.

18. Richard P. Burke, S.J., to Rev. Raymond J. Swords, S.J., Report on August 14, 1970, interview with Philip A. Carey, S.J., August 18, 1970, Institute of Industrial Relations Papers, Special Collections and Archives, College of the Holy Cross. Philip A. Carey, S.J., died on May 27, 1989. Xavier Labor School had closed in 1988 after years of dwindling enrollments.

19. Budd Schulberg to Ann Brown, May 20, 1987, box 6, folder 59, XIIR; Ken Hickman, "The Christening of the 'Rev. John M. Corridan, S.J.,'" *Regis Alumni News* (Winter 2006–7): 12–13.

Index

Page numbers with an *f* indicate figures.

A volume in the series
CUSHWA CENTER STUDIES OF CATHOLICISM IN TWENTIETH-CENTURY AMERICA
Edited by R. Scott Appleby

A list of titles in this series is available at www.cornellpress.cornell.edu.